CULTURAL ANTHROPOLOGY

CULTURAL ANTHROPOLOGY

A Perspective on the Human Condition

THIRD EDITION

EMILY A. SCHULTZ

Macalester College

ROBERT H. LAVENDA

St. Cloud State University

MAYFIELD PUBLISHING COMPANY

Mountain View, California

London • Toronto

Library of Congress Cataloging-in-Publication Data
Schultz, Emily A.
    Cultural anthropology: a perspective on the human condition /
  Emily A. Schultz, Robert H. Lavenda—3rd ed.
        p.   cm.
    Includes bibliographical references (p.   ) and index.
    ISBN 1-55934-387-7
    1. Ethnology.   I. Lavenda, Robert H.   II. Title.
GN316.S38   1995   94-17596
306--dc20   CIP

Manufactured in the United States of America
10   9   8   7   6   5   4   3   2

Mayfield Publishing Company
1280 Villa Street
Mountain View, California 94041

Sponsoring editor, Janet M. Beatty; production editor, Lynn Rabin Bauer; manuscript editor, Andrea McCarrick; text and cover designer, Anna Post George; cover photograph: © 1994 Gianni Vecchiato; art editors, Robin Mouat and Jean Mailander; photo editor, Melissa Kreischer; illustrators, Patricia Isaacs and Judith Ogus; manufacturing manager, Aimee Rutter. The text was set in 10/12 Berkeley Oldstyle by ColorType and printed on 45# Glatfelter Restorecote by R. R. Donnelley and Sons.

Acknowledgments and copyrights continue at the back of the book on pages 486–487, which constitute an extension of the copyright page.

 This book is printed on recycled paper.

For Daniel and Rachel

Preface

The photograph on the cover of this book appears to be a stereotypical image of the subject matter of anthropology: women, dressed in what seems to the western eye to be exotic clothing and engaged in a seemingly exotic occupation—backstrap weaving. Indigenous Guatemalan women, the picture seems to say, live in a colorful, peaceful, "traditional" world distant from the "modern" world of the presumed observer of the photograph. But images can be deceiving. In 1992, an indigenous Guatemalan woman, Rigoberta Menchú, dressed in "traditional" Guatemalan clothing, stood before the King of Sweden to receive the Nobel Peace Prize for her courageous dedication to defending human rights in her violence-wracked country. Indigenous Guatemalan people, like so many others, have been caught up in war, revolution, state-sponsored terrorism, massacres, and great political, religious, and social movements. The women on the cover may possibly have been unaffected by the decades of violence directed against indigenous people in Guatemala, but they may also be, like so many others, survivors of the violence. They may have lost husbands, brothers, or sons—killed by the Guatemalan army or by death squads. They, too, might have been involved in the struggle for autonomy, waged within the context of a modern state and world system.

The cloth the women weave carries a range of potential meanings. It may be fabric for themselves, their relatives, friends, or neighbors, but it may also be for the tourist market in Panajachel or Guatemala City, or for businesses that will make jackets to sell throughout Central America, the United States, Europe, and Japan. The weavers may be relatives or friends, or perhaps unrelated women who have organized themselves into a cooperative to market their cloth. To understand the photograph, we need to look beyond it. The ambiguities evoked by the photograph on the cover, and the task of looking beyond them, lie at the heart of our understanding of anthropology, and at the heart of this book.

APPROACH

Anthropology is no longer about the strange customs of exotic peoples (if it ever really was). In this text, our goal is to explore the interplay of cultural creativity, human agency, and material constraint in the shaping of human cultural traditions. While recognizing the importance of each of these factors, however, we do not reduce human culture to any one of them. We recognize that human experience of the world is fundamentally ambiguous. Human beings work to resolve that ambiguity through interaction with various aspects of the material world, including one another. Because ambiguous experiences can always be resolved in more than one way, individuals and groups must choose some interpretations rather than others simply to get on with living. As a result, human beings cannot avoid participating in the construction and reconstruction of cultural practices. Cultural practices that work become part of local traditions that serve as resources on which people can draw when faced with ambiguities in the future. However, the power struggles that go on in all societies always shape decisions about what works and what does not, further complicating the relationship between what people do and what ecology or economics or rationality is thought to require. The result is the tremendous variety of culturally constructed ways of life, none of which can easily be explained as the inevitable outcome of a single shaping force. Our book aims to show how human agents use cultural creativity to cope with the material constraints that circumscribe all human life.

WHAT'S NEW IN THE THIRD EDITION?

Many changes have been made to improve both the content and its presentation. We have listened closely to students and colleagues, and have made changes accordingly:

Chapter 2: Culture and the Human Condition. This chapter has been reorganized and shortened for clarity. Much of the philosophical discussion has been pared.

Chapter 3: Ethnographic Fieldwork. This chapter now includes a discussion of the Mead–Freeman case and incorporates material on communication in fieldwork based on the work of Nita Kumar and her fieldwork in her native country of India.

Chapter 4: History, Anthropology, and the Explanation of Cultural Diversity. Based on reviewers' suggestions, this chapter (formerly Chapter 8) has been retitled and extensively reworked.

Chapter 5: Language. This chapter includes a new discussion of ape language and additional material on male–female speech interaction based on the work of Deborah Tannen.

Chapter 6: Cognition. We have incorporated new material on syllogistic reasoning and emotion, revised the socialization/enculturation material, and presented material from recent Cuban research on children's development from a Vygotskian perspective.

Chapter 7: Play, Art, Myth, and Ritual. This chapter features a revised discussion of play and incorporates new material on the selective force of animal play behavior, on Chernobyl jokes as a form of political resistance, on Aymara joking, on dance and gender in northern Greece, and Samba schools in Rio. There is also a revised discussion of ritual with new examples.

Chapter 9: Kinship. There are new sections on sex, gender, and kinship (incorporating very recent supernumerary sex and gender studies), on the effect of new reproductive technologies on European-American kinship thinking, and on distinctive forms of kinship-like socioeconomic organization (the Japanese *Ie*).

Chapter 10: Marriage and the Family. This chapter includes new material on nonreproductive sexual practices, international migration and family structure, and micropolitics in polygynous families.

Chapter 12: Social Organization and Power. Opening with new material from recent events in El Salvador, this chapter also includes material on witchcraft and its connection with legitimacy and coercion among the Beng of Ivory Coast and new social movements, such as the *rondas campesinas* in highland Peru.

Chapter 14: The World System. This chapter incorporates new material on international aid for health care and the problems it creates in Costa Rica and a discussion of the critique of the development model in light of the end of the Cold War and the rise of new social movements.

Chapter 15: Anthropology in Everyday Life. The final chapter has been retitled and now includes new material on anthropology and human rights.

Innovative features of previous editions that are maintained in this edition include attention to issues in ethnographic representation; the dialogic nature of fieldwork; full coverage of linguistic anthropology, including discourse, pragmatics, schemas, prototypes, and metaphor; new directions in the study of cognition; treatment of play, art, myth, and ritual together; an entire chapter on worldview; forms of social organization based on metaphorical kinship (*compadrazgo* in Latin America; *Ie* in Japan); treatment of social organization and power together, along with attention to the power of imagination and power of negotiation; attention to human agency in the creation of cultural identity in a pluralistic world; thorough treatment of production, distribution, and consumption; world system and neomarxian approaches; colonialism and neocolonialism; and attention to anthropology and everyday life.

FEATURES AND LEARNING AIDS

- Material on gender and feminist anthropology is featured throughout the text. Discussions of gender are tightly woven into the fabric of the chapters on cultural and linguistic anthropology, and include (for example) material on supernumerary sexes and genders (such as Sambia *kwolu-aatmwol* and male and female berdaches in native North America), nonreproductive sexual practices, language and gender, dance and gender politics, and women and colonialism. Extensive material on gender is found in the chapters on Language; Cognition; Play, Art, Myth, and Ritual; Kinship; Marriage and the Family; Social Organization and Power; Making a Living; and The World System.
- We take an explicitly world-system approach in the text. We systematically point out the extent to which the current sociocultural situation of particular peoples has been shaped by their particular histories of contact with the world system and their degrees of incorporation in it. Cultures cannot be studied out of the broader context that shapes people's lives.
- New voices, including those of indigenous peoples, anthropologists, and nonanthropologists, are presented in the text in commentaries called "In Their Own Words." These short commentaries provide alternative perspectives—always readable and sometimes controversial—on topics featured in the chapter in which they occur.

- Carried over from earlier editions, the renamed EthnoProfiles provide a consistent, brief information summary for each society discussed at length in the text. They emerged from our sense as teachers that students could not be expected to know readily the locations of different societies, nor how many people might be involved. Each EthnoProfile includes data on the location of the society, the nation it is in, the population, the environment, the livelihood of the people, their political organization, and a source for further information. It also contains a map of the area in which the society is found. EthnoProfiles are not intended to be a substitute for reading ethnographies or for in-class lectures, but they provide a kind of consistent orientation for the reader.

- Additional learning aids include key terms that are boldfaced in the text and defined in a running glossary at the bottom of the page. Each chapter ends with a list of the key terms in the order they appeared in the text, a numbered chapter summary, and annotated suggested readings. We would particularly draw your attention to the maps that open each chapter, which include the locations of all societies discussed at length in the chapter.

- We have tried to indicate where the ideas of anthropology come from and have tried to avoid being omniscient narrators for three major reasons. First, students need to know about the heteroglossic nature of academic disciplines. Anthropology is constructed by the work of many, and no one should attempt to impose a single voice on our field. Second, we cannot expect students to take academic honesty seriously if their textbook authors do not cite sources. Third, we want students to see where anthropologists' conclusions come from. We have avoided, as much as we could, pre-digested statements that students must take on faith. We try to give them the information that they need to reach conclusions.

- A *Study Guide,* written with Margaret Rauch, director of the Academic Learning Center at St. Cloud State University, is unusual in that it is filled with hints and suggestions on improving study skills, strategies for studying this text, organizing information, writing essay exams, taking multiple-choice exams, and much more. Any student, even the best prepared, will find the information and strategies in the *Study Guide* valuable. Each chapter also contains a review of key terms, sample multiple-choice exams, and an innovative "Arguing Anthropology" section with questions for students to argue with their friends.

- An *Instructors' Manual* offers test-bank questions, chapter outlines, key terms, suggestions for class discussions, and film suggestions. The test-bank questions are also available to qualified adopters in a computerized class management system that provides all test items on computer disk for IBM-compatible and Macintosh computers. Instructors can select, add, or edit questions, randomize the question order for each exam and the answer order for each question, and print tests that meet the needs of their classes. The system also includes a gradebook module that enables the instructor to keep detailed performance records for individual students and for the entire class; maintain student averages; graph each student's progress; and set the desired grade distribution and curve, maximum score, and weight for each test. The system has extensive reporting options for tests, individual students, and entire classes.

We take students seriously. In our experience, although students may complain, they are also pleased when a course or a textbook gives them some credit for having minds and being willing to use them. We have worked very hard to make this book readable and to present anthropology in all of its diversity, as a vibrant, lively discipline full of excitement, contention, and intellectual value. We do not run away from the meat of the discipline with the excuse that it's too hard for students. Our collective teaching experience has ranged from highly selective liberal arts colleges to multi-purpose state universities, to semi-rural community colleges. We have found students at all of these institutions who are willing to be challenged and make an effort when it is clear to them that anthropology has something to offer. It is our hope that this book will be a useful tool in challenging students and convincing them of the value of anthropology as a way of thinking about, and dealing with, the world in which they live.

ACKNOWLEDGMENTS

Our thanks to Clark Baxter who provided the spark for this book. We would like to thank Jan Beatty, our editor at Mayfield, for bringing that spark to life. We appreciate her eagerness to publish both this book and our general anthropology book, and we value her support and advice. It has been a great pleasure to work with her and the superb production team at Mayfield, especially Lynn Rabin Bauer, production editor extraordinaire. We would also like to acknowledge the contributions of manuscript editor Andrea McCarrick, photo editor Melissa Kreischer, art editors Robin Mouat and Jean Mailander, permissions editor Pamela Trainer, editorial assistant Joanne Martin, and marketing manager Karen Murphy.

We continue to be impressed by the level of involvement of most of the reviewers of this manuscript. It is clear that reviewers understand how important they are to the authors of textbooks and recognize that authors may have more than time invested in their work. We have found that, even when we didn't follow reviewers' suggestions, their work caused us to think and rethink the issues they raised. We would like therefore to recognize Jill Brody, Louisiana State University; E. Paul Durrenberger, University of Iowa; Carole Glover, University of Maryland; Betsy Taylor, Albion College; and Daniel Yakes, Muskegon Community College.

We owe a special and profound debt to Ivan Karp, who has been our most important source of intellectual stimulation and support throughout this project.

We have found that textbook writing is a particularly solitary occupation, and that means that for our children, Daniel and Rachel, both Mom and Dad have had to spend an awful lot of time reading, taking notes, writing, revising, and attending to a seemingly unending stream of details. For a host of reasons, it is for our children that we undertook this project. When they finally come to read the result, we hope that they will understand why we spent so much time on it, and be pleased.

Contents in Brief

Contents

4   HISTORY, ANTHROPOLOGY, AND THE EXPLANATION OF CULTURAL DIVERSITY   *71*

5   LANGUAGE   *101*

EthnoProfiles

CULTURAL ANTHROPOLOGY

CHAPTER OUTLINE

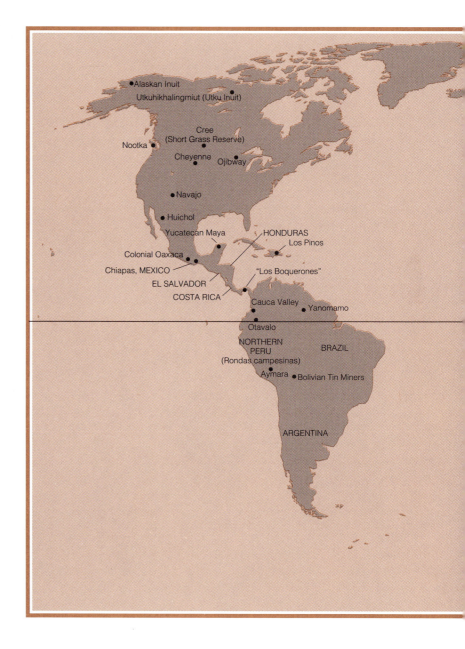

*Locations of peoples and places
discussed in this book.*

The Anthropological Perspective

I

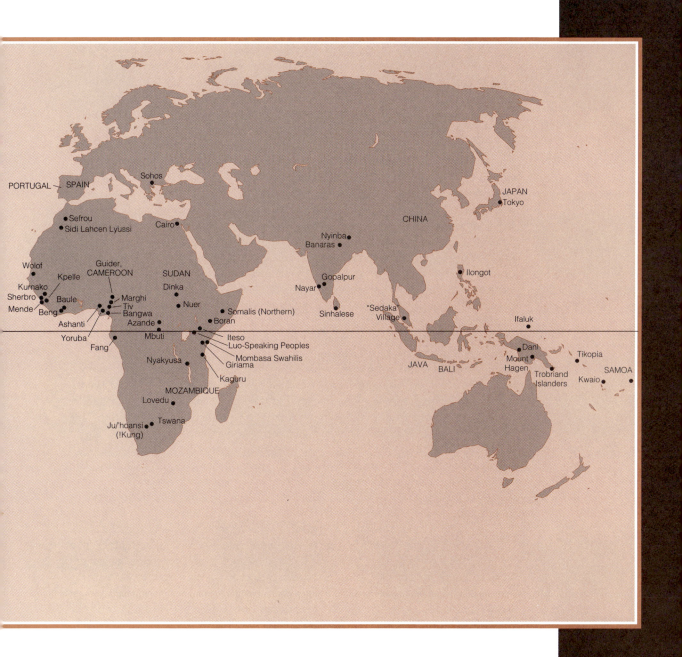

PORTUGAL — SPAIN

Sohos

JAPAN
Tokyo

CHINA

Sefrou
Sidi Lahcen Lyussi

Cairo

Nyinba
Banaras

Wolof

Guider,
CAMEROON

SUDAN

Ilongot

Kpelle

Dinka

Gopalpur

Kurnako

Nayar

Sherbro

Marghi

Baule

Tiv

Bangwa

Nuer

Sinhalese

"Sedaka"
Village

Mende

Beng

Somalis (Northern)

Azande

Boran

Ifaluk

Ashanti

Mbuti

Iteso

Yoruba

Luo-Speaking Peoples

Dani

Tikopia

Fang

Mombasa Swahilis

Mount

Nyakyusa

Giriama

Hagen

SAMOA

Kaguru

JAVA

BALI

Trobriand
Islanders

Kwaio

MOZAMBIQUE

Lovedu

Ju/'hoansi
(!Kung)

Tswana

*i*n early 1976, we (Emily Schultz and Robert Lavenda) traveled to northern Cameroon, in western Africa, to study social relations in the town of Guider, where we rented a small house. In the first weeks we lived there, we enjoyed spending the warm evenings of the dry season reading and writing in the glow of the house's brightest electric fixture, which illuminated a large, unscreened veranda. After a short time, however, the rains began, and with them appeared swarms of winged termites. These slow-moving insects with fat, two-inch abdomens were attracted to the light on the veranda, and we soon found ourselves spending more time swatting at them than reading and writing. One evening, in a fit of desperation, we rolled up old copies of the international edition of *Newsweek* and began an all-out assault, determined to rid the veranda of every single termite.

The rent we paid for this house included the services of a night watchman. As we launched our attack on the termites, the night watchman suddenly appeared beside the veranda carrying an empty powdered milk tin. When he asked if he could have the insects we had been killing, we were a bit taken aback but warmly invited him to help himself. He moved onto the veranda, quickly collected the corpses of fallen insects, and then joined us in going after those termites that were still airborne. Although we became skilled at thwacking the insects with our rolled-up magazines, our skills paled beside those of the night watchman, who simply snatched the termites out of the air with his hand, squeezed them gently, and dropped them into his rapidly filling tin can. The three of us managed to clear the air of insects in about ten minutes. We offered the night watchman our kill, which he accepted politely. He then returned to his post, and we returned to our books.

The following evening, soon after we took up our usual places on the veranda, the watchman appeared at the steps bearing a tray with two covered dishes. He explained that his wife had prepared the food for us in exchange for our help in collecting the termites. We accepted the food and carefully lifted the lids. One dish contained *nyiri,* a stiff paste made of red sorghum, a staple of the local diet. The other dish contained another pasty substance with a speckled, salt-and-pepper appearance, which we quickly deduced was termite paste prepared from the previous night's kill.

The night watchman waited at the foot of the veranda steps, an expectant smile on his face. Clearly, he did not intend to leave until we tasted the gift he had brought. We looked at each other. We had never eaten insects before or considered them edible in the North American, middle-class diet we were used to. To be sure, "delicacies" like chocolate-covered ants exist, but such items are considered by most North Americans to be food fit only for eccentrics. However, we understood the importance of not insulting the night watchman and his wife, who were being so generous to us. From our training, we knew that insects were a favored food in many human societies and that eating them brought no ill effects. With the watchman still standing there, smiling, waiting to see what we would do, we reached into the dish of *nyiri,* pulling off a small amount. We then used the ball of *nyiri* to scoop up a small portion of termite paste, brought the mixture to our mouths, ate, chewed, and swallowed. The watchman beamed, bid us goodnight, and returned to his post. We looked at each other in wonder. The sorghum paste had a grainy tang that was rather pleasant, and the termite paste tasted mild, like chicken, not unpleasant at all. We later wrote to our families about this experience, and when they wrote back, they described how they had recounted the details to our meal to a friend who was a home economist. Her response contained no shock whatsoever. She simply commented that termites were a good source of clean protein.

WHAT IS ANTHROPOLOGY?

Some of the central elements of the anthropological experience can be found in this anecdote. Anthropologists want to learn about as many different human ways of life as they can. Whether the people they come to know are members of their own society or live on a different continent, anthropologists are sometimes exposed to practices that startle them. However, as they take the risk of getting to know such ways of life better, they are often treated to the sweet discovery of familiarity. This shock of the unfamiliar becoming familiar—as well as the familiar becoming unfamiliar—is something anthropologists come to expect and is one of the real pleasures of the field. In this book, we share aspects of the anthropological experience in the hope that you, too, will come to find pleasure, insight, and self-recognition from an involvement with the unfamiliar.

Anthropology can be defined as the study of human nature, human society, and the human past (cf. Greenwood and Stini 1977). It is a scholarly discipline that aims to describe in the broadest possible sense what it means to be human.

Anthropologists are not alone in focusing their attention on human beings and their creations. Human biology, literature, art, history, linguistics, sociology, politics, economics—all these scholarly disciplines and many more—concentrate on one or another aspect of human life. Anthropology is unique because it draws on the findings of these other disciplines and attempts to fit them together with its own data in order to understand how human biology, economics, politics, religion, and kinship collectively shape one another to make human life what it is. That is, anthropology is **holistic;** holism is a central feature of the anthropological perspective.

---

anthropology The study of human nature, human society, and the human past.

holistic A characteristic of the anthropological perspective that describes how anthropology tries to integrate all that is known about human beings and their activities at the highest and most inclusive level.

To generalize about human nature, human society, and the human past requires evidence from the widest possible range of human societies. Thus, in addition to being holistic, anthropology is a **comparative** discipline. It is not enough, for example, to observe only our own social group, discover that we do not eat insects, and conclude that human beings as a species do not eat insects. When we compare human diets in different societies, we discover that insect eating is quite common and that our North American aversion to eating insects is nothing more than a dietary practice specific to our own society.

Anthropologists try to come up with generalizations about what it means to be human that are valid across space and over time. The field for comparison includes all human societies as well as all periods of the human past, from the emergence of humanlike primates some 5 million years ago to the present time. For this reason, anthropology also examines the biological evolution of the human species over time, including the study of human origins and genetic variety and inheritance in living human populations.

If evolution is understood broadly as change over time, then human societies and cultures may also be understood as having evolved from prehistoric times to the present day. One of anthroplogy's most important contributions to the study of human evolution has been to emphasize the critical differences that separate *biological evolution* (which concerns attributes and behaviors that are passed on by the genes) from *cultural evolution* (which concerns beliefs and behaviors that are *not* passed on by the genes but are transmitted through teaching and learning). Although this book emphasizes human culture rather than human biology, we wish to point out that the human species, human societies, and human cultures all change over time. Because anthropologists are interested in documenting and explaining these changes, the anthropological perspective is **evolutionary** at its core.

THE CONCEPT OF CULTURE

A consequence of human evolution that had the most profound impact on human nature and human society was the emergence of **culture,** which can be defined as sets of learned behavior and ideas that human beings acquire as members of society. Human beings use culture to adapt to and to transform the world in which we live.

Culture makes us unique among living creatures. Human beings are more dependent than any other species on learning for survival because we have no instincts that automatically protect us and find us food and shelter. Instead, we have come to use our large and complex brains to learn from other members of society what we need to know to survive. This teaching and learning process is a primary focus of childhood, which is longer for humans than for any other species.

In the anthropological perspective, the concept of culture is central to explanations of why human beings are what they are and why they do what they do. Anthropologists have frequently been able to show that members of a particular social group behave in a particular way because they *learned* to behave that way, not because the behavior was programmed by their genes. Typically, North Americans do not eat insects, but this behavior is not the result of genetic programming. Rather, North Americans have learned to label insects as "inedible" and avoid eating them. As we discovered personally, insects can be eaten by North Americans with no ill effects. Thus, this difference in social behavior can be explained in terms of culture rather than biology.

Interestingly, anthropologists have been able to demonstrate the power of culture precisely because they are also knowledgeable about human biology. Scholars who are trained in both areas, as has been traditional in many North American anthropology programs, understand how genes and organisms work and are acquainted with comparative information about a wide range of human societies. As a result, they are more realistic in evaluating the ways that biology and culture contribute to any particular form of human behavior. Indeed, most anthropologists reject explanations of human behavior that force them to choose between biology and culture as the cause. Instead, they prefer to emphasize that human beings are **biocultural organisms.** Our genetically guided biological makeup, including our brain, nervous system, and anatomy, makes us capable of creating and using culture. Without these biological endowments, human culture as we know it would not exist. At the same time, our survival as biological organisms depends upon learned cultural traditions that help us find food, shelter, and mates, and that teach us how to rear our offspring. This is because our biological endowment, rich as it is, does not provide us with instincts that would take care of these survival needs. Human biology makes culture possible; human culture makes human biological survival possible.

Anthropologists sometimes distinguish between *Culture* (with a capital *C*) and *cultures* (plural with a lowercase *c*). *Culture* is seen as an attribute of the human species as a whole—its ability to learn and to create sets of behaviors and ideas that allow members of the species to survive as biological organisms. By contrast, *cultures* are different traditions of learned behavior and ideas that specific groups of human beings learn because they are members of particular societies. Each tradition can be called a separate culture, although the boundaries separating one culture from another are often not easy to draw.

Although the human species as a whole can be said to have *Culture* as a defining attribute, anthropologists and other human beings have access 'only to particular human cultures. Ordinarily, anthropologists gain information about specific cultures by making direct contact with some other, particular way of life. Whether

---

comparative A characteristic of the anthropological perspective requiring that anthropologists consider similarities and differences in as wide a range of human societies as possible before generalizing about human nature, human society, or the human past.

evolutionary A characteristic of the anthropological perspective that requires anthropologists to place their observations about human nature, human society, or the human past in a temporal framework that takes into consideration change over time.

culture Sets of learned behavior and ideas that human beings acquire as members of society. Human beings use culture to adapt to and to transform the world in which we live.
biocultural organisms Organisms (in this case, human beings) whose defining features are codetermined by biological and cultural factors.

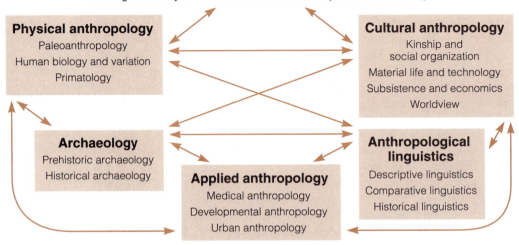

ANTHROPOLOGY

The integrated study of human nature, human society, and human history.

Physical anthropology
Paleoanthropology
Human biology and variation
Primatology

Cultural anthropology
Kinship and
social organization
Material life and technology
Subsistence and economics
Worldview

Archaeology
Prehistoric archaeology
Historical archaeology

Anthropological linguistics
Descriptive linguistics
Comparative linguistics
Historical linguistics

Applied anthropology
Medical anthropology
Developmental anthropology
Urban anthropology

FIGURE 1.1 *In the United States, anthropology is traditionally divided into four specialties: physical anthropology, cultural anthropology, anthropological linguistics, and archaeology. In recent years, another subfield has developed: applied anthropology, which draws on information provided by the other four specialties.*

living with a group of Fulbe in northern Cameroon, excavating an ancient Aztec site in Mexico, or studying the differences between men's and women's speech in Alabama, anthropologists must shift their perspectives away from the ones with which they are most familiar. Anthropologists who study chimpanzees or gorillas in the wild or who attempt to reconstruct the ways of life of the fossilized ancestors of modern human beings and apes push the boundaries of our understanding of what it means to be human. The results of their work frequently require us to reevaluate our commonsense notions about who we are. The experience of being "in the field" is central to modern anthropology and contributes profoundly to the anthropological perspective. All anthropology comes back to the mental, emotional, and physical experience of direct contact with a frequently unfamiliar world.

THE CROSS-DISCIPLINARY DISCIPLINE

Because the goal of anthropology is to describe what it means to be human, the discipline is extraordinarily diverse. At any given yearly meeting of the American Anthropological Association (the professional society to which most anthropologists belong), you will find research papers presented on such topics as the size and shape of the teeth of fossilized primates believed to be ancestral to modern human beings, patterns of marriage and divorce in Europe, biological and social factors involved with AIDS in Third World settings, traditional food-getting activities in Africa, and mat making in Polynesia. Because of its diverse interests, anthropology does not easily fit into any of the standard academic classifications. The discipline is usually listed as a social science, but it spans the natural sciences and the humanities as well.

Figure 1.1 brings some order to the variety of interests found under the anthropological umbrella. At the highest level, we may think of anthropology as the integrated study of human nature, human society, and human history. But traditionally, anthropologists have chosen to approach human nature from two different directions: physical and cultural.

Physical Anthropology (Biological Anthropology)

The first, and oldest, specialty within anthropology is **physical anthropology** (or **biological anthropology**). Physical anthropologists are most interested in looking at human beings as biological organisms to discover what makes us different from other living organisms and what we share with other members of the animal kingdom.

In the nineteenth century, when anthropology was developing as an academic field, physical anthropology flourished. Interest in this field was a by-product of centuries of exploration. Western Europeans had found tremendous variation in the physical appearance of peoples around the world and had long tried to make sense of these differences. Physical anthropologists invented a series of elaborate techniques to measure different observable features of human populations, including skin color, hair type, body type, and so forth. Their goal was to find scientific evidence that would allow them to classify all the peoples of the world into a set of unambiguous categories based on distinct sets of biological attributes. Such categories were called **races,** and many physical anthropologists were convinced that clear-cut criteria for racial classification would be discovered if careful measurements were made on enough people from around the world.

Of course, this early research in physical anthropology did not take place in a social and historical vacuum. The very peoples whom physical anthropologists were trying to assign to racial categories were in most cases non-European peoples who were coming under increasing political and economic domination by expanding European and European American capitalist societies. These peoples differed from "white" Europeans not only because of their darker skin color but also because of their unfamiliar languages and customs and because, in most cases, they possessed technologies that were no match for the might of the industrialized West. As a result, racial membership was understood to determine not just outward physical attributes of groups but their mental and moral attributes as well. Races were ranked in terms of these attributes. Unsurprisingly, "white" Europeans and North Americans were seen as superior, and the other races were seen to represent varying grades of inferiority. In this way, the first physical anthropologists helped develop theories that would justify the social practice of **racism:** the systematic oppression of

physical anthropology (or **biological anthropology**) The specialty of anthropology that looks at human beings as biological organisms and tries to discover what characteristics make us different from other living organisms and what characteristics we share.

races Social groupings based on perceived physical differences and cloaked in the language of biology.

racism The systematic oppression of one or more socially defined "races" by another socially defined "race" that is justified in terms of the supposed inherent biological superiority of the rulers and the supposed inherent biological inferiority of those they rule.

one or more socially defined "races" by another socially defined "race" that is justified in terms of the supposed inherent biological superiority of the rulers and the supposed inherent biological inferiority of those they rule.

As time passed, research techniques in physical anthropology improved. Physical anthropologists began to measure numerous internal features of populations, such as blood types, that they added to their calculations. They learned a tremendous amount about physical variation in human beings; however, they discovered that the external traits traditionally used to identify races, such as skin color, did not correlate well with other physical and biological traits. The more they learned about the biological attributes of human populations, the more they realized that races with distinct and unique sets of such attributes simply did not exist.

By the early twentieth century, some anthropologists and biologists concluded that the concept of "race" did not reflect a fact of nature but was instead a cultural label invented by human beings in order to sort people into groups. Anthropologists like Franz Boas, for example, who, in the early 1900s founded the first department of anthropology in the United States, had long been uncomfortable with racial classifications in anthropology. Boas and his students devoted much energy to debunking racist stereotypes, using both their knowledge of biology and their understanding of culture. As the discipline of anthropology developed in the United States, students were trained in both human biology and human culture to provide them with the tools to fight racial and ethnic stereotyping.

Rejecting the racial thinking of the nineteenth century, many modern anthropologists who study human biology prefer to call themselves **biological anthropologists** (Figure 1.2). They no longer study "race" and instead pay attention to patterns of variation within the human species as a whole. Some biological anthropologists trace chemical similarities and differences in the immune system, an inter-

FIGURE 1.2 *Some biological anthropologists are primatologists, such as Barbara Smuts (left), who studies olive baboons in Kenya. Other biological anthropologists, such as Carol Worthman (right), study human biological variation in a laboratory.*

est that has recently led into active work on AIDS (Acquired Immunodeficiency Syndrome). Others investigate the relationship between nutrition and physical development. There are **primatologists,** who specialize in the study of the closest living relatives of human beings, the nonhuman primates, as well as **paleoanthropologists,** who search the earth for the fossilized bones and teeth of our earliest ancestors. By comparing modern human beings with living and extinct nonhuman populations, biological anthropologists can illuminate what makes human beings similar to and different from other forms of life.

Whether they study human biology, primates, or the fossils of our ancestors, biological anthropologists have borrowed and developed methods and theories from the natural sciences—primarily biology, chemistry, and geology. What sets biological anthropologists apart from their nonanthropological colleagues is the holistic, comparative, and evolutionary perspective that has been part of their anthropological training. That perspective reminds them always to consider their work as only part of the overall story of human nature, human society, and the human past.

Cultural Anthropology

The second specialty within anthropology is **cultural anthropology,** which is sometimes called *sociocultural anthropology, social anthropology,* or *ethnology.* Once anthropologists realized that racial biology could not be used to explain why everyone in the world did not dress the same, speak the same language, pray to the same god, or eat insects for dinner, they knew that something else must be responsible for these differences. They suggested that this "something else" was culture: sets of learned behavior and ideas that human beings acquire as members of society. Because people everywhere use culture to adapt to and transform the wider world in which we live, the field of cultural anthropology is vast.

Cultural anthropologists tend to specialize in one or another domain of human cultural activity (Figure 1.3). Some study the ways human beings organize themselves to carry out collective tasks, whether economic, political, or spiritual. This focus within cultural anthropology bears the closest resemblance to the discipline of sociology, and from it has come the identification of anthropology as one of the social sciences. In fact, sociology and anthropology developed during the same period and share similar interests in social organization.

One important factor that first differentiated anthropology from sociology was the anthropological interest in comparing different forms of human social life. In the

---

biological anthropologists Anthropologists who specialize in the study of patterns of biological variation within the human species as a whole.

primatologists Anthropologists who specialize in the study of nonhuman primates, the closest living relatives of human beings.

paleoanthropologists Anthropologists who search the earth for fossilized remains of humanity's earliest ancestors.

cultural anthropology The specialty of anthropology that shows how variation in the beliefs and behaviors of members of different human groups is shaped by sets of learned behavior and ideas that human beings acquire as members of society, that is, by culture.

racist framework of nineteenth- and early-twentieth-century European and North American societies, some people viewed sociology as the study of "civilized" indus-trial societies and labeled anthropology as the study of all other societies, lumped together as "primitive." But modern anthropologists are concerned with studying *all* human societies, and they reject the labels "civilized" and "primitive" for the same reason they reject the term "race." Today, anthropologists do research in urban and rural settings around the world and among members of all societies, including their own.

Anthropologists have discovered that people in many non-Western societies do not organize bureaucracies or churches or schools, yet they still manage to carry out successfully the full range of human activity because they have developed the insti-tution of *kinship,* organizing themselves into social groups whose members are all considered "relatives." The study of kinship has become highly developed in anthropology and remains a focus of interest today. In addition, anthropologists have described a variety of non-kin forms of social organization that can be found outside the Western world. These include secret societies, age sets, and numerous forms of political organization.

Cultural anthropologists have investigated the patterns of material life found in different human groups. Among the most striking are worldwide variations in clothing, housing, tools, and techniques for getting food and making material goods. Some anthropologists specialize in the study of technologies in different societies or in the evolution of technology over time. Those interested in material life also describe the natural setting for which technologies have been developed and analyze the way technologies and environments shape each other.

Anthropologists who do comparative studies of language, music, dance, art, poetry, philosophy, religion, or ritual share many of the interests of specialists in the disciplines of fine arts and humanities. Of all these areas, the study of human language has been particularly important in cultural anthropology.

Anthropological Linguistics

Perhaps the most striking cultural feature of our species is **language:** the system of arbitrary vocal symbols we use to encode our experience of the world and of one another. People use language to talk about all areas of their lives, from material to spiritual. Thus, language is an important key to learning about a particular group of people and their way of life. **Anthropological linguistics** has become so highly developed that it is considered a separate specialty of anthropology. Many early anthropologists were the first people to transcribe non-Western languages and to produce grammars and dictionaries. Modern anthropological linguists are trained in both linguistics and anthropology, and many cultural anthropologists also receive linguistics training as part of their professional preparation. Anthropological linguists seek to understand language holistically in relation to the broader cultural, historical, and biological contexts that make it possible.

Fieldwork   Cultural anthropologists, no matter what their area of specialization, ordinarily collect their data during an extended period of close involvement with the people in whose language or way of life they are interested. This period of research is called **fieldwork,** and its central feature is the anthropologists' involvement in the everyday routine of those among whom they live. People who share information about their culture and language with anthropologists have traditionally been called

---

language The system of arbitrary vocal symbols we use to encode our experience of the world and of one another.

anthropological linguistics The specialty of anthropology concerned with the study of human languages.

fieldwork An extended period of close involvement with the people in whose language or way of life anthropologists are interested, during which anthropologists ordinarily collect most of their data.

In Their Own Words   **ANTHROPOLOGY AS A VOCATION: LISTENING TO VOICES**

James W. Fernandez, *(Ph.D., Northwestern University) is a professor of anthropology at the University of Chicago. He has worked among the Fang of Gabon and among cattle keepers and miners of Asturias, Spain. This is an excerpt from an essay about the anthropological vocation.*

For me, the anthropological calling has fundamentally to do with the inclination to hear voices. An important part of our vocation is "listening to voices," and our methods are the procedures that best enable us to hear voices, to represent voices, to translate voices.

By listening carefully to others' voices and by trying to give voice to these voices, we act to widen the horizons of human conviviality. If we had not achieved some fellow feeling by being there, by listening carefully and by negotiating in good faith, it would be the more difficult to give voice in a way that would widen the horizons of human conviviality. Be that as it may, the calling to widen horizons and increase human conviviality seems a worthy calling—full of a very human optimism and good sense. Who would resist the proposition that more fellow feeling in the world is better than less, and that to extend the interlocutive in the world is better than to diminish it?

At the same time, there is a paradox here, one that demands of us a sense of proportion. Although the anthropologist is called to bring diverse people into intercommunication, he or she is also called to resist the homogenization that lies in mass communication. We are called by our very experience to celebrate the great variety of voices in the human chorus. The paradox is that we at once work to amplify the scale of intercommunication—and in effect contribute to homogenization—while at the same time we work to insist on the great variety of voices in communication. We must maintain here too a sense of proportion. We must recognize the point at which wider and wider cultural intercommunication can lead to dominant voices hidden in the homogenizing process. Human intercommunication has its uses and abuses.

Source: Schultz and Lavenda 1990, 14–15.

informants; however, anthropologists use this term less today and prefer to describe these individuals as *teachers* or *friends* because these terms emphasize a relationship of equality and reciprocity. Fieldworkers gain insight into another culture by participating with members in social activities and by observing those activities as outsiders. This research method is known as participant-observation, which is central to cultural anthropology—and to human interaction in general.

Cultural anthropologists write about what they have learned in scholarly articles or in books and sometimes document the lives of their research subjects on film. An **ethnography** is a description of a particular culture; **ethnology** is the comparative study of many cultures. Thus, cultural anthropologists who write ethnographies are sometimes called *ethnographers,* and anthropologists who compare ethnographic information on many different cultures are sometimes called *ethnologists.*

Archaeology

Archaeology, another major specialty within anthropology, is a cultural anthropology of the human past involving the analysis of material remains. Through archaeology, anthropologists discover much about human history, particularly prehistory, the long stretch of time before the development of writing. In addition to under-standing physical and cultural anthropology, archaeologists must be able to identify any human remains they uncover and to interpret the nonhuman remains—such as postholes, garbage heaps, and settlement patterns. Moreover, they need to know about geology to be able to situate the sites of their digs correctly in time. Depending on the locations and ages of sites they are digging, archaeologists may also have to be experts on stone-tool manufacture, metallurgy, or pollen analysis.

The information uncovered by archaeologists is valuable to physical and cul-tural anthropologists. Archaeologists recover the bones and teeth used to recon-struct human and nonhuman primate evolution. The remains of material culture they find can lend historical depth to particular cultural traditions and trace the spread of cultural inventions over time from one site to another. If they are dealing with more recent sites—"recent" meaning within the last few thousand years—they may find evidence of ancient writing systems for anthropological linguists to decode and translate. Some contemporary archaeologists are excavating layers of garbage deposited by human beings within the last two or three decades, uncovering some-times surprising information about modern consumption patterns.

Applied Anthropology

In recent years, **applied anthropology** has come to be recognized as the fifth major field of anthropology (see Figure 1.1). Applied anthropologists use information gathered from the other anthropological specialties to solve practical cross-cultural problems. They may use a particular culture's ideas about illness and health to introduce new public health practices in a way that makes sense to and will be accepted by members of that culture. Other applied anthropologists may use knowl-edge of traditional social organization to ease the problems of refugees' trying to settle in a new land. Still others may use their knowledge of traditional and Western methods of cultivation to help farmers increase their crop yields. Given the growing concern throughout the world with the effects of different technologies on the envi-ronment, applied anthropology holds promise as a way of blending Western science and non-Western tradition in order to create sustainable technologies that minimize pollution and environmental degradation. Applied anthropology is so new and so interdisciplinary that it has not yet become a required part of graduate training, although increasing numbers of universities in the United States are developing programs in this specialty.

informants People in a particular cul-ture who work with anthropologists and provide them with insights about their way of life. Also called *teachers* or *friends*.

ethnography An anthropologist's writ-ten or filmed description of a particular culture.

ethnology The comparative study of many cultures.

archaeology A cultural anthropology of the human past involving the analysis of material remains left behind by ear-lier human societies.

applied anthropology A specialty of anthropology that uses information gath-ered from the other anthropological spe-cialties to solve practical cross-cultural problems.

USES OF ANTHROPOLOGY

Why take a course in anthropology? An immediate answer might be that human fossils or ancient potsherds or the customs of faraway peoples inspire a fascination that is its own reward. But the experience of being dazzled by seemingly exotic places and peoples carries with it a risk. As you become increasingly aware of the range of anthropological data, including the many options that exist for living a satisfying human life, you may find yourself wondering about the life you are living. Contact with the unfamiliar can be liberating, but it can also be threatening if it undermines your confidence in the absolute truth and universal rightness of your previous understanding of the way the world works.

The modern world is becoming increasingly interconnected. As people from different cultural backgrounds come into contact with one another, learning to cope with cultural differences becomes crucial. Anthropologists experience both the rewards and the risks of getting to know how other people live, and their work has helped to dispel many harmful stereotypes that sometimes make cross-cultural contact dangerous or impossible. Studying anthropology may help prepare you for some of the shocks you will encounter in dealing with people who look different from you, speak a different language than you, or do not agree that the world works exactly the way you think it does or should.

Anthropology involves learning about the kinds of living organisms that human beings are, the various ways we live our lives, and how we make sense of our experiences. Studying anthropology can equip you to deal with a different culture in a less threatened, more tolerant manner. You may never be called on to eat termite paste. Still, you may one day encounter a situation in which none of the old rules seem to apply. As you struggle to make sense of what is happening, what you learned in anthropology class may help you relax and dare to try something totally new to you. If you do so, perhaps you too will discover the rewards of an encounter with the unfamiliar that is at the same time unaccountably familiar. We hope you will savor the experience.

KEY TERMS

anthropology	races	fieldwork
holistic	racism	informants
comparative	biological anthropologists	ethnography
evolutionary	primatologists	ethnology
culture	paleoanthropologists	archaeology
biocultural organisms	cultural anthropology	applied anthropology
physical anthropology	language	
(biological	anthropological	
anthropology)	linguistics	

CHAPTER SUMMARY

1. Anthropology is a scholarly discipline that aims to describe in the broadest sense what it means to be human. To achieve this aim, anthropologists have developed a perspective on the human condition that is holistic, comparative, and evolutionary.

2. Because human beings lack instincts that automatically promote our survival, we must learn from other members of our society what we need to know to survive. For this reason, the concept of culture is central to the anthropological perspective.

3. Most anthropologists emphasize that human beings are biocultural organisms whose biological makeup allows us to make and use culture. Our biological survival depends on learned cultural traditions because human biology does not provide us with instincts that would otherwise ensure our survival.

4. Anthropology is a field-based discipline. All subdivisions of anthropological research bring anthropologists into direct contact with some other, particular way of life.

5. In the United States, anthropology is usually considered to have five major specialties: physical anthropology, cultural anthropology, anthropological linguistics, archaeology, and applied anthropology.

6. Physical anthropology began as an attempt to classify all the world's populations into different races, an undertaking that some people used to justify the social practice of racism. By the early twentieth century, however, most anthropologists had rejected racial classifications as scientifically unjustifiable. From the time of Franz Boas and his students, anthropologists have used information about human biology and human culture to debunk racist stereotypes.

7. Modern anthropologists who are interested in human biology include biological anthropologists, primatologists, and paleoanthropologists.

8. Cultural anthropologists study human diversity by focusing on sets of learned behaviors and ideas that human beings acquire as members of different societies. Because anthropology is comparative, research is done in Western and non-Western settings alike.

9. Anthropological linguists study linguistic diversity in different human societies, relating various forms of language to their cultural contexts.

10. Through fieldwork, cultural anthropologists gain insight into another culture by participating with their informants in social activities and by observing those activities as outsiders. Ethnographies are published accounts of what was learned during fieldwork. Ethnology involves comparing ethnographic information from many different cultures.

11. Archaeology is a cultural anthropology of the human past, but the material remains archaeologists recover can be of value to physical and cultural anthropologists. Archaeologists' interests range from research in human origins to what twentieth-century garbage dumps can tell us about the recent past.

12. Applied anthropologists use information gathered from the other anthropological specialties to solve practical cross-cultural problems in such areas as health care and economic development.

13. The study of human diversity may be threatening if it undermines your confidence in the truth and rightness of your own way of life. Yet it can also be liberating, enabling you to cope more realistically and tolerantly with people whose appearance or behavior is unfamiliar to you.

SUGGESTED READINGS

Barrett, Richard A. 1984. *Culture and conduct: An excursion in anthropology.* Belmont, CA: Wadsworth. *A short, well-written introduction to some of the most interesting questions in contemporary anthropology.*

Fagan, Brian M. 1991. *Archaeology: A brief introduction.* 4th ed. New York: Harper-Collins. *An up-to-date, engaging introduction to the techniques, assumptions, interests, and findings of modern archaeology.*

Freilich, Morris. 1983. *The pleasures of anthropology.* New York: New American Library, Mentor Book. *A wide-ranging collection of accessible articles arranged into eight sections. Most of the articles are from the 1960s to the early 1980s, but some enduring classics are also reprinted. All are a pleasure to read and are thought provoking.*

Johanson, Donald, and Maitland Edey. 1981. *Lucy: The beginnings of humankind.* New York: Simon and Schuster. *A well-written, exciting introduction to one aspect of physical anthropology: human origins. This book reads like a good thriller and is highly recommended.*

CHAPTER OUTLINE

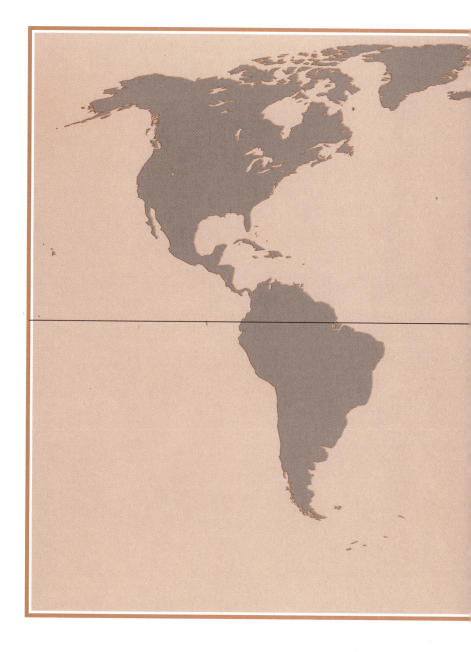

Culture and the Human Condition

2

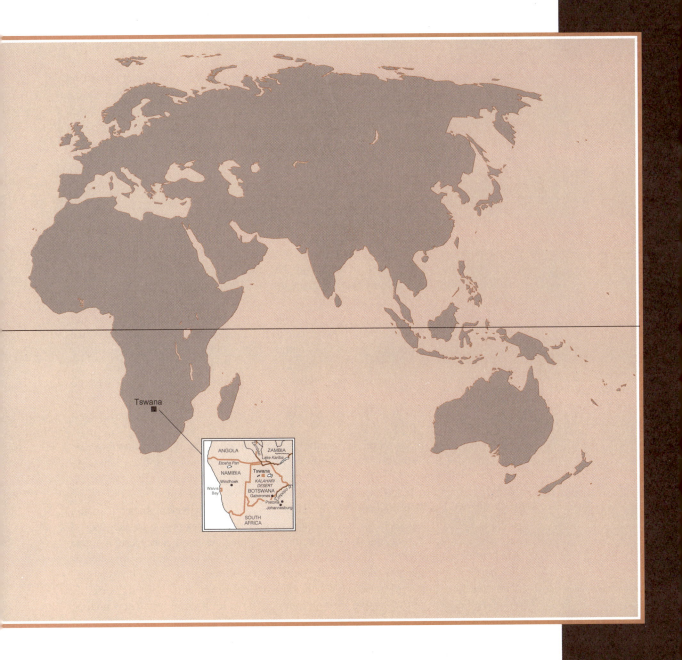

Tswana

ANGOLA
ZAMBIA
Lake Kariba
Etosha Pan
NAMIBIA
Tswana
KALAHARI
DESERT
Windhoek
BOTSWANA
Walvis
Bay
Gaborones
Pretoria
Johannesburg
SOUTH
AFRICA

*t*he human condition is distinguished from the condition of other living species by **culture.** Other living species are open systems, as we are, and other living species learn. But the openness of the human condition and the extent to which we depend upon learning to survive are unique in the animal kingdom. Because our brains are capable of open symbolic thought and our organs such as our hands are capable of manipulating matter powerfully or delicately, we interpenetrate the wider world more deeply than does any other species. This characteristic human relationship with the wider world makes cultural creation not only possible but necessary for our very survival. Apart from sucking, grasping, and crying, human newborns have no instincts or innate responses to ensure their survival; even those elementary responses fade after a few weeks, and they must be replaced by learned responses. Our dependence on culture is total. Without it, we cannot survive as biological organisms.

We begin cultural learning as infants from other members of our group. Therefore, culture is shared as well as learned. Culture is not reinvented by each generation; rather, the majority of what we learn comes from older members of our society, although we may later modify this heritage in some way. The transmission and enriching of cultural traditions depend on culture being shared, just as human survival depends on social living.

There can be no society without individuals, but society is more than just the sum of the individuals that make it up. According to this perspective, society and individual create each other. There can be no society without individual human beings, but without society we can never come to have a sense of self, of being distinct from others.

Culture is also our species' way of adapting to the wider environment. We have no biological instincts that would ensure our survival. Instead, we depend on the shared tradition that we learn from other members of society and the shared labor on which our existence depends (Figure 2.1).

Finally, culture is symbolic. A **symbol** is something that stands for something else. The letters of the alphabet, for example, symbolize the sounds of spoken language. There is no necessary connection between the shape of a particular letter and the speech sound it represents. Indeed, the same or similar sounds are represented symbolically by very different letters in the Latin, Cyrllic, Hebrew, Arabic, and Greek alphabets to name but five. Even the sounds of spoken language are symbols for meanings a speaker tries to express. The fact that we can translate from one language to another suggests that the same or similar meanings can be expressed by different spoken symbols in different languages. But language is not the only domain of culture that depends on symbols. Everything we do in society has a symbolic dimension, from how we conduct ourselves at the dinner table to the way we go about burying the dead. It is our heavy dependency

FIGURE 2.1 *Of all living organisms, human beings are the most dependent upon learning for their survival. From a young age, girls in northern Cameroon learn to carry heavy loads on their heads.*

on symbolic learning that sets human culture apart from the apparently nonsymbolic learning on which other species rely.

Culture is learned, shared, adaptive, and symbolic. Elements of culture can be learned by anyone from anyone and anywhere. But for most people, most of the time, culture is learned and practiced among a relatively limited group of people who share relatively close social ties. For example, any group of people who regularly interact must

culture Sets of learned behavior and ideas that human beings acquire as members of society. Human beings use culture to adapt to and to transform the world in which we live.

symbol Something that stands for something else. A symbol signals the presence of an important domain of experience.

21

negotiate some ground rules that everyone accepts to ensure communication and cooperation. If members of the group have grown up together and speak the same language, these ground rules are usually taken for granted and rarely made explicit. For these reasons, local cultural traditions tend to be coherent, in part because culture is a social product. The boundaries around a cultural tradition are always fuzzy, being determined not only by our customs but also by how different our customs are from somebody else's customs. Nevertheless, members of a society who share a common culture tend to think and talk about themselves in the same conceptual terms and tend to organize their activities by the same principles. If thus becomes possible to speak of the characteristic patterns of belief and behavior that distinguish one cultural tradition from another.

THE HUMAN CONDITION AND CULTURE

What is the world like? And what is the human condition within the world? Not only anthropologists but members of all societies pose questions like these. And all societies, including those that trace their origins to western Europe, develop their own answers. If asked what they believe about human nature, for example, many North Americans would answer that human nature has two parts: sometimes called *mind* and *matter, soul* and *body,* or *spirit* and *flesh.* The belief that human nature, or reality as a whole, is made up of two radically different elements, or essences, is called **dualism.** Dualistic thinking is deeply rooted in Western thought; for millennia, people have debated the importance of each half of our nature. Perhaps the oldest attempt to resolve this debate can be traced to the ancient Greek philosopher Plato.

Plato divided all reality into mind and matter: mind is higher and finer and belongs to the celestial realm of ideal forms; matter is lower and cruder and corruptible, belonging to the earthly realm. Human nature is dualistic because each person is made up of an earthly material body inhabited by a spirit whose true home is the realm of ideal forms. According to Plato, the drama of human existence consists in the internal struggle between the body, drawn naturally to base, corruptible matter, and the mind or soul, drawn naturally to pure, unchanging forms. Christian theology later incorporated the view that each human being consists of a soul that seeks God and a physical body that is tempted by the material world. This view of earthly life as a struggle between flesh and spirit is sometimes called *conflict dualism.*

The Platonic and Christian theories of human nature argue that although human beings are equipped with material bodies, their true nature is spiritual, not material; the body is a material impediment that frustrates the full development of the mind or spirit. This view is known as **idealism.** Platonic idealism was the source of essentialistic thinking about species up until Darwin's day.

However, it is equally possible to make the contrary argument: that matter—the material activities of our physical bodies in the material world—constitutes the essence of human nature. From this perspective, human existence becomes the struggle to exercise our physicality as fully as we can; to put spiritual values above bodily needs would "go against human nature." People would not seek spiritual salvation, it is sometimes argued, if their material needs were satisfied. This view is known as **materialism.**

Reductionism is the attempt to explain something complex by showing that complexity is *nothing but* the outcome of simpler causal forces. Idealists are reductionists because they claim that human nature is nothing but mind or spirit; materialists are reductionists because they claim that human nature is nothing but the product of genes or anatomy or biology. Reductionism is synonymous with **determinism.** Consequently, idealism and materialism are often called *deterministic theories.*

Although both idealism and materialism have been defended since the time of the pre-Socratic Greeks, Western materialism gained more support during the seventeenth-century Enlightenment, as science and technology developed and the Industrial Revolution got underway. As a result, materialist views of the human condition gradually replaced idealist views among scientists and the highly educated.

The nineteenth century was the great century of evolutionary thought in the Western world, and Charles Darwin was probably its most famous evolutionary thinker. Darwin was not the first to argue that change over time was the rule for biological species. Drawin's innovation was to propose a materialist explanation for such change. Natural selection is a two-step, random material process in which organisms possessing varied material traits are "tested" by forces of the material environment in which they live. Organisms whose material traits help them to withstand this environmental test survive; other organisms perish. There is no need for mind or God in this process. The material world, if left to its own devices, automatically improves the various living species by fitting them ever more perfectly into their respective environments.

Long before Darwin wrote about the origin of species through natural selection, other Western thinkers had speculated about the evolution of human society. Indeed, the expression "survival of the fittest," long associated with Darwin, was first used by Herbert Spencer, whose main interest was the evolution of society. Spencer believed that the material forces of evolution would inevitably produce a better world if they were allowed to operate without interference. It was all a matter of survival of the fittest. For Spencer, the present arrangements of society came about by the necessity of material evolution. Thus, social inequality and the suffering of the poor, however unjust or cruel they might appear, must be understood as the best of all possible social arrangements. Attempts to tamper with these arrangements involve going against the grain of evolutionary destiny and are doomed to failure.

Spencer's views contributed to a perspective called *biological determinism,* which was responsible for the racist classifications of human groups by nineteenth-century anthropologists and sociologists. Biological determinists claim that complex human social life is nothing more than the by-product of the simpler actions of many individual human

---

dualism The philosophical view that reality consists of two equal and irreducible forces.

idealism The philosophical view (dating back at least as far as Plato), that ideas—or the mind that produces such ideas—constitute the essence of human nature.

materialism The philosophical view that the material activities of our physical bodies in the material world constitute the essence of human nature.

reductionism The philosophical view that explains all evidence in terms of (or "reduces" it to) a single set of explanatory principles.

determinism The philosophical view that one simple force (or a few simple forces) causes (or determines) complex events.

beings, each of whom does nothing more than follow the dictates of his or her genes or hormones. In other words, biological determinists claim that genes or hormones determine the behavior of individual human organisms and that complex human society is nothing but the sum total of all these simpler, individual actions.

Other materialists subscribe to a second form of materialist reductionism called *environmental determinism*. Environmental determinists who look at human societies argue that the important material forces that shape our lives exist outside our bodies in the surrounding natural world. Rich soil, a temperate climate, too little rainfall, or the absence of domesticable animals are examples of environmental forces that shape society and determine forms of social organization, political arrangements, and religious beliefs.

For the followers of Karl Marx, social forces play a critical role. The collective material actions of people in society, shaped by the interests of the dominant class, are responsible for the human condition at any point in history. Progress is still possible, indeed inevitable, as historical necessity works itself out. Marx and his followers believe, however, that progress comes only through revolution. The old and the worse have to be overthrown forcibly to make way for the new and the better. This view is known as *historical materialism*.

An extreme, idealist reaction against these forms of materialism is called *cultural determinism*. Cultural determinists argue that the ideas, meanings, beliefs, and values that people learn as members of society become the determining agents of the human condition. In this view, "you are what you learn." Optimistic versions of cultural determinism place no limits on the abilities of human beings to be or do whatever they want. This perspective became very popular among many anthropologists in the 1940s and 1950s, who held out the hope that, if human nature is infinitely malleable, then human beings can mold themselves into the kinds of people they want to be. Pessimistic versions of cultural determinism rule this out: "You are what you learn" becomes "you are what you are conditioned to be," something over which you have no control. In this view, human beings are passive creatures who have no choice but to do what their culture tells them to do.

HOLISM

Materialists and idealists have battled with one another for centuries, neither side ever yielding to the other for long. To some observers, this unresolvable conflict is rooted in the dualistic view of human nature on which it is based. Many anthropologists have long argued that there is yet another point of view on the human condition that is less distorting than dualism and less simplistic than materialism or idealism. The anthropological point of view called **holism** does not assume that sharp boundaries separate mind from body, bodies from the environment, individuals from society, my ideas from our ideas, or their traditions from our traditions; rather, it assumes that mind and body (bodies and the environment, and so on) interpenetrate each other and even define each other. From a holistic perspective, attempts to divide reality into mind and matter are able, at most, to isolate and pin down certain aspects of a process that, by its very nature, resists isolation and dissection. A contribution of unique and lasting value has been made by anthropologists who have struggled throughout the history of the discipline to develop a holistic perspective on the human condition. Holism continues to hold great appeal for those who seek a theory of human nature that is rich enough to do justice to its complex subject matter.

One traditional way of expressing the holistic insight is to say that the whole (that is, a human being, a society, a cultural tradition) is more than the sum of its parts. Individual human organisms are not just *x* percent genes and *y* percent culture added together. Rather, human beings are what they are because the interpenetration of genes and culture has produced something new, something whose attributes cannot be reduced to the materials that were used to construct it. Similarly, a society or a culture is not just the sum of the behaviors of its individual members. Instead, human beings living in groups become different kinds of creatures. They are so deeply affected by shared cultural experiences that they become different from what they would have been had they matured in isolation from other people. Clifford Geertz notes that human beings raised in isolation would be neither failed apes nor "natural" people stripped of their veneer of culture; they would be "mental basket cases" (1973, 40). Indeed, we have discovered that human beings subjected to tragic isolation do not behave in ways that appear recognizably human. Social living and cultural sharing are necessary for individual human beings to develop what we recognize as a *human* nature.

We can enrich our understanding of the relationships among the parts that make up a whole by approaching those relationships in a dialectical manner. **Dialectical relationships** refer to a network of cause and effect, in which the various causes and effects affect each other. A dialectical approach to the human condition, therefore, emphasizes that biology and culture are neither separable nor antithetical nor alternatives, but complementary to one another. Lewontin, Rose, and Kamin observe that all causes of the behavior of organisms "are simultaneously social and biological . . . chemical and physical" (1984, 282). Put another way, the properties of parts and wholes *codetermine* one another. This was what we meant in Chapter 1 when we stated that anthropologists see human nature as *biocultural*.

We are proposing a holistic and dialectical view of human nature, a view that rejects dualism and reductionism. Dialectical holism is based on the view that human beings are open systems, and that the wider world, the environment, is also open to modification by the objects (including people) that inhabit it. For human beings, part of the wider world is human society, so human society too must be considered an open system. Figure 2.2 offers a comparison of this holistic perspective with the other alternatives discussed so far.

---

holism A perspective on the human condition that assumes that mind and body, individuals and society, and individuals and the environment interpenetrate and even define one another.

dialectical relationships A network of cause and effect in which the various causes and effects affect each other.

FIGURE 2.2 *Perspectives on the human condition.*

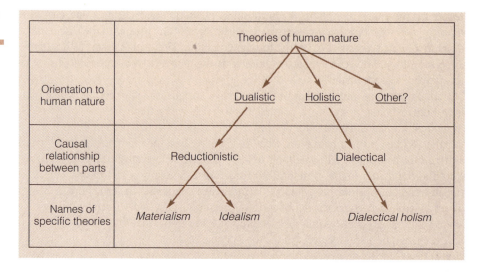

In the late twentieth century, scientists have become increasingly aware that the codetermination of organisms and environment involves information as well as matter. Recent work in particle physics reminds us how mysterious matter is, and work in information theory and computer intelligence suggests that information is no less mysterious. The transformation of signals from the wider world into information that an organism can process and the exchange of information between organisms are usually what we are referring to when we talk about "learning."

Of all living organisms, human beings are the most dependent upon learning for their survival, and what they learn concerns both the physical and social environments in which they live. We tend to think of learning primarily as a mental process, a capacity of mind. However, a holistic, dialectical view of the human condition would describe human beings as creatures whose bodies, brains, actions, and thoughts are equally involved in the learning process, codetermining one another. The result of their constant association would be the production of a human nature embedded in a wider world that also helps to define the human condition. A most important aspect of that wider world, which shapes us and is shaped by us, is culture.

CULTURAL DIFFERENCES

The same objects or events frequently mean different things to people in different cultures. In fact, what counts as an object or event in one tradition may not be recognized as such in another. This powerful lesson of anthropology was illustrated by the experience of some Peace Corps volunteers working in southern Africa.

In the early 1970s, the Peace Corps office in Botswana was concerned by the number of volunteers who seemed to be "burned out," failing in their assignments, and increasingly hostile to their Tswana hosts. (See EthnoProfile 2.1: Tswana.) The Peace

EthnoProfile 2.1 • **TSWANA**

REGION: Southern Africa

NATION: Botswana

POPULATION: 1,200,000 (also 1,500,000 in South Africa)

ENVIRONMENT: Savanna to desert

LIVELIHOOD: Cattle raising, farming

POLITICAL ORGANIZATION: Traditionally, chiefs and headmen; today, part of a modern nation-state

FOR MORE INFORMATION: Alverson, Hoyt. 1978. *Mind in the heart of darkness.* New Haven: Yale University Press.

Corps asked American anthropologist Hoyt Alverson, who was familiar with Tswana culture and society, for advice. Alverson (1977) discovered that one major problem the Peace Corps volunteers were having involved exactly this issue of similar actions having very different meanings.

In one instance, the volunteers complained that the Tswana would never leave them alone. Whenever they tried to "get away" and sit by themselves for a few minutes to have some "private time," one or more Tswana would quickly join them. This made the Americans angry. From their perspective, everyone is entitled to a certain amount of privacy and time alone. To the Tswana, however, human life is social life; the only people who want to be alone are witches and the insane. But these young Americans did not seem to be witches or lunatics, so the Tswana who saw them sitting alone "naturally" assumed that there had been a breakdown in hospitality and that the volunteers would welcome some company. Here, one type of behavior—a person walking out into a field and sitting by himself or herself—had two very different meanings.

Even within a single culture, the meaning of an object or an action may differ depending on the context. Quoting philosopher Gilbert Ryle, anthropologist Clifford Geertz notes that there is a world of difference between a wink and a blink, as anyone who has ever mistaken one for the other has undoubtedly learned.

Thus, human experience is inherently ambiguous. To resolve the ambiguity, experience must be interpreted. Human beings turn to their own cultural traditions in search of an interpretation that makes sense and is coherent. They do this daily as they go about life among others with whom they share traditions. But their interpretive activity does not cease at the boundary of the culture because there are no clear-cut boundaries. Self and other need not belong to the same society or share the same traditions, and yet the attempt to communicate and the interpretive activity continue. Serious misunderstandings may arise when two individuals are unaware that their ground rules differ. At this point, the concepts of ethnocentrism and cultural relativism become relevant.

Ethnocentrism

Ethnocentrism is the term anthropologists use to describe the opinion that one's own way of life is natural or correct, indeed the only true way of being fully human. Ethnocentrism arises when a person encounters another way of life that, compared with his or her own, appears unnatural, incorrect, or nonhuman.

Ethnocentrism is one solution to the inevitable tension between cultural self and cultural other. It is a form of reductionism; it reduces the other way of life to a distorted version of one's own. If our way is right, then their way can only be wrong. At best, their truth is a distorted truth; at worst, it is an outright falsehood. (Of course, from their perspective, our way of life may seem equally to be a distortion of theirs.)

The members of one tradition may go beyond merely interpreting another way of life in ethnocentric terms. They may decide to do something about the discrepancies they observe. They may, for example, conclude that the other way of life is wrong but not fundamentally evil and that the members of the other group need to convert to their own point of view. If the others are unwilling to change their ways, however, the failed attempt at reduction may enlarge into an active dualism: we versus they, civilization versus savagery, good versus evil. The ultimate result may be war and *genocide*—the deliberate attempt to exterminate an entire "people" based on race, religion, national origin, or other cultural features.

The Cross-Cultural Relationship

Is it possible to avoid ethnocentric bias? A holistic approach to relationships between ourselves and other people, across as well as within cultural traditions, holds promise. This approach views cross-cultural relationships as not being fundamentally different from intracultural relationships. Although cross-cultural relationships are often much more difficult to negotiate because the people involved have so much to learn about each other, they are possible. Like all human relationships, they affect all parties involved in the encounter, changing them as they learn about each other.

This sort of interwoven learning experience is common to all human relationships, but it is potentially much more radical when it involves parties from different cultural backgrounds. People from another culture may help you see possibilities for belief and action that are drastically at odds with everything your tradition considers possible. By becoming aware of these unsuspected possibilities, you become a different person. Knowledge changes people, and change (learning) is only possible as a result of contact with someone different from yourself. People from the other culture are likely to be affected in the same way. None of you will be the same again.

Cross-cultural learning is at once enormously hopeful and immensely threatening; once it occurs, we can no longer claim that any single cultural tradition has an exclusive monopoly on truth. Although this does not mean that the traditions in question must therefore be based entirely on illusion or falsehood, it does mean that the truth embodied in any cultural tradition is bound to be partial, approximate, and open to further insight and growth.

In Their Own Words   **THE PARADOX OF ETHNOCENTRISM**

Ethnocentrism is usually described in thoroughly negative terms. As Ivan Karp points out, however, ethnocentrism is a more complex phenomenon than we might expect.

Anthropologists usually argue that ethnocentrism is both wrong and harmful, especially when it is tied to racial, cultural, and social prejudices. Ideas and feelings about the inferiority of blacks, the cupidity of Jews, or the lack of cultural sophistication of farmers are surely to be condemned. But can we do without ethnocentrism? If we stopped to examine every custom and practice in our cultural repertoire, how would we get on? For example, if we always regarded marriage as something that can vary from society to society, would we be concerned about filling out the proper marriage documents, or would we even get married at all? Most of the time we suspend a quizzical stance toward our own customs and simply live life.

Yet many of our own practices are peculiar when viewed through the lenses of other cultures. Periodically, for over fifteen years, I have worked with and lived among an African people. They are as amazed at our marriage customs as my students are at theirs. Both American students and the Iteso of Kenya find it difficult to imagine how the other culture survives with the bizarre, exotic practices that are part of their respective marriage customs. Ethnocentrism works both ways. It can be practiced as much by other cultures as by our own.

Paradoxically, ethnographic literature combats ethnocentrism by showing that the practices of cultures (including our own) are "natural" in their own setting. What appears natural in one setting appears so because it was constructed in that setting—made and produced by human beings who could have done it some other way. Ethnography is a means of recording the range of human creativity and of dem-

onstrating how universally shared capacities can produce cultural and social differences.

This anthropological way of looking at other cultures—and, by implication, at ourselves—constitutes a major reason for reading ethnography. The anthropological lens teaches us to question what we assume to be unquestionable. Ethnography teaches us that human potentiality provides alternative means of organizing our lives and alternative modes of experiencing the world. Reading ethnographies trains us to question the received wisdom of our society and makes us receptive to change. In this sense, anthropology might be called the subversive science. We read ethnographies in order to learn about how other peoples produce their world and about how we might change our own patterns of production.

Source: Karp 1990.

Cultural Relativism

Anthropologists must come to terms with the consequences of cross-cultural learning as they do their fieldwork. One result has been the formulation of the concept of **cultural relativism.** Definitions of cultural relativism have varied as different anthropologists have tried to draw conclusions based on their cross-cultural experience. One definition

ethnocentrism The opinion that one's own way of life is natural or correct and, indeed, is the only true way of being fully human.

cultural relativism Understanding another culture in its own terms sympathetically enough so that the culture appears to be a coherent and meaningful design for living.

FIGURE **2.3** *Was Nazism due to the perversion of German morality by a charismatic madman who wished to rule the world, or was its appeal rooted in long-standing social, historical, and cultural patterns?*

that attempts a holistic approach is the following: "[Cultural relativism involves] understanding another culture in its own terms sympathetically enough so that the culture appears to be a coherent and meaningful design for living" (Greenwood and Stini 1977, 182).

According to this definition, the goal of relativism is understanding. For example, cultural relativism demands that we try to understand how the Nazi attempt to exterminate the Jews was conceived and implemented as a meaningful course of action in German society in the early part of the twentieth century (Figure 2.3). Knowledge about German culture in particular (including its history) and European culture in general (including the rise of fascism outside Germany) can help us understand these events. An explanation based on this knowledge implies that the Nazi Holocaust was not a momentary aberration brought on by a handful of madmen who managed to seize power in Germany for a few years and implement policies totally at odds with German culture and history; rather, Nazism was intimately related to certain cultural patterns and historical processes that are deeply rooted in German, and European, society.

Therefore, to understand Nazism from a relativistic point of view, we must ask why the Nazis were able to achieve power and why Jews were the chosen scapegoats. Answering these questions involves investigating the historical roots of anti-Semitism and nationalism in Germany. Moreover, the success of the Nazis in achieving their program, insofar as they did accomplish what they set out to do, is not explained in terms of German culture and society alone. Such boundaries are never clear, and it is unlikely that so many Jews would have died without the overt and covert assistance rendered Germany by the other countries of Europe. Even the United States is implicated because the American government refused to accept Jews as political refugees and, as a result, helped deliver them into the hands of their enemies.

This relativistic understanding accomplishes several things. It makes Nazi Germany comprehensible and even coherent. It reveals to us, to our horror, how the persecution and murder of human beings can appear perfectly acceptable when placed in a particular context of meaning. One thing this relativistic understanding does not do, however, is allow us to easily excuse or condemn the Nazis for what they did on the grounds that "it was all due to their culture." For many people, a deterministic interpretation would be preferable: for some, it would absolve Germans of any blame because it would mean they had no choice but to do what German culture dictated; for others, it would absolve non-Germans of blame—after all, if German culture had led to the Nazi Holocaust, then responsibility for its horrors would lie squarely on the German people.

These attempts to contain the evil of Nazi Germany by placing blame on one or another group of people are understandable. After all, the active, leading roles were played by Germans, in particular by members of the Nazi party. But to leave matters here is to give an incomplete account of a complex historical phenomenon. And to call the incomplete account "relativistic," as some critics have done, is to vulgarize the holistic understanding of cultural relativism that makes a complex historical explanation possible.

To accept the argument that "their culture made them do it" is to accept the position of cultural determinism. Cultural determinism, in turn, requires us to accept three assumptions about human nature and human society. First, we are asked to assume that cultures have neat boundaries between them and are sealed off from one another, neither overlapping nor interpenetrating. Second, we are asked to assume that every culture, within its closed world, offers people only one way to interpret their experience. That is, we are asked to accept the notion that cultures are monolithic and permit no variety, harbor no contradictions, and allow no dissent. Third, we are asked to assume that human beings living in these closed cultural worlds are passively molded by culture, helpless to resist indoctrination into a single worldview, and incapable of inventing alternatives to that view.

All three assumptions, however, are belied by human experience. Cultures are not sealed off from one another. Their boundaries are fuzzy; their members exchange ideas and practices. Cultures are not monolithic. Even without the alternatives introduced from the outside, every cultural tradition offers a variety of ways to interpret experience, although official sanction may be accorded to only one. Finally, human beings are not passive lumps shaped unresistingly to fit a single cultural mold. There is no such thing as a single cultural mold in a society acquainted with variety, be that variety internally or externally generated. Furthermore, in a society where options exist, choices must be made.

In fact, abundant evidence suggests that German society in the early twentieth century did not conform to the sealed off, monolithic model. Germany was not closed to the rest of the world. Moreover, German cultural tradition had more than one strand. Some Germans supported fascism, some lay low, others resisted actively—but all were Germans and drew on German tradition to justify their choices—suggesting that there was (and is) more to German culture than those aspects that the Nazis made use of. It suggests that Nazism could have been (and was) denounced by Germans as well as non-Germans. And this suggests that the recognition of evil is not simply a matter of condemning what your culture teaches you to condemn. Some Germans clearly understood why the Nazi program appealed to many of their fellow citizens, and they still condemned it in terms of traditional German values.

Understanding something is not the same as approving of it or excusing it. Often we are repelled by unfamiliar cultural practices when we first encounter them. Sometimes when we understand these practices better, we change our minds. We may conclude that the practices in question are more suitable for the people who employ them than our own practices would be. We might even recommend that they be adopted in our own society. But the opposite may also be the case. We may understand perfectly the cultural rationale behind such practices as slavery, infanticide, head-hunting, or genocide—and still refuse our approval. We may not be persuaded by the reasons offered to justify these practices, or we may be aware of alternative arrangements that could achieve the desired outcome using less drastic methods. Moreover, it is likely that any cultural practice with far-reaching consequences for human life will have critics as well as supporters within the society where it is practiced. This is certainly the case in American society, which is far from achieving moral consensus on such sensitive topics as abortion, capital punishment, or nuclear weapons.

Cultural relativism makes moral reasoning more complex. It does not, however, require us to abandon every value our own society has taught us. Our culture, like every other culture, offers us more than one plausible way of evaluating our experiences. Exposure to the traditional interpretations of an unfamiliar culture forces us to reconsider the possibilities our culture recognizes in light of new alternatives and to search for areas of intersection as well as areas of disagreement. What cultural relativism does discourage is the easy solution of refusing to consider alternatives from the outset. It also does not free us from sometimes facing difficult choices between alternatives whose "rightness" or "wrongness" is less than clear-cut. In this sense, "cultural relativism is a 'tough-minded' philosophy" (Herskovits [1951] 1973, 37).

CULTURE, HISTORY, AND HUMAN AGENCY

The human condition is rooted in time and shaped by history. As part of the human condition, culture is also historical, being worked out and passed on from one generation to the next. As paleoanthropologists have shown, the human species is itself a product of millions of years of evolution. Hence, human history is an essential aspect of the human story.

Anthropologists sometimes disagree about how to approach human history. Nineteenth-century thinkers such as Herbert Spencer argued that the evolution of social structures over time was central to the study of the human condition. Other anthropologists, often sensitive to the excesses of people like Spencer, were not interested in change over time. In the 1930s, A. R. Radcliffe-Brown justified this lack of interest by pointing out that, in societies without written records, knowledge about past life is nonexistent; any attempt to reconstruct such past life would be an unfounded attempt at "conjectural history."

For other anthropologists, history has been without interest for a different reason. Western capitalist culture, with its eye on the future and its faith in progress, has had little use for the past. It is therefore no wonder that some anthropologists built clock-

In Their Own Words   **CULTURE AND FREEDOM**

Finding a way to fit human agency into a scientific account of culture has never been easy. Hoyt Alverson describes some of the issues involved.

One's assumptions concerning the existence of structure in culture, or the existence of freedom in human action, determine whether one believes that there can be a science of culture or not. Note that the possibility of developing a science of culture has nothing to do with the use of mathematics, the precision of one's assertions, or the elegance of one's models. If a phenomenon actually has structure, then a science of that phenomenon is at least conceivable. If a phenome-

non exhibits freedom and is not ordered, then a science of that phenomenon is inconceivable. The human sciences, including anthropology, have been debating the issue of structure versus freedom in human cultural behavior for the past two hundred years, and no resolution or even consensus has emerged.

Some persuasive models of culture, and of particular cultures, have been proposed, both by those working with scientific, universalist assumptions, and by those working with phenomenological, relativistic assumptions.

To decide which of these approaches is to be preferred, we must have a specific set of criteria for evaluation. Faced with

good evidence for the existence of both structure and freedom in human culture, no coherent set of criteria for comparing the success of these alternative models is conceivable. The prediction of future action, for example, is a good criterion for measuring the success of a model that purports to represent structure: it must be irrelevant to measuring the success or failure of a model that purports to describe freedom. For the foreseeable future, and maybe for the rest of time, we may have to be content with models that simply permit us to muddle through.

Source: Alverson 1990.

work models of social structures that could be trusted to run reliably without "losing time." In these models, human beings and societies are both likened to machines. If a living organism is used as the model of society, and if organisms are nothing but machines, then a machine model of society, with individuals as robotlike moving parts, is not at all farfetched. A holistic and dialectical approach to human history, however, rejects these clockwork models. Culture is part of our biological heritage. Our biocultural heritage has produced a living species that uses culture to surmount biological and individual limitations. The result has been the emergence of creatures who are capable of studying themselves and their own biocultural evolution.

When human beings exercise at least some control over their own behavior, they are said to be *agents*. A holistic, dialectical approach to the human condition recognizes the existence and importance of human agency. Human agents are not isolated from the cultural and historical context within which they act. But this does not mean that the role of human choice may be safely ignored. Reductionist schemes assume that nothing can resist—or even tries to resist—whatever force is seen to be the prime mover, whether that force is the environment, biology, ideas, or history. However, human beings frequently have to select a course of action, even when the "correct" choice is unclear and the outcome uncertain.

Human beings live in environments that are complex, fluctuating, and ambiguous. It is in such contexts, with their ragged edges, that human beings make their interpretations and construct their actions. Some anthropologists even liken human existence to a mine field, which we must painstakingly try to cross without blowing ourselves up. As a result, human agents play a vital role as they work to interpret the behavior of others and to construct their own. The continuation of society and culture depends on such mentally and physically (holistically) active individuals.

THE PROMISE OF THE ANTHROPOLOGICAL PERSPECTIVE

The anthropological perspective on the human condition is not easy to maintain. It forces us to question the commonsense assumptions with which we are most comfortable. It only increases the difficulty we encounter when faced with moral and political decisions. It does not allow us an easy retreat back to ethnocentrism when the going gets rough. For once we are exposed to the kinds of experience that the anthropological undertaking makes possible, we are changed—for better or worse. We cannot easily pretend that these new experiences never happened to us. Once we have had a genuine glimpse of the other, seen his or her full humanity, there is no going back, except in bad faith.

So, anthropology is guaranteed to complicate your life. Nevertheless, the anthropological perspective can give you a broader understanding of human nature and the wider world, of society, culture, and history and thus help you construct more realistic and authentic ways of coping with those complications.

KEY TERMS

culture	materialism	dialectical relationships
symbol	reductionism	ethnocentrism
dualism	determinism	cultural relativism
idealism	holism	

CHAPTER SUMMARY

1. Culture distinguishes the human condition from the condition of other living species. Culture is learned, shared, adaptive, and symbolic. It also tends to be coherent.
2. The belief that human nature has two parts is known as dualism. Mind-matter dualism is deeply rooted in Western thought, dating back to such figures as Plato.
3. Many dualist thinkers have tried to reduce mind to matter, or matter to mind. Idealism reduces human nature to ideas or the mind that produces them. Materialism reduces human nature to our genes, hormones, or biology. Biological determinism, environmental determinism, and historical materialism are all forms of materialist determinism.
4. The most extreme position against the various forms of materialist reductionism, cultural determinism argues that the ideas, meanings, beliefs, and values that people learn in society determine their behavior. Optimistic versions of cultural determin-

ism hold out the hope that we can change these determining agents and make ourselves whatever we want to be. Pessimistic versions conclude that "you are what you are conditioned to be," something over which you have no control.

5. In preference to dualism, anthropologists have suggested holism, which assumes that objects and environments interpenetrate and even define each other. Thus, the whole is more than the sum of its parts. Human beings and human societies are open systems that cannot be reduced to the parts that make them up. Holism is dialectical rather than deterministic: the parts and the whole mutually define, or codetermine, each other. This book adopts a holistic and dialectical approach to human nature, human society, and human history.

6. Because human experience is often ambiguous, adaptation requires cultural interpretation, which is a constant, necessary process, whether it is carried on among members of a single cultural tradition or between members of very different cultural traditions.

7. Ethnocentrism is a form of reductionism. Anthropologists believe it can be countered by a commitment to cultural relativism, a concept that makes moral decisions more difficult because it requires us to take into account many things before we make up our minds. Cultural relativism does not require us to abandon every value our society has taught us; however, it does discourage the easy solution of refusing to consider alternatives from the outset.

8. Human history is an essential aspect of the human story, a dialectic between biology and culture. Culture is worked out over time and passed on from one generation to the next. Because human beings must interpret their experience in order to act, the story of our species also involves human agency. Because interpretations may differ from one agent to another, the outcome of human interaction is open.

SUGGESTED READINGS

Gamst, Frederick, and Edward Norbeck. 1976. *Ideas of culture: Sources and uses.* New York: Holt, Rinehart & Winston. *A useful collection of important articles about culture. The articles are arranged according to different basic approaches to culture.*

Garbarino, Merwyn S. 1977. *Sociocultural theory in anthropology: A short history.* New York: Holt, Rinehart & Winston. *A short (114-page) chronological consideration of the development of anthropological thought. Evenhanded and clear.*

Geertz, Clifford. 1973. Thick description: Towards an interpretive theory of culture; *and* The impact of the concept of culture on the concept of man. In *The interpretation of cultures.* New York: Basic Books. *Two classic discussions of culture from a major figure in American anthropology. These works have done much to shape the discourse about culture in anthropology.*

Lewontin, Richard. 1982. *Human diversity.* New York: Scientific American. *Although Lewontin is an evolutionary biologist, not an anthropologist, this work is of great value to the anthropology student. It is highly anthropological in outlook, particularly in terms of the dialectical holism discussed in this chapter.*

Voget, Fred. 1975. *A history of ethnology.* New York: Holt, Rinehart & Winston. *A massive, thorough, and detailed work. For the student seeking a challenging read.*

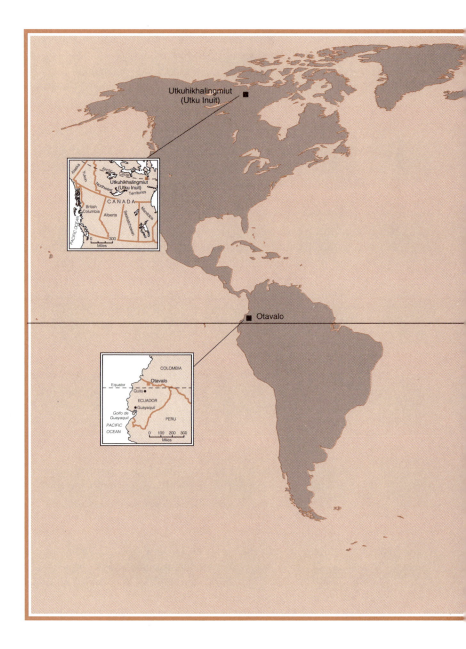

Ethnographic Fieldwork

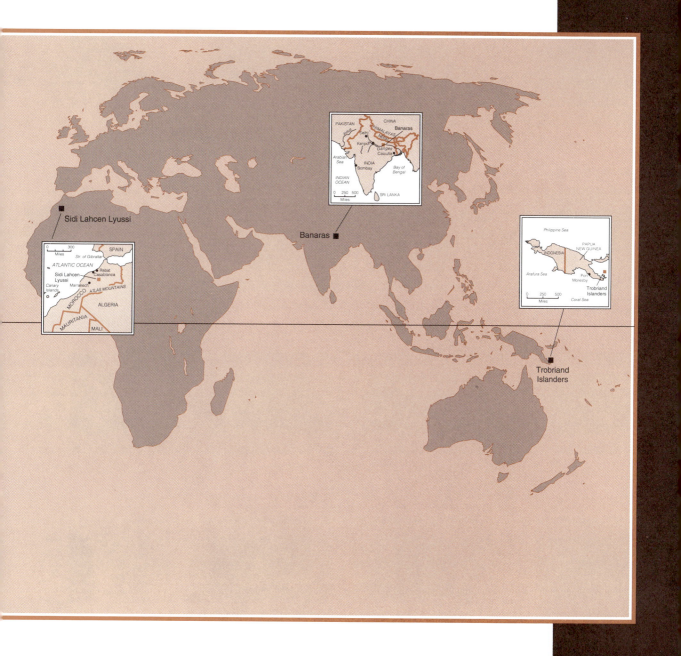

*t*he late Lawrence Carpenter was a linguistic anthropologist who worked for a number of years among the Quichua-speaking indigenous people who live in and around the town of Otavalo in highland Ecuador (Figure 3.1). (See EthnoProfile 3.1: Otavalo.) He established close ties with a number of the people, became a ritual coparent to their children, participated in weddings and wakes, and in many other ways became a semipermanent member of the village to which he returned nearly every year. But his participation in the life of that village was not originally a foregone conclusion.

Carpenter used to tell a story about the first time he was invited to attend a feast in the village itself, early in his first field trip. Traditional feasting among the indigenous peoples of highland Ecuador involves heavy consumption of alcoholic beverages. Sometimes the drink is *chicha,* a locally brewed corn beer; other times it is a powerful sugarcane alcohol approaching 100 proof called *trago* or *aguardiente.* In either case, the object of alcohol consumption is to achieve a state of communion with the spirit world; traditional celebrations cannot be successfully carried out in any other state.

FIGURE 3.1 *Anthropological linguist Lawrence Carpenter (center) drinks trago with his Otavalan informants and friends.*

EthnoProfile 3.1 • **OTAVALO**

REGION: South America (Andes)

NATION: Ecuador

POPULATION: 45,000 (late 1970s)

ENVIRONMENT: Mountain valleys and uplands, 9,000 feet and above

LIVELIHOOD: Agriculture, weaving

POLITICAL ORGANIZATION: Villages within a national political system

FOR MORE INFORMATION: Meisch, Lynn. 1987. *Otavalo: Weaving, costume, and the market.* Quito: Ediciones Libri Mundi.

Eager to "establish rapport" with the people whose way of life interested him, Carpenter was pleased to accept the invitation. He ate, drank, and smoked cigarettes with them. Afterward they accompanied him down the mountain to his apartment. His introduction into their society seemed to have gone off smoothly, and he was pleased that he had been accepted so easily.

Some weeks later, when research was well under way, one of the villagers reminisced about that first party with Carpenter. "You know," the young man added casually, "we had decided ahead of time that if you had not drunk with us, we were going to beat you up. You would have ended up at the bottom of the mountain."

Carpenter was shocked. What he had originally taken as a gesture of acceptance by the villagers had been, for them, nothing of the kind. They had been testing his honesty. They knew that most outsiders, especially missionaries and tax collectors, were always seeking acceptance into their society and would approach them much the same way Carpenter had. They resented missionizing and the patronizing interference that seemed to come with it. And so they had devised their test. They knew that missionaries frowned on drinking and smoking cigarettes, so they would see whether Carpenter was willing to drink. If not, they would know that he was really just a missionary or a tax collector in disguise, and they would show him what they thought of his hypocrisy by beating him up.

Carpenter experienced the kind of delayed shock one often feels after narrowly escaping a serious automobile accident. He had come close not only to losing the opportunity to do research in that community but also to possibly serious injury. How fortunate that he had not been prevented from drinking alcohol with his hosts because of medical reasons or because he was a recovering alcoholic or even because of personal reasons having nothing to do with religion. None of those reasons for sobriety might have made any difference to his hosts, and he might still have ended up at the foot of the mountain.

A MEETING OF CULTURAL TRADITIONS

In ethnographic **fieldwork**—the classical method of cultural anthropological research—such shocks are to be expected. Anthropologists use the expression **culture shock** to refer to the jolt that often accompanies an encounter with cultural practices that are unexpected and strange to us. Culture shock is unsettling because it calls into question our previous understanding of the way the world works, yet it also creates a new context for learning and discovery. Fieldwork institutionalizes culture shock (Karp and Kendall 1982, 262). It deliberately brings together people from different cultural traditions. From their confrontation, fieldwork generates much of what anthropologists can claim to know about people in other societies.

Gathering data while living for an extended period in close contact with members of another society is called **participant-observation.** Anthropologists also gather data by consulting archives and previously published literature relevant to their research topics. But participant-observation, which relies primarily on face-to-face contact with people as they go about their daily lives, was pioneered by cultural anthropologists and remains characteristic of anthropology as a discipline. Participant-observation allows anthropologists to interpret what people say and do in the wider context of social interaction and cultural beliefs and values. Sometimes they administer questionnaires and psychological tests as part of their fieldwork, but they would never rely solely on such methods because such information alone cannot be contextualized and may be highly misleading. The fieldwork experience of participant-observation is perhaps the best method available to scholars who seek a holistic understanding of culture and the human condition.

THE MECHANICS OF FIELDWORK

Anthropologists sometimes gain field experience as undergraduates or early in their graduate studies, working on research projects or in field schools run by established anthropologists. For most anthropologists, an extended period of fieldwork is the final phase of formal training. It is also the experience that characterizes and defines the discipline. Most anthropologists hope to return frequently to the field throughout their careers.

During graduate school, beginning anthropologists usually decide where they wish to do their research and on what topic. Next, they must obtain funding for their research. In the United States, this generally requires submitting grant proposals to private foundations or government agencies. Some anthropologists have begun to pay for their research themselves—sometimes through employment in the field research area—or by supplementing small grants from their universities out of their own pockets.

Once funding is secured, the anthropologist must get permission to carry out research in the geographical region chosen. For research outside the United States, this means contacting the government of the country where the research site is located, a research center or local university, or both. If the research project is approved, the researcher will establish professional ties with local scholars and institutions while the project is under way. In many countries, such professional affiliation is required by law.

Anthropologists view this affiliation as a significant part of their fieldwork. Colleagues at the appropriate institution can provide useful contacts, information, and shoptalk. Anthropologists must also consider what they can give to the people and the nation hosting them. The least they can do is share their work with host colleagues. Once affiliation is granted, the appropriate visa must be obtained. This accomplished, the anthropologist is ready to leave for the field.

Living conditions in the field depend both on the nature of the host society and the kind of research being undertaken. Participant-observation requires living as closely as possible to the people whose culture you are studying. Cultural anthropologists or biological anthropologists who work among remote peoples in rain forests, deserts, or tundra may need to bring along their own living quarters; the same is true for archaeologists and paleontologists whose most promising excavation sites are remote from contemporary settlements. Research funding is not designed to support luxurious living, but many anthropologists are surprised to discover how many amenities they can happily live without.

Here, as elsewhere in anthropology, there is room for personal variation. Some anthropologists are entirely comfortable living with nomadic herders, carrying all their possessions in a backpack. Others cannot get on with their work without a bed, electricity, plumbing, and a means of shutting out the unfamiliar world from time to time. Ethnographic fieldwork is a way of learning about another culture, and camping out is not always helpful or even necessary, particularly because much fieldwork is carried out today in urban settings.

In any case, living conditions in the field can themselves provide major insights into the culture under study. This is powerfully illustrated by the experiences of Charles and Bettylou Valentine, whose field site was a poor neighborhood they called *Blackston,* located in a large city in the northern United States. (See EthnoProfile 3.2: Blackston.) The Valentines lived for the last field year on one-quarter of their regular income; during the final six months, they matched their income to that of welfare families: "For five years we inhabited the same decrepit rat- and roach-infested buildings as everyone else, lived on the same poor quality food at inflated prices, trusted our health and our son's schooling to the same inferior institutions, suffered the same brutality and intimidation from the police, and like others made the best of it by some combination of endurance, escapism, and fighting back. Like the dwellings of our neighbors, our home went up in flames several times, including one disaster caused by the carelessness or ill will of the city's 'firefighters.' For several cold months we lived and worked in one room without heat other than what a cooking stove could provide, without hot water or windows, and with only one light bulb" (C. Valentine 1978, 5).

---

fieldwork An extended period of close involvement with the people in whose language or way of life anthropologists are interested, during which anthropologists ordinarily collect most of their data.

culture shock The feeling, akin to panic, that develops in people living in an unfamiliar society when they cannot understand what is happening around them.

participant-observation The method anthropologists use to gather information by living as closely as possible to the people whose culture they are studying while participating in their lives as much as possible.

EthnoProfile 3.2 • **BLACKSTON**

REGION: North America

NATION: United States

POPULATION: 100,000

ENVIRONMENT: Urban ghetto

LIVELIHOOD: Low-paying full-time and temporary jobs, welfare

POLITICAL ORGANIZATION: Lowest level in a modern nation-state

FOR MORE INFORMATION: Valentine, Bettylou. 1978. *Hustling and other hard work.* New York: Free Press.

Not all field sites offer such a stark contrast to the middle-class backgrounds of many fieldworkers, and indeed some can be almost luxurious. But physical and mental dislocation and stress can be expected anywhere. People from temperate climates who find themselves in the tropics have to adjust to the heat; workers in the Arctic have to adjust to the cold. In hot climates especially, many anthropologists encounter plants, animals, insects and diseases (such as malaria) with which they have had no previous experience. In any climate, fieldworkers need to adjust to local water and food.

In addition, there are the cultural differences—which is why they came. Yet the immensity of what they will encounter is difficult for them to anticipate. Initially, just getting through the day—finding a place to stay and food to eat—may seem an enormous accomplishment; but there are also supposed to be data to gather, research to do!

Early in their stay, it is not uncommon for fieldworkers to feel that the adjustments are too great. With time, however, they discover that the great process of human survival begins to assert itself: they begin to adapt. The rhythms of daily activity become familiar. Their use of the local language improves. Faces of the local inhabitants become the faces of neighbors. And incredibly, the time comes when they are able to turn their attention to the research questions that brought them there.

SCIENTIFIC FIELDWORK?

When anthropology began to take on its own identity as an intellectual discipline during the nineteenth century, it aspired to be "scientific." Anthropology still aims to be scientific in its study of human nature, human society, and human history. However, twentieth-century scientists and philosophers have grown increasingly aware that the traditional "scientific method," based on the success of the physical sciences, is only one way of doing science. Consequently, many scholars of physics, chemistry, biology, as well as the social sciences, have begun to question the assumptions on which that traditional scientific method is based. Likewise, attempts to do anthropology based on the traditional methods of physical science have also been questioned.

The Positivist Approach

The traditional method of physical science, which early social scientists tried to imitate, is now often called *positivistic science*. Its proponents based their view of science on a set of principles most fully set out in the writings of a group of influential thinkers known as positivists, who were active in the late nineteenth and early twentieth centuries. Today, **positivism** is a label for a particular way of looking at the world and a particular set of proposals for studying the world scientifically.

First of all, positivists are materialists. They hold that reality can be known through the five senses (sight, smell, touch, hearing, and taste). Second, positivists separate facts from values. For them, facts relate to the nature of physical, material reality—what *is*—and values are speculation about what *ought to be*. To the positivist, scientific research into subatomic structure, genetic engineering, in vitro fertilization, or human sexual response is all part of a disinterested quest for knowledge, a quest that cannot be compromised because it offends some people's moral or political sensibilities. Truth remains the truth, whether people like it or not, whether it conforms to their idea of what is good and proper or not. These examples illustrate a third point of the positivist outlook: the belief that a single scientific method can be used to investigate any domain of reality, whether it be planetary motion or chemical reactions or human life. Their hope is that all scientific knowledge will ultimately be unified.

The traditional goal of the positivist program has been to produce **objective knowledge,** knowledge about reality that is true for all people in all times and places. Positivist science has been viewed as the route to that objective knowledge, providing theories that are true because they describe the way the world is, independent of its meaning for human groups. For the positivist, there is a single structure to reality, and science can lay it bare.

Applying Positivist Methods to Anthropology

What happens when positivist principles are used to guide scientific investigation in anthropology? It might seem that the positivist approach is particularly well suited to biological anthropology and archaeology, which focus on fossils, material bodies, and artifacts. Positivism seems to claim that material facts speak for themselves. However, most paleoanthropologists and archaeologists would deny this claim: the significance of any individual material "fact"—a bone, a potsherd—is far from clear unless it can be placed in some kind of interpretive context.

---

positivism The view that there is a reality "out there" that can be known through the senses and that there is a single, appropriate set of scientific methods for investigating that reality.

objective knowledge Knowledge about reality that is absolute and true.

These difficulties are only compounded in cultural anthropology. For the positivist, the prototypical research scenario involves a physical scientist in a laboratory. This prototype creates obstacles for those who study human life by means of participant-observation in a natural setting. Early cultural anthropologists were aware of these obstacles, and they tried to devise ways to get around them. Their first step was to approximate lab conditions by testing their hypotheses in a series of different cultural settings. These settings were carefully selected to exhibit naturally the same range of variation that a laboratory scientist could create artificially. As a result, the field could be seen as a "living laboratory." Each research setting would correspond to a separate experimental situation, a method called *controlled comparison*. Margaret Mead used this method in the 1930s, when she studied four different societies in an attempt to discover the range and causes of gender roles (Figure 3.2).

Positivistically inclined anthropologists were encouraged by the enormous successes that the physical sciences had attained by following these principles. They were convinced that a similar commitment on their part would help them unlock the secrets of human social life. In fact, a great deal was learned by fieldworkers committed to the positivistic view of science in anthropology. Research carried out from the middle of the nineteenth century through the middle of the twentieth century was clearly superior to much of the slipshod, impressionistic writing on other cultures that had preceded it. For decades, anthropologists following this research program traveled into the remote corners of the world. They recorded as accurately as they could the ways of life of peoples their contemporaries had neither heard of nor cared to know. Their research was systematic, accurate, and sometimes insensitive.

What does it mean to accuse scientists of insensitivity? Positivist scientists regard the behavior of human beings as no different from the behavior of rocks or molecules, which have no thoughts or feelings, no freedom or dignity. Anthropologists can be charged with being insensitive to the humanity of their research subjects when their positivistic reports treat such human beings as if they, too, lacked thoughts, feelings, dignity, and the freedom to choose. We must emphasize that anthropologists often developed close personal ties to the people whose lives they studied. Many anthropologists became their friends and advocates, defending their full humanity to outsiders and sometimes intervening on their behalf with the government. But in their books and articles, those same anthropologists felt compelled to write as though they had been invisible in the village, recording and analyzing data objectively, like machines, with no human connection to the "subjects."

Many positivists have responded to charges of insensitivity by asserting that human consciousness is simply an illusion. It is a concept invented to stand for material processes that are internal to human beings, a concept that nonscientists cannot understand. Rocks and molecules might have minds and consciousness and as a result thoughts and feelings, but their inner lives are not accessible to scientific measurement. Why should scientists assume that it is any easier to measure the inner life of human organisms? Yet the charge of insensitivity is troubling, for the subject matter of the social sciences differs in one major respect from that of all the physical sciences: it involves human beings who belong to the same species (and possibly to the same society) as the scientists themselves. Scientists experience their own inner consciousness, have their own thoughts and feelings, and are often more concerned than most people with their own freedom and dignity. If the subjects of their study are also human beings, how can they justify denying to those human subjects the same "inner life" they claim for themselves?

Generations of anthropologists have attempted scientific fieldwork in the spirit of positivism. But more recently, anthropologists have come to reexamine some of the assumptions that underlie positivistic fieldwork. For example, they question the notion that the knowledge gained through positivistic fieldwork is based on an objective sample of reality that automatically reveals its meaning to an unbiased observer. Positivists claim that our five senses put us into direct contact with reality. The human brain, however, cannot form a clear picture of the world if the sensory impressions it receives are complex or ambiguous. In such situations, we are forced to make the facts speak by relying on socially learned rules of thumb designed to resolve ambiguities. But rules of thumb, useful as they are, can be inaccurate and misleading. Contemporary cultural anthropologists are actively devising new ways of writing about their cross-cultural experiences that reject the pose of total objectivity and instead focus on the ways they and their informants use culture to construct their interpretations of the world and of each other.

Anthropologists are also more aware that even those who tried the hardest to do positivistic fieldwork often gained some of their deepest insights in ways not recognized by the positivist program. Is the shape of this toothless fossil jaw more apelike or more humanlike? Was that a wink or just an involuntary blink? Interpretations of ambiguous signals are inevitably influenced by assumptions about the way the world works. Thus, the particular assumptions of positivist science must have contributed to the creation of the knowledge that positivist fieldworkers offer as a result of their labors; different observers working from different assumptions would have produced different knowledge.

In the 1980s, for example, an intense debate erupted in anthropology over conflicting views regarding adolescence in Samoa. (See EthnoProfile 5.2: Samoa.) Research done in the 1920s by Margaret Mead, one of the founding mothers of cultural anthropology, was harshly criticized by the Australian anthropologist Derek Freeman. Mead had argued that adolescence in Samoa was much less stormy than it was in the United States, and hence it was not possible to argue that the emotional and physical tone of U.S.-style adolescence was universal and biologically based. Freeman argued that the data on Samoan adolescence he had collected and interpreted were the opposite: Samoan adolescence was stormy, even violent. Mead's data, according to Freeman, were flawed, and she had, as it were, gotten it all wrong, because she had gone to the field convinced that culture was more important than biology. Mead's supporters (she herself had been dead for a decade by the time Freeman made his claims) asserted that Freeman misinterpreted Mead's work, primarily because he went into the field convinced that biology was more important than culture but also because much of his information came from different informants living lives rather removed from those of the teenage girls who were Mead's informants decades earlier. This debate, remarkable for its viciousness, illustrates clearly how different assumptions lead not just to different conclusions but to entirely different assessments of "the facts" (see Holmes 1989).

By contrast, consider the fieldwork of Annette Weiner in the Trobriand Islands carried out in the 1970s, nearly sixty years after Bronislaw Malinowski did his original and celebrated fieldwork there. Like Mead and Freeman, Weiner and Malinowski were anthropologists of different nationalities and different sexes working in different villages with different informants during different historical periods. Weiner made an important contribution to our understanding of Trobriand life by describing and explaining activities involving Trobriand women's "wealth" that were absolutely central to the continued healthy functioning of Trobriand life but about which Malinowski had written nothing (see Chapter 13). Weiner might have published her findings by declaring that

EthnoProfile 3.3 • TROBRIAND ISLANDERS

REGION: Oceania

NATION: Papua New Guinea

POPULATION: 8,500 (1970s)

ENVIRONMENT: Tropical island

LIVELIHOOD: Yam growing

POLITICAL ORGANIZATION: Traditionally, chiefs and others of rank; today, part of a modern nation-state

FOR MORE INFORMATION: Weiner, Annette. 1988. *The Trobrianders of Papua New Guinea.* New York: Holt, Rinehart and Winston.

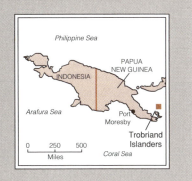

Malinowski had "got it wrong." But this route did not appeal to her, primarily because, as she puts it, he got so very much right. Malinowski's own preoccupations led him to write about aspects of Trobriand life different from those that interested Weiner. As a result, he left behind a portrait of Trobriand society that Weiner later felt obliged to correct. Nevertheless, Weiner found that much of Malinowski's work remained valid and insightful in her day. She quoted long passages from his ethnographies in her own writings about the Trobriands, in tribute to him (see Weiner 1988, 1976; see also EthnoProfile 3.3: Trobriand Islanders).

The discrepancies in the ethnographic reports of Mead and Freeman, or Weiner and Malinowski, seem to suggest at best that ethnographic knowledge is difficult to establish and at worst that all ethnographic knowledge is contaminated or distorted and thus not knowledge at all. But this pessimistic conclusion seems unwarranted. Clearly, much of what we call knowledge serves us well and is not based on total falsehood. But this is not the same as saying that all knowledge is therefore completely true, objectively true, for everyone everywhere and at all times. There are many ways of understanding the world; each way embodies some truth, but no one way is immune to correction. In other words, all knowledge is a product of the dialectic between observation and reflection. On the one hand, what we pay attention to is guided by the assumptions we make about the world, and no observation can be made without some set of assumptions that frame the observation. On the other hand, we are open creatures. We may detect (or someone else may point out to us) signals in the wider world that call into question our traditional assumptions.

Science was born centuries ago when some members of our society decided to pay systematic attention to material signals that tended to be downplayed or ignored by the dominant religious outlook. As scientists increased their experience with these previously unknown phenomena, they began to develop a new set of assumptions about the way the world works. The history of science in our own culture, particularly its struggle with religion, shows vividly that cultures offer alternatives. Both "science" and "religion" are equal parts of Western culture.

Thus, positivism encourages us to pay attention to certain kinds of material behavior. This emphasis has without question brought much truth to light. But only dialogue with alternative points of view can put positivistic truth in proper perspective. The dialogue may be internal to our own culture, but the potential for enrichment increases enormously when we enter into dialogue with members of another culture.

All this means that we must carefully reexamine exactly what anthropologists have been up to. A sound scientific study of human beings seems to require more than becoming involved, in human terms, with our informants. It also requires viewing this involvement not as a necessary evil but as central to our method. If the "objects" of anthropological investigation are actually "subjects" (that is, human beings like ourselves), then scientific accuracy demands that we treat these objects of study as if they really were human beings.

Field methods and knowledge are thus intimately connected. In cultural anthropology, a person studies other persons, subjects study other subjects. Is fieldwork just one person's subjective impressions of other people? No, because the fieldwork experience is a dialogue, not a solitary activity. Not only are anthropologists trying to figure out the locals, the locals are also trying to figure out the anthropologists.

For anthropologists in different specialities, fieldwork may not involve interaction with living human beings. Nevertheless, archaeologists always remember that the artifacts they uncover were made and used by living human beings; this is why they frequently employ ethnographic analogies when trying to interpret them. Still, the further back into the human past we go, the more problematic these analogies become. At some point, paleoanthropologists recognize that the fossils they are describing are so different from modern human beings that they seriously question whether more can be gained than lost by likening them to ourselves. This problem is even more acute for primatologists.

Despite its difficulties, fieldwork in a living society offers the fullest encounter possible between anthropologists and a group of human beings whose way of life interests them. It is not just the humanity of the informants that must not be overlooked; anthropologists must remember that they themselves are people. Understanding the way of life of another human society "requires interpretation, imagination, insight, perceptivity, human sympathy, humility, and a whole series of qualities—human qualities. It requires, fundamentally, that the student be himself or herself a human person" (Smith 1982, 68). For these reaons, we will pay particular attention in the remainder of this chapter to the unique requirements, and opportunities, offered by fieldwork in cultural anthropology.

To gather data about a culture, anthropologists are obliged to interact closely with the sources of that data: their **informants.** As a result, field data are not subjective but *intersubjective:* they are the product of long dialogues between researcher and informant (Figure 3.3). These dialogues are often patient and painstaking collaborative attempts to sort things out, to piece things together. When successful, the outcome is a new understanding of the world that both anthropologist and informant can share. Recognizing the humanity of one's informants in this way has nothing to do with trying, through sheer imagination, to reproduce the inner psychological states of those informants—which is what positivists have often accused their critics of trying to do. Such an imag-

FIGURE 3.3 *Advances in computer technology have simplified the recording of field data for anthropologists. Napoleon Chagnon uses a solar-powered computer to record creation myths of the Yanomamo of Brazil.*

inative effort, assuming it is possible, is solitary, whereas fieldwork is a dialogue. The focus of fieldwork is the range of **intersubjective meanings** that informants share. Fieldworkers can come to understand these meanings by sharing activities and conversations with their informants. This is what participant-observation is all about.

Reflexivity

The intersubjective meanings on which informants rely are public not private. Informants take them for granted, but they may not be obvious to an outsider. In order to make these meanings explicit, anthropologist and informant together must occasionally step back from the ordinary flow of daily life and examine them critically. They must think about the way members of the culture normally think about their lives. This

---

informants People in a particular culture who work with anthropologists and pro-vide them with insights about their way of life. Also called *teachers* or *friends*.

intersubjective meanings The shared, public symbolic systems of a culture.

"thinking about thinking" is known as **reflexivity;** thus, fieldwork in cultural anthropology is a reflexive experience. Both anthropologists and their informants have important reflexive roles to play in the fieldwork that generates anthropological knowledge. Anthropological theory has come to acknowledge this reflexivity, recognizing it as the least distorting path to knowledge about human social life. The best ethnographies have always been reflexive, whether they were done in 1935 or 1985 and whether or not the ethnographers realized this explicitly.

The commitment to reflexivity has had far-reaching implications for the ways anthropologists carry out their research. Fieldworkers do not merely participate and observe and let it go at that. They are scientifically obligated to make public the way in which they gather data. Some anthropologists have argued that they must also share their conclusions with their informants and even include their informants' reflections on those conclusions in their published ethnographies. Some have even coauthored their work with their informants. This may appear to be reflexivity with a vengeance: anthropologists thinking about how their informants think, thinking about the way they think about the way their informants think, asking their informants to think about the way a particular anthropologist thinks about the way anthropologists in general think about how their informants think. But this kind of mutual reflexivity is at the heart of anthropological knowledge.

Let us look at one anthropological attempt to maximize reflexivity in a published ethnography. Charles Valentine (1978, 7–8) notes that his wife, Bettylou Valentine, persuaded several of her informants to comment on her manuscript before publication. She visited them for lengthy discussions and found that, in general, they agreed with her conclusions. In the published volume, Valentine states her own conclusions, based on her own research and analysis. She also allows her informants a voice, permitting them, in a final chapter, to state where and why they disagree with her. Valentine's ethnography presents a vivid experience of the open-endedness of the dialogue between anthropologist and informant: no single interpretation of human experience is final.

THE DIALECTIC OF FIELDWORK: INTERPRETATION AND TRANSLATION

Fieldwork is a risky business. Fieldworkers not only risk offending their informants by misunderstanding their way of life, they also face the shock of the unfamiliar and their own vulnerability. Indeed, they must embrace this shock and cultivate this vulnerability if they are to achieve any kind of meaningful understanding of their informants' culture.

In the beginning, fieldworkers can be reassured by some of the insights that anthropological training has provided. Basic to these is the working assumption of *pan-human rationality*. Over a century of research in biological anthropology has demonstrated that all human beings are members of the same biological species. This means that with regard to such human potentialities as intelligence, we should expect to find the same range of variation in all human groups. We can therefore resist ethnocentric impulses by recalling "that if what we observe appears to be odd or irrational, it is probably because we do not understand it and not because it is a product of a 'savage' culture in which such nonsense is to be expected" (Greenwood and Stini 1977, 185).

In Their Own Words   THE SITUATION OF THE BRAZILIAN ANTHROPOLOGIST

Contemporary anthropologists come from many places other than Europe or the United States. Anthropologist Roberto da Matta explores what it means for him to be a Brazilian anthropologist working in Brazil.

In order to grasp deep motivations in ethnographic styles, one has to deal with how natives are represented as "others"—as different, as distinct—in divergent national contexts. In Brazil, the "other" is incarnated by a small native population, scattered in the empty Amazon and Central Brazil, a population generically called by the name, "Índio" (Indian). But the "Indian" is not alone, for with the cate-gory "Negro" they form the basis of a singular and intriguing view of the immediate human diversity for Brazilians. The "Negro" (who is fundamentally the ex-slave) is an intrinsic element of Brazilian social structure, haunting with his massive presence the "whiteness" of a bourgeois life-style. The "Indian" is an outsider, giving rise to the romantic fantasies of the noble savage who has to be either isolated and protected from the evils of civilization or be eliminated from the national landscape for incapacity to take part in modern progress.

In this context, to be with "Indians" is, for a Brazilian anthropologist, more than having the opportunity of living with another humanity. It is also to have the privilege of getting in touch with a mythical other. And by doing so, have the honor of being the one to overcome all manner of discomforts in order to describe a new way of life in the midst of Brazilian civilization. Thus, for Brazilian anthropologists, "to be there" is also an opportunity of being a *witness* to the way of life of a different society. This is particularly true when that way of life runs the risk of succumbing to a contact situation that is brutally unequal in political terms.

Source: da Matta 1994.

Interpreting Actions and Ideas

The problem becomes how to interpret our observations. But what exactly does **interpretation** involve? Jean Paul Dumont offers the following suggestion: "Interpretation . . . can refer to three rather different matters: an oral recitation, a reasonable explanation, and a translation from another language. . . . In all three cases, something foreign, strange, separated in time, space or experience is made familiar, present, comprehensible: something requiring representation, explanation or translation is somehow 'brought to understanding'—is interpreted" (1978, 4, quoting Palmer).

How does one go about interpreting the actions and ideas of other human beings? We need a form of interpretation that does not turn our informants into objects. That is, we need a form of interpretation based on reflexivity rather than objectivity. Paul Rabinow suggests that what we require has already been set forth in the philosophy of the French thinker Paul Ricoeur: "Following Ricoeur, I define the problem of hermeneutics (which is simply Greek for "interpretation") as 'the comprehension of self by the detour of the comprehension of the other.' It is vital to stress that this is not psychology of any sort. . . . The self being discussed is perfectly public. . . . [It is] the culturally

reflexivity Critically thinking about the way one thinks; reflecting on one's own experience.

interpretation The process of "bringing to understanding."

mediated and historically situated self which finds itself in a continuously changing world of meaning" (Rabinow 1977, 5–6).

For the anthropologist in the field, then, interpretation becomes a task of coming to comprehend the *cultural self* by the detour of comprehending of the *cultural other*. The self being discussed is public because it is intersubjectively constructed, using elements drawn from the cultural systems of anthropologist and informant alike. As we come to grasp the meaning of the other's cultural self, we simultaneously learn something of the meaning of our own cultural identity.

Learning to understand what makes other people tick may seem plausible among people from the same culture. After all, members of the same culture share at least some of the same intersubjective symbolic language and therefore have at least some foundation on which to build. But the anthropologist in the field and his or her informants cannot be assumed to share such a language. On what can they build their intersubjective understanding? The gulf between self and other may seem unbridgeable. Yet anthropologist and informant engaged in participant-observation do share something: the fieldwork situation itself.

Anthropologist and informant find themselves in physical proximity, observing and discussing the same material activities. At first, they may talk past one another, as each describes these activities from a different perspective using a different language. However, all cultures and languages are open enough to entertain a variety of viewpoints and a variety of ways to talk about them. Continued discussion allows anthropologist and informant to search for areas of intersection in possible ways of understanding and describing the same strip of behavior. Any intersection, however small, can form the foundation on which anthropologist and informant may then build a new intersubjective symbolic language. This process of building a bridge of understanding between self and other is what Rabinow refers to as "the dialectic of fieldwork" (1977, 39).

The Dialectical Process

Both fieldworker and informant begin with little or nothing in the way of shared experience that could allow them to "figure one another out" with any accuracy. But if they are motivated to make sense of one another and willing to work together, steps toward understanding and valid interpretation—toward recognition—can be made.

For example, traditional fieldwork often begins with collecting data on kinship relations in the host society. A trained anthropologist comes to the field with certain ideas about kinship in mind. These ideas derive in part from the anthropologist's own experience of kinship in his or her own culture. They are also based on ideas about kinship that the anthropologist has taken from professional research into the subject. As the fieldworker begins to ask kinship questions of informants, he or she may discover that the informants have no word in their language that accurately conveys the range of meaning carried by the anthropological term *kinship*. This does not mean that all is lost. At this point, successful fieldwork seems to involve entry into the dialectic process of interpretation and translation.

The dialectic process works something like this. The anthropologist poses a question about kinship using whatever term in the informants' language comes closest to it in meaning. The informants do their best to interpret the anthropologist's question in a way that makes sense to them. That is, each informant is required to exercise reflexivity, thinking about the way members of his or her society think about a certain domain of experience. Having formulated an answer, the informant responds to the anthropologist's question in terms he or she thinks the anthropologist will understand. Now it is the anthropologist's turn to interpret this response, to decide whether it carries the kind of information the anthropologist was looking for.

Translating

In the dialectic of fieldwork, both anthropologist and informant are active agents. Each party tries to figure out what the other is trying to say. If there is goodwill on the part of both, each party also tries to provide responses that make sense to the other. As more than one anthropologist has remarked (see, for example, Rabinow 1977; Crick 1976), anthropological fieldwork is **translation.** Moreover, the informant is just as actively engaged in translation as is the anthropologist. As time passes and the partners in this effort learn from their mistakes and successes, their ability to communicate increases. Each participant learns more about the other: the anthropologist gains skill at asking questions that make sense to the informant, and the informant becomes more skilled at answering those questions in terms that are relevant to the anthropologist. The validity of this ongoing translation is anchored in the ongoing cultural activities in which both anthropologist and informant are participant-observers.

The Dialectic between Self and Other

Out of this mutual translational activity comes knowledge about the informant's culture that is meaningful to both anthropologist and informant. This is new knowledge. And this is what dialectical holism is all about: the whole (knowledge about the culture) is more than the sum of its parts (the anthropologist's knowledge and the informant's knowledge). Knowledge of the culture arises out of the collaboration of anthropologist and informant, who create a world, usually thin and fragile, of common understandings and experiences.

It is possible to argue that all learning about another human being is the result of a dialogue between self and other. We have suggested that informants are equally involved in this dialogue and may end up learning as much or more about anthropologists as anthropologists learn about them. But it is important to emphasize that in field situations, the dialogue is initiated by anthropologists. Anthropologists come to the field with their own sets of questions, which are determined not by the field situation but by the

translation In anthropological fieldwork, the process of learning to describe one culture in terms that can be understood by members of another culture.

discipline of anthropology itself (see Karp and Kendall 1982, 254). Furthermore, when anthropologists are finished with a particular research project, they are free to break off the dialogue with informants and resume discussions with fellow professionals. The only link between these two sets of dialogues—between particular anthropologists and the people with whom they work, and among anthropologists in general—are the particular anthropologists themselves. Professional colleagues have relied on fieldworkers to speak for informants, traditionally assuming that informants would not speak for themselves. In recent years, members of indigenous societies have begun to speak powerfully on their own behalf, as political advocates for their people. However, language barriers still often prohibit informants from speaking to an audience of professional scholars on complex topics.

Fieldwork therefore involves differences of power and places a heavy burden of responsibility on researchers. Anthropologists feel strongly that their informants' identities should be protected. The need for protection is all the greater when informants belong to marginal and powerless groups that might suffer retaliation from more powerful members of their society. However, because some informants wish to express their identity and their ideas openly, anthropologists have experimented with forms of ethnographic writing in which they serve primarily as translators and editors of the voices and opinions of individual informants (see, for example, Keesing 1983; Shostak 1981). Increasingly, anthropologists working in their own societies write about their fieldwork both as observers of others and as members of the society they are observing (see, for example, Kumar 1992; Foley 1989).

COMMUNICATION IN FIELDWORK: CONSTRUCTING MEANING

Meaning in culture is never fully self-evident; rather it is constructed by those who use it and negotiated between them, sometimes with great difficulty. Nowhere is the problematic nature of human communication more obvious than in anthropological fieldwork. Finding informants and establishing rapport with them has always been seen as an indispensable first step, but there are no foolproof procedures that guarantee success. Nita Kumar is an anthropologist from Delhi, India, who chose to do research in a region of India very different from where she grew up. (See EthnoProfile 3.4: Banaras.) "Banaras was such a mystery to me when I arrived there in 1981 ironically *because* I was an Indian and expected to have a privileged insight into it. In fact, from Banaras I was *thrice* removed: through my education and upbringing, than which there is no greater molder of attitudes; by language and linguistic culture; and by region and regional culture" (1992, 15). Although her social connections smoothed the way for her in official circles, she had no special advantage when trying to make contact with the artisans in Banaras whose way of life interested her.

In her fieldwork memoir, *Friends, Brothers, and Informants,* Kumar shares the four failed attempts she made to contact weavers. The first time, the weavers she "discovered" turned out to have well-established ties to rickshaw pullers and taxi drivers who regularly brought tourists to visit their shop and buy souvenirs. Not wishing to become just another business contact, she left. Her second contact was with the Muslim owner of a weaving establishment nearby whose suspicions of her motives caused her to turn else-

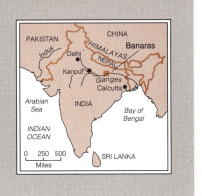

EthnoProfile 3.4 • **BANARAS**

REGION: Southern Asia

NATION: India

POPULATION: 1,000,000

ENVIRONMENT: Tropical monsoon region

LIVELIHOOD: Arts, weaving silk, handicrafts; pilgrimage center; urban occupations, education

POLITICAL ORGANIZATION: City in a modern nation-state

FOR MORE INFORMATION: Kumar, Nita. 1992. *Friends, brothers, and informants: Fieldwork memories of Banaras.* Berkeley: University of California Press.

where. Her third attempt was made through a sari salesman who took her to a market where silk weavers sold their wares. Unfortunately for her, he would periodically announce to all assembled who she was and invite weavers to come up and speak with her, a procedure she found deeply embarrassing.

Her fourth attempt followed her accidental discovery that two members of a team of three brothers and their uncle who were selling holiday firecrackers were also weavers. When she was invited to see one brother's loom, however, she grew "uncomfortable with all the obvious evidence of bachelor existence and their readiness to welcome me into it. . . . I just went away and never came back" (1992, 99). On her fifth attempt, she was introduced by a silk-yarn merchant to weavers living in a government-subsidized housing project next to his house. In the home of a weaver named Shaukatullah, surrounded by members of his family, she finally found a setting in which she felt welcome and able to do her work. "In a matter of weeks I was given the status of a daughter of Shaukatullah" (1992, 105).

Jean Briggs is an anthropologist who was also "adopted" by a family of informants. Briggs worked among the Utkuhikhalingmiut (Utku, for short), an Inuit (Eskimo) group in Alaska. (See EthnoProfile 3.5: Utkuhikhalingmiut [Utku Inuit].) She outlines the steps her informants took in their attempts to figure her out once she took on the role of "daughter" in the home of her new "father," Inuttiaq, and "mother," Allaq: "From the moment that the adoption was settled, I was 'Inuttiaq's daughter' in the camp. [They] drilled me in the use of kin terms appropriate to my position, just as they drilled [Inuttiaq's] three-year-old daughter, who was learning to speak" (Briggs 1980, 46). The context of their interactions had clearly changed as a result of the adoption, and Briggs's family had new expectations both of Briggs and of themselves: "Allaq, and especially Inuttiaq . . . more and more attempted to assimilate me into a proper adult parent-daughter relationship. I was expected to help with the household work . . . and I was expected to obey unquestioningly when Inuttiaq told me to do something. . . . Inevitably, conflicts, covert but pervasive, developed" (47).

EthnoProfile 3.5 • **UTKUHIKHALINGMIUT (UTKU INUIT)**

REGION: North America

NATION: Canada (Northwest Territories)

POPULATION: 35

ENVIRONMENT: Tundra

LIVELIHOOD: Nomadic fishing, hunting, gathering

POLITICAL ORGANIZATION: Communal

FOR MORE INFORMATION: Briggs, Jean. 1989. *Kapluna daughter: Adopted by the Eskimo.* In *Conformity and conflict: Readings in cultural anthropology,* 7th ed., edited by J. Spradley and D. McCurdy, Glenview, IL: Scott, Foresman & Co., 44–62.

Briggs began to sense that all was not as it should be, and she found herself taking on a reflexive stance. She began to realize that part of the problem had to do with differences between her ideas of how parents ought to relate to their daughters and Utku beliefs on these matters. She also experienced contradictions between her roles as "daughter" and "anthropologist." The dialectic of fieldwork brought sharply to awareness—aided in the construction of—her understanding of the meaning of "daughter" and "anthropologist" in her own culture. Perhaps only in a context like that of fieldwork would any of us be forced by the necessities of everyday life to spell out for ourselves exactly what our own cultural background consists of.

Briggs was not the only person who had to be reflexive. Her Utku informants were forced to reconsider how they had been dealing with her since her arrival. As she was able to reconstruct it, their understanding of her went through three stages. At first, her informants thought she was strange, anomalous. After her adoption, they saw her as educable. But when the communication breakdown occurred, they concluded that she was "uneducable in important ways . . . a defective person" (1980, 60–61). Either her informants could find no further way of making clear what was expected of her, or else it became obvious to them that she was unwilling to do what she knew they expected of her. Either conclusion on their part might have meant the end of Briggs's fieldwork were it not for the timely intervention of a third party. An Utku woman, who knew both Briggs and her adoptive family, was able to explain to Briggs's informants the aspects of her behavior that had been most distressing.

THE EFFECT OF FIELDWORK ON INFORMANTS

Because informants play active roles in the fieldwork enterprise, it is appropriate to discuss the role of informant in more detail. Many fieldworkers have long considered "informant" to be a term of respect for those who agree to try to explain their way of life to an anthropologist. Unfortunately, the term has taken on a sinister connotation in recent years as law enforcement professionals have used it to describe those who betray their partners in crime. Consequently, some anthropologists have searched for a new term—"teacher" or "friend," for example—that might be free of taint, although no alternatives have yet gained widespread acceptance. Regarding the term "informant," Rabinow observes: "The present somewhat nasty connotations of the world do apply at times, but so does its older root sense 'to give form to, to be the formative principle of, to animate.' . . . The informant gives external form to his own experiences, by presenting them to meet the anthropologist's questions, to the extent that he can interpret them" (1977, 153).

Strictly speaking, any member of a culture with whom an anthropologist speaks or interacts can be considered an informant. But most fieldworkers soon discover that some informants seem more interested in the anthropologist's work and are better able to understand what he or she is trying to accomplish than do others. According to Rabinow, these "key informants" have "the ability to explain even the simplest and [to them] most obvious things in a variety of ways." The best informants not only are patient and intelligent, but also have "an imaginative ability to objectify [their] own culture for a foreigner, so as to present it in a number of ways" (1977, 95).

Informants tend to be somewhat marginal to their own communities. They are likely to be as curious about the anthropologist's way of life as he or she is about their way of life. This is the unsettling part of informant-anthropologist interactions: the feeling that one's informants are shrewder than oneself, more aware, and in greater control of what is going on. But again, it is only ethnocentrism that prevents us from expecting this. After all, our informants are human beings, and, as Malcolm Crick reminds us, "to be a person requires the exercise of considerable anthropological skills. It requires self-understanding, communicative ability, and other-understanding. Thus it is that in all the social sciences those being investigated possess exactly the same powers as those doing the investigating" (1976, 104).

Fieldwork changes both the anthropologist and the informants. What kinds of effects can the fieldwork experience have on informants? Anthropologists have not always been able to report on this. In some cases, the effects of fieldwork on informants cannot be assessed until long after the anthropologist has returned home. In other cases, it becomes clear in the course of fieldwork that the anthropologist's presence and questions have made the informants aware of their own cultural selves in new ways that are both surprising and uncomfortable.

As he reflected on his own fieldwork in Morocco, Rabinow recalled some cases in which his informants' new reflexivity led to unanticipated consequences. One key informant, Malik, agreed to help Rabinow compile a list of landholdings and other possessions of the villagers of Sidi Lahcen Lyussi. (See EthnoProfile 3.6: Sidi Lahcen Lyussi.) As a first step in tracing the economic status of the middle stratum in society, Rabinow suggested that Malik list his own possessions. Malik appeared to be neither rich nor poor; in fact, he considered himself "not well off." "As we began to make a detailed list of his possessions, he became touchy and defensive. . . . It was clear that he was not as impoverished as he had portrayed himself. . . . This was confusing and troubling for him. . . . Malik began to see that there was a disparity between his self-image and my classification system. The emergence of this 'hard' data before his eyes and through his own efforts was highly disconcerting for him" (1977, 117–18).

EthnoProfile 3.6   •   **SIDI LAHCEN LYUSSI**

REGION: Northern Africa

NATION: Morocco

POPULATION: 900

ENVIRONMENT: Mountainous terrain

LIVELIHOOD: Farming, some livestock raising

POLITICAL ORGANIZATION: Village in a modern nation-state

FOR MORE INFORMATION: Rabinow, Paul. 1977. *Reflections on fieldwork in Morocco.* Berkeley: University of California Press.

Malik's easy understanding of himself and his world had been disrupted, and he could not ignore the disruption. He would either have to change his self-image or find some way to assimilate this new information about himself into the old self-image. In the end Malik managed to reaffirm his conclusion that he was not well-off by arguing that wealth lay not in material possessions alone. Although he might be rich in material goods, his son's health was bad, his own father was dead, he was responsible for his mother and unmarried brothers, and he had to be constantly vigilant in order to prevent his uncle from stealing his land. He was indeed not well-to-do, as he had always known, but his experiences with Rabinow had forced him to define his situation in a new way in order to maintain his old self-image (Rabinow 1977, 117–19).

Bettylou Valentine was determined from the outset to acknowledge the point of view of her informants in Blackston. Yet before the publication of her ethnography, she discovered that some informants were not pleased with what she had said about them. One woman read in the manuscript about her own illegal attempts to combine work and welfare to better her family's standard of living. Angry, she denied to Valentine that she had ever done such a thing. Valentine talked to her informant at some length about this matter, which was well documented in field notes. It gradually became clear that the woman was concerned that if the data about her illegal activities were published, her friends and neighbors on the block would learn about it. In particular, she was afraid that the book would be sold on corner newsstands. Once Valentine explained how unlikely this was, her informant relaxed considerably: "The exchange made clear how different interests affect one's view. From my point of view, corner newsstand distribution would be excellent because it would mean the possibility of reaching the audience I feel needs to read and ponder the implications of the book. Yet Bernice and Velma [the informant and her friend] specified that they wouldn't mind where else it was distributed, even in Blackston more generally, if it could be kept from people on Paul Street and the surrounding blocks" (B. Valentine 1978, 122).

THE EFFECT OF FIELDWORK ON THE RESEARCHER

What does it feel like to be in the field, trying to figure out the workings of an unfamiliar way of life? What are the consequences of this experience for the fieldworker? Graduate students in anthropology who have not yet been in the field often develop an idealized image of field experience: At first, the fieldworker is a bit disoriented, and his or her potential informants are suspicious. But uncertainty soon gives way to understanding and trust as the anthropologist's good intentions are made known and accepted. The fieldworker succeeds in establishing rapport. In fact, the fieldworker becomes so well loved and trusted, so thoroughly accepted by the locals, that he or she is adopted into their family, treated as one of them, and allowed access to the tribal secrets. Presumably, all this happens as a result of the personal attributes of the fieldworker. If you have what it takes, you will be taken in and treated like one of the family. If this doesn't happen, you are obviously cut out for some other kind of work.

But much more than the anthropologist's personality is responsible for successful fieldwork. Establishing rapport with the people being studied is an achievement of anthropologist and informants together. Acceptance is problematic, rather than ensured, even for the most gifted fieldworkers. After all, fieldworkers are usually outsiders with no personal ties to the community in which they will do their research. It is therefore not just naive to think that the locals will accept you as one of them without any difficulty, it is also bad science (Karp and Kendall 1982).

It is remarkable that anthropologists can still be seduced by such an idealized image in that they are trained by experienced fieldworkers and should know better. Rabinow recalled the relationship he formed with his first Moroccan informant, a man called Ibrahim, whom he hired to teach him Arabic. Rabinow and Ibrahim seemed to get along well together, and, because of the language lessons, they saw each other a great deal, leading Rabinow to think of Ibrahim as a friend. When Rabinow planned a trip to another city, Ibrahim offered to go along as a guide and stay with relatives. This only confirmed Ibrahim's friendliness in Rabinow's eyes.

But things changed once they arrived at their destination. Ibrahim told Rabinow that the relatives with whom he was to stay did not exist, that he had no money, and that he expected Rabinow to pay for his hotel room. When Rabinow was unable to pay for Ibrahim's room, Ibrahim pulled out his wallet and paid for it himself. Rabinow was shocked and hurt by this experience, and his relationship with Ibrahim was forever altered. Rabinow remarks: "Basically I had been conceiving of him as a friend because of the seeming personal relationship we had established. But Ibrahim, a lot less confusedly, had basically conceptualized me as a resource. He was not unjustly situating me with the other Europeans with whom he had dealings" (1977, 29).

Rabinow's experience illustrates what he calls the "shock of otherness." Fieldwork institutionalizes this shock. Having to anticipate culture shock at any and every turn, anthropologists sometimes find that fieldwork takes on a tone that is anything but pleasant and sunny. For many anthropologists, the mood that characterizes fieldwork, at least in its early stages, is one of anxiety—the anxiety of an isolated individual with nothing familiar to turn to, no common sense on which to rely, and no relationships that can be taken for granted. There is a reason anthropologists have reported holing up for weeks at a time reading paperback novels and eating peanut-butter sandwiches. I (Emily Schultz) recall how difficult it was every morning to leave my compound in Guider, Cameroon. Despite the accomplishments of the previous day, I was always convinced that no one would want to talk to me *today*. (See EthnoProfile 8.1: Guider.)

Seeing one's informants as fully human requires anthropologists to allow their own humanity to express itself. But expressing their humanity is exceedingly difficult, for most anthropologists do not wish to offend their informants. The situation is complicated, particularly at the beginning, by the fieldworker's imperfect awareness of the sorts of behavior that are likely to offend informants or even what constitutes an offense in their culture. As a result, the first rule of thumb for fieldworkers has long been, "The informant is always right." Many fieldworkers therefore forbid themselves to express anger or disgust or disagreement. But this behavior is likely to cause problems for both them and their informants. After all, what sort of human being is always smiling, never angry, without opinions? Anthropologists who refuse to challenge or be challenged by their informants dehumanize both themselves and their informants. Clearly, it takes a good deal of diplomatic skill to walk a fine line between ethnocentrism and depersonalization. Sometimes this may not be possible, and the fieldwork itself may be put in jeopardy.

Rabinow came face to face with the consequences of the fieldworkers' motto in his relations with his informant Ali, who had agreed to take Rabinow to a wedding at some distance from town; they were to go in Rabinow's car. Unfortunately, Rabinow was ill the day of the wedding. He did not want to break his promise to attend and thus risk offending Ali and ruining any future chances to attend weddings, but he felt terrible. Ali agreed to stay only a short time at the wedding and then leave.

Once they arrived, however, Ali would disappear for long stretches, returning to announce that they would definitely be leaving soon, only to wander off again and leave Rabinow to his own devices. Rabinow found himself feeling worse, trying to smile at members of the wedding party, and growing angrier and angrier with Ali. At last, many hours after their arrival, Rabinow managed to get Ali into the car and they headed for home.

Things did not improve. Rabinow was certain that his annoyance must be obvious to Ali as they drove along, yet Ali kept asking him if he was happy, which was the sign of a pleased guest and a good host. When Rabinow steadfastly refused to answer him, Ali then declared that if Rabinow was unhappy, he, Ali, was insulted and would get out of the car and walk back to town. Rabinow had had enough. He stopped the car to let his companion out and then drove on without him.

Rabinow was sure he had sabotaged his fieldwork completely. In retrospect, he acknowledges that this event led him to question seriously whether or not the informant is always right. He says, "If the informant was always right, then by implication the anthropologist had to become a sort of non-person. . . . He had to be willing to enter into any situation as a smiling observer. . . . One had to completely subordinate one's own code of ethics, conduct, and world view, to 'suspend disbelief' . . . and sympathetically and accurately record events" (1977, 46). The quarrel with Ali forced him to shuck the anthropologist's all-accepting persona and allow the full force of his personality through. Rabinow chose to be true to himself on this occasion, regardless of the consequences for his fieldwork.

In Their Own Words **THE RELATIONSHIP BETWEEN ANTHROPOLOGISTS AND INFORMANTS**

Many anthropologists have developed warm, lasting relationships with their informants. However, as Allyn Stearman points out, the nature of the anthropologist-informant relationship is not always unproblematic.

While doing fieldwork among the Ik (pronounced "eek") of Uganda, Africa, anthropologist Colin Turnbull challenged the old anthropological myth that the researcher will like and admire the people he or she is studying. A corollary of this assumption is that to the uninformed outsider who does not "understand" the culture, a group may seem hostile, unresponsive, or stoic, or may have any number of less admirable characteristics; but to the trained observer who truly knows "his or her" people, these attributes are only a façade presented to outsiders. What Turnbull finally had to concede, however, was that overall the Ik were not a very likable people. His portrait of the Ik as selfish, uncaring, and uninterested even in the survival of their own children is understandable when he describes their history of displacement, social disruption, and the constant threat of starvation. Nonetheless,

an intellectual understanding of the factors contributing to Ik personality and behavior did not make it any easier for Turnbull to deal emotionally with the day-to-day interactions of fieldwork.

For me, knowing of Turnbull's situation alleviated some of my own anxieties in dealing with the Yuquí. As was Turnbull's, my previous field experiences among other peoples had been very positive. In the anthropologist's terms, this meant that I was accepted quite rapidly as a friend and that my informants were open and cooperative. The Yuquí did not fit any of these patterns. But like Turnbull, I understood something of the Yuquí past and thus on an intellectual level could comprehend that since they were a hunted, beleaguered people being threatened with extinction I could not expect them to be warm, friendly, and welcoming. Still, on an emotional level it was very difficult to cope with my frequent feelings of anger and resentment at having to put up with their teasing, taunting, and testing on an almost daily basis. My only consolation was that while I was often the brunt of this activity, so were they themselves. I am uncertain whether I finally

came to understand the Yuquí, or simply became hardened to their particular way of dealing with the world. By doing favors for people, I incurred their indebtedness, and these debts could be translated into favors owed. How I chose to collect was up to me. As favors mounted, I found that relationships with individual Yuquí were better. Then came the challenges. Could I be easily duped or taken advantage of? At first, I extended kindnesses gratuitously and was mocked. I learned to show my anger and stubbornness, to demand something in return for a tool lent or a service provided. Rather than alienate the Yuquí, this behavior (which I found difficult and distasteful throughout my stay) conferred prestige. The more I provided and then demanded in return, the more the Yuquí were willing to accept me. In the Yuquí world, as in any other, respect must be earned. But unlike many other peoples, for the Yuquí, kindness alone is not enough. In the end it is strength that is valued and that earns respect.

Source: Stearman 1989.

The results could have been disastrous, but Rabinow was lucky. This rupture of communication with Ali was the prelude to Rabinow's experiencing one of his most significant insights into Moroccan culture. After his anger had cooled, he attempted to make up with Ali. To his great surprise, after only a few hours of warm apologies, his relationship with Ali was not only restored but even closer than before! How was this possible? Rabinow had unwittingly behaved toward Ali in the only manner that would impress him, in Moroccan terms. Rabinow learned that Moroccan men test each other all the time to see how far they can assert dominance before their assertions are challenged. In this world, anyone who is all-accepting, such as an anthropologist, is not respected or admired but viewed as weak. "There was a fortuitous congruence between my breaking point and Moroccan cultural style. Perhaps in another situation my behavior might have proved irreparable. . . . By standing up to Ali I had communicated to him" (1977, 49).

Jean Briggs's experience among the Utku illustrates how the same behavior in different cultural circumstances can be interpreted differently. Briggs seemed to be receiving from her informants the message that anger was dangerous and must never be shown. She also became aware of the various ways her informants diverted or diffused angry feelings. Nevertheless, she remained ignorant of the full power of this value in Utku interpretations of behavior until she found herself in the position of having violated it seriously.

Beginning a few years before her fieldwork, Briggs relates, sportsmen from the United States and Canada had begun to charter planes to fly into the inlet where her informants lived during July and August. Once there, these sportsmen borrowed canoes belonging to the Utku. Although there had at one time been several usable canoes in the community, only two remained during the summer she was there. Some sportsmen borrowed one canoe, but ran it onto a rock. They then asked the Utkus if they could borrow the one remaining canoe, which happened to belong to Briggs's "father," Inuttiaq.

Briggs translated the request to Inuttiaq. She was annoyed that the sportsmen's carelessness had led to the ruin of one of the last two good canoes. Because canoes are used for practical subsistence activities and are not pleasure craft, the loss of one canoe spelled serious economic consequences for her informants. So when the outsiders asked to use the last canoe afloat, Briggs says, "I exploded." She lectured the sportsmen about their carelessness and insensitivity, explaining how important canoes were to the Utku. Then, remembering Inuttiaq's often-repeated admonition never to lend his canoe, she told the sportsmen that the owner of the one remaining canoe did not want to lend it. You may imagine her shock and surprise, then, when Inuttiaq insisted that the canoe be lent.

But this was only the beginning. Briggs discovered that, following her outburst, her informants seemed to turn against her rather than against the sportsmen. "I had spoken unbidden and in anger. . . . Punishment was a subtle form of ostracism. . . . I was isolated. It was as though I were not there. . . . But . . . I was still treated with the most impeccable semblance of solicitude" (1980, 56–57).

Unlike Rabinow, Briggs discovered just how much at odds her breaking point was with Utku cultural style. This breach might well have ended her fieldwork if a Westernized Utku friend, Ikayuqtuq, had not by chance come to her rescue. "I had written my version of the story to Ikayuqtuq, had told her about my attempt to protect the Utku from the impositions of the kaplunas [white men] and asked her if she could help to explain my behavior to the Eskimos" (1980, 58). Ikayuqtuq did write to Allaq and Inuttiaq, although the letter did not arrive until three months later. During that time, Briggs seemed to be frozen out of Utku society.

Once the letter arrived, everything changed. Briggs's friend had found a way to translate the intentions behind her behavior into terms that Allaq and Inuttiaq could understand. As Briggs recalls, "the effect was magical." Inuttiaq began to tell the others what a dangerous task Briggs had taken on to defend the Utkus against the white men.

The ice melted. And Briggs knew that things had truly been restored (and perhaps deepened) when Inuttiaq called her "daughter" once again.

Ruptures of communication between anthropologists and their informants can ultimately lead to a deepening of insight and a broadening of intersubjective understanding. This is what all fieldworkers hope for—and dread, because negotiating the rupture can be dangerous and no happy outcome is ensured. The risks may seem greater when the informants' culture is very different from the anthropologist's, and consequently, it might seem that the resulting insights must also be more startling. Yet Bettylou Valentine discovered that fieldwork in the United States, among African Americans like herself, also held surprises: "At the start of fieldwork I assumed at a subconscious level that my college education . . . would enable me, unlike many ghetto residents, to handle successfully any problem resulting from the impact of the larger society on my family, myself, or any less-skilled ghetto resident I chose to help. This assumption was proved totally wrong many, many times" (1978, 132).

THE HUMANIZING EFFECT OF FIELDWORK

Anthropological knowledge is the fruit of reflexivity produced by the mutual attempts of anthropologist and informant to understand one another. As a result, anthropological knowledge ought to be able to provide answers to questions about human nature, human society, and human history. Somehow, good ethnography should not only be able to persuade its readers, on intellectual grounds, that the ethnographer's informants were human beings. It should also allow readers to experience the informants' humanity.

Charles Valentine explicitly states this as the ultimate aim of his wife's ethnography about life in Blackston: "This book . . . reports how those who are both Black and poor persist in being human despite inhumane conditions" (1978, 2). One important element in retaining their humanity was institutionalized celebrating. By middle-class standards, Blackstonians had little money to spend. Bettylou Valentine was initially surprised at how much of their cash was used on food, drink, and such items as stereos, all used in entertaining friends and relatives: "Some people might characterize such lavish entertainment in the face of limited resources as improvident and likely to keep people from saving enough to escape from the slum. Yet the amounts of money spent could not really make a difference in the basic circumstances of inadequate housing, racial discrimination, limited job opportunities, poor city services, and all the other things that Blackstonians escape from, at least temporarily, through dancing and partying. The social life of Blackston, willingness to share, free and easy access to whatever liquor and food there was among friends, neighbors, and kin are the features that those who moved away commented on most often and said they missed" (B. Valentine 1978, 122).

The "practical ethic"—bourgeois or marxian—that many Western ethnographers bring with them into the field often leads to frustration. Researchers are discouraged by the sight of their informants' "wasting" resources that ought to be invested either in individual self-betterment (the bourgeois option) or in the collective overthrow of the oppressing classes (the marxian option). In either case, there seems to be the unspoken judgment that people who are poor, powerless, and rational ought to have more self-control. They should live frugally, devoting what energy and resources they do have either to prudently accumulating capital or to furthering the revolution. This judgment would seem to deny the poor and powerless the right to celebrate, the right to escape from their lot. It seems to be based on the questionable premise that, "rationally" and "objectively" speaking, the poor and powerless have nothing to celebrate and no right to attempt, irresponsibly, to escape from their condition. The poor and powerless who do celebrate or escape thus run the risk of being considered irrational, or unworthy of sympathy or support.

Judgments such as these, conscious or unconscious, reveal the gulf that separates the observer from the observed. The gulf is only widened by language referring to "them" and "us," particularly when such terms reveal no reflexive awareness. Perhaps the most powerful lesson fieldwork teaches is the realization, in the mind and in the gut, that "there is no primitive. There are other [people] living other lives" (Rabinow 1977, 151).

Fieldworkers find themselves in a privileged position, enjoying as they do the opportunity to experience "the other" as human beings. This experience comes neither easily nor automatically. It must be cultivated, and it requires cooperation and effort between one's informants and oneself. Those who have achieved a measure of cross-cultural understanding find themselves—or should find themselves—less willing to talk about "us" and "them." Indeed, the appropriate language should be "not 'they,' not 'we,' not 'you,' but 'some of us' are thus and so" (Smith 1982, 70).

COMING UP WITH THE FACTS OF ANTHROPOLOGY

If anthropological knowledge is the intersubjective creation of fieldworker and informant together, so too are the facts that anthropologists collect. The **facts** of anthropology are not ready-made, existing out there in the real world only waiting for someone to come along and pick them up. The facts of anthropology are created and recreated (1) in the field, (2) when the fieldworker, back home, reexamines field notes and is transported back into the field experience, and (3) when the fieldworker discusses his or her experiences with other anthropologists.

Facts do not speak for themselves. They "speak" only when they are interpreted and placed in a context of meaning that makes them intelligible. What constitutes a cultural fact is ambiguous. Anthropologists and informants can disagree; anthropologists can disagree among themselves; informants can disagree among themselves. The facts of anthropology exist neither in the culture of the anthropologist nor in the culture of the informant. "Anthropological facts are cross-cultural, because they are made across cultural boundaries" (Rabinow 1977, 152).

ANTHROPOLOGICAL KNOWLEDGE AS OPEN-ENDED

The idea that anthropological knowledge is open-ended is disconcerting. We have suggested that there is no such thing as purely objective knowledge and that when human beings are both the subject and object of study, we must speak in terms of reflexivity rather than objectivity. The cultivation of reflexivity allows us to produce less-distorted

In Their Own Words   THE SKILLS OF THE ANTHROPOLOGIST

Anthropologists cannot avoid taking their own cultural and theoretical frameworks into the field. However, as Stephen Gudeman observes, fieldwork draws their attention in unanticipated directions, making them aware of new phenomena that constantly challenge those frameworks.

According to the accepted wisdom, poets should be especially facile with language and stretch our vision with freshly cut images. Historians, with their knowledge of past events, offer a wise and sweeping view of human change and continuities. Physical scientists, who have analytical yet creative minds, bring us discoveries and insights about the natural world.

What about anthropologists? Have we any finely honed talents and gifts for the world?

Because anthropology is the study of human life, the anthropologist needs to know a little something about everything—from psychology to legal history to ecology. Our field equipment is primitive, for we rely mainly on the eye, the ear, and the tongue. Because ethnographers carry few tools to the field and the tools they have can hardly capture the totality of the situation, the background and talents of the researcher strongly determine what is "seen" and how it is understood. But the field experience itself has a special impact, too. I studied economic practices in Panama because I was trained to do so, but the field research forced me to alter all the notions I had been taught. Most of them were useless! Anthropologists try to open themselves up to every facet of their field situation and to allow its richness to envelop them. In this, the tasks of the anthropologist are very unlike those of the normal laboratory scientist: the anthropologist can have no predefined hypothesis and testing procedures. The best equipment an ethnographer can possess is a "good ear" and patience to let the "data talk."

This is not all. In the field, anthropologists carry out intense and internal conversations with themselves. Every observation, whether clearly seen or dimly realized, must be brought to consciousness, shuffled about, and questioned. Only by recognizing and acknowledging their own incomprehension can anthropologists generate new questions and lines of inquiry. In the solitude of the field, the anthropologist must try to understand the limits of her or his knowledge, have the courage to live with uncertainty, and retain the ambition to seize on openings to insight.

But field studies constitute only a part of the total research process. Once home, the field notes have to be read and reread, put aside, and then rearranged. The anthropologist is a pattern seeker, believing that within the data human designs are to be found. The task is like solving a puzzle, except that there is no fixed solution and the puzzle's pieces keep changing their shapes! With work and insight, however, a picture—an understanding or an explanation—begins to emerge.

Eventually, the results of all these efforts are conveyed to others, and so anthropologists also need to have expository skills and persuasive powers, for they have to convince others of their picture and their viewpoint about how cultures and social lives are put together.

Source: Gudeman 1990.

views of human nature and the human condition, and yet we remain human beings interpreting the lives of other human beings. We can never escape from our humanity to some point of view that would allow us to see human existence and human experience from the outside. Instead, we must rely on our common humanity and our interpretive powers to show us the parts of our nature that can be made visible.

facts In anthropology, facts are created and recreated (1) in the field, (2) when the fieldworker, back home, reexamines field notes and is transported back into the field experience, and (3) when the fieldworker discusses his or her experiences with other anthropologists.

If there truly is "no primitive," no subsection of humanity that is radically different in nature or in capacity from the anthropologists who study it, then the ethnographic record of anthropological knowledge is perhaps best understood as a vast commentary on human possibility. As with all commentaries, it depends on an original "text"—in this case, human experience. But that experience is ambiguous, speaking with many voices, capable of supporting more than one interpretation. Growth of anthropological knowledge is no different, then, from the growth of human self-understanding in general. It ought to contribute to the domain of human wisdom that concerns who we are as a species, where we have come from, and where we may be going.

Like all commentaries, the ethnographic record is and must be unfinished: human beings are open systems; human history continues; and problems and their possible solutions change. There is no one, true version of human life. For anthropologists and for others, the true version of human life, from the narrowest to the broadest senses, consists of all versions of human life.

This is a sobering possibility. It makes it appear that "the anthropologist is condemned to a greater or lesser degree of failure" in even trying to understand another culture (Basham 1978, 299). Informants would equally be condemned to never know fully even their own way of life. And the scientific attitude, cultivated in the Western world, resists any admission that, ultimately, the exhaustive understanding of anything is impossible. But total pessimism does not seem warranted. We may never know everything, but it does not follow that we can learn nothing from our efforts. "Two of the fundamental qualities of humanity are the capacity to understand one another and the capacity to be understood. Not fully certainly. Yet not negligibly, certainly. . . . There is no person on earth that I can fully understand. There is and has been no person on earth that I cannot understand at all" (Smith 1982, 68–69).

Moreover, as our contact with the other is prolonged and as our efforts to communicate are rewarded by the construction of intersubjective understanding, we can always learn more. Human beings are open organisms, and we have a vast ability to learn new things. This is significant, for even if we can never know everything, it does not seem that our capacities for understanding ourselves and others is likely to be exhausted soon. This is not only because we are open to change, but also because our culture can change, our wider environment can change, and all will continue to do so as long as human history continues. The ethnographic enterprise will never be finished, even if all nonindustrial ways of life disappeared forever, if all human beings moved into cities, if everyone ended up speaking English. Such a superficial homogeneity would mask the vast heterogeneity beneath its bland surface. In any case, given the dynamics of human existence, nothing in human affairs can remain homogeneous for long.

KEY TERMS

fieldwork
culture shock
participant-observation
positivism

objective knowledge
informants
intersubjective meanings
reflexivity

interpretation
translation
facts

CHAPTER SUMMARY

1. Anthropological fieldwork traditionally involves extended periods of close contact with members of another society. This form of research, called participant-observation, institutionalizes culture shock. Anthropological knowledge is a product of reflection on the experiences of culture shock generated by fieldwork.

2. The nineteenth century saw the birth of positivistic science in Western intellectual circles. Positivism is based on the assumption that reality can be known through the five senses. Positivists believe that a single scientific method can be used to investigate any domain of reality, and they expect that all scientific knowledge will eventually be unified. They argue that facts have nothing to do with values. Positivists' aim is to produce knowledge about reality that is true for all people in all times and places.

3. Early anthropologists who wanted to be scientific attempted to adapt positivism to their needs. They adopted a view of controlled laboratory research as the prototype of scientific investigation and attempted to apply the prototype to the field situation. They also tried to record objectively only observable human behavior and explain that behavior in material terms. In this way, highly accurate data were systematically collected in many parts of the world.

4. Anthropologists with a positivistic outlook have been charged with insensitivity to the humanity of their research subjects. The positivist program in anthropology attempts, metaphorically, to turn human beings into objects, similar to the rocks and molecules that physical scientists study. This attempt has dehumanized both the informants (who are reduced to objects) and the fieldworkers (who are reduced to intelligent recording machines).

5. When human beings study other human beings, research is inevitably colored by the context and cultural presuppositions of both the anthropologists and the people they study. Positivism views this as contamination of the data. However, if the objects of anthropology are human beings, then scientific accuracy requires that we relate to them as human beings.

6. We suggest that a concern with objectivity be replaced with a concern for reflexivity: that anthropologists must think about the way they think about other cultures. Successful fieldwork involves informants who also must think about the way they think and try to convey their insights to the anthropologist.

7. The dialectic of fieldwork is a reflexive interchange between anthropologist and informant. It is a collaborative undertaking involving dialogue about the meaning of experience in the informant's culture. The outcome of this dialogue is an intersubjective understanding (an understanding between two subjects, anthropologist and informant) of the informant's culture.

8. Fieldwork is human experience. Knowledge of informants and their culture is gained in the same way as human beings gain knowledge about other human beings in any circumstances, even in their own cultures. Meaning must always be negotiated. There is no such thing as a final set of meanings or a final interpretation that cannot be renegotiated at some future date.

9. Fieldworkers must face the shock of the unfamiliar and their own vulnerability. As a result, fieldwork can be a profoundly alienating experience. The only remedy for

this alienation is to construct, with the aid of one's informants, an intersubjective world of meaning.

10. Because cultural meanings are intersubjectively constructed during fieldwork, cultural facts do not speak for themselves. The facts of anthropology are made and remade every time they are subjected to a fresh analysis and interpretation.

11. Learning about another culture is often greatest following a rupture of communication between anthropologist and informant. Ruptures occur when current intersubjective understandings prove themselves inadequate to account for experience. A rupture always carries the possibility of bringing research to an end. But when the reasons for the rupture are explored and explanations for it are constructed, great insights are possible.

12. Fieldwork has the potential to change both fieldworkers and informants by expanding their experiences of human possibility. This growth in self-awareness is not always comfortable. Nevertheless, the deepening of insight that it makes possible—the opportunity to experience the humanity of one's informants (or one's interviewer!)—can be immensely satisfying.

13. The ethnographic record of anthropological knowledge is perhaps best understood as a vast commentary on human possibility. Like all commentaries, it is—and must be—unfinished. We may never learn all there is to know, but we can always learn more.

SUGGESTED READINGS

Briggs, Jean. 1970. *Never in anger: Portrait of an Eskimo family.* Cambridge: Harvard University Press. *A moving, insightful study of fieldwork and of an Utku family.*

Kumar, Nita. 1992. *Friends, brothers, and informants: Fieldwork memories of Banaras.* Berkeley: University of California Press. *A moving and thought-provoking reflection on the experience of fieldwork in the author's own country but in a culture quite different from her own.*

Lévi-Strauss, Claude. 1974. *Tristes Tropiques.* New York: Pocket Books. *Originally published in French in 1955, this book (with an untranslatable title) is considered by some to be the greatest book ever written by an anthropologist (although not necessarily a great anthropology book). This is a multifaceted work about voyaging, fieldwork, self-knowledge, philosophy, and much more. It is a challenging read in some places but highly rewarding overall.*

Rabinow, Paul. 1977. *Reflection on fieldwork in Morocco.* Berkeley: University of California Press. *An important, brief, powerfully written reflection on the nature of fieldwork. Very accessible and highly recommended.*

Valentine, Bettylou. 1978. *Hustling and other hard work.* New York: Free Press. *An innovative, provocative study of African American inner-city life. Reads like a good novel.*

Lake Michigan
(Ojibway)

History, Anthropology, and the Explanation of Cultural Diversity

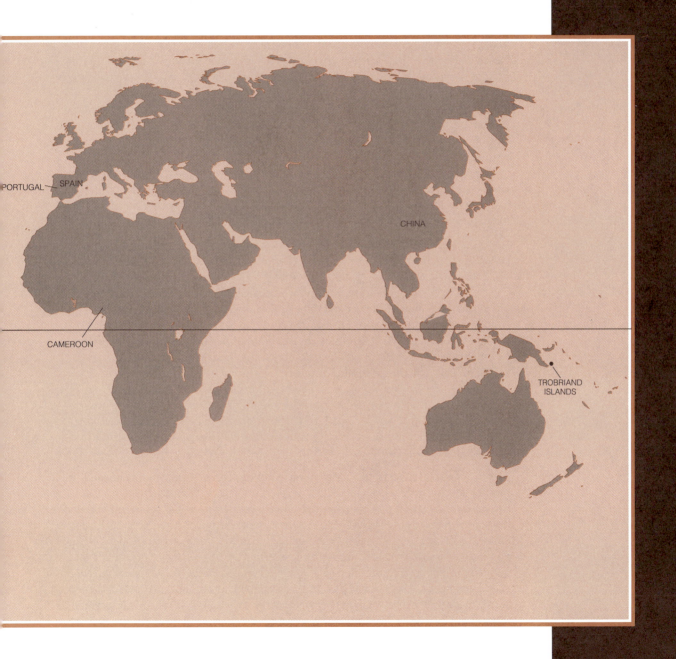

*t*he five-element theory, which dates to the third century B.C., was one of the bases of all Chinese scientific thought. The five "elements" that make up the world were said to be water, fire, wood, metal, and earth. These elements were understood not as substances but as processes, differentiated from one another by the kinds of changes they underwent. Water was associated with soaking, dripping, and descending. Fire was allied with heating, burning, and ascending. Wood was connected with that which accepted form by submitting to cutting and carving instruments. Metal was affiliated with that which accepted form by molding when in the liquid state and had the capacity to change form by remelting and remolding. Earth was associated with the production of edible vegetation.

In Han times (about 200 B.C. to A.D. 200), the theory achieved a final form, which has been passed down through the ages. According to Colin Ronan and Joseph Needham in their *Shorter Science and Civilisation in China,* one aspect of the theory, the mutual conquest order,

> described the series in which each element was supposed to conquer its predecessor. It was based on a logical sequence of ideas that had their basis in everyday scientific facts: for instance that Wood conquers Earth because, presumably, when in the form of a spade, it can dig up earth. Again, Metal conquers Wood since it can cut and carve it; Fire conquers Metal for it can melt or even vaporise it; Water conquers Fire because it can extinguish it; and, finally, Earth conquers Water because it can dam it and contain it—a very natural metaphor for people to whom irrigation and hydraulic engineering were so important. This order was also considered significant from the political point of view; it was put forward as an explanation for the course of history, with the implication that it would continue to apply in the future and was, therefore, useful for prediction. . . . The Five Elements gradually came to be associated with every conceivable category of things in the universe that it was possible to classify in fives (1978, 142ff.).

This included the seasons, the points of the compass, tastes, smells, numbers, kinds of musical notes, heavenly bodies, planets, weather, colors, body parts, sense organs, affective states, and human psychological functions. It also included the periods of dynastic history, the ministries of government, and five styles of government. The styles of government included relaxed, enlightened, careful, energetic, and quiet, corresponding respectively to wood, fire, earth, metal, and water.

"As we might imagine," Ronan and Needham conclude, "these correlations met with criticism, sometimes severe, because they led to many absurdities. . . . Yet in spite of such criticisms, it seems that in the beginning these correlations were helpful to scientific thought in China. They were certainly no worse than the Greek theory of the elements that dominated European mediaeval thinking, and it was only when they became over-elaborate and fanciful, too far removed from the observation of Nature, that they were positively harmful" (1978, 156–57).

These observations are relevant to any apt metaphor or good scientific theory. Just as the Chinese were obsessed by fives, so we in the West have often been obsessed by threes. In anthropology, this has repeatedly been the case when the task involves making sense of human cultural diversity. Like the Chinese sages, anthropologists' first step was to sort human cultures into different categories based on their similarities and differences. Over time, the purposes and the categories have been modified in ways that reflect changes in the wider world and changing research interests among anthropologists. This chapter considers some of the influential classifications, placing them in the context of the historical development of anthropology as a discipline.

HUMAN IMAGINATION AND THE MATERIAL WORLD

We argued in Chapter 2 that culture is an aspect of human nature that is as much a source of freedom as it is a requirement for our survival. This is the paradox of the human condition. Human imagination can suggest which aspects of the material world to pay attention to, and these suggestions can become part of a cultural tradition. Once any group accepts these suggestions, however, it commits itself to paying attention to some parts of the material world while ignoring or downplaying others. As a result, it locks itself into a set of relationships with the material world that it may not be able to abandon freely. These relationships can and do exert a determinant pressure on future choices.

What parts of the material world do human beings pay attention to, and what parts do they ignore? To answer this question, we can begin by considering how the need to make a living in different "natural" environments has led to the development of a range of different forms of human social organization. At the same time, because people can make a living in different ways in the same enviroment, or in much the same way in different environments, we must also pay attention to those cultural and social factors that cannot be predicted on the basis of natural environment alone. Some of these factors arise out of the internal traditions of the group itself; others depend on external and unpredictable historical encounters with other human groups. By looking at both sets of factors, we will understand better why anthropologists classify forms of human society as they do and what these classifications suggest about the forces shaping human society and human history.

CROSS-CULTURAL CONTACTS BETWEEN THE WEST AND THE REST OF THE WORLD

The wider social environment cannot be forgotten when we consider the history of contact by anthropologists with cultures in the non-Western world. If we look carefully, we see that the arrival of anthropologists was only the most recent phase of centuries-long contact by Western cultures with cultures of the wider world. This contact dates from the so-called *Age of Exploration,* when Western explorers such as Columbus ven-

FIGURE 4.1 *In the late fifteenth and sixteenth centuries, Western explorers such as Columbus ventured beyond the boundaries of the world known to Europe. This sixteenth-century engraving depicts Columbus meeting the inhabitants of Hispaniola, the first territory colonized by Spain in the New World.*

tured beyond the boundaries of the world known to Europe and first encountered the inhabitants of Africa, America, and Asia (Figure 4.1).

These early explorers, and the traders and settlers who followed them, were not motivated to travel such distances and take great risks merely for exotic experience. They were in the pay of European monarchs whose interest in new worlds was political and economic. Historians have shown that nearly every contact made between the West and the outside world sooner or later turned into conquest, leading to the establishment of far-flung colonial empires centered in Europe. Thus, contact between western Europe and the rest of the world neither began nor continued in neutral terms.

By the time anthropologists appeared on the scene in the late nineteenth century, contact between their world and the world of the peoples whose lives they wanted to study had long since been established. The anthropologists and the societies from which they came were in a superior economic and political position. They were not, for the most part, paying visits to independent, autonomous, thriving cultures. They came as representatives of a conquering society to observe remnants of a population that had been conquered.

Members of the conquered societies did recall and describe their past. Most had rallied in the aftermath of conquest to reconstitute their cultures under changed circumstances. Such is the strength and resilience of human beings in adversity. But we would be naive to believe, as many early anthropologists and other observers did, that these societies and cultures were "living fossils," intact representatives of ancient ways of life as yet untouched by history.

Anthropologist Eric Wolf (1982) discusses this tendency of Western observers to assume that people in the non-Western world are "people without history." The imperialist expansion of Europe, which coincided with the rise of industrial capitalism, was the central force leading to cross-cultural contact between the West and the rest of the world. Many of the "tribes" or "peoples" whom anthropologists later would study are relatively recent creations, forged in the field of contact between indigenous populations and Europeans. Before Europeans arrived in North America and Africa, such tribes—for example, the North American Ojibway or the African Baluba—had no separate identity and did not exist as autonomous societies. They became a product of the historical contact—and clash—between aggressive Europeans and local populations. In response to the European presence, these populations had to regroup and reshape their cultures.

Our survey of the forms of human society will therefore also involve an ethnography of ethnography. That is, anthropologists now pay a lot of attention to the social, cultural, and political circumstances that shape their relationships with informants. Anthropologists realize that no societies have ever been totally isolated in time and space, unaffected by the world around them, and cut off from history. We agree with Dennis Tedlock that "there is no such thing as 'pre-contact' ethnography" (1982, 161).

THE EFFECTS OF WESTERN EXPANSION

To understand these changes among non-Western peoples, we must look at European history, too. Certain key commercial linkages underlay European expansion into the rest of the world. Central to the European Age of Exploration, which began in the fifteenth century, was the attempt by various European rulers to gain independent access to sources of wealth outside their own territories. The earliest explorations were undertaken by Portugal. Castile and Aragon, the two kingdoms that formed the core of what later would be called Spain, followed soon thereafter. At the time, these kingdoms on the Iberian Peninsula were among the weakest and poorest territories in Europe. Any hopes they might have had for expansion within Europe were blocked to the north by France. Moreover, until the end of the fifteenth century, most Iberian Christian leaders were engaged in protracted warfare, both among themselves and against the Muslim overlords who had controlled the Iberian Peninsula for the previous 800 years.

Portugal managed to free itself from Muslim control in 1249. By the late 1300s, the kingdom was united enough to undertake attempts at expansion. Checked to the north and east by continuing conflicts between their neighbors, the Portuguese chose to move southward. Their official aim was to discover an ocean passage to the mythical Christian kingdom of Prester John, supposedly located somewhere southeast of Egypt. This was of interest to the Portuguese because gold and other riches that were coming into Europe from Africa were controlled by non-Portuguese middlemen. If the Portuguese found this kingdom, or any other kingdoms on the African continent, they would have direct access to this treasure. The Portuguese explorers never did find Prester John. During the fifteenth century, however, they "discovered" the entire Atlantic coast of Africa. Establishing trading posts as they went, they rounded the Cape of Good Hope in 1488.

In the last half of the fifteenth century, Castile and Aragon, united by the marriage of their rulers Isabella and Ferdinand, were actively involved in the "reconquest" of the remaining Muslim-ruled areas of the Iberian Peninsula. As victory neared, they too began to support voyages of exploration. One such voyage, that of Columbus, led to the European discovery of the New World. This occurred in 1492, the same year that the Muslims were decisively expelled from Spain. By this time, the Portuguese had already explored the eastern coast of Africa and were shortly to establish direct sea trade with India. Competition between Spain and Portugal led to the Treaty of Tordesillas, in 1494, in which the pope divided the non-Christian world between them. The dividing line was intended to leave the Western Hemisphere to the Spanish and the Eastern Hemisphere to the Portuguese. Later exploration revealed that the South American coastline of what is now Brazil fell on the Portuguese side of the line. This gave Portugal a foothold in the New World too.

The Iberians were the first to make European pressures felt in the New World, but their supremacy did not persist unchallenged. Holland, England, and France—the richer and more powerful European states—eventually turned their interests beyond Europe. In part, this was a result of their success in controlling European territory and trade relationships within it. Holland and especially England were at the forefront of the mercantile development that fueled the growth and expansion of capitalism. Although the Portuguese were the first to round the tip of Africa and make maritime contact with India, they were soon ousted by the Dutch, for whose better fleets and stronger commerce the Portuguese were no match.

The Dutch also ventured into the New World, establishing colonies in North America and vying again with the Portuguese (and other Europeans) for control of the Brazilian coast. However, the Dutch eventually withdrew from North America in favor of the English. Instead, they devoted themselves to consolidating their holdings in what is now Indonesia. The English also soon assumed control of trade with India. The French—not to be left behind—moved into North America, competing intensely with the English for access to territory and to trade goods.

Expansion in Africa and the Americas

Both in Africa and in America, the Europeans established commercial relations with the indigenous inhabitants they encountered. The nature of those relations differed radically. In Africa, first the Portuguese and later the Dutch, British, and French found themselves confined to the coast. Often their trading posts were built on the coast or on offshore islands; for more than 400 years, they were allowed to penetrate no farther inland. Instead, they made their interests known to the local peoples living along the coast, who in turn set out to procure the trade goods sought by their European partners.

This long-lasting arrangement shows at least two important things about the Africans whom Europeans first contacted. First, their societies were resilient enough to adapt to the European presence and strong enough to keep Europeans and their commercial interests at arm's length for several centuries. In other words, the terms of trade were not dictated solely by the Europeans. Second, the European presence on the coast reshaped coastal society, stimulating the growth of hierarchical social forms in some areas where there had been none before. These changes in coastal African society had repercussions farther inland. Peacefully or by force, the new coastal kingdoms sought trade goods for their new partners from the people of the African hinterland. Only in the second half of the nineteenth century did this relationship between Europeans and Africans change.

The situation in America was quite different. The European conquest was immediate and disastrous for many Native American populations. It was not merely a matter of armed force: European-borne diseases such as measles and smallpox effectively wiped out large portions of local populations who lacked immunity. (In Africa, the situation was often just the reverse; Europeans succumbed to tropical maladies such as malaria to which coastal African populations had greater resistance.) In Central America and South America, Spanish conquerors and then settlers arrived close on the heels of the first explorers. Thirty years after the arrival of Columbus, the two complex civilizations of the Americas—the Aztec in Mexico and the Inca in Peru—had been conquered.

Indigenous American societies disrupted by disease and conquest suffered further dislocation after Spanish colonial administration was established. The government in Spain was determined to control the exploitation of the new territories. It strove to check the attempts of colonists to set themselves up as feudal lords commanding local Native American groups as their peasants. These efforts were far from successful. Conquered Native Americans were put to work in mines and on plantations. Hard labor further reduced their numbers and fractured their traditional forms of social organization. By the time the worst of these abuses were finally curtailed, in the early seventeenth century, the nature of Native American society in New Spain had been drastically reshaped. Throughout the more settled years of subsequent centuries, these reshaped societies affected, and were strongly affected by, the social forms and the culture of their conquerors. Indeed, it would be inaccurate to think of many postconquest Native American societies as separate societies at all. In the areas of greatest Spanish penetration and control, Native American groups were reduced to but one component in the complex hierarchy of colonial society.

The Fur Trade in North America

The nature of European penetration of North America was shaped in important ways by the early development of the fur trade. Fur trappers and traders are part of American folklore, but most European Americans today are not aware of the fur trade's effect on indigenous forms of society in North America.

Background   Eric Wolf points out that trade in furs did not begin with the discovery of the New World (1982, 158ff.). For several centuries before Europe discovered America, furs had been an important source of wealth for early states in what is today Russia. In addition to fur collecting, fur processing became an important industry in Russia. When the Dutch first began to trade with Native Americans for furs, they already had trading links to eastern Europe, and the fur they obtained in North America was later traded with Russia. The fur trade was thus an international phenomenon, and the strong stimulus that Native American populations experienced to seek fur was shaped by the demand of the fur-processing industry in eastern Europe.

The most eagerly sought fur was that of the beaver, which was used to make felt for cloth and especially hats. So the hatmaking industry also contributed to the search for fur in North America, so much so that hats took on important social roles as symbols of superior status: rich Europeans could afford beaver hats, the poor had to be content with cloth caps. Native American populations found their fortunes waxing as long as beaver flourished in their lands; however, once the beaver were gone, their fortunes waned, often suddenly, as their European trading partners moved on too. Involvement in the fur trade significantly modified the traditional ways that Native American groups made a living. While the beaver supply lasted, they could obtain many of the material items they needed by exchanging pelts for them at the trading post. This gave them a strong incentive to neglect or even abandon the activities that previously had supplied those items and to devote themselves more completely to fur trapping. Over the generations, trapping itself became part of "tradition," and people came to depend on it for their livelihood, just as they had formerly depended on hunting or farming. Once the beaver were gone, however, people discovered that their highly successful new adaptation had become obsolete virtually overnight. They also discovered that a return to the old ways was impossible, either because those ways had been forgotten or because the new circumstances of life made them impossible to carry out. The result often was, and can be in similar circumstances, severe social dislocation.

Regrouping and Reworking Traditions   Native American societies did not remain passive in the face of the European challenge. They regrouped. They reworked their traditional understandings of human nature and human society to minimize the negative impact of European pressures.

The Iroquois confederacy is one example of such reworking. Wolf argues that the Native American groups in the confederacy tried to create a form of society that was similar to and could counter the European trading companies with which they dealt. In forming the confederacy, however, the groups did not simply borrow the social organization of the European traders. They drew on traditional kinship forms and reworked these into new and broader-reaching structures that, for a time at least, functioned well to keep the Europeans at bay. The Iroquois confederacy was not an unchanging, timeless structure, predating the coming of Europeans to America. Quite the contrary; it was new. This structure was like the coastal trading kingdoms in Africa mentioned earlier. Both developed in response to a new state of social, political, and economic affairs initiated by European contact.

As the fur trade moved westward, competition between France and England for fur increased. This, in turn, led to rivalry between local groups for lucrative trading relationships. There were casualties. Some Native American groups, such as the Huron, were wiped out. Other new groups, such as the Ojibway and Salteaux came into being. The creation of these new identities was not a passive development; rather it is best understood as a positive effort by the group's members to rework their social forms in the face of new experiences. We can see that these new groups did develop a positive sense of who they were when we look at changes in their ritual life.

A new cult known as the *Midewiwin* grew up among the Ojibway and their neighbors toward the end of the seventeenth century. Replacing more localized rituals, the

Midewiwin united numerous local groups. It emphasized individuals and their member-ship in a hierarchical association that went beyond their traditional territories and kin-ship groups. Wolf writes that this was an important change: older measures of worth and value were based on status relationships in local kinship groups; by contrast, status in the new association depended on wealth acquired in war or in trade. The cult accepted the existence of outside Europeans such as traders and missionaries, and its leaders were empowered to represent the members in dealings with them. For this reason, the Mide-wiwin is an example of a creative, adaptive response on the part of Native Americans to cope with a new and potentially threatening social experience.

The Slave and Commodities Trades

The fur trade and its effects on forms of human society in North America is but one early example of the effect of western European expansion into the non-Western world. Other later ventures included the slave trade and the trade in commodities such as cotton, which accompanied the rise of capitalist industry. These ventures not only continued to affect social life in the rest of the world; they also drew various parts of that world ever closer together into what would eventually constitute a capitalist world system.

The slave trade dominated commerce between Europeans and coastal Africans by the eighteenth century. The nature of the merchandise sought for this trade—human beings—had a devastating effect on the societies of the African hinterland whose mem-bers were captured and sold to meet European demand. The response by these societies was parallel to the North American response just reviewed. The survivors sought refuge beyond the slavers' reach, regrouping themselves into new societies with new names and reworking their collective traditions into new forms.

The slave trade did not alter the social fabric in Africa alone. Once they arrived in the New World, the slaves had to be fitted into a niche between local Native American inhabitants and European colonists. The growth of plantation economies in areas that had been used by hunters or gatherers or small-scale farmers altered the local ecology as well as local society. And the wealth produced in these economies transformed both the local gentry and the European nations who claimed sovereignty over them. As a result, Africa, America, and Europe became inextricably intertwined in one another's fate.

TOWARD CLASSIFYING FORMS OF HUMAN SOCIETY

The preceding historical sketch is important to keep in mind as we begin a survey of the various forms human society has taken. It reminds us that the societies ethnographers began to investigate in the mid-nineteenth century had all been affected in some way by several centuries of contact and conflict with western Europe. In many cases, they were conquered populations administered as colonial subjects of the ethnographers' own soci-eties. This alone may have made it difficult for an ethnographer to carry out research that the colonial administration did not find relevant. Actually, studying what the researcher thought was important and gaining permission to do research could be mutually exclu-

FIGURE 4.2 *Far from being static survivors of a timeless past, Australian aborigines such as Big Bill Neidjie and his son Jonathan Yarramarna are coping actively with contemporary problems and opportunities, such as the presence of uranium miners on traditional clan land.*

sive enterprises. As former colonies have become independent, these problems have not disappeared, for now the new nations' rulers have their own plans for their citizens and may be suspicious of the ethnographer's motives.

We can draw three general conclusions at this point. First, there are on this planet various human societies whose natures were radically affected by their "discovery" by Europeans. As physicists learned at the beginning of the twentieth century when they sought to observe electrons, the very act of observation alters the nature of the entity being observed. When the act involves considerably more than observation, as was the case of contact between the West and the rest of the world, the changes are even more dramatic. Thus, although life in the non-Western world today is undoubtedly culturally patterned, this patterning does not necessarily represent a timeless, unchanged way of life, unaffected by history or our own presence. Extant non-Western societies have not escaped the historical forces that have shaped everyone else.

Second, remnants of precontact societies survive today. These groups have not been absorbed without a trace into the society and culture of their conquerors. They have maintained a separate identity. Against high odds, they have regrouped and reshaped new identities. They have devised new social forms to deal with the effects of contact and conquest. Far from being static survivors of a timeless past, they are made up of people who are coping actively with contemporary problems and opportunities, people whose history is also our history (Figure 4.2). In some cases, these new social forms draw on very ancient traditions, which have been actively reworked to meet the demands of new experiences. In other cases, certain domains of traditional life have been

In Their Own Words   THE ECOLOGICALLY NOBLE SAVAGE?

Part of the stereotype of the "primitive," as Paul Rabinow pointed out, includes the belief that "primitives" live in total harmony with their environment. Kent Redford explores how this stereotype has been recycled in recent years into the image of an idealized "ecologically noble savage."

To live and die with the land is to know its rules. When there is no hospital at the other end of the telephone and no grocery store at the end of the street, when there is no biweekly paycheck nor microwave oven, when there is nothing to fall back on but nature itself, then a society must discover the secrets of the plants and animals. Thus indigenous peoples possess extensive and intensive knowledge of the natural world. In every place where humans have existed, people have received this knowledge from their elders and taught it to their children, along with what has been newly acquired. . . . Writings of several scientists and indigenous rights advocates echo the early chroniclers' assumption that indigenous people lived in "balance" with their environment. Prominent conservationists have stated that in the past, indigenous people "lived in close harmony with their local environment." The rhetoric of Indian spokespersons is even stronger: "In the world of today there are two systems, two different irreconcilable 'ways of life.' The Indian world—collective, communal, human, respectful of nature, and wise—and the western

world—greedy, destructive, individualist, and enemy of nature" (from a report to the International NGO Conference on Indigenous Peoples and the Land, 1981). The idealized figure of centuries past had been reborn, as the *ecologically* noble savage.

The recently accumulated evidence, however, refutes this concept of ecological nobility. Precontact Indians were not "ecosystem men"; they were not just another species of animal, largely incapable of altering the environment, who therefore lived within the "ecological limitations of their home area." Paleobiologists, archaeologists, and botanists are coming to believe that most tropical forests have been severely altered by human activities before European contact. Evidence of vast fires in the northern Amazonian forests and of the apparently anthropogenic origins of large areas of forest in eastern Amazonia suggests that before 1500, humans had tremendously affected the virgin forest, with ensuing impacts on plant and animal species. These people behaved as humans do now: they did whatever they had to to feed themselves and their families.

"Whatever they had to" is the key phrase in understanding the problem of the noble savage myth in its contemporary version. Countless examples make it clear that indigenous people can be either forced, seduced, or tempted into accepting new methods, new crops, and new technologies. No better example exists than the near-universal adoption of

firearms for hunting by Indians in the Neotropics. Shotguns or rifles often combined with the use of flashlights and outboard motors, change completely the interaction between human hunters and their prey.

There is no cultural barrier to the Indians' adoption of means to "improve" their lives (i.e., make them more like Western lives), even if the long-term sustainability of the resource base is threatened. These means can include the sale of timber and mining rights to indigenous lands, commercial exploitation of flora and fauna, and invitations to tourists to observe "traditional lifestyles." Indians should not be blamed for engaging in these activities. They can hardly be faulted for failing to live up to Western expectations of the noble savage. They have the same capacities, desires, and perhaps, needs to overexploit their environment as did our European ancestors. Why shouldn't Indians have the same right to dispose of the timber on their land as the international timber companies have to sell theirs? An indigenous group responded to the siren call of the market economy in just this spirit in Brazil in 1989, when Guajajara Indians took prisoners in order to force the government Indian agency, FUNAI, to grant them permission to sell lumber from their lands.

Source: Redford 1993, 11–13.

less affected by outside forces. Where this is the case, a contemporary ethnographer can glimpse ways of life that were invented long ago and continue to prove their worth by being reproduced today (see, for example, Lee 1992). Sometimes, modes of living that have endured successfully for centuries are at last falling before the advance of Western technology and the rigors of the capitalist world system. But this should not be taken to mean that such modes of living are primitive or incomplete or lacking. These modes of living proved their adequacy by allowing human groups employing them to flourish, sometimes for millennia.

Finally, an impressive variety of forms of human society remains—in spite of the Western onslaught. Anthropologists have been able to document this variety through archaeological reconstruction, by recording the memories of old people, and also through fieldwork. Many similarities that people seem increasingly to show throughout the world turn out to be far less important than the continuing differences in worldview and social organization that lie below the surface.

Making sense of the variety of forms of human society across space and over time is an ongoing task for anthropologists. One way they do this is by devising a **typology** to identify those societies that are most distinct from one another based on certain criteria and then to sort known societies by their resemblance to these exemplars. This effort has much in common with the procedures used by paleoanthropologists sorting fossils. As in the paleontological case, such procedures are useful not only when they seem successful but also when they fail. The sections that follow examine some common classifications of forms of human society. They point out both the commonalities those classifications help us to see and the differences they help to obscure.

Evolutionary Typologies: The Nineteenth Century

A system of classification reflects the features that its creator believes to be most significant. As a result, different assessments of what is significant can lead to different classifications. In the early years of anthropology, most Westerners who compared non-Western societies with their own were struck by certain features that set apart the world of conquering Europeans from those of the various peoples they conquered. Non-Western society identified these differences as *deficiencies:* lack of a state, lack of sophisticated technology, lack of organized religion, and so forth. Perhaps without realizing it, observers took Western industrial capitalist society as the universal standard against which to measure all other human societies. Having done this, they often assumed that the alleged defects of non-Western societies were too obvious to require comment.

This approach to cultural differences was persuasive, particularly in the nineteenth century. It spoke directly to the cross-cultural experience that Western nations were having with the non-Western peoples they had colonized or with whom they traded. A colonial ruler eager to establish a smoothly working administration in New Spain or the operator of a trading post anxious to make maximum profits in the fur trade would be most aware of the facets of a people's life that kept him from reaching his goals. How do you successfully collect taxes in a colony that has poor roads, lacks government officials who can read and write, and is populated by subjects who do not speak your language? How do you "pay" for beaver pelts when the "sellers" are not interested in money? Or how do you ensure a steady supply and motivate your trading partners to stay with you, rather than the competition, in the absence of strong government and strong armies? Europeans faced with such practical problems were bound to see life outside Europe in terms of a series of deficiencies compared with what they could count on in the home country.

Observers of a more philosophical nature, too, were bound to wonder why there should be such "deficiencies" in societies outside western Europe (or in the more provincial areas of Europe outside the capital cities). Although their research usually never took them outside their libraries, they studied the reports of travelers and missionaries as well as history. They learned that many of the social and technological patterns they took for granted had not always existed, even in the West. They became aware of the "advances" that had occurred and were continuing in all areas of European social life since the Middle Ages.

It seemed clear that their ancestors too had once lacked the tools and ideas and social forms that made them powerful today. If they went back far enough, perhaps they would discover that even more distant ancestors of the Europeans had lived much as many peoples of America or Africa were living at that time. Writers such as Julius Caesar, who had visited ancient Europe, painted a picture of indigenous life there that resembled the contemporary customs of Native Americans and Africans. As archaeology developed, particularly in the nineteenth century, researchers could supplement written records with ancient artifacts presumably made by the primitive ancestors of modern Europeans.

Unilineal Cultural Evolutionism   For many nineteenth-century thinkers, the experience of social change, together with historical and archaeological evidence of past social change, was suggestive. Perhaps the ways of life of the non-Western peoples they were reading about were similar to, and even repeats of, the ways of life of European generations long past. That is, perhaps the West had already moved through periods of history in which ways of life had been the same as those of contemporary non-Western societies. According to these scholars, if non-Western societies were left to themselves and given enough time, they would make the same discoveries and change socially the same way that western Europe had.

This way of thinking about social and cultural change has been called **unilineal cultural evolutionism.** It reached its most elaborate development in the nineteenth century, when evolutionary ideas were popular in all areas of Western thought. Unilineal cultural evolutionism was one way to explain the widespread cultural diversity that Europeans had been finding since the Age of Exploration. It proposed to account for this diversity by arguing that the different kinds of society existing at that time were not randomly different. In fact, they represented different stages of societal evolution through which every human society either had passed or would pass, if it survived. Unilineal

typology A classification system based on, in this case, forms of human society.

unilineal cultural evolution A nineteenth-century theory that proposed a series of stages through which all societies must go (or had gone) in order to reach "civilization."

cultural evolutionists saw their own world as the summit of evolution. For them, late-nineteenth-century European capitalist industrial society was the most advanced stage of cultural evolution yet. Societies that had not already reached this level were living relics of more primitive stages that the West had already successfully left behind.

Today, anthropologists find this approach to the classification of forms of human society to be inadequate if not totally misleading in most respects. Nevertheless, it is a powerful scheme, and its continuing popularity among ordinary members of Western societies is not difficult to understand: it offers a coherent framework for classifying all the societies of the world.

Unilineal cultural evolutionism gave scholars the tools to organize different types of living societies into a sequence based on the discoveries of history and archaeology. For example, contemporary groups who made a living by gathering, hunting, and fishing were assumed to represent the way of life that had once existed universally, before farming and herding were invented. By the nineteenth century, however, it was clear that agriculture and animal husbandry had been invented only a few thousand years ago, whereas human beings had been around far longer than that. Researchers concluded that contemporary foragers had somehow gotten stuck in the earliest stage of human cultural development, while other societies had managed to move upward by domesticating plants and animals. Putting societies in this kind of order was, to a great extent, based on educated guessing. Appropriate historical texts were not always available or reliable, and archaeological dating techniques were poorly developed.

Many of the non-Western groups with which nineteenth-century Europeans and Americans were familiar did farm or herd for a living. Their societies were usually larger than those of the foragers and technologically more complex. In addition to having the technology of cultivation and the tools to go with it, farmers usually also built permanent structures and made objects, such as pottery and woven cloth, that were unknown among foragers. Their social patterns too were often more complex. They developed elaborate kinship terminologies and strong lineage organization. These peoples clearly seemed to be a rung above the foragers. But they were also very different from Europeans. In most cases they did not have writing. Their societies were not organized in anything that looked at all like a hierarchical political state. For such reasons, this group of societies, midway between the foragers and the society of Europe, were given their own category. They seemed to typify the stage through which gatherers and hunters had to pass—through which Europe's ancestral populations had already passed—before attaining modern "civilization."

In this manner, the first important anthropological typology of human social forms emerged. It had three basic categories, corresponding to the preceding distinctions. But the labels given these categories indicated more than "objective" differences; they also carried social and moral implications. The foragers—peoples who neither farmed nor herded—were called *savages.* Groups that had domesticated plants and animals but had not yet invented writing or the state were called *barbarians. Civilization* was limited to the early states of the Mediterranean basin and southwestern Asia (such as Mesopotamia and Egypt), their successors (such as Greece and Rome), and certain non-Western societies boasting a similar level of achievement (such as India and China). However, the advances that Europe had experienced since antiquity were seen to be unique, unmatched by social changes in other civilizations, which were understood to be in decline. That decline seemed proven when representatives of Western civilization found they could conquer the rulers of such civilizations, as the English did in India.

Unilineal cultural evolution was sweeping and powerful. Yet even its proponents were aware that the simple three-part typology was too crude to capture important differences among members of one category. They also saw that their theory sometimes missed important similarities that linked members of different categories. An early American anthropologist, Lewis Henry Morgan, devoted himself to organizing these similarities and differences. His modifications of the unilineal sequence had great and far-reaching influence.

Morgan's Ethnical Periods   In his book *Ancient Society,* published in 1877, Morgan summarized the basic orientation of unilineal evolutionism: "The latest investigations respecting the early condition of the human race are tending to the conclusion that mankind commenced their career at the bottom of the scale and worked their way up from savagery to civilization through the slow accumulations of experimental knowledge" (3). Morgan described this evolutionary career in terms of a series of stages, or *ethnical periods,* "connected with each other in a natural as well as necessary sequence of progress" (3). The major categories in this sequence were savagery, barbarism, and civilization. But Morgan felt the need to distinguish additional levels within savagery and barbarism in order better to classify the variety of social forms known in his day. He was fully aware that some human groups might not easily fit into these categories. Hoping that future research would help resolve such ambiguities, however, he concluded that for his purposes "it will be sufficient if the principal tribes of mankind can be classified, according to the degree of their relative progress, into conditions which can be recognized as distinct" (9).

Table 4.1 shows the sequence of ethnical periods suggested by Morgan. Note that, almost without exception, the criteria used to separate one period from another have to do with changes in the "arts of subsistence"—that is, in techniques for getting food. In some cases, however, the transformation from one stage to the next is not clearly marked by changes in the food-getting techniques. Morgan sought other criteria in these cases,

TABLE 4.1

MORGAN'S ETHNICAL PERIODS

Period	Begins with
Savagery	
Lower	Origins of human race
Middle	Fishing, knowledge of use of fire
Upper	Invention of bow and arrow
Barbarism	
Lower	Invention of pottery
Middle	Domestication of animals and plants, invention of irrigation, use of adobe brick and stone
Upper	Smelting of iron ore, use of iron tools
Civilization	Invention of phonetic alphabet, use of writing

such as the invention of pottery or writing, to mark the transition. Later scholars criticized him for these inconsistencies, but he himself was aware of the difficulty. For example, in discussing his choice of the invention of pottery to divide savagery from barbarism, Morgan wrote: "The invention or practice of the art of pottery, all things considered, is probably the most effective and conclusive test that can be selected to fix a boundary line, necessarily arbitrary, between savagery and barbarism. The distinctness of the two conditions has long been recognized, but no criterion of progress out of the former into the latter has hitherto been brought forward. All such tribes, then, as never attained to the art of pottery will be classed as savages, and those possessing this art but who never attained a phonetic alphabet and the use of writing will be classed as barbarians" (1887, 10).

This quotation highlights the standard procedure of unilineal evolutionism when faced with ambiguity in the classification of forms of human society. Although Morgan could find no consistent, unambiguous cultural feature to indicate progress from one stage to another, he did not abandon the classification of forms of human society by evolutionary stage as an invalid undertaking. Quite the contrary; from his perspective, the unilineal scheme did such a good job making sense of cultural variation that he was convinced that exceptions or inconsistencies could only be due to inadequate data. Surely better research in the future would eliminate them!

This hope is shared by scientists of all kinds who are committed to persuasive theories that cannot resolve every anomaly. It is, indeed, a widespread human hope. Worldviews, like scientific theories in general, cannot explain everything we experience in a totally consistent manner. Yet we usually do not abandon them for that reason. As long as they continue to make sense of our experience, we remain willing to hope that—if only we knew more—the contradictions or inconsistencies will disappear.

Social Structural Typologies: The British Emphasis

As time passed, scrupulous attention to detail and better information on more societies led anthropologists to become dissatisfied with grand generalizations about cultural diversity and cultural change. This change in perspective was the outcome of improved scholarship and better scientific reasoning, but it was also a consequence of the changes taking place in the world itself.

Origins in the Colonial Setting   At the turn of the twentieth century, relationships between the Western and non-Western worlds changed. For one thing, the last quarter of the nineteenth century ushered in the final phase of Western colonialism. The territory of Africa and much of Asia, which until then had remained nominally independent, was divided up among European powers. At the same time, the United States assumed a similarly powerful and dominating role in its relationships with the indigenous peoples of the United States and eventually with the former colonies of Spain. Unilineal cultural evolutionism may have justified the global ambitions of Europe and made colonial rule appear inevitable and just. However, it was inadequate for meeting the practical needs of the rulers once they were in power.

Effective administration of subject peoples required accurate information about them. For example, one goal of a colonial administrator in Africa was to keep peace among the various groups over which he ruled. To do so, he needed to know how those people were accustomed to handling disputes. Most colonies included several societies with various customs about dispute resolution. Administrators had to be aware of the similarities and differences among their subjects in order to develop successful government policies.

At the same time, colonial officials planned to introduce certain elements of European law uniformly throughout the colony. Common examples were commercial laws permitting the buying and selling of land on the open market. They also tried to eliminate practices like witchcraft accusations or local punishment for capital crimes. Reaching these goals without totally disrupting life in the colony required firsthand understanding of local practices. The earlier "armchair anthropology" was wholly incapable of providing that understanding.

These changes in the relationships between the West and the rest of the world encouraged the development of a new kind of anthropological research. Under the colonial "peace," anthropologists found that they could carry out long-term fieldwork. Earlier, the unsettled conditions had made such work difficult. Anthropologists also found that colonial governments would support their research when persuaded that the work was scientific and could contribute to effective colonial rule. This did not mean that anthropologists who carried out fieldwork under colonial conditions supported colonialism. To the contrary, their sympathies often lay with the colonized peoples with whom they worked. For example, Sir E. E. Evans-Pritchard, who worked in central Africa for the British government in the 1920s and 1930s, saw himself as an educator of colonial administrators. He tried to convey to them a persuasive picture of the humanity and rationality of Africans. His goal was to combat the racism and oppression that seemed an inevitable consequence of colonial rule. For just these reasons, colonial officials were often wary of anthropologists and distrustful of their motives. It was all too likely that the results of anthropological research might make colonial programs look self-serving and exploitative.

Nevertheless, anthropologists working under colonial rule provided a vast amount of detailed, accurate information about aspects of indigenous life that the colonial administration needed to understand. Sometimes, the needs of colonial rulers seem to have shaped the direction of the studies undertaken, particularly among the British. Perhaps the most important information to a colonial ruler was accurate data about traditional political arrangements among the conquered people. Colonial bureaucracies were thinly staffed. Colonial officers quickly learned that their task would be easier if they could rely on traditional rulers to keep the peace among their traditional subjects through traditional means (Figure 4.3). Thus developed the British policy of *indirect rule*. Colonial officials were at the top of the hierarchy. Under them, the traditional rulers (elders, chiefs, and so on) served as intermediaries with the common people.

How could anthropologists contribute to the effectiveness of indirect rule? The information they gathered about a group's traditional political structures helped them suggest the best way to adapt indirect rule to that group. Of course, the advice of anthropologists was not always heeded, for the needs of the colonial power often clashed with anthropologically "appropriate" colonial policy.

FIGURE 4.3 *Colonial officers often relied on traditional rulers to keep the peace among their subjects through traditional means. This 1895 photograph shows the British governor of the Gold Coast (seated on the right) together with a contingent of native police.*

The work anthropologists did in the colonial setting came to emphasize certain aspects of non-Western social organization and to ignore others. This led, in turn, to new ways of classifying human social forms. The goal of colonial governments was to have the conquered societies contribute more efficiently to the prosperity of the colonial power. One way to do this was to restructure the societies they had conquered. And so we see developing, particularly among British anthropologists, a focus on the **social structure,** especially the political structure, of groups under colonial rule. That British anthropologists came to call themselves social anthropologists reflects these developments.

In 1940, in a classic work on African political systems, Meyer Fortes and E. E. Evans-Pritchard distinguished between state and stateless societies. Within these two basic categories, they made further distinctions having to do with similarities and differences among various states or among societies that have no state. Note that this basic distinction between state and stateless societies describes many non-Western societies in terms of what they lack: no centralized institutions to collect taxes, field an army, or defend a territory. This distinction is similar to Morgan's unilineal evolutionary classifications in terms of ethnical periods. However, there is a significant difference in the social structural classification of Evans-Pritchard and Fortes: it makes no mention of "progress" from "lower" to "higher" forms of society.

Evolutionism had not been decisively refuted by this time. Nevertheless, given the new approach to society that was taking shape, it had become irrelevant. The labels "savagery," "barbarism," and "civilization" had not even been officially expunged from the vocabulary of anthropology. For example, Malinowski was quite comfortable referring to

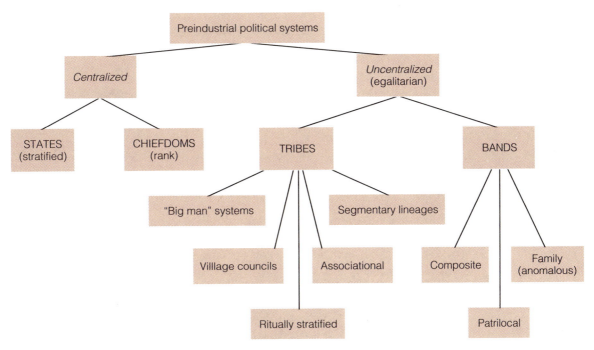

FIGURE 4.4 *A typical classification of forms of human society.* (From *Lewellen 1983, 16*)

the inhabitants of the Trobriand Islands, among whom he had worked, as *savages*. But the emphasis on contemporary social structures was bringing rich new insights to anthropology. Questions of evolution and social change took a back seat as social anthropologists concerned themselves with figuring out the enduring traditional structures of the societies in which they worked. A detailed knowledge of social structures was supposed to allow the anthropologist to identify the social type of any particular society. These types were treated as though unchanging. They were compared for similarities and differences, and out of this comparison emerged a new classification of social forms.

The Classification of Political Structures   A contemporary example of a typical social structural classification of forms of human society is shown in Figure 4.4. Here, the major distinction is between *centralized* political systems and *uncentralized,* or *egalitarian,* political systems. This distinction is similar to the one Evans-Pritchard and Fortes made between state societies and stateless societies; only the labels have been changed, perhaps so that societies without states can be identified in a positive fashion rather than in terms of what they lack. Still, uncentralized systems have no distinct, permanent institution exclusively concerned with public decision making. This is another way of saying that groups (and perhaps even individuals) within egalitarian systems enjoy rela-

social structure The enduring aspects of the social forms in a society, including its political and kinship systems.

tive autonomy and equal status and are not answerable to any higher authority.

In this scheme, egalitarian political systems can be further subdivided into two types. A **band** is a small social grouping whose members, like Morgan's savages, neither farm nor herd but depend on wild food sources. A **tribe** is a group that, like Morgan's barbarians, lies somewhere between a band and a centralized political system. A tribe is generally larger than a band and has domesticated plants and animals, but its political organization remains largely egalitarian and uncentralized. Ted Lewellen refers to three subtypes of band, including the *family band,* which are cases that do not fit into the other two subtypes. He also identifies five subtypes of tribe but comments that they hardly exhaust the variety of social arrangements that tribes display (Lewellen 1983, 26).

Centralized political systems are different from egalitarian systems because they have a central, institutionalized focus of authority such as a chief or a king. These systems also involve hierarchy; that is, some members of centralized societies have greater prestige, power, or wealth than do other members. Centralized systems are divided into two types. In a **chiefdom,** usually only the chief and his family are set above the rest of society, which remains fairly egalitarian. In a **state,** different groups suffer permanent inequality of access to wealth, power, and prestige, which signals the presence of social stratification.

Lewellen's typology does not attempt to make any hypotheses about evolutionary relationships. Tracing change over time is not its purpose; time has no place in such a typology. Instead, the focus is on social structural differences and similarities observed at one point in time: the here and now. This is not accidental. Remember that classifications of this kind were made in response to practical needs, originally those of the colonial administrators. Colonial rulers assumed that they were "civilized" and that their colonial subjects were "primitive," and they cared little about such matters as the origin of the state. The pressing questions for them were more likely, "How do African states work today?" "What do we need to know about them to make them work for us?"

Nevertheless, a typology that ignores change over time can be converted into an evolutionary typology with little difficulty. If you compare Table 4.2 with Table 4.1 (Morgan's ethnical periods), you will notice a rough correlation between bands and savagery; between tribes and lower and middle barbarism; between chiefdoms and upper barbarism; and between states and civilization. However, Lewellen's classification in Table 4.2 includes additional detail that was unknown in Morgan's day.

Structural-Functional Theory   British social anthropologists did not spend all their intellectual energy on the practical concerns of colonial officials, but their theoretical work was still affected by those concerns. Their theories dealt increasingly with how particular social forms function from day to day in order to reproduce their traditional structures. Such **structural-functional theory** was perhaps most highly developed in the work of A. R. Radcliffe-Brown, whose major theoretical work was done in the 1930s and 1940s.

In this way, social anthropology began to ask why things stayed the same, rather than why they changed. Why do some social structures last for centuries (Roman Catholic church) and others disappear quickly (the utopian communities of nineteenth-century America)? Why did some societies abandon foraging for agriculture thousands of years ago, while others are still gathering and hunting in the twentieth century? Both sets of questions are equally puzzling. However, an emphasis on social stability tends to downplay or ignore questions of change, just as an emphasis on social change tends to downplay or ignore questions of stability.

This new focus in British social anthropology, which is still with us today, has produced a succession of nonevolutionary classifications of human social forms. As data on more and more varieties of social structure grow, however, these typologies seem to overflow with more and more subtypes. It is not surprising that some anthropologists have begun to question the point of it all. In this, they are like the earlier generation that questioned the point of creating increasingly elaborate and unwieldy unilineal evolutionary schemes.

Doing without Typologies: Culture Area Studies in America

Anthropologists in the United States began to voice dissatisfaction with unilineal evolutionism at about the same time their British colleagues began to do so, and for similar reasons. The most important figure in this movement was Franz Boas, the man usually referred to as the father of American anthropology. Boas and his students worked primarily among the Native American populations of North America. They began to collect more and better data about these societies, especially data relating to the histories of individual groups. Change over time had not progressed through uniform stages for all these societies. For example, two societies with similar forms of social organization might have arrived at that status through different historical routes: one through a process of simplification, the other through a process of elaboration.

Boas emphasized that new forms of social life seemed to be more often borrowed from neighboring societies than invented independently. He and his followers were quick to note that if cultural borrowing, rather than independent invention, played an important role in culture change, then any unilineal evolutionary scheme was doomed.

---

band The characteristic form of social organization found among foragers, a band is a small group of people usually with 50 or fewer members. Labor is divided according to age and sex, and social relations are highly egalitarian.
tribe A form of social organization generally larger than a band; members usually farm or herd for a living. Social relations in a tribe are relatively egalitarian, although there may be a "chief" who speaks for the group or organizes group activities.

chiefdom A form of social organization in which the leader (the "chief") and his close relatives are set apart from the rest of the society and allowed privileged access to wealth, power, and prestige.

state A stratified society that possesses a territory that is defended from outside enemies with an army and from internal disorder with police. A state, which has a separate set of governmental institutions designed to enforce laws and collect taxes and tribute, is run by an elite who possesses a monopoly on the use of force.
structural-functional theory A position that explores how particular social forms function from day to day in order to reproduce the traditional structure of the society.

TABLE 4.2

PREINDUSTRIAL POLITICAL SYSTEMS: AN EVOLUTIONARY TYPOLOGY

	Uncentralized		Centralized	
	Band	Tribe	Chiefdom	State
Type of subsistence	Hunting-gathering; little or no domestication	Extensive agriculture (horticulure) and pastoralism	Extensive agriculture; intensive fishing	Intensive agriculture
Type of leadership	Informal and situational leaders; may have a headman who acts as arbiter in group decision making	Charismatic headman with no "power" but some authority in group decision making	Charismatic chief with limited power based on bestowal of benefits on followers	Sovereign leader supported by an aristocratic bureaucracy
Type and importance of kinship	Bilateral kinship, with kin relations used differentially in changing size and composition of bands	Unilineal kinship (patrilineal or matrilineal) may form the basic structure of society	Unilineal, with some bilateral; descent groups are ranked in status	State demands suprakinship loyalties; access to power is based on ranked kin groups, either unilineal or bilateral
Major means of social integration	Marriage alliances unite larger groups; bands united by kinship and family; economic interdependence based on reciprocity	Pantribal sodalities based on kinship, voluntary associations, and/or age grades	Integration through loyalty to chief, ranked lineages, and voluntary associations	State loyalties supersede all lower-level loyalties; integration through commerce and specialization of function
Political succession	May be hereditary headman, but actual leadership falls to those with special knowledge or abilities	No formal means of political succession	Chief's position not directly inherited, but chief must come from a high-ranking lineage	Direct hereditary succession of sovereign; increasing appointment of bureaucratic functionaries
Major types of economic exchange	Reciprocity (sharing)	Reciprocity; trade may be more developed than in bands	Redistribution through chief; reciprocity at lower levels	Redistribution based on formal tribute and/or taxation; markets and trade

Focusing on cultural borrowing as a major source of culture change also emphasized the links between different societies that made such borrowing possible.

The view of society that developed in the United States was therefore quite different from the one taking shape in Great Britain at the same time. Some American anthropologists no longer saw societies as isolated representatives of universal stages, closed to outside influences, responsible on their own for progressing or failing to progress. This had been the evolutionists' view. But neither did they see societies as bounded, atemporal social types that could be classified in a social structural matrix. Instead, Boas and his followers saw social groups as fundamentally open to the outside world; change over time was considered more a result of idiosyncratic borrowing from neighbors than of inevitable, law-governed, self-generated progress. Consequently, they focused their attention on the patterns of cultural borrowing over time, a form of research called *cultural*

	Uncentralized		Centralized	
	Band	Tribe	Chiefdom	State
Social stratification	Egalitarian	Egalitarian	Rank (individual and lineage)	Classes (minimally of rulers and ruled)
Ownership of property	Little or no sense of personal ownership	Communal (lineage or clan) ownership of agricultural lands and cattle	Land communally owned by lineage, but strong sense of personal ownership of titles, names, privileges, ritual artifacts, and so on	Private and state ownership increases at the expense of communal ownership
Law and legitimate control of force	No formal laws or punishments; right to use force is communal	No formal laws or punishments; right to use force belongs to lineage, clan, or association	May be informal laws and specified punishments for breaking taboos; chief has limited access to physical coercion	Formal laws and punishments; state holds all legitimate access to use of physical force
Religion	No religious priesthood or full-time specialists; shamanistic	Shamanistic; strong emphasis on initiation rites and other rites of passage that unite lineages	Inchoate formal priesthood, hierarchical, ancestor-based religion	Full-time priesthood provides sacral legitimization of state
Recent and contemporary examples	!Kung* Bushmen (Africa), Pygmies (Africa), Eskimo (Canada, Alaska) and Shoshone (U.S.)	Kpelle (W. Africa), Yanomamo (Venezuela), Nuer (Sudan), and Cheyenne (U.S.)	Precolonial Hawaii, Kwakiutl (Canada), Tikopia (Polynesia), and Dagurs (Mongolia)	Ankole (Uganda), Jimma (Ethiopia), Kachari (India), and Volta (Africa)
Historic and prehistoric examples	Virtually all paleolithic societies	Iroquois (U.S.) and Oaxaca Valley (Mexico), 1500–1000 B.C.	Precolonial Ashanti, Benin, Dahomy (Africa), and Scottish Highlanders	Precolonial Zulu (Africa), Aztec (Mexico), Inca (Peru), and Sumeria (Iraq)

Source: From Lewellen 1983, 20–21.
*Ju/'hoansi

area studies. Anthropologists developed lists of **culture traits,** or features, characteristic of a particular social group. They focused on only part of a society's culture, part of its heritage or customs: a particular ritual, a musical style, a way of making pots. They then searched the ethnographic record carefully to determine how widely those cultural traits had spread into other societies. A **culture area** was defined by the limits of borrowing, or the diffusion, of a particular trait or set of traits (Figure 4.5).

---

culture traits Particular features or parts of a cultural tradition (such as a dance, a ritual, or style of pot making).

culture area The limits of borrowing, or the diffusion, of a particular cultural trait or set of traits.

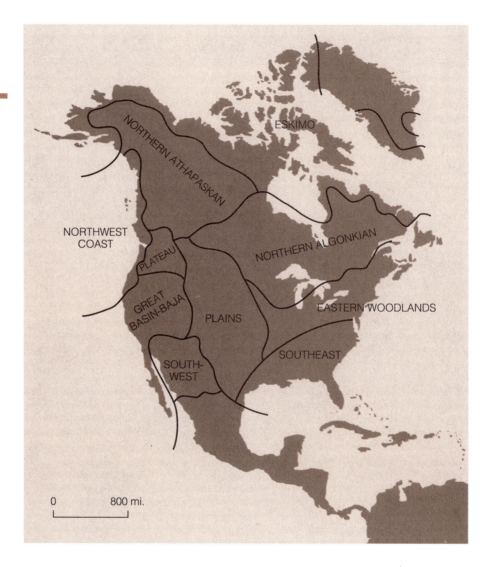

FIGURE 4.5 *This map shows the native American culture areas for North America north of Mexico.* (After Oswalt 1972)

This emphasis in anthropological research had consequences for typologies of social forms. If borrowing allowed societies to skip evolutionary stages entirely, then any classification of universal stages was meaningless. Furthermore, even timeless classificatory schemes, like those of the social anthropologists, were of limited value. They depended on the assumption that societies were airtight entities with clear-cut social structures. But what if societies are not closed but are perpetually open to cultural borrowing? It is then impossible to describe their structures in clear-cut terms. And indeed, the efforts of American anthropologists turned away from placing whole societies in categories and toward identifying culture traits and their regions of diffusion. Area studies created cultural classifications that were either broader than an individual society (culture areas) or narrower than an individual society (culture traits). The end product was a list of traits and a map of cultural areas in which the traits are found. Boundaries around particular societies were ignored.

Postwar Realities

Then the world changed again. World War II was closely followed by the breakup of European colonial empires in Africa and Asia and by the civil rights movement in the United States. Former colonies were now independent states. Their citizens rejected the traditional Western view of them as savages or barbarians. They intended to prove that they could govern their countries in a manner as "civilized" as that of Western nations.

Political realities thus created for Westerners new experiences of the non-Western "other." These experiences made the pretensions of unilineal evolutionism even less plausible. As well, the leaders of the new states set out to consolidate national consciousness among the supposedly structurally separate societies within their borders. This effort made the structural focus of preindependence social anthropologists seem increasingly misguided. Such efforts at nation building led some Western anthropologists to recognize that the "traditional" societies they had been studying had not, in fact, been structurally separate even under colonialism. The experience of decolonization forced anthropologists to pay direct attention to colonialism itself. They began to see it as a form of social organization that had essentially eliminated the autonomy of indigenous social groups and forcibly restructured them into subordinate positions within a larger social, political, and economic entity.

At the same time, anthropologists with roots in the non-Western world began to add their voices to those of Western anthropologists. They were and continue to be highly critical of the cultural stereotypes institutionalized by unilineal evolutionism and structural-functionalism. As a result, rankings of human social forms that seemed clearcut and persuasive in the late nineteenth and early twentieth centuries appear blurred and questionable today. But this does not mean that typologies have disappeared altogether in contemporary cultural and social anthropology. The problem posed for the analyst by cultural diversity has not disappeared. Most anthropologists, for some purposes, still need to classify the known societies of the world in one way or another, depending on the problems they are investigating.

Studying Forms of Human Society Today

It is probably fair to say that the field of anthropology as a whole is not committed to classification as an ultimate goal. In fact, among anthropologists themselves, opinions about the importance of classifying forms of human society vary greatly. Some anthropologists, especially those interested in political and economic issues, continue to find typologies useful. Others—for example, those studying art or religion—are not much concerned with the classification of the society in which they work. More important to them are similarities that overlap cultural boundaries.

Modern anthropologists have not found universally accepted answers to the seemingly unanswerable questions of social origins, social stability, and social change. But many have come to see the similarities and differences between the West and the rest of the world in terms of "more or less" rather than "present or absent." As a result, many modern anthropologists are no longer interested in whether a society is organized on the basis of "primitive" kinship or "civilized" social class; they understand "kinship" and "class" as culturally constructed idioms for organizing people and for thinking about the nature of human nature and human society.

This does not mean that the choice of a kinship idiom as opposed to a class idiom makes no difference or is without historical or cultural motivation. Many anthropologists would insist that a shift from organization by kinship to organization by class marks an important watershed in social organization. They would argue that the differences generated by this divide far outweigh any similarities that remain. Still, most anthropologists would agree that an emphasis on similarities or differences in different types of society is closely related to the questions anthropologists are investigating and the theoretical assumptions they bring with them to their research. Different schools of anthropology, not to mention different social sciences, have different professional "worldviews" that define for them what is worth paying attention to and what is safe to ignore. What remain are the phenomena to be classified.

Let us turn again to Lewellen's classification of social types. How meaningful is it? What does it reflect? Lewellen argues that it is designed to reflect structural, organizational similarities and differences. To defend such criteria, he employs a house metaphor: "Two houses built of different materials but to the same floor plan will obviously be much more alike than two houses of the same materials but very different designs (say, a town house and a ranch house). . . . In short, a house is defined in terms of its organization, not its components, and that organization will be influenced by its physical environment and the level of technology of the people who designed it" (1983, 17).

Because he assumes that structural similarities and differences are both supremely significant and objectively obvious, it seems that Lewellen is affiliated with the tradition of British social anthroplogy. Similarities and differences concerning the materials out of which the houses are made can safely be ignored. We suggest that structural similarities and differences are "obviously" supremely significant only if classification is approached with a previous set of assumptions concerning what is important and what is not.

"A house is defined in terms of its organization, not its components." For certain purposes, and for certain observers, this may be true. But *organization* is an ambiguous term. Is a house's organization manifested in its floor plan or in the way the various rooms are used regardless of floor plan? Is a bedroom "objectively" a bedroom wherever it occurs, whether in a town house or a ranch house? Is a bedroom still a bedroom, whether in a town house or a ranch house, when the people living in that house use it to store equipment or to cook in? Is an American living room still a living room, in any objective sense, when its primary role is to provide sleeping space for an extended family of southeastern Asian immigrants? Does that immigrant family's ideas of how living space should properly be used change when the family moves from a thatched hut to an apartment with wooden floors and plaster walls?

Structural similarities and differences that seem obvious to many political anthropologists in the British tradition lead those anthropologists to set off states and chiefdoms sharply from tribes and bands. Would these similarities and differences seem so sharp to an anthropologist interested in classifying the ways different societies make a living? As we shall see in Chapter 13, anthropologists interested in making such a classification employ concepts like *subsistence strategy* or *mode of production* to order their typologies. These concepts focus on what has been called the *material life process of society*. These are the strategies and technologies for organizing the production, distribution, and consumption of food, clothing, housing, tools, and other material goods. They therefore define a domain of relevance that may be quite different from that of political anthropologists. Not surprisingly, they yield different typologies.

It is possible to preserve the fourfold distinction among states, chiefdoms, tribes, and bands and yet to group them differently. Consider, for example, the subsistence strategies that each category of society typically employs: bands depend on foraging—gathering, fishing, hunting—to meet subsistence needs; by contrast, tribes, chiefdoms, and states depend on food production—plant cultivation and herding. On this basis, bands can be set off from tribes, chiefdoms, and states. Now consider these social organizations in terms of their political organization: tribes and bands are both egalitarian organizations, yet they differ substantially in their subsistence strategies (see Table 4.2). Neither the set of similarities (political organization) nor the set of differences (subsistence strategies) is objectively more obvious than the other. Both depend on the topic of research as well as prior assumptions, made by the researchers, concerning what is worth paying attention to and what can be safely downplayed or ignored.

The situation gets even more complicated. Many social typologists are confident about separating bands from tribes, chiefdoms, and states because, in an overwhelming number of ethnographic cases, a foraging subsistence strategy is not found together with developed lineages or social ranking or settled villages. But there are troublesome exceptions to this pattern, notably among the various societies of the northwest coast of North America: such groups as the Tlingit and Kwakiutl neither farmed nor herded (they fished, hunted, and gathered), but they created complex, settled societies with developed lineages and social ranking. Moreover, archaeological evidence from the Andes and elsewhere suggests that foraging societies were responsible for some of the earliest monumental architecture, the construction of which seems to imply a fair degree of social complexity (Keatinge 1988b).

Lewellen acknowledges the problems these societies pose for any political typology: "Indian societies of the Northwest Coast of North America are usually categorized as chiefdoms . . . but the fit is far from perfect. . . . Perhaps all the cultures of the Northwest Coast would seem to represent a blending of elements of both tribes and chiefdoms" (1983, 33–34).

It is also possible that the existence of such societies reveals the limits of a particular typology. They might represent an authentic social form in their own right, one that the prototypes of traditional classification systems are unable to characterize unambiguously. Such societies fall between the categories of a classification and may only be recognized when new evidence, in this case from archaeology, supports their validity. This should remind us that typologies are human cultural constructions, not pure reflections of objective reality, and that we may change them as our understanding changes.

Although it is sometimes easy to emphasize the shortcomings of past classificatory schemes in anthropology, it is important not to overlook the lasting contributions they have made. Despite its excesses, unilineal cultural evolutionism highlights the fact that cultures change over time and that our species has experienced a broad sequence of cultural developments. Structural-functionalist typologies may seem overly rigid and static, but the ethnographic investigation of the structural-functionalists shows just how intricate the social institutions and practices of so-called "simple" societies can be. The culture-area studies of Boas and his students deemphasize boundaries between separate societies, but the attention they pay to diffusion makes clear that indigenous people have never been unthinking slaves to tradition. On the contrary, they have been alert to their surroundings, aware of cultural alternatives, active to adopt new ways from other people when it has suited them. It is indeed the cultural creativity of all human beings, in all societies, that keeps anthropologists busy. In the following chapters, we will look first at various dimensions of cultural creativity and then at the forms of material constraint against which it struggles.

KEY TERMS

typology	band	structural-functional
unilineal cultural	tribe	theory
evolutionism	chiefdom	culture traits
social structure	state	culture area

CHAPTER SUMMARY

1. Cultural traditions take shape as a result of the dialectic between human imagination and the material world. Forms of human society are shaped by both the nonhuman natural environment and the human social environment.

2. The imperialist expansion of Europe, which coincided with the rise of industrial capitalism, was the central force leading to cross-cultural contact between the West and the rest of the world. Many of the peoples whom anthropologists would later study were relatively recent creations, forged in the field of contact between indigenous populations and Europeans. An anthropological survey of the forms of human society needs to investigate the historical circumstances surrounding the contacts between anthropologists and their informants.

3. Non-Western societies have not escaped the historical forces that have influenced everyone else, yet remnants of precontact societies survive today, showing that conquered peoples can actively cope with contemporary problems and opportunities to reshape their own social identities. An impressive variety of forms of human society remains.

4. Anthropologists have created typologies of the forms of human society. They first identify those societies that are most distinct from one another based on certain

criteria and then sort known societies by their resemblance to these exemplars. Depending upon an anthropologist's analytical purposes, the same social forms can be classified in different ways.

5. The earliest important anthropological typology of forms of human society was that proposed by unilineal cultural evolutionists. They tried to explain contemporary cultural diversity by arguing that different kinds of society existing in the nineteenth century represented different stages of societal evolution. Every human society either had passed or would pass through the same stages, if it survived. Societies in stages lower in the typology than Europe were viewed as living relics of the past. This typology contained three basic categories: savagery, barbarism, and civilization.

6. Anthropologists doing research in a colonial setting in the first half of the twentieth century collected a vast amount of detailed, accurate information about aspects of indigenous life, which the colonial administration needed to understand. Their research led them to set aside questions about cultural evolution and to focus on social structural differences and similarities observed at a single point in time.

7. In American anthropology, the classification of forms of human society was ignored almost totally in the early part of the twentieth century. Following Boas, American anthropologists rejected unilineal cultural evolutionism on the grounds that societies could easily borrow cultural forms from one another, thus skipping stages. Consequently, the aim of research shifted to making lists of culture traits and to mapping the culture areas in which they were found.

8. Classifying forms of human society is not an ultimate goal for most anthropologists today, although some anthropologists find typologies useful. Classifications differ, depending upon the problems to be solved. Thus, societies grouped together because of similarities in political organization may be separated from one another because of differences in subsistence strategies. The fuzziness of category boundaries reminds us that taxonomies are human cultural constructions, not pure reflections of objective reality.

SUGGESTED READINGS

Lewellen, Ted. 1983. *Political anthropology.* South Hadley, MA: Bergin and Garvey. *Contains much useful information about the different kinds of societies that different scholars have identified.*

Weatherford, Jack. 1988. *Indian givers. How the Indians of the Americas transformed the world.* New York: Fawcett Columbine.

————. 1991. *Native roots. How the Indians enriched America.* New York: Fawcett Columbine.

————. 1994. *Savages and civilization.* New York: Random House. *All three of these books are engaging accounts of the consequences of contact between the Old World and New World in the past and in the present.*

Wolf, Eric. 1982. *Europe and the people without history.* Berkeley: University of California Press. *A classic text about the connection of European expansion to the rest of the world. This work also discusses the effect of European contact on indigenous societies.*

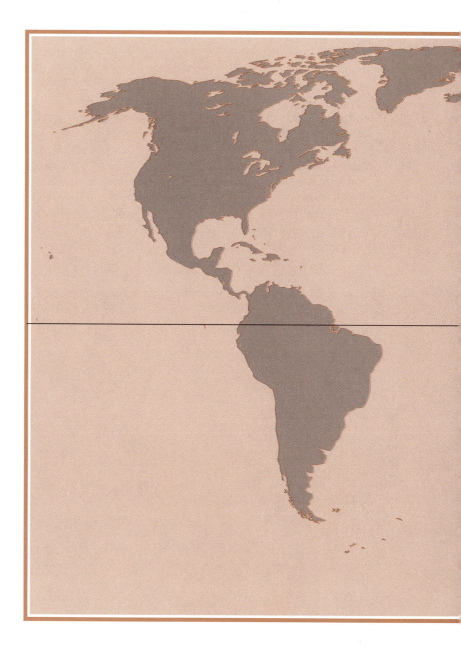

Language

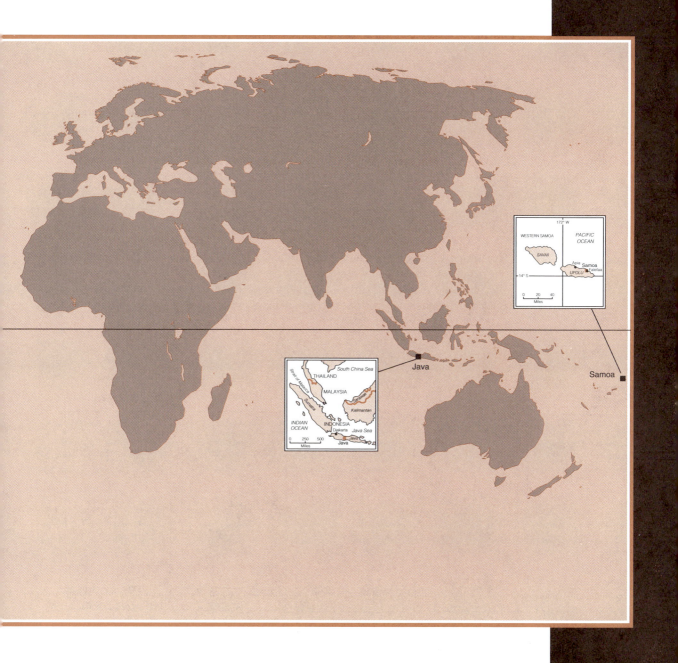

he system of arbitrary vocal symbols human beings use to encode and communicate about their experience of the world and of one another is called **language.** It is a unique faculty that sets human beings apart from other living species. It provides basic tools for human creativity, making possible the cultural achievements that we view as monuments to our species' genius. And yet, despite all that language makes possible, its tools are double edged. Language allows people to communicate with one another, but it also creates barriers to communication. One major barrier is linguistic diversity (Figure 5.1). There are some 3,000 mutually unintelligible languages spoken in the world today. Why should there be such barriers to communication? This chapter will explore the ambiguity, limitations, and power of human language.

LANGUAGE AND CULTURE

Human language is a biocultural phenomenon. The human brain and the anatomy of our mouth and throat make language a biological possibility for us. At the same time, every human language is clearly a cultural product. It is shared by a group of speakers, encoded in symbols, and historically transmitted through teaching and learning; it tends to be coherent, thus making communication possible.

FIGURE 5.1

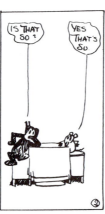

by George Herriman

Anthropological Interest in Language

Language is of primary interest to anthropologists for at least three reasons. First, field-workers need to be able to communicate with their informants, whose languages are often unwritten. This means that anthropologists must possess a certain level of linguistic skill, especially those who must learn their informants' languages without formal instruction.

Second, anthropologists can transcribe or tape-record speech and thus lift it out of its cultural context to be analyzed on its own. What is learned about the inner workings of language can then be applied to the analysis of other domains of culture. The motto seems to be this: "What is true about language is true about the rest of culture." Some schools of anthropological theory take this motto especially seriously, basing their analyses of culture explicitly on ideas taken from **linguistics**, the scientific study of language.

Third, and most important, all people use language to encode their experience and to structure their understanding of the world and of themselves. By learning another society's language, we learn something about their culture as well. In fact, learning another language inevitably provides unsuspected insights into the nature of our own language and culture, often making it impossible to take language of any kind for granted ever again.

It is useful to distinguish *Language* from *languages. Language* with a capital *L* (like *Culture* with a capital *C*) is an abstract property belonging to the human species as a whole. Anthropologists deduced this when they realized that all human groups had their own particular *languages*. It is also useful to distinguish *Language* (or *languages*) from *speech* and *communication.* We usually think of spoken language (speech) when we use the term *language,* but in fact, a language like English can be communicated in writing, Morse code, or American Sign Language, to name just three nonspoken media. *Human communication* can be defined as the transfer of information from one person to another, but communication clearly can take place without the use of words, spoken or otherwise. People communicate with one another nonverbally all the time, sending messages with the clothes they wear, the way they walk, or even how long they keep other people waiting for them.

In fact, even linguistic communication depends on more than words alone. Native speakers of one language share not just vocabulary and grammar but also a number of assumptions about how to speak that may not be shared by speakers of a different language. Students learning a new language discover early on that word-for-word translation from one language to another does not work. Sometimes there are no equivalent words in the second language; but even when there appear to be such words, word-for-word translation may not mean in language B what it meant in language A.

---

language The system of arbitrary vocal symbols we use to encode our experience of the world.

linguistics The scientific study of language.

Here are two examples: (1) When we have eaten enough, we say in English, "I'm full." This may be translated directly into French as *Je suis plein*. To a native speaker of French, this sentence (especially when uttered at the end of a meal) has the nonsensical meaning "I am a pregnant [male] animal." Alternatively, if uttered by a man who has just consumed a lot of wine, it means "I'm drunk." (2) In Spanish, a common expression that means "She gave birth" is *Ella dio a luz*. Translated word-for-word into English, it means "She gave to light."

Speaking a second language is often frustrating and even unsettling; someone who once found the world simple to talk about suddenly turns into a babbling fool. Studying a second language, then, is less a matter of learning new labels for old objects than it is of learning how to identify new objects that go with new labels. The student must also learn the appropriate contexts in which different linguistic forms may be used: a person can be "full" after eating in English, but not in French. Knowledge about context is cultural knowledge. The linguistic system abstracted from its cultural context must be returned to that context if a holistic understanding of language is to be achieved.

Talking about Experience

Language, like the rest of culture, is a product of human attempts to come to terms with experience. Each natural human language is adequate for its speakers' needs, given their particular way of life. Speakers of a particular language tend to develop larger vocabularies to discuss those aspects of life that are of importance to them. The Aymara, who live in the Andes of South America, have invented hundreds of different words for the many varieties of potato they grow (see EthnoProfile 7.1: Aymara.) By contrast, speakers of English have created an elaborate vocabulary for discussing computers. However, despite differences in vocabulary and grammar, all natural human languages ever studied by linguists prove to be equally complex. Just as there is no such thing as a "primitive" human culture, there is no such thing as a "primitive" human language.

Traditionally, languages are associated with concrete groups of people called *speech communities*. Nevertheless, because all languages possess alternative ways of speaking, members of particular speech communities do not all possess identical knowledge about the language they share, nor do they all speak the same way. Individuals and subgroups within a speech community make use of linguistic resources in different ways. Consequently, there is a tension in language between diversity and commonality. Individuals and subgroups attempt to use the varied resources of a language to create unique, personal voices. These efforts are countered by the pressure to negotiate a common code for communication within the larger social group. In this way, language is produced and reproduced through the activity of its speakers. Any particular language that we may identify at a given moment is a snapshot of a continuing process.

The resources of language stretch to accommodate the experiences of its speakers. There are many ways to communicate our experiences, and there is no absolute standard favoring one way over another. Some things that are easy to say in language A may be difficult to say in language B, yet other aspects of language B may appear much simpler than equivalent aspects of language A. For example, English ordinarily requires the use of determiners (*a, an, the*) before nouns, but this rule is not found in all lan-

FIGURE 5.2 *Him'be boi 'don nder luumo.*

guages. Likewise, the verb *to be,* called the *copula* by linguists, is not found in all languages, although the relationships we convey when we use *to be* in English may still be communicated. In English, we might say "There *are* many people in the market." Translating this sentence into Fulfulde, the language of the Fulbe of northern Cameroon, we get *Him'be boi 'don nder luumo,* which, word-for-word, reads something like "people-many-there-in-market" (Figure 5.2). No single Fulfulde word corresponds to the English *are* or *the.*

Differences across languages are not absolute. In Chinese, for example, verbs never change to indicate tense; instead, separate expressions referring to time are used. English speakers may conclude that Chinese speakers cannot distinguish between past, present, and future. This structure seems completely different from English structure. But consider such English sentences as "Have a hard day at the office today?" and "Your interview go well?" These abbreviated questions, used in informal English, are very similar to the formal patterns of Chinese and other languages of southeastern Asia (Akmajian, Demers, and Harnish 1984, 194–95).

This kind of overlap between two very different languages demonstrates at least three important things. First, it shows the kind of cross-linguistic commonality that forms the foundation both for learning new languages and for translation. Second, it highlights the variety of expressive resources to be found in any single language. We learn that English allows us to use either tense markers on verbs (*-s, -ed*) or unmarked verbs with adverbs of time (*have* + today). In addition, we learn that the former grammatical pattern is associated with formal usage, whereas the latter is associated with informal usage. Finally, it shows that the same structures can have different functions in different languages.

As anthropological linguist Elinor Ochs observes, most cross-cultural differences in language use "turn out to be differences in *context* and/or *frequency of occurrence*" (1986,

10). In the preceding example, the verbal pattern associated with formal usage in Chinese is associated with informal usage in English. This discovery leads us to suspect that Chinese must have informal usage as well and to wonder how the grammatical patterns of informal usage differ from those of formal usage. These are the kinds of questions anthropological linguists are continually asking about the languages they study.

DESIGN FEATURES OF HUMAN LANGUAGE

One anthropological linguist, Charles Hockett, has spent many years thinking about human language and how it differs from the communication systems of other animals. In 1966, he listed sixteen different **design features** of human language that, in his estimation, set it apart from other forms of animal communication. Six of these design features seem especially helpful in defining what makes human language distinctive: openness, displacement, arbitrariness, duality of patterning, semanticity, and prevarication.

Openness, probably the most important feature, emphasizes the same point that the celebrated linguist Noam Chomsky emphasized (1965, 6): human language is creative. Speakers of any given language can not only create new messages, they can also understand new messages created by other speakers. Someone may have never said to you, "Put this Babel fish in your ear," but knowing English, you can understand the message.

The importance of openness for human verbal communication is striking when we compare, for example, spoken human language to the vocal communication systems (or *call systems*) of monkeys and apes. Nonhuman primates can communicate in rather subtle ways using channels of transmission other than voice. However, these channels are far less sophisticated than, say, American Sign Language, and their call systems are very different from spoken human language. The number of calls are few and are produced only when the animal finds itself in a situation including such features as the presence of food or danger, friendly interest and the desire for company, the desire to mark the animal's location, or to signal pain, sexual interest, or the need for maternal care. If the animal is not in the appropriate situation, it does not produce the call. At most, it may refrain from uttering a call in a situation that would normally trigger it. In addition, nonhuman primates cannot emit a signal that has some features of one call and some of another. For example, if the animal encounters food and danger at the same time, one of the calls will take precedence. For these reasons, the call systems of nonhuman primates are said to be *closed* when compared to open human languages.

Openness is not the only feature of human language missing in the call system of apes. *Displacement,* which can be understood as an extension of openness, is also not found. Human beings can talk about absent or nonexistent objects and past or future events as easily as they discuss their immediate situations. Although nonhuman primates clearly have good memories, and some species, such as chimpanzees, seem to be able to plan social action in advance (such as when hunting for meat), they cannot use their call systems to talk about such events. Closed call systems lack displacement: for apes, out of sight is, if not out of mind, at least out of speech.

Closed call systems also lack the feature of *arbitrariness,* also connected with openness, which refers to the open nature of the link between sound and meaning: there is no necessary link between any particular sound and any particular meaning. For example, the sound sequence /boi/ refers to a "young male human being" in English, but means "more" or "many" in Fulfulde. One aspect of linguistic creativity is the free, creative production of new links between sounds and meanings. Thus, arbitrariness is the flip side of openness: if all links between sound and meaning are open, then the particular link between particular sounds and particular meanings in a particular language must be arbitrary. In primate call systems, by contrast, links between the sounds of calls and their meanings appear to be fixed and under considerable direct biological control.

Arbitrariness is evident in another design feature of language—*duality of patterning*. Human language, Hockett claimed, is patterned on two different levels: sound and meaning. On the first level, the small set of significant sounds (or *phonemes*) that characterize any particular language are not random but are systematically patterned. On the second level of patterning, however, grammar puts the sound units together according to an entirely different set of rules: the resulting sound clusters are the smallest meaning-bearing units of the language called *morphemes*.

Since Hockett first wrote, many linguists have suggested that there are more than just two levels of patterning in language. (We will discuss some additional levels later in the chapter.) In all cases, the principle relating levels to each other is the same: units at one level, patterned in one way (sounds), can be used to create units at a different level, patterned in a different way (morphemes, or units of meaning). The rules governing morphemes, in turn, are different from the rules by which morphemes are combined into sentences, which are different from the rules combining sentences into discourse. Today, linguists recognize many levels of patterning in human language, and the patterns that characterize one level cannot be reduced to the patterns of any other level. By contrast, ape call systems lack multilevel patterning (Wallman 1992).

Arbitrariness shows up again in the design feature of *semanticity*—the association of linguistic signals with aspects of the social, cultural, and physical world of a speech community. People use language to refer to and make sense of objects and processes in the world. Nevertheless, any linguistic description of reality, however accurate, is always somewhat arbitrary. This is because all linguistic descriptions are selective, highlighting some features of the world and downplaying others.

Perhaps the most striking consequence of the open, arbitrary nature of human language is the design feature *prevarication*. Hockett's remarks about this design feature deserve particular attention: "Linguistic messages can be false, and they can be meaningless in the logician's sense." In other words, not only can people use language to lie, but utterances that seem perfectly well formed grammatically may yield semantic nonsense. As an example, Chomsky offered the following sentence: "Colorless green ideas sleep furiously" (1957, 15). This is a grammatical sentence on one level—the right kinds of words are used in the right places—but on another level it is completely illogical. Prevarication makes this possible. It also makes the formation of scientific hypotheses possi-

---

design features Those characteristics of language that, when taken together, differentiate it from other known animal communication systems.

ble. The ability of language users to prevaricate—to make statements or ask questions that violate convention—is a major consequence of open symbolic systems. Apes using their closed call systems can neither lie nor formulate theories.

Opening Closed Call Systems

Charles Hockett and Robert Ascher (1964) hypothesize that the major switch in human evolution occurred when the closed call systems of our apelike ancestors opened up. When this happened, different sounds could be freely associated with the same meaning or the same meaning could be freely associated with different sounds. Multilevel patterning became possible. As a result, semanticity widened and became more complex and ambiguous. In addition, sounds and meanings became further detached, and detachable, from the immediate context in which they were being used, giving birth to displacement.

LANGUAGE AND COGNITION

Cognition refers to the mental processes by which human beings gain knowledge. The study of human language and the study of human cognition have long gone hand in hand. In particular, as more has been learned about language, psychologists and other social scientists have applied that knowledge to other areas of human mental functioning. (Unfortunately, some have attempted to reduce human knowledge to the structures of language.) Today, even nonanthropologists document the many ways that the nonlinguistic cognitive activity of human beings can affect their language development, particularly when both are studied in the context of language use.

Consequently, scholars are increasingly aware of the influence of context on what people choose to say. The results of this change in focus have been dramatic and are potentially quite radical. Alison Elliot reports, for example, that studies of child language no longer amount to a list of errors that children make when attempting to gain what Chomsky calls **linguistic competence,** or mastery of adult grammar; instead, linguists study children's verbal interactions in social and cultural context and draw attention to what children can do very well. "From an early age they appear to communicate very fluently, producing utterances which are not just remarkably well-formed according to the linguist's standards but also appropriate to the social context in which the speakers find themselves. Children are thus learning far more about language than rules of grammar. [They are] acquiring communicative competence" (Elliot 1981, 13).

Communicative competence, or mastery of adult rules for socially and culturally appropriate speech, is a term coined by American anthropological linguist Dell Hymes (1972). As an anthropologist, Hymes was sensitive to the role of context in shaping successful language use; he therefore objected to Chomsky's notion that linguistic competence consisted only of being able to make correct judgments of sentence grammaticality (Chomsky 1965, 4). Hymes observed that the meaning of the words and sentences that adults utter cannot be exhaustively described solely in grammatical terms. Competent adult speakers are able to choose words and topics of conversation appropri-

In Their Own Words   CULTURAL TRANSLATION

Linguistic translation is complicated and beset with pitfalls, as we have seen. Cultural translation, as David Parkin describes, requires not just knowledge of different grammars but also of the various, different cultural contexts in which grammatical forms are put to use.

Cultural translation, like translation from one language to another, never produces a rendering that is semantically and stylistically an exact replica of the original. That much we accept. What is not often recognized, perhaps not even by the translators themselves, is that the very act of having to decide how to phrase an event, sentiment, or human character engages the translator in an act of creation. The translator does not simply represent a picture made by an author. He or she creates a new version, and perhaps in some respects a new picture—a matter that is often of some great value.

So it is with anthropologists. But while this act of creation in reporting on "the other" may reasonably be regarded as a self-sustaining pleasure, it is also an entry into the pitfalls and traps of language use itself. One of the most interesting new fields in anthropology is the study of the relationship between language and human knowledge, both among ourselves as professional anthropologists and laypeople, and among peoples of other cultures. The study is at once both reflexive and critical.

The hidden influences at work in language use attract the most interest. For example, systems of greetings have many built-in elaborations that differentiate subtly between those who are old and young, male and female, rich and poor, and powerful and powerless. When physicians discuss a patient in his or her presence and refer to the patient in the third-person singular, they are in effect defining the patient as a passive object unable to enter into the discussion. When anthropologists present elegant accounts of "their" people that fit the demands of a convincing theory admirably, do they not also leave out [of] the description any consideration of the informants' own fears and feelings? Or do we go too far in making such claims, and is it often the anthropologist who is indulged by the people, who give him or her the data they think is sought, either in exchange for something they want or simply because it pleases them to do so? If the latter, how did the anthropologist's account miss this critical part of the dialogue?

Source: Parkin 1990.

ate to their social position, the social position of the person they are addressing, and the social context of interaction.

For example, children as well as adults need to know how to use personal pronouns appropriately when talking to others. This is particularly important in languages in which a speaker's choice of pronouns of address depends on his or her own status and the status of the person being addressed. For native speakers of English, the problem almost never arises with regard to pronoun choice because we address all people as "you." But any English speaker who has ever tried to learn a European language— French, for example—has struggled with the rules about when to address an individual using the second-person plural (*vous*) and when to use the second-person singular (*tu*).

cognition (1) The mental process by which human beings gain knowledge; (2) the nexus of relations between the mind at work and the world in which it works.

linguistic competence A term coined by linguist Noam Chomsky to refer to the mastery of adult grammar.

communicative competence A term coined by anthropological linguist Dell Hymes to refer to the mastery of adult rules for socially and culturally appropriate speech.

EthnoProfile 5.1 • JAVA

REGION: Southeastern Asia

NATION: Indonesia

POPULATION: 85,000,000

ENVIRONMENT: Tropical island

LIVELIHOOD: Intensive rice cultivation

POLITICAL ORGANIZATION: Highly stratified state

FOR MORE INFORMATION: Geertz, Clifford. 1960. *The religion of Java.* New York: Free Press.

To be safe, most students use *vous* for all individuals because it is the more formal term and they want to avoid appearing too familiar with native speakers whom they do not know well. But if you are dating a French person, at which point in the relationship does the change from *vous* to *tu* occur, and who decides? Moreover, sometimes—for example, among university students—the normal term of address is *tu* (even among strangers); it is used to indicate social solidarity. Native speakers of English who are learning French wrestle with these and other linguistic dilemmas. Rules for the appropriate use of *tu* and *vous* seem to have nothing to do with grammar, yet the choice between one form and the other indicates whether the speaker is someone who does or does not know how to speak French.

The French case is quite simple compared with other cases. Clifford Geertz has written about the Javanese language, in which all the words in a sentence must be carefully selected to reflect the social relationship between the speaker and the person addressed. (See EthnoProfile 5.1: Java.) Even a simple request like, "Are you going to eat rice and cassava now?" requires that speakers know at least five different varieties of the language in order to communicate socially as well as to make the request (Figure 5.3). It is impossible to say anything in Javanese without also communicating your social position relative to the person to whom you are speaking. This example illustrates the range of diversity present in a single language and how different varieties of a language are related to different subgroups within the speech community.

In summary, the design feature of openness is central to linguistic creativity. In fact, human cognition in general may operate on a design feature of openness. Openness would seem to be a necessary precondition for any creative use of symbols. What would the concept of *cognitive openness* refer to? One suggestion is that it would stand for the "central aspect of human thought and cognition, namely, *the ability to understand the same thing from different points of view*" (Ortony 1979, 14; emphasis added). In language, this means being able to talk about the same experiences from different perspectives, to paraphrase using different words and various grammatical constructions; at its most radical, it means that the experiences themselves can be differently conceived, labeled,

Speaking to persons of:	Level	"Are	you	going	to eat	rice	and	cassava	now?"	Complete sentence
Very high position	3a	menapa	pandjenengan	badé	dahar	sekul	kalijan	kaspé	samenika	Menapa pandjenengan badé dahar sekul kalijan kaspé samenika?
High position	3	menapa	sampéjan	badé	neda	sekul	kalijan	kaspé	samenika	Menapa sampéjan badé neda sekul kalijan kaspé samenika?
Same position, not close	2	napa	sampéjan	adjéng	neda	sekul		kaspé	saniki	Napa sampéjan adjéng neda sekul lan kaspé saniki?
Same position, casual acquaintance	1a		sampéjan		neda		lan	kaspé	saniki	Apa sampéjan arep neda sega lan kaspé saiki?
Close friends of any rank; also to lower status (basic language)	1	apa	kowé	arep	mangan	sega			saiki	Apa kowé arep mangan sega lan kaspé saiki?

FIGURE 5.3 *The dialect of nonnoble, urbanized, somewhat educated people in central Java.* (From Geertz 1960)

and discussed. In this view, no single perspective would necessarily emerge as more correct in every respect than all others.

THE SAPIR-WHORF HYPOTHESIS

During the first half of the twentieth century, two American anthropological linguists noted that the grammars of different languages often described the same situation in different ways. Edward Sapir and Benjamin Whorf were impressed enough to conclude that language has the power to shape the way people see the world. This claim has been called the *linguistic relativity principle*, or the **Sapir-Whorf hypothesis.** This hypothesis has been highly controversial because it is difficult to test and the results of testing have been ambiguous.

Sapir-Whorf hypothesis A position, associated with Edward Sapir and Benjamin Whorf, that asserts that language has the power to shape the way people see the world.

In Their Own Words   **ESKIMO WORDS FOR SNOW**

Word-for-word translation from one language to another is often difficult because the vocabulary referring to a given topic may be well developed in one language and poorly developed in another. However, as Laura Martin shows, we may draw erroneous conclusions from these differences without a deeper knowledge of the grammars of the languages concerned.

The earliest reference to Eskimos and snow was apparently made by Franz Boas. Among many examples of cross-linguistic variation in the patterns of form/ meaning association, Boas presents a brief citation of four lexically unrelated words for snow in Eskimo: *aput* 'snow on the ground,' *qana* 'falling snow,' *piqsirpoq* 'drifting snow,' and *qimuqsuq* 'a snow drift.' In this casual example, Boas makes little distinction among "roots," "words," and "independent terms." He intends to illustrate the noncomparability of language structures, not to examine their cultural or cognitive implications.

The example became inextricably identified with Benjamin Whorf through the popularity of "Science and Linguistics," his 1940 article (see Carroll 1956: 207–219) exploring the same ideas that interested Boas, lexical elaboration not chief among them. Although for Boas the example illustrated a similarity between English and "Eskimo," Whorf reorients it to contrast them (1956: 216). It is a minor diversion in a discussion of pervasive semantic categories such as time and space, and he develops it no further, here or elsewhere in his writings.

Of particular significance is Whorf's failure to cite specific data, numbers, or sources. His English glosses suggest as many as five words, but not the same set given by Boas. Although Whorf's source is uncertain, if he did rely on Boas, his apparently casual revisions of numbers and glosses are but the first mistreatments to which the original data have been subjected.

Anthropological fascination with the example is traceable to two influential textbooks, written in the late 1950s by members of the large group of language scientists familiar with "Science and Linguistics," and adopted in a variety of disciplines well into the 1970s. One or both of these were probably read by most anthropologists trained between 1960 and 1970, and by countless other students as well during that heyday of anthropology's popularity.

In the first, *The Silent Language,* Edward Hall mentions the example only three times, but his treatment of it suggests that he considered it already familiar to many potential readers. Hall credits Boas, but misrepresents both the intent and extent of the original citation. Even the data are misplaced. Hall inexplicably describes the Eskimo data as "nouns" and, although his argument implies quite a large inventory, specific numbers are not provided. Hall introduces still another context for the example, using it in the analysis of cultural categories.

Researchers devised two versions of the hypothesis. The so-called "strong" version, known as *linguistic determinism,* implies that the grammars of our native language determine how we think about the world. It reduces patterns of thought and culture to the patterns of the grammar that supposedly cause them. If a grammar classifies nouns in male and female gender categories, linguistic determinism concludes that speakers of that language must be forced to think of male and female human beings as radically different kinds of living beings. By contrast, a language that makes no grammatical distinctions on the basis of gender presumably trains its speakers to treat male and female human beings as equal. If linguistic determinism is correct, then a change in grammar could change thought patterns: if English speakers simply stopped using *he* and *she* and invented a new, gender-neutral, third-person singular pronoun, such as *te,*

At approximately the same time, Roger Brown's *Words and Things* (1958) appeared, intended as a textbook in the "psychology of language." Here the example is associated with Whorf and thoroughly recast. Brown claims precisely "three Eskimo words for snow," an assertion apparently based solely on a drawing in Whorf's paper. Psychological and cognitive issues provide still another context in Brown's discussion of a theory about the effects of lexical categorization on perception.

Brown's discussion illustrates a creeping carelessness about the actual linguistic facts of the example; this carelessness is no less shocking because it has become so commonplace. Consider Brown's application of Zipf's Law to buttress arguments about the relationship between lexicon and perception. Since Zipf's Law concerns word length, Brown's hypothesis must assume something about the length of his "three" "Eskimo" "snow" words; his argument stands or falls on the assumption that they must be both short and frequent. Eskimo words, however, are the products of an extremely synthetic morphology in which all word building is accomplished by multiple suffixation. Their length is well beyond the limits of Zipf's calculations. Furthermore, precisely identical whole "words" are unlikely to recur because the particular combination of suffixes used with a "snow" root, or any other, varies by speaker and situation as well as by syntactic role.

A minimal knowledge of Eskimo grammar would have confirmed the relevance of these facts to the central hypotheses, and would, moreover, have established the even more relevant fact that there is nothing at all peculiar about the behavior or distribution of "snow words" in these languages. The structure of Eskimo grammar means that the number of "words" for snow is literally incalculable, a conclusion that is inescapable for any other root as well.

Any sensible case for perceptual variation based on lexical inventory should, therefore, require reference to distinct "roots" rather than to "words," but this subtlety has escaped most authors. Brown, for example, repeatedly refers to linguistic units such as "verbal expression," "phrase," and "word" in a way that underscores the inadequacy of his understanding of Eskimo grammar. His assumption that English and "Eskimo" are directly comparable, together with his acceptance of pseudo-facts about lexical elaboration in an unfamiliar language, cause him to construct a complex psychocultural argument based on cross-linguistic "evidence" related to the example with not a single item of Eskimo data in support. This complete absence of data (and of accurate references) sets a dangerous precedent because it not only prevents direct evaluation of Brown's claims but suggests that such evaluation is unnecessary.

Source: Laura Martin 1986.

---

then, linguistic determinists predict, they would begin to treat men and women as equals in society.

There are a number of problems with linguistic determinism. In the first place, there are languages such as Fulfulde in which only one third-person pronoun is used for males and females (*o*); however, male-dominant social patterns are prominent among Fulfulde speakers in Cameroon. In the second place, if language determined thought in this way, it would be impossible to translate from one language to another or even to learn another language with a different grammatical structure. Because human beings do learn foreign languages and translate from one language to another, the strong version of the Sapir-Whorf hypothesis cannot be correct. Third, even if it were possible to draw firm boundaries around speech communities (which it isn't), every language contains within it a range of ways of speaking that provides its native speakers with alternative ways of describing the world. In any case, in most of the world's societies, monolingualism is the exception rather than the rule. Finally, people who grow up bilingual do not also grow up schizophrenic, as if trying to reconcile two contradictory views of reality. Indeed, bilingual children ordinarily benefit from knowing two languages, do not confuse them, can switch readily from one to another, and even appear to demonstrate greater cognitive flexibility on psychological tests than monolinguals (Elliot 1981, 56).

In the face of these objections, other researchers offer a "weak" version of the Sapir-Whorf hypothesis that rejects linguistic determinism for the preceding reasons but continues to claim that language shapes thought and culture. Thus, grammatical gender might not determine a male-dominant social order, but it might facilitate the acceptance of such a social order because the grammatical distinction between *he* and *she* might make separate and unequal gender roles seem "natural." However, if grammar merely "shapes" thought in this way, it would seem far too weak a force to merit any scientific interest, especially given that many native speakers of English turn out to be strong promoters of gender equality.

Neither Sapir nor Whorf favored linguistic determinism. Sapir argued that language's importance lies in the way it directs attention to some aspects of experience rather than to others. He was impressed by the fact that human beings cannot experience reality except as it is mediated by cognitive processes. Language is only one manifestation, although an important one, of these processes. As a result, he observed that "it is generally difficult to make a complete divorce between objective reality and our linguistic symbols of reference to it" (E. Sapir [1933] 1966, 9, 15).

Whorf's views have been more sharply criticized by later scholars. His discussions of the linguistic relativity principle are complex and ambiguous. At least part of the problem arises from Whorf's attempt to view grammar as the linguistic pattern that shapes culture and thought. Whorf's contemporaries understood grammar to refer to rules for combining sounds into words and words into sentences. Whorf did not reject this definition of grammar, but he believed that linguistic investigation showed that grammar needs to be thought of in broader terms. Some of Whorf's texts suggest that he was working to extend grammar to include a new level of patterning that went beyond words and sentences (Schultz 1990). Unfortunately, Whorf died before working out the theoretical language to describe such a level.

COMPONENTS OF LANGUAGE

Anthropologists are very interested in how human languages are put together. Originally, they hoped that coming to understand the sound patterns of language would be sufficient. But it soon became apparent that patterns in other areas of language cannot be reduced to patterns governing speech sounds. They recognized that languages have different levels, or components, each with its own particular rules. The duality-of-patterning design feature acknowledges the discovery that the rules governing speech sounds are different from the rules governing word formation and sentence structure.

Edward Sapir once commented that "all grammars leak." The history of linguistic study illustrates this statement: Over time, linguists came to recognize a growing number

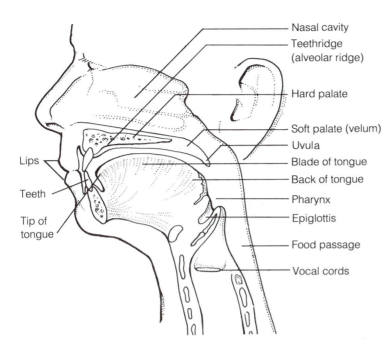

FIGURE 5.4 *The speech organs.*

of language components; each new component served as an attempt to plug the "leaks" in an earlier theory. Aspects of language that seemed to escape phonological explanation leaked out of that component, and morphology was developed to contain the leak—to explain what had previously resisted explanation. So it goes with all the remaining components of grammar. By the time the component of pragmatics is reached, however, the linguistic phenomena that resist explanation begin to spill over into the domain of culture. Let us examine each component of language in turn. The following discussion pinpoints the various leaks linguists have recognized (as well as their attempts to plug the leaks) and demonstrates how culture and language influence each other.

Phonology: Sounds

The study of the sounds of language, **phonology**, is a biocultural study from the outset. The sounds of human language are special because they are produced by a set of organs, the speech organs, that belong only to the human species (Figure 5.4). These organs are primarily for ingestion and breathing and secondarily for the production of speech. The actual sounds that come out of our mouths are called *phones*, and they vary continuously in acoustic properties. However, we hear all the phones within a particular range of variation as functionally equivalent *allophones* of the same *phoneme*, or

phonology The study of the sounds of language.

characteristic speech sound in the language. Part of the phonologist's job is to map out possible arrangements of speech organs that human beings may use to create the sounds of language. Another part is to examine individual languages to discover the particular sound combinations they contain and the patterns into which those sound combinations are organized.

The sounds of language can be studied from the perspective of the speaker, the hearer, or the sound medium itself. Most work in phonology has been done from the perspective of the speaker, who produces, or *articulates,* the sounds of language using the speech organs. No language makes use of all the many sounds the human speech organs can produce. For example, American English uses only 38 sounds, traditionally referred to as *consonants* and *vowels.*

Although all languages rely on only a handful of phonemes, no two languages use exactly the same set. Furthermore, different speakers of the same language often differ from one another in the way their phonemes are patterned, producing "accents," which constitute one kind of variety within a language. This variety is not random; the speech sounds characteristic of any particular accent follow a pattern. Speakers with different accents are usually able to understand one another in most circumstances, but their distinctive articulation is a clue to their ethnic, regional, or social-class origins. The sound changes that occur over time within any particular phonemic system (accent) are equally orderly.

Phonemes were originally conceived of as the building blocks of language, little atoms that could not be further broken down or analyzed. But phonologists discovered that it is possible to analyze the elements that constitute phonemes, just as atomic physicists discovered that atoms can be smashed to reveal subatomic particles. These smaller, subphonemic elements are called *distinctive features* of phonemes. Each phoneme of a language can be conceived of as a bundle of distinctive features.

Morphology: Word Structure

Morphology, the study of how words are put together, developed as a subfield of linguistics as soon as linguists realized that the rules they had devised to explain sound patterns in language could not account for meaning patterns as well. This became obvious when they began to study the structure of words.

What is a word? In some languages, such as English, a word might be defined as a short, meaning-bearing stretch of speech, clearly separable from other similar stretches of speech, and capable of being moved around in sentences or reappearing in different sentences. English speakers tend to think of words as the building blocks of sentences and of sentences as strings of words. But words are not all alike: some words (*book*), cannot be broken down into smaller elements; other words (*bookworm*) can.

The puzzle deepens when we try to translate words from one language into another. Sometimes expressions that require only one word in one language (*préciser* in French) require more than one word in another language (*to make precise* in English). Other times, we must deal with languages whose utterances cannot easily be broken down into words at all. Consider the utterance *nikookitepeena* from Shawnee (a Native American language), which translates into English as "I dipped his head in the water" (Whorf

TABLE 5.1

MORPHEMES OF SHAWNEE UTTERANCE AND THEIR GLOSSES

ni	*kooki*	*tepe*	*en*	*a*
I	immersed in water	point of action at head	by hand action	cause to him

1956, 172). Although the Shawnee utterance is composed of parts, the parts do not possess the characteristics we attribute to words in, say, English or French.

To make sense of the structure of languages such as Shawnee, anthropological linguists needed a concept that could refer to both words (like those in the English sentence above) and the parts of an utterance that could not be broken down into words. This led to the development of the concept of *morphemes,* which have traditionally been defined as "the minimal units of meaning in a language." The various parts of a Shawnee utterance can be identified as morphemes, and so can many English words. Describing minimal units of meaning as morphemes, and not as words, allows us to compare the morphology of different languages.

In a language like Shawnee, the rules for putting morphemes together are different from the rules used in English. A morphological analysis of the Shawnee utterance would subdivide it into five morphemes: *ni-kooki-tepe-en-a.* Each morpheme can be described as belonging to a separate class of morphemes defined in terms of its function in the whole utterance. In other words, *ni* not only means "I," it also belongs to the class of morphemes that occur at the beginning of an utterance and refer to the subject of a sentence (Table 5.1). Because the morphemes of Shawnee cannot stand alone, as English words can, their position in the utterance determines the function they play and the meaning they bear.

The words of English utterances are more independent than are the parts of Shawnee utterances, yet even English words must be ordered in a particular sequence to convey particular meanings. Consider the differences among the following sentences: "The dog is on the rug," "The rug is on the dog," and "Rug the the on is dog." Only certain ways of ordering morphemes are possible in English. Certain English words (known as complex words because they are made up of more than one morpheme) often contain morphemes that can never stand alone: consider the words *walked* and *unhappy.* English morphemes such as the past tense marker *-ed* and the negative prefix *un-* both carry meaning and affect the meaning of the words to which they are joined, yet they cannot be joined to just any words and they cannot stand alone; their use is patterned.

There are languages in which individual words carry so much meaning that their order in a sentence becomes almost irrelevant. In Latin, for example, each word indicates its function in the sentence. The sentence "Catullus loved Clodia" can be expressed in Latin six different ways: (1) *Catullus Clodiam amabat,* (2) *Catullus amabat Clodiam,* (3)

---

morphology In linguistics, the study of word structure.

Clodiam Catullus amabat, (4) *Clodiam amabat Catullus,* (5) *Amabat Clodiam Catullus,* and (6) *Amabat Catullus Clodiam* (Lyons 1969). To change the sentence so that "Clodia loved Catullus" would require not a shift in word order but a change in the function markers: *Clodia Catullum amabat,* and so on.

The study of morphemic patterning in a language such as Shawnee seems hopelessly complicated to native English speakers, yet the patterning of morphemes in English is equally complex. Why is it that some morphemes can stand alone as words (*sing, red*) and others cannot (*-ing, -ed*)? What determines a word boundary in the first place? Words, or the morphemes they contain, are the minimal units of meaning. Thus, they represent the fundamental point at which the arbitrary pairing of sound and meaning occurs.

Syntax: Sentence Structure

A third component of language is **syntax,** or sentence structure. Linguists began to study syntax when they discovered that certain patterns of word use could not be explained by morphological rules alone. In languages like English, words in sentences cannot occur in just any order (recall the preceding examples about the rug and the dog). But rules governing word order cannot explain everything puzzling about English sentences. For example, one thing we usually know about a word is the part of speech (noun, verb, adjective, and so on) to which it belongs. In many cases, we cannot know to which part of speech a word belongs unless we know the structure of the sentence in which the word appears.

In English, the following sentence is perfectly acceptable: "Smoking grass means trouble." For many native speakers of American English, this sentence exhibits what linguists call *structural ambiguity.* That is, we must ask ourselves what *trouble* means: the act of smoking grass (marijuana) or the act of noticing grass (the grass that grows on the prairie) that is giving off smoke. Either reading of the sentence is possible. To distinguish them from each other, we need to invent a way of distinguishing the use of *smoking* as a noun (and *smoking grass* as a noun phrase) and *smoking* as an adjective modifying the noun *grass* (producing again the noun phrase *smoking grass*).

We can explain the different meanings carried by structurally ambiguous sentences if we assume that the role a word plays in a sentence is not determined by the structure of the word itself. Rather, it depends on the overall structure of the sentence in which the word is found. We conclude that sentences are ordered strings of words and that those words must be classified as parts of speech in terms of the function they fulfill in a sentence.

Even these two assumptions are not sufficient to account for other acceptable English sentences. "The father of the girl and the boy fell into the lake" is a sentence that also exhibits structural ambiguity, but the ambiguity cannot be explained simply by classifying the words as parts of speech. How many people fell into the lake? Just the father, or the father and the boy? Each reading of the sentence depends on how the words of the sentence are grouped together. That is, should we group the words *of the girl and the boy* together, understand them to modify *father,* and conclude that one person fell into the lake? Or should we conclude that *of the girl* modifies *father,* group together *the father (of the girl) and the boy,* and conclude that two people fell into the lake?

This sort of grouping, called *structural grouping,* separates the various parts of speech into categories that represent the building blocks of the sentence itself. In the previous example, we had to decide which noun phrase was the *subject* of the sentence because there were two noun phrases that might have filled that role.

We are now able to define sentences as ordered strings of words that belong to different classes and that may be assigned various structural roles in the string where they occur. But even these three features do not account for the structure of all well-formed English sentences. Chomsky (1965) noted that native speakers of English understand that sentences such as (1) "The boy watered the garden" and (2) "The garden was watered by the boy" are related to one another. He argued that this perceived connection could be explained if we could show that these two sentences have something in common even though they appear to be structured differently.

Chomsky called the visible (or audible) appearance of a sentence its *surface structure.* But he argued that all sentences also possess a *deep structure,* which cannot be seen (or heard). He claimed that native speakers sense that two sentences are related because the sentences share the same deep structure. In the preceding example, the surface structure of the first sentence accurately reflects its deep structure. The second sentence, however, has been derived from the first by applying a *transformational rule.* In this case, the rule is called the *passive transformation.* That is, it transforms an active sentence ("The boy watered the garden") into a passive one ("The garden was watered by the boy").

By assuming both the existence of a deep structural level to syntax and the existence of transformational rules that can derive one grammatical sentence from another, Chomsky could account for the native speaker's intuitions about related sentences. Chomsky's transformational linguistics has inspired many years of active research into the structure of sentences in English and other languages.

Semantics: Meaning

Semantics, the study of meaning, was avoided by linguists for many years because *meaning* is a highly ambiguous term. What do we mean when we say that a sentence means something? We may be talking about what each individual word in the sentence means or what the sentence as a whole means or what I mean when I utter the sentence.

We sometimes talk about words meaning what they refer to in the "real world." That is, we think of meaning as *reference.* Understanding meaning as reference leads to the creation, for example, of *operational definitions* in which a term is defined by describing the operations one would have to perform in order to experience whatever the term refers to. For example, the term *monkeys* might be defined operationally as "the animals you will observe if you drive to the zoo and look inside the first cage from the entrance."

---

syntax The study of sentence structure.   **semantics** The study of meaning.

One problem with thinking of meaning as reference is that it is difficult to indicate unambiguously exactly what a particular term refers to. Consider the monkey example: the operational definition given is adequate only until we ask what the word *animals* means. Let's say we define *animals* as "all living creatures capable of growth and locomotion." We go to the zoo and discover that within the first cage from the entrance are several animals so defined. Some are crawling on the ground between the blades of grass, others are flying from their perches on the bars of the cage to the trees growing within the cage. Still others are scampering up the tree or sitting in the branches, are covered with fur, and occasionally approach the bars and reach out toward their human observers. If this were not enough, in a second cage are much larger animals that resemble some of the ones in the first cage in many ways, except that they have no tails. And in a third cage are yet other animals, far smaller than the four-limbed animals in the first two cages. They resemble the other animals, except that they use their long tails to swing from the branches of a tree. Which of these animals are monkeys?

To answer this question, the observer must decide which features of similarity or difference are important and which are not. Having made this decision, it is easier to decide which animals in cage 1 are monkeys and whether the animals in cages 2 and 3 are monkeys as well. But such decisions are not easily come by. Biologists have spent the last 300 years or so attempting to classify all living things on the planet into mutually exclusive categories. To do so, they have had to decide, of all the traits that living things exhibit, which ones matter.

To a large degree, this mania to classify has also been a central focus of *formal semantics,* which began with the goal of linking words to the world by specifying unambiguously what each word refers to. It soon became apparent that this effort could not succeed until linguistic classification systems themselves were refined. Consequently, attention shifted away from how words are linked to the world and instead focused on how words are linked to each other. Analysts had to specify how the words of a language are meaningful. Then they traced the meaning relations that link words to one another within the language. Typical meaning relations include *synonymy,* or "same meaning" (*old* and *aged*); *homophony,* or "same sound, different meaning" (*would* and *wood*); and *antonymy,* or "opposite meaning" (*tall* and *short*).

Formal semantics has taught us much about linguistic meaning that we might never have learned without abstracting language from the hurly-burly conditions of its everyday use. But abstract analyses cannot tell us all there is to know about language as a cultural creation of human societies. For instance, formal semantics has traditionally been preoccupied with a form of meaning called *denotation,* which refers to what a word means "in itself," how it is different from all other words in the language. To find a word's denotation, we might consult a dictionary. According to the *American Heritage Dictionary,* for example, a pig is "any of several mammals of the family Suidae, having short legs, cloven hoofs, bristly hair, and a cartilaginous snout used for digging."

A formal definition of this sort is useful if you are relating the word *pig* to other words in English, such as *cow* or *chicken*. Each word can be related to the others in terms of semantic features they do or do not share. Moreover, these meaning relations would hold even if all real pigs, cows, and chickens were wiped off the face of the earth. But difficulty arises as soon as we recognize that words never just mean what they denote.

Words also have *connotations,* additional meanings that derive from the typical contexts in which they are used in everyday speech. In the context of student antiwar demonstrations in the 1960s, for example, a *pig* was a police officer.

Formal semantics avoided having to reconcile the frequent lack of harmony between denotations and connotations of the same word. Denotations were said to be language based and rulelike, independent of the ways speakers choose to use them. Connotation was an idiosyncratic and unpredictable by-product of speaker use. Put in terms used earlier, formal semantics tried to reduce meaning to denotation. Reduction seemed unproblematic because denotational definitions are supposedly based on clear-cut features of the objects to which they refer. It was assumed, for instance, that acquaintance with real pigs would make it obvious that the traits listed in the dictionary definition of pig are the traits that matter.

However, knowing which traits matter and which do not is never self-evident. Everyday experience teaches us that no single classification is adequate for all our needs. As our purposes for classifying change, so too will the objects that are grouped together as similar or different. Bats and birds both have wings, and in this respect they can be put together in the same category. But bats give birth to live young, and birds lay eggs. In this respect they differ, and so they can be assigned to different categories. The ability to classify and reclassify our experiences is the hallmark of openness. And a focus on purpose is at the same time a focus on the context for which such a purpose is appropriate. This suggests that much of the referential meaning of language escapes us if we neglect the context of language use.

Pragmatics: Language in Contexts of Use

Pragmatics can be defined as the study of language in the context of its use. This definition has a double focus. On the one hand, it emphasizes the purposes of the user—the different functions to which the speaker puts language in the various contexts of daily life. On the other hand, pragmatics emphasizes that every attempt to use language occurs in a *context.* This context offers limitations and opportunities concerning what we may say and how we may say it. Everyday language use is thus often characterized by a struggle between speakers and listeners over definitions of context and appropriate word use.

Traditional formal semantics had only the narrowest view of context: that provided by the formal definitions of other words and phrases in the language. Pragmatics forces us to look outside individual sentences to determine the referential meanings of words. Pragmatics therefore requires us to pay attention to discourse, which refers to a stretch of speech longer than a sentence, united by a common theme. *Discourse* can be defined as a series of sentences uttered by a single individual or as a series of rejoinders in a conver-

pragmatics The study of language in the context of its use.

sation among two or more speakers. In fact, if we accept the persuasive arguments of such theorists of discourse as M. M. Bakhtin and V. N. Voloshinov (see, for example, Voloshinov [1929] 1986), the series of rejoinders in conversation are the primary form of discourse. In their view, the speech of any single individual, whether a simple yes or a book-length dissertation, is only one rejoinder in an ongoing dialogue with others on a particular theme.

Anthropological linguists such as Michael Silverstein (1976, 1985) have shown that the referential meaning of certain expressions in language cannot be determined unless we go beyond the boundaries of a sentence and place the expressions in question inside a wider context. Two kinds of context must be considered. *Linguistic context* refers to the other words, expressions, and sentences that surround the expression whose meaning we are trying to determine. The meaning of *it* in the sentence "I really enjoyed it" cannot be determined if the sentence is considered on its own. However, if we know that the previous sentence was "My aunt gave me this book for my birthday," we have a linguistic context that allows us to deduce that *it* refers to *this book*.

Nonlinguistic context consists of objects and activities that are present in the situation of speech at the same time we are speaking. Consider the sentence, "Who is that standing by the door?" We need to inspect the actual physical context at the moment this sentence is uttered to find the door and the person standing by the door and thus give a referential meaning to the words *who* and *that*. Furthermore, even if we know what a door is in a formal sense, we need the nonlinguistic context to specify for us what counts as a door in this instance (for example, a rough opening in the wall).

Once we begin to study the nonlinguistic context, we begin to notice other things, especially if we compare the way two different speakers, or speakers of two different languages, choose to represent the objects and activities that are before them as they are speaking. The same situation can be represented differently by different speakers of the same language, by different speakers of different languages, by the same speaker to different audiences, and so forth. Consider the monkey example referred to earlier in the chapter. A person who knew little about nonhuman primates might be inclined to group the four-limbed creatures in all three cages together and call them monkeys. Primatologists would distinguish apes from monkeys, and New World monkeys from Old World monkeys. They would be able to supply a separate label and a formal definition for the creatures in each cage: baboon (an Old World monkey), gorilla (an ape), spider monkey (a New World monkey).

Or consider a famous cross-linguistic example described by anthropologist Harry Hoijer, who discusses the Chiricahua Apache place name "*tonoogah,* for which the English equivalent (not the translation) is 'Dripping Springs.' Dripping Springs, a noun phrase, names a spot in New Mexico where the water from a spring flows over a rocky bluff and drips into a small pool below; the English name, it is evident, is descriptive of one part of this scene, the movement of the water. The Apache term is, in contrast, a verbal phrase and accentuates quite a different aspect of the scene. The element *to,* which means 'water,' precedes the verb *noogah,* which means, roughly, 'whiteness extends downward.' *Tonoogah,* as a whole, then, may be translated 'water-whiteness extends downward,' a reference to the fact that a broad streak of white limestone deposit, laid down by the running water, extends downward on the rock" (1953, 559).

The point of view that guides a speaker in deciding how to represent nonlinguistic experiences in language is called the speaker's *referential perspective* (Wertsch 1985, 168). Both examples above show how different speakers may adopt different referential perspectives on the same nonlinguistic context, with the result that contextual information is encoded differently in their speech. Sometimes different referential perspectives may seem to have so little in common with each other that we might conclude the speakers are talking about completely different matters. Much confusion is eliminated if we can establish that all speakers are attending to the same context. Once we know that this is the case, we can inspect that context for clues that make sense of each speaker's description.

Further dialogue about a common context often allows speakers to make their alternative referential perspectives comprehensible to one another. Thus, a professional primatologist understands why amateur observers might think all nonhuman primates look alike. However, a conversation at the zoo between professional and amateur, full of pointing at the various organisms in the three cages mentioned earlier, might be enough to lead the amateur to recognize the differences important to the professional and to learn the linguistic expressions that mark those differences. Similarly, if Apache speakers and English speakers know enough of one another's languages to interpret their respective names for the same place, they should have no difficulty appreciating the alternative referential perspectives represented in each place name. Moreover, with a little creativity, both referential perspectives might be represented in a single language; for example, *tonoogah* might be translated into the English place name "Limestone Streak."

In the course of anthropological fieldwork, individuals equipped with different languages and different cultural backgrounds work collaboratively to arrive at an understanding of shared nonlinguistic events. The more they learn, the more proficient each becomes in adopting the referential perspective of the other. When successful, the fieldwork experience teaches informant and anthropologist alike how to describe the same event from more than one referential perspective. However, such understanding is not limited to cross-cultural and cross-linguistic situations. All languages contain a variety of resources upon which their speakers may draw to articulate different referential perspectives on the same nonlinguistic events.

The choice of perspective can have far-reaching consequences. In the early 1980s, different groups of observers described the guerrilla army fighting the Sandinista government in Nicaragua as "contras," "freedom fighters," "right-wing thugs," and "the guerrilla army fighting the Sandinista government in Nicaragua." The descriptive expression chosen by a speaker provided a powerful clue to that speaker's political sympathies. If *ideology* is defined as the set of beliefs that justify a person's political commitments, then it is clear that referential perspectives are at the same time *ideological perspectives*. As Wertsch comments, "Just as one must use some referential perspective when speaking of objects and events, one must also use some ideological perspective. The fact that certain voices seem to be ideologically neutral to a particular audience . . . stems from a particular sociohistorical setting" (1985, 229).

Thus, Nicaraguans who suffered at the hands of the Sandinistas might well find the "freedom fighter" label to be an obvious, ideologically neutral description and might object to any supposedly neutral referential perspective (such as "guerrilla army fighting the Sandinista government") that does not take their suffering into account. Nicaraguans who suffered at the hands of the guerrilla army might be equally likely to deny the accuracy of a value-free perspective, but they would certainly reject the description of the guerrillas as "freedom fighters." The only way to resolve these seemingly irresolvable referential (and ideological) perspectives would involve intense collaborative negotiation, not unlike what goes on between informant and anthropologist in the field. But such negotiation can be extremely difficult to bring about, as recent Central American history has shown.

And so we begin to see, in outline, the complex dialectic between language and culture. We cannot use language without in some way considering the context of use. But taking context into consideration means adopting a referential perspective with respect to that context. And adopting a referential perspective means adopting an ideological perspective as well. But ideological perspectives are cultural creations, selectively drawing upon the varied resources available in any language to construct a coherent point of view on lived experience. This means, as Wertsch concludes, that anyone's characteristic way of speaking "carries with itself a great deal of sociohistorically specific ideological baggage" (1985, 229).

This might be seen as an argument for linguistic or cultural determinism, but it is not. Every language and culture can support many points of view and ways of talking about them. Members of every culture, speakers of every language, must come to terms with these alternatives in their respective societies. Thus, all people have the potential to master a variety of referential and ideological perspectives, to develop a *multilingual consciousness*. Here, the insights of Whorf, for example, become suggestive. Much of Whorf's writing on linguistic relativity can be seen as an attempt not only to describe but to create in the minds of his readers the experience of multilingual consciousness (Schultz 1990).

LINGUISTIC INEQUALITY

People who make value judgments about the different language varieties used by various individuals or groups in their society illustrate the fact that referential perspectives are ideological perspectives. We might call such judgments *linguistic ethnocentrism*—one language variety is taken as the standard against which all other varieties are measured.

The linguistic features that distinguish one language variety from another are rarely viewed neutrally. As a college undergraduate during the turbulent 1960s, I (Emily Schultz) vividly recall attending a political address given by a militant African American from a northern inner-city community. After his speech was over, the speaker accepted questions from the audience. A young European American woman asked respectfully what people such as herself ought to do to help the African American cause. Unfortunately, she spoke with a very definite southern accent, which was obvious to all, especially the speaker. The atmosphere in the room was electric with danger even before the speaker opened his mouth to reply, and his response, the contents of which are now forgotten, bristled with hostility and anger. The young woman's words were relatively innocuous, but her accent was not. The questioner's accent was that of the oppressors;

the speaker's accent was that of the oppressed. In the context of his speech, which urged that oppression be overthrown, the questioner's accent made her the enemy no matter what she said.

This example illustrates one kind of *linguistic inequality:* passing value judgments about other people's speech. African American speech and southern European American speech were each evaluated with reference to a context of dominance and subordination. When African Americans were slaves, and for a long time after, their speech was considered to be unquestionably inferior, just as European American speech was considered superior. With the civil rights movement of the 1960s this evaluation was reversed for militant African Americans. Their accents, legacies of oppression, were viewed positively, whereas their oppressors' accents were devalued. In neither case, however, was anything being claimed about what the linguist would label strictly linguistic or communicative matters. Both the African American militant and the European American woman in the audience observed the grammatical rules of standard English. Indeed, the audience understood both people without difficulty—in addition to being able to understand the speaker's hostile reaction to the European American woman's accent.

Speech in the Inner City

Strictly linguistic inequality is normally measured in different ways. Studies in the 1960s by William Labov and his colleagues dealt with such strictly linguistic matters in the speech of African American children living in urban areas of the northern United States (Labov 1972). Previous researchers had claimed that these children suffered from *linguistic deprivation.* The researchers had said that these children started school with a limited vocabulary and no grammar and thus could not perform as well as European American children in the classroom. Labov's response to this series of assertions demonstrated two things. First, he proved that the form of English spoken in the inner city was not defective pseudolanguage. Second, he showed how a change in research context permitted inner-city African American children to display a level of linguistic sophistication that previous European American researchers had never dreamed they possessed.

When African American children were in the classroom (a European American–dominated context) being interrogated by European American adults about topics of no interest to them, they said little. This did not necessarily mean, Labov argued, that they had no language. Rather, their minimal responses were better understood as defensive attempts to keep threatening European American questioners from learning anything about them. For the African American children, the classroom was only one part of a broader racist culture existing beyond the classroom. The previous European American investigators had been ethnocentrically oblivious of the effect this context might have on the results of their research.

Reasoning that reliable samples of African American speech had to be collected in contexts where the racist threat was lessened, Labov conducted fieldwork in the homes and on the streets of the inner city. He and his colleagues recorded enormous amounts of speech in *Black English Vernacular* (BEV) produced by the same children who had nothing to say when questioned in the classroom. Labov's analysis demonstrated that BEV

FIGURE 5.5 *Phonological, morphological, syntactic, semantic, and pragmatic differences associated with different varieties of a language such as English become markers of a speaker's membership in a particular speech community. Rappers like Heavy D and the Boys draw on the resources of a variety of American English that linguists call "Black English Vernacular."*

was a variety of English that had certain rules not found in Standard English. This can be seen as a kind of strictly linguistic difference in that most middle-class speakers of Standard English would not use these rules whereas most African American speakers of BEV would. However, neither variety of English is "defective" as a result of this difference. This kind of linguistic difference, which is apparent when speakers of two varieties talk with one another, is a marker of the speaker's membership in a particular speech community. Such differences can exist in phonology, morphology, syntax, semantics, or pragmatics (Figure 5.5).

Speech of Women and Men

Strictly linguistic differences in language knowledge or language use are not the sole preserve of ethnic groups; they also exist in the speech of men and women. In American society, women and men are expected to behave differently in many of the same situations. Carole Edelsky (1977) hypothesized that these different expectations might include different speech norms as well. She suggested that adult communicative competence might include rules for "talking like a lady" as well as for "talking like a man."

Edelsky set out to discover what these rules were and when they appeared in the speech of growing children. She tested first graders, third graders, sixth graders, and adults to measure their knowledge of the norms. The test presented the research subjects with such sentences as, "Won't you pretty please hand me that hammer" or "Damn it, get me that perfume!" She discovered that by the sixth grade, children were aware that linguistic usages displaying weakness or elaborateness are marked for females, whereas casual profanity is marked for males. Adults in Edelsky's sample applied these rules as a formula and persisted in defending them as literally descriptive of their own or other people's actual speech, even when faced with direct evidence to the contrary. "One subject, male, said men would not use *Oh dear* 'because it's a protected word, more passive, that men don't use.' This statement was separated by an interval of about 10 minutes from the following one, made by the same subject, 'I can't come up with anything. Oh dear, I'm just going to run the tape down'" (Edelsky 1977, 237).

Sociolinguist Deborah Tannen (1990) has gained much popular attention in the media for her recent study of speech patterns of men and women in the United States. Like Edelsky, Tannen focuses on typical male and female styles of discourse, arguing that men and women use language for different reasons: men tend to use language as a competitive weapon in public settings, whereas women tend to use language as a way of building closeness in private settings. Tannen shows what happens when men and women each assume that their rules are the only rules without realizing that the other gender may be defining appropriate language use from a different referential perspective. For example, when a husband and wife get home from work at the end of the day, she may be eager to talk while he is just as eager to remain silent. She may interpret his silence as a sign of distance or coldness and be hurt. He, by contrast, may be weary of the day's verbal combat and feel he has the right not to speak once he is at home. He may resent his wife's attempts at conversation, not because he is rejecting her personally, but because he believes he has a right to remain silent that she is violating.

THE DIALECTIC BETWEEN LANGUAGE AND CULTURE

If different groups in society have characteristically different histories and experiences, they are likely to develop characteristically unique referential perspectives to talk about those histories and experiences. By what processes, then, do linguistic expressions become so heavily laden with cultural meanings? Through learning processes that depend on schemas, prototypes, and metaphors.

Schemas

In any human society, experience itself tends to be patterned. We repeatedly experience the change of seasons or the transformation of water into ice and ice into water. We repeatedly experience other people around us; we watch them perform similar activities, and we watch them grow, one after another, from childhood to adulthood to old age.

EthnoProfile 5.2 • **SAMOA**

REGION: Oceania

NATION: Western Samoa

POPULATION: 182,000

ENVIRONMENT: Tropical island

LIVELIHOOD: Horticulture, fishing, wage labor in capital

POLITICAL ORGANIZATION: Ranked, with linguistic markers for high- and low-status people; now part of a modern nation-state

FOR MORE INFORMATION: Platt, Martha. 1986. Social norms and lexical acquisition: A study of deictic verbs in Samoan child language. In *Language socialization across cultures,* edited by Bambi Schieffelin and Elinor Ochs, 127–52. Cambridge: Cambridge University Press.

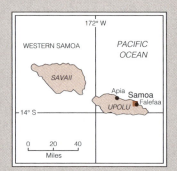

Schemas are simplified interpretive frameworks used to understand events (D'Andrade 1992, 48). Schemas might also be understood as chunks of experience that appear to hang together as wholes, exhibiting the same properties in the same configuration whenever they recur. As human beings grow up in any society, they gradually become aware of the chunks of experience that their culture (or subculture) recognizes. Language often provides labels for these culturally relevant experiential chunks, as well as a variety of grammatical means for describing how these chunks relate to one another. A child's first words are deeply embedded in the schemas to which they refer. Language is thus embedded in experience, and the experiences that shape language are culturally patterned schemas.

A schema important for many Western children is *Christmas,* a term that refers to a chunk of experience with recognizable characteristics recurring regularly once every year. The Christmas schema might involve the nature of the weather at Christmastime (cold and snowy) and particular events (baking cookies, singing carols, going to church, putting up a Christmas tree, buying and wrapping gifts, and so on). In the experience of a child, all these attributes may be equally relevant parts of a larger whole. It takes time and conditioning for parents to persuade children what the "true meaning of Christmas" really is. Sometimes adults who celebrate Christmas disagree about the "true meaning" depending, for example, on whether or not they are religious Christians. Likewise, non-Christian members of Western societies may experience Christmas in a very different way.

But it is not just objects and events, like potatoes or holidays, that are organized and categorized linguistically. Children learn that people, too, can be categorized in terms of status and that certain linguistic forms may be used by some people but not by others. Martha Platt (1986) expected that Samoan children would actively use the verb *sau* ("to come") before they used the verb *aumai* ("to bring/give") because *sau* is semantically simpler than *aumai*. She discovered, however, that Samoan children actively used the verb *aumai* before they used *sau*. (See EthnoProfile 5.2: Samoa.)

Why would children apparently master a more difficult word before a simpler one? Platt answered this question once she noted that Samoan children frequently encounter both words in everyday speech in the form of commands ("Come here!" "Bring me this!" "Give her that!"). They also quickly learn that high-status persons may use *sau* to summon a person of equal or lower status. *Aumai,* by contrast, may be used to address low-status and high-status persons alike. Status is closely related to age in Samoa; thus, children ordinarily use *sau* only when summoning children younger than they are or when conveying the request of a high-status person (such as a parent) to a third party.

Prototypes

Human beings accept without question most of the schemas that their culture recognizes. In other words, we take the experiences that our culture pays attention to as **prototypes** of human experiences. We use them as a baseline for judging other experiences as typical or not, human or not. This is the ground out of which ethnocentrism sprouts.

Prototypes of various sorts appear to be central to the way meaning is organized in human language. The words of our language refer to typical instances, typical elements or relations, typical experiences within one or another culturally relevant domain.

If the prototype we are using is well established in our culture and our language, ordinarily we should be able to use it and have other people understand our use of it without trouble. The term *idiom* is often used to refer to these well-worn ways of talking about our daily experiences. When we organize experience and assign meaning on the basis of prototypes, however, the categories we use have fuzzy boundaries. And because our experiences do not always neatly fit our prototypes, often we are not sure which prototype applies. Is a tossed salad a prototypical tossed salad if in addition to lettuce and tomatoes and onions it also contains raisins and apple slices? Is a library still a prototypical library when it contains fewer books than microfilms and videotapes and computer diskettes? In cases like this, suggests linguist R. A. Hudson (1980), a speaker must simply recognize the openness of language and apply linguistic labels creatively.

Metaphors

A central aim of linguistic theory is to account for ambiguity. The traditional approach has been to handle ambiguity by eliminating it, by "disambiguating" ambiguous utterances. However, an analysis of meaning based on prototypes accepts ambiguity from the outset as part of human experience and therefore as part of language as well.

---

schemas Patterned, repetitive experiences.

prototypes Examples of a typical instance, element, relation, or experience within a particular, culturally relevant semantic domain.

Linguistic ambiguity is most clearly illustrated by various forms of figurative or nonliteral language, of which **metaphor** is the most striking example. Metaphors proclaim the existence of a meaningful link between two expressions from different semantic domains. For example, we usually think of human beings and birds as belonging to separate semantic domains, so how should we interpret the statement, "Arnold is a turkey"? Perhaps someone has a pet turkey named Arnold. However, if Arnold is a human being, this assertion creates ambiguity: are people and birds (or Arnold and a turkey) alike or different? We cannot know until we place the statement "Arnold is a turkey" into some kind of context. If we know, for example, that Arnold is characteristically inept, ignorant, and annoying and that turkeys are prototypically stupid and clumsy, the metaphor "Arnold is a turkey" becomes intelligible and apt.

When we place ambiguous linguistic utterances in a particular context, we can often resolve their apparent ambiguity, but this resolution does not reveal the literal meaning of a sentence. The same sentence can literally and unambiguously mean different things in different contexts. When we use metaphor, we are suggesting that the world as we understand it might be otherwise understood. This is the radical threat posed by metaphor. Ambiguous and metaphorical utterances shock our ears because they violate convention in a manner similar to the way profanity in the speech of small children violates convention. Nevertheless, apt metaphors, particularly when they are linked to one another systematically, have the power to reshape our view of the world.

PIDGIN LANGUAGES: NEGOTIATING MEANING

We have been looking at contexts of language use in which speakers and listeners are able, for the most part, to draw upon overlapping ranges of linguistic variety in order to communicate, however imperfectly. In some instances, however, potential parties to a verbal exchange find themselves sharing little more than physical proximity to one another. Such situations arise when members of communities with radically different language traditions and no history of previous contact with one another come face to face and are forced to communicate with each other. There is no way to predict the outcome of such enforced contact on either speech community, yet from these new shared experiences, new schemas and possibly a new form of language—**pidgin**—may develop.

"When the chips are down, meaning is negotiated" (Lakoff and Johnson 1980, 231). The study of pidgin languages is the study of the radical negotiation of new meaning, the dialectical production of a new whole (the pidgin language) that is different from and reducible to neither of the languages that gave birth to it. The shape of a pidgin reflects the context in which it arises—generally one of colonial conquest or commercial domination. Vocabulary is usually taken from the language of the dominant group, making it easy for the dominant group to learn. Syntax and phonology may be similar to the subordinate language (or languages), however, making it easier for subordinated speakers to learn. Morphological complexity tends to disappear (Holm 1988).

Pidgins are considered to be reduced languages that have no native speakers. They develop, in a single generation, between groups of speakers that possess distinct native languages. When speakers of a pidgin language pass that language on to a new generation, linguists refer to the language as a *creole*. The creolization of pidgins normally involves growing complexity in phonology, morphology, syntax, semantics, and pragmatics, such that the pidgin comes to resemble conventional languages.

The distinction seems straightforward: pidgins are not real languages, but creoles, which develop out of pidgins, are real languages. In fact, this distinction is far from clearcut. "There is no moment at which a particular pidgin suddenly comes into existence, but rather a process of variety creation called pidginization, by which *a pidgin is gradually built up out of nothing*. We might well ask whether this process is essentially different from what happens in everyday interaction between people who think they speak the same language but who are in fact constantly accommodating their speech and language to each other's needs" (Hudson 1980, 70; emphasis added).

LANGUAGE AND TRUTH

For Thomas Kuhn, a philosopher of science, metaphor lies at the heart of science: changes in scientific theories are "accompanied by a change in some of the relevant metaphors and in corresponding parts of the network of similarities through which terms attach to nature" (1979, 416). Kuhn argues that these changes in the way scientific terms link up to nature are not reducible to logic or grammar. "They come about in response to pressures generated by observation or experiment"—that is, by experience and context. And there is no neutral language into which rival theories can be translated and subsequently evaluated as unambiguously right or wrong (416). Kuhn asks the question, "Is what we refer to as 'the world' perhaps a product of mutual accommodation between experience and language?"

If our understanding of reality is the product of a dialectic between experience and language (or, more broadly, culture), then ambiguity will never be permanently removed from any of the symbolic systems that human beings invent. Ambiguity is part of the human experience from the outset, and human beings must work to limit it within cultural boundaries. Reflexive consciousness makes human beings aware of ambiguity and of alternatives. The experience of doubt is never far behind.

This is not merely the experience of women and men in Western societies. E. E. Evans-Pritchard (1963) describes the same sort of disorientation among the Azande of central Africa. (See EthnoProfile 8.3: Azande.) The Azande people are well aware of the ambiguity inherent in language, and they exploit it by using metaphor (what they call *sanza*) to disguise speech that might be received badly if uttered directly. For example, "A man says in the presence of his wife to his friend, 'Friend, those swallows, how they flit about in there.' He is speaking about the flightiness of his wife and in case she should understand the allusion, he covers himself by looking up at the swallows as he makes his seemingly innocent remark" (Evans-Pritchard 1963, 211). Evans-Pritchard later observes that *sanza* "adds greatly to the difficulties of anthropological inquiry. Eventually the anthropologist's sense of security is undermined and his confidence shaken.

---

metaphor A form of thought and language that asserts a meaningful link between two expressions from different semantic domains.

pidgin A language with no native speakers that develops in a single generation between members of communities that possess distinct native languages.

He learns the language, can say what he wants to say in it, and can understand what he hears, but then he begins to wonder whether he has really understood . . . he cannot be sure, and even they [the Azande] cannot be sure, whether the words do have a nuance or someone imagines that they do" (228).

However much we learn about language, we will never be able to exhaust its meanings or circumscribe its rules once and for all. Historian of religions Wilfred Cantwell Smith speaks of the temple of Madurai, which he came to know during his years of research in India (1982, 65). He asks what it means to refer to this particular structure as a *temple*. The first Europeans who saw it apparently assigned the term because it was, from their perspective, a pagan religious structure not to be confused with a Christian church building. This first labeling of Hindu temples was rather slipshod, impressionistic, and ethnocentric. Later Western scholars who were scientifically trained were able to provide a much fuller definition for the expression *Hindu temple*. These scholars systematically and accurately recorded and analyzed the temple's architectural configuration and the artwork with which it was decorated, compared it with other similar structures, and so on. Scholars who followed them noticed that the temple could not be fully understood without also paying attention to the people who performed rituals there, the markets set up around it, and so on. Eventually, some Western scholars even developed reflexive consciousness and began to incorporate into their understanding of this temple, and others like it, the opinions of Hindu informants. We have never known so much about Hindu temples as we know today, and presumably this knowledge will increase in the future. Nevertheless, "it is still the case today that *no one on earth, neither Hindu nor outsider, yet fully knows what a temple is*" (65). Human language and human cognition are open systems, and as long as human history continues, new forms will be created and old forms will continue to be put to new uses.

KEY TERMS

language	Sapir-Whorf hypothesis	schemas
linguistics	phonology	prototypes
design features	morphology	metaphors
cognition	syntax	pidgin
linguistic competence	semantics	
communicative competence	pragmatics	

CHAPTER SUMMARY

1. Language is a uniquely human faculty that, on the one hand, permits us to communicate but, on the other hand, sets up barriers to communication. It is a part of culture that people use to encode their experience and structure their understanding of the world and of themselves. The study of different languages reveals the shared nature of language and culture and the contextual assumptions that speakers make and share.

2. Of the sixteen design features of language, six are particularly important: openness, arbitrariness, duality of patterning, displacement, semanticity, and prevarication.

3. The Sapir-Whorf hypothesis suggests that language has the power to shape the way in which people see the world. The strong version of this hypothesis amounts to linguistic determinism; the weak version makes the shaping force of language too weak to be of interest. Neither Sapir nor Whorf favored linguistic determinism.

4. Today, the study of language is usually subdivided into five specialties: phonology, morphology, syntax, semantics, and pragmatics.

5. Pragmatics requires us to pay attention to discourse and nonlinguistic contexts. Different speakers may take up different referential perspectives with regard to the same nonlinguistic context. Referential perspectives are ideological perspectives that carry heavy burdens of cultural and historical meaning. Successful communication occurs when a speaker and a listener are able to understand the same event from each other's referential perspectives. The study of linguistic inequality focuses on the study of language in context and the negotiation of meaning.

6. Language is embedded in experience, and we usually generalize on the basis of experiences we know well. The schemas that our culture recognizes become unquestionably true and appropriate for us, and we tend to take those experiences as prototypical human experiences. These prototypes are central to how we organize meaning in language.

7. Linguistic ambiguity can only be resolved in context, which means that there is no one literal meaning of a word or sentence. Thus, metaphor is a particularly important domain of linguistic inquiry. Metaphor poses a radical threat to our conventional understanding, because it calls into question the prototypes by which we live.

8. The study of pidgin languages is the study of the radical negotiation of new meaning. In pidgins, two groups of language speakers who come in contact (often as a result of colonization or commercial domination) invent a new language that is different from either of its parent languages.

SUGGESTED READINGS

Akmajian, A., R. Demers, A. Farmer, and R. Harnish. 1991. *Linguistics*. 3d ed. Cambridge: MIT Press. *A fine introduction to the study of language as a formal system. This text is particularly informative on the topics of phonology, morphology, and syntax.*

Lakoff, George and Mark Johnson. 1980. *Metaphors we live by*. Berkeley: University of California Press. *An important, clear, and very accessible book that presents a radical and persuasive view of metaphor.*

Salzmann, Zdenek. 1993. *Language, culture, and society: An introduction to linguistic anthropology*. Boulder, CO: Westview. *An up-to-date and thorough text on linguistic anthropology.*

Smitherman, Geneva. 1977. *Talking and testifying. The language of Black America*. Detroit: Wayne State University Press. *An engaging introduction to Black English Vernacular, for native and nonnative speakers alike, with exercises to test your mastery of BEV grammar.*

Trudgill, Peter. 1982. *Sociolinguistics*. 2d ed. Baltimore: Penguin. *An excellent, thorough, and very readable introduction to language in its social context.*

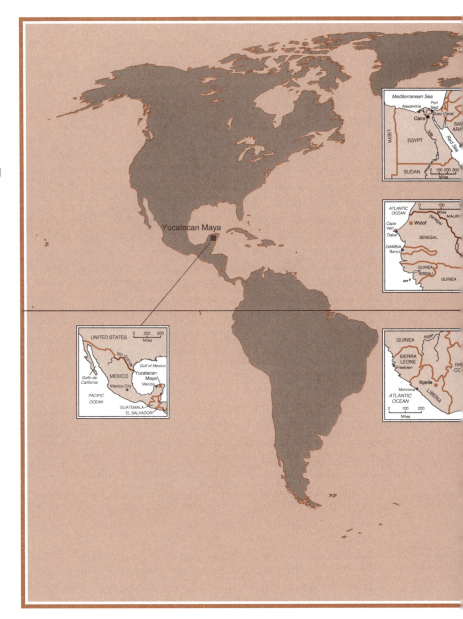

Cognition

6

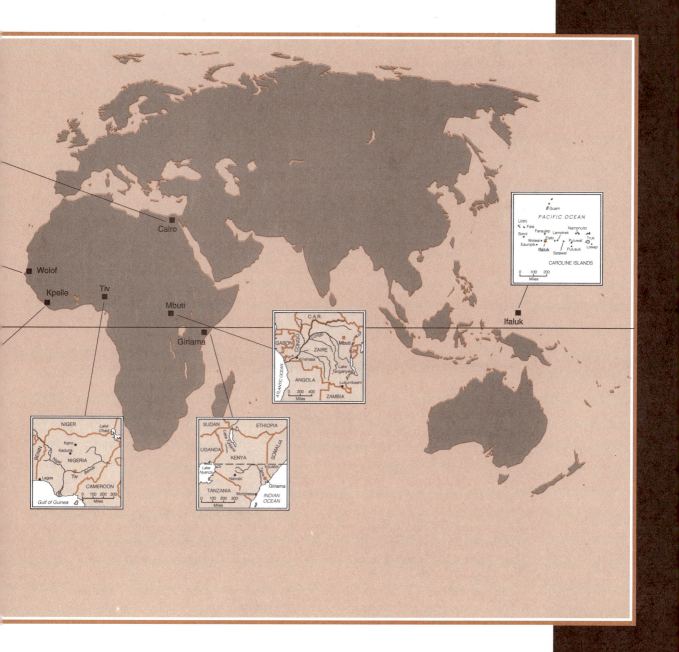

hapter 5 illustrated how we cannot easily separate language from the other processes we possess for making sense of the world around us; these other processes are generally referred to as **cognitive capacities.** In this chapter, we will explore the nature of human cognition and its relationship to culture.

If you examine Figure 6.1, you will see that marks on a piece of paper can be ambiguous. The signals we receive from the outside world tend to be open to more than one interpretation, be they words, patterns of light and dark striking the retinas of our eyes, smells, tastes, or shapes we feel with our hands.

Culture organizes different kinds of signals and directs our attention to the resulting bundle, or schema, to which a linguistic label is often applied. When we learn from this culturally shaped experience, we can use preexisting categories to help us interpret new experiences. The bundles of signals to which we pay attention and our interpretation of them together build our picture of the world.

COGNITION AS AN OPEN SYSTEM

Cognition was defined in Chapter 5 as the mental processes by which human beings gain knowledge. Like language, cognition is an open system. Human beings not only talk about the world in a variety of ways, they also think about the world in a variety of ways; if no one way of thinking is obligatory, then any particular way of thinking must be arbitrary. What we think about depends greatly on what we have learned to pay attention to in the past. Thus, how we think about a new situation depends on an entire collection of experiences from prior situations, which we use to help us make sense of what we experience at the present moment. This is called *displacement*. Not only our eyes but also all our senses can play tricks on us. If they are artful enough, people can trick other people into perceiving something that "does not exist." Prevarication is thus a built-in feature of cognition just as it is of language.

If we take language as a model of cognition in general, then cognition is a symbolic process. Language and visual perception, for example, both require human beings to construct symbolic representations of their experiences in order to make sense of them. As a result, the meaning of what we see, touch, smell, taste, or hear depends on context. In fact, two contexts are normally invoked: the immediate context of the perception itself and the displaced context stored in memory and shaped by culture. As with sentences, so too with the objects of perception. The "same" object can mean different things in different contexts. Consider what seeing a butcher knife means (1) lying on a cutting board in your kitchen next to a pile of mushrooms or (2) in the hand of a burglar who has cornered you in your kitchen at midnight.

FIGURE **6.1** *Ambiguous marks.*

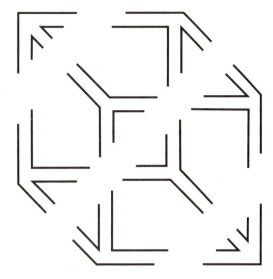

Cognition is often thought to have three aspects: perceptual, intellectual, and emotional. Perception as a cognitive process has been thought to link people to the world around them or within them: we perceive size, shape, color, pain, and so on. Intellect and emotion have referred to the two principal ways in which perceptions might be dealt with: rationally and logically on the one hand, passionately and intuitively on the other. Anthropologists and some psychologists suggest, however, that this approach to cognition is highly problematic. Particularly troubling is the traditional split between reason and emotion, accompanied by the overvaluing of reason and neglect of other cognitive capacities.

Cognitive Capacities and Intelligence

What makes it possible for human beings to receive signals from the outside world (or from within our own bodies) and then interpret those signals in a way that makes appropriate action possible? One traditional answer has been that every person either possesses at birth or develops over time certain basic cognitive capacities. At one time, these hypothetical capacities were thought of as substances or properties, and the goal of psychological testing was to measure how much of each cognitive capacity an individual had. Consequently, intelligence has traditionally been "measured" using an "instrument" called the *intelligence test;* the "amount" of intelligence measured is assigned a number called the *Intelligence Quotient,* or *IQ.* In the past, some researchers were quick to equate differences in performance on intelligence tests with differences in intelligence,

cognitive capacities The mental characteristics that enable us to receive signals from the outside world (or from within our own bodies) and to interpret these signals in a way that makes appropriate action possible.

no further questions asked. Today, such a reductionist approach is subjected to intense scrutiny.

It is difficult enough to identify and measure cognitive capacities in individuals. Michael Cole and Sylvia Scribner are two psychological anthropologists who have extensive experience in cross-cultural psychological testing. In their fieldwork, they repeatedly encountered situations in which the same psychological test produced results that differed between Western and non-Western subjects. They rejected the classical interpretation of these differences, which was that non-Western subjects were just less intelligent. Their knowledge of their informants was not limited to the narrow laboratory setting in which the psychological tests were administered. In the broader social and cultural context of everyday life, their informants' intelligence and full humanity were obvious.

So why do intelligent informants often perform poorly on psychological tests? In the work of the Russian psychologist Lev Vygotsky, Cole and Scribner (1974) found an approach that pointed toward an answer. Vygotsky distinguished between **elementary cognitive processes** and the higher **functional cognitive systems** into which these processes are organized. Elementary cognitive processes include the ability to make abstractions, to categorize, to reason inferentially, and so forth. All normal human beings everywhere are equipped with these abilities. Different cultures, however, organize these elementary processes into different functional systems. Culture also assigns different functional systems to different tasks in different contexts.

Consider once again the African American children whose "speech capacity" was measured by European American psychologists. The same test was used, the same instructions were given, and the same controlled testing situation was employed for African American children and for European American children. The European American children responded easily and fluently, whereas the African American children re-

FIGURE 6.2 *Pictures used for the study of depth perception in Africa.*

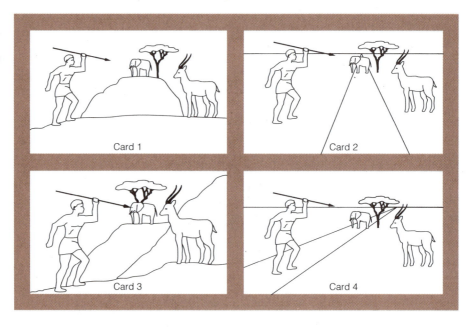

sponded in monosyllables or not at all. Following Vygotsky, we have no reason to doubt that both groups of children possessed the same range of elementary cognitive processes: they all could categorize, reason inferentially, and make abstractions. The difference in group performance was related to how the members of each group combined these elementary cognitive processes to interpret the testing situation and to function within it. The European American children interpreted the test and the testing situation as a nonthreatening opportunity to display their verbal ability, which they did. The African American children interpreted the same test and situation as a threatening personal and social attack, and they responded by refusing to respond. When interviewed in a non-threatening context, however, these same children displayed considerable verbal ability.

If we accept this analysis, the concept of schema introduced in Chapter 5 takes on a greater complexity. Culture not only identifies and labels recurring schemas for us, it also guides us in deciding how to cope cognitively with different categories of schemas. In other words, there are different ways of defining tasks, and once tasks are defined there are different strategies for carrying them out. Administering an adequate psychological test is as difficult as doing good anthropological fieldwork, with the same rewards and pitfalls.

PERCEPTION

Perception can be defined as the "processes by which people organize and experience information that is primarily of sensory origin" (Cole and Scribner 1974, 61). Identifying the nature of perception has long been central to understanding human cognition. As we saw in Chapter 3, the only evidence recognized by traditional positivist science is the evidence of our five senses. In this view, a suitably objective observer should be able to see and describe the world as it truly is. If other people describe the world differently from the scientific observer, then they must have perceptions that are in some way distorted. Either they are not being objective, or their ability to discriminate among sensations is impaired, or perhaps they are attempting to trick and mislead.

Most modern researchers are far less certain about what perception entails. True, our perception is sometimes impaired, either for physical reasons (we are not wearing our glasses) or because our observations aren't disinterested (our child's forehead feels "cool" because we are terrified he or she might have a fever). And people do sometimes play jokes on one another, insisting that they have seen things they really have not seen. But what about people whose physiological equipment is functioning properly, who have no stake in the outcome, and who are not trying to deceive?

Many investigators have begun to ask questions that attempt to relate people's descriptions of their experiences, or their performances on psychological tests, to their understandings of context. For example, nonliterate South African mine workers were tested using two-dimensional line drawings of three-dimensional objects (Figure 6.2).

---

elementary cognitive processes The ability to make abstractions, reason inferentially, and categorize.

functional cognitive systems Culturally linked sets of cognitive processes that guide perception, conception, reason, and emotion.

perception The processes by which people organize and experience information that is primarily of sensory origin.

FIGURE 6.3 *Drawings used for the construction of models in the depth-perception test in Africa.*

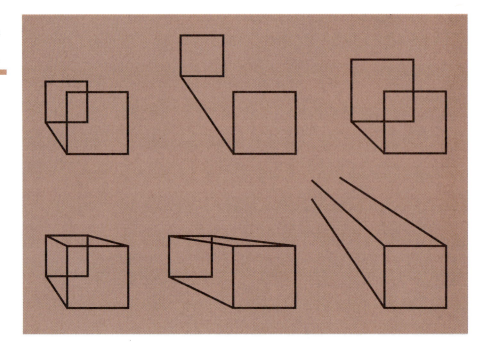

The tests results indicated that the mine workers persistently interpreted the drawings in two dimensions. When asked at which animal the man was pointing his spear on Card 1, subjects would usually respond, "the elephant." The elephant is, in fact, directly in line with and closest to the spear point in the drawing. However, the elephant ought to be seen as standing on top of the distant hill if the subjects interpret the drawings three-dimensionally. Did their responses mean that these Africans could not perceive in three dimensions?

J. B. Deregowski devised the following test. He presented different African subjects with the same drawings, asked them to describe what they saw, and got two-dimensional verbal reports. Next, he presented the same subjects with the line drawings in Figure 6.3. This time, he asked his subjects to construct models based on the drawings using materials he provided. His subjects had no difficulty producing three-dimensional models.

In these tests, the "correct" solution depended on the subject's mastery of a Western convention for interpreting two-dimensional drawings and photographs. For the drawings in Figure 6.2, the Western convention includes assumptions about perspective that relate the size of objects to their distance from the observer. Without such a convention in mind, it is not obvious, particularly in a drawing, that the size of an object has any connection with distance. Far from providing us with new insights about the African perceptual abilities, perhaps the most interesting result of tests like these is what they teach us about Western perceptual conventions. That is, drawings do not necessarily speak for themselves. They can make sense to us only once we accept certain rules for interpreting them. In the West, a major rule involves clearly separating what one sees from what one knows (Cole and Scribner 1974, 74).

FIGURE 6.4 *An example of distortion: the Ponzo illusion.*

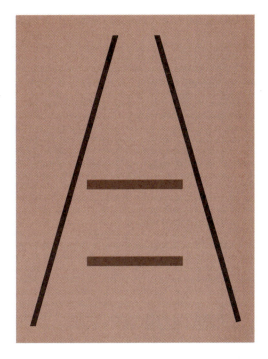

Illusion

Just as studies of metaphor provide insight into the nature of literal language, so too studies of visual illusions provide insight into the nature of the visual perception of reality. Indeed, the contrast between literal and metaphorical language is not unlike the contrast between reality and illusion as it relates to perception. In both cases, knowledge of context permits us to distinguish between the literal and the metaphorical, the real and the illusory.

Richard Gregory is a cognitive psychologist who has spent over 30 years studying visual illusions. In his view, illusions are produced by *misplaced procedures:* perfectly normal, ordinary cognitive processes that have somehow been inappropriately selected and applied to a particular set of visual signals. For him, perceptions are symbolic representations of reality, not direct samples of reality. Perceivers must often work very hard to make sense of the visual signals they receive. When they are wrong, they are subject to illusion.

Gregory (1983) describes four types of visual illusion. The first is *distortion:* what you see appears larger or smaller, longer or shorter, and so on, than it really is. Consider the Ponzo illusion in Figure 6.4. Typically, the upper parallel line appears to be longer than the lower parallel line. The standard explanation of this illusion is that we are looking at a two-dimensional drawing but interpreting it as if it were in three dimensions. In other words, the Ponzo illusion plays on our ability to see three-dimensional space in a two-dimensional drawing.

This explanation helps us understand the responses of the African mine workers in reference to Figure 6.2. Western observers interpret that drawing as a two-dimensional

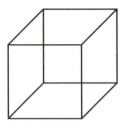

FIGURE 6.5 *An example of ambiguity: the Necker cube.*

representation of three-dimensional reality. In the Ponzo illusion, the shapes trick us because they are very similar to what we perceive when we stand on a railroad track and look toward its vanishing point on the horizon. Africans are also familiar with railroad tracks, but they did not attempt to interpret the Ponzo-like lines on Card 2 of Figure 6.2 as representations of three-dimensional reality. On the contrary, they seemed to work very hard to keep the relationships between objects in two dimensions, even if this meant that the sizes of the objects themselves appeared distorted. When we compare the Western interpretation of the Ponzo illusion with the African interpretation of the pictures in Figure 6.2, we discover something important: both sets of drawings are ambiguous, and both are potentially open to distortion. How people interpret them depends on preexisting cultural conventions.

The second type of visual illusion, *ambiguity,* occurs when a set of visual signals is constant but the perceiver's awareness of it flips from one image to another. Consider the Necker cube in Figure 6.5. As you stare at this pattern, it seems to move. First one face of the Necker cube is in front; a second later it pops to the back. Experiments demonstrate that this flipping back and forth of the image has nothing to do with the visual signals themselves; the pattern of lines on the retina remains fixed. What seems to be

FIGURE 6.6 *An example of paradox:* Relativity, *by M. C. Escher (lithograph, 1953).*

happening is that the mind is confronting a pattern that can be interpreted in at least two equally probable ways. It keeps hopping between each probable interpretation, testing various interpretive hypotheses in an attempt to resolve the ambiguity. But because the signals are so perfectly ambiguous, no resolution is possible. The image appears to flip endlessly from one possibility to the other.

Gregory's third type of illusion is *paradox:* a contradiction in terms, or at least an image that appears to be visually contradictory. Consider Figure 6.6. Here we are tripped up again and again as we apply a given set of cognitive procedures to make sense of the visual signals we are receiving. We seem to make sense of the image only to encounter some other part of it that upsets our previous theory.

Gregory's fourth type of illusion is *fiction:* seeing things that are not there. Consider the Kanizsa illusion in Figure 6.7. The white triangle's sides appear to curve inward and its points block out portions of three black circles beneath them. This illusion is fiction because nothing—no change in brightness across the edges of the "overlapping triangles," for example—signals to us that there are overlapping triangles rather than six separate black shapes arranged in a ring on a white background.

Gregory argues that we respond as we do to illusions of this kind because our experience in the world has made us familiar with certain patterns we come to expect. For example, when we encounter surprising gaps where we would normally expect to encounter continuous edges, we tend to assume that something is getting in the way of those continuous edges.

Perceptions are shaped by our habitual experience, by the schemas in terms of which we order our lives. We all encounter visual illusions from time to time in the everyday world. Unlike the drawings used for psychological tests, the sources of these illusions are not often abstract patterns devoid of context. And unlike subjects in a laboratory, we usually are free to use our other senses, to move our bodies in space, to manipulate the source of the puzzling signals until we resolve the ambiguity to our satisfaction. As with figurative language, however, we resolve the ambiguity only with respect to that particular context. Technically, according to Gregory, we are making hypotheses about what those visual signals most probably represent in the world we know, a world that is culturally shaped.

FIGURE 6.7 *An example of fiction: a Kanizsa illusion.*

Cognitive Style

The term **cognitive style** refers to a recurring pattern of perceptual and intellectual activity. Cultures provide people with a range of cognitive styles that are appropriate for different cognitive tasks in different contexts. Psychological anthropologists have attempted to compare cognitive styles cross-culturally. Some have argued that the styles of individuals and of groups can be located on a continuum between a global style and an

cognitive style Recurring patterns of cognitive activity that characterize an individual's perceptual and intellectual activities.

articulated style. People who use a **global style** tend to view the world holistically; they see first a bundle of relationships and only later the bits and pieces that are related. They are said to be *field dependent*. By contrast, people who use an **articulated style** tend to break up the world into smaller and smaller pieces, which can then be organized. They also tend to see a sharp boundary between their own bodies and the outside world. People using an articulated style are able to consider whatever they happen to be paying attention to apart from its context and so are said to be *field independent* (Cole and Scribner 1974, 82).

On this continuum, people in Western societies appear to be field independent, whereas most people in most non-Western cultures appear to be field dependent. However, more detailed research shows that these generalizations are misleading. For instance, the preferred cognitive style of an individual often varies from task to task and from context to context. People who use articulated styles for some tasks also use global styles for other tasks. In fact, they may bring a range of different styles to bear on a single task.

Research by Jean Lave and her colleagues (1988) demonstrated that middle-class North Americans are not field independent in every task in all contexts, even when the task involves mathematics, which would seem to be the most field independent of all cognitive activities. Lave and her associates wanted to test the widespread assumption that cognitive style does not vary across contexts. In particular, they wanted to find out whether ordinary people use the same mathematical skills in the supermarket and the kitchen that they use in the classroom. As part of the research, subjects were given a pencil-and-paper math test to determine how well they could solve certain problems in a schoolroomlike context. Researchers also observed how the same subjects used mathematics while making buying decisions at the grocery store. Finally, the subjects were presented with paired grocery items and asked to calculate the best buy.

The results of this research were surprising. First, the subjects averaged only 59 percent correct on the pencil-and-paper test but achieved averages of 98 percent on the supermarket experiment and 93 percent on the best-buy experiment. Second, the researchers found that the high scores on the last two experiments were achieved with very little reliance on the formal mathematical strategies taught in school. Many observers would have expected subjects trained in formal mathematics to rely on its infallible methods to help them make wise economic decisions. On the contrary, the test results suggest that shoppers were better able to make wise economic decisions using informal calculation strategies. The three most common informal strategies were *inspection* (recognizing that one item was both lower in price and larger in volume), *best-buy calculations* (comparing two quantities and two prices first and choosing the better value), and a *difference strategy* (deciding whether a marginal difference in quantity was worth the marginal difference in price; Lave 1988, 107ff.).

Lave notes that some psychologists would conclude from these results that there was something "primitive" or "illogical" about the informal strategies—and, by extension, about the people who used them (see, for example, Lave 1988, 79ff., 107ff.). In the terms we used earlier, these strategies are all closer to the global, field-dependent end of the cognitive-style continuum. Should we conclude, therefore, that ordinary middle-class North Americans fail to think rationally when they shop for groceries? This conclusion is contradicted by the experimental evidence showing that the shoppers' informal strategies were exceptionally accurate. In addition, shoppers did occasionally use formal mathematics as an alternative to the other informal strategies, but they did so only when the numbers for quantity and price were easy to transform into unit-price ratios. This did not happen very often, however, because units and prices in supermarkets are often given in prime numbers, making rapid mental calculation tedious and complicated. Rather than waste time dividing $5.27 by 13 oz. to obtain the price per ounce, the shoppers preferred to rely on other calculation strategies.

This last observation points to a major difference between "school" math and "grocery store" math. In school, the only purpose of a mathematical exercise is to obtain a single correct answer. "The puzzles or problems are assumed to be objective and factual. . . . Problem solvers have no choice but to try to solve problems, and if they choose not to, or do not find the correct answer, they 'fail' " (Lave 1988, 35). Matters are otherwise outside the classroom. Shoppers do not visit supermarkets as an excuse to practice formal mathematics; they go to buy food for their families. Consequently, the choices they make are influenced not merely by unit-price ratios but by the food preferences of the other family members, the amount of storage space at home, the amount of time they can spend shopping, and so on. In the supermarket, as Lave puts it, " 'problems' are dilemmas to be resolved, rarely problems to be solved" (20). Formal mathematics may help resolve some dilemmas, but in other cases it can be more trouble than it is worth. Shoppers, unlike students in the classroom, are free to abandon calculation, to use means other than formal mathematics to resolve a dilemma (58).

One feature all Lave's subjects shared was the knowledge that pencil-and-paper tests in schoollike settings required an articulated, field-independent style. In non-Western societies, attending a European- or American-style school seems to impart the same knowledge to non-Western people. But even Western subjects may reserve that cognitive style for the classroom, preferring a variety of more global strategies to resolve the dilemmas of everyday life. We have seen how some of these dilemmas can be generated by a lack of fit between the background information we take for granted and sensory signals that are ambiguous. This lack of fit may be between, say, our family's food preferences and confusing price ratio information on two products we are comparing. It may be between our expectation that straight edges are normally continuous and surprising gaps in our visual field. In any case, our awareness of the cognitive dilemmas we face should make us more sympathetic to cognitive "errors" we see being made by people from different cultures who may be employing different cognitive styles.

Colin Turnbull is an anthropologist who worked for many years among the Mbuti of northeastern Zaire. (See EthnoProfile 6.1: Mbuti.) He discovered that people who

---

global style A way of viewing the world that is holistic. People who use such a style first see a bundle of relationships and only later see the bits and pieces that are related. They are said to be *field dependent*.

articulated style A way of viewing the world that breaks it up into smaller and smaller pieces, which can then be organized. People who use such a style consider whatever they happen to be paying attention to apart from its context. They are said to be *field independent*.

EthnoProfile 6.1 • **MBUTI**

REGION: Central Africa

NATION: Zaire (northeastern)

POPULATION: 40,000

ENVIRONMENT: Dense tropical forest

LIVELIHOOD: Nomadic hunting and gathering

POLITICAL ORGANIZATION: Traditionally, communal bands of 7 to 30 families (average 17 families); today, part of a modern nation-state

FOR MORE INFORMATION: Turnbull, Collin. 1961. *The forest people.* New York: Simon and Schuster.

live all their lives in a dense forest have no experience of distance greater than a few feet and are therefore not accustomed to taking distance into consideration when estimating the size of an object in the visual field. Turnbull took one of his informants, Kenge, on a trip that brought them out of the forest and into a game park. For the first time in his life, Kenge faced vast, rolling grasslands nearly empty of trees and backed by a huge inland lake. Kenge's response to this experience was dramatic: "When Kenge topped the rise, he stopped dead. Every smallest sign of mirth suddenly left his face. He opened his mouth but could say nothing. He moved his head and eyes slowly and unbelievingly" (1961, 251).

When Kenge finally saw the animals grazing on the plain, he asked Turnbull what insects they were. When told that the "insects" were buffalo, Kenge laughed and accused Turnbull of lying. Then he strained to see better and inquired what kind of buffalo could be so small. Later, when Turnbull pointed out a fishing boat on the lake, Kenge scoffed at him and insisted it was a floating piece of wood (1961, 252).

Cole and Scribner had a similar experience with one of their informants, a young Liberian who had lived his entire life inland. He had never seen the ocean until they took him to Monrovia, the Liberian capital, which is also a large port city. On seeing specks in the distance that the anthropologists insisted were boats, he observed that men who put out to sea in such small boats must be very brave (1974, 97).

When people in another culture fail to see similarities between people or objects that we think ought to be obvious to any observer, we are apt to become impatient. Yet in the United States, where racist stereotypes influence perceptions of mixed peoples, many of us are subject to similar kinds of "blindness." In North America, where African Americans have been a minority, anyone with the slightest African ancestry has been classified as "black." This is just the opposite of the tendency in a place like Jamaica, for example, where Europeans have been a minority since the first Africans were brought to the island as slaves centuries ago. In Jamaica, the slightest phenotypic evidence of European ancestry is noted and can be used to link a person more closely with the "white" elite than with the "black" majority. This ambiguity in visual perceptions of similarity and difference eventually helped to undermine attempts by early anthropologists to classify humanity into mutually exclusive "races."

The study of illusion thus raises all kinds of questions about the nature of reality, just as the study of metaphor raises questions about the nature of literal language. It demonstrates that there can be a gulf between what we see and what we know, what we perceive and what we conceive. Nevertheless, in the ordinary contexts of everyday life, these discrepancies seem to be manageable: there is coherence between what we perceive and what we conceive. Moreover, because our link with the world is a dialectical one, there is no sharp boundary between what we perceive and what we conceive. Not only can new perceptions lead us to modify our conceptions (that is, we learn), but new conceptions can also lead us to perceive aspects of the world around us that we didn't pay attention to before. As a result, **cognition** is perhaps best understood as "a nexus of relations between the mind at work and the world in which it works" (Lave 1988, 1).

CONCEPTION

One way to illustrate the link between perception and conception, between what we see and what we know, is to compare the way different societies classify various phenomena. Patricia Greenfield carried out a study among the Wolof of Senegal using sets of pictures mounted on cards (Figure 6.8). (See EthnoProfile 6.2: Wolof.) Each subject was asked to select the two pictures in a set that were most alike and then to explain why they were most alike. This test was administered to three different groups: traditional rural Wolof people who had never been to school, ranging from six years of age to adulthood; schoolchildren from the same rural town from which the first group was taken; and schoolchildren from Dakar, the capital of Senegal.

The most striking correlation existed between the amount of Western-style schooling a subject had received and the kinds of classifications made. All the schoolchildren, whether urban or rural, performed much the same way American schoolchildren did. That is, the greater the number of years in school, the greater the children's preference to classify the objects in terms of form (shape and size) or function and the lesser their preference to classify them in terms of color. In addition, children with more schooling tended to explain their classifications in terms of conceptual categories ("round ones"). Those who had never been to school, regardless of age, preferred to classify in terms of color. Greenfield concluded that this difference could be attributed to the experience of Western schooling, in which people with normal perceptual abilities were trained in "European habits of perceptual *analysis*." Presumably Wolof, who do not receive such

---

cognition (1) The mental process by which human beings gain knowledge; (2) the nexus of relations between the mind at work and the world in which it works.

FIGURE 6.8 *Three picture displays used in the Wolof classification study, with their attributes.*

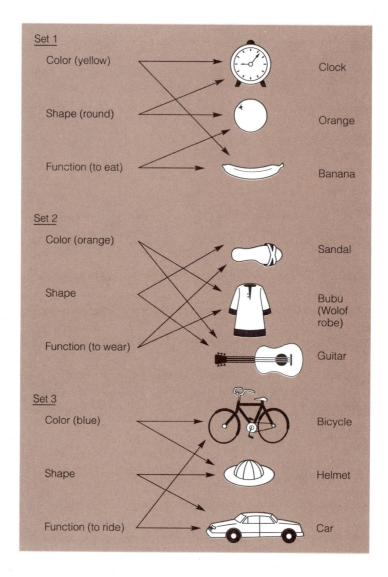

training, have little need or motivation (at least in the testing situation, as they understood it) to pay attention to features other than color to create a classification (Cole and Scribner 1974, 103–5).

The probable influence of Western-style education on ways of classifying appeared in another study by D. W. Sharp and Michael Cole in Yucatán, Mexico. (See EthnoProfile 6.3: Yucatecan Maya.) Using the cards pictured in Figure 6.9, they tested four groups of rural children and young adults: first graders, third graders, sixth graders, and teenagers who had attended no more than three years of school during their lives. They discovered that not all subjects were able to sort all the cards successfully according to a single rule (color, shape, or number). However, the third graders were more successful than the first graders, and the sixth graders were more successful than the third graders.

EthnoProfile 6.2 • **WOLOF**

REGION: Western Africa

NATION: Senegal

POPULATION: 2,700,000

ENVIRONMENT: Savanna

LIVELIHOOD: Farming

POLITICAL ORGANIZATION: Traditionally, a highly stratified kingdom; today, part of a modern nation-state

FOR MORE INFORMATION: Gamble, David P. *The Wolof of Senegambia*. London: International African Institute.

EthnoProfile 6.3 • **YUCATECAN MAYA**

REGION: Middle America

NATION: Mexico and Guatemala

POPULATION: 2,000,000 (all Maya; 1960s)

ENVIRONMENT: Arid semidesert

LIVELIHOOD: Corn farming

POLITICAL ORGANIZATION: Peasant society in modern nation-states

FOR MORE INFORMATION: Steggerda, Morris. [1941] 1984. *Maya Indians of Yucatán*. New York: AMS Press.

Given these data alone, it might seem that age is the important variable. But the teenagers with three years of school or less performed successfully at a level between that of the first graders and the third graders. Sharp and Cole concluded: "It seems quite possible that one consequence of educational experience is to instill the notion that any set of objects can be treated (classified) in a variety of ways—there is no 'one correct way,' regardless of the task at hand." That would explain the teenagers' level of performance (Cole and Scribner 1974, 106–8).

Douglas Price-Williams (cited in Cole and Scribner 1974, 116–17) suspected that the performance of African children on classification tests had been negatively affected because the children had been asked to sort unfamiliar abstract shapes. In his research among the Tiv of Nigeria, he decided to choose as test items ten different kinds of animals (represented mostly by plastic toys) and ten different kinds of plants familiar to

FIGURE 6.9 *Cards used in the Mexican reclassification study.*

Tiv children. (See EthnoProfile 6.4: Tiv.) With each set of objects, he asked the children to pick out the ones that belonged together and to tell him why they had chosen as they did. Each child was then asked to regroup the objects again and again until the child found no other groupings possible.

The results were impressive. The youngest children (six years old) could classify and reclassify all the objects three or four different ways, whereas the oldest children (eleven years old) found five or six ways to do so, and it made no difference whether they had attended school or not. Price-Williams also observed how the children had gone about constructing their classifications. Although they grouped the animals primarily in terms of concrete attributes, such as size, color, or place where they are found, they grouped the plants primarily in terms of the abstract attribute of edibility.

These studies, taken together, reinforce the conclusion that competent members of all societies employ a range of cognitive styles. We cannot speak of abstract thinking and concrete thinking as mutually exclusive. Anthropologists have found that many non-Western peoples are not used to thinking about things without relating them to some kind of context. Members of those societies can learn to use such a context-free cognitive style if they attend school, but, as the Tiv research illustrates, this does not mean that they never use abstract categories outside the classroom. Paradoxically, the Tiv children were able to display sophisticated classifying skills when the experimental task was made more, rather than less, context dependent: when they sorted the animals and plants on the basis of which could be eaten and which could not. But perhaps the paradox is not so great after all. In Lave's research, the full range of her shoppers' calculating skills were displayed only when she studied mathematics in the supermarket, rather than in the classroom, and became aware of the range of factors in addition to price (from available storage space to personal food preferences) that influenced buying decisions.

Cross-cultural research in cognition is a delicate business. For the researcher, the trick is first to devise a test that will give people who use different cognitive styles an opportunity to show what they know and what they can do. The researcher must also discover whether different groups of subjects understand the tasks they are being asked

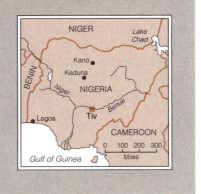

EthnoProfile 6.4 • **TIV**

REGION: Western Africa

NATION: Nigeria (northern)

POPULATION: 800,000

ENVIRONMENT: Undulating plain—wooded foothills to sandbanks

LIVELIHOOD: Farming

POLITICAL ORGANIZATION: Traditionally, egalitarian; today, part of a modern nation-state

FOR MORE INFORMATION: Bohannon, Laura, and Paul Bohannon. 1969. *The Tiv of central Nigeria.* 2d ed. London: International African Institute.

to perform in the same way. In recent years, a number of researchers have worked to develop methods to assess cognition that are not bound to the traditional psychological testing laboratory or to the classroom.

Reason and the Reasoning Process

As we have just seen, one great example of Western dualism is between what we see and what we know. Another, at least equally great, is between what we think and what we feel.

From the earliest days of the West's discovery of other societies, there has been a debate about the extent to which nonliterate non-Western peoples might be said to possess reason. How might one go about determining whether or not the members of a particular society are "rational" or "irrational"? To begin, we need to explore what we mean by **thinking**.

Most cognitive psychologists have adopted Jerome Bruner's famous definition of thinking as "going beyond the information given." This means that thinking is different from remembering (which refers to information already given) and also from learning (which involves acquiring information that was not given beforehand). Going beyond the information given thus implies a dialectic between some information already at hand and the cognitive processes of the person who is attempting to cope with that information. This definition highlights the "nexus of relations between the mind at work and the

thinking An active cognitive process that involves going beyond the information given.

world in which it works" (Lave 1988, 1). Thinking is open and active, and it has no predetermined outcome.

Many psychologists and anthropologists have tried to assess the levels of rational thinking in non-Western populations. One frequently used measure is the test of *conservation*. Swiss psychologist Jean Piaget devised this test as a way of measuring children's cognitive development. Children who "conserve" are able to recognize that the quantity of some substance remains constant even when its shape changes. According to Piaget, attaining this ability is an important step toward mature rational thought.

A classic conservation experiment would proceed in the following way. Children are shown a short, squat beaker of water. The experimenter pours the water from this beaker into a tall, thin beaker. Naturally the water level rises much higher in the tall, thin beaker. The experimenter then asks each child whether the amount of water has changed. It seems that not until Western children reach the age of six or seven do they become aware that the amount of water remains the same, or is "conserved." Before this time, they tend to argue that the tall, thin beaker has more water in it. The results of this experiment can be used to demonstrate concept formation (that is, the concept of volume). But they have often been used to demonstrate the presence or absence of rational thought. This is presumably because to conclude that the same volume changes in amount as it is poured from one beaker into another is "irrational" in any normal adult (Cole and Scribner 1974, 146ff.).

Conservation tests have been tried in several different societies, always with ambiguous results. Some people are able to "pass" the test, others are not, and there is no clear way to predict who will be successful and who will not be. "Until we have some better idea of what induces some members of traditional societies to solve conservation problems while their neighbors do not, we cannot be certain about the significance of conservation tests as a tool for understanding the relation between culture and cognitive development" (Cole and Scribner 1974, 156).

Culture and Logic

Another set of cognitive tests has to do with verbal reasoning ability. These tests present subjects with three statements in the form of a syllogism—for example, "All men are mortal, Socrates is a man, therefore Socrates is mortal." The first two propositions are called the *premises,* and the third statement is the *conclusion.* For a syllogism to be sound, the conclusion must follow from the premises.

Syllogistic reasoning is enshrined in Western culture as the quintessence of rational thought. Researchers thus suggested that the rational capacities of non-Western peoples could be tested using logical problems in syllogistic form. Presumably their rationality would be confirmed if they could deduce correctly when the conclusion followed logically from the premises and when it did not.

Cole and Scribner presented logical problems involving syllogistic reasoning to their Kpelle subjects. (See EthnoProfile 6.5: Kpelle.) Typically, the logical problem was embedded in a folktalelike story. The experimenter read the story to the subjects and then asked them a series of follow-up questions designed to reveal whether the subjects could draw a correct conclusion from the premises given.

EthnoProfile 6.5 • **KPELLE**

REGION: Western Africa

NATION: Liberia (central and western)

POPULATION: 86,000

ENVIRONMENT: Tropical forest

LIVELIHOOD: Rice farming

POLITICAL ORGANIZATION: Traditionally, chiefdoms; today, part of a modern nation-state

FOR MORE INFORMATION: Bellman, Beryl. 1975. *Village of curers and assassins: On the production of Fala Kpelle cosmological categories.* The Hague: Mouton.

Here is one story Cole and Scribner prepared: "At one time Spider went to a feast. He was told to answer this question before he could eat any of the food. The question is: Spider and Black Deer always eat together. Spider is eating. Is Black Deer eating?" (1974, 162). The syllogism is contained in the question at the end of the story. Given the two premises, the conclusion should be that Black Deer is eating.

Now consider a typical Kpelle response to hearing this story:

SUBJECT: Were they in the bush?

EXPERIMENTER: Yes.

SUBJECT: Were they eating together?

EXPERIMENTER: Spider and Black Deer always eat together. Spider is eating. Is Black Deer eating?

SUBJECT: But I was not there. How can I answer such a question?

EXPERIMENTER: Can't you answer it? Even if you were not there, you can answer it. (Repeats the question.)

SUBJECT: Oh, oh, Black Deer is eating.

EXPERIMENTER: What is your reason for saying that Black Deer was eating?

SUBJECT: The reason is that Black Deer always walks about all day eating green leaves in the bush. Then he rests for a while and gets up again to eat. (Cole and Scribner 1974, 162)

The subject's answer to the question and subsequent justification for that answer seem to have nothing whatever to do with the logical problem the subject is being asked to solve. One simplistic way to interpret this response would be to call it "irrational," but reread the original story. The story itself contains an element of paradox: Spider will not

---

syllogistic reasoning A form of reasoning based on the syllogism, a series of three statements in which the first two statements are the premises and the last is the conclusion, which must follow from the premises.

be allowed to eat until he answers a question, yet the question he is to answer presumes that he is already eating! Of course, the paradox exists only if the subjects assume that the contextual material about the feast is relevant to the logical problem they are being asked to solve. Yet it is precisely this that we cannot assume. As we have seen, people have to be trained to exclude context from their judgments of truth or falsity, literality or figurativeness.

The experimenters devised this story the same way schoolteachers devise mathematical word problems. That is, the contextual material is nothing more than a kind of window dressing. Students quickly learn to disregard the window dressing and seek out the mathematical problem it hides. In the same way, the Kpelle subjects hearing the story about Spider and Black Deer are supposed to demonstrate "logic" by disregarding the contextual material about the feast and seeking out the syllogism embedded within it. However, Kpelle subjects did not understand that they were being read this story in a testing situation for which considerations of context or meaningfulness were irrelevant. In the preceding example, the subject seemed to have difficulty separating the logical problem both from the introductory material about the feast and from the rest of his experiential knowledge.

Cole and Scribner interpreted their subject's response to this problem as being due not to irrationality but to a "failure to accept the logical task" (Cole and Scribner 1974, 162). In a follow-up study, Cole and Scribner discovered that Kpelle high school children responded "correctly" to the logical problems 90 percent of the time. This suggests a strong correlation between Western-style schooling and a willingness to accept context-free analytic tasks in testing situations (164).

But this is not all. David Lancy, one of Cole and Scribner's colleagues, discovered that Western-style syllogisms are very similar to certain forms of Kpelle riddles. Unlike syllogisms, however, those riddles have no single, "logically correct" answer. "Rather, as the riddle is posed to a group, the right answer is the one among many offered that seems most illuminating, resourceful, and convincing as determined by consensus and circumstance. This emphasis on edification as a criterion for 'rightness' is found in Kpelle jurisprudence as well" (Lancy cited in Fernandez 1980, 47–48). In other words, the "right" answer cannot be extracted from the form of the riddle by logical operations. Rather, it is the answer that seems most enlightening and informative to the particular audience in the particular setting where the riddle is posed.

Enlightening answers, moreover, appear to be rooted in shared cultural schemas. Roy D'Andrade has shown that college undergraduates at the University of California, San Diego, are unable to complete syllogisms similar to the Spider–Black Deer story when the content is arbitrary. Only 53 percent of UCSD undergraduates (a result only slightly above chance) selected the correct answer to the following syllogism:

1. *Given:* If Tom is drinking a Pepsi then Peter is sitting down.
2. *Suppose:* Peter is not sitting down.
3. Then:
   a. It must be the case that Tom is drinking a Pepsi.
   b. Maybe Tom is drinking a Pepsi or maybe he isn't.
   c. It must be the case that Tom is not drinking a Pepsi.

The correct answer (c.) exactly parallels the correct answer to the Spider–Black Deer story. And, indeed, the reasoning processes of the undergraduates bear a striking similarity to those of Cole and Scribner's Kpelle informants: "When arbitrary relations are presented, the typical respondent does not seem to integrate the state of affairs described by the first. Respondents say . . . 'So what if *Peter* is not sitting down. That doesn't have anything to do with *Tom's* drinking a Pepsi' " (D'Andrade 1992, 49). By contrast, 86 percent of UCSD undergraduates chose the correct answer to the same kind of syllogism that involved a well-formed North American cultural schema (that cities are located within states). There is no reason to doubt that Liberians, North Americans, and other human beings come equipped with the same elementary cognitive processes: the ability to make abstractions, to create conceptual categories, and to reason inferentially. The difficulty is to understand how these elementary cognitive processes are put to work within culturally shared schemas to produce different, functional cognitive systems known as **reasoning styles**.

If "riddle interpretation" is a reasoning style characteristic of Kpelle culture, then formal Western **logic** is perhaps best understood as a reasoning style characteristic of Western culture. Given D'Andrade's evidence, it would seem that formal logic is different from both informal Western reasoning styles and many non-Western reasoning styles, and for the same reason. That is, formal logic requires thinkers to draw conclusions in the absence of context without the aid of helpful cultural schemas. Non-Western reasoning and informal Western reasoning are rooted in cultural schemas and therefore depend upon cultural context. If this were not the case, there would be no need to take college courses in logic. Traditionally, logicians have scorned the "illogical, irrational" thought processes used in everyday life. But everyday reasoning clearly has its own order, as Lave's grocery shoppers and D'Andrade's undergraduates illustrate.

Logical systems represent objects and relationships between objects in the world. But the objects and relationships we experience in our lives can always be represented in more than one way. As Barry Barnes and David Bloor put it, "Just as our experience of a shared material world does not itself guarantee shared verbal descriptions of it, so our shared rationality does not guarantee a unique logical system" (1982, 44). Barnes and Bloor prefer to view traditional Western logic as "a learned body of scholarly lore, growing and varying over time" (45). This is not to claim that the rules of formal Western logic are useless. On the contrary, because they are in part engendered by careful attention to human experience of the world, they are hardly random in origin. But other "logics," rooted in different cultural schemas, may be equally useful in different cultural contexts. Formal Western logic, like literal language, does not offer us the only plausible, meaningful, or useful perspective on the human condition.

---

reasoning styles How we understand a cognitive task, how we encode the information presented to us, and what transformations the information undergoes as we think. Reasoning styles differ from culture to culture and from context to context within the same culture.

logic A symbolic system used to represent objects and relationships between objects in the world.

EMOTION

Psychological anthropologists who try to define **emotion** in cross-cultural terms run into a familiar problem: they discover not just that different cultures talk about emotion in different languages but that not all languages even possess a term that might be translated as "emotion." To get out of this tangle, they have tried to develop a theory of cognitive functioning that accounts for the experiences that some cultures recognize as "emotional."

In Their Own Words   **THE MADNESS OF HUNGER**

Medical anthropologist Nancy Scheper-Hughes describes how symptoms of a rural Brazilian folk ailment can be understood as a form of protest against physical exploitation and abuse.

Among the agricultural wage laborers living in the hillside shantytown of Alto do Cruzeiro, on the margins of a large, interior market town in the plantation zone of Pernambuco, Brazil, and who sell their labor for as little as a dollar a day, socioeconomic and political contradictions often take shape in the "natural" contradictions of angry, sick, and afflicted bodies. In addition to the wholly expectable epidemics of parasitic infections and communicable fevers, there are the more unexpected outbreaks and explosions of unruly and subversive symptoms that will not readily materialize under the health station's microscope. Among these are the fluid symptoms of *nervos* (angry, frenzied nervousness): trembling, fainting, seizures, hysterical weeping, angry recriminations, blackouts, and paralysis of face and limbs.

These nervous attacks are in part coded metaphors through which the workers express their dangerous and unacceptable condition of chronic hunger and need (see Scheper-Hughes, 1988) and in part acts of defiance and dissent that graphically register the refusal to endure what is, in fact, unendurable and their protest against their availability for physical exploitation and abuse. And so, rural workers who have cut sugarcane since the age of seven or eight years will sometimes collapse, their legs giving way under an *ataque de nervos*, a nervous attack. They cannot walk, they cannot stand upright; they are left, like Oliver Sacks (1984), without a leg to stand on.

In the exchange of meanings between the body personal and the body social, the nervous-hungry, nervous-angry body of the cane cutter offers itself as metaphor and metonym of the nervous sociopolitical system and for the paralyzed position of the rural worker in the current economic and political dis-order. In "lying down" on the job, in refusing to return to the work that has overly determined their entire lives, the cane cutters' body language signifies both surrender and defeat. But one also notes a drama of mockery and refusal. For if the folk ailment *nervos* attacks the legs and the face, it leaves the arms and hands intact and free for less physically ruinous work. Consequently, otherwise healthy young men suffering from nervous attacks press their claims as sick men on their various political bosses and patrons to find them alternative work, explicitly "sitting down" work, arm work (but not clerical work for these men are illiterate).

The analysis of *nervos* does not end here, for nervous attack is an expansive and polysemic form of dis-ease. Shantytown women, too, suffer from *nervos*—both the *nervos de trabalhar muito*, "overwork" nerves from which male cane cutters suffer, and also the more gender-specific *nervos de sofrir muito*, the nerves of those who have endured and suffered much. "Sufferers' nerves" attacks those who have endured a recent, especially a violent, tragedy. Widows of husbands and mothers of sons who have been abducted and violently "disappeared" are prone to the mute, enraged, white-knuckled shaking of "sufferers' nerves."

Source: Scheper-Hughes 1994.

In traditional Western dualism, reason and thought are associated with the mind and emotion with the body. Any attempt to explain emotion must deal with the nature of the bodily arousal we associate with it. But there is more to emotion, as commonly understood, than mere bodily arousal. Recall the butcher knife referred to earlier in this chapter. What do we feel when we see a butcher knife sitting beside mushrooms on a cutting board in our kitchen? What do we feel when we see that same knife in the hands of a burglar who is bent on attacking us? The knife alone does not trigger our feeling. The situation, or context, in which we encounter the knife is equally important. The context itself is often ambiguous, and our emotional experience changes as our interpretation of the context changes.

Thus, emotion can be understood as the product of a dialectic between bodily arousal and cognitive interpretation. Cognitive psychologist George Mandler suggests that bodily arousal can trigger an emotional experience by attracting our attention and prompting us to seek the source of arousal (1975, 97). Conversely, a particular interpretation of our experience can trigger bodily arousal. Arousal may heighten or diminish, depending on how we interpret what is happening around us.

Mandler's discussion of emotion, like Cole and Scribner's discussion of cognition, describes emotions as *functional systems*. Each links elementary processes that involve the body's arousal system to other elementary processes that are involved in the construction of perception, conception, and reasoning. "Emotions are not something that people 'have,' they are constituted of people's states, values and arousals" (Mandler 1983, 151). Approaching emotion from this perspective accomplishes three things: (1) it integrates mind and body in a holistic fashion; (2) it acknowledges ambiguity as a central feature of emotional experience, just as we have argued it is central to linguistic, perceptual, and conceptual experience; and (3) it suggests how different cultural interpretive frameworks might shape not only what we think but also what we feel.

Why should we experience emotion at all? The role of emotion in human life may be rooted in the evolutionary history of a highly intelligent species that is capable of thinking before acting. Bodily arousal alerts us to something new and unexpected in our environment, something that does not easily fit into any of our conventional schemas. Once our attention is caught in this way, the rest of our cognitive processes focus on the interrupting phenomenon. From this perspective, a person would be foolish to ignore his or her guts when trying to sort out a confusing experience. Indeed, the guts are usually what alert us to confusion in the first place. The need of "whole-body" experience for understanding also becomes more comprehensible. Mandler reminds us, "Just telling people what a situation is going to be like isn't enough, and it isn't good enough training when you encounter the real situation" (1983, 152). Generations of new spouses, new parents, and anthropological fieldworkers can testify to the overwhelming truth of this statement.

emotion The product of a dialectic between bodily arousal and cognitive interpretation, emotion comprises states, values, and arousals.

EthnoProfile 6.6   •   **GIRIAMA**

REGION: Eastern Africa

NATION: Kenya

POPULATION: 150,000

ENVIRONMENT: Varied; coastal to desert, lush, hilly, flat

LIVELIHOOD: Farming and herding

POLITICAL ORGANIZATION: Traditionally, men of influence but no coercieve power; today, part of a modern nation-state

FOR MORE INFORMATION: Parkin, David. 1991. *Sacred void: Spatial images of work and ritual among the Giriama of Kenya.* Cambridge: Cambridge University Press.

In sum, we experience bodily arousal when our familiar world is somehow interrupted. That arousal may either fade away or develop into an emotional experience depending on the meaning we assign to it. Possible meanings arise out of cultural interpretations of recurring experiential schemas. We should not be surprised to find some overlap in the categories of feeling recognized by different cultures. After all, certain experiential schemas that interrupt the familiar world—birth and death, for example—are human universals. At the same time, we should expect that the wider cultural context will in each case modify the angle from which such experiences are understood and, thus, the categories of feeling associated with them.

Emotion in an Eastern African Culture

David Parkin (1984) has studied the cultural construction of emotion among the Giriama of coastal Kenya. (See EthnoProfile 6.6: Giriama.) We must explain several features of Giriama thinking before considering their understanding of what we call emotion. First, the Giriama theory of human nature does not recognize a mind-body dualism of the Western sort. Indeed, the Giriama are unwilling to set up sharp, mutually exclusive oppositions of any kind when discussing human nature. Parkin tells us that such behavior as spirit possession, madness, hysteria, witchcraft, persistent violence, drunkenness, and thieving are explained "as the result of what we might call imbalances in human nature. . . . I call them imbalances because the Giriama do not believe that a person can be intrinsically or irredeemably evil: at some stage, usually remarkably quickly, he will be brought back into the fold, even if he subsequently leaves it again. A large number of terms, roughly translatable as greed, lust, envy, jealousy, malice, resentment, anger, are used to refer to these imbalances of character and the accompanying behavior" (1984, 14).

As with us, the Giriama associate different feelings with different parts of the body. In the West, we conventionally connect the brain with reason and the heart with emotion. For the Giriama, however, the heart, liver, kidneys, and eyes are the seat of reason and emotion. Although the Giriama may distinguish thinking from feeling in discussing the actual behavior of real people, they nevertheless presume a common origin for both (Parkin 1984, 17). Indeed, the Giriama framework for understanding human cognition has much in common with the anthropological perspective described throughout this chapter.

What about particular emotions? Although the categories of feeling recognized by Giriama overlap in some respects with the experiences labeled by English terms for emotions, Parkin suggests that there are important differences that stem from the nature of the schemas that Giriama culture conventionally recognizes and from the prototypical thoughts and feelings that are appropriate to those schemas. Consider what the term *utsungu* means as a label for a category of feeling: "Utsungu means poison, bitterness, resentment, and anger, on the one hand, but also grief on the other. It is the feeling experienced at a funeral of a loved or respected relative or friend. A man or woman is grieved at the loss but also bitter that it has happened at all, and angry with the witch who caused the death. Since the witch will be made to pay, the sentiment carried with it both the consequences of the loss of a dear one and the intention to avenge his or her death" (1984, 118).

We too feel "grief" at the death of a loved one. But the prototypical Western experience of grief does not contain the additional meaning involving anger at witchcraft and the desire for vengeance. One would have to be a Giriama—or have lived in another culture in which witchcraft was understood as the usual cause of death and in which such wrongful death could be avenged—to experience the particular emotional configuration that Parkin describes for the Giriama.

Emotion in Oceania

Catherine Lutz (1988) is concerned with situating understanding and reasoning about emotion more fully within the social structures and social behaviors that drive it. Lutz did fieldwork among the Ifaluk of the Caroline Islands in the Pacific. (See EthnoProfile 6.7: Ifaluk.) While not denying the links of emotion to the body, she emphasizes how emotions can be understood as a form of social discourse. That is, people's use of the language of emotion can be understood as a way of talking about social relationships. Like the Giriama, the Ifaluk do not distinguish sharply between thought and emotion; they understand events in a way that is simultaneously cognitive and affective. Saying that they are experiencing *song* (justifiable anger) is not just the description of an internal bodily state, it is also a comment about someone else's failure to observe appropriate social behavior. That is, inappropriate social behavior interrupts the world of social expectations, producing an emotional response. The Ifaluk expect that the person who provoked *song* in another will naturally experience *metagu* (fear/anxiety) once he or she finds out. Indeed the Ifaluk often link categories of thought/feeling in pairs: *song* and *metagu, gafago* (neediness) and *fago* (compassion/love/sadness).

EthnoProfile 6.7 • IFALUK

REGION: Micronesia

NATION: Caroline Islands

POPULATION: 430 (1988)

ENVIRONMENT: Coral atoll

LIVELIHOOD: Taro cultivation, government employment

POLITICAL ORGANIZATION: Traditionally, chiefdoms; today, a U.S. Trust Territory

FOR MORE INFORMATION: Lutz, Caroline. 1988. *Unnatural emotions*. Chicago: University of Chicago Press.

Lutz writes, "the mental state of *any* mature individual is seen as having fundamentally social roots. Others can then be held responsible for the social conditions that produce the state" (1988, 101). Consequently claiming to be justifiably angry is the first step in a process of negotiation about the meaning of other people's actions in relation to oneself. Claims of *song* made by people of higher status or greater power (such as lineage heads and chiefs) tend to be accepted publicly, and the responsible party is expected to experience *metagu* as a result. Claims made by people concerning others of similar status or power, however, may involve more negotiation over whether or not they have the right to use the concept *song* in a particular situation. Extended negotiation is also common when Ifaluk are unsure of what to feel/think about a newly introduced cultural item like cash, which does not fit into traditional schemas about proper social behavior and yet must be dealt with.

Lutz relates the Ifaluk's particular configuration of emotion/thought to the natural and political conditions of everyday life on a small coral atoll where a high rate of infant mortality and the threat of sudden devastation and death from typhoons are ever present. The emotion of *fago,* for example, motivates people to share food, adopt one another's children, and provide close personal care to those who are ill or in some other way *gafago* (needy).

THE PROCESS OF SOCIALIZATION AND ENCULTURATION

Acquiring the functional cognitive systems characteristic of a culture takes time. Cognitive learning is similar to language learning; it involves a dialectical interaction between organism and environment, and the people around us are an important part of that environment. Children use their own bodies and brains to explore their world. But from their earliest days, other people are actively working to steer their activity and attention in particular directions. Consequently, their exploration of the world is not merely trial and error: the path is cleared for them by others who shape their experiences—and their interpretations of their experiences—for them.

Two terms in the social sciences refer to this process of culturally and socially shaped cognitive development. The first term, **socialization,** originated in sociology. It focuses on the organizational problems facing human beings as material organisms who must live with each other. Organisms with material bodies must learn to pattern and adapt their behavior according to the appropriate behavioral rules established by their respective societies. The second term, **enculturation,** originated in anthropology. It focuses on the cognitive problems facing human beings as intelligent, reflexive creatures who must live with each other. These organisms must learn to pattern and adapt their ways of thinking and feeling to the ways of thinking and feeling that are considered appropriate in their respective cultures. The process of becoming human requires both these processes. After all, children learn how to act, think, feel, and speak at the same time, as they participate in the characteristic activities of their respective groups. We will use the term *socialization/enculturation* to represent this holistic experience.

Socialization/enculturation is a process whose product is a socially and culturally constructed **self** capable of functioning successfully in society. Anthropologists do not have any global theory of socialization/enculturation. However, important thinkers have addressed the issues involved and have devised theories that attempt to account for at least some of the processes through which mature human selves are produced. Four theorists have significantly influenced anthropological approaches to cognitive development and socialization/enculturation: Sigmund Freud (1856–1939), Jean Piaget (1896–1980), George Herbert Mead (1863–1931), and Lev Vygotsky (1896–1934).

Freud and Emotional Development

Freud's theory of personality development emphasizes in particular the patterning of the emotions in early childhood. Freud argued that all human children pass through a universal sequence of experiences within the family. How they negotiate those experiences has a lifelong impact on their emotional health.

According to Freud, human beings are, first and foremost, physical organisms. Their action in the world is guided by an innate predisposition to seek pleasure and avoid pain. This instinctive desire takes the form of drives for food and for sex. The drives exist in the unconscious, in a domain of the personality that Freud called the *id.* If the drives go unsatisfied for too long, the pressure will cause psychological damage. In this way, Freud, who was far from optimistic about human destiny, saw murder and rape as natural responses of human beings (he was thinking primarily of male human beings) whose natural drives are frustrated.

---

socialization The process by which human beings as material organisms, living together with other similar organisms, must learn to pattern and adapt their behavior according to the appropriate behavioral rules established by our respective societies.

enculturation The process by which human beings as intelligent, reflexive creatures, living with each other, must learn to pattern and adapt their ways of thinking and feeling to the ways of thinking and feeling that are considered appropriate in our respective cultures.

self The result of the process of socialization/enculturation for an individual.

Initially, newborn children are at the mercy of the id; Freud saw them as demanding and egocentric. Gradually, however, children discover that their demands will not all be met instantly and that their caretaker's will is not under their control. As this awareness emerges, the child's *ego*—the domain of the personality that embodies reason and common sense—develops. As children grow older and learn more about the wider social world, they develop within their personalities a third domain: the *superego*.

The superego is an internalized representation of the rules of the social group. It corresponds to what we refer to as a person's conscience and can redirect drives into socially acceptable channels. But society's rules may be very demanding and offer little satisfaction. Freud argued that people unable to withstand the social forces that channel or repress their innate drives may suffer psychological disturbances. They may seek pleasure in bizarre or unconventional ways in an attempt to satisfy *repressed* drives whose demands their egos are too weak to control.

Piaget and Rational Development

In contrast to Freud, the Swiss psychologist Jean Piaget placed primary emphasis on the development of reason in children. He proposed four stages of development in children's reasoning powers.

The earliest stage is the *sensorimotor stage* (birth to age two). Children in this stage learn about the environment through their senses by exploring and manipulating the physical world around them. They cannot yet speak and thus cannot rely on language to teach them about the world. As a result of their explorations in this stage, children begin to develop schemas, or recognizable, recurring configurations of experience.

As soon as children begin to learn language, they embark on the *preoperational stage* (about age two to age seven). Children at this stage have developed schemas about the world, but their schemas are not yet mature. For example, during the preoperational stage children are consistently misled by the illusions of greater volume, length, or weight in tests of conservation.

The third stage is that of *concrete operations* (age seven to age eleven). Children who reach this stage have mastered the illusions that misled them at their previous level of development. During this stage, they construct an increasingly sophisticated understanding of the structure and operation of the material world around them. They have difficulty, however, in abstracting from concrete experience.

Piaget's fourth stage is that of *formal operations*. It usually appears about the time children enter their teens. Children at this stage become able to manipulate abstract concepts. They can carry out calculations using the symbols of mathematics, for example, without direct reference to the concrete world that the symbols represent. Eventually, they become able to discuss concepts, such as negative numbers, for which there is no concrete reference in the world of experience. The stage of formal operations is the highest level of rational development. Piaget believed that not everyone would necessarily achieve this stage.

The theories of Freud and Piaget are stimulating and suggestive, yet they pose problems for anthropologists who attempt to use them in sociocultural research. Both Freud and Piaget take a highly individualistic approach to socialization/enculturation.

For both, children come into the world as independent individuals, able to begin making sense of the world around them without the guidance of others.

In the case of Freud, the id is an autonomous natural force propelling each individual toward egotism. Left on their own, human beings aim only to satisfy themselves, and they relate to other people only as means to this end. When human beings curb their biologically rooted egotism in order to live together in society, they are violating their own natures and will therefore suffer. And there is no remedy because we can neither eliminate our natural selfishness nor survive without other human beings. For Piaget, too, human beings are naturally self-centered and for the same "biological" reasons. For him, early childhood is a time when young, independent human animals develop, on their own, the inborn capacity for rational thought given to them in the genes. Socialization/enculturation is necessary for a child to learn how to get along with other members of the group, but it cannot help the child learn how the world works and may even interfere with such learning.

Mead and Vygotsky: Social and Sociohistorical Development

The theories of Freud and Piaget assume that the important factors influencing development are rooted in the biological characteristics of individual organisms. As a result, both theories are intended to explain social and cultural patterns as by-products of the efforts of self-contained individuals to come to terms with the wider world. Both theories are therefore reductionistic.

Anthropologists need a theory of cognitive development that is holistic; therefore, many psychologists and anthropologists have been attracted to the ideas of George Herbert Mead (1863–1931) and, more recently, to the work of Soviet psychologist Lev Vygotsky (1896–1934). Although both men were contemporaries, Vygotsky's work has become influential in the West only recently. Before his early death, Vygotsky had helped to found a major school of Soviet psychology that continues to thrive. The writings of this *sociohistorical school* have inspired some of the most interesting recent research in cognitive anthropology.

For Mead and Vygotsky alike, human life is social from the outset, and individual identity can be acquired only in a social context. As Vygotsky wrote, "The social dimension of consciousness is primary in time and in fact. The individual dimension of consciousness is derivative and secondary" (1978, 30). Like Vygotsky, Mead believed that human nature is completed and enhanced, not curtailed or damaged, by socialization and enculturation. Indeed, the successful humanization of human beings lies in people's mastery of symbols, which begins when children start to learn language. As children come to control the symbolic systems of their cultures, they gain the ability to distinguish objects and relationships in the world. Most important, they come to see themselves as objects as well as subjects.

For Mead, this ability is acquired through the process of *role playing*. Very young children are at first unaware that they and the world around them are not continuous with one another. Gradually, however, they come to recognize, for example, that their parent's point of view is different from their own. Children then enter a stage of development in which they imitate the roles of those few people—the *particular others*—with whom they are well acquainted. We observe this imitative play when children begin to talk and scold their toys the same way they are scolded.

As children grow older, they move into the *game stage,* wherein they have become expert enough at taking the roles of other people to be able to enter into complex interactions with others. They can keep in mind not only their own role in the game but also the roles of all the other participants. At the same time, their experience of other people widens beyond the immediate family, and they develop the ability to take the role of the *generalized other,* or society at large. Being able to play games and take the role of the generalized other successfully requires a mastery of symbolism, because the games' rules and society's point of view are both highly abstract and mediated by language.

Mead's analysis focused primarily on face-to-face interactions among people. Anthropologists need a theoretical framework that goes beyond face-to-face interactions and accounts for the social, cultural, and historical contexts in which those interactions unfold. Here Vygotsky's work becomes important, for Vygotsky's understanding of context goes beyond Mead's. Vygotsky wanted to create a psychology that was compatible with a marxian analysis of society. His ideas are far from doctrinaire; indeed, during the Stalin years in Russia, his work was censored. At the same time, his marxian orientation required that he pay attention to the social, cultural, and historical context in which individual action is embedded.

At the beginning of the chapter, we introduced one of Vygotsky's theoretical contributions: the distinction between elementary cognitive processes and functional cognitive systems. This distinction is useful to anthropology because it provides a way of describing the similarities and differences we observe when we compare how people from different cultures think and feel. These differences have implications for cognitive development as well. The functional systems employed by adult members of society must be acquired during childhood. For Vygotsky, acquisition takes place in a context of face-to-face interaction between, typically, a child and an adult. When children learn about the world in such a context, they are not only—or even primarily—working on their own; on the contrary, they are learning about the world as they learn the symbolic forms (usually language) that others use to represent the world.

This learning process creates in the child a new plane of consciousness based on the dialogical, question-and-answer format of social interaction. From this, Vygotsky inferred that our internal thought processes would also have a dialogical format. Mead suggested something similar when he spoke of every person as being able to carry on internal conversations between the *I* (the unsocialized self) and the *me* (the socially conditioned self). Only on this basis can an individual's sense of identity develop as the self comes to distinguish itself from the conversational other.

One interesting Vygotskian concept is the *zone of proximal development,* which is the distance between a child's "actual development level as determined by independent problem solving" and the level of "potential development as determined through problem solving under adult guidance or in collaboration with more capable peers" (Vygotsky 1978, 86). Psychologists everywhere have long been aware that children can often achieve more when they are coached than when they work alone. Western psychologists, with their individualist bias, have viewed this difference in achievement as contamination of the testing situation or as the result of cheating. Vygotsky and his followers, however, have seen it as an indispensable measure of potential developmental growth that simultaneously demonstrates how growth is rooted in social interaction, especially in educational settings (Moll 1990).

The concept of the zone of proximal development enables us to describe the inadequacies of traditional IQ tests. It also enables anthropologists and comparative psychologists to link cognitive development to society, culture, and history. This conclusion is based on Vygotsky's explicit association of coaching or formal instruction with, as he put it, the "historical characteristics of humans" (Wertsch 1985, 71). That is, the size of the zone of proximal development is shaped by social, cultural, and historical factors. To the extent that these factors vary from society to society, we can expect cognitive development to vary as well.

IS COGNITIVE DEVELOPMENT THE SAME FOR EVERYONE?

The theories of development reviewed here picture the development process as a progression through a series of stages. With the exception of Vygotsky's theory, these theories also tend to assume that the stages are the same for all human beings, or at least all human beings in a particular society. We have seen some of the problems that arise when anthropologists try to account for cross-cultural differences with reference to a universal scheme of development; we must not forget that each culture harbors variation within itself. A Vygotskian perspective helps us explain not only cross-cultural differences in development, but also differences in the cognitive development of different subgroups in a single society.

For example, since their birth in 1973 through the late 1980s, a sample of 4,299 children have been followed by a team of Cuban researchers who periodically collected information on their cognitive, social, economic, physical, and academic development (Gutierrez Muñiz, López Hurtado, and Arias Beatón n.d.). The researchers identified a series of correlations between levels of education, wage employment, living standards, and health of mothers and levels of development and achievement of their children. Put in Vygotskian terms, the data show that the zone of proximal development is greater for children of mothers with higher levels of education and participation in the paid work force than it is for children of mothers with lower educational levels who do not work outside the home. These findings contradicted popular beliefs that the children of educated working mothers would suffer as a result of their mothers' activities (Arias Beatón, personal communication).

Carol Gilligan (1982) carried out a comparative study on the moral development of women and men in North American society. She argues that middle-class boys and girls in the United States begin their moral development in different sociocultural contexts. Boys are encouraged from an early age to break away from their mothers and families and make it on their own. In this context, they learn that independence is good, that dependency is weakness, and that their first duty is to themselves and what they stand for. By contrast, girls mature in a sociocultural context in which their bond to their mothers and families is never sharply ruptured. They learn that connection to others is good, that the destruction of relationships is damaging, and that their first responsibility in any difficult situation is to ensure that nobody gets hurt.

In Their Own Words   AMERICAN PREMENSTRUAL SYNDROME

Anthropologist Alma Gottlieb explores some of the contradictions surrounding the North American biocultural construction known as PMS.

To what extent might PMS be seen as an "escape valve," a means whereby American women "let off steam" from the enervating machine of the daily domestic grind? To some extent this explanation is valid, but it tells only part of the story. It ignores the specific contours of PMS and its predictable trajectory; moreover it puts PMS in a place that is peripheral to the American vision of womanhood, whereas my contention is that the current understanding of PMS (and, before its creation, of the menstrual period itself) is integral to how we view femininity. Even if it occupies a small portion of women's lives (although some women may see the paramenstruum as occupying half the month), and even if not all women suffer from it, I contend that the contemporary vision of PMS is so much a part of general cultural consciousness that it constitutes, qualitatively, half the female story. It combines with the other part of the month to produce a bifurcated vision of femininity whose two halves are asymmetrically valued.

Married women who suffer from PMS report that during the "normal" phase of the month they allow their husbands' myriad irritating acts to go uncriticized. But while premenstrual they are hyper-critical of such acts, sometimes "ranting and raving" for hours over trivial annoyances. Unable to act "nice" continually, women break down and are regularly "irritable" and even "hostile." Their protest is recurrent but futile, for they are made to feel guilty about it, or, worse, they are treated condescendingly. "We both know you're going to have your period tomorrow so why don't we just go to bed?" one husband regularly tells his wife at the first sign of an argument, thereby dismissing any claim to legitimate disagreement. Without legitimacy, as Weber taught us long ago, protests are doomed to failure; and so it is with PMS.

I suggest that these women in effect choose, however unconsciously, to voice their complaints at a time that they know those complaints will be rejected as illegitimate. If complaints were made during the non-premenstrual portion of the month, they would have to be taken seriously. But many American women have not found a voice with which to speak such complaints and at the same time retain their feminine allure. They save their complaints for that "time of the month" when they are in effect permitted to voice them yet by means of hormones do not have to claim responsibility for such negative feelings. In knowing when their complaints will not be taken seriously yet voicing them precisely during such a time, perhaps women are punishing themselves for their critical thoughts. In this way, and despite the surface-level aggression they display premenstrually, women continue to enact a model of behavior doomed to failure, as is consistent with what some feminists have argued is a pervasive tendency among American women in other arenas (Horner 1972).

So long as American society recreates its unrealistic expectations of the female personality, it is inevitable that there will be a PMS, or something playing its role: a regular rejection of the stringent expectations of female behavior. But PMS masks the protest even as it embodies it: for, cast in a biological idiom, PMS is made to seem an autonomous force that is often uncontrollable (see Martin 1987, 132–3); or if it can be controlled, it is only by drugs not acts of personal volition. Thus women's authorship of their own states of mind is denied them. As women in contemporary America struggle to find their voices, it is to be hoped that they will be able to reclaim their bodies as vehicles for the creation of their own metaphors, rather than autonomous forces causing them to suffer and needing to be drugged.

Source: Gottlieb 1988.

Gilligan did not adopt a Vygotskian perspective in this study, although she was influenced by Mead. But the Vygotskian concept of the zone of proximal development provides a useful tool for describing how the differential moral development of boys and girls is accomplished. In Vygotskian terms, the moral development of boys and girls proceeds in different directions as a result of the coaching each receives from more mature members of society. When faced with the same dilemmas and unsure of how to act, boys are encouraged to make one set of choices, girls another. In this way, each gender category builds up a different set of schemas as to what constitutes the "good." As a result, American men and women consistently see one another acting immorally. For example, when men and boys try to be true to themselves and strike out on their own, women and girls may condemn such action as being highly destructive to personal relationships. When women and girls try to encourage intimacy and closeness, men and boys may view such ties as confining and repressive.

As Gilligan reminds us, men as a group hold power over women as a group in American society. Men therefore insist that their moral perspective is the correct one. This observation is very much in keeping with Vygotsky's insistence that explanations of cognitive development be situated in a wider social and historical setting. Changes in that wider setting, moreover, may be expected to affect the developmental paths embedded within it. As American women gain power and begin to articulate their own position, Gilligan suggests, women's "different voice" will increasingly make itself heard to challenge the male definition of morality.

COGNITION AND CONTEXT

Human cognition is a holistic phenomenon that involves perceiving, thinking, feeling, and acting in the world. Each cognitive domain shapes the others. What we perceive triggers thoughts and feelings and suggests possible actions. At the same time, how we think and feel and act shapes our perceptions. This is so, it appears, because "any fact, or small set of facts, is open to a wide variety of interpretations" (Cole and Scribner 1974, 172). The question then becomes one of trying to explain the different interpretations.

There are no clear-cut answers to this question. However, cross-cultural studies of cognition make us increasingly aware of the importance of context—not just the immediate context of the laboratory situation but also the displaced context of culture (that of the subjects and that of the experimenters), which may be invisible in the lab but is present in people's minds. We must also consider historical context. When administering a psychological test on visual illusions to the Fang, James Fernandez (1980) discovered that many questioned his explanation of the "real" reason behind such a bizarre activity as psychological testing. (See EthnoProfile 7.5: Fang.) Years of colonial domination and exploitation at the hands of outsiders made their suspicions of the anthropologist's motives far from irrational.

A further conclusion can be drawn: if human understanding of the world is holistic, then the anthropologist's understanding of another culture is also achieved holistically, whether the anthropologist is explicitly aware of it or not. Anthropological understanding involves not just perception, not just rational analysis, but the entire range of interacting human cognitive processes, including those we label "emotional."

EthnoProfile 6.8 • **CAIRO**

REGION: Southwestern Asia

NATION: Egypt

POPULATION: 11,000,000

ENVIRONMENT: Capital city; delta and desert

LIVELIHOOD: Modern stratified society

POLITICAL ORGANIZATION: City in a modern nation-state

FOR MORE INFORMATION: Gilsenan, Michael. 1982. *Recognizing Islam: Religion and society in the modern Arab world.* New York: Pantheon.

An excellent description of just this kind of holistic experience is given by anthropologist Michael Gilsenan (1982), who worked for a time among urban Muslims in Cairo, Egypt. (See EthnoProfile 6.8: Cairo.) Gilsenan spent many hours with his informants in the local mosque observing their prayers. During these sessions, he himself attempted to assume a properly reverential attitude. Along the inside wall of the mosque were verses from the Qur'an. These were not painted but were formed of bright green neon tubing. Green is the color of the prophet Muhammad, so finding that color used prominently in mosque decoration is not surprising. However, Gilsenan's experiences in Western culture did not include schemas in which neon light and serious worship went together. For several months he struggled to rid himself of his traditional associations. Then one day, Gilsenan reports, "I turned unthinkingly away from the swaying bodies and the rhythms of the remembrance of God and saw, not neon, but simply greenness. . . . No gaps existed between color, shape, light, and form. From that unreflecting and unsuspecting moment I ceased to see neon at all" (1982, 266).

Nothing had happened to Gilsenan's eyes or his other senses. They were still receiving the same signals they had always received in this context. But the meaning of the signals had been altered. Experience in the mosque had established for Gilsenan a new context for neon light, and increasing familiarity with that context made it seem less out of place and more natural. Eventually, Gilsenan's attention was attracted not by the medium but by what it represented: the color green. Gilsenan was still able to report that the green light he saw had been produced by green neon tubing; however, that fact seemed irrelevant given the new context he had come to use to interpret his experience. That experience was shaped by history, the faith of the worshipers, and numerous displaced cultural associations invisible to an ignorant, inexperienced outsider.

These transformations of perception and understanding remain mysterious, but they seem to occur whenever we have an insight of any kind. Insights, like apt metaphors, reshape the world for us, throwing new aspects into sharp focus and casting other aspects into the background. Our ability to achieve insights, like our ability to create apt metaphors, remains the most central and most mysterious aspect of human cognition.

KEY TERMS

cognitive capacities

elementary cognitive
   processes

functional cognitive
   systems

perception

cognitive style

global style

articulated style

cognition

rational thinking

syllogistic reasoning

reasoning styles

logic

emotion

socialization

enculturation

self

CHAPTER SUMMARY

1. We cannot easily separate our capacity for language from the other capacities we possess for making sense of our world. These other capacities—cognitive capacities—share many of the design features of language. The evidence of our senses depends upon context: both immediate context and cultural context.

2. Researchers have often pictured human intelligence metaphorically as a substance that could be measured by intelligence tests. Today, however, it is unclear exactly what the results of intelligence tests represent. Consequently, research has shifted its focus to cognitive processes and the way these are organized into culturally shaped functional systems.

3. Psychological anthropologists have tried to explain why intelligent informants perform poorly on Western intelligence tests that require subjects to interpret drawings and photographs. Western subjects are able to separate an object from a particular context, but the elimination of context is a Western perceptual convention that may not be shared by non-Western people. Drawings and photographs do not speak for themselves and can only make sense to us once we have mastered a particular group's conventions for interpreting them.

4. Illusions may be understood as the result of normal cognitive processes that have somehow been inappropriately selected and applied to a particular set of visual signals. Four important types of visual illusion are distortion, ambiguity, paradox, and fiction.

5. Some anthropologists argue that people in different cultures have different cognitive styles that can be located on a continuum ranging from global style at one end to articulated style at the other. Research suggests that an individual may use a global style for some tasks and an articulated style for other tasks. Indeed, one culture may use an articulated style for a task that another culture would approach with a global style. Jean Lave has shown that cognitive activity outside the laboratory often involves the use of a variety of cognitive strategies. In these everyday situations, the goal of cognition is not to solve a problem by finding the single correct answer. Instead, people try to resolve dilemmas in a way that allows them to get on with life. Cognition is thus best understood as the relations that link the mind at work to the world in which it works.

6. We may become impatient with people from a different culture if they fail to see similarities or differences that we think ought to be obvious to any observer. Yet the obviousness of particular features depends upon what any given culture chooses to emphasize and what it chooses to ignore. People may be perfectly aware of certain features if asked about them and simply ignore those features in ordinary circumstances because they carry no cultural relevance. Western schooling trains people to pay attention to a wider variety of perceptual features than are ordinarily culturally relevant.

7. Several attempts have been made to measure the levels of rational thinking in non-Western populations. The results are mixed. There seems to be no way to predict who will perform well or poorly on Piaget's conservation test, and tests of syllogistic reasoning require background knowledge that subjects may not have. In addition, informants may have a hard time interpreting syllogisms with arbitrary content.

8. Rational thinking is not the same as logic. Formal Western logic is better understood as a learned reasoning style that is characteristic of Western culture. Rules of Western logic can be very useful in reasoning, but other logics may be equally valid in other societies, particularly if they do not require the elimination of context for their application.

9. Our emotions, like our thoughts, are not just something we have; they are culturally constructed of our state of mind, our cultural interpretations, and our levels of bodily arousal. Different cultures recognize different domains of experience and different categories of feeling as being appropriate to these domains. For this reason, it is difficult to translate what emotions mean from one culture to another.

10. Human beings must learn to pattern and adapt our behavior and our ways of thinking and feeling to the standards considered appropriate in our respective cultures. The result of this process is the formation of a socially and culturally constructed self. Freud emphasized the patterning of emotions in the development of the self. Piaget emphasized the development of reasoning. Mead and Vygotsky argued that society and culture enhance and complete the development of the self, which occurs as language is mastered. Vygotsky's concept of the zone of proximal development stresses that cognitive development is a dialogic process. Children progress through that process at different rates and in different directions, depending on the amount and kind of coaching they receive by others. This concept makes it possible to explain why people in different cultural subgroups are socialized and enculturated in different ways.

SUGGESTED READINGS

Barnouw, Victor. 1985. *Culture and personality.* 4th ed. Homewood, IL: Dorsey. *An enduring classic, this book is an encyclopedia of psychological anthropology prior to the rise of the cognitive science approach.*

Cole, Michael, and Sylvia Scribner. 1974. *Culture and thought: A psychological introduction.* New York: Wiley. *A clear, readable survey of the literature and case studies on the cultural shaping of cognition.*

Miller, Jonathan. 1983. *States of mind.* New York: Pantheon. *A series of interviews in which Jonathan Miller (English actor, writer, physician, director) talks to several of the most interesting scholars on the mind, including George Mandler, Richard Gregory, and Clifford Geertz. This book is witty and enjoyable.*

Schwartz, Theodore, Geoffrey M. White, and Catherine A. Lutz, eds. 1992. *New directions in psychological anthropology.* Cambridge: Cambridge University Press. *An up-to-date survey of psychological anthropology with articles by experts in the fields of cognition, human development, biopsychological studies, and psychiatric and psychoanalytic anthropology.*

CHAPTER OUTLINE

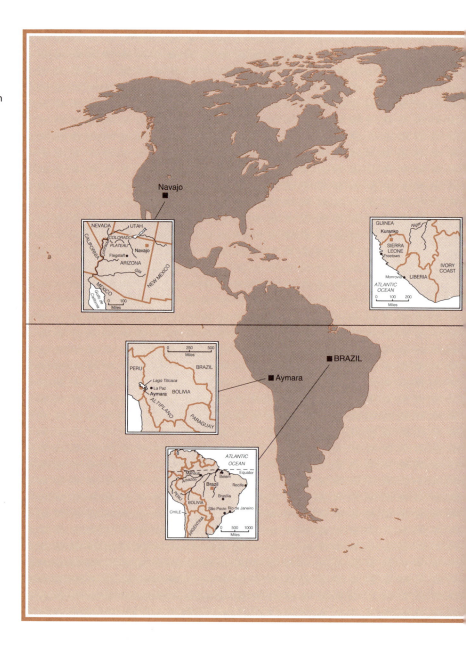

Play, Art, Myth, and Ritual

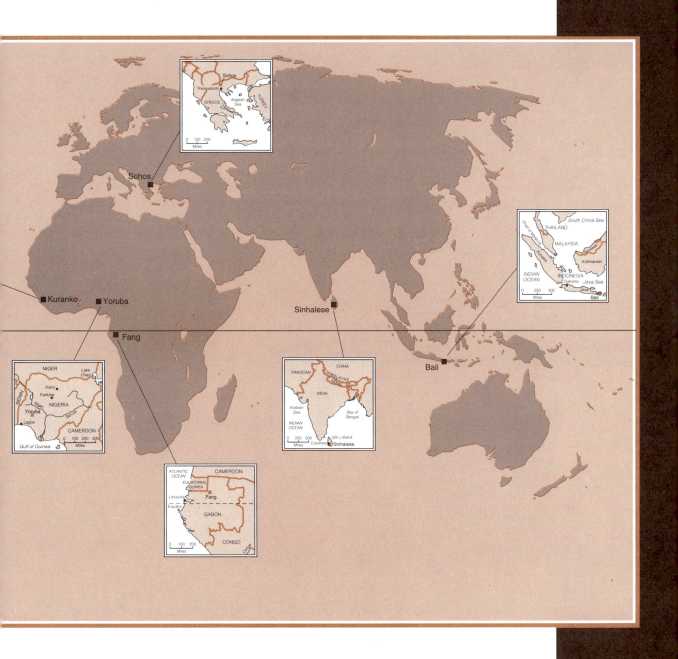

O ne of the authors of this book, Robert Lavenda, carried out fieldwork in Caracas, Venezuela. He writes:

Toward the end of October 1974, excitement about the heavyweight boxing championship featuring George Foreman and Muhammad Ali began to build. Boxing is extremely popular in Venezuela, and the Caracas newspapers devoted a great deal of attention to this bout. They gave Ali little chance of winning. It was late in his career, and he had already lost once to Foreman. Too old, they said, too out of shape, too big a mouth, too strong an opponent.

I managed to resist interest in the fight until the last moment. I had other work to do and didn't care for boxing. Besides, I didn't have a television in my apartment. On the night the fight was to be telecast on the national network, I went out to dinner alone. On my way home, I was surprised to see the city almost deserted. Then I remembered that the fight was about to start. I was feeling lonely, and my curiosity got the better of me. I passed a bar that had a television, so I stopped in. The preliminaries, native dancing from Zaire, were just ending. The bar gradually filled up. A couple of people seemed to know each other, but the rest were strangers.

As the fight began, I became aware that we were all Ali fans. As he did better and better, we became increasingly excited, and communication among the patrons increased. When finally, miraculously, Ali won, pandemonium broke loose. The crowd seemed to explode into a paroxysm of *abrazos* ("embraces," appropriate to men in Latin America), tears, cries of joy, and calls for rounds of beer. Strangers before, all were now united in a feeling of oneness and joy. None of us had any idea who the others were or what they did, but it didn't matter—we had witnessed something wonderful, and felt a comradeship that transcended our strangerness.

In this chapter, we consider how anthropologists go about trying to make sense of events similar to the event in the bar. We will examine play, art, myth, and ritual—four elements of human experience related to each other in some interesting and provocative ways. Indeed, their interrelationships are the focus of some of the most exciting work being done in anthropology today.

PLAY

Western natural and social scientists have shown little interest in the study of play. The traditional Western definition of play is negative: play is not work, not real, not serious, not productive, and so on (see Schwartzman 1978, 4); consequently, "serious" researchers have tended to devalue research on play. Play seems senseless, admitting the very chaos and misrule that social structures are meant to control. In recent years, however, researchers' attitudes about play have shifted, in part because their understanding of play has changed. In the previous two chapters, for example, we explored the concept of *openness* in linguistic and cognitive settings. Openness was defined as the ability to talk about, or think about, the same thing in different ways and different things in the same way. If we expand openness to include all behavior—that is, the ability not just to talk or think about, but also to *do* the same thing in different ways or different things in the same way—we begin to define **play**. All mammals play, and human beings play the most and throughout their lives.

Some of the most interesting work on animal play tries to understand play as the product of natural selection. Robert Fagen (1981, 1992) points out that young animals that play (including young human beings) get the exercise they need to build up their bodies for the rigors of adulthood. Play trains them in activities necessary for physical survival: fighting, hunting, or running away when pursued. During a brief period of neural development, peak brain development associated with motor skills and peak periods of play occur at the same time. Some scholars have proposed that play may be important for the development of cognitive and motor skills involving the brain. In species with more complex brains, play seems to aid in the development of other parts of the brain as well. Playful exploration of the environment aids learning and allows for the development of behavioral versatility (see Fagen 1981, 350–55). It also seems to have a connection with the repair of developmental damage caused either by injury or trauma. All of these functions of play may have significant value for the evolutionary life chances of individuals of various species.

Fagen proposes an additional function of play: the communication of the message "all's well" (1992, 48–49). There may be significant benefits to members of nonhuman species if they can communicate about their physical, cognitive, and emotional well-being from an early age. Just as messages of distress in infants—crying, tantrums, whining, depression—affect the behavior of older animals, so too do messages of positive well-being. "It seems likely that a frequent consequence and possible biological function of play is to convey information about short-term and long-term health, general well-being, and biological fitness to parents, littermates, or other social companions" (51).

Play also requires cooperation, which is of tremendous selective value. In good times, when resources are plentiful, play occurs repeatedly and in ways that are mutually beneficial for the animals involved. However, Fagen notes that it is possible to observe something in all animal play that he calls *fun*, or conscious pleasure. In fact, there may be neuropeptides (chemicals that influence different brain activities) that are released during play. Endorphins—one kind of neuropeptide—are associated with such play-related events as the "runner's high."

---

play A framing (or orienting context) that is (1) consciously adopted by the players, (2) somehow pleasurable, and (3) systemically related to what is nonplay by alluding to the nonplay world and by transforming the objects, roles, actions, and relations of ends and means characteristic of the nonplay world.

In terms of evolutionary adaptiveness, play may need to occur only rarely in order to repair developmental damage or to exercise inactive strengths and skills. In circumstances where frequent play is possible, however, animals might do so simply because play is so pleasurable. Years after early childhood, play gradually reemerges among young adult animals seeking mates. At this point, choice of play partners and frequency of play are based on the operations of the system of opiatelike neuropeptides alone. In situations where mate choice is possible, such as large primate troops, particular play partners might regularly prefer to mate with each other, leading to differential reproduction of genes connected with play and thus increasing the next generation's propensity to play. Put another way, choosing more playful partners becomes selection for openness.

Thinking about Play

We defined play as a generalized form of behavioral openness: the ability to think about, speak about, and do different things in the same way or the same thing in different ways. Don Handelman (1977) offers one way of thinking about such openness. He suggests that play is a way of organizing activities in which the ends and the means are altered. Consider a secretary typing a letter. In the nonplay world, the end of this activity is a legible business communication that furthers the goals of the company. The means to this end is the translation of shorthand notes to paper via touch typing. But sitting and typing letters all day can get boring. Suppose the secretary starts to pay attention to creating a scallop pattern in the right margin of the letters by varying the length of each typed line.

When the workday is over, the secretary has produced a single pile of legible business communications "designed to further the goals of the company." That is, the secretary has done the "same thing"—typing letters—both before and after getting bored. However, in the course of the workday, the secretary did this same thing in two "different ways": at first, seriously (solely to further the goals of the company) and later playfully (to create a design with the lines of type). In the first case, the typing was a means to produce a business letter; in the second case, the rules for typing business letters became for the secretary the means to achieve a private goal: creating a design in the right-hand margin.

The consequences of changing the relationships of means and ends can be dramatic. For example, in a nonplay context, saying "You bastard" to someone can lead to an argument, separation, or even a fight. If said in play, however, the same words imply something different—perhaps admiration for someone who is clever; delivering an insult in play may establish or enhance closeness between two people. Because means and ends are altered in play, players are permitted a high degree of freedom. Play activity dissolves many role boundaries that would otherwise separate participants from one another. Instead of being a college student, a Unitarian, a Jaycee, a son, a fraternity brother, or a factory worker, you and the other participants are simply "players."

Joking, a kind of play that can be verbal or physical (practical jokes, pranks, horseplay), is a good example of how play operates overall and in its cultural context. Anthropologist Andrew Miracle discusses joking behavior among Aymara people in Bolivia. (See EthnoProfile 7.1: Aymara.) He notes that ordinarily Aymara do not laugh in the

EthnoProfile 7.1 • AYMARA

REGION: South America

NATION: Bolivia

POPULATION: 500,000

ENVIRONMENT: High mountain lake basin

LIVELIHOOD: Peasant farmers

POLITICAL ORGANIZATION: Preconquest state societies conquered first by Incas and later by Spanish; today, part of a modern nation-state

FOR MORE INFORMATION: Miracle, Andrew. 1991. Aymara joking behavior. *Play and Culture* 4:144–52.

presence of strangers because that is considered disrespectful. They laugh and joke only within a circle of acquaintances and friends. This kind of joking serves to reinforce existing social bonds (1991, 151).

Much of the joking Miracle observed took place on the crowded buses or trucks that transport rural people around the country. Ordinarily, Aymara personal space extends about one arm's length. Where there is any choice, people do not get any closer to one another. They also show respect and honor other people's privacy by not staring. Miracle notes that in everyday situations, "when stared at, the Aymara may yell at the one staring and become quite rude" (1991, 146). On buses or trucks, however, the context changes, and people who are strangers to one another are forced into artificial intimacy. They must sit or stand very close to one another for long periods of time, frequently looking right at one another. Their response, Miracle writes, is often to joke and laugh, behavior normally reserved for intimates. Put another way, they choose to do "different things" (passing time with close friends and passing time with strangers in unusually close quarters) in the "same way," by joking. This altered definition of context gives joking among strangers a new meaning, playfully changing strangers into friends and thus making a socially unpleasant situation more tolerable.

Play does have limits, however. It is true that when friends insult one another in play, they may end up feeling even closer than they were before, but because playful insults and serious insults sound "the same," there is often a lingering undertone of ambiguity. If someone chooses to take offense, play is threatened. When the everyday roles reassert themselves, play ends.

Another way of thinking about the shift from seriousness to playfulness is to describe it as a shift from one form of reality to another. For example, a person shifts from the serious, everyday reality of a 9-to-5 job to a playful reality where drudge work becomes a means to artistic expression. Put another way, moving from everyday reality to the play reality requires a radical transformation of referential perspective. This movement may remain hidden, as with the secretary typing letters; to an outside observer, the switch from everyday reality to play reality may go undetected. However, sometimes the

FIGURE 7.1 *When dogs show each other their play faces, their fangs are bared and one animal attacks the other, but the bites are harmless nips.*

switch from one reality to the other can have serious consequences for other people and their activities. In this case, play and nonplay must be signalled clearly, so that one is not mistaken for the other. According to Gregory Bateson (1972), this shift requires a level of communication that is more abstract than either everyday reality or play. This level of communication, called **metacommunication,** is communication about communication. It provides information about the relationship between those who are communicating.

Consider the remark, "Open the window." This is a simple statement, but it can communicate a variety of messages about the relationship between the speakers. It can be an order: the metacommunication is "I have the right to compel you to open the window." It can also be a plea: "You are able to open this window. I am not." Or it can be an admission of equality: "You are now at the point of doing something that I too can do."

In play there are two kinds of metacommunication. The first, called **framing,** is a cognitive boundary that marks certain behaviors as "play" or as "ordinary life." Dogs, for example, have the *play face,* a signal understood by other dogs (and recognizable by humans beings too) indicating a willingness to play (Figure 7.1). If dogs agree to play, their fangs are bared, and one animal attacks the other. But the bite is not consummated; it becomes a nip. Both dogs have agreed to enter the *play frame,* an imaginary world in which bites don't mean bites. To put it another way, a basic element of Western logic—that A = A—does not apply in play; or, the "same" thing is being treated in "different" ways. Human beings have many ways of marking the play frame: a smile, the phrase "Just joking," a particular tone of voice, a referee's whistle, the words "Let's play" or "Let's pretend" or "You can be the king." The marker says that "everything from now until we end this activity is set apart from everyday life."

The second kind of metacommunication involves **reflexivity.** Play offers us the opportunity to think about the social and cultural dimensions of the world in which we find ourselves. This opportunity comes from the way play creates a perspective on reality that contrasts with the perspective of everyday life. Because play suggests that ordinary life can be understood in more than one way, play can be a commentary on the nature of ordinary life (Handelman 1977, 186). We often say, for example, that jokes keep us from taking ourselves too seriously. What does this mean? Through jokes we are able to see that there are alternative, even ridiculous, explanations for our experience. A satiric monologue by a stand-up comedian forces us to stand back from the events being commented on. As we follow the comedian's performance, we too take those events out of their usual context and realize that they can be understood in other ways. We may even conclude that perhaps this comedian takes nothing seriously. Anything can be understood differently. This too is a characteristic of all play. It communicates about "what can be" rather than about "what should be" or about "what is" (186).

Play, Morality, and Resistance   The openness of play—the way it encourages us to look at the world from different perspectives—suggests that play is the source of human creativity. This does not mean, however, that play is unambiguously good or bad. Play is about possibilities, but what those possibilities may be and whom they benefit are never guaranteed. Play can just as easily lead to degradation as to uplift, to humiliation as to creative triumph. It can distract from the critical problems of life as well as solve them. It can just as easily destroy the social structure as it can creatively construct it.

Societies contain the threat posed by play by defining it as "unserious," "untrue," "pretend," "make-believe," "unreal," and so forth (Handelman 1977, 189). Many political figures recognize that play can undermine the established political order. Repressive political regimes frequently attempt to censor humor critical of the rulers, with the result that such humor becomes an accepted mode of political resistance. There is an entire literature in folklore and anthropology about humor and resistance in the former Soviet Union and its client states. Láslö Kürti discusses jokes told in eastern Europe about the 1986 nuclear plant disaster at Chernobyl, outside Kiev in Ukraine. Examples include: "What is the price of cabbage and lettuce at the Kiev market? Life"; and "What were the first two announcements [from the government] concerning radiation? The first: there is no radiation. The second: The radioactivity during the second week has subsided considerably, being only one half of the first week's"; and "What's the best antiradiation device in Eastern Europe? TASS, the official Soviet news agency" (1988, 324–34). Bitingly humorous, these jokes also criticized the policies of both the Ukrainian government and the central government in Moscow.

Some Effects of Play   Even though play is defined in some societies (including our own) as unserious or unreal, it may still have real-life effects. Play is a major cause of death or serious injury in young mammals; they expose themselves to predators, attempt dangerous maneuvers in dangerous surroundings, and use up lots of energy. Among human beings, various play activities regularly account for serious injuries and deaths. There is even a medical specialty—sports medicine—dedicated to treating the consequences of play.

Some scholars see play as rehearsal for the "real world." Animals play at fighting so they will know how to fight for their lives when their survival is at stake. Similarly,

metacommunication Communicating about the process of communication itself.

framing A cognitive boundary that marks certain behaviors as "play" or as "ordinary life."

reflexivity Critically thinking about the way one thinks; reflecting on one's own experience.

children play house as a way of learning the appropriate sex roles and skills needed for adulthood. This anthropological approach commonly views children's play as an imitation of adult activities and therefore as a way of learning culture (see Schwartzman 1978, 100, 101). Others have suggested that play (especially make-believe play) increases children's creativity and originality by allowing children to overcome their limitations of age, experience, and maturity and by permitting a richer reproduction of adult life (Sarah Smilansky, cited in Schwartzman 1978, 116).

Psychologist Brian Sutton-Smith has examined children's play and games that reverse the regular world. He suggests that these "games of order and disorder" (for example, ring-around-a-rosy, in which an orderly circle is formed and then destroyed) are not always enculturative; they may seek to challenge and reverse the social order. In these games, the social order is created only to be destroyed as everyone first acts together and then collapses. In his research (summarized in Schwartzman 1978, 124ff.), Sutton-Smith suggests that play activities are important not because they provide a socializing force for society but because they allow for innovation, a point made by Fagen (1992) for the possible evolutionary power of play in any species.

The idea that play is a source for changing ordinary life is a long way from the idea that play teaches adult roles. Helen Schwartzman has demonstrated how play, through satire and clowning, may allow children to comment on and criticize the world of adults (1978, 232–45). Certain adult play forms, such as the pre-Lenten Carnival (discussed later in this chapter), also act as a commentary on the "real world." They sanction insults and derision of authority figures, inversions of social status, clowning, parody, satire, and the like (124).

FIGURE 7.2 *The Balinese cockfight has been interpreted as a form of deep play involving stakes that are so high that, from a practical perspective, it is irrational for anyone to engage in it at all.*

EthnoProfile 7.2 • **BALI**

REGION: Southeastern Asia

NATION: Indonesia

POPULATION: 3,000,000

ENVIRONMENT: Large tropical island: mountains, ridges, slopes, plains

LIVELIHOOD: Intensive rice cultivation (irrigation); animal raising

POLITICAL ORGANIZATION: Highly stratified state; now an Indonesian province

FOR MORE INFORMATION: Geertz, Hildred, and Clifford Geertz. 1975. *Kinship in Bali.* Chicago: University of Chicago Press.

Play and Alternative Views of Reality   In the case of children, we think we can see the difference between play and the real world. What about adults who climb rocks? "Is climbing a vertical face of rock at the risk of one's life play, or is it done in earnest?" (Csikszentmihalyi 1981, 16). Indeed, a rock climber risks serious consequences. Is rock climbing, then, not play? It fits the definition of play—it is consciously adopted by the player, it is somehow pleasurable, it transforms the relations of ends and means characteristic of the non-play world—and yet "the climber is as immersed in reality as anyone can be in this world." But this suggests that there is no uniform reality "out there." Each person's view of reality "is relative to the goals that cultures and individuals create" (17). Reality is defined in terms of the goals toward which each player directs attention at any given time. In rock climbing, the goal is to find hand and toe holds in order to get to the top of the rock; it is to put one's body at risk rather than to *avoid* putting one's body at risk. In other words, people do not always submit to the rules of the "paramount reality" of ordinary life, which is their basic referential perspective.

Play allows us to recognize that no referential perspective is absolute. Play exists when there is an awareness of alternatives, "of two sets of goals and rules, one operating here and now, one that applies outside the given activity" (Csikszentmihalyi 1981, 19). Unless we are aware that we can act according to a set of rules that are different from those of our paramount reality, we cannot play. More important, without play there is no awareness of alternatives. Play demonstrates the openness in human experience. But openness in play is like openness in any other aspect of human life: it is ambiguous.

Deep Play

Clifford Geertz (1972) discusses a particularly gripping form of play, the Balinese cockfight (Figure 7.2). (See EthnoProfile 7.2: Bali.) He sees this "popular obsession of consuming power" as a story that the Balinese tell themselves about themselves. The cockfight is so deeply embedded in Balinese culture that, at least for men, the language of everyday moralism is filled with imagery of the fighting cock, the masculine symbol par excellence. But the cocks are not just symbolic expressions of the owner's self. For the Balinese, they also express, on every level, the direct inverse of the human: the animal.

Geertz tells us that this Balinese opposition between human beings and animals cannot be overemphasized. In identifying with his cock (a pun that Geertz intends), the Balinese man is also identifying with what he most fears, hates, and is fascinated by: the powers of darkness. The connection of cocks and cockfighting with these powers is explicit. The cockfight is understood as a blood sacrifice to the demons, and the appropriate rituals and chants are carried out before each fight. When Geertz was in Bali in the early 1960s, public responses to natural evils—illness, crop failure, volcanic eruptions—almost always involved cockfights (Geertz 1972, 7).

The fight itself is held in a ring about 50 feet square. It begins in the late afternoon, runs until sunset, and is usually made up of nine or ten separate matches. After cocks have been matched, a steel spur, 4 to 5 inches long and razor sharp, is attached to the leg of each animal. At a signal, the two animals usually fly at each other in "a wing-beating, head-thrusting, leg-kicking explosion of animal fury so pure, so absolute, and in its own way so beautiful, as to be almost abstract, a Platonic concept of hate" (Geertz 1972, 8–9). The round is usually over in less than 30 seconds, as one cock lands a solid blow with the spur. The action then stops for about 2 minutes. The handler of the injured bird works on it, trying to keep it alive for the second and final round. The fight is over when one of the animals dies. No matter how badly wounded, a bird has won if it is still standing at the death of its opponent. Fights usually last between 15 seconds and 5 minutes.

Cockfighting involves gambling. There are two major kinds of wagers: the first is a central bet between the owners of the cocks; the second involves many separate bets by spectators. The Balinese try to create an interesting, or *deep,* match by making the central bet as large as possible. This is not because someone expects to win a great deal of money; rather, it ensures that the cocks will be as equal and as fine as possible, which in turn ensures that the outcome will be as unpredictable as possible (Geertz 1972, 15).

Why is such a match interesting to the Balinese? To answer this question, Geertz borrows the concept of deep play from the philosopher Jeremy Bentham. **Deep play** involves stakes that are so high that, from a practical perspective, it is irrational for anyone to engage in it at all. In deep play, both players are in over their heads; together they stand to lose more than either might gain. The alternative reality, which is assumed for pleasure, overtakes them. It inevitably leads to pain when the paramount reality, which is their regular state, resumes.

Why do they do it? For the Balinese, betting can be very costly. But not only money is at stake in a cockfight. Equally at stake in deep matches are esteem, honor, dignity, and respect, which the money represents. These are at stake "playfully," for the outcome does not actually change a bettor's status. But the cockfight is a metacommunication about how things might be. "What the cockfight talks about is status relationships, and what it says about them is that they are matters of life and death" (Geertz 1972, 25).

The cockfight is a Balinese reflection on violence and the aspects of Balinese culture associated with violence: "animal savagery, male narcissism, opponent gambling, status rivalry, mass excitement, blood sacrifice. . . . Balinese go to cockfights to find out what a man, usually composed, aloof, almost obsessively self-absorbed . . . feels like when, attacked, tormented, challenged, insulted, and driven in result to the extremes of fury, he has totally triumphed or been brought totally low" (Geertz 1972, 27).

Deep play is not unknown in American society. Sutton-Smith suggests that sexual activity without the use of contraceptives among college students is deep play (1984, 3; 1980, 5). Here—where images of manhood, chastity, competition, spontaneity, and lust rage—a play frame is created in which the potential for loss is far higher than that of the Balinese in their cockfights. Since the appearance of Acquired Immunodeficiency Syndrome (AIDS), the stakes for unprotected sex have escalated. To a potential loss of esteem, honor, dignity, and economic opportunity must now be added the loss of life. Nevertheless, for some of those most at risk, for complex reasons, the play continues.

Sport

Sport is a kind of constrained play: "a physically exertive activity that is aggressively competitive within constraints imposed by definitions and rules. A component of culture, it is ritually patterned, gamelike, and of varying amounts of play, work and leisure. In addition, sport can be viewed as having both athletic and nonathletic variations, *athletic* referring to those activities requiring the greater amount of physical exertion." (Blanchard and Cheska 1985, 60)

Play is only one component of sport. Sport can be work for the players and an investment for the owners of professional teams. It is also a form of personal and social identification for fans, who are invited into a make-believe world in which they may playfully identify with their heroes, rage at the opponents, imagine coaching the team, suffer, and rejoice. The play element in sport draws a frame around the activity. Conflict in games and sports is different from conflict in ordinary life. Competitors agree "to strive for an incompatible goal—only one opponent can win—within the constraints of understood rules" (Lever 1983, 3). Conflict becomes the whole point of the activity rather than the means of settling a disagreement. As with all forms of play, the relationships of means and ends in sport are altered. Sport is struggle for the sake of struggle. "Athletes and teams exist only to be rivals; that is the point of their relationship. In the world of sport, there should be no purpose beyond playing and winning. Unlike rivals in the real world, who have opposing political, economic, or social aims, sports competitors must be protected, not persuaded or eliminated" (4). Indeed, sport is play, but it is embedded in the prevailing social order to a far greater degree than open play.

The Effect of Culture on Sport   "Even a sport that has been introduced from a foreign source is very quickly redefined and adjusted to fit the norms and values of tradition"

---

deep play Play in which the stakes are so high that, from a utilitarian perspective, it is irrational for anyone to engage in it at all.

sport A physically exertive activity that is aggressively competitive within constraints imposed by definitions and rules. Sport is

a component of culture that is ritually patterned, gamelike, and consists of varying amounts of play, work, and leisure.

EthnoProfile 7.3 • **NAVAJO**

REGION: North America

NATION: United States (northwestern New Mexico, northeastern Arizona, southeastern Utah)

POPULATION: 100,000

ENVIRONMENT: Rugged landscape

LIVELIHOOD: Farming, sheepherding, silver work and arts

POLITICAL ORGANIZATION: Traditionally, clans, public consensus; today, a tribal council

FOR MORE INFORMATION: Witherspoon, Gary. 1975. *Navajo kinship and marriage.* Chicago: University of Chicago Press.

(Blanchard and Cheska 1985, 55). Sports reflect the basic values of the cultural setting in which they are performed, and they are transformed when they are translated into a new cultural setting. Navajo basketball is different from the original game introduced to the Navajo by the Mormon Anglos. (See EthnoProfile 7.3: Navajo.) "Behaviorally, [Navajo basketball] is less aggressive, structured, outwardly enthusiastic, and morally educative; while at the same time it is more individualistic, kin-oriented, and pure good times than that of the town's Anglo-Mormon population" (Blanchard 1974, cited in Blanchard and Cheska 1985, 55).

An even more striking example of how a sport can transform from one culture to another is found in the Trobriand Islands. (See EthnoProfile 3.3: Trobriand Islanders.) An English missionary introduced the sport of cricket to the Trobrianders in the very early years of the twentieth century. By the 1970s, in the more rural parts of the islands, it had become a different game. Played between two villages, it became a substitute for warfare and a way of establishing political alliances. If the hosts had 40 men ready to play and the visitors had 36, then there were 36 to a side instead of the "correct" 11. The game was always won by the home team—but not by too many runs because that would shame the visitors. War magic was employed to aid batsmen and bowlers. Teams had dances and chants for taking the field, leaving it, and celebrating outs. These dances and chants were used to comment on current events and became fertile ground for additional competition beyond that of the sporting event itself. The bat was redesigned for greater accuracy, and the entire activity was associated with the ceremonial exchange of food and other goods. Cricket, the sport of empire, was radically transformed.

From the perspective of some Trobrianders, in fact, their cricket was a way of taking the English colonizers' favorite game—a game that was supposed to teach Trobrianders how to become "civilized"—and using it to express their rejection of the colonial world. As one Trobriand leader says in the film *Trobriand Cricket* (1974), "we rubbished the white man's game; now it's our game."

FIGURE 7.3 *In Brazil, soccer provides a mechanism for creating national unity, or a sense of "Brazilianness," among fans.*

The Function of Sport in the Nation-State   The full institutionalization of sport seems to have taken place in the nation-state, and only fairly recently. The most important and universal feature of sport in the nation-state is that it helps complex modern societies cohere (Lever 1983, 3). In her study of soccer in Brazil, aptly titled *Soccer Madness,* Janet Lever argues that large-scale organized sport presents a mechanism for building political unity and allegiance to the nation (Figure 7.3). (See EthnoProfile 7.4: Brazil.) "Sport's paradoxical ability to reinforce societal cleavages while transcending them makes soccer, Brazil's most popular sport, the perfect means of achieving a more perfect union between multiple groups . . . [by giving] dramatic expression to the strain between groups while affirming the solidarity of the whole" (5, 9).

In Brazil, there is at least one professional soccer team in every city. The larger cities have several teams, representing different fundamental social groups. In Rio de Janeiro, for example, separate teams tend to be supported by the old rich, the modern middle class, the poor, the blacks, the Portuguese, and a number of neighborhood communities. The teams come to represent these different groups in a concrete, visible fashion. Through these teams, separate groups maintain their identities. At the same time, the teams bring their opposing fans together through a shared enthusiasm for soccer. City and national championships work similarly to unify the socioeconomically and geographically diverse groups of Brazil.

For many Brazilians—indeed for many people around the world—the experience of supporting a soccer team may be their first and perhaps only experience of a loyalty

EthnoProfile 7.4 • BRAZIL

REGION: South America

NATION: Brazil

POPULATION: 157,000,000

ENVIRONMENT: Varied; coastal to tropical rain forest

LIVELIHOOD: Industry, farming, mining, manufacturing, and so on

POLITICAL ORGANIZATION: Modern nation-state

FOR MORE INFORMATION: Lever, Janet. 1983. *Soccer madness.* Chicago: University of Chicago Press.

beyond the local community. Unity is achieved by demonstrating that different teams, and the groups they represent, are in conflict only at one level. At a higher level, the fans of those teams are really united; for example, fans of all Rio teams support the team that goes on to represent Rio in the national championships. This process reaches a climax in international competition, as the supporters of many local soccer teams back the national team. At this highest level of significant integration, soccer provides a way of affirming one's "Brazilianness." When the Brazilian national team goes to the World Cup competition, the team and its exploits become a focus and a means for expressing national feelings.

There is one important exception to the global mass culture of sport: it regularly separates women from men. Soccer is incredibly important to Brazilian men, and to many other men in the rest of the world, but it is much less important to women. The sex segregation of the sport has significant consequences for the experience of growing up male or female. It also affects relationships later in life between men and women who do not share the same fundamental experiences. This is beginning to change in Brazil; more teenage girls are joining fan clubs and accompanying boys, without chaperones, to professional games (Lever 1983, 154). But there seems to be a long way to go. There is a fundamental ambiguity in the relation of sports and integration: as sports join people together in one domain, they separate them in another. Sports can maintain and sharpen distinctions that are already significant in many other areas of a culture.

ART

In Western societies, art prototypically includes sculpture, drawing, painting, dance, theater, music, and literature; it also often encompasses similar processes and products such as film, photography, mime, oral narrative, festivals, and national celebrations. When anthropologists talk about art in non-Western societies, they begin by focusing on activities or products that resemble art in the West. Whether non-Western peoples refer to such activities or products as "art," the activities and products themselves are universal. They seem rooted in playful creativity, a birthright of all human beings. And yet, like sport, those activities defined as "art" differ from free play because they are circumscribed by rules. Artistic rules direct particular attention to, and provide standards for evaluating, the *form* of the activities or objects that artists produce.

A Definition of Art

Anthropologist Alexander Alland defines **art** as "play with form producing some aesthetically successful transformation-representation" (1977, 39). For Alland, "form" refers to the rules of the art game: the culturally appropriate restrictions on the way this kind of play may be organized in time and space. We can also think about form in terms of style. A style is a schema (a distinctive patterning of elements), that is recognized within a culture as appropriate to a given medium. Certain things make a painting a portrait: it depicts a person, it resembles the person in some appropriate way, it is done with paint, it can be displayed, and more. By "aesthetic," Alland means appreciative of, or responsive to, form in art or nature (xii). "Aesthetically successful" means that the creator of the piece of art (and possibly its audience as well) experiences an emotional response.

It might be more accurate, however, to characterize aesthetic response as holistic, as involving all our faculties including emotion, especially as these are shaped by our social and cultural experience. V. N. Voloshinov argued that our aesthetic response to form in a work of art is based largely on our culturally shaped evaluation of the appropriateness of form to content. "Through the agency of artistic form the creator takes up *an active position with respect to content*. The form in and of itself need not necessarily be pleasurable . . . what it must be is a *convincing evaluation* of the content. So, for instance, while the form of 'the enemy' might even be repulsive, the positive state, the pleasure that the contemplator derives in the end, is a consequence of the fact that the form is *appropriate to the enemy* and that it is *technically perfect* in its realization" ([1926] 1987, 108). Evaluations of appropriateness and of technical perfection clearly involve a broad range of intellectual, emotional, and moral judgments on the part of the viewer.

Aesthetic value judgments guide the artist's choice of form and material; they also guide the observers' evaluations. It is therefore a mistake to think of art in terms of works (of objects) alone. Voloshinov argues that art is a creative "event of living communication" involving the work, the artist, and the artist's audience ([1926] 1987, 107). Artists create their works with an audience in mind, and audiences respond to these works as if they were addressed to them. Sometimes the response is enthusiastic; sometimes it is highly critical. In either case, the aesthetic event does not leave its participants indifferent.

This view also suggests that aesthetic creation involves more than the end product, such as a painting or a poem. Art also includes the *process* through which some product is made. James Vaughan (1973, 186) points out, for example, that the Marghi of north-

art Play with form producing some aesthetically successful transformation-representation.

eastern Nigeria do not appreciate a folktale as a story per se but rather enjoy the *performance* of it. (See EthnoProfile 11.7: Marghi.) Similarly, a photographer may feel that the "art" is in the taking of a picture—seeing it, setting it up in the viewfinder, taking it, and printing it—not the final print.

Transformation-Representation   To understand the term **transformation-representation** in Alland's definition of art, we must recall that symbols represent something other than themselves. They are arbitrary in that they have no necessary connection with what they represent. This means that they can be cut away from the object or idea represented and can be appreciated for their own sake. They may also be used to represent a totally different meaning. Consider the tone poem *Also Sprach Zarathustra,* by Richard Strauss. This orchestral work originally represented themes from a philosophical book of the same name by the nineteenth-century German philosopher Friedrich Wilhelm Nietzsche. Classical music lovers came to appreciate the musical interpretation on its own terms, quite apart from the book. (Since 1967, this piece of music is more commonly known as the theme from the film *2001: A Space Odyssey.*)

Because transformation and representation depend on each other, Alland (1977, 35) suggests that they be referred to together (as *transformation-representation.*) Transformation-representation is another way of talking about metaphor. A drawing, for example, is a metaphoric transformation of experience into visible marks on a two-dimensional surface. Similarly, a poem metaphorically transforms experience into concentrated and tightened language. This process is one place where the technical skill of the artist is involved.

Reflecting and Affecting Culture

Alland's definition of art attempts to capture something universal about human beings and their cultures. This is different from a definition that describes art narrowly as aesthetic objects produced by refined minds in high civilizations.

In the Western prototype of art, there is a distinction between art and nonart. Some paintings, songs, stories, carvings, dances, and the like are considered art; some are not. From this perspective, the *Mona Lisa* is art, but a painting of Elvis Presley on black velvet is not. Why? Part of the answer involves the high degree of specialization in Western societies, which has led to the emergence of an "art establishment" that includes critics, art historians, art teachers, journalists, schools, museums, and the like—as well as professional artists. These people define what art is and what it is not, sometimes by invoking universal standards. In doing so, they are responding to the stratification and divisions embedded in their culture.

Thus, to them, Elvis on velvet is not art because it does not address problems in art theory, because it does not refer to the beautiful and the true, because it does not portray the artist's struggle to produce a new expressive style distinct from all other styles that have come before, or, indeed, because the artist seems ignorant or disdainful of the stylistic experimentation that makes up Western art history. That the artist may, in fact, have created a work that is important and meaningful to many people does not change the art world's opinion of these paintings. As a result, it is rare to find "art-establishment art" in Western societies that reflects the central symbols of the wider culture. Rather, Western "art-establishment art" tends to reflect symbols meaningful to individuals within the art establishment itself, or to particular elites in society, who have appropriated the power of art for their own purposes.

One dramatic counterexample that demonstrates the power of art is the Vietnam Veterans Memorial in Washington, D.C. This is a work that has not only impressed the art critics but continues to have a profound aesthetic and emotional impact on hundreds of thousands of visitors. The memorial continues to draw offerings by visitors, not just wreaths or flowers but messages of all kinds remembering those memorialized and even communicating with them. Letters from friends and families, a hand-lettered sign from a thirtieth high school reunion in a small Indiana town, tracings of names, intensely private grief, a respectful silence are testimony to the success of this piece of art.

The division into categories of art and nonart is not universal. In many cultures, there is no category of art distinct from other human activities. Only in a few societies are there people who earn a living by telling other people what is and what is not "art." This is not to say that aesthetic judgments are not made in other societies, for they are. The aesthetic categories that people employ, however, are culture specific.

All art is embedded in culture. It "will reflect or be controlled by culture to a greater or lesser degree, depending on the nature of the relationships between art and other cultural areas" (Alland 1977, 120). Artists in nonliterate societies produce and use symbols that are of central importance to their societies. Art becomes a means for presenting and representing the basic metaphors of a culture. For this reason, art works to maintain the social order in many societies, and artists do not see themselves as (nor are they understood to be) alienated critics of society.

In Western society, however, "art is strongly affected by those market factors which pervade every other aspect of our daily life" (Alland 1977, 120). Because artistic objects have become commodities—objects created for sale on the market—artists' livelihoods depend on their ability to sell what they produce. Consequently, artists may be tempted to produce "safe" works that people want to buy because they are comfortable, un-challenging of the status quo. Producing "safe" art, however, contradicts modern West-ern views of artists as alienated geniuses whose mission is to serve society by criticizing it in original new ways. For this reason, artists also may experience intense pressure to produce something "new and different" that attracts attention, creating publicity that will increase sales. In either case, the Western artist's aesthetic values may be compromised by the need to make money. Unfortunately, audiences and critics sometimes have a hard time distinguishing work at the cutting edge of aesthetic achievement from lesser efforts designed merely to shock and to sell. Recent debates in the United States concerning the difference between breakthrough high art and pornography illustrate this situation. Of course, if art can progress only by undermining one restriction after another, it risks losing the very aesthetic standards that define it as a distinct social activity.

transformation-representation The process in which experience is transformed as it is represented symbolically in a different medium.

FIGURE 7.4 *This Fang sculpture by Eye Meugeh is a mask representing a forest spirit.*

Is Art a Universal Language?   A common claim in Western society is that art is a universal language. The preceding discussion implies that if that claim is true, it is true only at a remote level. Although it is possible to describe how members of a given culture manipulate form in space or time, to understand why they do what they do requires more. To understand art in American society, we can examine the works of art themselves and how they were made, but we must also look at who the artists are, at their positions in society, at the social groups they form, and at the relationship of their social groups to other groups in American society. We must look at the consumers of art: how they understand art, what they use art for, the extent of their influence on artists, and more. To understand the art world of any culture requires this same process of investigation; all art is embedded in culture and can be understood only in context.

Consider how music loses meaning when divorced from its culture. All we hear are sounds and rhythms arranged in time. The sounds of the Javanese gamelan (a percussion orchestra made up of various-sized gongs and xylophones) are recognizable as music to Western listeners, but we may not like the sounds because they are unfamiliar. Moreover, not only is the structure of this music unfamiliar to us, but we also lack the host of associations that the Javanese have with their music.

Talking about art as a kind of play has several implications. Like play, art presents its creators and participants with alternative realities, a separation of means from ends, and the possibility of commenting on and transforming the everyday world. However, art is

EthnoProfile 7.5 • FANG

REGION: Central Africa

NATION: Gabon

POPULATION: 400,000 (1978)

ENVIRONMENT: Tropical forest with intense rainfall

LIVELIHOOD: Farming, hunting

POLITICAL ORGANIZATION: Traditionally, village councils, headmen; today, part of a modern nation-state

FOR MORE INFORMATION: Fernandez, James. 1982. *Bwiti: An ethnography of the religious imagination.* Princeton: Princeton University Press.

play subject to limitations of form and content. That is, art must conform to culturally appropriate rules if it is to be considered art. This means that art enjoys a different position in the social system than does play. Most significantly, art is taken more seriously than pure play, with the result that challenges to its rules are culturally far more threatening.

Fang Sculpture and the Social Structure   In studying the aesthetics of the Fang of central Africa, James Fernandez discovered that they had very definite ideas about what was pleasing to them in their own sculpture (Figure 7.4). (See EthnoProfile 7.5: Fang.) Fernandez arranged a set of statues in a row and asked the Fang which figures they liked the most and why. The Fang commented on the finished or unfinished quality of each object—whether it was smooth or rough. They talked about the balance of the object, especially whether its quadrants were balanced with one another. If one leg or one arm or one shoulder was different in its proportions from the opposite, this was always mentioned and criticized ([1966] 1971, 363). People said there should be balance in the figure, or else it would not be real—it would have no life or vitality. They sometimes preferred statues that were, to Western eyes, stolid, formal, even suppressed.

The Fang are well aware that the proportions of these statues are not those of living people. For them, "what the statue represents is not necessarily the truth, physically speaking, of a human body but a vital truth about human beings, that they keep opposites in balance. Both the statues and men have this in common and therefore the statues in this sense are accurate portrayals—accurate representations of living beings" (Fernandez [1966] 1971, 363).

Fernandez goes on to demonstrate that both Fang social structure and aesthetic life elaborate on two basic sets of oppositions—one spatial (right and left; northeast and southwest) and one qualitative (male and female)—and create vitality in so doing. He further suggests that in this, the social structure is the expression of aesthetic principles at work. In other words, art provides a way of understanding social structure. Instead of being a mere reflection of social structure, art plays a significant role in people's creation of and commentary about social structure.

Dance and Gender in Northern Greece   Jane Cowan has explored how dance may play a role in the social construction of gender in northern Greece. (See EthnoProfile 7.6: Sohos.) She considers three different kinds of dance-events in the town of Sohos: the wedding dance, the formal evening dance, and a private dance at a home. In the dance-event, individuals present themselves publicly by eating, drinking, and talking, as well as dancing, and other people at the event evaluate them. Men and women, however, do not present themselves in the same way, nor are they evaluated in the same way. They perform and experience themselves as gendered subjects—that is, as males or females, as these are defined in Sohos. "In dance-events associated with pleasure, sensual intensity, and public sociability, gender inequalities and other social hierarchies are constituted and even celebrated" (1990, 4).

Contrasting, culturally specific images of male and female sexuality in northern Greece are given a particular public form in the dance. From the perspective of women in northern Greece, dances are places where they can "escape" and "forget" their relatively restricted everyday lives. Everyone at the dance—men and women alike—encourages them to do this in order to be good, carefree celebrants. But dance presents problems for women: they are keenly aware that they are being watched, that they not only act but are acted upon. So, at the dance, women know they must retain control of themselves emotionally and physically. The limits of appropriate bodily expression, both for women and for men, are learned early in life and continue to be internalized throughout life. A woman's expressions of "letting go" may be at the boundaries of those limits but rarely overstep them in any fundamental way (Cowan 1990, 228).

Dance provides a place where northern Greek women play with the boundaries of "good" and "bad" female sexuality. Should she take the first position in a circle dance, or is that too forward? How intense should her *tsifte teli* (belly dance) be? Should she move

EthnoProfile 7.6 • **SOHOS**

REGION: Europe

NATION: Greece

POPULATION: 3,500

ENVIRONMENT: Rugged mountainside

LIVELIHOOD: Farming, commerce

POLITICAL ORGANIZATION: Commercial and administrative center within a modern nation-state

FOR MORE INFORMATION: Cowan, Jane K. 1990. *Dance and the body politic in northern Greece.* Princeton: Princeton University Press.

In Their Own Words   TANGO

Anthropologist Julie Taylor describes the traditional cultural understandings that inform the contexts in which the Argentine tanguero, *or tango-man, dances the tango.*

Traditionally, Argentines will not dance to a tango that is sung. If they danced they could not attend properly to the music and lyrics, or hear their own experience and identity revealed in the singer's and musicians' rendering of quintessential Argentine emotions. The singer of the tango shares his personal encounter with experiences common to them all. He does not need bold pronouncement or flamboyant gesture. His audience knows what he means and his feelings are familiar ones. They listen for the nuances—emotional and philosophical subtleties that will tell them something new about their guarded interior worlds.

When they dance to tangos, Argentines contemplate themes akin to those of tango lyrics, stimulating emotions that, despite an apparently contradictory choreography, are the same as those behind the songs. The choreography also reflects the world of the lyrics, but indirectly. The dance portrays an encounter between the powerful and completely dominant male and the passive, docile, completely submissive female. The passive woman and the rigidly controlled but physically aggressive man contrast poignantly with the roles of the sexes depicted in the tango lyrics. This contrast between two statements of relations between the sexes aptly mirrors the insecurities of life and identity.

An Argentine philosophy of bitterness, resentment, and pessimism has the same goal as a danced statement of machismo, confidence, and sexual optimism. The philosopher elaborates his schemes to demonstrate that he is a man of the world— that he is neither stupid nor naive. In the dance, the dancer acts as though he has none of the fears he cannot show—again proving that he is not *gil.* When an Argentine talks of the way he feels when dancing a tango, he describes an experience of total aggressive dominance over the girl, the situation, the world—an experience in which he vents his resentment and expresses his bitterness against a destiny that denied him this dominance. Beyond this, it gives him a moment behind the protection of this facade to ponder the history and the land that have formed him, the hopes he has treasured and lost. Sábato echoes widespread feeling in Argentina when he says "Only a gringo would make a clown of himself by taking advantage of a tango for a chat or amusement."

While thus dancing a statement of invulnerability, the som-ber tanguero sees himself, because of his sensitivity, his great capacity to love, and his fidelity to the true ideals of his childhood years, as basically vulnerable. As he protects himself with a facade of steps that demonstrate perfect control, he contemplates his absolute lack of control in the face of history and destiny. The nature of the world has doomed him to disillusionment, to a solitary existence in the face of the impossibility of perfect love and the intimacy this implies. If by chance the girl with whom he dances feels the same sadness, remembering similar disillusion, the partners do not dance sharing the sentiment. They dance together to relive their disillusion alone. In a Buenos Aires dance hall, a young man turned to me from the fiancee he had just relinquished to her chaperoning mother and explained, "In the tango, together with the girl— and it does not matter who she is—a man remembers the bitter moments of his life, and he, she, and all who are dancing contemplate a universal emotion. I do not like the woman to talk to me while I dance tango. And if she speaks I do not answer. Only when she says to me, 'Omar, I am speaking,' I answer, 'And I, I am dancing.' "

Source: Taylor 1987.

closer to her partner, lean toward him, and playfully shimmy her shoulders? When a man dances an intense *tsifte teli*, should she break plates at his feet, a conventional statement of deep understanding of and empathy with the dancer's inner state? "In this dance space, ambivalent attitudes toward female sexuality are juxtaposed. Girls and women are not necessarily expected to mute or hide their sexuality. Flirtation, energy, the display of beauty, even subtle seduction are acknowledged and valued aspects of female performance in these events" (Cowan 1990, 228). But there is always a potential problem: a female who is thought to lack control in these displays can be censured. "A female celebrant's experience of the dance, then, is rooted in her position in gender relations, but it is not only men who keep her 'in her place.' Women do, as well. Only when she believes that everybody is truly 'all together' can the female celebrant really feel free to let go; for girls, everybody being 'all together' is both the precondition for and the expression of collective *kefi* [high spirits]" (229).

Oral Narrative and Moral Perception: The Kuranko   Folktales are often studied as examples of verbal art. Anthropologist Michael Jackson observed how the Kuranko of western Africa use the art of folktales to help them resolve some of the ethical problems they encounter in everyday life. (See EthnoProfile 7.7: Kuranko.) Tellers of folktales encourage ethical discussion by performing in ways that dramatize uncertainty, promote ambivalence, and exploit ambiguity, thus stimulating listeners to resolve problems by thinking them through and reaching judgments that everyone can agree on. Through the play element of these narratives, individual narrators may vary the content as seems appropriate. In addition, because of the play element, the narratives "break free of the constraints and organizations of everyday life and entertain new possibilities of thought and action" (1982, 51). The child listening to the folktales learns that the social world is contingent, that it is not something external and preexisting but the product of human activity.

EthnoProfile 7.7 • KURANKO

REGION: Western Africa

NATIONS: Sierra Leone and Guinea

POPULATION: 125,000; 45,000 in Guinea (1970s)

ENVIRONMENT: Foothills, margins of the Guinea highlands, and savanna

LIVELIHOOD: Shifting cultivation of upland rice

POLITICAL ORGANIZATION: Traditionally, chiefs and councils of elders; today, part of nation-states

FOR MORE INFORMATION: Jackson, Michael. 1977. *The Kuranko.* New York: St. Martin's Press.

The Revolutionary Potential of Art

Art has a revolutionary potential as well. The potential for overthrowing existing social systems is inherent in public celebrations such as Carnival (the three days of riotous celebration before Ash Wednesday, including Mardi Gras). In countries where Carnival is celebrated, authorities have long recognized this revolutionary potential and have frequently tried to control it or to use it for their own ends. The Brazilian military government and conservative media tried to control Carnival between 1964 and 1985 by encouraging the Samba Schools (associations for dancing samba during Carnival) to hire middle-class designers, lawyers, and accountants and to feature media stars in order to make their performances more elaborate and television oriented. They built an immense, ugly stadium for the great Carnival parades, seating 80,000 people at very high prices. But this new Carnival has not yet silenced the poor Afro-Brazilians, who were samba's originators. Samba Schools' parades in recent years have featured criticisms of the legacy of military dictatorship, the external debt, and the destruction of the Amazon; they have examined the legacy of slavery on the 100th anniversary of its abolition; and they have proclaimed the solidarity of African peoples (Rowe and Schelling 1991; Guillermoprieto 1990).

MYTH

We have suggested that play lies at the heart of human creativity. However, because the openness of play is random and thus just as likely to undermine the social order as to enhance it, societies tend to circumscribe play with cultural rules, channeling it in directions that appear less destructive. Rules designed to limit artistic expression are one result of this channeling process. As we have seen, artists in various media are permitted a wide range of expression as long as they adhere to rules governing the form that expression takes. Societies differ in how loose or strict the rules of artistic form may be. Artists who challenge the rules, however, are often viewed negatively by those in power who believe they have the right to restrict artistic expressions that question social, religious, or sexual precepts that ought not to be questioned.

In fact, all societies depend on the willingness of their members not to question certain assumptions about the way the world works. Because the regularity and predictability of social life might collapse altogether if people were free to imagine, and act upon, alternatives to the local version of paramount reality, most societies find ways to persuade their members that the local version of paramount reality is the only reality, period. The most venerable way of doing this is through the use of myth. **Myths** are stories whose truth seems self-evident because they do such a good job of integrating our personal experiences with a wider set of assumptions about the way society, or the

myths Stories whose truth seems self-evident because they do such a good job of integrating our personal experiences with a wider set of assumptions about the way society, or the world in general, must operate.

world in general, must operate. As stories we are told and tell others, myths are products of high verbal art. Frequently the official myth tellers are the ruling groups in society: the elders, the political leaders, the religious specialists. The content of myths usually concerns past events (usually at the beginning of time) or future events (usually at the end of time). Myths are socially important because, if they are taken literally, they tell people where they have come from and where they are going and, thus, how they should live right now.

Societies differ in the degree to which they permit speculation about key myths. In complex Western societies, like that of the United States, many different groups, each with its own mythic tradition, often live side by side. Because our government permits freedom of conscience in such matters, it regularly prohibits one group from silencing an opposing group. But this does not mean that the United States is without a myth justifying the existence of such a marketplace of ideas within its borders. Consider the Declaration of Independence and its "self-evident truths": that all men are created equal and are endowed by their Creator with certain inalienable rights, among them life, liberty, and the pursuit of happiness. It is precisely in order to defend these self-evident truths that the government refuses to compromise its citizens' freedom of expression.

Myths and related beliefs that are taken to be self-evident truths are sometimes codified in an explicit manner. When this codification is extreme and deviation from the code is not treated lightly, we sometimes speak of **orthodoxy** (or "correct doctrine"). Although societies differ in the degree to which they require their members to adhere to orthodox interpretations of key myths, they are rarely wholly indifferent, because myths have implications for action. They may justify past action, explain present action, or generate future action. To be persuasive, myths must offer plausible explanations for our experience of human nature, human society, and human history. The power of myths comes from their ability to make life meaningful for those who accept them.

The success of Western science has led many members of Western societies to dismiss nonscientific myths as flawed attempts at science or history. Only recently have some scientists come to recognize the similarities between scientific and nonscientific storytelling about such events as the origin of life on earth. Scientific stories about origins—*origin myths*—must be taken to the *natural* world to be matched against material evidence; the success of this match determines whether they are accepted or rejected. By constrast, nonscientific origin myths get their vitality from how well they match up with the *social* world. But the social significance of mythic storytelling is usually missing when most of us in the Western world first encounter myths from other traditions, such as the Trobriand origin myth discussed in the next section. Schoolchildren may learn about such tales, but the versions they read are usually censored and are presented as isolated tales, divorced from the social context in which they originated. At best, such stories present the imaginative potential of the human mind; at worst, they are viewed as expressions of ignorance or forbidden unconscious desires.

Myth as a Charter for Social Action

Early in the twentieth century, anthropologist Bronislaw Malinowski introduced a new approach to myth. He believed that to understand myths, we must understand the social context in which they are embedded. Malinowski argued that myths serve as "charters" or "justifications" for present-day social arrangements. In other words, a myth operates much like the Declaration of Independence or the United States Constitution. That is, the myth contains some "self-evident truth" that explains why society is as it is and why it cannot be changed. If the social arrangements justified by the myth are challenged, the myth can be used as a weapon against the challengers.

Malinowski's famous example is of the origin myths of the Trobriand Islanders ([1926] 1948). (See EthnoProfile 3.3: Trobriand Islanders.) Members of every significant kinship grouping know, mark, and retell the history of the place from which their group's ancestress and her brother emerged from the depths of the earth. These origin myths are set in the time before history began. Each ancestress-and-brother pair brought a distinct set of characteristics that included special objects and knowledge, various skills, crafts, spells, and the like. On reaching the surface, the pair took possession of the land. That is why today the people on a given piece of land have rights to it. It is also why they possess a particular set of spells, skills, and crafts. Because the original sacred beings were a woman and her brother, the origin myth can also be used to endorse present-day social arrangements. Membership in a Trobriand clan depends on a person's ability to trace kinship links through women to that clan's original ancestress. A brother and a sister represent the prototypical members of a clan because they are both descended from the ancestress through female links. Should anyone question the wisdom of organizing society in this way, the myth can be cited as proof that this is indeed the correct way to live.

In Trobriand society, clans are ranked relative to one another in terms of prestige. To account for this ranking, Trobrianders refer to another myth. In the Trobriand myth that explains rank, one clan's ancestor, the dog, emerged from the earth before another clan's ancestor, the pig, thus justifying ranking the dog clan highest in prestige. To believe in this myth, Malinowski asserted, is to accept a transcendent justification for the ranking of clans. Malinowski made it clear, however, that if social arrangements change, the myth changes too—in order to justify the new arrangements. At some point, the dog clan was replaced in prominence by the pig clan. This social change resulted in a change in the mythic narrative. The dog was said to have eaten food that was taboo. In so doing, the dog gave up its claim to higher rank. Thus, to understand a myth and its transformations, one must understand the social organization of the society that makes use of it.

For some years, anthropological studies of myth did not go beyond Malinowski's mode of analysis. But things began to change in the mid-1950s following the appearance of a series of books and articles by the French anthropologist Claude Lévi-Strauss ([1962] 1967), who transformed the study of myth. He argues that myths have meaningful structures that are worth studying in their own right, quite apart from the uses to which the myths may be put. He suggested that myths should be interpreted the way we interpret musical scores. In a piece of music, the "meaning" emerges not just from the

orthodoxy "Correct doctrine"; the prohibition of deviation from approved mythic texts.

melody (reading across), but also from the harmony (reading up and down). In other words, the structure of the piece of music, the way in which each line of the music contributes to the overall sound and is related to other lines, carries the meaning.

Myth as a Conceptual Tool

For Lévi-Strauss, myths are tools for overcoming logical contradictions that cannot otherwise be overcome. They are put together in an attempt to deal with the oppositions of particular concern to a particular society at a particular moment in time. Using a linguistic metaphor, Lévi-Strauss argues that myths are composed of smaller units—phrases, sentences, words, relationships—that are arranged in ways that give both narrative (or "melodic") coherence and structural (or "harmonic") coherence. These arrangements represent and comment upon aspects of social life that are thought to oppose each other. Examples include the opposition of men to women; opposing rules of residence after marriage (living with the groom's father or the bride's mother); the opposition of the natural world to the cultural world, of life to death, of spirit to body, of high to low, and so on.

Lévi-Strauss also made a stronger claim that the oppositional structure of myth represents the way the human mind itself operates in dealing with experience. The human mind, he asserted, processes information about the world in opposed pairs. The complex syntax of myth works to relate those opposed pairs to one another in an attempt to overcome their contradictions. However, these contradictions can never be overcome; for example, the opposition of death to life is incapable of any earthly resolution. But myth can transform an insoluble problem into a more accessible, concrete form. Mythic narrative can then provide the concrete problem with a solution. The solution may be the traditionally accepted, "self-evident" solution, or it may be a solution that is totally unacceptable. In either case, the concrete problem is resolved. By analogy, believers in a myth may conclude that the more abstract contradiction is resolved as well.

For example, a culture hero may bridge the opposition between death and life by traveling from the land of the living to the land of the dead and back. Alternatively, a myth might propose that the beings who transcend death are so horrific that death is clearly preferable to eternal life. Perhaps a myth describes the journey of a bird that travels from the earth, the home of the living, to the sky, the home of the dead. This is similar to Christian thought, where the death and resurrection of Jesus may be understood to resolve the opposition between death and life by transcending death.

From this point of view, myths do not just talk about the world as it is, they describe the world as it might be. To paraphrase Lévi-Strauss, myths are good to think with; mythic thinking can propose other ways to live our lives. Lévi-Strauss insists, however, that the alternatives myths propose are ordinarily rejected as impossible. Thus, even though myths allow for play with self-evident truths, this play remains under strict control.

Is Lévi-Strauss correct? There has been a great deal of debate on this issue since the publication in 1955 of his article "The Structural Study of Myth" (see Lévi-Strauss [1962] 1967). But even those who are most critical of his analyses of particular myths agree that mythic structures are meaningful because they display the ability of human beings to play with possibilities as they attempt to deal with basic contradictions at the heart of human experience.

For Malinowski, Lévi-Strauss, and their followers, those who believe in myths are not conscious of how their myths are structured or of the functions their myths perform for them. More recent anthropological thinking (such as the work of Michael Jackson, cited earlier) takes a more reflexive approach. This research recognizes that ordinary members of a society often are aware of how their myths structure meaning, allowing them to manipulate the way myths are told or interpreted in order to make an effect, to prove a point, or to buttress a particular referential perspective on human nature, society, or history.

RITUAL

Play allows unlimited consideration of alternative referential perspectives on reality. Art permits consideration of alternative perspectives, but certain limitations restricting the form and content are imposed. Myth aims to narrow radically the possible referential perspectives and often promotes a single, orthodox perspective presumed to be valid for everyone. It thus offers a kind of intellectual indoctrination. But because societies aim to shape action as well as thought to orient all human faculties in the approved direction, art, myth, and ritual are often closely associated with one another.

A Definition of Ritual

Our definition of **ritual** has four elements. First, ritual is a repetitive social practice composed of a sequence of symbolic activities in the form of dance, song, speech, gestures, the manipulation of certain objects, and so forth. Second, it is set off from the social routines of everyday life. Third, rituals in any culture adhere to a characteristic, culturally defined ritual schema. This means that members of a culture can tell that a certain sequence of activities is a ritual even if they have never seen that particular ritual before. Finally, ritual action is closely connected to a specific set of ideas that are often encoded in myth. These ideas might concern the nature of evil, the relationship of human beings to the spirit world, and so forth. The purpose for which a ritual is performed guides how these ideas are selected and symbolically enacted.

The Western prototype of ritual includes the notion that it is "religious." However, in anthropological terms, ritual includes a much broader range of activities. According to the definition given in the preceding paragraph, a scientific experiment, a college gradu-

ritual A repetitive social practice composed of a sequence of symbolic activities in the form of dance, song, speech, gestures, or the manipulation of objects, adhering to a culturally defined ritual schema, and closely connected to a specific set of ideas that are often encoded in myth.

ation ceremony, procedures in a court of law, and a child's birthday party are rituals just as much as weddings, bar mitzvahs, and the Catholic mass.

Consider a young child's birthday party. Several children are formally invited to help celebrate the birthday. Each brings a wrapped gift, which is handed to the birthday child and then set aside. The children often put on birthday hats. Some group activities are performed such as pin-the-tail-on-the-donkey (or a modern equivalent). The games culminate in the appearance of a birthday cake, illuminated by candles (one for each year of the child's life) and accompanied by the singing of "Happy Birthday." The birthday child makes a wish and blows out the candles. Following the cake and ice cream, the birthday child opens the presents. There is much commotion as the guests urge the birthday child to open theirs first. As the birthday child opens each gift, he or she examines it and thanks the guest (often with an adult's prompting). Shortly after the presents are opened, the guests' parents or guardians appear, the guest receives a bag of party favors and leaves. The ritual order of these events matters. The central events of the party—the giving of gifts, the events associated with the cake, candles, the wish, and the singing of "Happy Birthday," and the opening of the gifts—must occur in that order.

In the birthday party, children (both hosts and guests) learn to associate receiving gifts with important moments in life. They discover the importance of exchanging material objects in defining significant social relations. They learn to defer gratification (the presents cannot be opened immediately). They live out patterns of sociability and friendship (as anyone knows who has heard the ultimate preschool threat, "I'm not inviting you to my birthday party") while recognizing the centrality of the individual (there are few things worse than sharing your birthday party with someone else!). Finally, the children participate in patterns of sharing, of celebrating the self, and of recognizing relationships with friends and kin that are important in other areas of American life.

Ritual as Action

A ritual has a particular sequential ordering of acts, utterance, and events: that is, ritual has a *text*. Because ritual is action, however, we must pay attention to the way the ritual text is performed. The *performance* of a ritual cannot be separated from its text; text and performance shape each other dialectically. Through ritual performance, the ideas of a culture become concrete, take on a form, and, as Bruce Kapferer (1983) puts it, give direction to the gaze of participants. At the same time, ritual performance can serve as a commentary on the text to the extent of transforming it. For example, Jewish synagogue ritual following the reading of Torah (the handwritten Five Books of Moses, the Hebrew Bible) includes lifting the Torah scroll, showing it to the congregation, and then closing it and covering it. In some synagogues, a man and a woman, often a couple, are called to lift and cover the Torah: the man lifts and, after he seats himself, the woman closes the scroll, places the tie around it, and covers it with the mantle that protects it. One of the authors once observed a performance of this ritual in which the woman lifted the Torah and the man wrapped it; officially, the ritual text was carried out, but the performance became a commentary on the text—on the role of women in Judaism, on the Torah as an appropriate subject of attention for women as well as for men, on the roles of men and women overall, and so on. The performance was noteworthy—indeed, many of the

In Their Own Words · VIDEO IN THE VILLAGES

Patricia Aufderheide describes how indigenous peoples of the Amazonian rain forest in Brazil have been able to master the video camera and use it for their own purposes.

The social role and impact of video is particularly intriguing among people who are new to mass-communications technologies, such as lowlands Amazonian Indians. One anthropologist has argued persuasively that a naive disdain for commercial media infuses much well-meaning concern over the potential dangers of introducing mass media and that "indigenous media offers a possible means—social, cultural, and political—for reproducing and transforming cultural identity among people who have experienced massive political, geographic, and economic disruption" (Ginsburg 1991, 96). In two groups of Brazilian Indians, the Nambikwara and the Kayapo, this premise has been tested.

The Nambikwara became involved with video through Video in the Villages, run by Vincent Carelli at the Centro de Trabalho Indigenista in São Paulo. This project is one example of a trend to put media in the hands of people who have long been the subjects of ethnographic film and video (Ruby 1991). While some anthropologists see this resort as a "solution" to the issue of ethnographic authority, others have focused on it as part of a struggle for indigenous rights and political autonomy (Moore 1992). Many of the groups Carelli has worked with have seized on video for its ability to extensively document lengthy rituals that mark the group's cultural uniqueness rather than produce a finished product (V. Carelli, personal communication, January 23, 1992).

Carelli coproduced a project with a Nambikwara leader, documenting a cultural ritual. After taping, the Nambikwara viewed the ritual and offered criticisms, finding it tainted with modernisms. They then repeated the ritual in traditional regalia and conducted, for the first time in a generation, a male initiation ceremony—taping it all. (This experience is recounted in a short tape, *Girls' Puberty Ritual*, produced by Carelli with a Nambikwara leader for outsiders.) Using video reinforced an emerging concept of "traditional" in contrast to Brazilian culture—a concept that had not, apparently, been part of the Nambikwara's repertoire before contact but that had practical political utility.

The Kayapo are among the best-known Brazilian Indians internationally, partly because of their video work, promoted as a tool of cultural identification by the anthropologist who works most closely with them. Like other tribes such as the Xavante who had extensive contact with Brazilian authorities and media, the Kayapo early seized on modern media technologies (Turner 1991b). Besides intimidating authorities with the evidence of recording equipment (Smith 1989), the Kayapo quickly grasped the symbolic expectations of Brazilian mass media for Indians. They cannily played on the contrast between their feathers and body paint and their recording devices to get coverage. Even staging public events for the purpose of attracting television crews, they were able to insert, although not ultimately control, their message on Brazilian news by exploiting that contrast (Turner 1991a; Moore 1992). Using these techniques, Kayapo leaders became international symbols of the ironies of the postmodern age and not incidentally also the subjects of international agitation and fundraising that benefited Kayapo over other indigenous groups and some Kayapo over others.

Kayapo have also used video to document internal cultural ceremonies in meticulous detail; to communicate internally between villages; to develop an archive; and to produce clips and short documentaries intended for wide audiences. Their video work, asserts anthropologist Terence Turner, has not merely preserved traditional customs but in fact transformed their understanding of those customs as customs and their culture as a culture. Turner also found that video equipment, expertise, and products often fed into existing factional divisions. Particular Kayapo leaders used the equipment in their own interests, sometimes as a tool to subdue their enemies, sometimes as evidence of personal power (Turner 1991a: 74).

Source: Aufderheide 1993.

regular members of the congregation seemed quite surprised—precisely because it violated people's expectations and in so doing directed people's gaze toward men and women in religious ritual at the end of the twentieth century as well as toward the Torah as the central symbol of the Jewish people.

FIGURE 7.5 *Rites of passage are rituals, such as the initiation of the Apache girl pictured here, in which people move from one position in the social structure to another.*

Ritual performers are not robots but active individuals whose choices are guided by, but not rigidly dictated by, previous ritual texts (see, for example, Margaret Drewel's 1992 study of Yoruba ritual, discussed later). This is what we should expect, if human behavior is fundamentally open. Rituals highlight the fact that human understanding of the world is not just mental, or not just physical, but is a holistic coming together of mind and body, thought and feeling. By performing our ideas, by feeling the implications of our myths, their truth becomes self-evident.

Rites of Passage

Let us examine this process by looking at one kind of ritual performance: the **rite of passage.** At the beginning of the twentieth century, the Belgian anthropologist Arnold Van Gennep noted that certain kinds of rituals around the world had similar structures. These were rituals associated with the movement (or passage) of people from one position in the social structure to another. They included births, initiations, confirmations, weddings, funerals, and the like (Figure 7.5).

Van Gennep (1960) found that all these rituals began with a period of *separation* from the old position and from normal time. During this period, the ritual passenger left behind the symbols and practices of his or her previous position. For example, in induction into military service, recruits leave their families behind and are moved to a new place. They are forced to leave behind the clothing, activities, and even the hair that marked who they were in civilian life.

The second stage in rites of passage involves a period of *transition,* in which the ritual passenger is neither in the old life nor yet in the new one. This period is marked by rolelessness, ambiguity, and perceived danger. It is often a period in which the person or persons involved are subjected to ordeal by those who have already passed through. In the military service, this is the period of basic training, in which the recruits (not yet soldiers but no longer civilians) are forced to dress and act alike. They are subjected to a grinding-down process, after which they are rebuilt into something new.

During the final stage—*reaggregation*—the ritual passenger is reintroduced into society but in his or her new position. In the military, this involves the graduation from basic training and the visit home, but this time in uniform, on leave, and as a member of the armed forces, a new person.

The work of Victor Turner has greatly increased our understanding of rites of passage. Turner concentrated on the period of transition, which he saw as important both for the rite of passage and for social life in general. Van Gennep referred to this part of a rite of passage as the liminal period, from the Latin *limen* ("threshold"). During this period, the individual is on the threshold, betwixt and between, neither here nor there,

---

rite of passage A ritual that serves to mark the movement and transformation of an individual from one social position to another.

neither in nor out. Turner notes that the symbolism accompanying the rite of passage often expresses this ambiguous state. **Liminality,** he tells us, "is frequently likened to death, to being in the womb, to invisibility, to darkness, to bisexuality, to the wilderness, and to an eclipse of the sun or moon" (1969, 95). People in the liminal state tend to develop an intense comradeship in which their nonliminal distinctions disappear or become irrelevant. Turner calls this modality of social relationship **communitas,** which is best understood as an unstructured or minimally structured community of equal individuals.

Turner goes on to suggest that liminality and communitas are not just characteristic of rites of passage. The same sense of communitas seems to occur in other kinds of societal positions: positions of marginality (at the edges of structure) and inferiority (beneath structure). Prostitutes and slaves are, respectively, marginals and inferiors who are located outside the structure. They challenge the structure of society by their existence but maintain the structure by "knowing their place" and accepting it.

Turner contends that all societies need some kind of communitas as much as they need structure. Communitas gives "recognition to an essential and generic human bond, without which there could be no society" (1969, 97). That bond is the common humanity that underlies all culture and society. However, periods of communitas (often in ritual context) are brief. Communitas is dangerous, not just because it threatens structure but because it threatens survival itself. Lost in a world of communitas, the things structure ensures—production of food and physical and social reproduction of the society—cannot be provided. Someone always has to take out the garbage and clean up after the party. Communitas gives way to structure, which in turn generates a need for the release of communitas. The feeling of oneness reported in the earlier anecdote about the Ali-Foreman fight is communitas, and communitas is also possible in play.

Play and Ritual as Complementary

How does ritual differ from play? Play and ritual (like metaphorical and literal language) are complementary forms of metacommunication (Handelman 1977). Just as the movement from nonplay to play is based on the premise of metaphor ("Let's make-believe"), the movement to ritual is based on the premise of literalness ("Let's believe"). From the perspective of paramount reality (the everyday social order), the result of these contrasting premises is the "inauthenticity" of play and the "truth" of ritual.

Because of the connection of ritual with self-evident truth, the metacommunication of the ritual frame ("This is ritual") is associated with an additional metacommunication: "All messages within this frame are true." Both the frame and the messages within the frame become imbued with morality and thus contrast with the amoral metacommunication of play. It is ritual that asserts *what should be* to play's *what can be*. The ritual frame is more rigid than the play frame. Consequently, ritual is the most stable liminal domain, while play is the most flexible. Players can move with relative ease into and out of play, but such is not the case with ritual.

Finally, play usually has little effect on the social order of ordinary life. This permits play a wide range of commentary on the social order. Ritual is different: its role is

EthnoProfile 7.8 • YORUBA

REGION: Western Africa

NATION: Nigeria

POPULATION: 24,000,000

ENVIRONMENT: Coastal and forest

LIVELIHOOD: Farming, commerce, modern professions

POLITICAL ORGANIZATION: Traditionally kingdoms; today, part of a modern nation-state

FOR MORE INFORMATION: Bascom, William. 1969. *The Yoruba of Southwestern Nigeria.* New York: Holt, Rinehart and Winston.

explicitly to maintain the status quo, including the prescribed ritual transformations. Societies differ in the extent to which ritual behavior alternates with everyday, nonritual behavior. When nearly every act of everyday life is ritualized and other forms of behavior are strongly proscribed, we sometimes speak of **orthopraxy** ("correct practice"). Traditionally observant Jews and Muslims, for example, lead a highly ritualized daily life, attempting from the moment they awaken in the morning until the moment they fall asleep at night, to carry out even the humblest of activities in a manner that is ritually correct. In their view, ritual correctness is the result of God's law, and it is their duty and joy to conform their every action to God's will.

Ritual may seem overwhelming and all powerful. Yet individuals and groups within a society can sometimes manipulate ritual forms to achieve nontraditional ends. This can range from pushing against tradition as far as it can go without actually destroying the ritual (as when a bride and groom have an "alternative" wedding outdoors, write their own vows, and still have a priest officiating) to emphasizing the importance of one ritual and ignoring or downplaying another (as when Protestant Baptists downplayed the communion ritual and emphasized the baptism ritual as a way of articulating their challenge to Roman Catholicism) to exchanging one set of rituals for another (as when lone rural migrants to the cities of northern Cameroon convert to Islam shortly after their arrival, abandoning their traditional rituals together with the rural way of life into which they were born).

Margaret Drewal argues that, at least among the Yoruba, play and ritual overlap. (See EthnoProfile 7.8: Yoruba.) Yoruba rituals combine spectacle, festival, play, sacrifice,

liminality The ambiguous transitional state in a rite of passage in which the person or persons undergoing the ritual are outside their ordinary social positions.

communitas An unstructured or minimally structured community of equal individuals found frequently in rites of passage.

orthopraxy "Correct practice"; the prohibition of deviation from approved forms of ritual behavior.

and so on and integrate diverse media—music, dance, poetry, theater, sculpture (1992, 198). They are improvisatory events, spontaneous individual moves, in which the mundane order is not only inverted and reversed but may also be subverted through power play and gender play. In Yoruba life, gender roles are rigidly structured. Yoruba rituals, however, allow some cross-dressing by both men and women, providing institutionalized opportunities for men and women to cross gender boundaries and to express the traits that Yoruba consider to be characteristic of the opposite sex, sometimes as parody but sometimes seriously and respectfully (190).

COMBINING PLAY, ART, MYTH, AND RITUAL

Many anthropologists have suggested that play, art, myth, and ritual may be, and often are, experienced together. Bruce Kapferer has made these connections clear in a study of demon exorcism in Sri Lanka. (See EthnoProfile 7.9: Sinhalese.) The demon exorcism ceremonies of the Sinhalese Buddhist working class and peasantry last an entire night and are designed to cure disease. The performance combines in "a marvelous spectacle" ritual, comedy, music, and dance. Its goal is "to change the experiential condition of [the] patients and to bring patients back into a normal conception of the world" (1983, 177, 236). In other words, the entire performance is transformative. During the course of the ceremony, a demonic reality is created and then destroyed.

At the beginning of the exorcism, the patient and the audience are in different realities. The audience is in the paramount reality of everyday life, the patient is in the alternative reality of his or her illness. In that reality, demons are central and powerful actors. During the Evening Watch, through music, song, and eventually dance, the audience becomes increasingly engaged in this alternative reality. In this part of the ceremony, the demons are portrayed as figures of horror.

EthnoProfile 7.9 • SINHALESE

REGION: Southern Asia

NATION: Sri Lanka (city: Galle)

POPULATION: 12,580,000 (population of Galle: 115,000)

ENVIRONMENT: Tropical island

LIVELIHOOD: Farming, urban life

POLITICAL ORGANIZATION: Highly stratified state

FOR MORE INFORMATION: Kapferer, Bruce. 1983. *A celebration of demons*. Bloomington: Indiana University Press.

At midnight, the process is complete: the audience has joined the patient's reality. The demons, played by actors, appear. At this point, the Midnight Watch begins. This part of the ceremony is a comic drama that will last until nearly 3:00 A.M. The eruption of comedy into what had been an intensely serious ceremony transforms the demons into figures of ridicule. Through the comedy, the demonic reality begins to fragment as the gods appear and reassert their dominance. As this occurs, the sick person begins to see that the demons are really subordinate to the gods, not superior to them.

The last part of the exorcism is the Morning Watch, which continues until 6:00 A.M. During this period, the patient and audience become reengaged in the reality of ordinary life. The final comic drama of the performance "confirms the demonic absurdity, and destroys the demonic as powerful and relevant to normal experience in daily life" (Kapferer 1983, 220). Having played on the mind, body, and emotions of the patient and the audience, the performance ends.

To understand the performance as a whole, the interactions of all aspects of the performance must be grasped. Kapferer calls this the ceremony's *aesthetics*. He argues that the ceremony succeeds because it is composed of many different parts that fit together in a way that is satisfying to the Sinhalese. Only in the aesthetic realm are ideas, symbolic objects, and actions brought into the relationship from which their meaning comes.

Play, art, myth, and ritual are different facets of the holistic human capacity to construct and view the world from a variety of perspectives. The human capacity to play is channeled in different directions in different cultures, but it is always present. When the products of this containment process come together in key cultural productions, such as the Sinhalese curing ceremony, they display both the opportunities and dangers that result from open human creativity.

KEY TERMS

play	art	ritual
metacommunication	transformation-	rite of passage
framing	representation	liminality
reflexivity	myths	communitas
deep play	orthodoxy	orthopraxy
sport		

CHAPTER SUMMARY

1. Play is a generalized form of behavioral openness: the ability to think about, speak about, and do different things in the same way or the same thing in different ways. Play is common to all mammals, but it reaches greatest development in human

beings, who play throughout their lives. Play can be thought of as a way of organizing activities, not merely a set of activities.

2. Bateson argues that play is framed differently from the activities of ordinary life. We put a frame that consists of the message "this is play" around certain activities, thereby transforming them into play. This is a kind of metacommunication. Play also permits reflexive consideration of alternative realities by setting up a separate reality and suggesting that the perspective of ordinary life is only one way to make sense of experience.

3. The functions of play include exercise, practice for the real world, increased creativity in children, learning by children that behavior occurs in context, and commentary on the real world.

4. Deep play is a variety of play in which the stakes are so high that it appears irrational for anyone to engage in it at all; the alternative reality of play becomes all-consuming.

5. When sports are translated from one culture to another, they are frequently transformed to fit the patterns appropriate to the new culture.

6. Art is a kind of play that is subject to certain culturally appropriate restrictions on form and content. It aims to evoke a holistic, aesthetic response from the artist and the observer. It succeeds when the form is culturally appropriate for the content and is technically perfect in its realization. Aesthetic evaluations are culturally shaped value judgments. We recognize art in other cultures because of its family resemblance to what we call art in our own culture.

7. Myths are stories whose truth seems self-evident because they do such a good job of integrating our personal experiences with a wider set of assumptions about the way the world works. As stories, myths are the products of high verbal art. A full understanding of myth requires ethnographic background information. Orthodoxy refers to the prohibition of deviation from approved mythic texts. Malinowski viewed myths as social charters. Lévi-Strauss argued that myths are tools people use to overcome logical contradictions that cannot otherwise be overcome. Myths can serve both purposes.

8. Ritual is a repetitive social practice composed of sequences of symbolic activities such as speech, singing, dancing, gestures, and the manipulation of certain objects. In studying ritual, we pay attention not just to the symbols but to how the ritual is performed. Cultural ideas are made concrete through ritual action.

9. Rites of passage are rituals in which members of a culture move from one position in the social structure to another. These rites are marked by periods of separation, transition, and reaggregation. During the period of transition, individuals occupy a liminal position and regularly develop an intense comradeship and a feeling of oneness, or communitas.

10. Ritual and play are complementary. Play is based on the premise "Let us make-believe," while ritual is based on the premise "Let us believe." As a result, the ritual frame is far more rigid than the play frame. When nearly every act of everyday life is ritualized and other forms of behavior are strongly proscribed, we sometimes speak of orthopraxy. Although ritual may seem overwhelming and all powerful, individuals and groups can sometimes manipulate ritual forms to achieve nontraditional ends.

SUGGESTED READINGS

Alland, Alexander. 1977. *The artistic animal.* New York: Doubleday Anchor. *An introductory look at the biocultural bases for art. This work is very well written, very clear, and fascinating.*

Blanchard, Kendall, and Alyce Cheska. 1985. *The anthropology of sport.* South Hadley, MA: Bergin and Garvey. *An excellent introduction to the field.*

Fagen, Robert. 1981. *Animal play behavior.* New York: Oxford University Press. *The definitive work.*

Kapferer, Bruce. 1983. *A celebration of demons.* Bloomington: Indiana University Press. *An advanced text that is well worth reading.*

Lever, Janet. 1983. *Soccer madness.* Chicago: University of Chicago Press. *A fascinating study of soccer in Brazil.*

Schwartzman, Helen. 1978. *Transformations: The anthropology of children's play.* New York: Plenum. *A superlative work that considers how anthropologists have studied children's play, with some insightful suggestions about how they might do this in the future.*

Turner, Victor. 1969. *The ritual process.* Chicago: Aldine. *An important work in the anthropological study of ritual, this text is an eloquent analysis of rites of passage.*

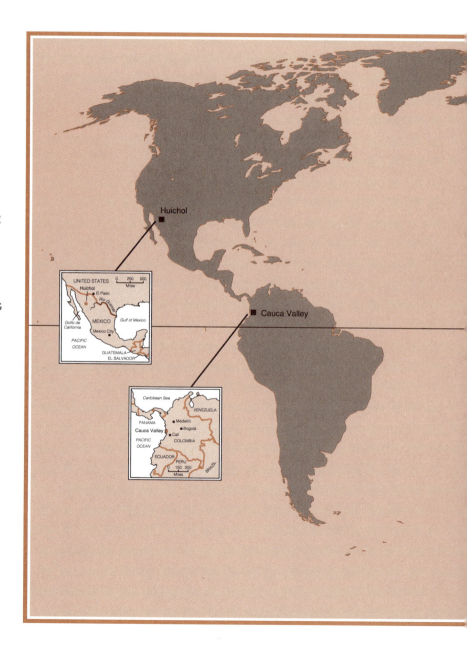

Worldview

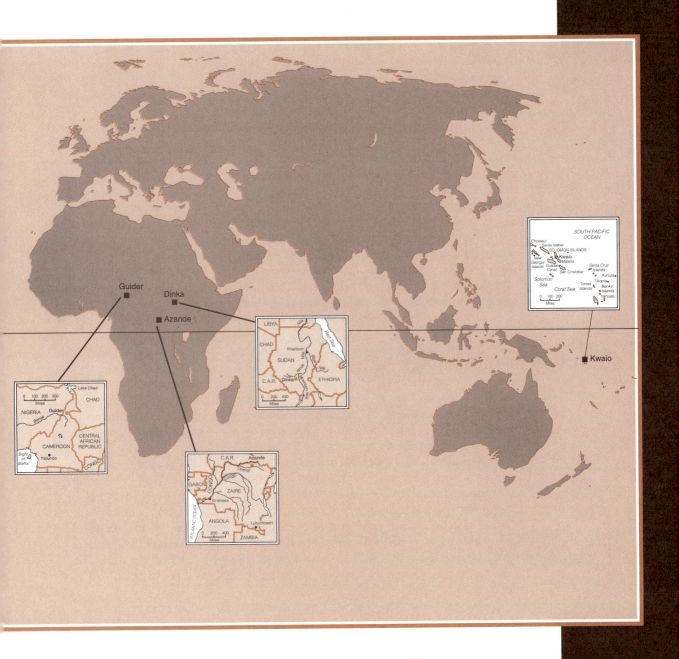

*i*n 1976, soon after the authors of this book, Emily Schultz and Robert Lavenda arrived in Guider, Cameroon, we bought a bicycle. (See Ethno-Profile 8.1: Guider.) About a month later, it was stolen. The thief had been seen and was well known. We went directly to the *gendarmerie,* where we swore out a complaint.

A month later, I (Robert Lavenda) was talking to Amadou, a 19-year-old member of the Ndjegn ethnic group. Amadou mentioned that the Ndjegn were famous for the power of their magic (Figure 8.1). I asked him if he knew any magic. Amadou replied that he was too young but that his older brother was a powerful magician. I asked what kinds of magic his brother was best at. Amadou began to list them—one of the first was magic to return stolen property. "Why didn't you mention this when our bike was stolen?" I inquired. "Well, I talked it over with my best friend. We agreed that you white people don't believe in any of that and would laugh at us." But I wanted to know what would happen to the thief if Amadou's brother made the magic against him. "His stomach will begin to hurt," Amadou explained, "and if he doesn't return the bicycle within two weeks, his stomach will swell up until it explodes and he will die." I thought this was a good idea and said I wanted the magic made.

Amadou went home and told his brother, who agreed to cast the spell. Word quickly went around Guider that the two "white visitors" had caused magic to be made against the bicycle thief. The days passed, but the bicycle did not reappear. After three weeks, I asked Amadou what had happened.

"Here's the problem, Monsieur," Amadou explained. "We waited too long after the theft to cast the spell. It works better when the magic is made right after the theft. Also, the thief is in Nigeria now. He's too far away for the magic to reach him."

Why do people believe—or not believe—in magic? Amadou was bright, suspicious of fakery, far from gullible. He had attended primary and secondary school. How could he remain convinced that his brother's magic worked? Why would many Americans be convinced that he was wrong?

Anthropologists are interested in what makes magic work because it occasionally does work: people are cursed, they sicken, and sometimes they die. How can this be? The usual anthropological explanation is that magic works when the people who believe in its power find out that it has been made against them. After all, people do often get stomachaches in northern Cameroon. Many people in Guider knew that the magic had been made and by whom. Only a fool or a desperate person would take the chance of having his or her stomach swell up until it exploded. But in this case, the thief, long gone, did not know that magic had been made, and the magic's effect was neutralized by distance.

Amadou's explanation of why magic succeeds or fails is just as coherent as the traditional anthropological explanation. But each explanation is based on a different set

EthnoProfile 8.1 • **GUIDER**

REGION: Western Africa

NATION: Cameroon

POPULATION: 18,000 (1976)

ENVIRONMENT: Savanna

LIVELIHOOD: Farming, commerce, civil service, cattle raising

POLITICAL ORGANIZATION: Traditionally an emirate; today, part of a modern nation-state

FOR MORE INFORMATION: Schultz, Emily. 1984. From Pagan to Pullo: Ethnic identity change in northern Cameroon. *Africa* 54 (1): 46–64.

FIGURE **8.1** *This man from northern Cameroon is believed to know powerful magic.*

of assumptions about what the world is like. Where do these ideas about the world come from? Why don't all people share the same ideas? This chapter suggests some answers to these questions.

FROM EVERYDAY EXPERIENCE TO WORLDVIEW

In our earlier discussions of language and cognition, we looked at some of the ways human beings use culture to construct rich understandings of everyday experiences. In this chapter, we build on those insights and describe how human beings use cultural creativity to make sense of the wider world on a comprehensive scale.

Anthropologists have good evidence that culture is not just a hodgepodge of unrelated elements. The directions in which cultural creativity goes may differ widely from one group to the next, but in any particular society, culture tends to be coherent and patterned; thus, an individual's everyday attempts to account for experience are not isolated efforts. Members of the same society make use of shared assumptions about how the world works. As they interpret everyday experiences in light of these assumptions, they make sense of their lives and their lives make sense to other members of the society. The encompassing pictures of reality that result are called **worldviews.** Anthropologists are interested in how worldviews are constructed and how people use them to make sense of their experiences in the broadest contexts. To do this, anthropologists must pay attention to the role of metaphor, metonymy, and symbol.

THE ROLE OF METAPHOR, METONYMY, AND SYMBOL

In Chapter 5, we argued that a **metaphor** asserts the existence of a meaningful link between two expressions from different semantic domains. Metaphorical statements such as "Arnold is a turkey" create an ambiguity that can only be resolved in context. If we know Arnold is characteristically inept, ignorant, and annoying and that turkeys are prototypically stupid and clumsy, our metaphor becomes intelligible and apt.

Why not simply say, "Arnold is inept, ignorant, and annoying"? Why resort to metaphor to represent our opinion of Arnold? When we choose to use metaphoric language instead of literal language, it is usually because literal language is not equal to the task of expressing the meaning we intend. Perhaps it is not just that Arnold is inept, ignorant, and annoying. Perhaps we think he is funny looking, with a tiny head and a vast, cumbersome body. Perhaps his voice reminds us of the gobbling sound turkeys make. Perhaps his neck is loose and wobbles when he walks. There is something about the image of a turkey that encompasses more of what we think about Arnold than can ever be represented by a list of adjectives.

Put another way, our experience of Arnold is complex and difficult to pin down in literal language. We therefore select a figurative image whose features are more familiar and use it as a tool to help us understand what kind of person Arnold is. The metaphor does not demonstrate unequivocally that Arnold *is* a turkey. It simply asserts that the link exists and invites those who know both Arnold and turkeys to decide (and perhaps to debate) the extent to which the metaphor is apt. Similarly, the metaphor "The Lord is my shepherd" links a subject we have trouble describing (the Lord) to an image (my shepherd) that is familiar and well understood. This metaphorical statement is an invitation to ponder what it means to be a shepherd, to be my shepherd, and then apply this knowledge to one's understanding of the Lord.

Worldviews aim to encompass the widest possible understanding of how the world works. In constructing worldviews, people tend to examine what they already know for clues that might help them make sense of what puzzles them. Metaphor is a powerful tool for constructing worldviews because it clarifies areas of human experience that are vague or poorly understood. The first part of a metaphor, the **metaphorical subject,** represents the domain of experience that needs to be clarified (the Lord). The second part of a metaphor, the **metaphorical predicate,** suggests a domain of experience that is familiar (sheepherding) and may help us understand what the Lord is all about (Figure 8.2).

To understand the metaphor, we have to list for ourselves every conceivable attribute of shepherds and then decide which attributes might aptly describe the Lord. Those attributes might include the love a shepherd has for his sheep or a shepherd's tireless vigilance in protecting his flock from the danger of wild animals. In addition, because the metaphor suggests that the Lord is *my* shepherd, I must think of myself as a sheep in relation to my shepherd, the Lord. Consequently, I must list all the conceivable attributes of sheep: that they are not very intelligent, that they are likely to go astray and get themselves into trouble if left on their own, or even that they are destined to die at the shepherd's hands.

These attributes of shepherds and sheep are called **metaphorical entailments.** They suggest what follows from, or is entailed by, our calling the Lord a shepherd. If we were to assert that "the Lord is my friend," an entirely different set of metaphorical entailments would follow: that my relationship with the Lord is a relationship between equals, for example, or that both of us have to make an effort if our friendship is to succeed.

Metaphors direct attention to certain aspects of experience and downplay or ignore others. As a result, different metaphors establish different referential perspectives. In so doing, metaphors assert different hypotheses and thus have the power to create different "realities." The creation of multiple realities through metaphor generates ambiguity. Most of us avoid being overwhelmed by this ambiguity by choosing one referential perspective as the paramount reality. We take this paramount reality to represent the "literal truth." The recurring patterns of experience, or schemas, found in paramount reality form domains of meaningful experience (or semantic domains). The boundaries of these domains appear so stable to us that we take them for granted.

---

worldviews Encompassing pictures of reality created by the members of cultures.

metaphor A form of thought and language that asserts a meaningful link between two expressions from different semantic domains.

metaphorical subject The first part of a metaphor that indicates the domain of experience that needs to be clarified.

metaphorical predicate The second part of a metaphor that suggests a familiar domain of experience that may clarify the metaphorical subject.

metaphorical entailments All the attributes of a metaphorical predicate that relate it to the culturally defined domain of experience to which it belongs.

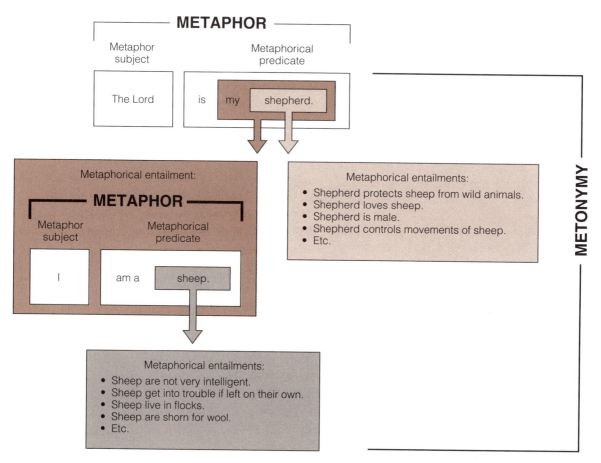

FIGURE 8.2 *An analysis of the metaphor "The Lord is my shepherd," illustrating the links of metaphor and metonymy.*

Metonymy is the relationship that links the parts of a semantic domain to one another. In the metaphor "The Lord is my shepherd," the link between the metaphorical subject shepherd and its metaphorical entailments is a link of metonymy. The word *shepherd* can stand for any and all attributes connected to the semantic domain defined by sheepherding. At the same time, any of these attributes (such as protecting sheep from wild animals) may entail the word shepherd. Because semantic domains are culturally defined, the meaningful elements that are linked by metonymy are also culturally defined. Sheepherding occurs in many different societies, and yet the range of meanings associated with sheepherding may vary: compare a society in which shepherds are women, sheep graze freely, and mutton is primarily for family consumption with a different society in which shepherds are men, sheep graze in enclosed fields, and most animals are sold on the market for cash.

Of course, members of the first society may think that theirs is the only sensible way to herd sheep, and vice versa. Put another way, in any society, semantic domains defined by links of metonymy are viewed as "true" or "literal" associations. By contrast, the semantic links set up by metaphor are viewed as "hypothetical" or "false." Nevertheless, an apt metaphor may suit the situation it describes more fully than any literal expression. If, in addition, the metaphor illuminates other areas of our experience, we may conclude that the metaphor enlarges our understanding. We then assimilate what we learn into the domain of truth. In this way, metaphor is converted into metonymy. Old metaphors become new truths that we can use as metaphorical predicates of yet other shadowy domains of experience.

Everyday experience may seem chaotic and meaningless until we are able to assign it to some familiar semantic domain. As we explore the elements that make up this semantic domain, we may conclude that our personal situation is illuminated when we view it in terms of the semantic domain we have chosen. We may decide that the sense of helplessness we feel is exactly described by the image of a "lost sheep." Further pondering what it might mean to be a lost sheep, we may conclude that a lost sheep was lost by someone, the shepherd to whom it belonged. This reflection, in turn, may lead us to ask who our "shepherd" might be. To someone who has experienced such reflection, the discovery that some religious groups believe that "the Lord" is their shepherd would seem most apt. Thus, by exploring the links of metonymy within a semantic domain, we may understand the validity of a particular metaphor. Such reflections probably play as important a role in cases of religious conversion as they do in science when a new theory is adopted in place of an old one (see Poewe 1989; Kuhn 1970).

People increase their understanding of themselves and the wider world by creating apt metaphors, which they may then convert into metonyms. Along the way, it is helpful to establish benchmarks that facilitate organizing this knowledge. People devise symbols to remind themselves of their significant insights and the connections between them. A **symbol**—be it a word, image, or action—is something that stands for something else. Symbols signal the presence and importance of given domains of experience. They are special cases of metonymy. Some symbols—what Sherry Ortner (1973) calls *summarizing symbols*—represent a whole semantic domain and invite us to consider the various elements within it. Other symbols—what Ortner calls *elaborating symbols*—represent only one element of a domain and invite us to place that element in its wider semantic context.

Summarizing symbols sum up, express, represent for people "in an emotionally powerful . . . way what the system means to them" (Ortner 1973; 1339). To many people, for example, the American flag stands for "the American way." But the American way is a complex collection of ideas and feelings that includes such things as patriotism, democracy, hard work, free enterprise, progress, national superiority, apple pie, and motherhood. As Ortner points out, the flag focuses our attention on all these things at once. It does not encourage us, say, to reflect on how the American way affects non-Americans. The symbolic power of the flag is double-edged. For some people, Americans included, this same flag stands for imperialism, racism, opposition to the legitimate struggle of Third World peoples, and support for right-wing dictatorships. Perhaps

---

metonymy The culturally defined relationship of the parts of a semantic domain to the domain as a whole and of the whole to its parts.

symbol Something that stands for something else. A symbol signals the presence of an important domain of experience.

FIGURE 8.3 *For pastoral peoples such as the Dinka and their neighbors the Nuer, cattle are elaborating symbols of paramount power.*

stranger still, for many Americans who came of age during the 1960s, the flag sums up all these things at once, contradictory though they are!

Elaborating symbols are essentially analytic. They allow people to sort out and label complex and undifferentiated feelings and ideas into comprehensible and communicable language and action. Elaborating symbols provide people with categories for thinking about how their world is ordered. Consider the Dinka, a cattle-herding people of eastern Africa (Figure 8.3). (See EthnoProfile 8.2: Dinka.) According to Godfrey Lienhardt, cattle provide the Dinka with most of the categories they use for thinking about and responding to experience. For instance, Dinka perceptions of color, light, and shade are connected to the colors they see in cattle. They even liken how their society is put together to how a bull is put together (Lienhardt 1961; Ortner 1973).

A WORLDVIEW IN OPERATION

Anthropologists often say that people of different cultures live in different worlds. This itself is a metaphorical statement. It asserts that our world depends on culture, particularly on the referential perspectives that our specific culture embodies. Every culture contains subcultures, each of which teaches us what the world is like from a different point of view. The experience of multiple referential perspectives that we gain in our own society helps us to understand the referential perspectives of different societies.

We have been discussing how worldviews are constructed. But now we consider how anthropologists and others encounter fully worked out worldviews when they come face-to-face with other societies. As outsiders, we discover a rich tapestry of sym-

EthnoProfile 8.2 • **DINKA**

REGION: Eastern Africa

NATION: Sudan

POPULATION: 2,000,000

ENVIRONMENT: Savanna

LIVELIHOOD: Principally cattle herding, also agriculture

POLITICAL ORGANIZATION: Traditionally, egalitarian with noble clans and chiefs; today, part of a modern nation-state

FOR MORE INFORMATION: Deng, Francis Madeng. 1972. *The Dinka of the Sudan.* New York: Holt, Rinehart and Winston.

EthnoProfile 8.3 • **AZANDE**

REGION: Central Africa

NATIONS: Sudan, Zaire, Central African Republic

POPULATION: 500,000

ENVIRONMENT: Sparsely wooded savanna

LIVELIHOOD: Farming, hunting, fishing, chicken raising

POLITICAL ORGANIZATION: Traditionally, highly organized, tribal kingdoms; today, part of modern nation-states

FOR MORE INFORMATION: Evans-Pritchard, E. E. [1937] 1976. *Witchcraft, oracles and magic among the Azande.* Abridged ed. Oxford: Oxford University Press.

bols and rituals and everyday practices linked to one another in what often appears to be a seamless web. Where do we begin to sort things out?

Anthropologist E. E. Evans-Pritchard, in his classic work *Witchcraft, Oracles, and Magic Among the Azande* ([1937] 1976), shows how Azande beliefs and practices concerning witchcraft, oracles, and magic are related to one another. (See EthnoProfile 8.3: Azande.) He describes how Azande use witchcraft beliefs to explain unfortunate things that happen to them and how they employ oracles and magic to exert a measure of control over the actions of other people. Evans-Pritchard was impressed by the intelligence, sophistication, and skepticism of his Azande informants. For this reason, he was all the more struck by their ability to hold a set of beliefs that, to a European, were superstitious at best.

Azande Witchcraft Beliefs

The Azande believe that children inherit **witchcraft** from their parents. Witchcraft is believed to be a substance in the body of witches, generally located under the sternum. For the Azande, all deaths are due to witchcraft and must be avenged by **magic.**

Being part of the body, the witchcraft substance grows as the body grows; therefore, the older the witch, the more potent his or her witchcraft. Men and women may both be witches. Men are believed to practice witchcraft against other men, women against other women. The Azande believe that a "soul" of witchcraft removes the soul of a certain organ in the victim's body, usually at night, causing a slow, wasting disease. Suffering such a disease is therefore an indication that an individual has had witchcraft directed against him or her.

Besides death, any other failure or misfortune is believed to be caused by witchcraft unless there is a better reason (perhaps the victim is incompetent, has broken a taboo, or has failed to observe a moral rule). Suppose I am an incompetent potter and my pots break while I am firing them. I may claim that witchcraft caused them to break, but everyone will laugh at me because they know I lack skill.

Witchcraft is an idiom the Azande use to describe and to explain all genuine misfortunes. Witchcraft is believed to be so common that the Azande are neither surprised nor awestruck when they encounter it. Quite the contrary: their usual response is anger. Witchcraft is a basic concept for the Azande, one that shapes their experience of misfortune.

The Azande are aware that there are "natural" causes for events. Consider the classic case of the collapsing granary. Azandeland is hot, and people seeking shade often sit under traditional raised granaries, which rest on logs. Termites are common in Azandeland, and sometimes they destroy the supporting logs, making a granary collapse. Occasionally, when a granary collapses, people sitting under it are killed. Why does this happen? The Azande are well aware that the termites chew up the wood until the supports give way, but to them that is not answer enough. Why, after all, should that particular granary have collapsed at that particular moment? To Westerners, the only connection is coincidence in time and space. We do not provide any explanation for why these two chains of causation intersect. But the Azande do: witchcraft causes the termites to finish chewing up the wood at just that moment, and that witchcraft must be avenged.

Witchcraft, Oracles, and Magic among the Azande

How to expose the witch? For this task, the Azande employ **oracles** (invisible forces to which people address questions and whose responses they believe to be truthful.) Preeminent among these is the poison oracle. The poison is a strychninelike substance imported into Azandeland. The oracle "speaks" through the effect the poison has on chickens. When witchcraft is suspected, a relative of the afflicted person will take a certain number of chickens into the bush along with a specialist in administering the poison oracle. This person will feed the chickens the poison and ask the oracle to identify the witch. A series of names will be presented twice to the oracle. The first time, the oracle will be asked to kill the chicken if the named person is the witch; the second time the oracle will be asked to spare the chicken. Thus, the Azande double-check the oracle carefully; a witchcraft accusation is not made lightly.

People do not consult the oracle with a long list of names. Because witchcraft is malevolent, people need only consider those who might wish them or their families ill: people who have quarreled with them, who are unpleasant, who are antisocial, and whose behavior is somehow out of line. Moreover, witches are always neighbors, because neighbors are the only people who know you well enough to wish you and your family ill.

Once the oracle has identified the witch, the Azande removes the wing of the chicken and has it taken by messenger to the compound of the accused person. The messenger presents the accused witch with the chicken wing and says that he has been sent concerning the illness of so-and-so's relative. "Almost invariably the witch replies courteously that he is unconscious of injuring anyone, that if it is true that he has injured the man in question he is very sorry, and that if it is he alone who is troubling him then he will surely recover, because from the bottom of his heart he wishes him health and happiness" (Evans-Pritchard [1937] 1976, 42). The accused then calls for a gourd of water, takes some in his mouth, and sprays it out over the wing. He says aloud, so the messenger can hear and repeat what he says, that if he is a witch he is not aware of it and that he is not intentionally causing the sick man to be ill. He addresses the witchcraft in him, asking it to become cool, and concludes by saying that he makes this appeal from his heart, not just from his lips (42).

People accused of witchcraft are usually astounded; no Azande thinks of himself or herself as a witch. However, the Azande strongly believe in witchcraft and in the oracles, and if the oracle says someone is a witch, then that person must be one. The accused witch is grateful to the family of the sick person for letting this be known. Otherwise, if the accused had been allowed to murder the victim, all the while unaware of it, the witch would surely be killed by vengeance magic. The witchcraft accusation carries a further message: the behavior of the accused is sufficiently outside the bounds of acceptable Azande behavior to have marked him or her as a potential witch. Only the names of people you suspect wish you ill are submitted to the oracle. The accused witch, then, is being told to change his or her behavior.

---

witchcraft The performance of evil by human beings believed to possess an innate, nonhuman power to do evil, whether or not it is intentional or self-aware.

magic A set of beliefs and practices designed to control the visible or invisible world for specific purposes.

oracles Invisible forces to which people address questions and whose responses they believe to be truthful.

Patterns of Witchcraft Accusation

Compared with the image we have of sixteenth- and seventeenth-century European-American witchcraft—old hags dressed in black, riding on broomsticks, casting spells, causing milk to sour or people to sicken—Azande witchcraft seems quite tame. We in the West have the impression that witchcraft and witch-hunting tear at the very fabric of society. Yet anthropological accounts like Evans-Pritchard's suggest that practices such as witchcraft accusation can sometimes keep societies together.

Anthropologist Mary Douglas looked at the range of witchcraft accusations worldwide, and discovered that they fall into two basic types (1970, xxvi–xxvii): in some cases, the witch is an evil outsider; in others, the witch is an internal enemy, either the member of a rival faction or a dangerous deviant. These different patterns of accusation perform different functions in a society. If the witch is an outsider, witchcraft accusation can strengthen in-group ties. If the witch is an internal enemy, accusations of witchcraft can weaken in-group ties; factions may have to regroup, communities may split, and the entire social hierarchy may be reordered. If the witch is a dangerous deviant, witchcraft accusation can be seen as an attempt to control the deviant in defense of the wider values of the community. Douglas concludes that the way people understand witchcraft is based on social relations in the society where witchcraft is practiced. In each case, members of the society are asserting, metaphorically, that the invisible realm operates the same way their society does.

KEY METAPHORS FOR CONSTRUCTING WORLDVIEWS

Differences in worldview ultimately derive from differences in experience, which people try to explain to themselves by means of metaphor. Human beings are not content to take things as they come, to refrain from asking how or why things are the way they are. Worldview, then, is an attempt to answer the following question: What must the world be like for my experiences to be what they are?

Over the ages, thoughtful people in all cultural traditions have suggested a variety of answers to this question. Those suggestions that have become entrenched in any particular tradition are based on especially apt metaphors whose power to make sense of experience in a variety of circumstances and historical periods has been demonstrated repeatedly. But that power is limited. New metaphors that are appropriate for changed circumstances can provide insight when the old ways fail and can form the basis for new worldviews.

Anthropologist Robin Horton suggests that people who construct a worldview are "concerned above all to show order, regularity and predictability where primary theory [that is, commonsense experience] has failed to show them." As they search for key metaphors, therefore, they look at those areas of everyday experience that are most associated with order, regularity, and predictability (1982, 237). **Key metaphors** that have served as the foundation of worldviews in different societies include societal, organic, technological, and computer metaphors.

Societal Metaphors

In many societies, human action and interaction are the part of everyday experience that provides the greatest order, regularity, and predictability. In such societies, the model for the world is the social order. Such a **societal metaphor** is found among the Azande, for example. Horton argues that this has been the case in all traditional African societies, and that it was true of the Western world as well until the Renaissance (1982, 237).

Suppose the key metaphor of a society is, "The structure of the world is (the same as) the structure of our society." Members of this society will interpret the wider world in terms that derive from the structure of their own society. Thus, Horton suggests such a society will conceive of personalized beings, such as gods or ancestor spirits, who are believed to run the wider world the same way people run human society.

Worldviews that Western observers have called *religions* are ordinarily based on the societal metaphor. After all, the traditional hallmark of religion, from a Western perspective, is a belief in spirits or gods. Nevertheless, because societies are so different from one another, each will give rise to a rather different religion. Societies organized in strong groups based on kinship usually people the wider world with the spirits of powerful ancestor figures. By contrast, societies run by vast and complex bureaucratic hierarchies are apt to picture the universe as being run by an army of hierarchically ordered spirits, perhaps topped by a chief god. We can predict that "The Lord is my shepherd" is not likely to be accepted as an apt description of cosmic reality by people living in a society that lacks class distinctions between lords and peasants and has no experience of sheepherding.

Societal metaphors are not restricted to non-Western peoples. As Horton noted, before the rise of science (which conceived of the cosmos in terms of impersonal mechanical forces), the dominant Western worldviews stretching back to antiquity were all based on societal metaphors. All envisioned a universe run by personalized beings (or a personalized Being) in ways that paralleled human social organization. With the growth of science in the West, our understanding of society (and our use of societal metaphors) has changed. For example, biologist Richard Lewontin and his colleagues point out that biologists studying cells used a societal metaphor almost from the very beginning. They liken cells to a factory assembling the biochemical products needed to support the body's economy. This metaphor recurs in the twentieth-century work of Francis Crick, one of the discoverers of the structure of DNA (deoxyribonucleic acid). Lewontin and colleagues suggest, "Read any introductory textbook to the new molecular biology and you will find these metaphors as a central part of the cellular description. Even the drawings of the protein synthesis sequence are often deliberately laid out in 'assembly-line' style" (1984, 59).

Similarly, contemporary sociobiologists have borrowed certain concepts from modern economic thought and used them to describe the behavior of genes or of living

---

key metaphors Metaphors that serve as the foundation of a worldview.

societal metaphor A worldview metaphor whose model for the world is the social order.

organisms. Thus, sociobiologists describe the nurturing behavior of parents toward their offspring as "parental investment." They talk about the cost-benefit analyses that people make before deciding whether or not to sacrifice themselves for others and even describe genes as "selfish." To some sociobiologists, the natural world is just the capitalist market on a larger scale. Indeed, anthropologist Marshall Sahlins (1976b) and others have argued that, from its inception, modern biology took its key metaphors from the social world that was familiar to the biologists. That world, at its beginning in the late eighteenth century, was the world of early capitalism. As capitalism has changed over time, so too have the socioeconomic metaphors biologists use. The image of survival of the fittest was originally proposed in an attempt to explain how Western society worked. One wonders whether this image would have been viewed as an apt metaphor for the natural world in a society that did not have capitalist competition.

Organic Metaphors

An **organic metaphor** applies the image of a living body to social structures and institutions. The body of a living organism can be divided into different systems (digestive, reproductive, respiratory, and so on), each of which carries out a specialized task. Only when all these systems are functioning as they should, in harmony with one another, is the organism said to be healthy. If we compare society to a living organism, we look for the subsystems into which society can be divided, identify the tasks each subsystem is supposed to perform, and describe a "healthy" society as one in which all the subsystems are functioning as they should, in harmony with one another. Indeed, this metaphor is responsible for the social scientific theoretical perspective called *structural-functionalism*. Alternatively, we can use this metaphor to analyze the life course of a society or civilization in terms of its birth, youth, maturity, old age, and death.

Personification (attributing human characteristics to nonhuman entities) is an organic metaphor. The belief that rocks and trees have spirits or that soda pop machines have a personality that is both malevolent and greedy are examples of personification. James Fernandez states that organic metaphors are common in the Bwiti religion of the Fang of Gabon. (See EthnoProfile 7.5: Fang.) The human heart, for example, is an apt metaphor for Bwiti members because "(1) it is the heart which is the most alive of the bloody organs, (2) it is traditionally conceived by the Fang to be the organ of thought, and (3) in its bloodiness it is associated with the female principle. . . . Many meanings are at work in this metaphor, for that bloody organ, the heart, has a congeries of useful associations" (1977, 112).

Mary Douglas (1966) has much to say about the use of organic metaphors in the construction of a society's worldview. In her discussion of the worldview of the ancient Hebrews, she points out that the body was understood as a metaphor for their society. As a result, threats to society were interpreted as threats to the body, and bodily rituals were prescribed to deal with them. It is difficult to say whether this is a case of a societal metaphor or an organic metaphor. Perhaps it is an example of what George Lakoff and Mark Johnson (1980) call a *bi-directional metaphor:* that is, the ancient Hebrews may have used their knowledge of the body and its processes to illuminate society and its processes, and vice versa.

Technological Metaphors

A **technological metaphor** uses objects made by human beings as metaphorical predicates. One manufactured object that has stimulated the imagination in a variety of cultures, especially in the West, is the mirror: "the eyes are the mirror of the soul," "the mind mirrors the world," and so forth.

Technological metaphors that use machines as metaphorical predicates are rampant in the worldview (or worldviews) of Western society since the rise of science. In the seventeenth century, philosopher René Descartes popularized the notion that the human body was a machine, albeit one inhabited by an immortal soul. One of his near contemporaries, Julien La Mettrie, carried this analogy to its radical conclusion. In his book *L'homme machine* ("man-machine"), he argued that even the concept of the soul was superfluous because machines do not have souls.

As Western science and technology have grown in importance, machine metaphors have also become more widespread. Starting in the Renaissance, machines began to transform the world in unprecedented ways and stimulate people's imaginations. The increasing complexity of machines, coupled with their builders' intimate knowledge of how they were put together, made them highly suggestive as metaphorical predicates.

The metaphorical entailments that follow from a machine metaphor are very different from those that follow from organic or societal metaphors. "Bodies are indissoluble wholes that lose their essential characteristics when they are taken into pieces. . . . Machines, on the contrary, can be disarticulated to be understood and then put back together again. Each part serves a separate and analyzable function, and the whole operates in a regular, lawlike manner that can be described by the operation of its separate parts impinging on each other" (Lewontin, Rose, and Kamin 1984, 45). When we say that we are only cogs in a machine or talk about statuses and roles as interchangeable parts, we are using machine metaphors (Figure 8.4).

In the Western world, the clock has become a prototype for the ingenious mechanism. Indeed, in British English, the term *clockwork* is used as a synonym for *mechanical.* Other products of human industry have also lent themselves to metaphor. Technology seems to be responsible for what has been called the *conduit metaphor,* which is so deeply rooted in Western thought that its origin may be impossible to trace. In any case, it might be properly classed as a key metaphor in our Western worldview.

George Lakoff and Mark Johnson (1980) discuss the way the conduit metaphor is used to talk about language:

The Conduit Metaphor:

Ideas (or meanings) are objects.

Linguistic expressions are containers.

Communication is sending.

---

organic metaphor A worldview metaphor that applies the image of the body to social structures and institutions.

technological metaphor A worldview metaphor that employs objects made by human beings as metaphorical predicates.

FIGURE 8.4 *When we say that we are only cogs in a machine or talk about status and roles as interchangeable parts, we are using machine metaphors. Charlie Chaplin made use of technological metaphors in his film* Modern Times *(1936).*

Taken together, these three metaphorical statements create the image of a communication pipeline, or channel, along which message-containers filled with meaning-objects are sent back and forth. The conduit metaphor implies that words are containers that have their meanings inside them. Thus, understanding a word is simply a matter of unloading or unpacking the meaning contained within it. A failure to communicate is the result of choosing the wrong word-container to begin with (if you were the sender) or failing to empty the container properly once it arrived (if you were the receiver).

Computer Metaphors

A **computer metaphor** is a technological metaphor, but because of its significance in modern science, we will treat it separately. In the twentieth century, a major revolution in cognitive psychology was brought about by a shift in key technological metaphors. Psychologists rejected the steam engine metaphor (taken from nineteenth-century industrial technology) in favor of the computer metaphor (taken from twentieth-century cybernetic technology).

Computer jargon has become popular among scientists investigating the functions of the brain, the nervous system, and even the whole human body. It seems impossible to avoid such language, given the many suggestive insights into human mental functioning the computer metaphor makes possible. Using a computer (instead of a mirror, for example) as a model for the mind can produce varying interpretations. Everything depends on the kind of computer you choose as the metaphorical predicate or the aspects of computer operations you emphasize. For example, biological determinists might prefer to think of the mind as a "dedicated" computer, whose functions are fully specified and wired into the hardware, allowing little flexibility.

Psychologist Richard Gregory is impressed by the distinction between "hardware" and "software," between the machines themselves and the programs that run on them. In contrast to dedicated computers, Gregory's metaphor focuses on the sophisticated "general-purpose" computers. We cannot predict the specific tasks a general-purpose computer performs simply by knowing the design of its hardware; rather, by loading different software programs we direct the computer's hardware to perform different, particular tasks. If the brain is structured the way a computer is structured, according to Gregory, it resembles a general-purpose machine, not a dedicated machine. That is, "its functional processes cannot be guessed at from its design. . . . Although we may have biological origins, these may not be much more relevant than, say, soil for flowers. . . . Soil chemistry tells us remarkably little about orchids" (1981, 566).

Were we to pursue this kind of computer metaphor, we could argue that the brain is the hardware and culture is the software. The coevolution of brain and culture could be described as the process by which an applications program hungry for random-access memory (RAM) makes demands on hardware design. Random alterations that result in new central processing unit (CPU) chips and hardware design (mutations) allow more RAM applications to be developed. At a certain point, however, the capacity of the CPU chip to access RAM is reached. An external "swap file" to handle the users' ever increasing memory demands must be created in some sort of external storage system—on floppy or hard disks. The human cultural equivalent of this swap file would be oral tradition and later forms of symbolic inscription, such as writing.

METAPHOR AND WORLDVIEW AS INSTRUMENTS OF POWER

We have discussed the process that people use to build their worldviews and have noted how worldviews vary enormously from culture to culture. But within any particular culture—insofar as boundaries can be drawn—there are also often, perhaps always, differences of opinion about how the world truly works.

How does a particular picture of reality achieve the position of being the "official" worldview for a given culture? And once that position is achieved, how is it maintained? To be in the running for the official picture of reality, a worldview must be able, however minimally, to make sense of some people's personal and social experiences. Sometimes

---

computer metaphor A worldview metaphor that employs computers as metaphorical predicates.

minimally persuasive views of reality triumph over alternatives that seem far more plausible; at least this is how things seem from the perspective of other members of society. Thus, something more must be involved: that something is power. As Lakoff and Johnson put it, "People in power get to impose their metaphors" (1980, 157). Powerless people may be unable to dislodge the official worldview of their society. They can, however, refuse to accept the imposition of someone else's worldview and develop an unofficial worldview based on metaphors that reflect their own condition of powerlessness (Scott 1990). Such unofficial worldviews may even suggest appropriate action for transforming that condition.

How can metaphors, or the symbols that represent them, be used as instruments of power and control? First, a symbol can be used to refer to self-evident truths when people in power seek to eliminate or impose certain forms of conduct. Thus, a deceased parent, whose memory must be respected, may be invoked to block some actions or to stimulate others. Holy books, like the Qur'an, may also be used in this way. For example, a legal record from Guider indicates that a son once brought suit against his father for refusing to repay him a certain amount of money. The father claimed that he had paid. Both father and son got into an increasingly heated argument in which neither would give ground. Finally, the judge in the case asked the father to take a copy of the Qur'an in his hand and swear that he was telling the truth. This he did. The son, however, refused to swear on the Qur'an and finally admitted that he had been lying. In this case, the status of the Qur'an as the unquestioned word of God, which implied the power of God to punish liars, controlled the son's behavior.

Second, a symbol may be under the direct control of a person wishing to affect the behavior of others. Consider the role of official interpreters of religious or political ideology, such as priests or kings. Their pronouncements define the bounds of permissible behavior. As Roger Keesing points out: "Senior men, in Melanesia as elsewhere in the tribal world, have depended heavily on control of *sacred knowledge* to maintain their control of earthly politics. By keeping in their hands relations with ancestors and other spirits, by commanding magical knowledge, senior men could maintain a control mediated by the supernatural. Such religious ideologies served too, by defining rules in terms of ancient spirits and by defining the nature of men and women in supernatural terms, to reinforce and maintain the roles of the sexes—and again to hide their nature" (1982, 219).

Keesing's observations remind us that knowledge, like power, is not evenly distributed throughout a society. Just as some people speak or write or carve better than others, so too some people possess knowledge and control symbols to which others are denied access. Furthermore, this distribution of knowledge is not random in a society. Different kinds of people know different things. In some societies, what men know about their religious system is different from what women know, and what older men know may be different from what younger men know. Such discrepancies can have important consequences. Keesing suggested that men's control over women and older men's control over younger men are based on differential access to knowledge (1982, 14). It is not just that these different kinds of people know different things; rather, the different things they know (and don't know) enable them (or force them) to remain in the positions they hold in the society.

RELIGION

Many cultures assume that the universe operates according to the same principles as their society does. Those cultures tend to personify cosmic forces and deal with them as one deals with powerful human beings. Their societies possess what we in the West call **religion.**

Anthropologist A. F. C. Wallace has proposed a set of the "minimal categories of religious behavior" (1966, 53–67). These are, in a sense, design features of religion. For Wallace, religious activity involves one or more of the following:

1. *Prayer.* Every religious system in the world has a customary way of addressing personified cosmic forces, usually by speaking or chanting out loud and by holding the body in a conventional posture. Often, people pray in public, at a sacred location, and with special apparatus: incense, smoke, objects, and so on.

2. *Music.* Music is very often (perhaps universally) a part of religious ceremony; it may be in the form of singing, dancing, chanting, playing instruments, or reciting. Although addressing cosmic powers may be considered more effective in music, Wallace suggests that "musical media are preferred because of their effect upon the human performer and [his or her] audience and that sometimes . . . the participants are consciously aware that musical performance facilitates entry into a desired state of heightened suggestibility or trance in which possession and other ecstatic religious experiences can be expected to occur" (1966, 34–35).

3. *Physiological exercise.* The physical manipulation of psychological states to induce an ecstatic spiritual state is found in every religious system. Wallace suggests four major kinds of manipulation: (1) drugs; (2) sensory deprivation; (3) mortification of the flesh by pain, sleeplessness, and fatigue; and (4) deprivation of food, water, or air. In many societies, the experience of ecstasy, euphoria, dissociation, or hallucination seems to be a goal of religious effort.

4. *Exhortation.* In all religious systems, certain people are believed to have closer relationships with the invisible powers than others, and they are expected to use those relationships in the spiritual interests of others. They give orders, they heal, they threaten, they comfort, and they interpret.

5. *Reciting the code.* All societies have a sacred oral or written literature that asserts what is taken to be true. The code includes information about the nature of the cosmic forces and the universe as a whole, the religious myths, and the moral code of the religious system. At appropriate times, some or all of the code is told, recited, read, discussed, or studied.

6. *Simulation.* Ritual sometimes involves imitating things that are related to the cosmic realm. This may be in divination or witchcraft, but it frequently also has to do with the gods themselves. The painted or sculpted objects that are honored in some

---

religion A worldview in which cosmic forces are personified and dealt with as if they were powerful human beings.

FIGURE 8.5 *The joint pilgrimage by Hindu worshipers to the Ganges River is an example of the religious design feature* congregation.

religious systems are not usually considered divine themselves; rather, they imitate divinity and are treated as if they were divine. In certain kinds of theatrical ritual, people sometimes impersonate the gods.

7. *Mana.* Mana refers to an impersonal superhuman power that is sometimes believed to be transferable from an object that contains it to one that does not. The laying on of hands, in which the power of a healer enters the body of a sick person to remove or destroy an illness, is an example of the transmission of power. In Guider, some people believe that the ink used to copy passages from the Qur'an has power. Washing the ink off the board on which the words are written and drinking the ink transfers the power of the words into the body of the drinker. The principle here is that sacred things are to be touched so that power may be transferred.

8. *Taboo.* Objects or people that may not be touched are taboo. It is believed that the cosmic power in some objects or people may injure the toucher or "drain away" the power. Many religious systems have taboo objects. Traditionally, Catholics are not to touch the Host during communion; Jews may not touch the handwritten text of the biblical scrolls. In ancient Polynesia, commoners could not touch the chief's body; even an accidental touch resulted in the death of the commoner. Food may also be taboo; many societies have elaborate rules concerning the foods that may or may not be eaten at different times or by different kinds of people.

9. *Feasts.* Eating and drinking in a religious context is very common. The Catholic and Protestant Holy Communion are meals set apart by their religious context. The Passover Seder for Jews is another religious feast. For the Huichol of Mexico, the consumption of peyote is set apart by its religious context. (See EthnoProfile 8.4: Huichol.) Even everyday meals may be seen to have a religious quality if they begin and/or end with prayer.

10. *Sacrifice.* Giving something of value to the invisible forces or their agents is a feature of many religious systems. This may be an offering of money, goods, or services. It may also be the immolation of animals or, very rarely, human beings. Sacrifices may be made in thanks to the cosmic forces, in hopes of influencing them to act in a certain way, or simply to gain general religious merit.

11. *Congregation.* Religious behavior is always in part social. The people of a religious tradition sometimes come together as a group in the form of processions, meetings, or convocations (Figure 8.5). The joint performance of some ritual acts is part of all religious systems.

12. *Inspiration.* Not every member of a religious system may be possessed, undergo a dramatic conversion experience, or go into trance or other religious ecstasy. However, religious systems generally recognize that such states are the result of the intervention of cosmic forces in human life. "It is apparently the case that some persons in all human populations are subject to sudden, spontaneous interruptions of mood and thought. Whatever the reasons—psychodynamic or biochemical—for such alterations of mental activity, the belief in supernatural beings offers a ready and universally employed explanation. Religions differ in the extent to which they cultivate such experiences; all interpret them in religious terms" (Wallace 1966, 66).

13. *Symbolism.* Certain symbols in a society's repertoire are associated with cosmic forces, as they are understood in the society. They may directly represent the deity or deities, or they may symbolize major religious principles and beliefs. The Christian cross is an example of the latter.

Religious Organization

The most important entailment that follows from the societal metaphor is that forces in the universe are personalized. Thus, people seeking to influence those forces must handle them as they would handle powerful human beings. Communication is perhaps the central feature of how we deal with human beings. When we address each other, we expect a response. The same is true when we address personalized cosmic forces. Each design feature of religion that Wallace lists is related to human communication with personalized cosmic forces. These include not only gods, spirits, and ancestors, but also witches and oracles.

To address these forces effectively, worshipers must communicate as eloquently as possible, usually through religious rituals. Communication with the gods is enhanced by music and other aesthetic products and processes in which key religious symbols are highlighted. Worshipers seeking pity from the cosmic forces may offer sacrifices that testify to their seriousness of purpose. Physiological exercises—singing, chanting, dancing, rhythmic movements of the body—put worshipers in the right state of awareness to approach cosmic powers. Religious specialists may exhort believers in place of cosmic beings themselves as an entitlement of their special status or skill. These specialists may also be the ones who recite the code. To encourage a favorable response, a congregation may assume a humble body posture, touch certain objects, or refrain from touching others as they repeat together those actions known to please the gods. The response of the cosmic powers may be marked by communal feasts that allow worshipers to celebrate the fact that their prayers have been heeded. Alternatively, the response may be (1) recognized when worshipers or religious specialists experience spirit possession, (2) ascertained by divination, or (3) deduced from subsequent events.

Maintaining contact with invisible cosmic powers is thus a tremendously complex undertaking. It is not surprising, therefore, that some societies have developed complex social practices to ensure that it is done properly. In other words, religion becomes institutionalized. Social positions are created for specialists who supervise or embody correct religious practice.

Anthropologists have identified two broad categories of religious specialists: shamans and priests. A **shaman** is an individual, part-time religious practitioner who is believed to have the power to contact invisible powers directly on behalf of individuals or groups. Shamans are often thought to be able to travel to the cosmic realm to communicate with the beings or forces that dwell there. They often plead with those beings or forces to act in favor of their people and may return with messages for them. By contrast, a **priest** is skilled in the practice of religious rituals, which he or she carries out for the benefit of the group. Priests do not necessarily have direct contact with cosmic forces. Often their major role is to mediate such contact by ensuring that the required ritual activity has been properly performed.

Shamans are found even in societies where there are no other kinds of status outside kinship and gender. The Ju/'hoansi (!Kung), for example, recognize that some people are able to develop an internal power that enables them to travel to the world of the spirits—to enter "half death"—in order to cure those who are sick. (See EthnoProfile 9.1: Ju/'hoansi [!Kung].) Priests are found in hierarchical societies. Status differences separating rulers and subjects in such societies are reflected in the unequal relationship between priest and laity.

Mind, Body, and Emotion in Religious Practice: The Huichol

Barbara Meyerhoff (1974) discusses the peyote hunt of the Huichol (Figure 8.6). (See EthnoProfile 8.4: Huichol.) This ritual pilgrimage is a religious experience in which mind, body, and emotion all come together.

The Huichol are corn farmers who live in the Sierra Madre Occidental of northern Mexico. Annually, they travel to a desert about 350 miles from their homes to hunt peyote. Because peyote is sacred to the Huichol, this journey is also sacred, representing a pilgrimage to *Wirikuta,* the original Huichol homeland where the First People, both deities and ancestors, once lived. The journey is hard and dangerous, both physically

FIGURE 8.6 *A Huichol shaman's violin and arrows, together with a basket of freshly gathered peyote.*

and spiritually. The pilgrims seek to restore and experience anew the original state of unity that existed at the beginning of the world.

The original state of unity is symbolized by deer, maize, and peyote. The deer symbolizes the masculine, hunting past, and thus connects the Huichol with their ancestors. In Huichol thought, the deer gave them peyote and appears every year in the hunt in Wirikuta. Blood from a sacrificed deer makes the maize grow and makes it nourishing to people. The deer is more powerful than human beings but not as remote as the gods. It symbolizes independence, adventure, and freedom.

shaman An individual, part-time religious practitioner who is believed to have the power to travel to and/or contact supernatural forces directly on behalf of individuals or groups.

priest A religious practitioner skilled in the practice of religious rituals, which he or she carries out for the benefit of the group.

EthnoProfile 8.4 • **HUICHOL**

REGION: Latin America

NATION: Mexico

POPULATION: 9,000

ENVIRONMENT: Mountainous terrain

LIVELIHOOD: Corn farming, deer hunting in recent past

POLITICAL ORGANIZATION: Traditionally, no formal organization, some men with influence; today, part of a modern nation-state

FOR MORE INFORMATION: Meyerhoff, Barbara. 1974. *Peyote hunt.* Ithaca, NY: Cornell University Press.

Although the Huichol have only recently begun to grow maize, it is central to their present-day life. A life based on maize is precarious and tedious: the Huichol have to stay home to watch the crops when they would rather be visiting others or hunting. Even if they are careful, the maize may not grow. Maize symbolizes the labor of the present: food, domesticity, sharing between the sexes, routine, and persistent diligence. It also provides the Huichol with the language of beauty. "Maize," the Huichol say, "is our life."

Peyote, when gathered in the land of its origins, is sacred. It is used to induce private visions, which are not shared with others. It is also used ritually, in which case so little is eaten that no visions are produced. It seems that the purpose of ritual consumption is to reach communion with the deities. Peyote provides an unknowable, but private, experience for the Huichol, who think of it as plant and animal at once. At the climactic moments of the peyote hunt, it is hunted like the deer. For the Huichol, peyote is a quiet gift of beauty and privacy. "Peyote is neither mundane like maize, nor exotic and exciting, like deer. It is that solitary, ahistorical, asocial, asexual, nonrational domain without which [human beings] are not complete, without which life is a lesser affair" (Meyerhoff 1974, 227).

In Huichol religious thought, deer, maize, and peyote fit together: maize cannot grow without deer blood; the deer cannot be sacrificed until after the peyote hunt; the ceremony that brings the rain cannot be held without peyote; and the peyote cannot be hunted until maize has been cleaned and sanctified. The key event, then, is the peyote hunt.

In 1966, Barbara Meyerhoff and Peter Furst accompanied Huichol pilgrims on the peyote hunt. Each pilgrim was given the name of a Huichol god for the duration of the pilgrimage. The pilgrims, under the guidance of a shaman, all followed strict rules about sexual continence and other behaviors that served to separate them from their everyday routine.

Once the pilgrims entered Wirikuta, many ways of speaking and acting were reversed. "Stand up" meant "sit down"; "go away" meant "come here." The van in which they traveled that year became a "burro" that would stop "if he ran out of tequila." If a man wanted to talk to someone in front of him, he would turn to the rear. The shaman who led the pilgrimage told Meyerhoff that "on the peyote hunt, we change the names of things because when we cross over there, into Wirikuta, things are so sacred that all is reversed" (Meyerhoff 1974, 148).

In the sacred land, the pilgrims became hunters, searching for peyote. Once the first peyote cactus was found, it was trapped by two arrows. The pilgrims then encircled it and presented their offerings. The shaman cut it out of the ground, sliced sections, and put one section in each pilgrim's mouth.

> The little group was sharply etched against the desert in the late afternoon sun—motionless, soundless, the once-bright colors of their costumes now muted under layers of dust—chewing, chewing the bitter plant. So Sahagún described the ancient Indians who wept in the desert over the plant they esteemed so greatly. The success of the undertaking was unquestionable and the faces changed from quiet wonder to rapture to exaltation all without words, all at the same moment. . . . Their camaraderie, the completeness of their communion with one another was self-evident. The companions were radiant. Their love for life and for one another was palpable. Though they did not speak and barely moved, no one seeing them there could call the experience anything less than collective ecstasy. (Meyerhoff 1974, 155–57)

Following this moment of communitas, the pilgrims collected as much peyote as they would need for their community and hastened to depart. The reversals and other requirements remained in effect until they reached home.

The unification of deer, maize, and peyote gives the peyote hunt its power. As Meyerhoff puts it, "In the climactic moments of the rituals in Wirikuta, these symbols provide the Huichols with a formulation of the large questions dealt with by religion, the questions of ultimate meaning and purpose. In Wirikuta, a vision is attained by the operation of the deer, the maize, and the peyote; with lucidity and power, the symbols accomplish their sacred task of giving significance and order to [people's] lives" (1974, 229).

Meyerhoff writes that at the climax of the journey, several different unifications occur. On the societal level, the social barriers that separate the members of the group at home, and especially those that keep the shaman apart, are transcended. There are no longer distinctions between leader and follower, between male and female, between old and young. For a moment, people are distinct from their social roles. At the historical level, the Huichols' past life as free, male-dominated, desert-dwelling hunters is set apart from, but also reconciled with, their present settled life in the mountains, where men and women cooperate to grow maize.

Once in Wirikuta, the relationship of the Huichol to the natural environment changes. This is the home of the ancestors, and the landscape itself is sanctified. Time itself disappears. The Huichol become their ancestors and their gods, thus bridging the gap between past and present. The Huichol come to feel that they were always a single people with a distinctive, eternal way of life.

According to Meyerhoff, "this Huichol symbol complex takes up the problem of moral incoherence. By making possible the retention of the past as part of the present, it eliminates the need for dealing with the question of why the world changed, why the beauty and freedom of former times has passed away, why [people] lost touch with the gods, plants, and animals, why the Spaniards steal Huichol land, and why it is no longer possible to pursue 'the perfect life—to offer to the gods and chase the deer' " (1974, 261).

Meyerhoff suggests that the way the Huichol's religious system answers these problems is distinctive. Some religions explain present-day moral incoherence by asserting that an original paradise was lost following an ancient sin. Other systems assert that there is an afterlife in which all the suffering of the world will be set right. But the Huichol refuse to let go of their past. "Their most precious religious heritage—their beginnings—is idealized and recovered. Even if only for a little while, by means of the peyote hunt, Paradise may be regained. Through the deer-maize-peyote complex, the deer and a life dedicated to hunting the deer is still a fact of present-day life rather than a fading, shabby memory, chewed over by old men at the end of the day" (1974, 262).

In the terms we have been using so far, the deer-maize-peyote complex and the peyote hunt represent the union of mind, body, and emotion. Through a holistic ritual experience that is profoundly meaningful, deeply moving, and thoroughly physical, the Huichol reexperience the correctness of their way of life.

MAINTAINING AND CHANGING A WORLDVIEW

What makes a worldview stable? Why is a worldview rejected? These questions are related to general questions about the persistence and change in human social life. Anthropologists recognize that culture change is a complex phenomenon, and they admit that they do not have all the answers.

The first steps toward understanding culture change should involve attempts to relate any changes (or lack of them) to the experiences of a particular society. The kinds of experiences human beings have—of their bodies, their activities, their relationships with other people and with the natural environment—need to be accounted for. Stable, repetitive experiences reinforce the acceptability of any traditional worldview that has successfully accounted for such experiences in the past. When experiences become unpredictable and past experiences can no longer be trusted as guides for the future, traditional worldviews that cannot encompass these new experiences are undermined. During such periods, thinking people in any society become painfully aware that they face totally new situations. The age-old and time-tested theories that used to account successfully for experience now seem to be irrelevant (see Horton 1982, 252).

Coping with Change

Drastic changes in experience lead people to create new meanings that will help them cope with the changes. Sometimes these creative activities will involve *elaboration* of the old worldview, by adapting its organization and message to the needs of people living in changing circumstances. For example, the so-called world religions have persisted over

EthnoProfile 8.5 • **KWAIO**

REGION: Oceania (Melanesia)

NATION: Solomon Islands (Malaita)

POPULATION: 7,000 (1970s)

ENVIRONMENT: Tropical island

LIVELIHOOD: Horticulture and pig raising

POLITICAL ORGANIZATION: Traditionally, some men with influence but no coercive power; today, part of a modern nation-state

FOR MORE INFORMATION: Keesing, Roger. 1992. *Custom and confrontation.* Chicago: University of Chicago Press.

many centuries by adjusting to changing social conditions. For example, the Protestant Reformation adapted the Christian tradition to changing social circumstances in northern Europe during the Renaissance by breaking ties to the Pope, turning church lands over to secular authorities, allowing clergy to marry, and so forth. Protestants retained their identity as Christians even though their religious practices had changed.

But not all worldviews can evolve in this way, at least not under all social conditions. Some societies facing drastically changed circumstances have responded by discarding the old ways and embracing the new through *conversion.* In Guider, lone rural migrants to town frequently abandon their original religious practices, convert to Islam, and adopt urban customs. However, the conflict between new and old need not necessarily lead to conversion. Sometimes the result is a creative synthesis of the old religion and a new one, a process called **syncretism.** Under the pressure of Christian missionizing, indigenous people of Central America identified some of their own pre-Christian, personalized superhuman beings with particular Catholic saints. Similarly, Africans brought to Brazil identified Catholic saints with African gods, to produce the syncretistic religion Candomblé.

The Kwaio, living on the island of Malaita in the Solomon Islands, have responded to changed circumstances in yet a different way: by actively rejecting outside ideas and practices, they have engaged in cultural *resistance.* (See EthnoProfile 8.5: Kwaio.) Almost all their neighbors have converted to Christianity, and the nation of which they are a part is militantly Christian. Their neighbors wear clothing, work on plantations or in tourist hotels, attend schools, and some live in cities. The Kwaio have refused all this,

syncretism The synthesis of a traditional way of life and a new way of life that has been introduced by a different and usually more powerful culture.

In Their Own Words   CUSTOM AND CONFRONTATION

In the following passage, the late Roger Keesing recorded the words of one of his Kwaio informants, Dangeabe'u, who defends Kwaio custom.

The government has brought the ways of business, the ways of money. The people at the coast believe that's what's important, and tell us we should join in. Now the government is controlling the whole world. The side of the Bible is withering away. When that's finished, the government will rule unchallenged. It will hold all the land. All the money will go to the government to feed its power. Once everything—our lands, too—are in their hands, that will be it.

I've seen the people from other islands who have all become Christians. They knew nothing about their land. The white people have gotten their hands on their lands. The whites led them to forget all the knowledge of their land, separated them from it. And when the people knew nothing about their land, the whites bought it from them and made their enterprises. . . .

That's close upon us too. If we all follow the side of the Bible, the government will become powerful here too, and will take control of our land. We won't be attached to our land, as we are now, holding our connections to our past. If the government had control of our land, then if we wanted to do anything on it, we'd have to pay them. If we wanted to start a business— a store, say—we'd have to pay the government. We reject all that. We want to keep hold of our land, in the ways passed down to us.

Source: Keesing 1992, 184.

redoubling their commitment to the old ways: "Young men carry bows and arrows; girls and women, nude except for customary ornaments, dig taro in forest gardens; valuables made of strung shell beads are exchanged at mortuary feasts; and priests sacrifice pigs to the ancestral spirits on whom prosperity and life itself depend" (Keesing 1982, 1).

Why are the Kwaio different? Roger Keesing (1992) admits that he cannot really answer that question, although he suggests several possibilities. Perhaps there were some precolonial social and political differences between the Kwaio and their coastal neighbors that were crucial to later developments. The colonial encounter was certainly relevant. In 1927, Kwaio attacked a British patrol, killing the District Officer and 13 Solomon Island troops. The subsequent massacre of Kwaio by a police force of other Malaitans and their marginalization and persecution by the colonial government contributed to Kwaio resistance.

Keesing points out that although the Kwaio are aware of an alternative way of life, they choose to maintain their old ways. They find deep satisfaction in producing with their own hands and in family groups everything they need. They take pleasure in living amid ancient landmarks. They enjoy living, gardening, and worshiping where their parents, grandparents, and great-grandparents did. They perceive the richness and value in a traditional life (1982, 237). But "traditional" Kwaio life has become a life lived in a "modern" context. "In the course of anticolonial struggle, 'kastomu' (custom) and commitment to ancestral ways have become symbols of identity and autonomy" (240). In the eyes of the Kwaio, the many Solomon Islanders who became Christianized and acculturated lost their cultural ties and thereby their ties to the land and to their past. They have become outsiders—in their own homeland. For the Kwaio, "'kastomu' has become a symbol of personal and group identity. . . . Following the rules of the ancestors is a mode of political struggle, as well as a way of life" (240).

By maintaining their traditional ways, the Kwaio are consciously making a political statement. They are maintaining their traditional worldview, not just because they believe it is right but also because it is theirs. "The Kwaio have confronted the forces that have threatened them and their ancestors, not by culturally incorporating or encapsulating them but by marginalizing them, building walls and fighting to preserve them against breaches. It has been a cultural fencing operation, to keep the enemy without rather than encapsulating him within. The fencing has been possible only because . . . the Kwaio have lived in an isolated, mountainous terrain of no economic value to whites. Without the mountain wall there could have been no cultural fences" (Keesing 1992, 206).

Sometimes, a group's defense of its own way of life leads to a process that anthropologists call **revitalization**—a conscious, deliberate, and organized attempt by some members of a society to create a more satisfying culture (Wallace 1972, 75). Revitalization arises in times of crisis, most often in societies or subgroups within a society that are suffering radical transformations, usually at the hands of outsiders (such as colonizing powers). Put another way, revitalization movements emerge out of the experience of oppression. Sometimes revitalization takes the form of seeking a return to a golden age, when life was good, food was plentiful, and people knew their place. When a messiah is expected to lead believers to the new golden age, this movement is often called *revivalism, millenarianism,* or *messianism.* At other times, the idea is to rid the society of all alien influences. This is called *nativism.* Often both nativism and revivalism appear together in a social movement that produces leaders, followers, and significant changes in social action.

A classic New World example of a revitalization movement was the Ghost Dance of 1890, among Native Americans on the Great Plains of the United States. Independent life on the plains ended when the buffalo were exterminated and Native Americans were herded onto reservations by the numerically superior and better-armed European Americans. Out of this final crisis emerged Wovoka, a prophet, who taught that the existing world would soon be destroyed and that a new crust would form on the earth. All settlers and Native Americans who followed the settlers' ways would be buried at this time. But the Native Americans who abandoned the settlers' ways, led pure lives, and danced the Ghost Dance would be saved. As the new crust formed, the buffalo would return, as would all the ancestors of all believers. Together, all would lead lives of virtue and joy.

In contrast to some revitalization movements in other parts of the world, violence against the oppressors was not a necessary part of the Ghost Dance because the world was going to change by itself. Nevertheless, the movement frightened settlers and the

revitalization A conscious, deliberate, and organized attempt by some members of a society to create a more satisfying culture.

In Their Own Words   FOR ALL THOSE WHO WERE INDIAN IN A FORMER LIFE

Andrea Smith challenges members of the New Age movement who, in her view, trivialize the situation of women like herself "who are Indian in this life."

The New Age movement completely trivializes the oppression we as Indian women face: Indian women are suddenly no longer the women who are forcibly sterilized and tested with unsafe drugs such as Depo Provera; we are no longer the women who have a life expectancy of 47 years; and we are no longer the women who generally live below the poverty level and face a 75 percent unemployment rate. No, we're too busy being cool and spiritual.

This trivialization of our oppression is compounded by the fact that nowadays anyone can be Indian if s/he wants to. All that is required is that one be Indian in a former life, or take part in a sweat lodge, or be mentored by a "medicine woman," or read a how-to book.

Since, according to this theory, anyone can now be "Indian," then the term *Indians* no longer regresses specifically to those people who have survived five hundred years of colonization and genocide. This furthers the goals of white supremacists to abrogate treaty rights and to take away what little we have left. When everyone becomes "Indian," then it is easy to lose sight of the specificity of oppression faced by those who are Indian in *this* life. It is no wonder we have such a difficult time finding non-Indians to support our struggles when the New Age movement has completely disguised our oppression.

The most disturbing aspect about these racist practices is that they are promoted in the name of feminism. Sometimes it seems that I can't open a feminist periodical without seeing ads promoting white "feminist" practices with little medicine wheel designs. I can't seem to go to a feminist conference without the woman who begins the conference with a ceremony being the only Indian presenter. Participants then feel so "spiritual" after this opening that they fail to notice the absence of Indian women in the rest of the conference or Native American issues in the discussions. And I certainly can't go to a feminist bookstore without seeing books by Lynn Andrews and other people who exploit Indian spirituality all over the place. It seems that, while feminism is supposed to signify the empowerment of all women, it obviously does not include Indian women.

If white feminists are going to act in solidarity with their Indian sisters, they must take a stand against Indian spiritual abuse. Feminist book and record stores should stop selling these products, and feminist periodicals should stop advertising these products. Women who call themselves feminists should denounce exploitative practices wherever they see them.

Source: Smith 1994, 71.

U.S. Army, who suspected an armed uprising. Those fears and suspicions led to the massacre at Wounded Knee, in which the U.S. Cavalry killed all the members of a Sioux band, principally women and children, whom they encountered off the reservation.

CHANGING WORLDVIEWS: TWO EXAMPLES

Let us consider two detailed examples of change in worldview. We will pay particular attention to the circumstances surrounding the culture change these two societies have experienced.

FIGURE 8.7 *Fang women perform the Belebele dance during a Bwiti ceremony.*

The Fang

Caught by the French colonial presence and its Christianizing and civilizing mission since the late nineteenth century, the Fang in central Africa have faced three important challenges to their worldview. (See EthnoProfile 7.5: Fang.) First, the reality of "the far away," represented by the colonizers, came to challenge the reality of "the near" and familiar. Second, the protective traditional powers of "the below" were challenged by the missionaries' message of divinity in "the above." Third, the pluralism of colonial life was a double standard in which the colonized were treated differently from the colonizers (Fernandez 1982, 571).

For many Fang, the syncretistic Bwiti religion represents a response to colonization and the pressures put on their social system (Figure 8.7). Bwiti members cope with the first challenge by using the drug *eboga* to go out to the far and convert it into the near. In the second case, the Christian god of the above and the traditional gods of the below are both incorporated into the Bwiti pantheon, establishing a creative tension. Finally, in Bwiti, ritual promotes among members the communal feeling of "one-heartedness."

Bwiti has been successful in creating a worldview that allows many Fang to cope with the strains of social dislocation and exploitation (Fernandez 1982, 571). The Bwiti members have built a world in which some of the old metaphors (the forest, the body social, the kinship system) are reanimated and some new ones (red and white uniforms, a path of birth and death, the world as a globe or a ball) are created. The old and the new are fitted together in a satisfying and syncretistic way. This world has, however, closed itself off from the wider society of the Gabon Republic. Bwiti represents a kind of escape from the pressures of the outside world (566).

The Cauca Valley Peasants

Michael Taussig (1980) reports a very different response to change in the tropical Cauca valley of Colombia. (See EthnoProfile 8.6: Cauca Valley.) In the course of the twentieth century, the descendants of freed Colombian slaves have been transformed from independent peasant producers into landless laborers forced to work on rapidly expanding sugar plantations. Although none of them have ever seen it happen, these people believe that some of their fellows enter into contracts with the devil in order to increase their production and hence their wage. Peasants working on their own land are not believed to do this. The money gained by a contract with the devil can only be used for luxury items. It may not be used to purchase capital goods like land or livestock because

EthnoProfile 8.6 • CAUCA VALLEY

REGION: South America

NATION: Colombia

POPULATION: 700,000 outside the state capital, Popayán

ENVIRONMENT: Tropical jungle to river valley

LIVELIHOOD: Plantation agriculture, coffee, cocoa, subsistence crops

POLITICAL ORGANIZATION: Region within a modern nation-state

FOR MORE INFORMATION: Taussig, Michael. 1980. *The devil and commodity fetishism in Latin America.* Chapel Hill: University of North Carolina Press.

nothing will grow on land purchased with it, and any animals purchased will not reproduce and will die. Indeed, any sugarcane cut by a person who has such a contract will no longer sprout. In addition, many people say that a person who makes a contract with the devil will die prematurely and in pain (Taussig 1980, 13).

Given these consequences, why would anyone make such a contract? Taussig suggests that we must see these devil beliefs as both a commentary on and a protest against the imposition of capitalism. The "devil contract" represents a peasant interpretation of capitalism cast in an idiom drawn from peasant life and peasant understandings about labor. In other words, these people express their awareness of the threats that plantations pose to peasant independence by describing successful wageworkers as having made a bargain with the devil. "The religion of the oppressed can assuage that oppression and adapt people to it, but it can also provide resistance to that oppression" (Taussig 1980, 231). By representing to the peasant proletarians of the Cauca Valley (in language they understand) what capitalist agribusiness is doing to them, the metaphor of the devil contract sharpens the peasants' awareness of their plight. It may also engender resistance to that plight.

KEY TERMS

worldviews
metaphors
metaphorical subject
metaphorical predicate
metaphorical entailments
metonymy
symbol

witchcraft
magic
oracles
key metaphors
societal metaphor
organic metaphor
technological metaphor

computer metaphor
religion
shaman
priest
syncretism
revitalization

CHAPTER SUMMARY

1. People attempting to account for their experiences make use of shared cultural assumptions about how the world works. The encompassing pictures of reality that result are called worldviews. Metaphors are valuable tools for constructing worldviews, by directing attention to certain aspects of experience and downplaying or ignoring others.

2. The distinction between metonymy and metaphor may be said to correspond to the distinction between semantic linkages viewed as literal or true and semantic linkages viewed as hypothetical or false. If metaphors fit the rest of our experience, they may be converted into metonyms.

3. As people create apt metaphors that are transformed into metonyms, they mark semantic domains by symbols. Symbols that sum up an entire semantic domain are summarizing symbols. Elaborating symbols are analytic and allow people to sort out complex and undifferentiated feelings and ideas.

4. Witchcraft beliefs central to the Azande worldview provide an explanation for evil, illness, and misfortune. Witchcraft accusations also serve to indicate to the accused that his or her behavior has passed acceptable bounds.

5. Differences in worldview derive from differences in experience that people try to explain by means of metaphor. People use at least four kinds of key metaphors as foundations for a worldview: societal metaphors, organic metaphors, technological metaphors, and computer metaphors.

6. Within any culture there are differences of opinion about worldviews. Knowledge, like power, is not evenly distributed throughout a society. More powerful individuals and groups are often able to impose their preferred key metaphors on the rest of society. Those without power can resist this imposition by creating their own contrasting metaphors.

7. When people assume that the universe operates according to the same principles as their society does, they tend to personify cosmic forces. They then deal with those personified forces the same way they deal with powerful human beings. These societies possess what we in the West call *religion*. Religion can be described in terms of design features, all of which are related to the most important attribute of personalized cosmic forces: we can address cosmic forces symbolically, and we can expect them to respond. Maintaining contact with cosmic forces is very complex, and societies have complex social practices designed to ensure that this is done properly. Two important kinds of religious specialists are shamans and priests.

8. Drastic changes in peoples' experiences lead them to create new meanings to explain the changes and to cope with them. This can be accomplished through elaboration of the old system to fit changing times, conversion to a new worldview, syncretism, resistance, or revitalization.

SUGGESTED READINGS

Evans-Pritchard, E. E. [1937] 1976. *Witchcraft, oracles, and magic among the Azande.* Abridged ed. Oxford: Oxford University Press. *An immensely influential and very readable anthropological classic.*

Fernandez, James. 1982. *Bwiti: An ethnography of the religious imagination in Africa.* Princeton: Princeton University Press. *A book that is tremendously rewarding and demanding. A major study of a religious movement and its associated rituals in context.*

Geertz, Clifford. 1968. *Islam observed.* Chicago: University of Chicago Press. *A brief but important statement of several issues in the anthropology of religion. This work compares two Islamic worldviews that turn out to be rather different from each other, those of Java and Morocco.*

————. [1966] 1973. Religion as a cultural system. In *The interpretation of cultures.* New York: Basic Books. *An enduring classic article in anthropology. This is highly recommended.*

Keesing, Roger. 1992. *Custom and confrontation: The Kwaio struggle for cultural autonomy.* New York: Columbia University Press. *Based on 30 years of research, Keesing's final book provides a clear, readable, and committed discussion of Kwaio resistance.*

Meyerhoff, Barbara. 1974. *Peyote hunt.* Ithaca: Cornell University Press. *A remarkable account of the worldview and sacred journey of the Huichol Indians of Mexico, a journey in which the author participated. This work is accesible, very well written, and theoretically sophisticated.*

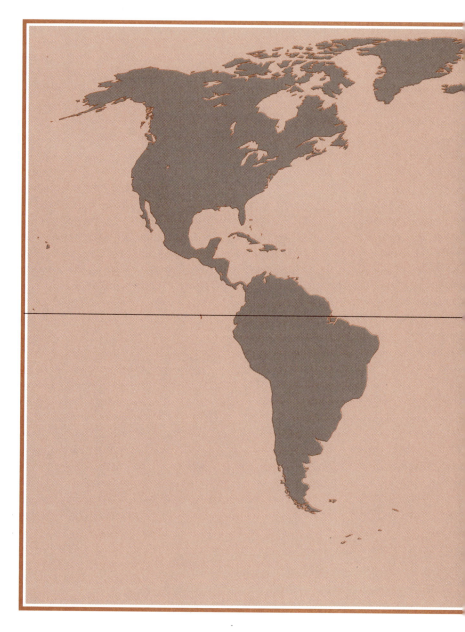

Kinship

9

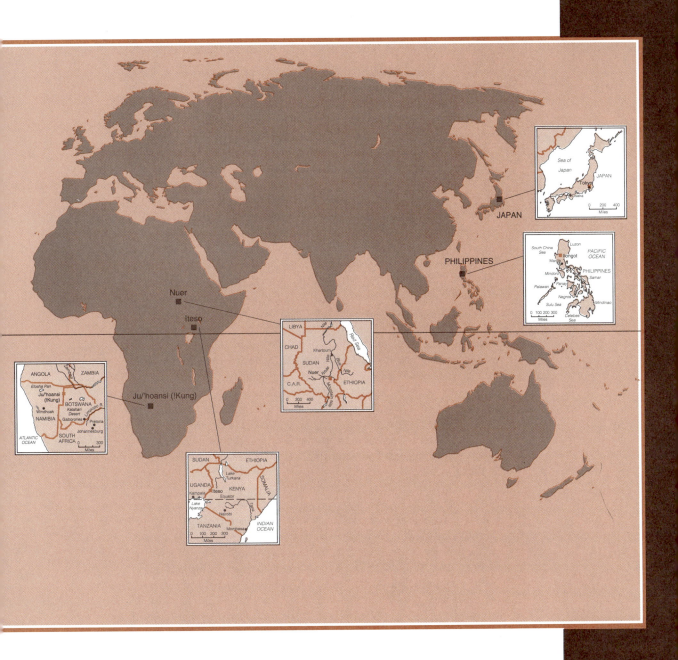

*m*artha Macintyre, an Australian anthropologist, did field research on the small island of Tubetube in Papua New Guinea from 1979 to 1983. She writes:

Like many anthropologists, I was initially taken in as "fictive kin." The explanations given to me for this were several. First, as I was going to stay on the island for a long time, I had to live in an appropriate place. I therefore needed to belong to the totemic "clan" that would enable me to live near to the main hamlet. This was a pragmatic decision. Secondly, as the only person who could translate for me was a young married man, I must become his "elder sister" in order to avoid scandal. Later a *post hoc* explanation emerged which drew on a long tradition of incorporating migrants and exiles into the community. My reddish hair, my habit of running my fingers through my hair when nervous, and the way that I hold my head at a slight angle when I listen to people intently, were indicators of my natural connection to Magisubu, the sea eagle clan. This view gained currency as I was "naturalised," and was proved to everybody's satisfaction when an elderly woman from another island pronounced that the lines on my hand proclaimed me as Magisubu.

An equally pressing reason for incorporating me was the need to minimize the disruption I caused by having no rightful place. People found it difficult to use my first name, as first names are used exclusively by spouses, or in intimate contexts. This left them with the honorific "sinabada," a form of address for senior women that was used in the colonial context for white women. It is now redolent of subservience and I hated being addressed in this way. In making me a part of the Magisubu clan, Tubetube leaders lessened my anomalous status and gave everyone on the island a way of speaking to me. Set in a large lineage with two older sisters, a mother and three powerful men as my mother's brothers, as well as numerous younger siblings, I could be managed, instructed, and guided in ways that did not threaten their dignity or mine. Although I was unaware of it at the time, there was a meeting of people who decided my fate in these terms within days of my arrival.

The adoption by Magisubu people carried with it numerous obligations, most of which were unknown to me until I was instructed as to their nature. In retrospect, they were advantageous to my research in the sense that I was given a role in various events affecting my adoptive family and so learned within a defined context. Usually, before any occasion where I might be expected to behave in some role appropriate to my (fictive) status, some senior person would explain to me what I should do. So, for example, I was told that I must on no account step over people's belongings nor stand so that I looked down on the head of a senior man or woman, nor sit close to any affines [in-laws]. . . .

On neighbouring islands I was treated as an honoured guest, unless I was accompanied by a group of Magisubu people, in which case the hosts would treat me in accordance with my fictive status within that clan. (1993, 51–52)

In many societies, kinship is so fundamental a way of defining who people are and how they connect with others that outsiders, even anthropologists, are made part of the system. Kinship enmeshes people in a web of relatives. Each person in the web is aware of his or her responsibilities and rights; the position of each in relation to all others is made clear. Life together becomes organized.

KINSHIP SYSTEMS: WAYS OF ORGANIZING HUMAN INTERDEPENDENCE

Human life is group life. Part of our primate heritage is sociability and gregariousness. A human infant is brought into the world able only to grasp, suck, and cry. To survive, it depends on other, older human beings. Even after childhood, however, human beings need other people. Human individuals would perish without culture and human companions to sustain them. Although people must live in groups, how they choose to organize themselves is open to creative variation.

Determining Group Membership and Relationships

Some human societies organize themselves on the basis of **kinship**—that is, on relationships that are prototypically derived from the universal human experiences of mating and birth. Relationships derived from mating are called **marriage** (discussed in Chapter 10), and relationships based on birth are called **descent**. Although marriage is based on mating and descent is based on birth, marriage is not the same thing as mating and descent is not the same thing as birth. The human experiences of mating and birth are multifaceted. The fascinating thing about human kinship systems is that different societies choose to highlight some features of those experiences while downplaying or even ignoring others. As we know from our own society, mating is not the same as marriage, although a valid marriage encourages mating between the married partners. Similarly, all births do not constitute valid links of descent. Children whose parents have not been married according to accepted legal or religious specifications do not fit the cultural logic

---

kinship Social relationships that are prototypically derived from the universal human experiences of mating and birth.

marriage An institution that prototypically involves a man and a woman, transforms the status of the participants, carries implications about permitted sexual access, gives the offspring a position in the society, and establishes connections between the kin of the husband and the kin of the wife.

descent The principle based on culturally recognized parent-child connections that defines the social categories to which people belong.

of descent, and many societies offer no positions that they can properly fill. Put another way, through kinship, a culture selects which aspects of human experience to emphasize, thereby reflecting that culture's particular theory of human nature.

Marriage and descent are thus selective. One society may emphasize that women bear children and base its kinship system on this fact, paying little formal attention to the mate's role in conception. Another society may trace connections through men, emphasizing the paternal role in conception and reducing the maternal role to that of a passive incubator for male seed. Even though they contradict one another, both understandings can be justified with reference to the human experience of mating and birth.

Consider the American kinship term *aunt*. This term seems to refer to a woman who occupies a unique biological position. In fact, it refers to a woman related to us in one of four different ways: as our father's sister, mother's sister, father's brother's wife, or mother's brother's wife. In our eyes, all those women have something in common, and we believe that they are related to us equally. "Aunt" is a category into which certain people perceived to be similar are placed. Prototypically, this is a woman one generation older than we are and a sister or sister-in-law of our parents.

However, we may also refer to our mother's best friend as "aunt." By doing so, we recognize the strength of this system of classification. Thus, kinship is an idiom. It is a selective interpretation of the common human experiences of mating and birth. The result is a set of coherent principles that allow people to assign one another group membership. These principles normally cover several significant issues: how to carry out the reproduction of legitimate group members (marriage); where group members should live after marriage (residence rules); how to establish links between generations (descent); and how to pass on positions in society (succession) or material goods (inheritance) in terms of descent. Taken together, kinship principles define social groups, locate people within those groups, and position the people and groups in relation to one another both in space and over time.

Sex, Gender, and Kinship

Kinship is based on but is not reducible to biology. It is a cultural interpretation of the culturally recognized "facts" of human reproduction. One of the most basic "facts" of human reproduction, recognized in some form in all societies, is that two different kinds of human beings must cooperate sexually in order to produce offspring. Anthropologists use the term **sex** to refer to the observable physical characteristics that distinguish the two kinds of human beings, females and males, needed for human biological reproduction. People everywhere pay attention to *morphological sex* (the appearance of external genitalia and observable secondary sex characteristics such as enlarged breasts in females). Scientists further distinguish females from males on the basis of *gonadal sex* (presence of ovaries in females, testes in males) and *chromosomal sex* (two X chromosomes in females, one X chromosome and one Y chromosome in males). At the same time, cross-cultural research repeatedly demonstrates that physical indicators of sex difference do not allow us to predict the roles that females or males will play in any particular society. Consequently, anthropologists distinguish sex from **gender**—the cultural

FIGURE 9.1 *Cross-cultural research repeatedly demonstrates that physical indicators of sex difference do not allow us to predict the roles that females or males will play in any particular society. In Hopi society, men were responsible for the weaving, whereas this woman of the Libinza people in Zaire is responsible for hunting.*

construction of beliefs and behaviors considered appropriate for each sex. As Barbara Miller puts it, "In some societies, people with XX chromosomes do the cooking, in others it is the XY people who cook, in others both XX and XY people cook. The same goes for sewing, transplanting rice seedlings, worshipping deities, and speaking in public. Even the exclusion of women from hunting and warfare has been reduced by recent studies from the level of a universal to a generality. While it is generally true that men hunt and women do not, and that men fight in wars and women do not, important counter cases exist" (1993, 5; Figure 9.1).

In fact, information from a number of different cultures suggests that the outward physical features used to distinguish females from males are frequently ambiguous. Sometimes genetic or hormonal factors produce ambiguous external genitalia, a phenomenon called *hermaphroditism*. Steroid 5-alpha reductase deficiency, for example, is a rare hormonal defect that causes males who are otherwise biologically normal to be born with ambiguous genitals, leading some to be categorized as male and others as female. At puberty, however, increased testosterone levels cause these individuals to experience changes typical of males: a deepening voice, muscle development, growth of the penis, and descent of the testicles. Gilbert Herdt (1994b) investigated cases of individuals with steroid 5-alpha reductase deficiency in the Dominican Republic and in New Guinea. In both places, the sexually anomalous individuals had been assigned to a locally recognized third sex, called *guevedoche* ("penis at twelve") in the Dominican Republic and *kwolu-aatmwol* ("changing into a male thing") among the Sambia of New Guinea.

sex Observable physical characteristics that distinguish two kinds of human beings, females and males, needed for human biological reproduction.

gender The cultural construction of beliefs and behaviors considered appropriate for each sex.

In other cases, however, anthropologists have documented the existence of *super-numerary* (that is, more than the standard two) sexes in cultures where the presence of ambiguous genitalia at birth seem to play no obvious role. In the Byzantine civilization of late antiquity, phenotypic differences were deliberately created in the case of eunuchs, whose testicles were removed or destroyed, often before puberty (Ringrose 1994). In the case of the hijras of Gujarat, India, adult males deliberately cut off both penis and testicles in order to become ritual performers dedicated to the Mother Goddess Bahuchara Mata (Nanda 1994). In both these cases, third gender roles distinct from traditional feminine and masculine gender roles are believed appropriate for third-sexed individuals.

Elsewhere, supernumerary gender roles developed that apparently had nothing to do with morphological sex anomalies. Perhaps the most famous case is that of the *berdache.* Male berdaches have been described in almost 150 indigenous North American societies and female berdaches in perhaps half that number. Will Roscoe points out that "the key features of male and female berdache roles were, in order of importance, *productive specialization* (crafts and domestic work for male berdaches and warfare, hunting, and leadership roles in the case of female berdaches), *supernatural sanction* (in the form of an authorization and/or bestowal of powers from extrasocietal sources) and *gender variation* (in relation to normative cultural expectations for male and female genders)," commonly but not always marked by cross-dressing (1994, 332). Although the sexual partners of berdaches were often nonberdache members of the same sex, some may have been what Westerners consider homosexual or bisexual. Berdaches were accepted and respected members of their communities, and their economic and religious pursuits seem to have been culturally more significant than their sexual practices.

For many people, the "natural" existence of only two sexes, each with its own gender role, seems too obvious to question. And yet, as Roscoe points out, "the presence of multiple genders does not require belief in the existence of three or more physical sexes but, minimally, a view of physical differences as unfixed, or insufficient on their own to establish gender, or simply less important than individual and social factors" (1994, 342). Herdt's survey of the ethnographic literature leads him to conclude that it is difficult for societies to maintain supernumerary sexes or genders. Still, a strong case can be made for the existence of a supernumerary sex (such as the Sambia *kwolu-aatmwol*) or supernumerary genders (such as male and female berdaches) when a culture defines for each "a symbolic niche and a social pathway of development into later adult life distinctly different from the cultural life plan set out by a model based on male/female duality" (1994a, 68).

Interestingly, supernumerary sexes and genders can coexist alongside strongly marked male-female duality, as is the case among the Sambia, perhaps serving to temper the absolutism of that duality. That male-female duality should be an issue for the Sambia reminds us that no human society is unconcerned about biological and social reproduction. However, kinship institutions, which build on gender duality, do more than provide for reproduction. Kinship not only classifies people, it also establishes and enforces the conventions by which different classes of people interact with one another. In this way, societies are able to maintain social order without central government.

Understanding Different Kinship Systems

Kinship practices, rather than written statutes, clarify for people what rights and obligations they owe one another. But to the first Westerners who encountered these practices, some of them seemed highly unusual. Western explorers discovered, for example, that some non-Western people distinguished among their relatives only on the basis of age and sex. To refer to people one generation older than the speaker required only two terms: one applying to men and one applying to women. The explorers mistakenly concluded that these people were unable to tell the difference between their fathers and their uncles, because they used the same kin term for both. They did not understand that *father* and *uncle* are not universally recognized kinship categories. The people whom the explorers met did not understand kinship the same way the explorers did; they had one category of male relative, where Europeans had two. For them, the man who was married to their mother, although known to them and personally important to them, was socially no more or less significant than that man's brothers or their mother's brothers. By referring to all these men by the same kin term, they were no more deluded than we are when we assert that our father's sister and our mother's brother's wife are equally our *aunts*.

Beyond that, the categories of feeling these people associated with different kin were as real as, but different from, the emotions we associate with kin. "Just as the word *father* in English means a great deal more than lineal male ancestor of the first ascending generation, *aita* in Basque has many local connotations not reducible to *father,* as we understand the term" (Greenwood and Stini 1977, 333). This takes us back to the rights and obligations associated with each category within a particular kinship system. Because the world of kin is a world of expectations and obligations, it is fundamentally a moral world charged with feeling. In some societies, a man's principal authority figure is his mother's brother and his father is a figure of affection and unwavering support. "God the Father" would not mean the same thing in those societies as it would in a society in which the father has life-and-death control over his children and a mother's brothers are without significant authority.

PATTERNS OF DESCENT IN KINSHIP

An important part of kinship is descent—the cultural principle that defines social categories through culturally recognized parent-child connections. Descent groups are defined by ancestry and so have a time depth. The descent principle involves transmission and incorporation: the transmission of membership through parent-child links and the incorporation of these people into groups. In some societies, descent group membership controls how people mobilize for social action.

Two major strategies are employed in establishing patterns of descent. In the first strategy, the descent group is formed by people who believe they are related to each other by connections made through their mothers and fathers *equally*. That is, they believe themselves to be just as related to their father's side of the family as to their mother's. Anthropologists call this **bilateral descent** (or *cognatic descent*). Two kinds of bilateral kinship groups are analyzed by anthropologists. One is made up of people who claim to be related to one another through ties either from the mother's or father's side to a common ancestor. This is called a *bilateral descent group* and is rare. The other kind, called a *bilateral kindred,* is much more common and consists of the relatives of one person or group of siblings.

The second major strategy, called **unilineal descent,** is based on the assumption that the most significant kin relationships must be traced through *either* the mother *or* the father. These descent groups are made up of people related to one another only through men or only through women and are the most common kind of descent group in the world today. Unilineal descent groups that are made up of links traced through one's father are called *patrilineal,* and those traced through one's mother are called *matrilineal.*

Bilateral Kindreds

The **bilateral kindred** is the kinship group that most Americans know. It is a group that forms around a particular individual and includes all the people who are linked to that individual through kin of both sexes—people whom we conventionally call *relatives* (Figure 9.2). These people form a group only because of their connection to the central person or persons, known in the terminology of kinship as *Ego.* In American society, bilateral kindreds assemble when Ego is baptized, confirmed, bar or bat mitzvahed, married, or buried. Each person within Ego's bilateral kindred has his or her own separate kindred. For example, Ego's father's sister's daughter has a kindred that includes people related to her through her father and his siblings. Ego, however, is not related to these people. This is simultaneously the major strength and major weakness of bilateral kindreds. That is, they have overlapping memberships and they do not endure beyond the lifetime of an individual Ego. But they are widely extended and can form broad networks of people who are somehow related to one another.

A classic bilateral kindred is found among the Ju/'hoansi (!Kung) of the Kalahari Desert in southern Africa. (See EthnoProfile 9.1: Ju/'hoansi [!Kung].) Anthropologist Richard Lee points out that for the Ju/'hoansi, every individual in the society can be linked to every other individual by a kinship term, either through males or through females. As a result, a person can expect to find a relative everywhere there are Ju/'hoansi. The Ju/'hoansi live in groups that are relatively small (10 to 30 people) but made up of a constantly changing set of individuals. "In essence, a Ju/'hoan [!Kung] camp consists of relatives, friends, and in-laws who have found that they can live and work well together. Under this flexible principle, brothers may be united or divided; fathers and sons may live together or apart. Further, during his or her lifetime a Ju/'hoan may live at many waterholes with many different groups" (1992b, 62). A wide range of kinspeople makes this flexibility possible. When someone wants to move, he or she has kin at many different waterholes throughout the area in which the Ju/'hoansi live and can choose to activate the appropriate kin tie. For the Ju/'hoansi, the bilateral kindred provides one of the many flexible aspects of their kinship system.

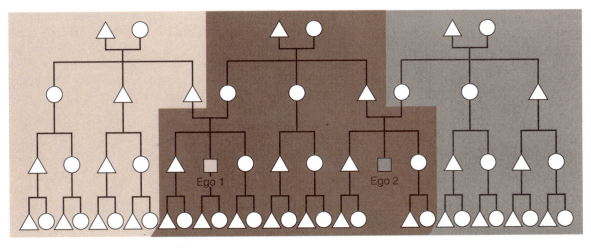

Marriage connection
| Descent
| Siblings

☐ Person, gender unspecified
△ Male
○ Female

FIGURE 9.2 *A bilateral kindred includes all recognized relatives on Ego's father's and mother's sides. The kindreds of Ego 1 and Ego 2 overlap.*

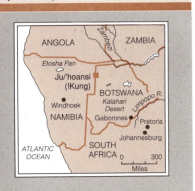

EthnoProfile 9.1 • **JU/'HOANSI (!KUNG)**

REGION: Southern Africa

NATIONS: Botswana and Namibia

POPULATION: 45,000

ENVIRONMENT: Desert

LIVELIHOOD: Hunting and gathering

POLITICAL ORGANIZATION: Traditionally, egalitarian bands; today, part of modern nation-states

FOR MORE INFORMATION: Lee, Richard B. 1992. *The Dobe Ju/'hoansi.* 2d ed. New York: Holt, Rinehart and Winston.

---

bilateral descent The principle that a descent group is formed by people who believe they are related to each other by connections made through their mothers and fathers equally (sometimes called *cognatic descent*).

unilineal descent The principle that a descent group is formed by people who believe they are related to each other by links made through men only or women only.

bilateral kindred A kinship group that consists of the relatives of one person or group of siblings.

In a society like that of the Ju/'hoansi, a bilateral kindred offers many advantages, yet the boundaries dividing the social groups that make up the society are ambiguous and problematic in at least four kinds of social circumstances: (1) where clear-cut membership in a particular social group must be determined, (2) where social action requires the formation of groups that are larger than individual families, (3) where conflicting claims to land and labor must be resolved, and (4) where people are concerned to perpetuate a particular social order over time. In societies that face these dilemmas, unilineal descent groups are usually formed.

Unilineal Descent Groups

Unilineal descent groups are found all over the world, from Australia to Africa to Asia to the Americas. They are all based on the principle that certain kinds of parent-child relationships are more important than others. Membership in a unilineal descent group is based on the membership of the appropriate parent in the group. In patrilineal systems, an individual belongs to a group formed through male sex links, the lineage of his or her father. In matrilineal systems, an individual belongs to a group formed by links through women, the lineage of his or her mother. *Patrilineal* and *matrilineal* do not mean that only men belong to one and women to the other; rather, the terms refer to the principle by which membership is conferred. In a patrilineal society, women and men belong to a **patrilineage** formed by father-child links (Figure 9.3); similarly, in a matrilineal society, men and women belong to a **matrilineage** formed by mother-child

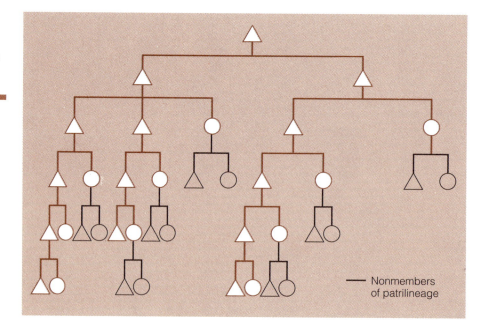

FIGURE 9.3 *Patrilineal descent: all those who trace descent through males to a common male ancestor are indicated in white.*

— Nonmembers of patrilineage

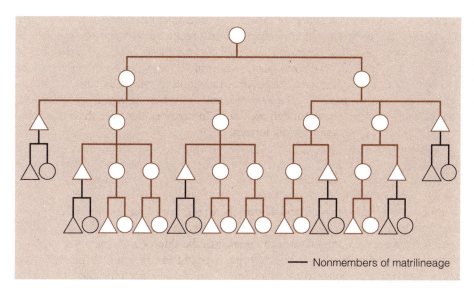

—— Nonmembers of matrilineage

connections (Figure 9.4). In other words, membership in the group is, on the face of it, unambiguous. An individual belongs to only one unilineage. This is in contrast to a bilateral kindred, in which an individual belongs to overlapping groups.

LINEAGES

The *lineal* in patrilineal and matrilineal refers to the nature of the social group formed. Anthropologists call these groups **lineages,** which are composed of people who believe they can specify the parent-child links that unite them. Although the abstract kinship diagrams that anthropologists draw include just a few people, lineages in the world vary in size, ranging from 20 or 30 members to several hundred. Some Chinese lineages were composed of more than 1,000 members.

Lineage Membership

The most important feature of lineages is that they are *corporate* in organization—that is, a lineage has a single legal "personality." As the Ashanti put it, a lineage is "one person" (Fortes 1953). To outsiders, all members of a lineage are equal *in law* to all others. For

---

patrilineage A social group formed by people connected by father-child links.

matrilineage A social group formed by people connected by mother-child links.

lineages The consanguineal members of descent groups who believe they can trace their descent from known ancestors.

example, in the case of a blood feud, the death of any opposing lineage member avenges the death of the person who started the feud. Lineages are also corporate in that they control property, specifically land. Such groups are found only in societies where rights to use land are crucial and must be monitored over time.

Lineages are also the main political associations in the societies that have them. Individuals have no political or legal status in such societies except through lineage membership. They have relatives who are outside the lineage, but their own political and legal statuses come through the lineage.

Because membership in a lineage comes through a direct line from father or mother to child, lineages can endure over time and in a sense have an independent existence. As long as people can remember from whom they are descended, lineages can endure. Most lineages have a time depth of about five generations: grandparents, parents, Ego, children, and grandchildren. When members of a group believe that they can no longer accurately specify the genealogical links that connect them but believe that they are "in some way" connected, we find the clan. A **clan** is usually made up of lineages that the society's members believe to be related to each other through links that go back into mythic times. Sometimes the common ancestor of each clan is an animal that lived at the beginning of time. The important point is that lineage members *know* who their common ancestor is, whereas clan members *believe* they have a common ancestor. The clan is thus larger than any lineage and also more diffuse in both membership and the hold it has over individuals.

The Logic of Lineage Relationships

The memories people have of their ancestry are not always correct and are often transmitted in the form of myth or legend. Thus, it is a mistake to approach them as if they were accurate historical records. Rather, as Malinowski observed, they are better understood as mythical charters, justifications from the invisible world for the visible social arrangements of the society. Fortes (1953, 165) quotes anthropologists Paul and Laura Bohannan, whose research was among the Tiv of Nigeria. (See EthnoProfile 6.4: Tiv.) The Bohannans observed Tiv people publicly rearranging their lineage relationships by recognizing that some mutual ancestors must have been relatives. This rearranging enabled them to bring their lineage relationships into line with changed legal and political relationships. It was not an exercise in deception; the Tiv assumed that traditional lineage relationships determined current social arrangements and that people did not consciously misrepresent tradition. But if current social arrangements and tradition conflicted, the Tiv concluded that the tradition was faulty. Tradition, therefore, needed to be revised to bring it into line with the current situation.

Indeed, genealogies and lineages might look solid and unchanging, but they are often more flexible than they appear. Lineages endure over time in societies in which no other form of organization lasts. Hence, they provide for the "perpetual exercise of defined rights, duties, office and social tasks vested in the lineage" (Fortes 1953, 165). In other words, the system of lineages becomes the foundation of social life in the society.

EthnoProfile 9.2   •   **NUER**

REGION: Eastern Africa

NATIONS: Ethiopia and Sudan

POPULATION: 300,000

ENVIRONMENT: Open grassland

LIVELIHOOD: Cattle herding and farming

POLITICAL ORGANIZATION: Traditionally, egalitarian tribes, no political offices; today, part of modern nation-states

FOR MORE INFORMATION: Evans-Pritchard, E. E. 1940. *The Nuer*. Oxford: Oxford University Press.

Patrilineages

By far the most common form of lineage organization is the patrilineage, which consists of all the people (male and female) who believe themselves to be related to each other because they are related to a common male ancestor by links through men. The prototypical kernel of a patrilineage is the father-son pair. Women who are members of patrilineages normally leave the lineages when they marry, but they do not relinquish their interest in their own lineages. In a number of societies, they play an active role in the affairs of their own patrilineages for many years.

An assumption of hierarchy exists in patrilineal societies: men believe they are superior to women, and many women seem to agree. However, there is a patrilineal puzzle at the heart of these societies. Women with little power, who are strangers to the lineage, nevertheless marry its members and produce the children who perpetuate the lineage. Ironically, the future of the patrilineage depends on people who do not belong to it! A second irony is that women must leave their own lineages to reproduce the next generation of somebody else's lineage. Women in patrilineal societies are often torn between conflicting interests and loyalties (see Karp 1986). Should they support their own children or their fathers and brothers?

A classic patrilineal system is found among the Nuer of the Sudan and Ethiopia. (See EthnoProfile 9.2: Nuer.) At the time of his fieldwork in the 1920s, English anthro-

clan A descent group formed by members who believe they have a common (sometimes mythical) ancestor, even if they cannot specify the genealogical links.

pologist E. E. Evans-Pritchard noted that the Nuer were divided into at least 20 clans. Evans-Pritchard defined *clan* as the largest group of people who (1) trace their descent patrilineally from a common ancestor, (2) cannot marry each other, and (3) consider sexual relations within the group to be incestuous. The clan is divided, or segmented, into lineages that are themselves linked to each other by presumed ties of patrilineal descent. The most basic stage of lineage segmentation is the minimal lineage, which has a time depth of three to five generations.

Evans-Pritchard observed that the Nuer kinship system worked in the following way: Members of lineages A and B considered themselves related because they believed that the founder of lineage A had been the older brother of the founder of lineage B. Thus, the living members of lineage A believed themselves to be related to the members of lineage B because the two brothers had a father in common. These two minimal lineages together formed the *minor lineage*. Minor lineages could be connected to other minor lineages by a presumed common ancestor, forming *major lineages*. These major lineages also were believed to share a common ancestor and thus formed a *maximal lineage*. The members of two maximal lineages believed their founders had been the sons of the clan ancestor; thus, all members of the clan were believed to be patrilineally related to each other.

According to Evans-Pritchard, disputes among the Nuer emerged along the lines created by lineages. Suppose a quarrel erupted between two men whose minimal lineages were in different minor lineages. Each would be joined in the quarrel by men who belonged to his minor lineage, even if they were not in his minimal lineage. The dispute would be resolved when the quarreling minor lineages recognized that they were all part of the same major lineage. Similarly, the minor lineages to one major lineage would ally if a dispute with an opposed major lineage broke out. This process, called **segmentary opposition,** is expressed in kinship terms but represents a very common process.

Evans-Pritchard noted that lineages were important to the Nuer for political purposes. Members of the same lineage in the same village were conscious of being in a social group with common ancestors and symbols, corporate rights in territory, and common interests in cattle. When a son in the lineage married, these people would help provide the **bridewealth** cattle. If the son were killed, they—indeed, all members of his patrilineage, regardless of where they lived—would avenge him and would hold the funeral ceremony for him. Nevertheless, relationships among the members of a patrilineage were not necessarily harmonious: "A Nuer is bound to his paternal kin from whom he derives aid, security, and status, but in return for these benefits he has many obligations and commitments. Their often indefinite character may be both evidence of, and a reason for, their force, but it also gives ample scope for disagreement. Duties and rights easily conflict. Moreover, the privileges of [patrilineal] kinship cannot be divorced from authority, discipline, and a strong sense of moral obligation, all of which are irksome to Nuer. They do not deny them, but they kick against them when their personal interests run counter to them" (1951, 162).

Although the Nuer were patrilineal, they recognized as kin people who were not members of their lineage. In the Nuer language, the word *mar* referred to "kin": all the people to whom a person could trace a relationship of any kind, including people on the mother's side as well as those on the father's side. In fact, at such important ceremonial occasions as a bridewealth distribution after a woman in the lineage had been married, special attention was paid to kin on the mother's side. Certain important relatives, such as the mother's brother and the mother's sister, were given cattle. A man's mother's brother was his great supporter when he was in trouble. The mother's brother was kind to him as a boy, and even in manhood the mother's brother provided a second home. If he liked his sister's son, a mother's brother would even be willing to help pay the bridewealth so that his sister's son could marry. "Nuer say of the maternal uncle that he is both father and mother, but most frequently that 'he is your mother' " (Evans-Pritchard 1951, 162). Ultimately, for a Nuer, every other Nuer he or she met was in some way a relative. If that person was not a relative, then he or she was believed to be an enemy.

Matrilineages

Matrilineages are often thought to be mirror images of patrilineages, and this certainly appears to be the case. In matrilineages, descent is traced through women rather than through men. Recall that in a patrilineage a woman's children are not in her lineage. In a matrilineage, a man's children are not in his. However, certain features of matrilineages make them more than just mirror images of patrilineages.

First, the prototypical kernel of a matrilineage is the sister-brother pair; a matrilineage may be thought of as a group of brothers and sisters connected through links made by women. Brothers marry out and often live with the family of their wives, but they maintain an active interest in the affairs of their lineage. Second, the most important man in a boy's life is not his father (who is not in his lineage) but his mother's brother, from whom he will receive his lineage inheritance. Third, the amount of power women exercise in matrilineages is still being hotly debated in anthropology. A matrilineage is not the same thing as a *matriarchy* (a society in which women rule). Brothers often retain what appears to be a controlling interest in the lineage. Some anthropologists claim that the male members of a matrilineage are supposed to run the lineage. These scholars have agreed that there is more autonomy for women in matrilineal societies than in patrilineal ones but that the day-to-day exercise of power is carried out by the brothers or sometimes the husbands. A number of studies, however, have questioned the validity of these generalizations. Trying to say something about matrilineal societies in general is difficult. The ethnographic evidence suggests that matrilineages must be examined on a case-by-case basis.

---

segmentary opposition A mode of hierarchical social organization in which groups beyond the most basic emerge only in opposition to other groups on the same hierarchical level.

bridewealth The transfer of certain symbolically important goods from the family of the groom to the family of the bride on the occasion of their marriage. It represents compensation to the wife's lineage for the loss of her labor and her child-bearing capacities.

In Their Own Words   WHAT DO MEN WANT?

Women and men in societies with patrilineal traditions, such as those of western Europe and the United States, are familiar with the attempts women have made to challenge social and legal rules that favor men's access to wealth, power, and prestige. Syed Zubair Ahmed writes here about the struggle of Khasi men in northeastern India against the rules of a matrilineal system that they believe places them at a disadvantage.

Shillong, India
The matrilineal Khasi society in northeastern India, one of the few surviving female bastions in the world, is making a fervent effort to keep men in their place.

Though an all-male organization that is battling the centuries-old matrilineal system has yet to make any significant dent, the rebels claim to have enlisted the support of some prominent Khasi

women. Their struggle to break free, they say, has resulted in small victories; some have begun to have a say in family affairs and are even inheriting property. But they constitute an insignificant minority in the 800,000-member Khasi society.

The men say the Khasi women are overbearing and dominating. "We are sick of playing the roles of breeding bulls and baby sitters," complains Mr. A. Swer, who heads the organization of maverick males. Another member laments: "We have no lines of succession. We have no land, no business. Our generation ends with us."

The demand for restructuring Khasi society in the patriarchal mold is a fallout from the growing number of women who are marrying outsiders. That, according to male opinion, has resulted in the bastardization of Khasi society.

Following custom, the youngest daughter inherits the property and after marriage her husband moves into the family house. Outsiders are said to marry the Khasi women for their property, while the women say they prefer to marry outsiders because their own tribesmen tend to be irresponsible in family matters.

In rebuttal, many Khasi men say the outsiders take advantage of the immaturity, youth and vulnerability of the youngest daughters and devour all their property and business. As a result, many Khasi men become paupers. And if the young men are often lazy and have no sense of a family, the rebels argue, it's the matrilineal system that is to blame.

Another problem caused by these marriages is the disintegration of families. About 27,000 Khasi women were divorced by their non-Khasi husbands in re-

The Navajo are a matrilineal people. (See EthnoProfile 7.3: Navajo.) The basic unit of Navajo social organization is the subsistence residential unit composed of a head mother, her husband, and some of their children with their spouses and children (Witherspoon 1975, 82; Figure 9.5). The leader of the unit is normally a man, usually the husband of the head mother. He directs livestock and agricultural operations and is the one who deals with the outside world: "He speaks for the unit at community meetings, negotiates with the traders and car salesmen, arranges marriages and ceremonies, talks to visiting strangers, and so on." He seems to be in charge. But it is the head mother around whom the unit is organized.

[The head mother] is identified with the land, the herd, and the agricultural fields. All residence rights can be traced back to her, and her opinions and wishes are always given the greatest consideration and usually prevail. In a sense, however, she delegates much of her role and prestige to the leader of the unit. If we think of the unit as a corporation, and the leader as its president, the

cent years, the highest number among India's northeastern tribes.

The identity crisis has led the Khasi Student Union to issue a stern warning to young Khasi women against marrying "non-tribals," saying they may be ostracized if they do. The Student Union is against switching over to the patrilineal system, however. So is a prominent Khasi scholar, H. W. Sten, who cautions that a patrilineal shift "would result in cross-marriages between clans, which is taboo in Khasi society," and adds, "Ultimately, it would lead to genetic defects in the offspring."

He points out that a Khasi son or daughter takes the surname of the mother. Therefore, if two sisters marry two men of different clans, in a patriarchal system the surnames of their children would be different and the marriages between cousins would be valid.

"This goes against the basic principle of Khasi custom," he said.

At the same time, Mr. Sten condemns those who are opposed to Khasi women's marrying outside the tribe. "Khasi culture is very flexible," he said. "No problem if a non-tribal wants to marry a Khasi girl as long as he is prepared to live with her and follow the Khasi custom. It will only add to the variety in Khasi society."

But Mr. Swer, president of the male group of social reformers, says such liberalism is the root cause of bastardization of his tribe. "Today, we have over 2,000 clans, but very few of them are pure Khasis," he observed. His demand for change, he adds, would stop outsiders from chasing Khasi young women, since under the patrilineal system their wives could not inherit property. But what about men marrying outside their tribe?

"The girls will be taken into the Khasi fold," he replied. "The children from the wedlock will automatically be Khasis."

While some men would like to end female domination, they do not support Mr. Swer's movement to abandon the deeply held tradition. "We Khasis underestimate the contributions of our fathers to the family," said Mr. H. T. Wells, a cousin of Mr. Sten. "Our fathers do a lot, but the credit goes to the mothers. I would love to have the patriarchal system but for the respect of our custom."

Mr. Swer admits that the Khasi men's demand for a patrilineal society is still a distant hope. But people like Mr. Wells, half converts to his idea, sustain his dream.

Source: Ahmed 1994.

head mother will be the chairman of the board. She usually has more sheep than the leader does. Because the power and importance of the head mother offer a deceptive appearance to the observer, many students of the Navajo have failed to see the importance of her role. But if one has lived a long time in one of these units, one soon becomes aware of who ultimately has the cards and directs the game. When there is a divorce between the leader and the head, it is always the leader who leaves and the head mother who returns, even if the land originally belonged to the mother of the leader. (Witherspoon, 1975, 82–83)

Anthropologists recognize that the European American habit of thinking hierarchically presents an obstacle to understanding matrilineal societies. Given any two things, European Americans want to know which is better; given any two groups of people, they want to know which is superior and which is inferior. Looking at matrilineal societies, we see groups of men and groups of women, and we "naturally"

FIGURE 9.5 *The head mother of a Navajo subsistence residence unit is identified with the land, the herd, and the agricultural fields.*

assume that either the women are in charge or the men are. But reality is more complex. Evidence from matrilineal societies reveals some domains of experience in which men and women are equal, some in which men are in control, and some in which women are in control. Observers and participants may disagree about which of these domains of experience is more or less central to Navajo life.

In discussing patrilineages, we referred to a patrilineal puzzle. In matrilineal societies, there is a paradox sometimes called the *matrilineal puzzle*. This is a contradiction between the rule of residence and the rule of inheritance. The contradiction is especially clear in societies that are strongly matrilineal and that encourage residence with the wife's matrilineage. Among the Bemba of Zambia, for example, a man is a stranger in his wife's house, where he goes when he marries. A man may feel great affection for his father, but he will not be his father's heir. He will inherit from his mother's brother, who lives elsewhere. And although a father may wish to have his son inherit from him, he must give to his sister's son (Richards 1954).

The classic case of the matrilineal puzzle comes from the Trobriand Islands, and Malinowski interpreted it in the way just described. (See EthnoProfile 3.3: Trobriand Islanders.) But research on the Trobriand Islanders by anthropologist Annette Weiner calls Malinowski's interpretation into question. Weiner argues that to understand matrilineal kinship in the Trobriand Islanders, one must begin by seeing the sister-brother pair as an integral unit: "[The sister-brother pair] makes complementary contributions both to a woman's brother's children and to a woman's own children. . . . In the former instance, a man and his sister (father and father's sister to a child) contribute their own [lineage] resources to the man's children, thus building up these children with resources that they may use, but may not subsequently pass on to their own children. . . . In the latter case, a woman and her brother (mother and mother's brother) contribute to the regeneration of [the matrilineage]—the woman through the process of conception and the man through the control and transmission of [matrilineage] property such as land and palm trees" (1980, 286–87). The result is that both a man and his sister "give" to the man's children, and his children return things to them later in life.

KINSHIP TERMINOLOGIES

People everywhere use special terms to refer to people they recognize as kin. Despite the variety of kinship systems in the world, anthropologists have identified six major patterns of kinship terminology based on how people categorize their cousins. The six patterns reflect common solutions to structural problems faced by societies organized in terms of kinship. They provide clues concerning how the vast and undifferentiated world of potential kin may be divided up. Kinship terminologies suggest both the external boundaries and internal divisions of the kinship groups, and they outline the structure of rights and obligations assigned to different members of the society.

Criteria for Distinctions

Kinship terminologies are built on certain widely recognized kinship criteria. From the most common to the least common, these criteria include the following:

- *Generation.* Kin terms distinguish relatives according to the generation to which the relatives belong. In English, the term *cousin* conventionally refers to someone of the same generation as Ego.
- *Sex.* The sex of an individual is used to differentiate kin. In Spanish, *primo* refers to a male cousin and *prima* to a female cousin. In English, cousins are not distinguished on the basis of sex, but *uncle* and *aunt* are distinguished on the basis of both generation and sex.
- *Affinity.* A distinction is made on the basis of connection through marriage, or **affinity.** In English, when we distinguish *mother-in-law* from *mother,* we use the criterion of affinity. In matrilineal societies, the mother's sister and the father's sister are distinguished from each other on the basis of affinity. The mother's sister is a

---

affinity Connection through marriage.

direct, lineal relative, and the father's sister is an affine. In English, the women are both called *aunt;* in matrilineal societies they are called by different terms.

- Collaterality. A distinction is made between kin who are believed to be in a direct line and those who are "off to one side," linked to Ego through a lineal relative. In English, the distinction of **collaterality** is exemplified by the distinction between *mother* and *aunt* and *father* and *uncle.* In kinship systems where collaterality is not employed, the same term is used for the mother and the mother's sister and the father and the father's brother.

- *Bifurcation.* The distinction of **bifurcation** is employed when kinship terms referring to the mother's side of the family are distinguished from those referring to the father's side of the family.

- *Relative age.* Relatives of the same category are distinguished on the basis of whether they are older or younger than Ego. Among the Ju/'hoansi, for example, speakers must separate "older brother" (*!ko*) from "younger brother" (*tsin*).

- *Sex of linking relative.* This criterion is related to collaterality. It distinguishes *cross relatives* (usually cousins) from *parallel relatives* (also usually cousins). Parallel relatives are linked to each other through two brothers or two sisters. **Parallel cousins,** for example, are Ego's father's brother's children or mother's sister's children. Cross relatives are linked to each other through a brother-sister pair. Thus, **cross cousins** are Ego's mother's brother's children or father's sister's children. The sex of either Ego or the cousins does not matter. The important feature is the sex of the linking relative (Figure 9.6). If this criterion is used in kinship systems in which collaterality is important, cross cousins and parallel cousins are called by separate kin terms.

Patterns of Kinship Terminology

The six major patterns of kinship terminology are based on how cousins are classified. These patterns have been named after the societies that represent the prototypes. The first two patterns are found in association with bilateral descent systems; the remaining four are found in association with unilineal descent.

Bilateral Patterns   The *Hawaiian* pattern is based on the application of the first two criteria: generation and sex (Figure 9.7). The kin group is divided horizontally by generation, and within each generation there are only two kinship terms, one for males and one for females. Consequently, siblings and "cousins" of the same sex are called by the same term. This terminological pattern emphasizes the equality of the father's and mother's sides. It is found in association with residence rules that allow a newly married couple to live with the husband's or wife's kin group. In this system, Ego maintains a maximum degree of flexibility in choosing the descent group with which to affiliate. Ego is also forced to look for a spouse in another kin group because Ego may not marry anyone in the same terminological category as a genetic parent, a genetic sibling, or a genetic offspring.

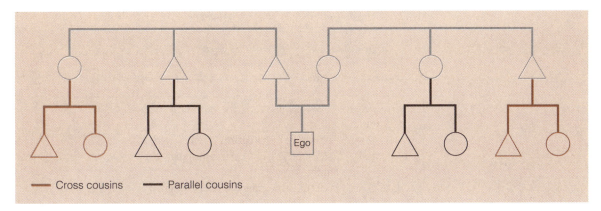

FIGURE 9.6 *Cross cousins and parallel cousins: Ego's cross cousins are the children of Ego's father's sister and mother's brother. Ego's parallel cousins are the children of Ego's father's brother and mother's sister.*

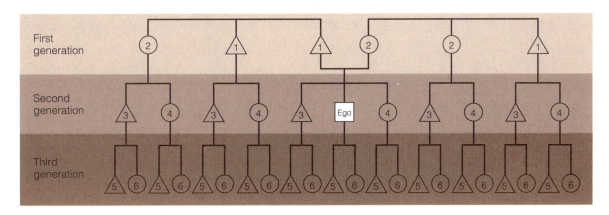

FIGURE 9.7 *Hawaiian kinship terminology: numbers represent kin terms. Ego uses the same kin term to refer to all those assigned the same number.*

collaterality A criterion employed in the analysis of kinship terminologies in which a distinction is made between kin who are believed to be in a direct line and those who are "off to one side," linked to the speaker by a lineal relative.

bifurcation A criterion employed in the analysis of kinship terminologies in which kinship terms referring to the mother's side of the family are distinguished from those referring to the father's side of the family.

parallel cousins The children of a person's parents' same-sex siblings (a father's brother's children or a mother's sister's children).

cross cousins The children of a person's parents' opposite-sex siblings (a father's sister's children or a mother's brother's children).

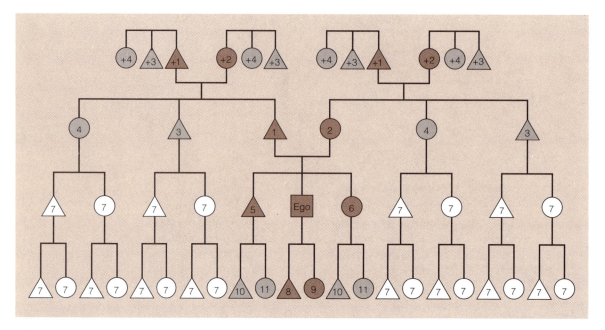

FIGURE 9.8 *Eskimo kinship terminology: all those indicated in brown represent Ego's lineal relatives; those in gray represent Ego's collateral relatives; and those in white are cousins. The symbol + equals grand (for example, +1 = grandfather).*

The terminological pattern called *Eskimo* is one of anthropology's little jokes because it is also the North American pattern (Figure 9.8). The Eskimo pattern reflects the symmetry of bilateral kindreds. A lineal core—the nuclear family—is distinguished from collateral relatives, who are not identified with the father's or the mother's side. Once past the immediate collateral line (aunts and uncles, great-aunts and great-uncles, nephews and nieces), generation is ignored. The remaining relatives are all "cousins," sometimes distinguished by *number* (second or third) or by *removal* (which marks generations away from Ego*). This is the only terminological system that sets the nuclear family apart from all other kin. If the Hawaiian system is like a layer cake made up of horizontal layers of kin, our system is like an onion with layers of kin surrounding a core (Fox 1967, 259).

Unilineal Patterns   The *Iroquois* pattern is sometimes known as *bifurcate merging,* because it merges Ego's mother's and father's parallel siblings with Ego's parents (Figure 9.9). This is so even though it is associated with unilineal, especially matrilineal, descent. The sex of the linking relatives is important in this system because the parents' parallel siblings are grouped together with the parents, whereas the cross siblings are set apart. This is repeated on the level of cousins. In a bilateral system, these distinctions

---

*A person's "first cousin once removed" can be one generation older or younger than that person. Your cousin Phil's daughter is your first cousin once removed, but so is your father's cousin Marlys. Her son, Marvin, is your second cousin.

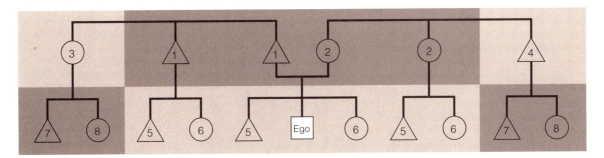

FIGURE 9.9 *Iroquois kinship terminology.*

would be meaningless, but in a unilineal system they mirror the lines of lineage membership. If Ego is a male, he will use one term to refer to all women of his matrilineage who are one generation older than he is. Their children are all referred to by another set of terms, one for males and one for females. Similarly, in his father's matrilineage, all men in the father's generation are referred to by one term. Their children are called by the same set of terms used for the cousins on the mother's side.

The pattern called *Crow* is a matrilineal system named after the Crow people of North America, but it is found in many other matrilineal societies, including the Trobriand Islands (Figure 9.10). The Crow system distinguishes the two matrilineages that are important to Ego: Ego's own, and that of Ego's father. As in the Iroquois system, the sex of the linking relative is important, and both parents and their same-sex siblings are grouped together. Their children—Ego's parallel cousins—are in the same category as Ego's siblings. The terms for cross cousins follow lineage membership, which is more important than generation. In Ego's own matrilineage, all the children of males are referred to by the same term regardless of their generation; in the Trobriand Islands, Ego's brother's daughter and mother's brother's daughter are called *latu* if Ego is male and *tabu* if Ego is female (Weiner 1979, 340). Their fathers are in Ego's matrilineage, but *they* are not. On the side of Ego's father's matrilineage, all male members are distin-

FIGURE 9.10 *Crow kinship terminology: members of Ego's matriline are represented in brown. Note the merging of generations and what follows as a result: all children of 3s are 1s and 3s; all children of 2s are 5s and 6s; all children of 5s are 9s and 10s; and all children of 4s and 6s are 7s and 8s—regardless of generation.*

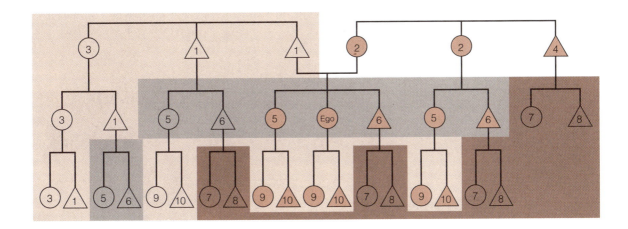

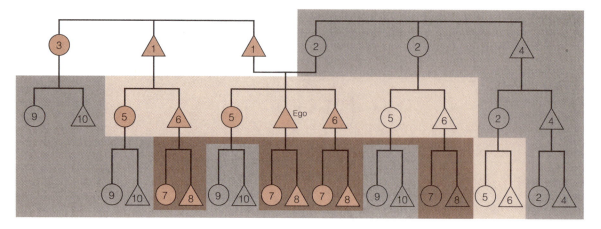

FIGURE 9.11 *Omaha kinship terminology: members of Ego's patriline are represented in brown. Note the merging of generations and what follows as a result: all children of 4s are 2s and 4s; all children of 1s are 5s and 6s; all children of 6s are 7s and 8s; and all children of 3s and 5s are 9s and 10s—regardless of generation.*

guished by one term and all female members by another, regardless of generational relationship to Ego.

Weiner (1979) suggests that three kinship pairs are crucial to the operation of the Trobriand system (and perhaps other matrilineal systems): mother and mother's brother, father and father's sister, and father and mother. Mother and mother's brother (*ina* and *kada*) are the basis for perpetuation of the matrilineage, but they must marry outsiders for that to happen. The "outsiders" are the father (*tama*) and father's sister (*tabu*), who must also cross the boundaries of their matrilineage in order to keep it alive. Finally, each father-mother pair (*tama* and *ina*) supplies the critical element for each matrilineage: children.

The system known as *Omaha* (Figure 9.11) is found among patrilineal peoples and represents the mirror image of the Crow system. All the members of Ego's mother's patrilineage are distinguished only by sex, and all the children of women in Ego's patrilineage are referred to by the same terms, one for males and one for females. Lineage membership again is more important than generation, a principle that is often hard for people living in bilateral kindreds to grasp.

FIGURE 9.12 *Sudanese kinship terminology: each person related to Ego is referred to by a separate term.*

Finally, in the *Sudanese* pattern, each related person is referred to by a separate term (Figure 9.12). This is a relatively rare terminological pattern. It is found in patrilineal societies, especially in northern Africa.

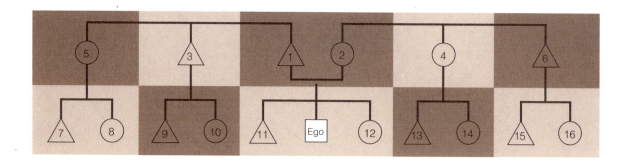

KINSHIP AND ALLIANCE THROUGH MARRIAGE

Any society divided into subgroups must devise a way to manage intergroup relations. It must also arrange for the continuation of those relations from one generation to the next. Societies based on kinship attempt to resolve these difficulties by connecting kinship with marriage. By promoting or *prescribing* certain kinds of marriage, such societies ensure the reproduction of their own memberships while establishing long-term alliances with other lineages.

Anthropologists find two major types of prescriptive marriage patterns in unilineal societies. One is a man's marriage with the father's sister's daughter. The more common is a man's marriage with the mother's brother's daughter.

In patrilineal societies, a "father's sister's daughter marriage" sets up a pattern of **direct exchange marriage.** In this pattern, a line that has received a wife from another line in one generation gives a wife back in the next generation. That is, if line A receives a wife for one of its members from line B in generation I, line A will provide a wife for a member of line B in generation II. But in generation I, the men of line B cannot marry women from line A. They must find wives from somewhere else, say line C. This pattern reverses itself in the next generation, when the obligation has been fulfilled and the original balance restored. This is called a *father's sister's daughter marriage* because, from a man's point of view, that woman is the prototypical spouse. However, any woman of the appropriate line is an eligible marriage partner for him. Before the marriage occurs, the men and women of the groom's line will negotiate with the men and women of the bride's line to determine the appropriate match.

A *mother's brother's daughter marriage* sets up a pattern of **asymmetrical exchange marriage.** Unlike direct exchange systems, this marriage pattern does not balance out after two generations. Instead, one line always gets wives from the same line and gives wives to a different line. Put another way, women always marry into the line their father's sisters married into, and men always find wives in the line their mothers came from. This pattern provides a permanent alliance among the lines involved. Here too the literal "mother's brother's daughter" is the prototypical wife for a man. However, she represents all women of the line from which the man's line gets wives. Notice that if a man in a matrilineal society actually does marry his mother's brother's daughter, he inherits doubly. He gets both what his mother's brother would give him and what his wife's father would give her husband. This is a wise strategy for conserving an inheritance.

Here, then, is the final piece in the lineage puzzle. People recognize certain *classes* of kin as potential marriage partners, and their kinship terminologies reflect this. Women whom anthropologists refer to as *mother's brother's daughters* form a category of women whom a man may marry. This is also the answer to the question that inevitably arises: "What happens if Ego doesn't have a mother's brother's daughter?" The answer is clear:

---

direct exchange marriage A line that receives a wife from a certain different line in one generation provides one back to the next generation (sometimes called a *father's sister's daughter marriage*).

asymmetrical exchange marriage A line that always gets wives from the same line and gives wives to a different line (sometimes called a *mother's brother's daughter marriage*).

Ego may not be looking for a literal mother's brother's daughter. He and the older members of his line are looking merely for a good match in the proper category.

INDIGENOUS VIEWS OF KINSHIP

Some anthropologists have studied how members of different cultures view their own kinship systems. For example, James Fernandez reports that the Fang use metaphors of the body to talk about lineage. (See EthnoProfile 7.5: Fang.) A generation is called a *joint*. The articulation of joints in the body from chest to extended fingers corresponds to the points of articulation in the generations of the lineage. "The clan itself was represented as rising in the chest or the heart . . . and as spreading out through one or both arms to its contemporary representatives, the fingertips" (1982, 88–89).

Evans-Pritchard noted that when drawing diagrams of related lineages on the ground, the Nuer sketched a number of lines running at angles from a common point (1940, 202). (See EthnoProfile 9.2: Nuer.) The Nuer saw their system as actual relations between groups of kin within local communities and not as a series of family trees. In their drawings, they placed lineages together on the basis of geography, showing which lineages lived near each other. For the Nuer, except for certain ritual situations, concrete spatial relations—who lived near whom—were more important than lineage theory.

Work by Marilyn Strathern on kinship and gender among the people of Mount Hagen, in Papua New Guinea, explores how Hageners use gender as a metaphor for thinking about different kinds of kinship attachments (1987, 274). (See EthnoProfile 10.6: Mount Hagen.) The person is essentially genderless. An adult is an autonomous, self-directed person whose commitment to the tasks of life reveals the operation of his or her will. But men and women vary, both in the tasks they perform and in their connection to their clans. When they marry, men stay in their home villages, whereas women move away from their clans. However, women who move away continue to carry their clan identity with them. This distinguishes a woman from her husband and members of his clan. As a result, women are seen as connected and disconnected at the same time.

Hageners' conceptions of kinship and gender are connected with prestige, wealth, and politics. For example, sources of male clan prestige include such items as shell valuables, pigs, and money. These items are thought to be "female" because, like a woman when she marries, they leave their place of origin and come into the clan from the outside, usually as gifts from the husband's clan when a woman of the clan marries. The significant feature of Strathern's analysis is the distinct way Hageners themselves use gender to understand kinship, politics, prestige, economics, and other social activity.

KINSHIP EXTENDED: LITERAL AND METAPHORICAL KIN

Kinship systems may appear to be fairly rigid sets of rules that people use to determine their relationships and hence their rights and obligations to one another. However, most kinship systems are flexible enough to accommodate many of the social dilemmas people must resolve in the real world.

Negotiation among the Ju/'hoansi (!Kung)

In presenting the Ju/'hoansi kinship system, Richard Lee demonstrates that "the principles of kinship constitute, not an invariant code of laws written in stone, but instead a whole series of codes, consistent enough to provide structure but open enough to be flexible." He adds: "I found the best way to look at [Ju/'hoansi] kinship is as a game, full of ambiguity and nuance" (1992b, 62). (See EthnoProfile 9.1: Ju/'hoansi [!Kung].)

The Ju/'hoansi have what seems to be a straightforward Eskimo system with alternating generations. Outside the nuclear core of the system, the same terms are used by Ego for kin of his or her generation, his or her grandparents' generation, and his or her grandchildren's generation. Likewise, the same terms are used for Ego's parent's generation and children's generation. These terms have behavioral correlates, which Lee calls "joking" and "avoidance." Anyone in Ego's own generation (except opposite-sex siblings) and in the grandparent's generation or the grandchildren's generation is joking kin. Anyone in Ego's parent's generation or children's generation is avoidance kin, as are Ego's same-sex siblings. Relatives in a joking relationship can be relaxed and affectionate and can speak using the familiar forms. In an avoidance relationship, however, respect and reserve are required, and the formal variety of the language must be used. Many of these relationships may be warm and friendly if the proper respect is shown in public; however, people in an avoidance relationship may not marry one another.

The "game," as Lee puts it, in the Ju/'hoansi system begins when a child is named. The Ju/'hoansi have very few names: 36 for men and 32 for women. Every child must be named for someone: a first-born son should get his father's father's name, and a first-born daughter should get her father's mother's name. Second-born children are supposed to be named after the mother's father and mother. Later children are to be named after the father's brothers and sisters and the mother's brothers and sisters. It is no wonder that the Ju/'hoansi invent a host of nicknames to distinguish among people who have the same name.

Ju/'hoansi naming practices impinge upon the kinship system because all people with the same name claim to be related. A man older than you with your name is called *!kun!a* ("old name") which is the same term used for *grandfather.* A man younger than you with your name is called *!kuna* ("young name"), the same term used for *grandson.* It does not matter how people are "really" related to others with the same name or even if they are related at all according to the literal kinship terminology; the name relationship takes precedence.

But the complications do not end here. By metaphorical extension, anyone with your father's name you call *father,* anyone with your wife's name you call *wife,* and so on. Worse, "a woman may not marry a man with her father's or brother's name, and a man may not marry a woman with his mother's or sister's name" (Lee 1992b, 74). Sometimes a man can marry a woman but because his name is the same as her father's she can't marry him! Further, you may not marry anyone with the name of one of your avoidance kin. As a result, parents who do not want their children to marry can almost always find a kinship-related reason to block the marriage. Once again, it does not matter what the exact genealogical relationships are.

The name relationship ties Ju/'hoansi society closer together by making close relatives out of distant ones. At the same time, it makes nonsense of the formal kinship system. How is this dilemma resolved? The Ju/'hoansi have a third component to their kinship system, the principle of *wi*, which operates as follows: Relative age is one of the few ways the Ju/'hoansi have of marking distinctions. Thus, in any relationship that can be described by more than one kin relationship, the older party chooses the kin term to be used. For example, a man may get married only to discover that his wife's aunt's husband has the same name he has. What will he and his wife's aunt call each other? According to the principle of *wi*, the aunt decides because she is older. If she calls him *nephew* (rather than *husband*), he knows he should call her *aunt*.

The principle of *wi* means that a person's involvement with the kinship system is continually changing over the course of his or her lifetime. For the first half of people's lives, they must accept the kin terms their elders choose, whether they understand why or not. After midlife, however, they begin to impose *wi* on their juniors. For the Ju/'hoansi, kinship connections are open to manipulation and negotiation rather than being rigidly imposed from the outside.

European American Kinship and New Reproductive Technologies

As Western medicine has developed new reproductive technologies—in vitro fertilization, sperm banks, and surrogate motherhood—the consequences are not only played out in legal and ethical debates, but they may also affect kinship systems. Marilyn Strathern (1992) has devoted some attention to exploring the effects of the new reproductive technologies on European American kinship. She observes that in the European American world, kinship is thought of as the social construction of natural facts, a logic that both combines and separates the social and natural worlds. Both worlds are necessary: European Americans recognize kin related by blood and those by marriage but also believe that the process—procreation—that brings kin into existence is part of nature. Within the kinship domain, individual kin roles repeat this overlap: an unambiguous kinsperson is both related by blood and is one whose relationship is acknowledged in forms of interpersonal interaction. "A mother both gives birth and nurtures her child; you share genes with your mother's sister, but she enters your life as an aunt because of the visits and presents" (19).

Previously, the term "natural parent" referred to someone who did not take on the social role of parent (Figure 9.13). Today, "natural parent" is increasingly used to refer to people who in the past would have been referred to as "social parents" or just "parents"—that is, to people who were both progenitors and caregivers—while the term "social parent" is increasingly used to refer to people who are not biologically responsible for the children they rear. Strathern suggests that these terms have shifted in meaning because, with the development of assisted reproduction, a third term has been introduced: the term "biological parent" is being applied to donors of sperm or ova, surrogate mothers, and the progenitors of children placed for adoption. As a result, the term "social parent" no longer applies to the positively viewed category of progenitor and caregiver and is being used for the less positively viewed category of parent who is unable to procreate. "So the 'natural' parent of the future . . . may well turn out to be the

FIGURE 9.13 *In-vitro fertilization, one of the new reproductive technologies, is already having an effect on what it means to be a "natural" parent. All of these babies are the result of in-vitro fertilization.*

one for whom no special techniques are involved and the one on whose behalf no special legislation is required" (Strathern 1992, 20). In that case it would be the natural, rather than the social, parent who combined both biological and legal attributes.

This may not be just a linguistic change. Strathern notes that medical technology is giving assistance to the natural facts of procreation. Legislation setting out the rights, obligations, and legal status of persons using the new reproductive technologies is transforming the social facts of kin recognition and relatedness and thus eliminating the distinctiveness of kinship as a social domain. "The rooting of social relations in natural facts traditionally served to impart a certain quality to one significant dimension of kin relations. For all that one exercised choice, it was also the case that these relations were at base non-negotiable" (Strathern 1992, 28). You might choose never to see your siblings again, but they could never stop being your siblings. Ties of kinship in general stand for what is unalterable in a person's social world by contrast to what is open to change. Yet the new reproductive technologies make clear that nothing is unalterable: even the world of natural facts is subject to social intervention. As Strathern concludes, "Whether or not all this is a good thing is uncertain. What is certain is that it will not be without consequence for the way people think about one another" (28).

Compadrazgo in Latin America

A metaphorical extension of kinship is found in the Latin American Roman Catholic practice of ritual coparenthood. This practice, which is also found in southern Europe, is called **compadrazgo.** The baptism of a child requires the presence of a godmother and a godfather as sponsors. By participating in this ritual, the sponsors become the ritual coparents of the child. In Latin America, godparents are expected to take an active interest in their godchildren and to help them wherever possible. However, the more important relationship is between the godparents and the parents. They become *compadres* ("coparents"), and they are expected to behave toward each other in new ways.

Although the godparents are sometimes already kin, a couple usually chooses godparents whose social standing is higher than their own. Frequently, the godparents are the owners of the land the parents farm or of the factory where they work. The connection of ritual coparenthood changes the social relationship of people who initially are unequal strangers. These people become ritual kin. Although their relationship is still unequal, it is now personalized, friendlier, more open. The parents will support the godparents when that support is needed (politically, for example) and the godparents will do favors for the parents. They even call each other *compadre* rather than, say, "Señor López" and "José."

Catherine Allen notes that the bonds of *compadrazgo,* in combination with marriage alliances and kinship, "form constellations of mutual obligation and dependence that shift with time as new *compadrazgo* relationships are formed, young relatives come of age, and old bonds fall into disuse through death or quarreling. Like kin ties, bonds of *compadrazgo* can become as much a burden as an asset, and like kin ties they can be ignored or honored in the breach" (1988, 90).

Ie in Contemporary Japan

In a study that focuses on a small family-owned factory in Japan, Dorinne Kondo (1990) discusses the *ie,* a kinshiplike organization. (See EthnoProfile 9.3: Japan.) *Ie* is sometimes translated as "household." In the past, prototypical households were highly organized, task-performance units based on work; they were sites of identity formation that commanded their members' loyalty and love. Today, the *ie* is a unit of production and/or consumption, encompassing the roles of corporation, enterprise, and household. The *ie* is not simply a kinship unit based on blood relationship; it is a corporate group based on social and economic ties. The *ie* holds property (land, a reputation, an art, and so on), it can serve primary religious functions, and it provides the primary form of social welfare in Japan, including care of the aged and infirm. The *ie* is better understood as a "task performance unit" in which the core of the group may be composed of people not necessarily related biologically.

Ie organization is based on a set of positions rather than on a set of kinship relations. In any given generation, there are only two people in permanent positions in the *ie*—a married couple. "They are, so to speak, the trustees of the corporation, who will take care of the family property and fortunes during the period of their tenure. They should do their best to ensure the survival and, ideally, the increasing prosperity of their *ie,*

EthnoProfile 9.3 • **JAPAN**

REGION: Northeastern Asia

NATION: Japan

POPULATION: 118,000,000

ENVIRONMENT: Temperate climate

POLITICAL ORGANIZATION: Highly urbanized nation-state

FOR MORE INFORMATION: Kondo, Dorinne. 1990. *Crafting selves.* Chicago: University of Chicago Press.

which they can then hand over to their successors" (Kondo 1992, 122). But of the children of the married couple, only one, along with his or her spouse, can be the successors. Thus, the household of birth may not be the household a person joins as a permanent member.

The difference between *ie* and true kinship-based groups emerges more clearly when examining succession to the permanent positions in the *ie*. Because the *ie* is a corporate group, like the unilineages examined earlier in this chapter, the overriding concern is the continuity of the group over time. Thus, two permanent *ie* members must be recruited in each generation. Kinship, in the sense of blood relationship, is only one of these recruitment mechanisms. The person(s) who take over the *ie* may in fact be totally unrelated by blood. Ideally, people would prefer not to take this latter course, but they may choose to do so if the continuity of the *ie* is sufficiently critical to them.

People prefer *primogeniture,* succession by the eldest son, but Kondo notes that the system of succession is composed of ranked preferences that can be modified according to economic and social conditions: "the presence of appropriate successors; their competence; the relationships with other households one may want to create through marriage, and so on" (1990, 125). Because the *ie* requires two permanent members, there are three strategies for recruitment: (1) the son of the married couple marries a woman from an out-group, the usual version of "marriage"; (2) the daughter of the married couple marries a man from an out-group, the so-called *adopted bridegroom;* (3) both the man and woman come from an out-group, the so-called *fufu yoshi,* or adoption of a married couple. The forms of adoptive marriage emphasize the desire for *ie* continuity. Unlike in the United States, where adoption generally takes place at a young age, in Japan, "adop-

compadrazgo Ritual coparenthood in Latin America and Spain, established through the Roman Catholic practice of having godparents for children.

EthnoProfile 9.4 • **ILONGOT**

REGION: Oceania

NATION: Philippines (Luzon)

POPULATION: 3,500 (1960s)

ENVIRONMENT: Lush, well-watered, relatively in-accessible highlands

LIVELIHOOD: Hunting and gardening

POLITICAL ORGANIZATION: Traditionally, loosely structured groups; today, part of a modern nation-state

FOR MORE INFORMATION: Rosaldo, Renato. 1980. *Ilongot headhunting, 1883–1974: A study in society and history.* Stanford: Stanford University Press.

tion" usually occurs in adulthood as a form of marriage. Indeed, the second most common form of marriage/succession is bringing in a man from the outside to marry into the family and take over the family name and, usually, the family business.

Kinship as Metaphor

Kinship offers an elaborate and nuanced set of categories for placing people in definite relationships with one another. Consequently, it can also be an apt and all-encompassing metaphor for dealing with outsiders (such as visiting ethnographers) who have no place in the literal kinship system. This metaphoric kinship is termed *fictive kinship* by anthropologists. The possibility of turning strangers into fictive kin demonstrates how kinship is culturally constructed. The idiom of mating and birth can be used to organize human interdependence quite apart from any biological "facts."

KINSHIP AND PRACTICE

Formal kinship systems are not straitjackets; rather, they provide a flexible series of opportunities for people to choose how to deal with others. They also provide multiple social vectors along which relations of alliance, association, mutual support, opposition, and hatred may develop.

The Ilongot of the Philippines illustrate this point. (See EthnoProfile 9.4: Ilongot.) Renato Rosaldo (1980) shows that Ilongot marriage and alliance decisions are not the product of a set of abstract, elegant rules. Instead, they emerge out of the social activities and historical context of Ilongot life. The Ilongot world is constantly changing. The nature of the relationships Ilongot have with one another and their feelings about those relationships are the result of previous alliances with other kin groups. Past interactions include head-hunting raids they have participated in together or been victims of, the shared background of colonialism (first Spanish and then American), and the shared experience of World War II and the Japanese army's flight into the Ilongot hills. More recently, Ilongot have had to cope with martial law in the Philippines and the penetration of soldiers into the Ilongot area, the arrival of members of other Philippine ethnic groups who have settled on the fringes of the Ilongot homeland, and the influence of New Tribes Missionaries.

All of these experiences are alive in the Ilongot mind. Rosaldo is able to show how they influence Ilongot decisions concerning feuding, head-hunting, marriage, and alliance. A dense web of affinal and **consanguineal** (connections through descent or "blood") ties links members of Ilongot groups to virtually any other person in Ilongot society. The Ilongot thus face opportunities as well as potential barriers as they pursue their interests: sometimes they get caught in the middle of conflicts because they are linked to all parties involved; at other times, their contradictory loyalties can bring peace to the feuding parties—but this is by no means guaranteed.

Rosaldo tells of a man named Lakay who was a member of both the Peknar and Pasigiyan groups of Ilongot. In 1924, the younger brother of a man named Pangpang beheaded a Pasigiyan woman who was Lakay's mother's sister's daughter (but whom he called by the term *sister*). Lakay was enraged and wanted to behead Pangpang's younger brother. Unfortunately, they were related to each other by the marriage of Lakay's maternal grandmother to a man of Pangpang's group, the Rumyads. Lakay could not resolve these conflicting loyalties. His solution was to organize a raid in which Peknars and Rumyads settled their differences by attacking a third group toward which both groups had a mutual animosity.

No kinship rules offer tried-and-true formulas for resolving such dilemmas. Resolutions are worked out in the context of the situations. As Rosaldo puts it, "In reflecting upon their own social order, the Ilongots themselves confirm that it is ever improvised anew, as they follow one another along shifting paths, at times gathering together and at times dispersing" (1980, 289). These tensions, decisions, and improvisations result in a social order that is flexible and changes from generation to generation. Contrary to stereotype, the Ilongot do not expect children to follow in their parents' footsteps.

In his work on the Iteso of Kenya, Ivan Karp discusses the options for action that a kinship system can provide (principally Karp 1978). (See EthnoProfile 9.5: Iteso.) Karp notes that among the Iteso, affinal and consanguineal kin have very different and even contradictory rights and obligations to one another. Two people who share both a link through marriage and a link through patrilineal descent must choose which tie to emphasize; it is often the affinal tie rather than the consanguineal tie. However, they may be ambivalent about the choice. Close members of a patrilineage often quarrel and may be ritually dangerous to one another, but they will—indeed, must—help one another in ritual and conflict situations. By contrast, affinal relatives are amiable and helpful but cannot be counted on in times of crisis.

consanguineal Kinship connections based on descent.

EthnoProfile 9.5 • **ITESO**

REGION: Eastern Africa

NATIONS: Kenya and Uganda

POPULATION: 150,000 in Kenya; 600,000 in Uganda (1970s)

ENVIRONMENT: High-rainfall savanna and hills

LIVELIHOOD: Agriculture, both subsistence and cash

POLITICAL ORGANIZATION: Traditionally, chiefs, subchiefs, headmen; today, part of modern nation-states

FOR MORE INFORMATION: Karp, Ivan. 1978. *Fields of change among the Iteso of Kenya.* London: Routledge and Kegan Paul.

Karp recounts a story that serves as an example. An Iteso man who was widowed and had remarried moved away from his lineage and was living with his maternal kin. His daughters by his first marriage were living with their mother's brother. One daughter was bitten by a snake and died. Karp was asked to help bring the body back to her father's house for burial. The father went to all his neighbors—his maternal kin—for help in burying her, but none would help. Only at the last moment did some members of his patrilineage arrive to help with the burial. This story illustrates the drawbacks associated with living apart from one's close lineage mates. The father had left himself open to a lack of support in a crisis by cutting himself off from his lineage and choosing to live with his maternal kin. As with the Ilongot, the Iteso kinship system provides no rule for resolving conflicting kinship loyalties to maternal and paternal kin. In fact, the system almost ensures the creation of overlapping loyalties that are difficult to resolve.

KINSHIP: A FRAMEWORK FOR INTERPRETING LIFE

Kinship may seem awesomely complete and utterly basic to the life of the societies just described; however, it varies in importance between societies and even between subgroups within the same society. In addition, the Nuer, the Ju/'hoansi, the Trobriand Islanders, and others have demonstrated that kinship categories can also be used metaphorically. To use kinship in this way is to experience one kind of thing—the division of labor, religion, political struggle, social order—in terms of another phenomenon that is better understood. Kinship is built on an interpretation of mating and birth. But our understanding of these basic human experiences is shaped by the principles of our kinship system. Kinship is "a variety of social idiom, a way of talking about and understanding, and thus of shaping, some aspects of social life" (Geertz and Geertz 1975, 169). There is more to life than kinship, but kinship provides one holistic framework for interpreting life.

KEY TERMS

kinship	patrilineage	bifurcation
marriage	matrilineage	parallel cousins
descent	lineages	cross cousins
sex	clan	direct exchange marriage
gender	segmentary opposition	asymmetrical exchange
bilateral descent	bridewealth	marriage
unilineal descent	affinity	*compadrazgo*
bilateral kindred	collaterality	consanguineal

CHAPTER SUMMARY

1. Human life is group life; we depend upon one another to survive. The idiom of kinship is one way all societies organize this interdependence. Kinship relations are based on, but not reducible to, the universal experiences of mating and birth. Kinship principles construct a coherent cultural framework by defining groups, locating people within those groups, and positioning people and groups in relation to one another in space and time. Although female-male duality is basic to kinship, many societies have developed supernumerary sexes and/or genders. Kinship systems help societies maintain social order without central government.

2. Kinship systems are selective. Matrilineal societies emphasize that women bear children and trace descent through women. Patrilineal societies emphasize that men impregnate.women and trace descent through men. Both of these contradictory ways of tracing descent can be understood in terms of the common human experiences of mating and birth.

3. Descent links members of different generations with one another. Bilateral descent results in the formation of groups called *kindreds*. Unilineal descent results in the formation of groups called *lineages*. Unlike kindreds, lineages are corporate groups. Lineages control important property, such as land, that collectively belongs to their members. The language of lineage is the idiom of political discussion, and lineage relationships are of political significance.

4. Kinship terminologies pay attention to certain attributes of people that are then used to define different classes of kin. The attributes most often recognized include generation, sex, affinity, collaterality, bifurcation, relative age, and the sex of the linking relative.

5. Anthropologists recognize six basic terminological systems according to their patterns of classifying cousins. These systems are named after societies that represent the prototype of each pattern: Hawaiian, Eskimo, Iroquois, Crow, Omaha, and Sudanese. The first two are found in association with bilateral descent systems, and the remaining four are found in association with unilineal descent.

6. By prescribing certain kinds of marriage, lineages are able to establish long-term alliances with one another. Two major types of prescriptive marriage patterns in

unilineal societies are (1) a father's sister's daughter marriage (which sets up a pattern of direct exchange marriage) and (2) a mother's brother's daughter marriage (which sets up a pattern of asymmetrical exchange marriage).

7. Alongside the literal kinship system defined in the terminology, there often exist relationships linking metaphorical kin. The opportunity to create metaphorical links with strangers adds flexibility to social relations in societies organized in terms of kinship. At the same time, the possibility of turning strangers into fictive kin demonstrates how kinship is a cultural construction that employs the idiom of mating and birth to organize human interdependence quite apart from the biological facts.

SUGGESTED READINGS

Bohannan, Paul, and John Middleton. 1968. *Kinship and social organization.* New York: Natural History Press. *A collection of important, classic articles from a wide range of theoretical perspectives.*

Collier, Jane, and Sylvia Yanagisako. 1987. *Gender and kinship: Essays toward a unified analysis.* Stanford: Stanford University Press. *An important collection of work on the connections of gender and kinship.*

Ginsburg, Faye D. 1989. *Contested lives: The abortion debate in an American community.* Berkeley: University of California Press. *A study of gender and procreation in the context of the abortion debate in Fargo, North Dakota, in the 1980s.*

Graburn, Nelson. 1971. *Readings in kinship and social structure.* New York: Harper and Row. *Another collection of essays, this one covering a wider range of topics and with little overlap.*

Weiner, Annette. 1979. Trobriand kinship from another view: The reproductive power of women and men. *Man* 14 (2): 328–48. *An important article, worthwhile reading.*

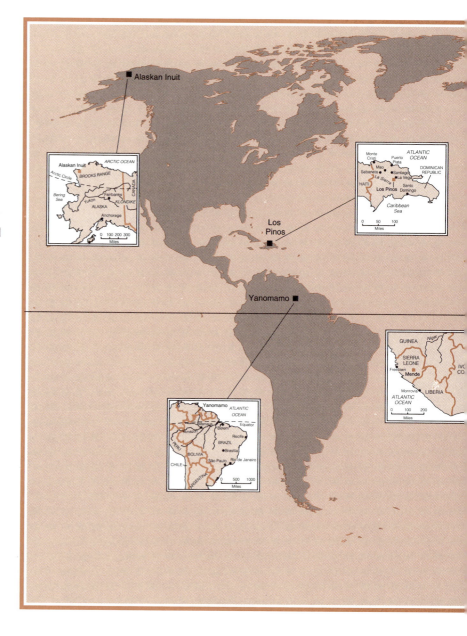

Marriage and the Family

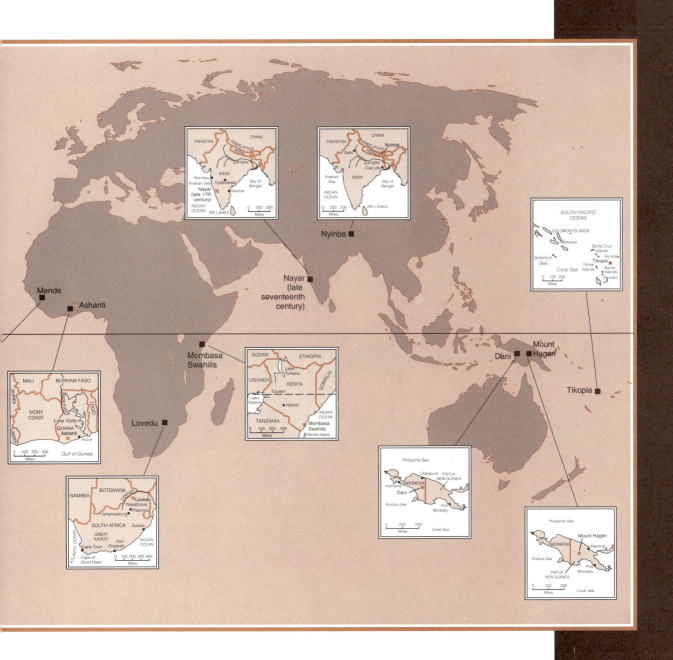

*t*he distinguished Indian novelist R. K. Narayan (b. 1908) writes in his autobiography about falling in love and getting married.

. . . In July 1933, I had gone to Coimbatore, escorting my elder sister, and then stayed on in her house. There was no reason why I should ever hurry away from one place to another. I was a free-lance writer and I could work wherever I might be at a particular time. One day, I saw a girl drawing water from the street-tap and immediately fell in love with her. Of course, I could not talk to her. I learned later that she had not even noticed me passing and repassing in front of her while she waited to fill the brass vessels. I craved to get a clear, fixed, mental impression of her features, but I was handicapped by the time factor, as she would be available for staring at only until her vessels filled, when she would carry them off, and not come out again until the next water-filling time. I could not really stand and stare; whatever impression I had of her would be through a side-glance while passing the tap. I suffered from a continually melting vision. The only thing I was certain of was that I loved her, and I suffered the agonies of restraint imposed by the social conditions in which I lived. The tall headmaster, her father, was a friend of the family and often dropped in for a chat with the elders at home while on his way to the school, which was at a corner of our street. The headmaster, headmaster's daughter, and the school were all within geographical reach and hailing distance, but the restraint imposed by the social code created barriers. I attempted to overcome them by befriending the headmaster. He was a booklover and interested in literary matters, and we found many common subjects for talk. We got into the habit of meeting at his school after the school-hours and discussing the world, seated comfortably on a cool granite *pyol* in front of a little shrine of Ganesha in the school compound. One memorable evening, when the stars had come out, I interrupted some talk we were having on political matters to make a bold, blunt announcement of my affection for his daughter. He was taken aback, but did not show it. In answer to my proposal, he just turned to the god in the shrine and shut his eyes in prayer. No one in our social condition could dare to proceed in the manner I had done. There were formalities to be observed, and any talk for a marriage proposal could proceed only between the elders of the families. What I had done was unheard of. But the headmaster was sporting enough not to shut me up immediately. Our families were known to each other, and the class, community, and caste requirements were all right. He just said, "if God wills it," and left it at that. He also said, "Marriages are made in Heaven, and who are we to say Yes or No?" After this he explained the difficulties. His wife and womenfolk at home were to be consulted, and my parents had to approve, and so on and so forth, and then the matching of the horoscopes—this last became a great hurdle at the end. . . .

What really mattered was not my economic outlook, but my stars. My father-in-law, himself an adept at the study of horoscopes, had consultations with one or two other experts and came to the conclusion that my horoscope and the girl's were incompatible. My horoscope had the Seventh House occupied by Mars, the Seventh House being the one that indicated . . . nothing but disaster unless the partner's horoscope also contained the same flaw, a case in which two wrongs make one right. . . .

In spite of all these fluctuations and hurdles, my marriage came off in a few months, celebrated with all the pomp, show, festivity, exchange of gifts, and the overcrowding, that my parents desired and expected.

Soon after my marriage, my father became bed-ridden with a paralytic stroke, and most of my mother's time was spent at his side upstairs. The new entrant into the family, my wife Rajam, was her deputy downstairs, managing my three younger brothers, who were still at school, a cook in the kitchen, a general servant, and a gigantic black-and-white Great Dane acquired by my elder brother, who was a dog-lover. She kept an eye on the stores, replenishing the food-stuffs and guarding them from being squandered or stolen by the cook. Rajam was less than twenty, but managed the housekeeping expertly and earned my mother's praise. She got on excellently with my brothers. This was one advantage of a joint family system—one had plenty of company at home. . . . (1974, 106–10)

Narayan had fallen in love, gotten married, and set up housekeeping with his wife. These are familiar phases in the relationship of a man and a woman, yet the details of his description seem exotic to a North American, perhaps even extraordinary. Narayan's essay illustrates how the patterns of courtship, marriage, and housekeeping in India engage people in the wider patterns of Indian life. They channel emotion and economic activity. They also link previously unrelated people while binding individuals firmly to groups. One individual, Narayan, fell in love with and married another individual, Rajam. But they could never have become a married couple without knowing how to maneuver within the cultural patterns that shaped their society. Neither could they have gotten married without the active intervention of the wider social groups to which they belonged—specifically, their families.

Human life is indeed group life, and in Chapter 9, we saw some of the ways human beings classify themselves and others. *Marriage* and the *family* are two concepts anthropologists use to describe how mating and birth are understood and organized in different societies.

TOWARD A DEFINITION OF MARRIAGE?

Each culture has its own definition of marriage, yet nowhere is *marriage* synonymous with *mating*. Marriage involves a change in the social position of two people and affects the social position of their offspring.

Some criteria for defining marriage are common in most societies; we will concentrate on these criteria in our own definition of marriage. A prototypical **marriage** (1) involves a man and a woman and (2) stipulates the degree of sexual access the married partners may have to each other, ranging from exclusive to preferential sexual access. It also (3) establishes the legitimacy of children born to the wife, and (4) creates relationships between the kin of the wife and the kin of the husband.

If a prototypical marriage involves a man and a woman, however, what are we to make of the following cases? Each offers an alternative way of understanding the combination of features that define appropriate unions in a particular society. Although the people who are allowed to marry may vary, the role of legitimacy in maintaining patterns of descent over generations does not.

Nuer Woman Marriage

Among the Nuer, as E. E. Evans-Pritchard observed during his fieldwork in the 1920s, a woman could marry another woman and become the "father" of the children the wife bore. (See EthnoProfile 9.2: Nuer.) This practice, which appears in some other parts of Africa, involved a distinction between pater and genitor: the *pater* was the legal "father" of a child; the *genitor* was the man who impregnated the child's mother. Put another way, "father" is a *gender* role that can be separated from the biological *sex* of the person who fills it.

The female husband had to have some cattle of her own to use for bridewealth payments to the wife's lineage. Once the bridewealth had been paid, the marriage was established. The female husband then got a male kinsman, friend, or neighbor to impregnate the wife and to help with certain tasks around the homestead that the Nuer believed could be done only by men.

Generally, Evans-Pritchard (1951) noted, a female husband was unable to have children herself, "and for this reason counts in some respects as a man." In other words, the Nuer metaphorically labeled such a woman as a near-man. Indeed, she played the social role of a man. She could marry several wives if she was wealthy. She could demand damage payment if those wives engaged in sexual activity without her consent. She was the pater of her wives' children. On the marriage of her daughters, she received the portion of the bridewealth that traditionally went to the father. Her brothers and sisters received the portions of the bridewealth that were supposed to go to the father's side. Her children were named after her, as though she were a man, and they addressed her as *Father.* She administered her compound and her herds as a male head of household would, and she was treated by her wives and children with the same deference shown to a male husband and father.

Nuer Ghost Marriage

Another unusual example of the split between sex and the legal characteristics of marriage also comes from the Nuer. (See EthnoProfile 9.2: Nuer.) A common feature of Nuer social life was what Evans-Pritchard called the *ghost marriage*. The Nuer believed that a man who died without male heirs left an unhappy and angry spirit who might trouble his living kin. The spirit was angry because a basic obligation of Nuer kinship was for a man to be remembered through and by his sons: his name had to be continued in his lineage. To appease the angry spirit, a kinsman of the dead man—a brother or a brother's son—would often marry a woman "to his name." Bridewealth cattle were paid in the name of the dead man to the patrilineage of a woman. She was then married to the ghost but resided with his living kinsman. In the marriage ceremonies and afterwards, this kinsman acted as though he were the true husband. The children of the union were referred to as though they were the kinsman's—but officially they were not. His children were considered children of the ghost husband. As the children got older, the name of their ghost father became increasingly important to them. The ghost father's name, not his stand-in's name, would be remembered in the history of the lineage.

In this case, biological paternity was divorced from legitimacy. But for the Nuer, legitimacy was a central attribute of marriage. The essential feature of the ghost marriage was the provision of children to the ghost husband's lineage. The social union between the ghost and the woman took precedence over the sexual union between the ghost's surrogate and the woman.

Ghost marriage served to perpetuate social patterns. Although it was common for a man to marry a wife "to his kinsman's name" before he himself married, it became difficult, if not impossible, for him to marry later in his own right. His relatives would tell him he was "already married" and that he should allow his younger brothers to use cattle from the family herd so they could marry. Even if he eventually accumulated enough cattle to afford to marry, he would feel that those cattle should provide the bridewealth for the sons he had raised for his dead kinsman. When he died, he died childless because the children he had raised were legally the children of the ghost. He was then an angry spirit, and someone else (in fact, one of the sons he had raised for the ghost) had to marry a wife to *his* name. Thus the pattern continued.

MARRIAGE AS A SOCIAL PROCESS

Marriages set up new relationships between the kin of the husband and the kin of the wife. These are called **affinal** relationships (based on *affinity*—relationships created via marriage) and contrast with **consanguineal** (or "blood") relationships. The two issues of affinity and consanguinity are centrally associated with the definition of marriage and the formation of social groups. Mating alone does not create in-laws, nor does it set up a way of locating the offspring in space and time as members of a particular social group. Marriage, however, does both.

Socially, marriage has four characteristics: (1) it transforms the status of the participants; (2) it alters the relationships among the kin of each party; (3) it perpetuates social

---

marriage An institution that prototypically involves a man and a woman, transforms the status of the participants, carries implications about permitted sex- ual access, gives the offspring a position in society, and establishes connections between the kin of the husband and the kin of the wife.

affinal Kinship connections through marriage, or affinity.
consanguineal Kinship connections based on descent.

patterns through the production of offspring, who also have certain kinds of rights and obligations (see Karp 1986); and (4) it is always symbolically marked in some way, such as an elaborate wedding or simply the appearance of a husband and wife seated one morning outside her hut. Marriage marks a major transformation of social position: two individuals become one married couple. In an important way, the third party to any wedding—the rest of the community—must acknowledge the legitimacy of the new union.

Every society has ways of matching the right groom with the right bride. Sometimes marriages must be contracted within a particular social group, a marriage pattern called **endogamy.** In other cases, marriage partners must be found outside a particular group, a marriage pattern called **exogamy.** In Nuer society, for example, a person had to marry outside his or her lineage. Even in North American society, we prefer people to marry within the bounds of certain groups. We are told to marry "our own kind," which usually means our own ethnic or racial group, religious group, or social class. In all societies, some close kin are off limits as spouses or as sexual partners. This exogamous pattern is known as the *incest taboo.*

Patterns of Residence after Marriage

Once married, a couple must live somewhere. There are four major patterns of post-marital residence. Most familiar to Americans is **neolocal** residence, in which the new couple sets up an independent household at a place of their own choosing. Neolocal residence tends to be found in societies that are more or less atomistic in their social organization, especially those with Eskimo kinship systems.

When the married couple lives with (or near) the husband's father's family, it is called **patrilocal** residence, the most common residence pattern in the contemporary world. It produces a characteristic social grouping of related men: a man, his brothers, and their sons, along with in-marrying wives, all live and work together. This pattern is common in both herding and farming societies; some anthropologists argue that survival in such societies depends on activities that are best carried out by groups of men who have worked together all their lives.

When the married couple lives with (or near) the family in which the wife was raised, it is called **matrilocal** residence, which is usually found in association with matrilineal kinship systems. Here, the core of the social group consists of a woman, her sisters, and their daughters, together with in-marrying men. This pattern is most common among horticultural groups.

Less common, but also found in matrilineal societies, is the pattern known as **avunculocal** residence. Here, the married couple lives with (or near) the husband's mother's brother. The most significant man in a boy's matrilineage is his mother's brother, from whom he will inherit. Avunculocal residence emphasizes this relationship.

There are other, even less common patterns of residence. In *ambilocal* residence, the couple shifts residence, living first with the family of one spouse and later with the family of the other spouse. At some point, the couple usually has to choose which family they want to affiliate with permanently. *Duolocal* residence is found where lineage membership is so important that husbands and wives continue to live with their own lineages even after they are married. The Ashanti of Ghana observe duolocal residence. (See EthnoProfile 10.5: Ashanti.) We will see later how this residence pattern affects other aspects of Ashanti social and cultural life.

Single and Plural Spouses

The number of spouses a person may have varies cross-culturally. Anthropologists distinguish, first of all, between a form of marriage that allows a person only one spouse (**monogamy**) and another that allows several spouses (**polygamy**). Within the category of polygamy are two subcategories: **polygyny**, or multiple wives, and **polyandry**, or multiple husbands. Most societies in the world permit polygyny.

Monogamy Monogamy is the only legal spousal pattern of the United States and most industrialized nations. (Indeed, in 1896, a condition of statehood for the territory of Utah was the abolition of polygyny, which had been practiced by Mormon settlers for nearly 50 years.) There are variations in the number of times a monogamous person can be married. Before the twentieth century, people in western European societies could marry only once unless death intervened. Today, some observers suggest that we practice *serial monogamy;* we may be married to several different people but only one at a time.

Polygyny Polygynous societies vary in the number of wives a man may have. Islam permits a man to have as many as four wives but only on the condition that he can support them equally. Other polygynous societies have no limit on the number of wives a man may marry. Nevertheless, not every man can be polygynous. There is a clear demographic problem: for every man with two wives, there is one man without a wife. Men can wait until they are older to marry and women can marry very young, but this imbalance cannot be eliminated. Polygyny is also expensive, for a husband must support all his wives as well as their children (Figure 10.1).

Polyandry Polyandry is the rarest of the three marriage forms. In some polyandrous societies, a woman may marry several brothers. In others, she may marry men who are not related to each other and who all will live together in a single household. Sometimes a woman is allowed to marry several men who are not related, but she will live only with

---

endogamy Marriage within a defined social group.

exogamy Marriage outside a defined social group.

neolocal A postmarital residence pattern in which a married couple sets up an independent household at a place of their own choosing.

patrilocal A postmarital residence pattern in which a married couple lives with (or near) the husband's father.

matrilocal A postmarital residence pattern in which a married couple lives with (or near) the wife's mother.

avunculocal A postmarital residence pattern in which a married couple lives with (or near) the husband's mother's brother (from *avuncular,* "of uncles").

monogamy A marriage pattern in which a person may be married to only one spouse at a time.

polygamy A marriage pattern in which a person may be married to more than one spouse at a time.

polygyny A marriage pattern in which a man may be married to more than one wife simultaneously.

polyandry A marriage pattern in which a woman may be married to more than one husband simultaneously.

FIGURE 10.1 *The wives and children of a polygynous family.*

the one she most recently married. Polyandry traditionally has gotten short shrift in anthropology and has sometimes been dismissed as an oddity; however recent studies have challenged our traditional understanding of polyandry and have shed new light on the dynamics of polygyny and monogamy.

Polyandry, Sexuality, and the Reproductive Capacity of Women

Different marriage patterns reflect significant variation in the social definition of male and female sexuality. Monogamy and polygyny are in some ways similar because both are concerned with controlling women's sexuality while giving men freer rein. Even in monogamous societies, men (but not women) are often expected to have extramarital sexual adventures. Polyandry is worth a closer look; it differs from polygyny or monogamy in instructive ways.

Polyandry is found in three major regions of the world: Tibet and Nepal, southern India and Sri Lanka, and northern Nigeria and northern Cameroon. The forms of polyandry in these areas are different, but all involve women with several husbands.

Fraternal Polyandry The traditional anthropological prototype of polyandry has been found among some groups in Nepal and Tibet, where a group of brothers marry one woman. This is known as *fraternal polyandry*. During one wedding, one brother, usually the oldest, serves as the groom. All brothers (including those yet to be born to the husbands' parents) are married by this wedding, which establishes public recognition of the marriage. The wife and her husbands live together, usually patrilocally. All brothers have equal sexual access to the wife, and all act as fathers to the children. In

292

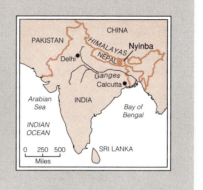

EthnoProfile 10.1 • **NYINBA**

REGION: Central Asia

NATION: Nepal

POPULATION: 1,200

ENVIRONMENT: Valleys

LIVELIHOOD: Agriculture, herding

POLITICAL ORGANIZATION: Traditionally, head-men; today, part of a modern nation-state

FOR MORE INFORMATION: Levine, Nancy. 1988. *The dynamics of polyandry: Kinship, domesticity, and population on the Tibetan border.* Chicago: University of Chicago Press.

some cases—notably among the Nyinba of Nepal (Levine 1980, 1988)—one of the brothers is always recognized as the genitor of each child. (See EthnoProfile 10.1: Nyinba.) In other cases, all the brothers are considered jointly as the father, without distinguishing the identity of the genitor.

Contrary to the Western male stereotype, there appears to be no sexual jealousy among the men, and the brothers have a strong sense of solidarity with one another. Levine (1988) emphasizes this point for the Nyinba. If the wife proves sterile, the brothers may marry another woman in hopes that she may be fertile. As with the first wife, all brothers will have equal sexual access to the new wife and will be treated as fathers by her children. In societies that practice fraternal polyandry, marrying sisters (or *sororal polygyny*) may be preferred or permitted. In this system, a group of brothers could marry a group of sisters.

According to Levine, Nyinba polyandry is reinforced by a variety of cultural beliefs and practices (1988, 158ff.). First, it has a special cultural value. Nyinba legendary ancestors are polyandrous, and they are praised for the harmony of their family life. Second, the solidarity of brothers is a central kinship ideal. Third, the corporate, landholding household, central to Nyinba life, presupposes polyandry. Fourth, the structure of Nyinba villages presupposes a limited number of households, and polyandry is highly effective in checking the proliferation of households. Finally, a household's political position and economic viability increase when its resources are concentrated.

Associated Polyandry   A second form of polyandry, known as *associated polyandry*, refers to any system in which polyandry is open to men who are not necessarily brothers (Levine and Sangree 1980). There is some evidence that associated polyandry was an acceptable marriage variant in parts of the Pacific and among some indigenous peoples of North and South America. The best-described form of associated polyandry, however, is from Sri Lanka. (See EthnoProfile 7.9: Sinhalese.) Among the Sinhalese of Sri Lanka, a woman may marry two, but rarely more than two, men. Unlike fraternal polyandry, which begins as a joint venture, Sinhalese associated polyandry begins monogamously.

EthnoProfile 10.2 • **NAYAR (LATE SEVENTEENTH CENTURY)**

REGION: Southern Asia

NATION: India (Kerala State)

POPULATION: About 30,000 to 40,000

ENVIRONMENT: Flatland between mountains and coast

LIVELIHOOD: Ruling and warrior caste

POLITICAL ORGANIZATION: Traditionally, a caste in a stratified kingdom; today, part of a nation-state

FOR MORE INFORMATION: Gough, Katherine. 1961. Nayar: Central Kerala. In *Matrilineal societies*, edited by David Schneider and Katherine Gough, 298–384. Berkeley: University of California Press.

The second husband is brought into the union later. Also unlike fraternal polyandry, the first husband is the principal husband in terms of authority. A woman and her husbands live and work together, although economic resources are held independently. Both husbands are considered fathers to any children the wife bears. This system allows many individual choices. For example, two husbands and their wife may decide to take another woman into the marriage—often the sister of the wife. Thus, their household becomes simultaneously polygynous and polyandrous, a marriage pattern called *polygynandry*. Thus, depending on relative wealth and the availability of economic opportunity, a Sinhalese household may be monogamous, polyandrous, or polygynandrous.

One famous anthropological example of polyandry, reconstructed from historical data, comes from the Nayar of India as they were until the end of the seventeenth century (see, for example, Gough 1961). (See EthnoProfile 10.2: Nayar [late seventeenth century].) The Nayar during this period were matrilineal, and each lineage was linked to two or three other lineages of the neighborhood. These linked lineages acted as partners in the ceremonies of life, including the marriage rites for prepubescent girls. Every 10 to 12 years, each lineage married all its immature girls to men of the linked lineages. At the ceremony, each groom tied a gold ornament around the neck of his bride, who had been chosen for him by the elders. Following the ceremony, each couple was secluded in a room in the ancestral house for 3 days and 3 nights. If the girl was old enough, sexual relations might occur. On the fourth day, the grooms left and had no further obligations to their brides.

At the end of the marriage rite, a girl had achieved the status of mature woman. She was permitted to establish sexual relations of a more or less enduring quality with one or more men of her own or an appropriate higher caste. These men could not be brothers, and a man could not have sexual relations with two women of the same household. The first of these relationships was marked by a brief ceremony, which might be repeated each time another of these relationships was established. Spouses lived separately, and the husband would come to visit his wife in the evening. While the relationship lasted, a husband was expected to give gifts to his wife at the three main festivals of the year. The husband's only other obligation came at the birth of a child. One or more of the husbands who had had sexual relations with the woman during the relevant time period had to acknowledge possible biological paternity. Their gifts, although very small and economically inconsequential, were of the utmost symbolic significance. If no man would give gifts to a wife, it was assumed that she had engaged in sexual relations with a man of lower caste or with a Muslim or Christian. She would be banished—if she were lucky.

In short, the Nayar marriage system did not include many of the characteristics we take for granted in marriage. Husbands and wives did not live together; women and men both had multiple spouses; no economic relationships existed between the husbands and wives as individuals; and no attempt was made to determine the biological father of the woman's children. Nevertheless, the children had a place within the society and seemed to lead satisfying lives, and the society survived and even prospered for many generations.

As we mentioned at the beginning of the chapter, one important aspect of marriage is the creation of ties between the bride's and the groom's families. The two forms of polyandry just discussed sharply curtail the potential network of ties created by marriage. This is particularly true where fraternal polyandry occurs with preferred or permitted sororal polygyny. For example, in a Tibetan household of four brothers married to one woman, the entire household is tied affinally only to the family of the wife. If these same brothers decided to take another wife—to engage in polygynandry—they might marry a sister of their first wife. In so doing, they would be giving up the possibility of establishing ties with other households in favor of fortifying the relationship already established by the first marriage. In the same way, Nayar polyandry concentrated relationships among lineages that were already associated before the marriages. Nancy Levine and Walter Sangree call this *alliance intensifying*.

Secondary Marriage   The final form of polyandry, sometimes referred to as *secondary marriage,* is found only in northern Nigeria and northern Cameroon. In secondary marriage, a woman marries one or more secondary husbands while staying married to her previously married husband (Levine and Sangree 1980, 400). The woman lives with only one husband at a time, but she retains the right to return to the first husband and to have legitimate children by him at a later date. No divorce is permitted in the societies that practice secondary marriage; marriage is for life.

In this system, as in the other polyandrous systems examined here, men are polygynous and women are polyandrous. A man marries a series of women and lives with one or more of them at his homestead. At the same time, the women independently pursue their own marital careers. Secondary marriage is really neither polyandry nor polygyny but rather a combination of the two, resulting from the overlap of men seeking several wives and women seeking several husbands. Secondary marriage is the opposite of Tibetan fraternal polyandry. It is *alliance proliferative,* leading to an extensive network of kinship and marriage-based ties throughout a region. It serves to unite rather than to concentrate groups.

The Distinction Between Sexuality and Reproductive Capacity   Polyandry demonstrates how a woman's sexuality can be distinguished from her reproductive capacity. This distinction is absent in monogamous or purely polygynous systems, in which polyandry is not permitted; such societies resist perceiving women's sexual and reproductive capacities as separable (except, perhaps, in prostitution), yet they usually accept the separability of men's sexual and procreative attributes without question. "It may well be a fundamental feature of the [worldview] of polyandrous peoples that they recognize such a distinction for *both* men and women" (Levine and Sangree 1980, 388). In the better-known polyandrous groups, a woman's sexuality can be shared among an unlimited number of men, but her childbearing capacities cannot be. Indeed, among the Nyinba (Levine 1980), a woman's childbearing capacities are carefully controlled and limited to one husband at a time. But she is free to engage in sexual activity outside her marriage as long as she is not likely to get pregnant.

Inuit Comarriage

The exotic popular image of Inuit marriage is one of "wife trading" and offering wives to strangers as an act of "hospitality." (See EthnoProfile 10.3: Alaskan Inuit.) Research by anthropologists has shown that neither of these images is true. Nevertheless, traditional Inuit marriage is of great interest. First, the Inuit are among the only peoples we know about who seem to have no marriage rituals. Second, until the turn of the twentieth century, the Inuit practiced a form of marriage that looked much like the polygynandrous marriage discussed earlier. Ernest Burch notes that a major feature of traditional Inuit marriage is what he calls *comarriage* (1975, 119). Comarriage had nearly disappeared by 1900, although when Burch was in the field in 1970, he knew a few older Inuit who were still part of a comarriage. Following Burch's example, our discussion is set at the end of the nineteenth century.

Traditional Inuit marriage was defined by three features. First, a couple began to live together, usually in the house of one spouse's parents. Second, the couple engaged in sexual intercourse. Third, the couple began to refer to one another using the terms *ui* and *nuliaq,* ("husband" and "wife"; Burch 1975, 81). Marriage was marked by no elaborate ritual, just by the socially accepted coresidence and sexual intercourse. The couple did not even have to live together very long for the relationship to be considered established by them or by the other members of the community.

Burch suggests that the lack of elaboration was due to the position marriage held in the Inuit view of their own social world: it was a more or less utilitarian relationship designed to meet as effectively as possible the problems of daily existence (1975, 82). Apart from activities primarily oriented toward economic or sexual matters, a husband and wife rarely saw much of each other. The woman stayed in the house; the husband hunted, visited male relatives and friends, or spent time in the community social center, which was dominated by men (85). Put another way, Inuit kinship favored consanguinity over affinity. Relationships based on birth were privileged over relationships created through marriage. In Inuit marriage, the *ui-nuliaq* relationship was the only one in which sexual intercourse had the specific aim of producing children.

EthnoProfile 10.3 • **ALASKAN INUIT**

REGION: North America

NATION: United States (northwestern Alaska)

POPULATION: 11,000 (1960s)

ENVIRONMENT: Arctic: mountains, foothills, coastal plain

LIVELIHOOD: Hunting, wage labor, welfare

POLITICAL ORGANIZATION: Traditionally, families; today, part of a modern nation-state

FOR MORE INFORMATION: Burch, Ernest S., Jr. 1975. *Eskimo kinsmen: Changing family relationships in northwest Alaska.* American Ethnological Society Monograph, no. 59. St. Paul: West.

One form of institutionalized marriage, and the main form of nonresidential marriage, was the so-called "wife-exchange" pattern. This is better understood as comarriage, or nonresidential polygynandry. Here, two *ui-nuliaq* pairs became associated with each other through sexual intercourse with each other's spouse. Burch notes that intercourse had to occur only once to establish the relationship in perpetuity. Intercourse validated the union of the two couples, a union that had been agreed on by all the parties involved beforehand.

The most important relationships in the comarriage were between the cowives and between the cohusbands, who now established strong bonds of friendship, mutual aid, and protection (Burch 1970). This is the key to understanding comarriage. These relationships were usually between couples living in different villages or even in different societies. Note that the Inuit, like us, did not have extensive networks of relatives spread out through their entire territory. Consequently, alternative ways of establishing trusting and close ties with other people of the same sex were vital. In fact, Burch's informants told him that cohusbands became like brothers and cowives like sisters. The sibling relationship was of profound importance to the Inuit. Siblings were morally bound to cooperate in almost all the major activities of life. Equally interesting was the effect of comarriage on the next generation. The children of these comarriages were all considered brothers or sisters of one sort or another, all of whom had to honor the obligations siblings had to one another. In the next generation, cousins were established, and so on, creating pockets of kinship throughout the region. Ultimately comarriage established long-term, interregional alliances where there were none before. As one northwestern Inuit put it: "In early days ago, Eskimo change wife in Arctic of Alaska to make big family and have lots of relatives. Suppose, here, man and wife from Kotzebue and man and wife from Point Hope. Them men they exchange wife, they agree everything among themself, and they claim their children just like one family. And when them children grow up, parents told their children they have half brother or half sister at Point Hope or Kotzebue" (Paul Green, cited in Burch 1975, 109).

Calling comarriage "wife swapping" or "wife exchange" distorts the practice and misses an essential point. These phrases imply that the husband initiated the practice and that the wife was traded between two men. Burch's data make it clear that husbands were exchanged as much as wives and that wives had just as much to say about the establishment of a comarriage as did the husbands. Indeed, wives could even take the initiative in establishing such a union.

It should be noted that although the sex act between cospouses was the symbolic validation of the marriage, it was also enjoyed. The sexual interaction between cospouses was believed to be considerably more elaborate and pleasurable than the conjugal relation between spouses who lived together (Burch 1975, 117–18). The important point is what the sex act meant *in this context*. It is clear that it meant more than sexual gratification with a new partner.

BRIDEWEALTH

Marriage is a transaction as well as a transformation. It is a flow of rights and obligations involving both sides in the union. Husband and wife gain these rights, but so do the groups from which they come. In certain societies, marriage involves the transfer of a young woman in one direction in exchange for certain symbolically important goods in the other direction. These goods are called **bridewealth.**

Bridewealth is most common in patrilineal societies that combine agriculture, pastoralism, and patrilocal marriage, although it is found in other types of societies as well. When it occurs among matrilineal peoples, usually a postmarital residence rule (avunculocal, for example) takes the woman away from her matrilineage.

The goods exchanged have significant symbolic value to the people concerned. They include shell ornaments, ivory tusks, brass gongs, bird feathers, cotton cloth, and animals. Bridewealth in animals is prevalent in eastern and southern Africa, where cattle have the most profound symbolic and economic value. In these societies, a man's father, and often his entire patrilineage, will give a specified number of cattle (often in installments) to the patrilineage of the man's bride. Bridewealth is usually understood as a way of compensating the bride's relatives for the loss of her labor and childbearing capacities. When the bride leaves her home, she goes to live with her husband and his lineage. She will be working and producing children for his people, not her own.

Bridewealth transactions create affinal relations in two directions. The obvious connection is between the relatives of the wife and those of the husband. However, the new wife's relatives will use the bridewealth they receive to establish ties with yet another kinship group—the one that provides a bride for the new wife's brother. Bridewealth therefore enables both sisters and brothers to find spouses. This connection is not lost on the people who practice it. The relationship between brothers and sisters in these societies is extremely important. In many societies in eastern and southern Africa, a woman gains power and influence over a brother because her marriage brings the cattle that allow him to marry and continue their lineage. As the Southern Bantu put it, "cattle beget children" (Kuper 1982, 3).

Bridewealth in Southern Africa: Linking Brothers and Sisters

Following Adam Kuper, let us consider bridewealth practices in southern Africa (Figure 10.2). Here, as ethnographers E. J. Krige and J. D. Krige (1943) noted at the time of their fieldwork, the fundamental bridewealth rule was that marital rights to a woman were transferred for cattle. Of particular importance was the right to the woman's childbearing capacities. If a wife was infertile, or if she died or deserted her husband before bearing children, then either the bridewealth had to be returned or the woman's lineage had to provide another wife to the husband. The transfer of control over the woman's childbearing was permanent; her children belonged to her husband's lineage and could not

FIGURE 10.2 *This photograph illustrates a bridewealth ceremony in southern Africa. Bridewealth is usually understood as a way of compensating the bride's relatives for the loss of her labor and childbearing capacities. Cash may also be used for bridewealth, as here among the Lese of Zaire.*

bridewealth The transfer of certain symbolically important goods from the family of the groom to the family of the bride on the occasion of their marriage. It represents compensation to the wife's lineage for the loss of her labor and her childbearing capacities.

EthnoProfile 10.4 • **LOVEDU**

REGION: Southern Africa

NATION: South Africa

POPULATION: 40,000 (1940s)

ENVIRONMENT: Savanna

LIVELIHOOD: Horticulture and gathering; little cattle herding

POLITICAL ORGANIZATION: Traditionally, a kingdom (queen) and class divisions between aristocrats and commoners; today, part of a modern nation-state

FOR MORE INFORMATION: Krige, E. J., and J. D. Krige. 1943. *Realm of a rain queen.* London: Oxford University Press.

be claimed by her own lineage for any reason, including divorce. If a husband and wife divorced, the children stayed with the husband's lineage; they did not follow their mother. As with the Nuer, even after the death of her husband, a widow was still expected to bear children in his name, usually by marrying his brother.

In southern Africa, when a brother used his sister's bridewealth cattle to get himself a wife, he and his sister became known as *cattle-linked siblings.* They were bound in a special relationship with effects lasting over several generations. Among the Lovedu, for example, the brother remained in his sister's debt because she had given him a wife. (See EthnoProfile 10.4: Lovedu.) The sister had ritual power to protect her brother's new village from witches. When she came to visit, she put her things in her brother's wife's house, and her brother's wife was obligated to wait on her. She could sometimes even control who her brother would marry. "The sister even wields a certain amount of authority in the house of her brother, as was well illustrated at a gathering we attended where the man of the house was quarreling with his wife about an uninvited guest. In the midst of the uproar a voice was heard: 'This is my village which I have built. I will have no unseemly behavior here.' It was the sister rebuking her brother, who subsided immediately and went on with the ceremonial as if nothing had happened." (Krige and Krige 1943, 75–76).

In other places in southern Africa, a woman could help herself to the clothing and household goods of the wife of her cattle-linked brother; she could even expect her younger brother's wife to wait on her and call her *female husband.* Furthermore, she often demanded a direct return from her brother. After all, she had obtained a wife for him; now he must do the same for her. In some cases, she would marry the wife herself, in a woman marriage. This wife would work as her subordinate and bear children for her lineage. More often, she would claim a daughter-in-law as a wife for her son. From the son's point of view, this is marriage with the mother's brother's daughter, a common form of preferential marriage. Notice how bridewealth set up ongoing ties of exchange and alliance among series of lineages. In this example, the wife's in-laws paid bride-wealth to her relatives for her. They then had to pay bridewealth to her relatives again, to obtain a wife for her son.

BROTHERS AND SISTERS IN CROSS-CULTURAL PERSPECTIVE

The previous examples suggest that the brother-sister relationship deserves special atten-tion. In American society, we tend to interpret all relationships between men and women in terms of the prototypical relationship between husbands and wives. Such an inter-pretation is unnecessarily limiting and overlooks the significant variations in how people view relationships (see Sacks 1979). In some cultures, the most important relationships a man and a woman have are those with their opposite-sex siblings. This is perhaps most clear in matrilineal societies, where, for example, a man's closest ties to the next generation are with his sister's children.

Brothers and Sisters in a Matrilineal Society

A classic illustration comes from the Ashanti of Ghana. (See EthnoProfile 10.5: Ashanti.) The central legal relationship in Ashanti society is the tie between brother and sister. A brother has power over his sister's children because he is their closest male relative and because Ashanti legal power is vested in males (Fortes 1950). A sister has claims on her brother because she is his closest female relative and represents the only source of the continuity of his lineage. In patrilineal societies like that of the Nuer, a man is centrally

EthnoProfile 10.5 • ASHANTI

REGION: Western Africa

NATION: Ghana

POPULATION: 200,000

ENVIRONMENT: Slightly inland, partly mountainous

LIVELIHOOD: Farming, fishing, market trading (women)

POLITICAL ORGANIZATION: Traditionally, a kingdom; today, part of a modern nation-state

FOR MORE INFORMATION: Fortes, Meyer. 1950. Kinship and marriage among the Ashanti. In *African systems of kinship and marriage,* edited by A. R. Radcliffe-Brown and Daryll Forde. Oxford: Oxford University Press.

concerned with his own ability to produce children. Among the Ashanti, a man is centrally concerned with his *sister's* ability to produce children. "Men find it difficult to decide which is more important to them, to have children or for their sisters to have children. But after discussion most men conclude that sad as it may be to die childless, a good citizen's first anxiety is for his lineage to survive" (274–75).

More than this, the Ashanti brother and sister are supposed to be close confidants:

> Quoting their own experiences, men say that it is to his sister that a man entrusts weighty matters, never to his wife. He will discuss confidential matters, such as those that concern property, money, public office, legal suits, and even the future of his children or his matrimonial difficulties with his sister, secure in the knowledge that she will tell nobody else. He will give his valuables into her care, not his wife's. He will use her as go-between with a secret lover, knowing that she will never betray him to his wife. His sister is the appropriate person to fetch a man's bride home to him, and so a sister is the best watch-dog of a wife's fidelity. Women, again, agree that in a crisis they will side with their brothers against their husbands. There is often jealousy between a man's sister and his wife because each is thinking of what he can be made to do for her children. That is why they cannot easily live in the same house. Divorce after many years of marriage is common, and is said to be due very often to the conflict between loyalties towards spouse and towards sibling. (Fortes 1950, 275)

Because Ashanti women may be sisters and wives simultaneously, they often experience conflict between these two roles. We Westerners must change our frame of reference to understand this. For us, the relationship of husband and wife takes precedence over the brother-sister relationship, which is attenuated at marriage. But for the Ashanti, the lineage comes first. In part, the closeness of brothers and sisters is tied to the Ashanti residence pattern: people live in their matrilineages' neighborhoods, and often husbands and wives do not live together.

The marriage agreement grants the husband exclusive sexual rights over his wife and legal paternity over any children born. The husband also has the right to domestic and economic services. Ashanti women also have rights within the marriage agreement. The wife is entitled to food, clothing, and housing if she needs it. She also expects sexual satisfaction, care in illness, debt coverage, and the right to approve or disapprove if her husband wishes to take another wife. For Ashanti, then, marriage grants rights in sexuality to both partners, and a man who wishes to take another wife must ask his first wife to share her sexual rights in him with another woman.

Brothers and Sisters in a Patrilineal Society

The relationship of brother and sister is important in patrilineal societies too, and even in some contemporary urban nation-states. Thomas Belmonte notes that in the slums of Naples, a brother still maintains over his sister a moral control that her husband does not have (1978, 193). In patrilineal societies, the strength of the relationship depends on how the kinship group is organized. Where sisters do not move too far from home upon

EthnoProfile 10.6 • **MOUNT HAGEN**

REGION: Southeastern Asia

NATION: Papua New Guinea (western highlands)

POPULATION: 75,000 (1960s)

ENVIRONMENT: Forested mountain slopes, grassy plains

LIVELIHOOD: Farming, pig raising

POLITICAL ORGANIZATION: Traditionally, some men of influence but no coercive power; today, part of a modern nation-state

FOR MORE INFORMATION: Strathern, Marilyn. 1972. *Women in between*. London: Academic Press.

marriage and where they are not incorporated into their husbands' lineages, a group of brothers and sisters may control the lineage and its economic, political, social, and religious aspects. The senior members of the lineage—males and females alike—exercise control over the junior members. Although the brothers generally have more control than the sisters (in part because they are the ones who stay in place while the sisters move when they marry), sisters still have influence.

In the Mount Hagen area of the New Guinea highlands, for example, women marry into many different subtribes, usually within a two-hour walk from home. (See Ethno-Profile 10.6: Mount Hagen.) However, they retain rights to the wealth of their own lineages and to its disposal. A clan sister married outside the clan is believed to remain under the control of her clan ghosts. At her death, in association with them, she is able to influence the affairs of her own lineage. Nevertheless, over the course of time, a woman becomes more interested and involved in the affairs of her husband's clan. As this happens, it is believed that she comes increasingly under the control of her husband's clan ghosts. After her death, in addition to her influence on her own clan as a ghostly sister, she is believed to have influence on her husband's clan as a ghostly mother (Strathern 1972, 124).

FAMILY STRUCTURE

The process by which a woman becomes gradually involved in her husband's clan or lineage was recorded by Evans-Pritchard during his fieldwork among the Nuer. (See EthnoProfile 9.2: Nuer.) Affinal ties gradually become kinship ties: *ruagh* (in-law relationship) became *mar* (kinship; Evans-Pritchard 1951, 96). The birth of a child gave the wife kinship with her husband's relatives, and it gave the husband kinship with the wife's relatives. In many patrilineal societies, a woman begins to identify with and become

FIGURE 10.3 *Cowives in polygynous households frequently cooperate in daily tasks, such as food preparation.*

more interested in the affairs of her husband's lineage, partly because she has been living there for many years and comes to be more intimate with the details of her husband's lineage. More significantly, however, her husband's lineage becomes her children's lineage. The children create a link to the lineage that is independent of her husband. This is one example of how family relationships inevitably transform over time. The transformations people experience vary from one society to the next according to how families are organized.

The Nuclear Family

The structure and dynamics of neolocal monogamous families are familiar to North Americans. We call them nuclear families and assume that most North Americans live in them. In fact, our families are monogamous, but they are not always nuclear. For anthropologists, a **nuclear family** is made up of two generations: the parents and their unmarried children. Each member of a nuclear family has a series of evolving relationships with every other member: husband and wife, parents and children, and children with each other. These are the principal lines along which jealousy, controversy, and affection develop in neolocal monogamous families.

The Polygynous Family

Polygynous families are significantly different in their dynamics. Each wife has a relationship with her cowives as individuals and as a group (Figure 10.3). Cowives, in turn, individually and collectively, interact with the husband. These relationships change over time, as we (Emily Schultz and Robert Lavenda) had occasion to learn in Guider, northern Cameroon. (See EthnoProfile 8.1: Guider.) The nine-year-old daughter of our landlord announced one day that she was going to become Lavenda's second wife. "Madame [Schultz]," she said, "will be angry at first, because that's how first wives are when their husbands take a second wife. But after a while, she will stop being angry and will get to know me and we will become friends. That's what always happens."

The differences in internal dynamics in polygynous families are not confined to the relationships of husband and wives. An important distinction is made between children with the same mother and children with a different mother. In Guider, people ordinarily refer to all their siblings (half and full) as brothers or sisters. When they want to emphasize the close connection with a particular brother or sister, however, they say that he or she is "same father, same mother." This terminology conveys a relationship of special intimacy and significance. Children, logically, also have different kinds of relationships with their own mothers and their fathers' other wives—and with their fathers as well.

Where there is a significant inheritance, these relationships serve as the channels for jealousy and conflict. The children of the same mother, and especially the children of different mothers, compete with one another for their father's favor. Each mother tries to protect the interests of her own children, sometimes at the expense of her cowives' children.

Competition in the Polygynous Family Although the relationships among wives in a polygynous society may be very close, among the Mende of Sierra Leone, cowives eventually compete with each other. (See EthnoProfile 10.7: Mende.) Caroline Bledsoe

nuclear family A family pattern made up of two generations: the parents and their unmarried children.

EthnoProfile 10.7 • **MENDE**

REGION: Western Africa

NATION: Sierra Leone

POPULATION: 12,000,000

ENVIRONMENT: Forest and savanna

LIVELIHOOD: Slash-and-burn rice cultivation, cash cropping, diamond mining

POLITICAL ORGANIZATION: Traditionally, a hierarchy of local chiefdoms; today, part of a modern nation-state

FOR MORE INFORMATION: Little, Kenneth. 1967. *The Mende of Sierra Leone.* London: Routledge and Kegan Paul.

(1993) explains that this competition is often focused on children: how many each wife has and how likely it is that each child will obtain things of value, especially education. Husbands in polygynous Mende households should avoid overt signs of favoritism, but wives differ from one another in status. First, wives are ranked by order of marriage. The senior wife is the first wife in the household, and she has authority over junior wives, each of whom is ranked in order of marriage. Marriage-order ranking structures the household but also lays the groundwork for rivalries. Second, wives are also ranked in terms of the status of the families from which they came. Serious problems arise if the husband shows favoritism toward a wife from a high-status family by educating her children ahead of older children of other wives or children of wives higher in the marriage ranking.

The level of her children's education matters intensely to a Mende woman because her principal claim to her husband's land or cash, as well as her expectations of future support after he dies, comes through her children. She depends not only on the income that a child may earn to support her but also on the rights her children have to inherit property and positions of leadership. Nevertheless, education requires a significant cash outlay in school fees, uniforms, books, and so on. A man may be able to send only one child to school, or he may be able to send one child to a prestigious private school only if he sends another to a trade apprenticeship. These economic realities make sense to husbands but can lead to bitter feuds—and even divorce—among cowives who blame the husband for disparities in the accomplishments of their children. In extreme cases, cowives are said to use witchcraft to make their rivals' children fail their exams. To avoid these problems, children are frequently sent to live with relatives who will send them to school. Such competition is missing in traditional monogamous households; however, it is a distinct possibility in monogamous households with adopted children or with spouses who already have children from a previous marriage.

Extended and Joint Families

Within any society, certain patterns of family organization are considered proper. In American nuclear families, two generations live together. In some societies, three generations—parents, married children, and grandchildren—are expected to live together in a vertical **extended family**. In still other societies, the extension is horizontal: brothers and their wives (or sisters and their husbands) live together in a **joint family**. These are ideal patterns, which not all families may be able or willing to emulate.

Individual families also change in their basic structures over time. In a polygynous society with extended families, consider a recently married husband and wife who set up housekeeping by themselves. They are monogamous. After a while, a child is born, and they become a monogamous nuclear family. Some time later, elderly parents come to live with them, and they become an extended family. Later the husband takes another wife, and the family becomes polygynous. Then the elderly parents die, and the family is no longer extended. After a time, the husband's younger brother and his wife and children move in, creating a joint household. One wife leaves, and the husband is monogamous again. His brother and his wife and children leave, the husband takes another wife, and the family is polygynous again. The eldest son marries and brings his wife to live in the household, and for the second time the household is an extended family. One wife dies, and the children all move away, and there is now a monogamous couple living in the household. Finally, with the death of the husband, there is a solitary family, made up of the widow, who is supported by her eldest son but lives alone in the household.

In this example, each household structure is different in its dynamics. These are not several nuclear families that overlap. A joint family is fundamentally different from an extended family with regard to the relationships it engenders.

TRANSFORMATIONS IN FAMILIES OVER TIME

Families change over time. They have a life cycle and a life span. The same family takes on different forms and provides different opportunities for the interaction of family members at different points in its development. New households are formed and old households dissolve through divorce, remarriage, and the breakup of extended families.

Divorce and Remarriage

Most human societies make it possible for married couples to separate. In some societies, the process is long, drawn out, and difficult, especially when bridewealth must be re-

---

extended family A family pattern made up of three generations living together: parents, married children, and grandchildren.

joint family A family pattern made up of brothers and their wives or sisters and their husbands (along with their children) living together.

In Their Own Words   **LAW, CUSTOM, AND CRIMES AGAINST WOMEN**

John van Willigen and V. C. Channa describe the social and cultural practices surrounding dowry payments that appear to be responsible for violence against women in some parts of India.

A 25-year-old woman was allegedly burnt to death by her husband and mother-in-law at their East Delhi home yesterday. The housewife, Mrs. Sunita, stated before her death at the Jaya Prakash Narayana Hospital that members of her husband's family had been harassing her for bringing inadequate dowry.

The woman told the Shahdara subdivisional magistrate that during a quarrel over dowry at their Pratap Park house yesterday, her husband gripped her from behind while the mother-in-law poured kerosene over her clothes.

Her clothes were then set ablaze. The police have registered a case against the victim's husband, Suraj Prakash, and his mother.

—Times of India, February 19, 1988

This routinely reported news story describes what in India is termed a "bride-burning" or "dowry death." Such incidents are frequently reported in the newspapers of Delhi and other Indian cities. In addition, there are cases in which the evidence may be ambiguous, so that deaths of women by fire may be recorded as kitchen accidents, suicides, or murders. Dowry violence takes a characteristic form. Following marriage and the requisite giving of dowry, the family of the groom makes additional demands for the payment of more cash or the provision of more goods. These demands are expressed in unremitting harassment of the bride, who is living in the household of her husband's parents, culminating in the murder of the woman by members of her husband's family or by her suicide. The woman is typically burned to death with kerosene, a fuel used in pressurized cook stoves, hence the use of the term "bride-burning" in public discourse.

Dowry death statistics appear frequently in the press and parliamentary debates. Parliamentary sources report the following figures for married women 16 to 30 years of age in Delhi: 452 deaths by burning for 1985; 478 for 1986 and 300 for the first six months of 1987. There were 1,319 cases reported nationally in 1986 (Times of India, January 10, 1988). Police records do not match hospital records for third degree burn cases among younger married women; far more violence occurs than the crime reports indicate.

There is other violence against women related both directly and indirectly to the institution of dowry. For example, there are unmarried women who commit suicide so as to relieve their families of the burden of providing a dowry. A recent case that received national attention in the Indian press involved the triple suicide of three sisters in the industrial city of Kanpur. A photograph was widely published showing the three young women hanging from ceiling fans by their scarves. Their father, who earned about 4000 Rs. [rupees] per month, was not able to negotiate marriage for his oldest daughter. The grooms were requesting approximately 100,000 Rs. Also linked to the dowry problem is selective female abortion made possible by amniocentesis. This issue was brought to national attention with a startling statistic reported out of a seminar held in Delhi in 1985. Of 3000 abortions carried out after sex determination through amniocentesis, only one involved a male fetus. As a result of these developments, the government of the state of Maharashtra banned sex determination tests except those carried out in government hospitals.

Source: van Willigen and Channa 1991.

turned; a man who divorces a wife in such societies, or whose wife leaves him, expects some of the bridewealth back. But for the wife's family to give the bridewealth back, a whole chain of marriages may have to be broken up. Brothers of the divorced wife may have to divorce to get back enough bridewealth from their in-laws. Sometimes a new husband will repay the bridewealth to the former husband's line, thus letting the bride's relatives off the hook.

Divorce in Guider   In other societies, divorce is easier. Marriages in Guider, for example, are easily broken up. (See EthnoProfile 8.1: Guider.) The Fulbe of Guider prefer that a man marry his father's brother's daughter. In many cases, such marriages are contracted simply to oblige the families involved; after a few months, the couple splits up. In other cases, a young girl (12 or 13 years old) is married to a man considerably her senior, despite any interest she may have had in men closer to her own age. Here too the marriage may not last long. In general, there is enough dissatisfaction with marriage in Guider to make household transformation through divorce quite common.

Among Muslims in Guider, divorce is controlled by men; women are not allowed legally to initiate divorces. A man wanting a divorce need only follow the simple procedure laid down in the Qur'an and sanctioned by long practice in Guider: he appears before two witnesses and pronounces the formula "I divorce you" three times. He is then divorced, and his wife must leave his household. She may take an infant with her, but any children at the toddler stage must stay with the father. If she takes an infant, she must return the child to the father's household by the time the child is 6 to 8 years old. In case she was pregnant at the time of the divorce, a woman must wait 3 months after she is divorced before she can remarry. After this time, the vast majority of women remarry.

Do women in Guider, then, have no power to escape from marriages that are unsatisfactory? Legally, perhaps not. But several conventionally recognized practices allow a woman to communicate her desire for a divorce. She can ask her husband for a divorce, and in some cases he will comply. If he does not or if she is unwilling to confront him directly, she can neglect household duties—burn his food or stop cooking for him entirely or refuse to sleep with him. Because these are the most important services a wife provides her husband, men usually get the hint quickly.

Grounds for Divorce   Divorce in most societies need not be elaborately public. Men usually give nagging and quarreling as their reasons for divorce, while women often claim cruelty and mistreatment or stinginess. Depending on the society, adultery is sometimes cause for divorce. In almost all societies, childlessness is grounds for divorce as well. For the Ju/'hoansi (!Kung), most divorces are initiated by women, mainly because they do not like their husbands or do not want to be married (Lee 1992b; Shostak 1983). (See EthnoProfile 9.1: Ju/'hoansi [!Kung].) After what is often considerable debate, a couple that decides to break up will merely separate. There is no bridewealth, no legal contract to be renegotiated. Mutual consent is all that is necessary. The children go with the mother. Ju/'hoansi divorces are cordial, Richard Lee (1992b) tells us, at least compared with the Western norm. Ex-spouses may continue to joke with each other and even live next to each other with their new spouses.

What about societies in which divorce is not recognized? There are very few such societies. In ancient Rome, for example, divorce was impossible. This followed from legal consequences of the marriage ritual. When she married, a woman was cut off from the patrilineage into which she was born and incorporated into her husband's patrilineage. Were she to leave her husband, she would have no place to go and no lineage to protect her.

Separation among the Inuit   Among the northwestern Inuit, the traditional view is that all kin relationships, including marital ones, are permanent (Burch 1970). (See EthnoProfile 10.3: Alaskan Inuit.) Thus, although it is possible to deactivate a marriage by separating, a marriage can never be permanently dissolved. (Conversely, reestablishing the residence tie is all that's needed to reactivate the relationship.) A husband and wife who stop living together and having sexual relations with each other are considered to be separated and ready for another marriage. This is when Inuit divorce becomes fascinating. If each member of a separated couple remarried, the two husbands of the wife would become cohusbands; the two wives of the husband, cowives; and the children of the first and second marriages, cosiblings. The result looks almost identical to comarriage! The only difference is that the relationship of cospouses would not be established in the case of divorce and remarriage. In effect, a "divorce" among the Inuit results in more, not fewer, connections.

Breaking up Complex Households

We now turn to the formation of new households following the breakup of extended families. This process is best illustrated in joint families. In a joint family, the pressures that build up among coresident brothers or sisters often increase dramatically on the death of the father. In theory, the eldest son inherits the position of head of the household from his father, but his younger brothers may not accept his authority as readily as they did their father's. Some of the younger brothers may decide to establish their own households, and gradually the joint family splits. Each brother whose household splits off from the joint stem usually hopes to start his own joint family; eventually, his sons will bring their wives into the household, and a new joint family will emerge out of the ashes of an old one.

Something similar happens among the Nyinba, the polyandrous people of Nepal discussed earlier. (See EthnoProfile 10.1: Nyinba.) In a family with many brothers widely separated in age, the corporation of brothers may take a second, fertile wife. At first, all brothers will have equal sexual access to her, but in time the brothers will tend to form groups around each wife, with some preferring the first and others preferring the second. At this point, the time is ripe for splitting the household in two. The Nyinba recognize that bringing a second fertile wife into the house sets in motion the transformation of the family into two polyandrous households and the division of land ownership. Hence, family systems contain within them the seeds of their own transformation.

In the northern Nigerian societies where secondary marriage is practiced, there is no divorce. However, both women and men recognize that there are good reasons for leaving one marriage and contracting a new one. The practice of secondary marriage allows for burgeoning affinal links and the establishment of many households. It also

EthnoProfile 10.8 • **LOS PINOS**

REGION: Caribbean

NATION: Dominican Republic

POPULATION: 1,000

ENVIRONMENT: Rugged mountain region

LIVELIHOOD: Peasant agriculture (tobacco, coffee, cacao) and labor migration

POLITICAL ORGANIZATION: Part of a modern nation-state

FOR MORE INFORMATION: Georges, Eugenia, 1990. _The making of a transnational community: Migration, development, and cultural change in the Dominican Republic._ New York: Columbia University Press.

makes it possible to maintain the older ties, so that a wife may always return to any of her previous husbands.

International Migration and the Family

Migration to find work in another country has become increasingly common worldwide and has important effects on families. Anthropologist Eugenia Georges (1990) examined its effects on people who migrated to the United States from Los Pinos, a small town in the Dominican Republic. (See EthnoProfile 10.8: Los Pinos.) Migration divided these families, with some members moving to New York and some members remaining in Los Pinos. Some parents stayed in the Dominican Republic while their children went to the United States. A more common pattern was for spouses to separate, with the husband migrating first and the wife staying home. Consequently, many migrant households in Los Pinos were headed by women. In most cases, however, the spouse in the United States worked to bring the spouse in Los Pinos to New York.

This sometimes took several years because it involved completing paperwork for the visa and saving money beyond the amount regularly sent to Los Pinos. Children of the couple who were close to working age also came to the United States, frequently with their mother, and younger children were sent for as they approached working age. Finally, after several years in the United States, the couple who started the migration cycle would take their savings and return home to the Dominican Republic. Their children stayed in the United States and continued to send money home. Return migrants tended not to give up their residence visas, and therefore had to return to the United States annually. Often they stayed for a month or more to work. This also provided them

In Their Own Words   WHY MIGRANT WOMEN FEED THEIR HUSBANDS TAMALES

Brett Williams suggests that the reasons why Mexican migrant women feed their husbands tamales may not be the stereotypical reasons that outside observers often assume.

Because migrant women are so involved in family life and so seemingly submissive to their husbands, they have been described often as martyred purveyors of rural Mexican and Christian custom, tyrannized by excessively masculine, crudely domineering, rude and petty bullies in marriage, and blind to any world outside the family because they are suffocated by the concerns of kin. Most disconcerting to outside observers is that migrant women seem to embrace such stereotypes: they argue that they *should* monopolize their foodways and that they should *not* question the authority of their husbands. If men want tamales, men should have them. But easy stereotypes can mislead; in exploring the lives of the poor, researchers must revise their own notions of family life, and this paper argues that foodways can provide crucial clues about how to do so.

The paradox is this: among migrant workers both women and men are equally productive wage earners, and husbands readily acknowledge that without their wives' work their families cannot earn enough to survive. For migrants the division of labor between earning a living outside the home and managing household affairs is unknown; and the dilemma facing middle-class wives who may wish to work to supplement the family's income simply does not exist. Anthropologists exploring women's status cross-culturally argue that women are most influential when they share in the production of food and have some control over its distribution. If such perspectives bear at all on migrant women, one might be led to question their seemingly unfathomable obsequiousness in marriage.

Anthropologists further argue that women's influence is even greater when they are not isolated from their kinswomen, when women can cooperate in production and join, for example, agricultural work with domestic duties and childcare. Most migrant women spend their lives within large, closely knit circles of kin and their work days with their kinswomen. Marriage does not uproot or isolate a woman from her family, but rather doubles the relatives each partner can depend on and widens in turn the networks of everyone involved. The lasting power of marriage is reflected in statistics which show a divorce rate of 1 percent for migrant farmworkers from Texas, demonstrating the strength of a union bolstered by large numbers of relatives concerned that it go well. Crucial to this concern is that neither partner is an economic drain on the family, and the Tejano pattern of early and lifelong marriages establishes some limit on the whimsy with which men can abuse and misuse their wives.

While anthropology traditionally rests on an appreciation of other cultures in their own contexts and on their own terms, it is very difficult to avoid class bias in viewing the lives of those who share partly in one's own culture, especially when the issue is something so close to home as food and who cooks it. Part of the problem may lie in appreciating what families are and what they do. For the poor, public and private domains are blurred in confusing ways, family affairs may be closely tied to economics, and women's work at gathering and obligating or *binding* relatives is neither trivial nor merely a matter of sentiment. Another problem may lie in focusing on the marital relationship as indicative of a woman's authority in the family. We too often forget that women are sisters, grandmothers, and aunts to men as well as wives. Foodways can help us rethink both of these problematic areas and understand how women elaborate domestic roles to knit families together, to obligate both male and female kin, and to nurture and bind their husbands as well.

Source: Williams 1984.

with the opportunity to buy clothing and household goods at a more reasonable cost, as well as other items—clothing, cosmetics, and the like—to sell to neighbors, friends, and kin in the Dominican Republic.

Georges observes that the absent family member maintained an active role in family life despite the heavy psychological burden of separation. Although he might be working in a hotel in New York, for example, the husband was still the breadwinner and the main decision maker in the household. He communicated by visits, letters, and occasional telephone calls. Despite the strains of migration, moreover, the divorce rate was actually slightly lower in migrant families. In part, this was because the exchange of information between Los Pinos and New York was both dense and frequent, but also because strong ties of affection connected many couples. Finally, "the goal of the overwhelming majority of the migrants [from Los Pinos] I spoke with was permanent return to the Dominican Republic. Achievement of this goal was hastened by sponsoring the migration of dependents, both wives and children, so that they could work and save as part of the reconstituted household in the United States" (1990, 201). This pressure also helped keep families together.

THE FLEXIBILITY OF MARRIAGE

It is easy to get the impression that marriage rules compel people to do things they really do not want to do. People have to marry someone in a certain category (either a cross or a parallel cousin or a mother's brother's daughter, for example). They have to marry into one group or out of another. Younger people seem compelled by parents and relatives to marry complete strangers. Women appear to be pawns in men's "deep play" of prestige and power.

Sometimes the anthropological evidence reinforces this impression. Napoleon Chagnon's description of Yanomamo marriage is a case in point. (See EthnoProfile 10.9: Yanomamo.) Chagnon writes: "Girls have almost no voice in the decisions reached by their elder kin in deciding whom they should marry. They are very largely pawns to be disposed of by their kinsmen, and their wishes are given very little consideration. . . . Marriage does not enhance the status of the girl, for her duties as wife require her to assume difficult and laborious tasks too menial to be executed by the men" (1983, 111). If Chagnon is correct, this is an extreme case.

Rigidity in marriage rules are sometimes a function of the anthropologist's desire to build an airtight analytic model. Marriage rules are always subject to some negotiation. We have seen how, among the Inuit, comarriage is negotiated by both husbands and wives. (See EthnoProfile 10.3: Alaskan Inuit.) Burch (1970) notes that although the husband officially has the final authority in the family, he will never do anything of any importance without consulting his wife and taking her opinion into account.

A clear and especially revealing example is the marriage practices of the Ju/'hoansi (!Kung) of the Kalahari Desert. (See EthnoProfile 9.1: Ju/'hoansi [!Kung].) Richard Lee (1992b) notes that all first marriages are set up by means of a long-term exchange of gifts between the parents of a bride and groom. As we saw in Chapter 9, the Ju/'hoansi

EthnoProfile 10.9 • **YANOMAMO**

REGION: South America

NATIONS: Venezuela and Brazil

POPULATION: 12,000

ENVIRONMENT: Tropical rain forest

LIVELIHOOD: Hunting, gathering, and gardening

POLITICAL ORGANIZATION: Traditionally, a headman with influence but no coercive power; today, part of modern nation-states

FOR MORE INFORMATION: Chagnon, Napoleon. 1983. *Yanomamo: The fierce people.* 3d ed. New York: Holt, Rinehart and Winston.

kinship system is as simple or as complex as people want to make it, and the game of kinship is extended to marriage. A girl may not marry a father, brother, son, uncle, or nephew, but neither may she marry a first or second cousin. She may also not marry a boy with her father's or brother's name, and a boy may not marry a girl with his mother's or sister's name. As well, neither a boy nor girl should marry someone who stands in an avoidance relationship.

Consequently, for the Ju/'hoansi, about three-quarters of a person's potential spouses are off limits. In practice, parents of girls tend to be quite choosy about whom their daughter marries. If they are opposed to a particular suitor, they will come up with a kin or name prohibition to block the match. Because the parents arrange the first marriage, it appears that the girl has very little to say about it. If she protests long and hard, however, her parents may well call it off. This clear and insistent assertion of displeasure is not uncommon in the world. Even when a young woman follows the wishes of her parents for her first marriage, that first marriage may well not be her last if her dissatisfaction persists. Despite the parents' quest to find ideal spouses for their children, close to half of all first marriages among the Ju/'hoansi fail. However, as in many societies, only about 10 percent of marriages that last five years or longer end in divorce (Lee 1992b, 83).

One promising direction for anthropological study centers on the contrast between the formal rules of marriage and the actual performance of marriage rituals. Ivan Karp (1987) asks why Iteso women laugh at marriage ceremonies. (See EthnoProfile 9.5: Iteso.) During his fieldwork, Karp was struck by a paradox. The marriage ritual is taken very seriously by the patrilineal Iteso; it is the moment of creation for a new household, and it paves the way for the physical and social reproduction of Iteso patrilineages. But the ritual is carried out entirely by women who are not consanguineal members of the patrilineage! Despite the seriousness of the occasion and although they are carrying out the ritual for the benefit of a lineage to which they do not belong, Iteso women seem to find the ceremony enormously funny.

To explain this apparently anomalous behavior, Karp suggests that the meaning of the marriage ritual needs to be analyzed from two different referential perspectives: that of the men and that of the women. The men's perspective constitutes the official ideology of Iteso marriage. It emphasizes how marriage brings the bride's sexuality under the control of her husband's lineage. It distinguishes between women of the mother-in-law's generation and women of the wife's own generation. It stresses the woman's role as an agent of reproduction who is equivalent, in a reproductive sense, to the bridewealth cattle.

The women's perspective constitutes an unofficial ideology of Iteso marriage. For the men and women of a given lineage to succeed in perpetuating that lineage, they must control women's bodies. But the bodies they must control belong to female outsiders who marry lineage men. These same female outsiders direct the two ritual events crucial to lineage reproduction: marriage and birth. And men of the lineage are not allowed to attend either of these rituals. In sum, female outsiders control the continued existence of a patrilineage whose male members are supposed to control them!

Iteso women, Karp says, can see the irony in this: they are at once controlled and controlling. In the marriage ritual itself, they comment on this paradox through their laughter. In so doing, they reveal two things to the men. First, they show that they know the men are dependent on them. Second, even as the men assert their control over women's bodies, the women's ritual actions escape the men's control. The official ideology of male control is subverted, at least momentarily, by the women's laughter. Even as they ensure that their husband's and son's lineages will continue, they are able to comment on the paradoxical relation of women to men.

SEXUAL PRACTICES

Some anthropologists seem to regard marriage as an abstract formal system, having little if anything to do with human sexuality. As a result, their discussions tend to ignore the carnal aspects of marriage. But sexual intercourse is part of almost all marriages. And because in many societies marriage is the formal prerequisite for becoming sexually active (at least for females), a desire for sex is a strong motivation for getting married (Spiro 1977, 212).

Ranges of Heterosexual Practices

The range of sexual practice in the world is vast. In many Oceanian societies—Tikopia, for example—the young are expected to have a great deal of sexual experience before marriage. (See EthnoProfile 10.10: Tikopia.) Young men and young women begin having sexual relations at an early age, and having several lovers is considered to be a normal activity of the young. Getting married, as in many societies, is considered to be the final step (or the beginning of the final step) in becoming an adult. The distinguished British anthropologist Sir Raymond Firth notes that for the Tikopia, marriage represents a great change for both partners in this regard. The woman must abandon sexual free-

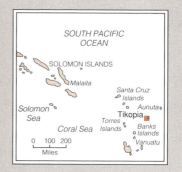

EthnoProfile 10.10 • **TIKOPIA**

REGION: Oceania (Polynesia)

NATION: Solomon Islands

POPULATION: 1,200 (1928)

ENVIRONMENT: Tropical island

LIVELIHOOD: Horticulture and pig raising

POLITICAL ORGANIZATION: Traditionally, chiefs; today, part of a modern nation-state

FOR MORE INFORMATION: Firth, Raymond. [1936] 1984. *We, the Tikopia.* Reprint. Stanford: Stanford University Press.

dom, but she replaces it with what Firth calls "a safe and legalized sexual cohabitation" ([1936] 1984, 434). The man is theoretically free to continue to have affairs, but in practice he will "settle down." This pattern is quite common cross-culturally.

The Ju/'hoansi (!Kung) also begin sexual activity at an early age. (See EthnoProfile 9.1: Ju/'hoansi [!Kung].) As a result, the social and sexual constraints of marriage represent quite a shock at first, especially for young women. Some Ju/'hoansi are strictly faithful to one another, but a significant minority take lovers. The Ju/'hoansi have no double standard; both men and women are free to take lovers, and women are sometimes eloquent about the time they spend with lovers. However, discretion is necessary when taking a lover because both husbands and wives can become very jealous and start fights. Sexual satisfaction is important to the Ju/'hoansi; female orgasm is known, and women expect both husbands and lovers to satisfy them.

This attitude toward sex is not universal. Robert Murphy and Yolanda Murphy (1974) note that for the Mundurucu, a group of about 1,250 gardening and hunting people in the Brazilian Amazon, female orgasm is more accidental than expected. Many societies require a woman's virginity at marriage; in some Arabian societies, bloodstained sheets must be produced the morning after the consummation of a marriage to demonstrate that the bride was a virgin.

Particularly interesting in this regard is Karl Heider's research (1979) among the Dani, a people of highland New Guinea. (See EthnoProfile 10.11: Dani.) Heider discovered that the Dani have extraordinarily little interest in sex. For five years after the birth of a child, the parents do not have sexual intercourse with each other. This practice, called a *postpartum sex taboo,* is found in all cultures. In most societies, however, it lasts for a few weeks or months (in the United States, we say that the mother needs time to heal; other societies have other justifications). In a few cases, the postpartum sex taboo is two years long, which is considered a very long time. Five years is hard to believe. What could explain it?

Heider points out that Westerners assume the sex drive is perhaps the most powerful biological drive of all. We believe that if this drive is not satisfied directly in sexual

EthnoProfile 10.11 • **DANI**

REGION: Oceania (New Guinea)

NATION: Indonesia (Irian Jaya)

POPULATION: 100,000 (1960s)

ENVIRONMENT: Valley in central highlands

LIVELIHOOD: Horticulture and pig raising

POLITICAL ORGANIZATION: Traditionally, some men with influence but no coercive power; today, part of a modern nation-state

FOR MORE INFORMATION: Heider, Karl. 1979. *Grand Valley Dani.* New York: Holt, Rinehart and Winston.

activity, then some other outlet will be found. Heider's study of the Dani calls this assumption about human sexuality into question. The Dani are not celibate, and they certainly have sexual intercourse often enough to reproduce biologically. But they do not seem very interested in sex; nor do they engage in much sexual activity (1979, 78–81).

Here again we encounter the *cultural construction of reality*—indeed, of a reality so basic that we consider it part of the biological nature of our species. Heider cannot explain why the Dani have such a low level of sexuality. He argues that it is connected with what he calls a low level of psychic energy (1979, 21). Nevertheless, the implications of this pattern for understanding the range of human sexual behavior are significant. The Dani, who are not abnormal physically or mentally, represent one extreme in the cultural construction of sexuality.

Nonreproductive Sexual Practices

The traditional anthropological focus on reproductive (hetero)sexuality is understandable. Every society is concerned about perpetuating itself, and most have developed complex ritual structures to ensure that this occurs. At the same time, much evidence shows that forms of sexual expression unconnected to heterosexual reproduction are far from rare in human societies. As we saw in the previous chapter, the cultural construction of sex and gender has not always decreed that reproductive sexuality be required of all members of society. Anthropological information about supernumerary sexes and genders has provided a cross-cultural context for understanding nonreproductive sexual practices such as homosexuality and bisexuality, that are found in Western societies.

Homosexuality at Initiation   In one part of New Guinea, several societies have institutionalized male homosexual practices as part of their initiation rituals. It is believed that females are physically complete at birth but that males are incomplete. For

EthnoProfile 10.12 • **MOMBASA SWAHILIS**

REGION: Eastern Africa

NATION: Kenya

POPULATION: 50,000 Swahili among 350,000 total population of city (1970s)

ENVIRONMENT: Island and mainland port city

LIVELIHOOD: Various urban occupations

POLITICAL ORGANIZATION: Part of a modern nation-state

FOR MORE INFORMATION: Shepherd, Gill. 1987. Rank, gender and homosexuality: Mombasa as a key to understanding sexual options. In *The cultural construction of sexuality,* edited by Pat Caplan, 240–70. London: Tavistock.

boys to grow, it is believed, they must ingest semen through either fellatio or anal intercourse (see the collected essays in Herdt 1982). This pattern is associated with a series of beliefs among men concerning the danger of women, the need for sexual separation, and the creation of men. An extreme example comes from the Marind Anim of New Guinea. During his fieldwork in the 1960s, Van Baal (1966) observed that heterosexual intercourse was sufficiently rare among the Marind Anim that they were unable to reproduce at a level high enough for their survival. To ensure that there would be enough people in the next generation, they captured children from neighboring societies during head-hunting raids.

Female Homosexuality in Mombasa   A contrasting example comes from Mombasa, Kenya. (See EthnoProfile 10.12: Mombasa Swahilis.) Anthropologist Gill Shepherd shows that both male and female homosexuality among Swahili Muslims can be understood as a rational decision, given traditional patterns of male-female interaction in Swahili society (1987, 240–70). Shepherd observes that men and women in Muslim Mombasa live in very different subcultures that are rich and satisfying for their members. Shepherd writes that the most enduring relationship in Swahili society is between mothers and daughters (249). This connection is imitated in the relationship between an older married sister and a younger unmarried sister. Men and women join a variety of sex-segregated groups for leisure-time activities such as dancing or religious study. Within these all-male or all-female groups, competition for social rank occurs. The relationships between brothers and sisters and mothers and sons are more distant, and the relationship of husband and wife (except in the case of young, modern, educated couples) is often emotionally distant (249). Because the world of men and the world of women overlap so little, relationships between the sexes tend to be one-dimensional.

Of the some 50,000 Swahili in Mombasa, about 5,000 could be called homosexual. The number is misleading, however, because men and women shift between homosexuality and heterosexuality throughout their lives. Women are allowed to choose other women as sexual partners only after they have been married. Therefore, all lesbians in Mombasa are married, widowed, or divorced. Both lesbians and homosexuals are open about their behavior. They fit regularly into everyday life, and "nobody would dream of suggesting that their sexual choices had any effect on their work capabilities, reliability, or religious piety" (Shepherd 1987, 241).

Lesbian couples in Mombasa are far more likely to live together than are male homosexual couples. Because there are plenty of all-female households that are not lesbian, the term *lesbian* implies an overt sexual relationship between two women. Lesbians are distinguished by two kinds of activity. First, they engage in private, sexual relationships with other women. Second, they form clublike groups. They meet regularly in one another's houses and choose women as their leaders. These groups form the context within which the women compete for power. Each group is composed of an inner circle of relatively wealthy older women who are friends. Their lovers, who are poorer and usually younger, make up the rest of the membership. The rule is that younger, lower-status women visit older, higher-status women. Wealthy lesbian women hold court in the afternoons, when domestic duties are done for a while and Swahili women have the chance to go visiting (Shepherd 1987, 254). When invited to weddings, wealthy lesbian women compete with each other by trying to dress their lovers as opulently as possible.

Women are drawn into lesbian relationships for a variety of reasons. Swahili women to whom Shepherd spoke were quite clear about the practical reasons: women with little money have little chance of marrying men who can offer them status or financial security; a lesbian lover, however, can offer them both. In Mombasa, jewelry, shoes, new dresses, and so on are significant markers in the women's prestige system. These are the things a wealthy lover can provide. A poor young woman in an unhappy marriage may have no way to support herself if she leaves her husband unless she has a lesbian lover.

> Very occasionally a wealthy lesbian woman will help a girl who has not married but remains miserably caught within the constraints of unmarried womanhood while all her peers have moved forward. Such a girl is usually of high birth, or so well educated, that men hesitate to make offers for her since the parents refuse all suitors. Slight miscalculations may find her still unmarried in her late twenties or early thirties, and the rigidity of the division between the never married and the married, among women, is such that adult freedoms can *only* come through marriage. A lesbian woman who wants to help such a girl will find a man prepared to make a marriage of convenience and give him the money with which to go to the girl's parents and make an offer. The couple are divorced shortly after the marriage and the girl goes to live with her lesbian benefactor. (Shepherd 1987, 256–57)

The wealthy partner in a lesbian relationship is freed from the extreme constraint normally placed on high-ranking women in Muslim societies. According to Islamic law, a wealthy, high-ranking Muslim woman can only marry a man who is her equal or superior. A marriage of this kind brings a great deal of seclusion, and her wealth is administered by her husband. "Thus if she wishes to use her wealth as she likes and has a taste for power, entry into a lesbian relationship, or living alone as a divorced or widowed woman, are virtually her only options" (Shepherd 1987, 257).

Financial independence for a woman offers the chance to convert wealth to power. If she pays for the marriages of other people or provides financial support in exchange for loyalty, a woman can create a circle of dependents. Shepherd points out that a few women, some lesbians, have achieved real political power in Mombasa in this way (1987, 257).

Still, it is not necessary to be a lesbian to build a circle of dependents. Why then do some women follow this route? The answer, Shepherd tells us, is complicated. It is not entirely respectable for a woman under 45 or 50 to be unmarried. Some women are able to maintain a good bit of autonomy by making a marriage of convenience to a man who already lives with a wife and then living apart from him. Many women, however, find this arrangement both lonely and sexually unsatisfying. Living as a lesbian is less respectable than being a second, nonresident wife, but it is more respectable than not being married at all. The lesbian sexual relationship does not reduce the autonomy of the wealthy partner "and indeed takes place in the highly positive context of the fond and supportive relationships women establish among themselves anyway" (1987, 258).

Clearly, homosexuality in Mombasa is accepted, and Shepherd suggests that rank is the most important reason why. Rank is built up out of wealth, the ability to claim Arab ancestry, and the degree of Muslim learning and piety. Men and women both expect to rise in rank over a lifetime. Rank determines marriage partners, as well as relations of loyalty and subservience. Although lesbian couples may violate the prototype for sexual relations, they do not violate relations of rank. Shepherd suggests that a marriage between a poor husband and a rich wife might be more shocking than a lesbian relationship between a dominant rich woman and a dependent poor one (1987, 262–63). It seems that rank takes precedence over sexual preference in Mombasa: it is less important that a woman's lover be male than it is for her to be a good Arab, a good Muslim, and a person of influence.

SEX, MARRIAGE, AND POWER

How can we understand these varied sexual practices? Or what are we to make of bridewealth, the exchange of young women and men by older lineage members, marriages arranged by parents, and marriages involving young women and much older men? The practice and control of sexuality may serve as a metaphor for expressing differential power within a society. Homosexuality in the New Guinean societies discussed earlier may be associated with an ideology of growth, development, and fear of women. However, it has two results: it enables senior men to establish and symbolize their control over younger men, and it sets men apart from women. Controlling children's marriages in lineage-based societies does something similar. It maintains and perpetuates the power of older members of the lineage (male or female) over younger members. Thus, sex can be used to embody relative social position. It is an enactment, in unmistakable physical terms, of inequality and differential power. This is a central component of date rape and family violence in America today.

The physical activity that we call sexual intercourse, like so much else in human life, does not "speak for itself," nor does it have only one meaning. Sexual activity, like marriage, can be used to give concrete form to more abstract notions we have about the place of men and women in the world. The example of the Ju/'hoansi (!Kung) is striking in this regard. In their sexual lives, Ju/'hoansi men and women are essentially equal. This sexual equality is symbolic of the relatively egalitarian relations between Ju/'hoansi men and women elsewhere in their society: in labor, in politics, and in the family.

This reminds us that marriage never occurs in a vacuum. Complex connections link marriage to other social practices such as food production, political organization, and kinship. Plural marriage, for example, is likely to be found where many hands in the field under one person's supervision bring in more food (and power) than those hands cost in food. We must not conclude from this, however, that the environmental determinists are right. Polyandry, for example, is embedded in a complex of connected cultural, social, economic, and historical factors. The natural environment is only one element among many that codetermine cultural practices. Other societies exploiting similar natural environments do not practice polyandry. The cultural construction of marriage and family represents the flexible interplay of culture and the natural environment.

KEY TERMS

marriage	patrilocal	polyandry
affinal	matrilocal	bridewealth
consanguineal	avunculocal	nuclear family
endogamy	monogamy	extended family
exogamy	polygamy	joint family
neolocal	polygyny	

CHAPTER SUMMARY

1. Marriage is a social process that prototypically involves a man and a woman, transforms the participants, alters the relationships among the kin of each party, and perpetuates social patterns through the production of offspring with certain rights and obligations.
2. Woman marriage and ghost marriage highlight several defining features of marriage and also demonstrate that the gender role of husband and father may not be dependent on the sex of the person who fills it.
3. There are four major patterns of postmarital residence: neolocal, patrilocal, matrilocal, and avunculocal.
4. A person may be married to only one person at a time (monogamy) or to several (polygamy). Polygamy can be further subdivided into polygyny, in which a man is married to two or more wives, and polyandry, in which a woman is married to two or more husbands.

5. The study of polyandry reveals a separation of a woman's sexuality and her reproductive capacity, an aspect not found in monogamous or polygynous societies. There are three main forms of polyandry: fraternal polyandry, associated polyandry, and secondary marriage.

6. Bridewealth represents a flow of rights and obligations in marriage. It is a payment of symbolically important goods by the husband's lineage to the wife's lineage. Anthropologists see this as compensation to the wife's family for the loss of her productive and reproductive capacities. A woman's bridewealth payment may enable her brother to pay bridewealth to get a wife. In some societies, this transfer of bridewealth produces a particularly strong relationship between brother and sister. A sister may have claims on her brother's possessions and may be able to demand a wife from him for her son; she may also be the brother's closest confidante and adviser.

7. Different family structures produce different internal patterns and tensions. There are three basic family types: nuclear, extended, and joint. Families may change from one type to another over time and with the birth, growth, and marriage of children.

8. Most human societies permit marriages to end by divorce, although it is not always easy. In most societies, childlessness is grounds for divorce. Sometimes nagging, quarreling, adultery, cruelty, and stinginess are causes. In some societies, only men may initiate a divorce, and in a very few societies, divorce is impossible.

9. Marriage rules are subject to negotiation, even when they appear rigid. This is illustrated by Iteso marriage. The Iteso depend upon women from the outside to perpetuate their patrilineages, and the women express their ironic awareness of this fact through ritualized laughter at marriage.

10. Sexual practices vary greatly worldwide, from the puritanical and fearful to the casual and pleasurable. In some societies, young men and women begin having free sexual relations from an early age until they are married. Attitudes toward nonreproductive sex vary widely, from disapproval to acceptance and institutionalization.

SUGGESTED READINGS

Bohannon, Paul, and John Middleton. 1968. *Marriage, family, and residence.* New York: Natural History Press. *A classic collection, with important and readable articles.*

Firth, Raymond. [1936] 1984. *We, the Tikopia.* Stanford: Stanford University Press. Reprint. *An enduring classic in anthropology set in the Pacific island of Tikopia. Firth writes engagingly and clearly about kinship and marriage.*

Sacks, Karen. 1979. *Sisters and wives.* Urbana: University of Illinois Press. *A marxian analysis of the notion of sexual equality. This book includes very important data and analysis on sister-brother relations.*

Shostak, Marjorie. 1981. *Nisa: The life and words of a !Kung woman.* New York: Vintage. *A wonderful book. The story of a Ju/'hoansi (!Kung) woman's life in her own words. Shostak provides background for each chapter. There is much here on marriage and everyday life.*

Suggs, David, and Andrew Miracle. 1993. *Culture and human sexuality.* Pacific Grove, CA: Brooks/Cole. *A collection of important articles from a variety of theoretical perspectives on the nature and culture of human sexuality.*

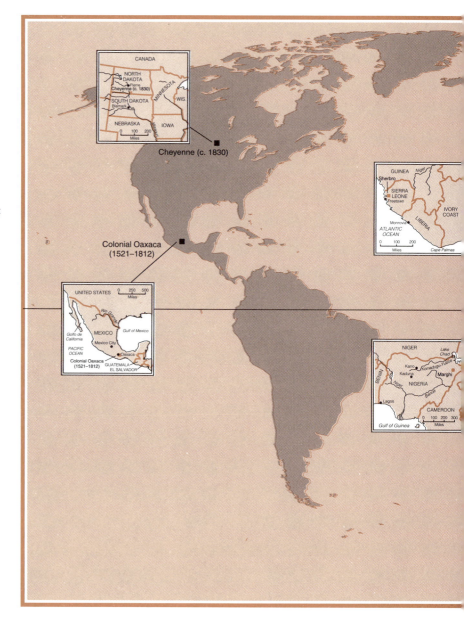

Cheyenne (c. 1830)

Colonial Oaxaca
(1521–1812)

Beyond Kinship

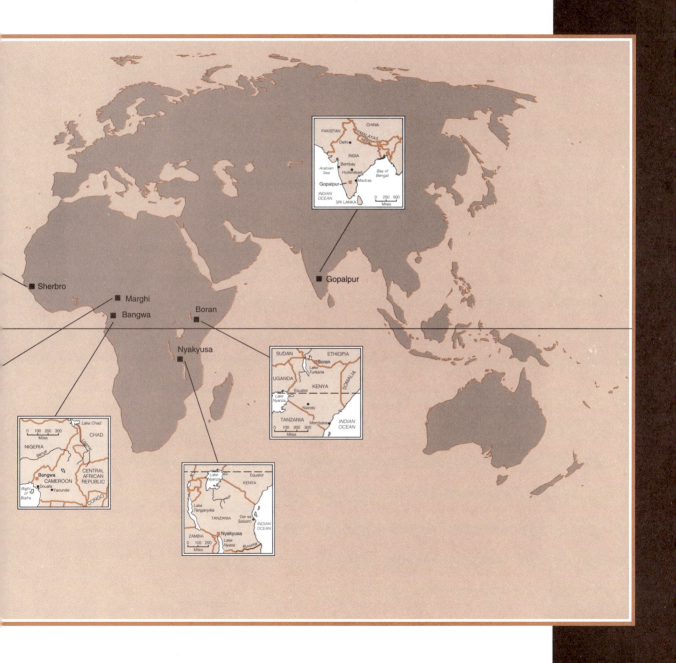

*h*umorist Garrison Keillor makes the following observation about life in the mythical small town of Lake Wobegon, Minnesota:

> When the Thanatopsis Club hit its centennial in 1982 and Mrs. Hallberg wrote to the White House and asked for an essay from the President on small-town life, she got one, two paragraphs that extolled Lake Wobegon as a model of free enterprise and individualism, which was displayed in the library under glass, although the truth is that Lake Wobegon survives to the extent that it does on a form of voluntary socialism with elements of Deism, fatalism, and nepotism. Free enterprise runs on self-interest. This is socialism, and it runs on loyalty. You need a toaster, you buy it at Co-op Hardware even though you can get a deluxe model with all the toaster attachments for less money at K-Mart in St. Cloud. You buy it at Co-op because you know Otto. Glasses you will find at Clifford's which also sells shoes and ties and some gloves. . . . Though you might rather shop for glasses in a strange place where they'll encourage your vanity, though Clifford's selection of frames is clearly based on Scripture ("Take no thought for what you shall wear. . . .") and you might put a hideous piece of junk on your face and Clifford would say, "I think you'll like those" as if you're a person who looks like you don't care what you look like—nevertheless you should think twice before you get the Calvin Klein glasses from Vanity Vision in the St. Cloud Mall. Calvin Klein isn't going to come with the Rescue Squad and he isn't going to teach your children about redemption by grace. You couldn't find Calvin Klein to save your life.
>
> If people were to live by comparison shopping, the town would go bust. It cannot compete with other places item by item. Nothing in town is quite as good as it appears to be somewhere else. If you live there, you have to take it as a whole. That's loyalty. (Keillor 1985, 95–96)

If human beings are social by nature, then no individual can be self-sufficient and autonomous. Patterns of kinship recognize and organize human interdependence in all societies. But even in societies where kinship considerations touch all social relationships, people are called on to deal with others who are not their kin. Every society would risk going bust if its members had no way of establishing links with nonkin. In this chapter we examine some of the ways nonkin loyalties are created and nurtured.

KIN-BASED VERSUS NONKIN-BASED SOCIETIES

In non-Western societies, kinship is central to social organization. As we have seen, an elaborate kinship system can regulate social life and organize behavioral patterns. In the Western world, however, kinship has long been reduced to the realm of personal and family relations. Separate and specialized social structures called *institutions* long ago took over such important social functions as government, religion, and education. In the nineteenth century, scholars of classical antiquity recognized that kinship groups had played roles in ancient European societies comparable to the role they play in many contemporary non-Western societies. Somehow, over time, those kin-ordered forms of social life had transformed themselves into the large-scale, impersonal, bureaucratically ordered forms of social life typical of a modern nation-state. What was responsible for this transformation?

Status Versus Contract Relationships

Sir Henry Maine, an English jurist who studied the roots of Roman law, described the shift as one from status to contract. In ancient societies organized on the basis of **status,** people's relationships with one another were specified by the particular position, or status, that each held within the group. Each status carried with it a bundle of rights and duties, which modern social scientists, using a theatrical metaphor, call a **role.** Statuses (and the roles attached to them) complemented one another: holders of each status were responsible for particular tasks and could rely on other members of the status system to perform different tasks. Ideally, the multiple statuses of the society fit together like pieces of a puzzle, ensuring that all tasks needed for group survival were carried out in an orderly fashion.

Societies organized on the basis of kinship were the prototype of status-based societies. For Maine, the crucial feature of status-based social organization was that people were not free to choose their own statuses, nor could they modify the rights and responsibilities associated with those statuses. Status-based societies contrasted in four major ways with societies organized on the basis of contract, such as modern nation-states. First, at least ideally, the parties to contractual relationships enter into them freely. Second, the contracting parties are equally free to specify the rights and obligations between them for the duration of the contract. Third, the range of possible statuses and roles is limitless, bound only by the imagination and interests of the contracting parties. Finally, once the terms of the contract are met, the parties may choose to terminate their relationship with one another. This would be impossible in a society based on status.

Mechanical Versus Organic Solidarity

French social thinker Emile Durkheim described the shift in terms of the social bonds that held societies together. For Durkheim, "primitive" societies (ancient and contemporary) were held together on the basis of **mechanical solidarity.** In this view, "primitive"

---

status A particular social position in a group.

role The rights and duties associated with a status.

mechanical solidarity The sense of fellow feeling and interdependence in so-called "primitive" societies, based on such similarities as language and mode of livelihood.

societies assigned the same social tasks to everybody who occupied the same kinship status. This meant that every kinship group—indeed, every family—could carry out the full range of tasks needed for survival. As a result, social solidarity, keeping kin groups together as parts of a larger whole, was problematic. Nothing bound these groups together except "mechanical" similarities in language, mode of livelihood, and so on. Mechanical solidarity, therefore, was brittle. Groups could split off and go their own way without seriously affecting their ability to survive.

"Modern" societies, according to Durkheim, were held together by **organic solidarity,** which was quite different from mechanical solidarity. "Modern" societies were still composed of groups, but each group specialized in a particular task needed for the survival of the larger whole. That is, organic solidarity depended on a highly developed **division of labor.** In societies with mechanical solidarity, the division of labor was limited to the division of kinship roles within each kinship group. Usually, this division was minimal, limited to task specializations based on age and sex. Each kinship group contained the full range of roles necessary to carry out subsistence activities without depending on outsiders. In societies with organic solidarity, however, the division of labor was much more elaborate. Some people specialized in food production, others in trade, others in government, and others in religion. Full-time specialization meant that each group had to depend on other groups to provide it with things it could not provide for itself. Very large societies could be held together on the basis of organic solidarity. Like the separate organs of a living creature, each specialized group had to contribute its activities if society as a whole were to survive. If any one specialized group were to disappear, the society as a whole would suffer.

Ascribed Status and Achieved Status

Based on the work of thinkers such as Maine and Durkheim, twentieth-century social scientists developed a model of the prototypical kin-based society. It is small in size and characterized by face-to-face relationships of a highly personal nature. Each group is basically autonomous and self-sufficient. Autonomy and self-sufficiency depend on the proper performance of basic survival tasks. In theory, the only way people know how to carry out these tasks is through the roles provided by the kinship system.

In a kin-based society, opportunities for success in life come through the kinship system. Each status has role obligations associated with it. People can perform their role obligations well or badly, but they have no control over the statuses they hold. These are called **ascribed statuses,** reflecting their fixed nature. People are "born into" ascribed statuses (such as *son* or *daughter*) or will "grow into" others (such as *wife, husband, mother,* or *father*). But even in kin-based societies, it is possible for people to attain personal distinction by their own efforts. Foragers, for example, will award the status of "good hunter" or "good gatherer" to persons who perform these activities outstandingly well. These are called **achieved statuses.** They depend not on tradition but on individual personal achievement. In kin-based societies, ascribed statuses outnumber and are more important than achieved statuses.

The shift from kin-based to "modern" society involves, among other things, a growth in the importance of achieved statuses. When two parties enter into a business contract, for example, they create or "achieve" new statuses, as defined by the terms of their contract. In a bureaucracy such as the United States Civil Service, for example, personal ties and ascribed status are excluded as the bases for opportunity and success. Rather, all statuses are explicitly defined as part of a complex formal hierarchy. Each position within the bureaucratic hierarchy is an achieved status that requires a certain level of mastery. Ideally, success and opportunity depend on this mastery.

METAPHORICAL KIN REVISITED

Kin-ordered societies depend on kinship to regulate the major areas of social life. But kinship relations are not the only social relations recognized and encouraged in such societies. All societies find ways to link people who are not "literal" kin. Perhaps the most widespread manner in which this is done is through the metaphorical extension of kinship status and roles to people who are not members of a given kinship group.

In Chapter 9, we discussed three instances of metaphorical kinship: the name relationship among the Ju/'hoansi (!Kung), the extension of lineage membership among the Nuer, and the Latin American Catholic ritual of coparenthood, or *compadrazgo*. What is the status of the people linked through such arrangements? They are not literal kin because they do not fit the prototypes of the formal kinship system, yet they treat one another according to roles associated with the formal kinship system, so they are not nonkin either. Metaphorical kin seem to be on the boundary of two categories: kin and nonkin.

Friendship

The metaphorical kin relationship makes unrelated strangers into friends. For anthropologist Robert Brain, institutions such as compadrazgo are cases of *institutionalized friendship*. Brain cites a dictionary definition of *friend* as "one joined to another in intimacy and mutual benevolence independent of sexual or family love" (1976, 15). He quickly points out that the Western belief that friendship and kinship are separate phenomena often breaks down in practice. Today, for example, some husbands and wives in Western societies consider each other "best friends." Similarly, we may become friends with some of our relatives while treating other relatives the same way we treat nonrelatives. Presumably, we can be friends with people over and above any ties we might have with them on the basis of kinship. Thus, *friendship* can be defined as love that is free of bias or self-interest, as "emotional and disinterested love" (28).

---

organic solidarity The sense of fellow feeling and interdependence in so-called "modern" societies, based on specializations of different social groups; like the organs in a body, contributions from each group are necessary for the survival of the society.

division of labor Work specialization within a society based on membership in a given group. The most basic human divisions of labor are by sex and age.

ascribed statuses Social positions assigned at birth.
achieved statuses Social positions attained by individual performance.

EthnoProfile 11.1 • **BANGWA**

REGION: Western Africa

NATION: Cameroon

POPULATION: 30,000 (1960s)

ENVIRONMENT: Broken, mountainous terrain

LIVELIHOOD: Agriculture, especially coffee growing

POLITICAL ORGANIZATION: Traditionally, kingdoms; today, part of a modern nation-state

FOR MORE INFORMATION: Brain, Robert. 1976. *Friends and lovers*. New York: Basic Books.

Bangwa Friendship   How do societies bring strangers together in mutual benevolence? Brain notes that people in many non-Western societies are far less haphazard about this than are Westerners. The Bangwa of Cameroon, among whom Brain did fieldwork, seal friendships with a ritual similar to that of marriage. (See EthnoProfile 11.1: Bangwa.) But the obligations of friendship are not the same as the obligations of kinship that derive from marriage. Friendship limits the risks that follow from close relationships with consanguineal kin.

> The Bangwa spoke of ideal friendship as one of equality and complete reciprocity, backed by moral, rather than supernatural and legal sanctions. He is my friend "because he is beautiful," "because he is good." Although there is in fact a good deal of ceremonial courtesy and gift exchange it is seen as a relationship of disinterested affection. Youths who are friends spend long hours in each other's company, holding hands when they walk together in the market. As they grow older friendships become increasingly valued—elders have little else to do but sit around with their friends, chatting about local politics, disputes over land boundaries, trouble with an obstreperous young wife. . . . Friendship is valued far above kinship; between kin there are niggling debts and witchcraft fears. Friendship lasts till death; kinship is brittle and involves inequalities of age and wealth and status. Friendship alone can cancel these out. A chief born on the same day as a slave automatically becomes his "best friend" and is bound to treat him in a friendly manner, at least in some contexts. The son who succeeds to a chief's position depends on the friends he made as a child—not his kin—in the crooked corridors of palace politics. (Brain 1976, 35)

Brain recognizes that certain relationships among literal kin may be viewed as prototypes of friendship in some societies. Even for the Bangwa, twins are ideal best friends, and other groups, such as the Kuma of New Guinea, see brothers-in-law as best friends.

But friendship can also be seen as a nonkin link that can correct the defects and limitations of literal kinship. If this is assumed, then all social structures above and beyond the boundaries of literal kinship may be viewed as kinds of institutionalized friendship.

American College Student Friendship and Friendliness   Between 1977 and 1987, anthropologist Michael Moffatt studied student culture at Rutgers University in New Jersey, where he teaches. Friendship was a central cultural feature for the American college students he knew in the 1980s. Friends were the only freely chosen companions of equal status in their lives; all other social connections—family, religion, work, race, ethnicity—were imposed on the self from the outside. Friends were those with whom you shared "who you really were," your authentic self. But proof of friendship was invisible, which was troubling to the students: "You and I are true friends if and only if both of us consider the other to be a true friend 'in our hearts,' and I am never entirely certain about what you really feel in your heart" (1989, 43). As a result, students spent hours thinking about and discussing the authenticity of their own friendships and those of other people they knew well. Not everyone, of course, could be a friend, but Moffatt found that the students he knew believed that normal Americans should be ready under certain circumstances to extend "real" friendship to any other person. To be otherwise is to be "snobbish," or to "think you are better than other people."

This attitude reflects what Moffatt sees as a central value of American daily life: friendliness. To act "friendly" is "to give regular abbreviated performances of the standard behaviors of real friendship—to look pleased and happy when you meet someone, to put on the all-American friendly smile, to acknowledge the person you are meeting by name (preferably by the first name, shortened version), to make casual body contact, to greet the person with one of the two or three conventional queries about the state of their 'whole self' ('How are you?' 'How's it goin'?' 'What's new?')" (1989, 43–44). Moffat observed that students were friendly to anyone they had met more than once or twice. This was even more strongly required among students who knew one another personally. "To violate 'friendly' in an apparently deliberate way was to arouse some of the strongest sentiments of distrust and dislike in Rutgers student culture" (1989, 43–44).

Kinship in Nonkin Relationships

The ambiguity between kin and nonkin remains. For the Bangwa, the closest kin—twins—are the best of friends. In general, however, kin are not trusted, and friends must be sought outside the kinship group. Nonkin patterns of social relations do not follow the rules of recruitment or enforce the traditional status distinctions and role obligations that are at the heart of kinship. And yet those involved in such nonkin social relations often use a kinship idiom to refer to each other and to the expectations each has concerning the other's behavior. Ritual coparents refer to themselves as coparents (*compadres*). Members of Catholic monastic orders, who may neither marry nor bear children, nevertheless continue to refer to one another as *brother, sister, father,* and *mother.* They also take as the prototype for these interpersonal relationships the literal role obligations of family members.

Anthropologist David Schneider (1968) argued that the prototypical emotion of kinship is the feeling of "diffuse and enduring solidarity." But this definition might just as well apply to friendship, as we discussed it earlier. Perhaps diffuse and enduring solidarity is something that human beings regularly seek to establish in their relations with other people—kin or not. The institution of kinship is one traditional means for cultivating such a sentiment. But so are the institutionalized friendships among the Bangwa. Indeed, all customary patterns of human interaction involve diffuse and enduring solidarity. As we saw in earlier chapters on kinship and marriage, this is true even for relationships characterized by respect and avoidance or by joking and license. In both cases, the individuals or groups who must avoid one another or joke with one another are people whose cooperation is essential to orderly social life. Order is preserved if people avoid confrontations with others who might disagree with them. But if it is agreed neither party may take offense at anything that is said or done, then order can be maintained by encouraging such confrontations. "Joking relatives," in particular, are ordinarily said to be the best of friends.

We now turn to some important forms of nonkin social relations. Not surprisingly, nonkin organizations in non-Western societies are often described by their members using a kinship idiom.

NONKIN TIES IN EGALITARIAN SOCIETIES: SODALITIES

The kind of social relationships that we have called nonkin ties are not randomly distributed throughout the societies of the world. In general, the larger the society, the more complex the division of labor within that society. The greater the specialization in the division of labor, the more likely nonkin social patterns will be found alongside or replacing kinship organization.

The simplest and most ancient form of human social organization is found among foraging societies such as the Ju/'hoansi (!Kung). (See EthnoProfile 9.1: Ju/'hoansi [!Kung].) Foragers typically live in groups of related nuclear families called *bands*. In these societies, literal kinship relations form the basis of all social relations. The division of labor is based entirely on tasks connected to kinship roles. And yet the Ju/'hoansi have developed a parallel system of metaphorical kinship linking people who share the same name. This metaphorical system undermines the literal kinship system even as it borrows principles of organization from it. The Ju/'hoansi case suggests that even in the small-scale society of foragers, the literal system can be bypassed in order to cultivate different forms of diffuse and enduring solidarity with strangers.

Once a society comes to depend on domesticated plants and animals for food, larger populations can be supported on less land. The cultivation of plants restricts a group's mobility, and most farmers settle in villages. Those who rely on domesticated animals may be mobile for part of the year, but their movements are dictated by the needs of their herds for pasture and water. Kinship organization is important in these societies, and unilineal kinship groups are common. Although one or two individuals may be accorded more prestige than everyone else, by and large social relations remain egalitarian. The term *tribe,* or *rank society,* is commonly used to refer to societies with these characteristics.

FIGURE 11.1 *The president of the Oruru Devil Fraternity (Bolivia), a sodality organized in honor of the Virgin of Socavon, wears the costume associated with his office, crowned by the devil mask.*

Despite its importance, kinship is not the only organizational principle in egalitarian societies. Nonkin forms of social organization have been created in many societies of foragers, farmers, and herders. Anthropologist Elman Service called these nonkin structures *pantribal sodalities* (1962, 113). David Hunter and Phillip Whitten define **sodalities** as "secondary groups or associations" in which membership may be voluntary or involuntary (1976, 362). Sodalities are "special-purpose groupings" that may be organized on the basis of age, sex, economic role, and personal interest. "[Sodalities] serve very different functions—among them police, military, medical, initiation, religious [Figure 11.1], and recreation. Some sodalities conduct their business in secret, others in

---

sodalities Nonkin forms of social organization; special-purpose groupings that may be organized on the basis of age, sex, economic role, and personal interest.

EthnoProfile 11.2 • **CHEYENNE (C. 1830)**

REGION: North America

NATION: United States (northern Colorado and southeastern Wyoming)

POPULATION: 3,500

ENVIRONMENT: Plains

LIVELIHOOD: Originally horticulture, later mounted nomadism

POLITICAL ORGANIZATION: Tribal council in the 1800s

FOR MORE INFORMATION: Hoebel, E. Adamson. 1960. *The Cheyennes.* New York: Holt, Rinehart and Winston.

public. Membership may be ascribed or it may be obtained via inheritance, purchase, attainment, performance or contract. Men's sodalities are more numerous and highly organized than women's and, generally, are also more secretive and seclusive in their activities." (Hunter and Whitten 1976, 362). Sodalities create diffuse and enduring solidarity among members of a large society, in part because they draw their personnel from a number of "primary" forms of social organization, such as lineages.

Cheyenne Military Societies

Sodalities are not limited to farmers and herders, as shown by the Cheyenne military societies. (See EthnoProfile 11.2: Cheyenne [c. 1830].) Toward the middle of the nineteenth century, the Cheyenne people of the Great Plains of North America were a foraging people whose main source of meat was the buffalo. They traced descent bilaterally and organized themselves into a number of kindreds. During the winter months, the Cheyenne lived in camps composed of several kindreds. During the summer months, everyone camped together in order to perform important rituals, including the Arrow Renewal and the Sun Dance. Cheyenne identity also rested in the council of 44 peace chiefs, in whom lay supreme authority for the people as a whole.

The Cheyenne had several sodalities whose membership cut across kindreds and bands (Figure 11.2). There were sodalities for women and men, but those for men were more numerous and their organization more complex. The most important of these were the seven military societies.

According to E. Adamson Hoebel, Cheyenne military societies "centered on the common experience of the warriors, with rituals glorifying and enhancing that experience, and with duties and services performed on behalf of the community at large" (1960, 33). All seven societies were of equal status. A Cheyenne boy who was ready to go to war could join any society he chose and become a full-fledged member imme-

FIGURE 11.2 *The Cheyenne had several sodalities whose membership cut across kindreds and bands.*

diately. Membership was usually for life. Each society had four leaders, two of whom were war chiefs and two of whom were considered "the bravest men in the society." In addition, each society had ritual paraphernalia, dress, dances, and songs that distinguished it from the other societies.

The military societies were charged with maintaining order during public ceremonies and during the communal buffalo hunt. They were also responsible for carrying out legal decisions of the council of chiefs, such as banishment of murderers from the community. The Cheyenne believed that any member of their community who killed another member began to rot internally, and that the stench drove the buffalo away; the expulsion of murderers rid the community of this pollution. The system also eliminated feuds between bands and kindreds because any retaliatory killing would only worsen the pollution and undermine the survival of the community as a whole.

The Cheyenne military societies were nonkin voluntary associations that cut across kinship groups. They were dedicated to glorifying and perpetuating the successes of fighting men. And yet they were not totally free of the influence of women and the idiom of kinship. A mythological female figure, Sweet Medicine, was believed to have given the Cheyenne the idea of military societies, together with their rituals. Five of the sodalities invited four virgin daughters of chiefs "to participate in their ceremonies and to sit in the midst of the circle of war chiefs when they meet in common council." These young girls were similar to mascots. They represented the sodality as a whole, and its warriors would be successful in battle only as long as these young women remained chaste. "All the members of a society call their four maids by the kin term 'sister,' and they may never marry one of their own maidens" (Hoebel 1960, 33–34).

EthnoProfile 11.3   •   **NYAKYUSA**

REGION: Eastern Africa

NATION: Tanzania

POPULATION: 160,000 (1930s)

ENVIRONMENT: Well-watered, fertile valley

LIVELIHOOD: Agriculture, especially bananas and millet, and stock raising

POLITICAL ORGANIZATION: Traditionally, small chiefdoms; today, part of a modern nation-state

FOR MORE INFORMATION: Wilson, Monica. 1951. *Good company*. Oxford: Oxford University Press.

Age Sets

All societies recognize in some way that people pass through stages as they grow from infancy to maturity to old age. Generational differences are marked in every kinship system. But some groups emphasize generational distinctions to an unusual degree and use them as the basis for forming sodalities. Although distinctions in age were not marked in the Cheyenne military sodalities, the situation is different in eastern Africa. A number of societies there assign men from different kinship groups to sodalities defined in terms of relative age.

Age sets are composed of young men born within a specific time span (five years, for example). Each age set is "one unit in a sequence of similar units" that succeed each other in time as their members pass through youth, maturity, and old age. "Sets are part of the formal social order blessed by tradition and membership is usually ascribed, and is always obligatory" (Baxter and Almagor 1978, 4). Age-set systems for women are not found in these societies. P. T. W. Baxter and Uri Almagor suggest that this may be because women are involved in domestic matters from an early age and marry shortly after puberty (11).

Age-set systems are like kinship systems in that they assign people membership in groups on the basis of generation and age. But age-set systems are built on two additional assumptions: that generations of fathers and sons will succeed one another regularly and that the succession will follow a uniform timetable. Unfortunately, experience belies both assumptions. Members of age-set systems must continually work to reconcile age, generation, and the passage of time. "Age systems which are based on measured units of time are unsuccessful attempts to tame time by chopping it up into manageable slices" (Baxter and Almagor 1978, 5).

The Eastern African Age-Set System   The classic study of eastern African age sets was by Monica Wilson (1951), who examined their role among the Nyakyusa. (See

EthnoProfile 11.3: Nyakyusa.) At the time of Wilson's fieldwork, the Nyakyusa were patrilineal and patrilocal. Their society was divided into many independent chiefdoms. Nyakyusa age sets initially included a group of boys from about 10 to 15 years old. When the members of this junior set were about 33 to 35 years old, an elaborate series of rituals was held to mark their "coming out." At that time, the reigning senior generation "handed the country over to them." At any point in time, there were three strata in the Nyakyusa age system: retired elders, active senior men who carried political and military responsibilities for the entire society, and immature juniors.

In precolonial times, members of junior eastern African age sets were as flashy as members of Cheyenne military societies. Each set had distinctive dress and titles and exhibited flamboyant behavior. According to Baxter and Almagor, however, it was unusual for age sets to take on political or military roles, even though they most often are found in societies with no central authority. Baxter and Almagor argue that the colorful activities of junior sets should not distract observers from recognizing that the seniors run things. If junior sets act, they usually act as agents of seniors. Indeed, the wildness of junior sets is conventional in many societies with age systems. Although this custom allows juniors to enjoy themselves, it also publicly reinforces traditional wisdom that places power and property in the hands of elders.

Fostering Solidarity with Age Sets   Age-set systems foster a sense of diffuse and enduring solidarity among their members. This is especially so if membership in a set comes after a rigorous initiation ritual. That age-mates are supposed to be the "best of friends" is illustrated by the widespread rule that forbids age-mates to accuse one another of adultery and demand compensation. This means, in practice, that a married man cannot prevent sexual relationships that might develop between his wife and his age-mates. This leads to a relationship among age-mates similar to that of "joking kin," who are forbidden to take offense at anything they say or do to each other. Here, the refusal to recognize adultery is institutionalized. It emphasizes that nothing, especially not sexual jealousy, must come between age-mates. The rule appears most onerous for the first members of junior sets who marry. Members of senior sets usually all have wives of their own (Baxter and Almagor 1978, 17).

Nyakyusa age sets were able to cultivate an unusual degree of solidarity among their members because each set was required to live in its own village. Indeed, the Nyakyusa believed that the main purpose of age villages was to allow set members to enjoy *ukwangala,* "good company"—the company of friends and equals. Wilson wrote that to attain *ukwangala,* "men must build not only in villages, rather than in scattered homesteads, but also with contemporaries rather than with kin, since there can be no free and easy intercourse and sharing of food and beer between fathers and sons. *Ukwangala* implies eating and drinking together frequently and cannot be fully enjoyed by people who do not live close to one another" (1951, 163).

---

age sets Nonkin forms of social organization that are composed of young men born within a specified time span and are part of a sequence of age sets that proceeds through maturity and old age.

EthnoProfile 11.4 • BORAN

REGION: Eastern Africa

NATIONS: Kenya and Ethiopia

POPULATION: 80,000 (1970s)

ENVIRONMENT: Adequate rangeland, scrub, and desert

LIVELIHOOD: Herding of cattle by preference, also sheep and goats

POLITICAL ORGANIZATION: Traditionally, a kinship-based organization with a set of six elders who have certain responsibilities for maintaining order; today, part of a modern nation-state

FOR MORE INFORMATION: Baxter, P. T. W., and Uri Almagor, eds. 1978. *Age, generation and time.* New York: St. Martin's Press.

Functions of Age-Set Systems Age-set systems may play an important cognitive role in the societies where they are found. For example, Baxter argues that the *gada* age-set system of the Boran of Kenya provides the idiom the Boran use to describe and debate social and political life. (See EthnoProfile 11.4: Boran.) The complex gada system recognizes five generation sets that succeed one another over a period of 40 years. Every 8 years, a new generation set is formed and the oldest generation set retires. The retirement of the most senior set is marked by an elaborate culmination ceremony called the *gaadamoji*. "The set organisation is said to be there to ensure that these ceremonies are held. From another point of view the organisation generates a set of men every eight years who, for their own ritual needs, require the opportunity, as they enter the condition of *gaadamoji*, to undergo the culmination ceremony" (Baxter 1978, 160).

Other explanations for age-set systems have been offered. Monica Wilson suggested that Nyakyusa age villages played an important role in controlling sexual behavior. Wilson noted that the Nyakyusa themselves argued that young men had to live apart from their fathers to prevent incest between the son's wife and his father. The same arrangement also prevented sexual involvements between a son and his father's wives. Such involvement was a real risk because a son traditionally inherited his father's wives (excluding his own mother) when his father died.

For Baxter, Boran discussions of gada reveal it to be a conceptual system that guides them in political and social matters. But Baxter rejects the suggestion that the gada system ever played a political role in Boran society. "Gada exists primarily . . . in the folk view as well as in mine, to ensure the well-being of the Boran and to regulate the ritual growth and development of individuals and to do so in such a way as to permit all men who survive life's full span to achieve responsible and joyful sanctity. It is this last, joyful aspect of *gada* as an institution which performs rituals that has struck intelligent non-professional observers . . . and not its political ones" (1978, 156).

Secret Societies in Western Africa

Several neighboring peoples in western Africa use **secret societies** as a way of drawing members of different kinship groups into crosscutting associations. The most famous secret societies are the Poro and Sande, which are found among the Mende, Sherbro, Kpelle, and other neighboring peoples of Sierra Leone, Ivory Coast, Liberia, and Guinea.

Membership and Initiation   Poro is a secret society for men; Sande, a secret society for women. Poro is responsible for initiating young men into social manhood; Sande, for initiating young women into social womanhood. These sodalities are secret in the sense that each has certain knowledge that can be revealed only to initiated members. Both sodalities are hierarchically organized. The higher a person's status within the sodality, the greater the secret knowledge revealed.

Poro and Sande are responsible for supervising and regulating the sexual, social, and political conduct of all members of the wider society. To carry out this responsibility, high-status sodality members impersonate important supernatural figures by donning masks and performing in public. One secret kept from the uninitiated is that these masked figures are not the spirits themselves.

Membership is automatic on initiation, and all men and women are ordinarily initiated. "Until he has been initiated in the society, no Mende man is considered mature enough to have sexual intercourse or to marry" (Little 1967, 245). (See EthnoProfile 10.7: Mende.) Each community has its own local Poro and Sande congregations, and a person initiated in one community is eligible to participate in the congregations of other communities. Initiates must pay a fee for initiation, and if they wish to receive advanced training and progress to higher levels within the sodality, they must pay additional fees. In any community where Poro and Sande are strong, authority in society is divided between a sodality of mature women and one of mature men. Together, they work to keep society on the correct path. Indeed, the relationship between men and women in societies with Poro and Sande tends to be highly egalitarian.

Anthropologist Beryl Bellman (1984) was initiated into a Poro chapter among the Kpelle of Liberia. (See EthnoProfile 6.5: Kpelle.) He describes initiation as a ritual process that takes place about every 16 to 18 years, about once each generation. One of the Poro's forest spirits, or "devils," metaphorically captures and eats the novices—only for them later to be metaphorically reborn from the womb of the devil's "wife." Marks incised on the necks, chests, and backs of initiates represent the "devil's teeth marks."

secret societies Nonkin forms of social organization that initiate young men or women into social adulthood. The se-crecy concerns certain knowledge that is known only to initiated members.

After this scarification, initiates spend a year living apart from women in a special village constructed for them in the forest. During this period, they carry out various activities under the strict supervision of senior Poro members. Female Sande initiates undergo a similar experience during their year of initiation, which normally takes place several years after the Poro initiation has been completed.

Use of the Kinship Idiom   In Kpelle society, the relationship between a mother's brother (*ngala*) and a sister's son (*maling*) describes the "literal" relationship between kin. There is also a metaphoric aspect to this connection that is used to describe relationships between patrilineages, sections of a town, and towns themselves. "Besides the serious or formal rights and obligations between *ngala* and *maling,* other aspects of the relationship are expressed as joking behavior between kinsmen. . . . The *ngala-maling* relationship is also the basis of labor recruitment, financial assistance, and a general support network" (Bellman 1984, 22–23). This kinship idiom is used within the Poro society to describe the relationships between certain members. For example, two important Poro officials involved in initiation are the *Zo* and the *kwelebah.* The Zo directs the ritual, and the kwelebah announces both the ritual death and the ritual rebirth of the initiates to the community at large. The Zo is said to be the ngala of the kwelebah, and the kwelebah is said to be the maling of the Zo.

The Thoma Secret Society: A Microcosm   Anthropologist Carol MacCormack (1980b) studied secret societies among the Sherbro. (See EthnoProfile 11.5: Sherbro.) In addition to Poro and Sande congregations, the Sherbro MacCormack studied have a third secret society called *Thoma,* which initiates both men and women. Members of one society cannot be initiated into the others, and families with several children usually try to initiate at least one child into each sodality.

MacCormack writes: "With Poro and Sande, the contrastive gender categories are split apart and the uniqueness of each gender is emphasized, but always with the final view that the complementarity of the two constitute human society, the full cultural unity. Thoma is a microcosm of the whole. Its local congregations or chapters are headed by a man and a woman, co-equal leaders who are 'husband and wife' in a ritual context but are not married in mundane life" (1980b, 97). The Sherbro are concerned with the reproduction of their society. *Reproduction* here means not just production of children but also continuation of the division of labor between men and women. The Sherbro say that the ritual function of the Thoma sodality is to "wash the bush"—that is, "to cleanse the land and the village from evil and restore its fertility and well-being" (98).

The purpose of Thoma initiation is to transform uninitiated, protosocial beings into initiated, fully social, adult human beings. The Thoma society has four masks representing two pairs of spirits: an animal pair and a humanoid pair. The masks, which are considered very powerful, appear when initiates are nearing the end of their ritual seclusion in the forest. They "symbolize that 'wild,' unsocialized children are being transformed into cultured adults, but will retain the fertile vigour of the animal world" (MacCormack 1980b, 100). The humanoid masks represent male and female ancestral spirits who appear when the initiates are about to be reborn into their new, adult status.

EthnoProfile 11.5 • SHERBRO

REGION: Western Africa

NATION: Sierra Leone

POPULATION: 15,000 (1970s)

ENVIRONMENT: Rainy, swampy coastal area with sandy soil

LIVELIHOOD: Shallow-water fishing and hoe cultivation of rice

POLITICAL ORGANIZATION: Chiefdoms that are part of a modern nation-state

FOR MORE INFORMATION: MacCormack, Carol. 1980. Proto-social to adult: A Sherbro transformation. In *Nature, culture, and gender,* edited by Carol MacCormack and Marilyn Strathern, 95–118. Cambridge: Cambridge University Press.

"Human beings must abide by ancestral rules of conduct if they are to be healthy and fertile. Indeed, they wish to be as healthy and strong as forest animals which give birth in litters. Only by becoming fully 'cultural,' vowing to live by ancestral laws, may they hope to avoid illness and barrenness" (116).

The Meaning of Secrecy in a Secret Society   Bellman was interested in the secrecy that surrounded membership in Poro and other similar sodalities. He discovered that Poro (and Sande) initiation rituals are primarily concerned with teaching initiates how to keep a secret. Discretion—knowing when, how, and even whether to speak about various topics—is a prized virtue among the Kpelle and is required of all mature members of their society. So learning how to "practice secrecy" is a central lesson of initiation. "It was always crucial for members to be certain whether they have the right to talk as well as the right to know. The two are not necessarily related. Nonmembers very often know some of the secrets of membership; yet they must maintain a description of the event comparable to that of nonmembers" (1984, 51).

Based on this interpretation of "secrecy" in the secret society he knew, Bellman analyzed what the secret societies meant to outsiders. What do the uninitiated actually believe about these societies? In the case of the Poro, the women speak of devils killing and eating novices as though they believe this to be literally true. Bellman and his informants believe that the women know perfectly well what is "really" happening when Poro novices are taken away into the forest. But women are not allowed to talk about what they know except in the language of ritual metaphor. In the context of the initiation ritual, participation of the "audience" of women and other noninitiates is as important as the participation of the Poro elders and the initiates themselves. In playing their appropriate ritual role, women show respect for traditional understandings concerning which members of society have the right to speak about which topics in which manner and under which circumstances. "The enactment of Poro rituals serves to establish the ways in which that concealed information is communicated. . . . It offers methods for mentioning the unmentionable" (1984, 141).

NONKIN TIES IN STRATIFIED SOCIETIES

Sodalities are most common in **egalitarian societies;** that is, societies where there is no central chief or king who rules over the entire group. People in these societies may gain the esteem of their fellows. Men might even have substantial support groups of wives, children, and retainers. But their status depends entirely on their own personal prowess. They cannot transform what they have achieved into permanent superiority of wealth, power, or prestige.

Permanent hierarchies do exist in other societies. Stratification may be minimal, as in *chiefdoms,* where perhaps only the office of chief is a permanently superior status. Privileges accrue to those who are closely related to the chief, while other members of the society must settle for less. In fully **stratified societies,** by contrast, some members of the society have permanent, privileged access to wealth, power, and prestige, and this privileged access can be inherited.

The stratified society, which can be much larger than tribes or chiefdoms, may be internally divided into a number of groups whose statuses relative to one another are carefully specified. In **caste** societies, membership in each ranked group is closed, and individuals are not allowed to move from one group to another. For anthropologists, India is the prototypical caste society. **Class** societies also have internally ranked subgroups, but these groups are open, and individuals can move upward or downward from one class to another. Modern Europe and the United States are classic examples of class societies.

Criteria for Membership in Levels of Society

In stratified societies, different criteria may be used to place people in one or another stratum. Karl Marx argued, for example, that class membership in capitalist society is determined by the relationship people have to the means of production: whether or not they own the tools and raw materials needed for industry. Capitalists who own the means of production make up the ruling class; those who work for capitalists for wages but do not own the means of production make up the proletariat, or subject class. Other criteria can also be important in assigning membership to the various levels in a stratified society. Occupational specialization is one such criterion and appears to be central to caste systems. **Race** and **ethnicity** involve other criteria that are based on biology or culture or both. These may complicate or contradict stratification based on other principles.

The various levels of a stratified society do not in themselves provide ties that link nonkin to one another. The key to social solidarity in stratified societies is the nature of the relationships uniting the levels. Again, in the marxian view of class, the links between capitalists and proletarians are purely economic; both classes must cooperate to produce goods for society as a whole. Their relationship is sealed by the transfer of money, either as wages to workers or as payment for goods. In caste societies, where each caste specializes in one kind of work, the cash nexus is traditionally less important. Instead, members of different castes are urged to continue to perform their appropriate tasks by a political system that justifies the division of labor in terms of religious doctrines reinforced by strict ritual prohibitions.

Economic or political links between different levels of a stratified society involve groups as wholes. In many of the stratified societies studied by anthropologists, however, levels are also linked by the institution of **clientage**. According to M. G. Smith, clientage "designates a variety of relationships, which all have inequality of status of the associated persons as a common characteristic" ([1954] 1981, 31). It is a relationship between individuals rather than groups. The party of superior status is the patron, and the party of inferior status is the client. For example, clientage is characteristic of compadrazgo relationships, especially when the ritual parents are of higher social status than the biological parents. In fact, the Latin American societies in which compadrazgo flourishes are class societies, and parents often do seek their social superiors as compadres.

Stratified societies united by links of clientage can be very stable. Often the stratified order is believed to be natural and not questioned. Those of low status believe their security depends on finding someone in a high-status group who can protect them. Clientage links individuals, yet the clients may be unaware that they belong to a group of people who are all similarly underprivileged. In marxian terms, they lack class consciousness. In other stratified societies, underprivileged groups do have a common sense of identity. Sometimes they even have organizations of their own, such as trade unions, that defend group members' interests in dealings with outsiders. This is also often the case for groups whose memberships depend on race or ethnicity.

Caste Societies

The word *caste* comes from the Portuguese word *casta,* meaning "chaste." Portuguese explorers applied it to the stratification system they encountered in India in the fifteenth century. Each group in society had to remain sexually pure, or chaste: both sexual and

---

egalitarian societies Societies in which no great differences in wealth, power, or prestige divide members from one another.

stratified societies Societies in which there is a permanent hierarchy that accords some members privileged access to wealth, power, and prestige.

caste A ranked group within a hierarchically stratified society that is closed and prohibits individuals to move from one caste to another.

class A ranked group within a hierarchically stratified society that is open and allows individuals to move upward or downward from one class to another.

race A social grouping based on perceived physical differences and cloaked in the language of biology.

ethnicity A set of prototypically descent-based cultural criteria that people in a group are believed to share.

clientage The institution linking individuals from upper and lower levels in a stratified society.

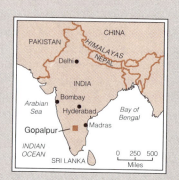

EthnoProfile 11.6 • **GOPALPUR**

REGION: Southern Asia

NATION: India

POPULATION: 540 (1960)

ENVIRONMENT: Center of a plain, some fertile farmland and pasture

LIVELIHOOD: Intensive millet farming, some cattle and sheep herding

POLITICAL ORGANIZATION: Caste system in a modern nation-state

FOR MORE INFORMATION: Beals, Alan. 1962. *Gopalpur, a south Indian village.* New York: Holt, Rinehart and Winston.

marital links between groups were forbidden. Ever since, the stratification system of India has been taken as the prototype of caste stratification. Some scholars have even argued that caste cannot properly be said to exist outside India. If we take the Indian system as a prototype, however, we may apply the term caste to systems of social stratification that bear a family resemblance to the Indian case. One important non-Indian example, which we examine later in this chapter, comes from Nigeria. (See EthnoProfile 11.7: Marghi.)

Caste in India   *Jati* is the Hindi word for the Portuguese *casta*. Villagers in the southern Indian town of Gopalpur defined a jati for anthropologist Alan Beals. (See Ethno-Profile 11.6: Gopalpur.) They said it was "a category of men thought to be related, to occupy a particular position within a hierarchy of jatis, to marry among themselves, and to follow particular practices and occupations" (Beals 1962, 25). Beals's informants compared the relationship between jatis of different rank to the relationship between brothers. Members of low-ranking jatis respect and obey members of high-ranking jatis just as younger brothers respect and obey older brothers.

Villagers in Gopalpur were aware of at least 50 different jatis, although not all were represented in the village. Because jatis have different occupational specialties that they alone can perform, villagers are sometimes dependent on the services of outsiders. For example, there was no member of the Washerman jati in Gopalpur. As a result, a member of that jati from another village had to be employed when people in Gopalpur wanted their clothes cleaned ritually or required clean cloth for ceremonies.

Jatis are distinguished in terms of the foods they eat as well as their traditional occupations. These features have a ritual significance that affects interactions between members of different jatis. In Hindu belief, certain foods and occupations are classed as pure and others as polluting. In theory, all jatis are ranked on a scale from purest to most polluted. For example, a vegetarian diet is purest, and vegetarian castes such as Carpenters and Blacksmiths are assigned a high rank. Below the vegetarians are "clean," or "pure," meat eaters. In Gopalpur, this group of jatis included Saltmakers, Farmers, and Shepherds, who eat sheep, goats, chicken, and fish but not pork or beef. The lowest-ranking jatis are "unclean" meat eaters, who include Stoneworkers and Basketweavers (who eat pork) and Leatherworkers (who eat pork and beef). Occupations that involve slaughtering animals or touching polluted things are themselves polluting. Jatis that traditionally carry out such activities as butchering and washing dirty clothing are ranked below jatis whose traditional work does not involve polluting activities. Ranked highest of all are the vegetarian Brahmins, who are pure enough to approach the gods.

Hindu dietary rules deal not only with the kinds of food that may be eaten by different jatis but also with the circumstances in which members of one jati may accept food prepared by members of another. Members of a lower-ranking jati may accept any food prepared by members of a higher-ranking jati. Members of a higher-ranking jati may accept only certain foods prepared by a lower-ranking jati. In addition, members of different jatis should not eat together.

In practice, these rules are not as confining as they appear. In Gopalpur, " 'food' refers to particular kinds of food, principally rice. 'Eating together' means eating from the same dish or sitting on the same line. . . . Members of quite different jatis may eat together if they eat out of separate bowls and if they are facing each other or turned slightly away from each other" (Beals 1962, 41). Members of jatis that are close in rank and neither at the top nor at the bottom of the scale often share food and eat together on a daily basis. Strict observance of the rules is saved for ceremonial occasions.

The way in which non-Hindus have been incorporated into the jati system in Gopalpur illuminates the logic of the system. For example, Muslims have long ruled the region surrounding Gopalpur; thus, political power is a salient attribute of Muslim identity. In addition, Muslims do not eat pork or the meat of animals that have not been ritually slaughtered. These attributes, taken together, have led the villagers in Gopalpur to rank Muslims above the Stoneworkers and Basketweavers, who eat pork. All three groups are considered to be eaters of unclean meat.

There is no direct correlation between the status of a jati on the scale of purity and pollution and the economic status of members of that jati. Jati membership may be advantageous in some cases. Beals notes, for example, that the high status of Brahmins means that "there are a relatively large number of ways in which a poor Brahmin may become wealthy" (1962, 37). Similarly, members of low-status jatis may find their attempts to amass wealth curtailed by the opposition of their status superiors. In Gopalpur, a group of Farmers and Shepherds attacked a group of Stoneworkers who had purchased good rice land in the village. Those Stoneworkers were eventually forced to buy inferior land elsewhere in the village.

In general, however, regardless of caste, a person who wishes to advance economically "must be prepared to defend his gains against jealous neighbors. Anyone who buys land is limiting his neighbor's opportunities to buy land. Most people safeguard themselves by tying themselves through indebtedness to a powerful landlord who will give them support when difficulties are encountered" (Beals 1962, 39).

Although the interdependence of jatis is explained in theory by their occupational specialties, the social reality is a bit different. For example, Saltmakers in Gopalpur are farmers and actually produce little salt—which can be bought in shops by those who need it. It is primarily in the context of ritual that jati interdependence is given full play. Recall that Gopalpur villagers require the services of a Washerman when they need *ritually* clean garments or cloth; otherwise, most villagers wash their own clothing. "To arrange a marriage, to set up the doorway of a new house, to stage a drama, or to hold an entertainment, the householder must call on a wide range of jatis. The entertainment of even a modest number of guests requires the presence of the Singer. The Potter must provide new pots in which to cook the food; the Boin from the Farmer jati must carry the pot; the Shepherd must sacrifice the goat; the Crier, a Saltmaker, must invite the guests. To survive, one requires the cooperation of only a few jatis; to enjoy life and do things in the proper manner requires the cooperation of many" (Beals 1962, 41).

Caste in Western Africa   Anthropologists often use the term *caste* to describe societies outside India when they encounter one of two features in a society: (1) endogamous occupational groupings whose members are looked down on by other groups in the society or (2) an endogamous ruling elite who set themselves above those over whom they rule. Both these features are present in Indian society. The problem is that, apart from these similarities, caste systems found outside the Indian subcontinent are very different indeed.

Anthropologist James Vaughan (1970) reviewed the data on western African caste systems. The first feature of non-Hindu caste described here was common in societies of the Sahara and in the western Sudan (the band of territory between Senegal and Lake Chad, south of the Sahara and north of the coastal rain forest). Vaughan also found castes in a second culture area located in the mountain ranges that lie along the modern border between Nigeria and Cameroon. In this region, many societies had endogamous groups of "blacksmiths" whose status was distinct from that of other members of society. These people were not despised, however; if anything, they were regarded with awe or feared.

EthnoProfile 11.7 • MARGHI

REGION: Western Africa

NATION: Nigeria

POPULATION: 100,000 to 200,000 (1960s)

ENVIRONMENT: Mountains and valley floor

LIVELIHOOD: Farming, selling surplus in local markets

POLITICAL ORGANIZATION: Traditionally, kingdoms; today, part of a modern nation-state

FOR MORE INFORMATION: Vaughn, James. 1970. Caste systems in the western Sudan. In *Social stratification in Africa*, edited by Arthur Tuden and Leonard Plotnikov. New York: Free Press.

FIGURE 11.3 *The Marghi* ngkyagu *are traditional craft specialists. The woman on the right holds a basket. The man in the left foreground is hammering a steel knife. The man in the center is making the scabbard for another knife out of crocodile skin. The man on the left (hidden by the child) is fashioning leather loin garments. Three pots in the left rear contain divining paraphernalia. Only members of the ngkyagu caste may perform these tasks.*

Vaughan studied such a caste of blacksmiths in a kingdom of the Marghi, whose traditional territory is in the mountains and nearby plains south of Lake Chad in present-day Nigeria. (See EthnoProfile 11.7: Marghi.) Members of the caste, who are called *ngkyagu,* are traditional craft specialists whose major occupation is the smithing of iron (Figure 11.3). They make a variety of iron tools for ordinary Marghi, the most important of which are the hoes they use for farming. They also make weapons and iron ornaments of various kinds. They work leather, fashioning traditional items of apparel, leather-covered charms, and the slings in which infants are carried. They work wood, making beds and carving stools. They are barbers, incising traditional tribal markings on Marghi women, and are responsible in some Marghi kingdoms for shaving the head of a newly installed king. They are morticians, responsible for assisting in the preparation of a body for burial, digging the grave, and carrying the corpse from the compound to the grave. They are musicians, playing a distinctive drum played by no one else. Some are diviners and "doctors." And female caste members are the potters of Marghi society.

Vaughan stresses that although regular Marghi and ngkyagu both recognize that ngkyagu are different, in most ways the ngkyagu do not stand out from other Marghi. All the same, Marghi and ngkyagu do not intermarry and will not share the same food. In an interesting parallel to the Indian case described above, ngkyagu can drink beer brewed by Marghi women as long as they provide their own drinking vessel. Marghi, however, will not drink beer brewed by female ngkyagu.

When Marghi described the differences between themselves and ngkyagu to Vaughan, they said that caste members were "different" and "strange." In Vaughan's opinion, this has to do in large part with the fact that ngkyagu do not farm: "To be a Marghi means to be a farmer. . . . A person who does not farm cannot in the Marghi idiom be considered an altogether normal person" (1970, 71). By contrast, ngkyagu attribute the difference between themselves and other Marghi to the division of labor and point out that both groups depend on one another. Marghi do their own smelting, but they require ngkyagu to use their skills as smiths to turn the smelted ore into implements. Thus, Marghi rely on members of the caste for their farming tools, but ngkyagu rely on Marghi for food.

Vaughan suggests that this division of labor and interdependence is not only practical but also ideological. It is part of the Marghi worldview and is further revealed in the domains of politics and ritual. For example, a curious relationship links ngkyagu to Marghi kings. The most remarkable feature of this relationship is that Marghi kings traditionally take a female member of the caste as a bride, thereby violating the rule of endogamy. Recall the role a member of the caste plays during the investiture of a new king; it is even more common for ngkyagu to bury deceased Marghi kings seated on an iron stool, surrounded by charcoal, which is the way ngkyagu themselves are buried. In addition, of all Marghi clans, only the ngkyagu clans are exempt from participating in the choice of a new Marghi king. Indeed, traditionally they had their own "king," the *ptil ngkyagu,* who decided disputes among ngkyagu without recourse to the legal advisers of the Marghi king.

All this suggests that the two categories *Marghi* and *ngkyagu* form the foundation of Marghi society. They are mutually interdependent. The ritual prohibitions that divide them, however, suggest that this interdependence carries symbolic overtones. According to Vaughan, the caste system allows the Marghi to resolve a paradox. They are a society of farmers who need to support full-time toolmaking nonfarmers in order to farm. Marghi dislike being dependent on others, yet their way of life requires them to depend on ngkyagu. The ritual prohibitions that separate ngkyagu from other Marghi also ensure that there will always be some caste specialists around to provide Marghi with the tools they cannot make themselves.

Class, Race, and Ethnicity

We now turn to the role of social class in human society, specifically as it relates to race and ethnicity. Recall that classes are levels in a socially stratified society whose boundaries are less rigid than those of the caste system. Unlike castes, classes are not endogamous, although members of a class often tend to choose other members of their class as spouses. Also unlike castes, the boundaries between classes are fluid enough for people to change their class membership within their lifetimes.

Social stratification is rarely a simple matter in societies as large and complex as nation-states. Social scientists mainly agree that the large-scale societies of the modern world are divided into classes. There is debate over the precise boundaries of the classes, as well as the distinctive features that indicate class membership. Position in the hierarchy depends not only on power, not only on wealth, not only on prestige, but on a

In Their Own Words   THE POLITICS OF ETHNICITY

Stanley Tambiah reflects on the late-twentieth-century upsurge in ethnic conflict that few people predicted because many assumed that ethnic particularisms would disappear within modern nation-states.

The late-twentieth-century reality is evidenced by the fact that ethnic groups, rather than being mostly minority or marginal subgroups at the edges of society, expected in due course to assimilate or weaken, have figured as major "political" elements and major political collective actors in several societies. Moreover, if in the past we typically viewed an ethnic group as a subgroup of a larger society, today we are also faced with instances of majority ethnic groups within a polity or nation exercising preferential or "affirmative" policies on the basis of that majority status.

The first consideration that confirms ethnic conflict as a major reality of our time is not simply its ubiquity alone, but also its cumulative increase in frequency and intensity of occurrence. Consider these conflicts, by no means an exhaustive listing, that have occurred since the sixties (some of them have a longer history, of course): conflicts between anglophone and francophone in Canada; Catholic and Protestant in Northern Ireland; Walloon and Fleming in Belgium; Chinese and Malay in Malaysia; Greek and Turk in Cyprus; Jews and other minorities on the one hand and Great Russians on the other in the Soviet Union; and Ibo and Hausa and Yoruba in Nigeria; the East Indians and Creoles in Guyana. Add, to these instances, up-

heavals that became climactic in recent years: the Sinhala-Tamil war in Sri Lanka, the Sikh-Hindu, and Muslim-Hindu, confrontations in India, the Chakma-Muslim turmoil in Bangladesh, the actions of the Fijians against Indians in Fiji, the Pathan-Bihari clashes in Pakistan, and last, but not least, the inferno in Lebanon, and the serious erosion of human rights currently manifest in Israeli actions in Gaza and the West Bank. That there is possibly no end to these eruptions, and that they are worldwide has been forcibly brought to our attention by a century-old difference that exploded in March 1988 between Christian Armenians and Muslim Azerbaijanis in the former U.S.S.R.

Most of these conflicts have involved force and violence, homicide, arson, and destruction of property. Civilian riots have evoked action by security forces: sometimes as counteraction to quell them, sometimes in collusion with the civilian aggressors, sometimes both kinds of action in sequence. Events of this nature have happened in Sri Lanka, Malaysia, India, Zaire, Guyana, and Nigeria. Mass killings of civilians by armed forces have occurred in Uganda and in Guatemala, and large losses of civilian lives have been recorded in Indonesia, Pakistan, India, and Sri Lanka.

The escalation of ethnic conflicts has been considerably aided by the amoral business of gunrunning and free trade in the technology of violence, which enable not only dissident groups to successfully resist the armed forces of the state, but also civil-

ians to battle with each other with lethal weapons. The classical definition of the state as the authority invested with the monopoly of force has become a sick joke. After so many successful liberations and resistance movements in many parts of the globe, the techniques of guerrilla resistance now constitute a systematized and exportable knowledge. Furthermore, the easy access to the technology of warfare by groups in countries that are otherwise deemed low in literacy and in economic development—we have seen what Afghan resistance can do with American guns—is paralleled by another kind of international fraternization among resistance groups who have little in common save their resistance to the status quo in their own countries, and who exchange knowledge of guerrilla tactics and the art of resistance. Militant groups in Japan, Germany, Lebanon, Libya, Sri Lanka, and India have international networks of collaboration, not unlike—perhaps more solidary than—the diplomatic channels that exist between mutually wary sovereign countries and the great powers. The end result is that professionalized killing is no longer the monopoly of state armies and police forces. The internationalization of the technology of destruction, evidenced in the form of terrorism and counterterrorism, has shown a face of free-market capitalism in action unsuspected by Adam Smith and by Immanuel Wallerstein.

Source: Tambiah 1989.

EthnoProfile II.8 • **COLONIAL OAXACA**

REGION: North America

NATION: Mexico

POPULATION: 18,000 (1792)

ENVIRONMENT: High mountain river basin; temperate

LIVELIHOOD: Administrative center, clothing and textile industries

POLITICAL ORGANIZATION: Colony of Spain

FOR MORE INFORMATION: Chance, John. 1978. *Race and class in colonial Oaxaca.* Stanford: Stanford University Press.

mix of all three elements. In a complex society, hierarchy may also be complicated or contradicted by the presence of nonclass groupings based on race or ethnicity. Caste systems are faced with similar contradictions: in the example from Gopalpur, social pressure and physical violence forced the Saltmakers to buy inferior land that was more in keeping with their caste status than their economic status.

Negotiating Social Status: Mexico 1521–1812 Anthropologist John Chance studied the role of class, race, and ethnicity in the city of Oaxaca, Mexico. (See Ethno-Profile 11.8: Colonial Oaxaca [1521–1812].) Oaxaca, known as *Antequera* during the colonial period, is a highland city founded in an area densely populated by Native Americans who participated in preconquest Mexican high civilization. Chance's research (1978) is a bit unusual in anthropology because it is entirely historical. He examined how social stratification changed from the period of Spanish colonial conquest, in 1521, to the early years of the Mexican war of independence, in 1812. Chance used an anthropological perspective to interpret census records, wills, and other archival materials preserved in Mexico and Spain. As a result, he was able to show that changes occurred both in the categories used to describe social stratification and in the meanings attached to those categories.

THE ESTATE SYSTEM   When the Spanish arrived in Mexico in 1521, they found a number of indigenous societies organized into states. The Aztecs, for example, were divided into an upper ruling stratum of nobles and a lower, commoner class. After the conquest, the stratification systems of the two societies—Spanish and indigenous—began to move toward unification. The Spanish conquerors tried to make sense of postconquest society by applying concepts based on the European system of estates. *Estates* were legally recognized social categories that were entitled to a voice in government. European estates prototypically included the nobility, the clergy, and the common people. In New Spain, estate membership was assigned on the basis of race. The clergy and nobility were reserved for the Spanish; conquered indigenous groups became the common people.

There were exceptions to this system, however. Indigenous nobles were given special status in postconquest society and were used by the colonial administration to control their own people. Moreover, the conquistadors, who brought no Spanish women with them, soon established sexual relationships with local indigenous women. In the early years, if these unions involved marriage, the offspring were usually considered Spanish, but if they were casual or clandestine the offspring were more likely to be considered indigenous. Thus a population of mixed descent was created. By 1529, African slaves had been brought to New Spain. These slaves ranked at the bottom of the colonial hierarchy. All three groups interbred, producing their own mixed offspring.

According to the system of estates, people of mixed race were not supposed to exist. By the mid-sixteenth century, however, their numbers and their economic importance in the colony made them impossible to ignore. As a result, the rulers of New Spain developed the *sistema de castas,* "a cognitive and legal system of ranked socioracial statuses" used to refer to all people of mixed racial heritage (Chance 1978, viii). The first castas recognized were the *mestizos* (people of mixed Spanish and indigenous descent) and the *mulattoes* (people who showed evidence of African ancestry).

Whether the Spanish word *casta* should be translated "caste" or "class" or "race" or "ethnic group" is an interesting question. The original "estates" whose interbreeding produced the castas were defined in terms of race. In addition, it was understood that races should not intermarry. That is, each estate was supposed to practice endogamy, like a caste. The sixteenth-century assumption that all people of mixed race were illegitimate demonstrated this belief. Because Spaniards monopolized wealth, power, and prestige in the new colony, they could be viewed as the ruling class—with everyone else making up the subject class. Finally, members of the original colonial estates initially differed from one another not only in terms of race but also in terms of culture. So they might also be seen as constituting separate ethnic groups within colonial society.

As soon as there were enough mestizos and mulattoes to attract attention, the colonial government tried to limit their social mobility by legal means. Yet their status was ambiguous. Mestizos were ranked above mulattoes because they had no African ancestry but were theoretically ranked below the Spanish because of their "illegitimacy." In cases where indigenous and Spanish spouses were legally married, their children were called *españoles* (creoles). They were distinguished from *españoles europeos* (Spaniards born in Spain). In later years, the term *creole (criollo)* was also used to refer to people of presumably "pure" European ancestry who were born in America. Some mestizos managed to obtain elite privileges, such as the right to carry arms. Most mulattoes were classed with Africans and could be enslaved. Yet free mulattoes could also apply for the right to carry arms, which shows that even their status was ambiguous.

During the seventeenth century, the castas were acknowledged as legitimate strata in the system of colonial stratification. A number of new castas were recognized: *castizo* (a person of mixed Spanish and mestizo descent), *mulato libre* ("free mulatto"), *mulato esclavo* ("mulatto slave"), *negro libre* ("free black"), and *negro esclavo* ("black slave"). Perhaps most striking is the castizo category. This seems to have been designed by the colonial elite to stem the tide of ever "whiter" mestizos who might be mistaken for genuine Spaniards. John Chance (1978, 126) points out that racial mixing was primarily an urban phenomenon and that the castas perceived themselves, and were perceived by the elite, as belonging to Hispanic rather than indigenous society (1978, 126). It is perhaps not surprising that lighter-skinned castas became increasingly indistinguishable from middle-class and lower-class creoles. In fact, census records in Oaxaca list creoles as the largest segment of the city's population throughout the entire colonial period.

OTHER STRATIFICATION SYSTEMS   As if the sistema de castas were not enough, colonial society recognized three additional systems of classification that cut across the castas. One distinguished groups required to pay tribute to the Spanish crown (indigenous groups, Africans, and mulattoes) from everyone else. The second distinguished *gente de razon* ("rational people," who practiced the Hispanic culture of the city) from *indios* (the rural, culturally distinct indigenous population). And a third distinguished *gente decente* ("respectable people") from *la plebe* (the "common people"). Chance suggests that the last distinction, which made most sense in the urban setting, represented an embryonic division into socioeconomic classes (1978, 127).

MOBILITY IN THE CASTA SYSTEM   Throughout the colonial period, the boundaries of the stratification system in Oaxaca were most rigid for those of pure indigenous, African, and European descent. These were the "unmixed" categories at the bottom and top of the hierarchy. Paradoxically, those of mixed background had the most ambiguous status and had the greatest opportunity to improve it. For example, when a couple married, the priest decided the casta membership of the bride and groom. The strategy for upward mobility called for choosing a marriage partner who was light-skinned enough for the priest to decide that both spouses belonged in a high-ranking casta. Over time, such maneuvering swelled the ranks of the creoles.

The growth of the casta population coincided with the transformation of the colonial economy from one based on tribute and mining to one based on commercial capitalism. The prosperity this transformation brought to Oaxaca was greatest in the eighteenth century. That was when the city became the center of an important textile and dye-manufacturing industry. Many castas were able to accumulate wealth, which together with a light skin and urban culture made it possible for them to achieve the status of creole within their lifetimes.

Chance argues that during the late colonial period, racial status had become an achieved, rather than an ascribed, status. By that time, the increasing rate of legitimacy in all castas meant that descent lost its importance as a criterion of group membership. Creole status could be claimed by anyone who was able to show that his or her ancestors had not paid tribute. At the same time, in a dialectical fashion, people's image of what high-status people looked like had changed. As people with indigenous and African ancestry moved up the social scale, their physical appearance, or phenotype, widened the range of phenotypes considered prototypical for people of their status.

Negotiating Social Status in Other Societies   Processes similar to those Chance describes continue to take place today. In many areas of Latin America where extensive racial mixing has occurred, "racial" status is an achieved status. Benjamin Colby and Pierre van den Berghe (1969) documented the process that occurred in Guatemala during the twentieth century. Members of indigenous groups who left their traditional communities, learned Spanish, dressed like Europeans, and took a "non-Indian" occupation might easily pass as *ladinos* (members of the "white" population) whether they wanted to or not. Colby and van den Berghe write: "A factor which probably contributes to ladinoization is the ambiguity in the ethnic status of the Indian who does not belong to the local majority group. Local Indians will regard him as a stranger, and, of course, unless he speaks the local Indian language, he will be forced to use Spanish as a lingua franca. Ladinoization and 'passing' of Indian 'strangers' are probably more the consequences of marginality than of any conscious desire to become assimilated to the ladinos. Rejection by local Indians makes ladinoization almost inevitable" (1969, 172).

I (Emily Schultz) encountered a similar process at work in Guider, Cameroon. (See EthnoProfile 8.1: Guider.) I found that people born outside the dominant Fulbe ethnic group could achieve Fulbe status within their lifetimes (1984). To do this, they had to be successful in three tasks: they had to adopt the Fulbe language (Fulfulde), the Fulbe religion (Islam), and the Fulbe "way of life," which was identified with urban customs and the traditional high culture of the western Sudan. Many Fulbe claimed that descent from one or another Fulbe lineage was needed in order to claim Fulbe identity. Nevertheless, they seemed willing to accept "Fulbeized Pagans" as Fulbe (for example, by giving their daughters to them as brides) because those people were committed defenders of the urban Fulbe way of life. Those who were "Fulbeizing," however, came from societies in which descent had never been an important criterion of group membership. For those people, ethnic identity depended on the language, customs, and territorial affiliation of the group to which they were currently committed. In becoming Fulbe, they had simply chosen to commit themselves to Fulfulde, Islam, and life in "Fulbe territory," the town.

THE DIMENSIONS OF GROUP LIFE

In looking at the range of nonkin social ties that people invent to link themselves across kinship boundaries, we have considered some features of the larger groups into which human beings have organized themselves. As an organization or society grows in size and complexity, changes inevitably occur in economic, political, and social patterns. This is particularly striking when societies come to be based on class divisions. Many anthropologists would argue, in fact, that transition to a class-based society marks a qualitative change in the nature of social life. That is, *class organization* marks a threshold where a change in *degree* of complexity is transformed into a change in *kind* of complexity. Anthropologists who hold this view embody yet another referential perspective on the striking differences between the society of Western anthropologists and many of the societies they study. In this way, the issues that occupied the attention of such figures as Maine and Durkheim are still alive.

The next chapters examine more closely the different ways human beings have coped with power relations, economic relations, and relations with their neighbors. In particular, we will focus on the role of European colonialism in shaping the forms of human society anthropologists encounter in the modern world.

KEY TERMS

status	achieved statuses	caste
role	sodalities	class
mechanical solidarity	age sets	race
organic solidarity	secret societies	ethnicity
division of labor	egalitarian societies	clientage
ascribed statuses	stratified societies	

CHAPTER SUMMARY

1. Early social scientists described and explained the differences they saw between "primitive" and "modern" human societies. They thought of "primitive" society as organized in terms of kinship and therefore characterized by personalized, face-to-face relationships, ascribed statuses, and mechanical solidarity. "Modern" society, by contrast, was characterized by impersonal relationships, achieved statuses, and organic solidarity. In "modern" society, kinship played a much reduced role, and most of the people with whom an individual dealt were nonkin.

2. Every society provides ways of establishing links with nonkin, such as the creation of metaphorical kin or the establishment of friendship. It is sometimes difficult to draw a neat line between kinship and nonkin relationships because kinship terms may be used between "friends" or kinship roles may be the prototypes for the roles expected of friends—or both. In any case, the relationships cultivate a sentiment of diffuse and enduring solidarity.

3. The larger a society is, the more complex its division of labor will be. The more specialized the division of labor is, the more likely institutionalized relationships will exist between nonkin. Such institutions are minimally developed in most band societies but become increasingly important in tribal societies, in the form of sodalities.

4. Cheyenne military societies, eastern African age sets, and western African secret societies are all examples of pantribal sodalities. These institutions tend to be found in nonhierarchical societies. Members of the sodalities, drawn from the various kinship groups, ordinarily take on responsibility for various public functions of a governmental or ritual nature. Membership in such sodalities is often a mark of adulthood and may be connected with initiation rituals.

5. In stratified societies, some groups have permanently privileged access to valued resources, while others have permanently restricted access. The relations between subgroups are carefully specified. Two common patterns of stratification are caste and class. Links between castes or classes may be based on such criteria as the relationship individuals have to the means of production and occupational specialization. These links may be complicated by race or ethnicity. In many stratified societies, individuals from different strata are linked by clientage.

6. In stratified societies, particularly those in which membership in one or another stratum is based on race or ethnicity, group membership is often a matter of negotiation. Data from colonial Oaxaca show how the recognized categories of society and the criteria used to assign membership change over time. These data and examples noted elsewhere demonstrate that individuals can manipulate the rules to advance in status, successfully "passing" as members of groups to which they do not "literally" belong. They illustrate that racial, ethnic, or class prototypes are selective cultural constructions that emphasize certain attributes of individuals while ignoring others.

SUGGESTED READINGS

Brain, Robert. 1976. *Friends and lovers.* New York: Basic Books. *A thorough, highly readable account of friendship taken very broadly, with excellent ethnographic examples. Brain draws provocative lessons for Western society from his research.*

Keillor, Garrison. 1985. *Lake Wobegon days.* New York: Viking. *The best-selling book about kinship and the other ties that bind in American small-town life.*

Nash, Manning. 1989. *The cauldron of ethnicity in the modern world.* Chicago: University of Chicago Press. *Nash looks at ethnicity in the postcolonial world and sees more of a seething cauldron than a melting pot. He examines the relations between Ladinos and Maya in Guatemala, Chinese and Malays in Malaysia, and Jews in the United States.*

Smith, Mary F. [1954] 1981. *Baba of Karo.* Reprint. New Haven: Yale University Press. *A remarkable document: the autobiography of a Hausa woman born in 1877. A master storyteller, Baba provides much information about the patterns of friendship, clientage, adoption, kinship, and marriage.*

CHAPTER OUTLINE

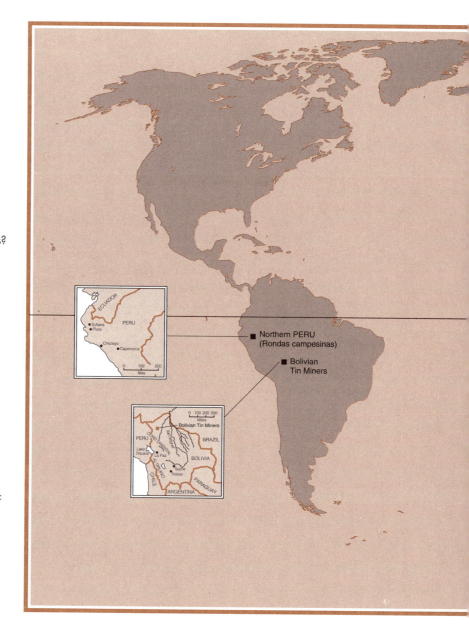

Social Organization and Power

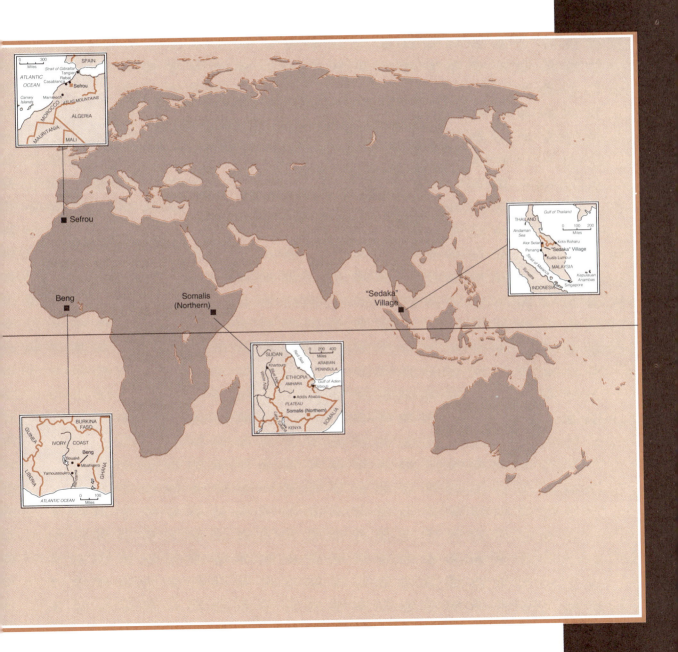

*a*t the beginning of 1992, following 12 years of civil war and 2 years of intensive negotiation, representatives of the government of El Salvador and representatives of the Salvadoran guerrilla movement known as the Faribundo Martí National Liberation Front (FMLN) signed a peace accord brokered by the United Nations. The civil war had cost over 75,000 lives and had turned a million other Salvadorans into refugees. By late 1989, both the government and the guerrillas had realized that neither side was close to victory.

How was it possible that so many years of fierce fighting could be ended at the negotiator's table? For the civil war in El Salvador was one of the bloodiest insurrections in twentieth-century Latin America. The roots of the conflict go back into the nineteenth century, when a tiny elite of Salvadoran landowners managed to monopolize 60 percent of the land in order to raise coffee for export. The result was one of the most highly polarized class structures in all Latin America. Some 98 percent of the citizens were forced to survive on plots too small to support them, lived as tenant farmers or laborers on land they did not own, or became landless migrants. When the coffee market crashed during the depression of the 1930s, the majority on the bottom rebelled against their exploitation, and the Salvadoran army crushed them in a brutal massacre known as *la matanza*.

During the cold war between the United States and the Soviet Union that began in the late 1940s, even comparatively mild efforts to reform the system were repressed. After 1958, Washington interpreted challenges to the Salvadoran government as signs that El Salvador might be vulnerable to a Cuban-style communist revolution and viewed Salvadoran repression of reformers and rebels as a fight against the spread of communism, an explanation the Salvadoran government willingly endorsed. By the late 1970s, convinced that peaceful forms of social change would never be tolerated, political moderates in El Salvador swelled the ranks of five guerrilla groups that united to form the FMLN. The government response in the 1980s was as brutal as it had been in the 1930s and included a new *matanza* in the peasant village of El Mozote, in which over 200 men, women, and children were massacred by government troops for their supposed collaboration with the guerrillas (Danner 1994).

By 1990, Salvadoran society was still polarized, but the prospect of endless war caused Salvadorans on both sides to rethink their positions. Government supporters of the National Republican Alliance Party (ARENA) had won national elections and seemed less hostile to democracy, whereas their elite supporters had become convinced that continued fighting would only hurt their business interests. The United States was also tiring of the war and could no longer ignore highly publicized human rights violations committed by the Salvadoran government. Furthermore, the notion that supporting the Salvadoran government was stemming the spread of communism lost its force following the collapse of communism in eastern Europe. At the same time, Salvadoran guerrillas concluded that military victory offered no permanent guarantees when the Sandinistas in neighboring Nicaragua, who had won their revolution a decade earlier, were voted out of office in 1990. Led by guerrilla leaders like Rubén Zamora, who had long favored a negotiated settlement, the FMLN eventually agreed to meet their enemies at the peace table.

What drives people to take up arms against powerful, well-armed government forces? What convinces battle-hardened fighters who believe that their cause is just to lay down their arms and negotiate? It is not as though the outcome of either decision can be predicted with any certainty. Historian Peter Winn observes that the 1992 U.N.-brokered accord in El Salvador "was a political compromise that allowed both sides to claim victory, while leaving the future in doubt" (1992, 535). Not all Salvadorans supported the negotiated settlement, and sporadic violence directed against some guerrillas-turned-politicians after 1992 threatened the fragile peace it brought about. In May of 1994, however, the first national elections held since the signing of the peace accord were peaceful. Armando Calderon Sol, the ARENA presidential candidate, won two-thirds of the vote against the left coalition whose candidate, Rubén Zamora, won one-third of the vote.

To be sure, the absence of violence at one moment of political crisis does not mean that violence will not be used later. The U.N. accord has not ended economic and political inequality in El Salvador, which leads some observers to expect that fighting could well resume. But the mere fact that violence is not automatic suggests that even the most thoroughgoing systems of political oppression have points of vulnerability and that the exercise of power, even in a highly stratified society, is more complicated than it may appear.

There are always choices to be made about how a society is to be organized or how that organization may be changed. Who has the power to make the choices? Where does that power come from? What is power? In this chapter, we examine how different ways of organizing society can be seen as different ways of answering these three questions.

VARIETIES OF SOCIAL ORGANIZATION

We have already described the variety of forms of human society and looked at some attempts by anthropologists to introduce order into that variety. Lewis Henry Morgan urged anthropologists to pay close attention to what he called the "arts of subsistence." He was confident that all cultural differences—in kinship patterns, marriage practices, religious beliefs, and ritual—could be explained in terms of the ways different societies went about making a living. But he ran into difficulties when he observed significant differences in ways of life that were *not* connected with significant differences in ways of making a living. In Morgan's scheme, for example, both "barbarians" and "civilized peoples" relied on farming and herding, and in many cases their technologies were quite similar. What did separate them were differences in social organization: in who did what to produce the fruits of cultivation and animal husbandry, how it was done, and for whom. **Social organization** refers to the patterning of human interdependence in a given society through the actions and decisions of its members. This chapter focuses on social organization and the powers that human beings have to reproduce or change that organization.

THE SEARCH FOR THE LAWS OF SOCIAL ORGANIZATION

Since before the birth of the social sciences, Western thinkers have searched for the inflexible laws of society that would explain differences in social organization. The following sections review the perspectives on the laws of social organization that anthropologists have traditionally considered.

The Historical Explanation

Morgan and other unilineal evolutionists believed that the laws of society are rooted in the dynamics of history and work themselves out over time for each human group. Karl Marx was inspired by Morgan's work. He also explained variation in social organization in terms of historical laws working themselves out through the activities of human beings in the course of time. For Marx, every new form of society emerges out of its predecessor. But every form of society contains internal contradictions. As the society develops, these contradictions become increasingly acute, finally leading to the overthrow of the social order. Modern evolutionary thinkers, whether marxian or not, continue to seek evolutionary laws whose operation would explain the appearance of similar forms of social organization in different parts of the world.

The Environmental Explanation

Other thinkers do not look to world history for the origins of lawful social process. They explain similarities and differences in social organization with reference to the local environment of a particular society. These scholars view social organization as the result of *adaptation* to material, ecological conditions. For example, a particular environment may be seen as "requiring" only small flexible groups to exploit its meager resources. A different environment, however, might "require" many people and a complex division of labor to ensure successful human adaptation. Here, the environment is thought to determine social organization.

The Biological Explanation

Unlike the historical and environmental approaches, the biological explanation looks for lawful processes operating deeply within human beings, forcing them to act in some ways and forbidding them to act in other ways. *Biological determinists* claim that human behavior is under close biological or genetic control and is little affected by the material environment. In the words of sociobiologist E. O. Wilson, human genes have culture "on a short leash." That is, we are altruistic, aggressive, and sexual because our genes make us so, and our social organizations must adjust to the iron requirements of genetics.

The Arbitrariness of Social Organization

Perhaps the most important and controversial contribution of anthropology to the debate about laws of social organization is the argument that social relations in any society are ultimately arbitrary. This does not mean that societies are free to do or be whatever they like; rather, there is no way to reduce the complexities of human societies to a single underlying cause.

For example, the demonstrated adaptive flexibility of the human brain and body would be impossible if our behavior were rigidly controlled by instinct. Environmental determinism is implausible because, historically speaking, no society has ever been left on its own long enough for so-called environmental pressures to exert their forces without outside human interference. European colonial conquest is an eloquent case in point. It demonstrates how the most delicately balanced societal adaptation to a given environment can be totally disrupted, if not destroyed, when outsiders arrive with plans of their own and the power to enforce them. Yet even if societies could be isolated from one another and left to work out their own destinies in their own environments, it is unlikely that identical societies would develop in "identical" environments. I. M. Lewis points out, for example, that the northern Somalis and the Boran Galla live next to each other in semiarid scrubland and even herd the same animals (goats, sheep, cattle, camels; 1976, 166ff.). (See EthnoProfile 12.1: Somalis [Northern]; see also EthnoProfile 11.4: Boran.) Despite these similarities, the Somali and the Boran are quite different in social structure: the Boran engage in much less fighting and feuding than the Somali; Boran families split up to take care of the animals, whereas the Somali do not; and lineage organization is less significant among the Boran.

THE POWER TO CHOOSE

So, human beings do not endure environmental pressures passively but actively work to reshape the environment to suit themselves. However, when human beings reshape the material world, they do so selectively. We choose which aspects of the material world we will depend on for our livelihood, and there is always more than one choice in any environment. Human choice is equally important in the domain of social organization.

social organization The patterning of human interdependence in a given society through the actions and decisions of its members.

EthnoProfile 12.1 • **SOMALIS (NORTHERN)**

REGION: Eastern Africa

NATIONS: Somalia, Djibouti, Ethiopia, Kenya

POPULATION: 600,000 (3,250,000 total; 2,250,000 in Somalia)

ENVIRONMENT: Harsh, semidesert

LIVELIHOOD: Herding of camels, sheep, goats, cattle, horses

POLITICAL ORGANIZATION: Traditionally, lineage-based, ad hoc egalitarian councils; today, part of modern nation-states

FOR MORE INFORMATION: Lewis, I. M. 1967. *A pastoral democracy: A study of pastoralism and politics among the northern Somali of the Horn of Africa.* London: Oxford University Press.

Some archaeologists suggest, for example, that population growth is a constant aspect of the human condition that determines forms of organization, yet population pressure determines nothing more than the number of people that can be supported when the environment is used in a particular way. Marshall Sahlins reminds us that the response of a particular society to this kind of pressure can be varied (1976a, 13). People can try to get along on less, intensify food production by inventing new technology, reduce their numbers by inventing new social practices (infanticide or other forms of birth control), transform previously ignored elements of the environment into new resources, or part of their group can migrate elsewhere. All these choices are open to them, and none is specified by the pressure of population.

Indeed, the manner in which a group might choose to implement any of these options is equally undetermined by population pressure. Which members of the group will have to do with less—everyone? men? women? certain lineages? commoners? Which members will be responsible for technological innovations or control them once they are made? Will all women and men equally be required to limit the number of their offspring or will the limitation apply only to certain societal subgroups (for example, poor women)? Who will be expected to take advantage of new resources—everyone? or only some members of society? if only some, which ones? If migration of part of the group to a new environment is the solution, who will migrate? Answers to all these questions are open. Population pressure alone cannot determine which or how many solutions a given society might choose.

Discussions of human choice raise the question of human responsibility. A society may be described as having collectively made a decision about how to cope, for example, with population pressure. But the potential solutions to this problem are many. How was the final choice made? Is compromise, as opposed to consensus, more likely in one society than in another and, if so, why? Who decides and according to what principles?

The ability to choose implies the ability to transform a given situation. Thus, the ability to choose implies **power,** which may be understood broadly as "transformative capacity" (Giddens 1979, 88). When the choice affects an entire social group, we speak of *social power.* Eric Wolf (1994) describes three different modes of social power. The first is *interpersonal power* and involves the ability of one individual to impose his or her will on another individual. The second, what he calls *organizational power,* highlights how individuals or social units can limit the actions of other individuals in particular social settings. The third mode he calls *structural power,* which organizes social settings themselves, and controls the allocation of social labor.

The prototype of power for most Americans is naked physical force, and this can be an important form of power for other peoples as well. In most societies at most times, however, power cannot be reduced to naked physical force. Power operates, and people allow it to operate, according to certain principles. These principles are cultural creations; they are therefore arbitrary and may differ from one society to another. "It may be in the nature of agricultural production that father and son *cooperate,* but it is not in the nature of agricultural production that *father* and *son* cooperate—as opposed to mother and daughter, mother's brother and sister's son, or Don Quixote and Sancho Panza" (Sahlins 1976a, 9). How a society actually organizes agricultural production is a cultural construction. Its appropriateness is recognized for cultural reasons. It will ordinarily be enforced, or renegotiated, by the culturally appropriate deployment of social power.

THINKING ABOUT SOCIAL POWER

The study of social power in human society is the domain of **political anthropology.** Over time, political anthropologists have investigated a broad series of problems having to do with power and social control. Ted Lewellen lists the following: "1) the classification of political systems, 2) the evolution of political systems, 3) the structure and functions of political systems in preindustrial societies, 4) the processes of politics in preindustrial or developing societies, 5) action, an outgrowth of the process approach with an emphasis on the manipulative strategies of individuals, 6) the modernization of formerly tribal societies and modern political institutions in industrial states" (1983, ix–x).

The Role of the State in Western Thought

Generations of Western thinkers have been interested in the topics studied by political anthropologists. As we noted in our discussion of kinship, these thinkers began with the assumption that the state was the prototype of "civilized" social power. The absence of a state therefore had to represent anarchy and disorder—what the English philosopher Thomas Hobbes (1588–1679) called the "war of all against all." What prompted Hobbes

---

power Transformative capacity; the ability to transform a given situation.

political anthropology The study of social power in human society.

to believe that disorder must reign in the absence of the state? For one thing, he lived during the English Civil War and its aftermath. Old institutions were losing the loyalty of citizens but had not yet been replaced by new institutions capable of regaining that loyalty. Hobbes viewed the confusion around him with alarm and was eager to find an explanation for it, as well as a solution. For Hobbes, the answer was that human beings were by nature selfish. They would war with one another to the death, destroying society in the process, unless they were forcibly prevented from doing so.

This was why the state was necessary. Its most significant role was to monopolize the use of force in order to protect the naturally weak from the naturally strong. The prototype of power—naked physical force—is the same in all cases. The assumption is that human beings will not cooperate unless they are coerced. If physical power ultimately decides all conflicts, it is better that the state control the use of such power. This is because the state presumably has the interests of everyone in mind. Thus, the state should be able to punish those who would use their own physical power to serve selfish individual interests. Although the state often perpetrated injustice or exploitation as a side effect of its monopoly of force, this was often viewed as a necessary price to pay for social order.

Social Power in Societies without States

These basic Western assumptions about human nature and the role of the state have often gone unquestioned by Western observers investigating social organization and power in the non-Western world. Early anthropologists such as Morgan, however, showed that kinship institutions organized social life in societies without states. A later generation of political anthropologists supplied a wealth of data on how this happened. They showed how different kinship institutions distribute power among their members. They also learned about nonkin institutions such as secret societies that, although less encompassing than the state, sometimes carry out important political roles. They were able to show repeatedly that societies without states are able to reach and carry out decisions affecting the entire social group by means of orderly traditional processes.

In the absence of a state that monopolizes physical force and can punish the disobedient, why do people cooperate? In order to answer this question, political anthropologists have had to reconsider many traditional Western assumptions about human nature and social power. As a consequence, they are keenly aware of the ambiguity of power both as a concept and as a phenomenon in everyday life.

POWER AS COERCION

The Role of Physical Force

The traditional Western prototype of power in human social relations is based on physical coercion. A fistfight might be seen as the typical "natural" manifestation of physical coercion. This prototype is based on an exceedingly pessimistic, even cynical, view of human nature. It argues that, left to their own devices, all human individuals would challenge any other human beings in order to establish power over them. In this view, human evolution took a giant leap forward when our ancestors first realized that sticks and stones could be used as weapons, not only against nonhuman predators but especially against human enemies. Human history is thus a chronicle of the production of better and better weapons. The civilizations we are so proud of have been born and sustained in violence.

Coercion in Societies without States?

Some political anthropologists would subscribe, more or less, to this approach to the human condition. As a result, they approach non-Western political organization in a characteristic way. They recognize that many stateless societies do not have governments with the ability to punish those who deviate. Nevertheless, they argue that other institutions have a similar function. Such societies fear not the king or the police but the ancestors, witchcraft, or the lineage elders. Power is still viewed as physical coercion, with cooperation resulting largely from the fear of punishment.

This is not a persuasive portrait of life in nonstate societies, however. Evans-Pritchard ([1937] 1976) argued that the Azande were not in a constant state of fear even though they lived in a stateless society and held a complex set of beliefs about witchcraft, oracles, and magic. (See EthnoProfile 8.3: Azande.) He observed that Azande people discussed witchcraft openly. If they believed they were bewitched, they were likely to be angry rather than afraid and so did not feel helpless. This kind of attitude was not irrational, because the threatening forces were seen as part of the fabric of the universe. Most people believed that witchcraft would not be directed against them, and in any case they had remedies to fight their own victimization. In such a context, the belief system and the institutionalization of power it implies seem natural and rational. For that reason, ordinary, rational people support it.

Coercion and Legitimacy

Here we encounter an ambiguity about power in human affairs. People may submit to institutionalized power because they fear punishment. But they may also submit to it because they believe that submitting is the right—perhaps the only—thing to do. Recognition of this problem has led political anthropologists to distinguish between power based on physical force, which we will call **coercion** (Figure 12.1), and power based on group consensus, which we will call **legitimacy**. The tricky thing for the analyst is deciding which motivation is operating at any one time.

After all, people may voluntarily submit to a system in which naked force is used against them if they accept the cultural principles that justify such a use of coercion.

---

coercion Power based on physical force.

legitimacy Power based on group consensus.

FIGURE 12.1 *Prior to colonial conquest by outsiders, Muslim emirs from northern Cameroon had coercive powers.*

Many citizens of modern nation-states support the right of the state to monopolize deadly force, even in the nuclear age. In some cases, it is probably futile to try to separate fear of punishment from consensus in determining why most people accept the principles upon which their society depends. People may fear the loss of personal physical integrity less than they fear the collapse of a meaningful, orderly understanding of the world if principles are abandoned. They may even be willing to sacrifice themselves physically—as soldiers do in battle—if they are convinced that doing so will preserve "the world as we know it," "keep the world safe for democracy," or the like.

Alma Gottlieb discusses witchcraft and its connection with legitimacy and coercion among the Beng of Ivory Coast. (See EthnoProfile 12.2: Beng.) The Beng are organized into two regions, each ruled by a king and a queen, who come from a specific matriclan. The king holds legitimate authority. He is said be the owner of the Earth, the primary focus for worship among the Beng. Violations of taboos concerning the Earth are believed to endanger the entire region and therefore must be dealt with by the king of the region. The king also is said to have the power to foresee natural calamities if they are interpreted as punishment for sins committed. In general, "the king is responsible

In Their Own Words　　**LEGITIMATE COERCION IN POSTCOMMUNIST RUSSIA**

Anthropologist Anatoly Khazanov reports on the political choices facing Russians following the collapse of the Soviet Union. He describes how their opportunity to choose new ways of organizing political life is constrained by old political traditions.

In some respects the situation in Russia is different from that in Central Asia and the Caucasus in that it has glimmers of hope. The highly industrialized and urbanized Russian society has a working class which has during the last years demonstrated much more maturity than might be expected; its post-Communist period has opened new avenues of economic and social mobility to many of its youth; and, last but not least, it has numerous educated middle strata. For many members of the latter, the economic hardships are still tolerable, while the liberalization of political life is an indisputable achievement. These people alone represent the guarantee for the continuation of the democratization process much better than the Russian political elite, even those parts of it who are in Yeltsin's camp but who nevertheless demonstrate some inclinations toward authoritarianism.

One should also take into account another circumstance. Most Russian families at present consist of only one or, at best, two children. This leads to an increasing appreciation of human life and to an aversion to bloody violence in all of its forms. To prove this point I can refer to the extreme unpopularity of military service or to the widespread resentment with the Russian army's involvement in inter-ethnic conflicts in the CIS [Commonwealth of Independent States] countries.

These are the positive factors. However one should not dismiss the negative ones. The Reds and Browns in Russian political parlance, i.e., the broad coalition of Communists, fascists, and all kinds of chauvinists is actively propagandizing violence as a way of changing the existing political, social, and economic conditions and restoring the Russian imperial glory of old. They find a receptive audience in a growing number of disoriented, pauperized, and lumpenized people to whom reforms turned out to be detrimental. Anti-democratic sentiments are very strong in the army, the Cossack movement, the Russian Orthodox church, and some other segments of Russian society.

The most dangerous moment in this development is that the society is again considering violence as an inevitable concomitant of the political process. Again the dispute is not over the question whether violence is legitimate but over who exactly has the legitimate right to use it.

Thus we face a vicious circle: the virtual absence of civil society and traditions and mechanisms for solving political, social, and ethnic conflicts through negotiation and compromise facilitates the spread of violence, and violence, in turn, makes the emergence of civil society much more difficult. Some recent events in Moscow prove this point. The opponents of Yeltsin's rule are certainly adversaries of the liberalization process, but they were suppressed by undemocratic means which soon resulted in violence. Thus the door is open for more violence or for essentially authoritarian rule. Only the future will tell whether Russia is capable of getting out of this circle.

Source: Khazanov 1993.

not only for the legal but also the moral and spiritual well-being of the people living in his region" (1989, 249).

The legitimate power of the king is in direct contrast to the power of witches, who are considered to be utterly immoral; using illegitimate power, working in secret, they kill and "consume" their close matrilineal kin. Nevertheless, when a man becomes the king, he has one year to bewitch three close relatives in his matriline. If he fails to do so, he himself will die. Rather than destroy his power, this exercise of illegitimate power legitimates his rule. By killing three close matrilineal relatives, the king shows his com-

EthnoProfile 12.2 • BENG

REGION: Western Africa

NATION: Ivory Coast

POPULATION: 10,000+

ENVIRONMENT: Savanna and forest

LIVELIHOOD: Farming, both subsistence and cash; hunting; gathering

POLITICAL ORGANIZATION: Traditionally, a kingdom; today, part of a modern nation-state

FOR MORE INFORMATION: Gottlieb, Alma. 1989. Witches, kings, and the sacrifices of identity *or* The power of paradox and the paradox of power among the Beng of Ivory Coast. In *Creativity of power*, edited by W. Arens and I. Karp, 245–72. Washington, DC: Smithsonian.

mitment to the greater public "good." He is demonstrating his control over, and independence from, the narrow interests of his own kinship group. Operating on a plane beyond that of common morality, the king, a man who has sacrificed part of himself, will rule the kingdom fairly. From the point of view of the Beng, including members of his own matriclan, his actions are legitimate. Indeed, they make it possible for him to rule.

The Ambiguity of Power

Violence has been part of human experience for as long as we can tell, but we cannot assume that its role is the same in all human societies. The occasional violent outburst of one member of a foraging society against another is not the same thing as the organized violence of one army against another in a conflict between modern nation-states. No one can deny that human beings can be violent with one another. But is this the whole story?

Anthropologist Richard Newbold Adams has said: "It is useful to accept the proposition that, while men have in some sense always been equal (i.e. in that each always has some independent power), they have in another sense never been equal (in that some always have more power than others)" (1979, 409). Political anthropologists who think of power as coercion have traditionally emphasized the universality of human inequality. Others have taken another route, concentrating on the first part of Adams's observation. Although aware of the role of the state in monopolizing physical force, they have been concerned with two additional matters: (1) they have reexamined the role of power in societies without states; and (2) they have reconsidered the nature of independent power available to individuals living in societies with states. The first focus involves looking at power as an independent entity. The second looks at the power of the human imagination to define the nature of social interactions and to persuade other actors to accept these definitions of the situation.

Self-Interest Versus Collective Obligation

Discussions of power as coercion tend to see political activity as a form of bargaining. Using a metaphor drawn from the marketplace, they describe political engagements as another form of haggling—not over material goods but over control. This description of political horse-trading sounds plausible to people familiar with Western political institutions. The basic assumption is that the parties to political negotiation are free agents. This means that, in making decisions, they are not and should not be duty-bound to consider the effect of their actions on anyone but themselves. No larger groups, no historical obligations, no collective beliefs can or ought to deter them from following what they perceive to be in their individual self-interest. People in America are free, so we believe, to become whatever they want to be, free of the shackles of ascribed status.

The "shackles" of kinship and community relationships, however, can be approached from a different point of view. Ascribed social ties can also be understood as necessary protection for society's weaker members, which the stronger members are obligated for humanitarian reasons to provide. Members of societies without states often have a strong sense of collective obligation for each other's welfare. Western observers have noted that members of such societies are not free agents. For example, individuals often must consult elders or community leaders or kin before entering into contracts with outsiders. Such collective obligations are often regarded by Westerners as backward. Anthropologists would argue that they represent an alternative understanding of the human condition and of the nature of social power.

POWER AS AN INDEPENDENT ENTITY

In the stateless societies of native North and South America, power is understood to be an entity existing in the universe independent of human beings. As such, it cannot be produced and accumulated through the interactions of human beings with one another. Strictly speaking, power does not belong to human beings at all. At most, people can hope to *gain access* to power, usually through ritual means. From this point of view, "control over resources is evidence of power, rather than the source of power" (Colson 1977, 382).

If we assume that power is part of the natural order of things yet is independent of direct human control, certain consequences seem to follow. First, we may be able to tap some of that power if we can discover how. Societies that see power as an independent entity usually know, through tradition, how to tap it.

Second, societies that see power as an independent force usually embed this understanding within a larger worldview in which the universe consists of a balance of different forces. Individuals may seek to manipulate those natural forces to their own ends, but they are enjoined not to tamper with the balance in doing so. The trick thus becomes tapping the power in the universe without upsetting the universal balance.

For this reason, as a third consequence, coercive means of tapping power sources are ruled out in such societies. Violence threatens to undo the universal balance. Thus, in many native North and South American societies, gentler measures were required. One approached power through prayer and supplication. The Native American vision

FIGURE 12.2 *For a Samoan "talking chief" from the island of Tutuila, verbal argument is the means to leadership.*

quest (as among the Lakota) is a good example of such an approach: through fasting and self-induced suffering, individuals hoped to move the source of power to pity so that the source might then freely bestow on them the power they sought in the form of a vision or a song or a set of ritual formulas. Power freely bestowed would not disrupt the balance of the universe. However, attempts to intimidate the power sources were viewed as wrong; not only would they have threatened the universal balance, they would have been ineffective for that very reason.

This leads to a fourth consequence: In such a worldview, violence and access to power are mutually contradictory. Physical coercion can only upset the natural balance of forces in the universe. This understanding of the role of violence has implications for its role in human affairs. If power is an independent entity that cannot be coerced, it must be approached gently; it must be supplicated. Cultures that conceive of power in this way also tend to view individual human beings as independent entities who cannot be coerced but must be supplicated. Although it may seem paradoxical from a Western point of view, individuals in such societies do exercise agency, despite their manifold obligations to one another. They are not "free agents" in the Western sense of freedom from social ties and responsibilities, but they are agents in the sense of possessing **autonomy**—that is, the power to resist being forced against their will to conform to someone else's wishes.

Recognizing the autonomy of individuals affects how stateless societies arrive at decisions. That is, a fifth consequence of viewing power as an independent entity is an emphasis on **consensus** as the appropriate means to decide issues affecting the wider

POWER AS AN INDEPENDENT ENTITY

group. In seeking consensus, proponents of a particular course of action must use **persuasion,** rather than coercion, to get other members of the group to support their cause. To make their case they must resort to verbal argument, not physical intimidation. As a result, the most respected members of stateless societies, those sometimes given the title "chief" by outsiders, are persuasive speakers (Figure 12.2). Indeed, as Pierre Clastres (1977) points out, such respected individuals are often referred to by other members of their society as "those who speak for us." The shamans (or *mara'akate*) of the Huichol Indians of northern Mexico serve this function. (See EthnoProfile 8.4: Huichol.) By virtue of their verbal ability, they see themselves (and are seen by their fellows) as especially well suited to negotiate for all the Huichol with outsiders, especially with representatives of the Mexican state.

The two different understandings of power we have discussed so far rest on different ideas of human nature and human freedom. When power is viewed exclusively as coercion, powerful individuals are those who are able to use the threat of violence to make others obey them. Such individuals are free agents because they are theoretically able to do anything their power makes possible. Nothing need restrain them from acting in any way at all except the limits of their personal ability to bend others to their will.

People who see power as an entity external to themselves have a different understanding of human nature. The only power individuals possess is the power accorded to all entities in the universe. This is the power of autonomy, the right not to be forced by violence or threat of violence to do the will of others. This does not mean that people in such societies always refrain from violence in their dealings with others; it does mean, however, that attempts to coerce are likely to meet with serious disapproval. Harmony is the desired goal—in the universe as in social relations. It can be attained only by respecting the autonomy of others, by respecting the cosmic balance, which is threatened whenever that autonomy is infringed.

Given this worldview, human beings must act in ways that preserve or restore harmony among people and within the universe. It is assumed that human beings are all free to choose how they act. They can choose responsibly, basing their actions on traditional wisdom, or they can choose irresponsibly, attempting to bend the universe and other people to their will through violence. Their lives entail a clear element of risk, for there is no way to prevent irresponsible choices and their destructive consequences. The best one can do is remind people, as the chief does, of their personal power to choose and their personal responsibility to choose wisely.

A classic example of this attitude toward power and leadership comes from the Pacific: the Big Man. Roger Keesing describes his Kwaio friend 'Elota as a *man with influence:* "When he spoke, in his hoarse voice, it was never loudly; he never shouted, never spoke in anger, never dominated conversation. Yet when he spoke people paid attention, deferred to his wisdom or laughed at his wit" (1983, 3). (See EthnoProfile 8.5: Kwaio.) He owed part of his influence to an extraordinary memory. Keesing thinks

---

autonomy The power to resist being forced against one's will to conform to someone else's wishes.

consensus An agreement to which all parties collectively give their assent.

persuasion Power based on verbal argument.

'Elota could recall genealogical information about some 3,000 to 4,000 people, as well as the details of 50 years' worth of the financial transactions that are at the heart of Kwaio feasts and marriages. In addition, "his wit and wisdom were a continuing guide towards the virtues of the past, towards thinking before rushing into action." Keesing tells us that 'Elota was "a master gamesman, in a system where prestige derives from manipulating investments and publicly giving away valuables." Finally, 'Elota also realized that the road to prominence lay in hard work devoted to producing goods that other Kwaio wanted. Those goods included taro for feasts, pigs, cane bracelets and anklets, and bark-cloth wrapping for valuables. For 'Elota, and for the Kwaio, prestige and influence come from giving away valued things. A Big Man is a master of this, especially in financing marriages and giving feasts.

Pierre Clastres suggests that stateless forms of social organization are strongly resistant to the emergence of hierarchy (1977, 35). Indeed, he argues that members of stateless societies struggle to prevent such authority from emerging. They sense that the rise of what we call state power spells the end of individual autonomy and disrupts beyond repair the harmonious balance between human beings and the forces of the wider world. Richard Lee agrees, arguing that band societies, and some farmers and herders, have found ways "to reproduce themselves while limiting the accumulation of wealth and power. Such societies operate within the confines of a metaphorical ceiling and floor: a ceiling above which one may not accumulate wealth and a floor below which one may not sink. These limits . . . are maintained by powerful social mechanisms known as leveling devices. . . . Such societies therefore have social and political resources of their own and are not just sitting ducks waiting to adopt the first hierarchical model that comes along" (1992a, 39–40). Leveling devices, such as institutionalized sharing, will be discussed at some length in Chapter 13.

THE POWER OF THE IMAGINATION

We have been looking at two ways of understanding power. The first view of power is typical in state societies: power is something that individuals, as free agents, can accumulate from their attempts to coerce other people to yield to their will. From this perspective, violence is a common and effective means to increase the power of individuals and groups. The second view of power is typical in stateless societies: individuals are not free agents who can accumulate power by coercive means. Power cannot be accumulated by coercive means without endangering the cosmic balance of forces. This means that power and coercion contradict each other. Nonviolent means of persuasion are the appropriate means for individuals to tap independent power, both from cosmic sources and from other people. Individual human beings, although not free agents, are nevertheless autonomous beings with the right to resist having another's will imposed upon them by force.

There is yet a third way of understanding power that is applicable to state societies and stateless societies alike. This approach suggests that power is defined too narrowly when it focuses on issues of physical coercion alone. To be sure, one cannot neglect the effects of physical force (or its absence) in determining the actions we may or may not undertake. But a more holistic view of power recognizes that behavior alone does not tell the whole story. We must also take into account how people make sense of the constraints and opportunities for action that are open to them. That is, an essential power of all human beings is the power of our imagination to invest the world with meaning.

All people everywhere have the power to interpret their experiences, regardless of the complexity of a social system and whether or not the power of coercion is monopolized by a central authority. This kind of power is a form of individual autonomy that may be preserved even under totalitarian dictatorship. It is notoriously difficult to erase from human consciousness, often to the frustration of political leaders, be they radical or reactionary. Hoyt Alverson argues that "a belief in one's power to invest the world with meaning (the 'will to believe') and a belief in the adequacy of one's knowledge for understanding and acting on personal experience are essential features of all human self-identity" (1978, 7). Only when human self-identity is irrevocably crushed, through extreme deprivation, is this essential human power extinguished. That may be one reason some contemporary political regimes have resorted to torture as a final means of violent coercion. Such regimes have a hard time persuading citizens with intact self-identities to follow them without question. They therefore try to coerce obedience by destroying human identity—when they do not destroy human life itself.

The power of the human imagination to invest the world with meaning is also the power to resist outside influences, material or rhetorical. This ability—not only to choose but also to reject alternative choices that others want to impose—forms the core of human self-identity. Indeed, Alverson defines self-identity as "those authentic beliefs a person holds about the *who-and-what-he-is* which resist variations in the outside forces that impel his various social actions" (1978, 3). This does not mean that individuals work out the meanings of their experiences in isolation. All human activities, including the growth and development of self-identity, take place in a social, cultural, and historical context. Nevertheless, each individual retains the power to interpret that context from his or her unique vantage point, in terms of his or her unique experiences.

The Power of the Weak

Cynics might argue that the power of the imagination must in the real world be restricted at most to private opinions; the mind can resist, but the body must conform. From this perspective, for example, the actions of a miner who labors underground daily for a meager wage are clear-cut and unmistakable: he works for money to buy food for his family. However, ethnographic data suggest that this may not be the whole story. To understand why, we need to explore more fully what is involved in political domination.

In the contemporary world, the prototype of the downtrodden and exploited human being is the industrial laborer. Workers in Western countries have managed to better their lot during the twentieth century. However, their achievements have been won with considerable struggle and sacrifice, and their situation is far from secure even today. It would seem that industrial workers in the non-Western world must be far worse off. After all, their inclusion in the industrial labor force is much more recent, and most of them have not benefited from the same gains as Western workers.

Some anthropologists who have studied patterns of industrial employment in non-Western societies interpret this industrialization as a recent consequence of Western colonial domination and exploitation. These scholars, focusing on the effects industrial employment might have on preindustrial social relationships, have wondered whether non-Western peoples respond to industrialization today the way Western people responded to industrialization in the past.

In western Europe and the United States, the Industrial Revolution of the eighteenth and nineteenth centuries brought profound social and cultural dislocation. Social scientists at that time observed those changes and tried to describe them. Emile Durkheim used the term **anomie** to refer to the pervasive sense of rootlessness and normlessness that people appeared to be experiencing. Karl Marx used the term **alienation** to describe the deep separation workers seemed to experience between their innermost sense of identity and the labor they were forced to do in order to earn enough money to live.

Do industrial workers in the Third World similarly suffer from anomie and alienation? The issue has been hotly debated. Some argue that their condition should be far worse than that of Western workers because the context of non-Western industrialization is so much more backward. This has been called the "scars of bondage" thesis. This thesis predicts that the more complete the political domination and exploitation of a people, the more deeply they will be scarred by the experience, brutalized, and dehumanized. For people suffering the twin exploitations of colonialism and industrialism, the outcome could only be the most bitter, unrelieved tragedy.

Hoyt Alverson (1978) set out to test the "scars of bondage" thesis in the field. He focused on migrant workers and their experiences in the gold mines of South Africa. His informants were Tswana living in the independent nation of Botswana, which forms part of South Africa's northern border. (See EthnoProfile 2.1: Tswana.) Botswana in the 1960s and 1970s was a poor country, and most of its families were supported only by the wages men received for working in South African mines. Here was a colonized population forced into industrial exploitation in order to survive. If the "scars of bondage" thesis were correct, the Tswana ought to be an alienated, brutalized, dehumanized lot.

Without question, the material standard of living of most of Alverson's Tswana informants was low. Without question, life in the South African mines was brutal. Without question, the difficulties families had to face when one or more of their male members was absent for months on a mining contract were considerable. And yet, for most of his informants, there was little evidence of the alienation, brutalization, and dehumanization Alverson had expected to find. On the contrary, his informants led coherent, meaningful lives. Despite their "objective" bondage to an exploitative system, "subjectively" they remained relatively unscarred. How could this be?

Were the Tswana merely happy savages, primitives without enough intelligence to understand what had been happening to them? Were they happy because they were ignorant? Such racist explanations were not persuasive to Alverson. On the contrary, the Tswana he knew struck him as particularly thoughtful people. How, then, could they have survived their experiences so well? As it turned out, the mine experience simply did not mean to the Tswana what outside observers assumed it meant: "All phenomena, including towns and gold mines, are ambiguous and can therefore be invested with manifold meanings" (1978, 215).

In most cases, Alverson's informants suffered from neither anomie nor alienation. Most had managed to come to terms with their experiences in a meaningful way. This was true both for those who were grateful to the mines and for those who hated the mines. Coming to terms with one's experiences involves mental effort. It is largely a question of finding an apt metaphor that links a person's traditional understandings with new experiences. Different people may choose different metaphors. "One Tswana may equate the relations of bosses and workers in the mine to the relationship of parent and child. If he authentically believes this analogy, then the meaning he invests in this 'inequality' will be different from that invested in it by a Tswana who defines the relationship in terms of a set of contractual exchanges made among people bound by the same set of general rights and duties" (1978, 258).

The Tswana encountered brutal inequality and discrimination outside the mines as well. Here again, however, many successfully drew on resources from their traditional culture to make sense of, and thereby transform, these experiences. For the migrant workers Alverson knew, the figure of the *Trickster* provided them with a prototype of the kind of person one had to be to survive in South Africa. The Trickster is a stock character in Tswana folklore. As his name implies, he lives by his wits, is basically amoral, and is happy to hoodwink anyone who tries to take advantage of him.

Older informants, recounting their life histories, saw themselves as Tricksters. Their greatest pride lay in the way they had managed to get by despite the traps and snares all around them. According to Alverson, the strength and genius of Tswana culture was highlighted by his informants' ability to make sense of their experiences in terms of traditional Tswana narratives.

June Nash (1979), working among Bolivian tin miners (Figure 12.3), has made similar observations about the power of human imagination to transform experiences by investing them with meaning. (See EthnoProfile 12.3: Bolivian Tin Miners.) If anything, the "objective" conditions under which these miners labor is worse than those encountered by Tswana migrants. The labor force in Bolivian mines has been drawn from local indigenous populations who, unlike the Tswana, have been effectively separated from their involvement in traditional indigenous communities. But like the Tswana of Botswana, the tin miners of Bolivia have been able creatively to combine elements of the dominant industrial culture with elements drawn from indigenous traditions. Bolivian miners have created new, cohesive cultural patterns; far from being dissonant and alienating, the miners' culture provides an intact sense of self and belonging and an ability to celebrate life because it is viewed as meaningful.

How can we explain—in the lives of Bolivian miners or Tswana migrants—this combination of what appears to be both genuine suffering and genuine celebration?

---

anomie A pervasive sense of rootlessness and normlessness in a society.

alienation A term used by Karl Marx to describe the deep separation that workers seemed to experience between their innermost sense of identity and the labor they were forced to perform in order to earn enough money to live.

FIGURE **12.3** *A woman shoveling ore at the tin mines in Bolivia.*

EthnoProfile 12.3 • BOLIVIAN TIN MINERS

REGION: South America

NATION: Bolivia (city of Oruro)

POPULATION: 28,000 miners; with families, about 180,000

ENVIRONMENT: Mountainous

LIVELIHOOD: Wage labor in the mines

POLITICAL ORGANIZATION: Unionized miners, part of a modern nation-state

FOR MORE INFORMATION: Nash, June. 1979. *We eat the mines, and the mines eat us.* New York: Columbia University Press.

Exploitation certainly leaves its mark on its victims: poor health, high infant mortality, intrafamilial abuse, shattered hopes. Yet neither the Bolivian miners nor Tswana migrants have been irrevocably brutalized by these experiences. Their powers to invest their experiences with meaning remain intact, virtually inextinguishable despite crushing conditions of exploitation.

This is the point: "The power the Tswana will think he has will not be defined in terms of what he can get the boss to do and vice versa, but rather in terms of how freely and effectively he invests his experience with the meaning *he chooses*" (Alverson 1978, 258). This power was noted by Nash for the Bolivian miners as well: "My experience living in mining communities taught me more than anything else, how a people totally involved in the most exploitative, dehumanizing form of industrialization managed to resist alienation" (Nash 1979, 319–20). Like Alverson, Nash argues that the events people experience are less important than how they interpret those events. Nash concludes that the ethnocentrism of Western observers has kept them from recognizing the creative, revolutionary potential embodied in syncretistic cultures like that of the Bolivian tin miners.

Human beings everywhere are active creatures who engage the wider world as well as respond to it. A Tswana mine-labor migrant is not helpless and passive in the face of hardship and suffering: "Almost immediately he begins to cope in consciousness. . . . What began as a collision can achieve a state of coherent integration" (Alverson 1978, 279). This power to cope in consciousness, to invest experience with one's own meanings, is a very real power, available to all even under the most repressive conditions of political domination.

And so we return to our original question: What does it mean to labor in the mines for a pittance? Western critics may continue to see it as dehumanizing drudgery imposed on the politically weak in a stratified society. The Tswana migrant would not necessarily deny this observation. Alverson's informants did not glorify the conditions in the mines, even though they knew they needed the mine wages to support their families. And yet they compartmentalized their involvement in mine labor, seeing it as only one temporary aspect of their life and not a particularly meaningful one at that. As a result, the impact of the mine experience on their sense of self was minimized and perhaps eventually transformed into material for a personalized Trickster tale. Mine labor was only one element in a larger picture, the Tswana worldview, that migrants drew upon successfully to infuse their experiences with meaning.

THE POWER OF PERSUASION

The power that people have to invest their experiences with meanings of their own choosing suggests that a ruler's power of coercion is limited. Thought alone may be unable to alter the material circumstances of coercion, yet it has the power to transform the meaning of those material circumstances.

Any political establishment runs the risk that the dominated may create new, plausible accounts of their experiences of domination. Political scientist James Scott (1990)

In Their Own Words   **THE STRUGGLE FOR INDIGENOUS RIGHTS IN ECUADOR**

Historian Peter Winn describes the recent history of CONAIE (Confederation of Ecuadorian Indigenous Nationalities), the first South American organization to unite indigenous highland and rain forest peoples in a common political struggle against a national government.

By 1980, when Fabián Muenala joined fifty-two educated young Indians in a bilingual Catholic University program in Quito, Ecuador's sierra Indians were ready to unite their efforts with those of the Amazonian Indians about whom they knew little.

During the early 1980s, that bilingual education project, based in part on the Shuar experience, served as a frame within which Ecuador's Indians became familiar with each other's cultures and histories. They also spent these same years working out common positions on controversial issues. "It was a difficult process," Muenala said. "There were many outside influences that tried to bend our interests to suit theirs: The Marxists wanted us to be part of a class-based peasant organization, the Chris-

tians wanted us to be part of a religious movement, the *indigenistas* wanted us to become dependent on foreign aid agencies, and the *indianistas* wanted us to reject everything Western and re-create the Inca empire. [But] in the end, we developed our own positions, in accordance with our own criteria and experience." After studying the examples of the United States, the Soviet Union, Canada, and Switzerland, the Ecuadorian Indians decided that they were "nationalities"—each with their own language, history, and "cosmovision"—living in a country that should recognize it was a multinational state. In 1986, they joined together in the Confederation of Ecuadorian Indigenous Nationalities (CONAIE), the first organization in South America to unite highland and rain forest Indians despite the many differences between them. "In the Amazon, we are trying to defend the lands of our ancestors," said Leonardo Viteri. "In the sierra they are trying to recover the lands taken from their ancestors. We agreed to support each other's struggle."

The formation of such a confederation was an historic event, but it marked the beginning of their struggle, not its end. The 1988 election of a center-left reform government led by Rodrigo Borja sparked Indian hopes: Borja had agreed during his campaign to CONAIE demands for the recognition of Ecuador as a multinational state and Quichua as one of its official languages, as well as to bilingual education, agrarian reform in the highlands, and the demarcation of Indian lands in the rain forest. Once in office, however, Borja dragged his feet on fulfilling his promises to CONAIE.

As a result, CONAIE decided on a dramatic protest. It began as a hunger strike in Quito's Santo Domingo church by two hundred Indian leaders, "to protest the government's refusal to grant our demands or even to discuss them with us," Fabián Muenala explained. The government responded by sealing off the church with troops. It backed down in the face of Church mediation and international pressure, but then refused to recognize the accord. In response,

refers to these unofficial accounts as "hidden transcripts." Occasionally, those who are dominated may be able to organize themselves socially in order to defend their hidden transcripts publicly against attacks from the political establishment. Under such conditions, those who are dominated may become considerably more than armchair revolutionaries. They may develop the ability to go beyond simply creating an unofficial account of their situation to actually "make their account count" in official public discussions (see Giddens 1979, 83). That is, they may be able to persuade some or all of those around them that their interpretation of social experience is better or truer than that of the current rulers. Their account "counts" if current rulers can no longer ignore it when making political choices. In some cases, making an alternative account count may even be the prelude to replacing the current rulers.

CONAIE called for peaceful protest marches throughout the country. The result was the Indian Uprising of June 1990, which galvanized Ecuador's indigenous people in Cayambe and other communities in the sierra and the rain forest. CONAIE's leaders "hadn't realized what the magnitude of response to its call would be," Muenala said. "The people exploded against the injustices they were suffering, and their energy and force paralyzed the entire country."

The scope and effectiveness of the Indian protests took Ecuador by surprise. The Church was sympathetic and offered to mediate with the government. Support from labor, women's, and peasant organizations poured in, along with expressions of solidarity from ordinary Ecuadorians—including mestizo taxi drivers, *chola* marketwomen, and creole intellectuals. Only the government refused to recognize the popular rebellion for what it was, accusing the Indians of being "agitators without a sense of nationality who want to divide the country." But after three days, "the cities were dying of hunger" and the government was forced to agree to a Church-brokered accord that committed it to negotiating Indian demands.

The Indian rebellion had brought the Ecuadorian government to the bargaining table, but had not persuaded it to compromise on substantive issues. As one official insisted on condition of anonymity: "The government can not allow a small group of Indians to control its development policies and oil revenues." Nor was the Borja government willing to confront the creole elite that controlled Ecuadorian politics over land reform in order to placate its Indians. A year later, CONAIE occupied the Chamber of Deputies to protest the slow pace of reform, the jailing of Indian leaders, and the failure to declare Ecuador a multinational state. In April 1992, a two-week march of seven thousand Shuar, Ashuar, and Quichua activists from the Amazon to Quito—retracing the 180-mile ascent of the Andes undertaken a century ago by indigenous chiefs for a similar purpose—dramatized the lack of progress on several of these issues.

By then it was clear that the struggle for indigenous rights in Ecuador was going to be a very long march. It was also evident that it was going to be an increasingly violent struggle. The government had intensified its repression, jailing leaders and harassing organizations. Even more ominous was the formation of paramilitary death squads by local landholders threatened with Indian land invasions. Kidnappings and murders of Indian activists confronted the movement with a new situation. "We do not want violence," Leonardo Viteri insisted. But neither he nor other Indian leaders would rule out violence in response to violence. "Indians have been dying for centuries," affirmed Shuar leader Rafael Pandam. "We are not afraid to die for our people." Viteri was conscious of the parallels to the experience of indigenous people elsewhere in the region: "We do not want another Guatemala," he stressed, "but it may not be up to us."

Source: Winn 1992, 261–63.

And so we find a fourth way of understanding power: the ability to make certain accounts count. This view of power combines elements of the three approaches already explored. When coercive power is monopolized by the state, the individual's power to choose and to resist the choices of others is curtailed, sometimes severely. But it is not wholly destroyed. What remains may be no more than the power of a martyr who views the sacrifice of her life as serving a higher moral purpose even though her executioners insist that her death is a just punishment for crimes she has committed. Nevertheless, a person's power may be considerably stronger than this. Individuals or groups may develop alternative accounts of a situation and mount direct or indirect challenges to the official account. Such challenges to incumbent political power are frequently too strong to be ignored and too widespread to be simply obliterated by force.

When coercion no longer works, what remains is a confrontation between alternative accounts of experience. Which account eventually comes to influence major decisions and shape people's lives on a grand scale will be determined by the power of persuasion. Physical force may be one element that influences how persuasive a particular account is. This is true not just in the cynical sense that "might makes right" but also in the sense that possession of physical power may be seen as a demonstration of the ability to tap the primal forces of the universe. This is the essential political dynamic noted by Pierre Clastres (1977) for stateless societies, but this time the action may be organized within or between states. When application of physical force is recognized as a cure worse than the political ills it seeks to remove, there is no alternative but negotiation.

Negotiation

Political activity in human society involves not just coercion by physical force or threat of force but also **negotiation** about when such coercion may or may not be legitimate. In other words, what is considered a legitimate exercise of power must be seen to conform to political principles that are consistent with the culture's worldview.

However, "political principles consistent with a culture's worldview" is a highly ambiguous category. Some principles may seem to be consistent with the worldview when taken individually but contradict one another when considered together. For example, U.S. citizens would probably agree that liberty and equality are key principles defining political legitimacy in our society. However, unrestricted liberty (as exemplified by laissez-faire capitalism) can lead to the domination of the weak by the strong, which seriously undermines the principle of equality. Yet enforcing equality (as in affirmative action programs) is seen by some as restricting important liberties by undermining incentives for individual self-betterment. It is also possible to agree on a principle and disagree on how to put the principle in practice. Does American "equality" properly refer to equality of opportunity or to equality of outcome? Does American "liberty" protect polygynists as well as Presbyterians?

In the United States, many consider the tension between the principles of liberty and equality as healthy and creative. Nevertheless, the existence of this tension reflects (1) our difficulty in deciding once and for all what liberty or equality "really" means and (2) an ongoing struggle in American society to define and redefine acceptable accounts of our shared situation in the world. Such accounts must not only be faithful to cultural principles but must also meet the practical needs of our social existence. Because different groups within a society (or different societies) may disagree about which account should prevail, negotiation among these groups is an inevitable part of ongoing social life.

Anthropologist F. G. Bailey paid close attention to the everyday workings of a non-Western political system. His research in a village in India suggested that physical coercion is normally not at issue in day-to-day politics; rather, he saw politics as a kind of game. Like games, political systems have rules, and those rules dictate who can play, which moves are legitimate and which are not, and what the reward is for winning. This orientation is reflected in the title of Bailey's book, *Stratagems and Spoils: A Social Anthro-*

EthnoProfile 12.4 • **"SEDAKA" VILLAGE**

REGION: Southeastern Asia

NATION: Malaysia

POPULATION: 300

ENVIRONMENT: Lush paddy land

LIVELIHOOD: Rice cultivation

POLITICAL ORGANIZATION: Village within a modern nation-state

FOR MORE INFORMATION: Scott, James. 1985. *Weapons of the weak.* New Haven: Yale University Press.

pology of Politics (1969). Bailey argued that much everyday political activity involves manipulating the rules of a given system in order to obtain the reward—or spoils—that success brings.

Bailey chose what he considered an apt metaphor for interpreting the moves of political actors for whom might alone does not make right. But even people who share the most basic principles can disagree over the proper application of those principles in any particular case. In addition, people often have to interact even if they do not have the same set of rules. How can such parties engage one another in political activity? Physical coercion, from fisticuffs to armed insurrection, is one way. But violence on an everyday basis is expensive and can backfire on the perpetrators. What occurs is more likely to be a metaphoric "fight," a war of words and covert resistance.

James Scott carried out two years of ethnographic research among peasant rice farmers in a Malaysian village called "Sedaka" (a pseudonym). (See EthnoProfile 12.4: "Sedaka" Village.) Poor Malaysian peasants are at the bottom of a social hierarchy dominated locally by rich farmers and nationally by a powerful state apparatus (Figure 12.4). These peasants are not kept in line by some form of state-sponsored terrorism; rather, the context of their lives is shaped by what Scott calls *routine repression:* "occasional arrests, warnings, diligent police work, legal restrictions, and an Internal Security Act that allows for indefinite preventive detention and proscribes much political activity" (1985, 274).

Scott wanted to find out how this highly restrictive environment affected political relations between members of dominant and subordinate classes in the village. He quickly realized that the poor peasants of Sedaka were not about to rise up against their oppressors. But this was not because they accepted their poverty and low status as

negotiation Reaching a settlement or agreement by means of verbal discussion.

FIGURE 12.4 *Until recently, rice harvesting in rural Malaysia was manual labor that regularly allowed poor peasants to earn cash and receive grain from their employers as a traditional form of charitable gift.*

natural and proper. For one thing, organized overt defense of their interests would have been difficult under the best of circumstances given the conflicting loyalties generated by local economic, political, and kinship ties. For another thing, even had such organization been possible, the peasants knew that overt political action in the context of routine repression would be foolhardy. And they had to feed their families. Their solution was to engage in what Scott calls *everyday forms of peasant resistance:* this included "foot dragging, dissimulation, desertion, false compliance, pilfering, feigned ignorance, slander, arson, sabotage, and so forth" (1985, xvi). These actions may have done little to alter the peasants' situation in the short run; however, Scott argues, in the long run they may have been more effective than overt rebellion in undercutting state repression.

What we find in everyday forms of peasant resistance are indirect attempts to make an alternative account of the social situation count. Scott says, "The struggle between rich and poor in Sedaka is not merely a struggle over work, property rights, grain, and cash. It is also a struggle over the appropriation of symbols, a struggle over how the past and present shall be understood and labeled, a struggle to identify causes and assess blame" (1985, xvii). When peasants criticize rich landowners or rich landowners find fault with peasants, the parties involved are not just venting emotion. According to Scott, each side is simultaneously constructing a worldview. Rich and poor alike are offering "a critique of things as they are as well as a vision of things as they should be. . . . [They are writing] a kind of social text on the subject of human decency" (23).

Scott describes the dynamics of this struggle during the introduction of mechanized rice harvesting in Sedaka. Traditionally, rice harvesting was manual labor. It regularly allowed poor peasants to earn cash and receive grain from their employers as a traditional form of charitable gift. In the late 1970s, however, the introduction of combine harvesters eliminated the rich farmers' need for hired labor, a loss that dealt poor families a severe economic blow. When the rich and poor talked about the harvesters, each side offered a different account of their effect on economic life in the village. The struggle of each side to make its account count illustrated the power of persuasion in practice.

Scott tells us that both sides recognized certain obvious facts about combine harvesters. They agreed, for example, that using the machines hurt the poor and helped the rich. When each side was asked whether the benefits of the machines outweighed their costs, however, consensus evaporated. The poor offered practical reasons against the use of combine harvesters: they claimed that the heavy machines were inefficient and that their operation destroyed rice paddies. They also offered moral reasons: they accused the rich of being "stingy," of ignoring the traditional obligation of rich people to help the poor by providing them with work and charity. The rich denied both the practical and the moral objections of the poor. They insisted that using harvesters increased their yield. They accused the poor people of bad faith. They claimed that the poor suffered because they were bad farmers or lazy, and they attributed their own success to hard work and prudent farm management.

Rich rice farmers would never have been able to begin using combine harvesters without the outside assistance of both the national government and the business groups who rented the machines to them at harvesttime. Poor peasants were aware of this, yet they did not expect the government or business organizations outside the village to help them out in times of need; that is, however, exactly what they expected from rich local farmers. After all, the rich farmers "are a part of the community and therefore *ought* not to be indifferent to the consequences of their acts for their neighbors" (Scott 1985, 161). The stinginess of the rich did not just bring economic loss. It also attacked the social identity of the poor, who vigorously resisted being turned into nonpersons. The poor insisted on being accorded the "minimal cultural decencies in this small community" (xviii). The only weapon they controlled in this struggle was their ability, by word and deed, to undercut the prestige and reputation of the rich.

And so they rejected the accounts rich people offered of themselves and their actions. Also, by offering an alternative account, they made it more difficult for those in power to ignore them. This strategy worked in Sedaka because rich local farmers were not ready to abandon the traditional morality that had regulated relations between rich and poor. They had not yet become so Westernized that they no longer cared what other villagers thought of them. A shrewd campaign of character assassination may have caused at least some of the rich to hesitate before ignoring their traditional obligations. If successful, the poor may have been able to persuade the rich of their right to work and charity. The improvement might have been minor in strictly economic terms, but it would have been major in terms of the ability of the poor to defend their claims to citizenship in the local community. In addition, the wider political arena could always change in the future. Scott was convinced that many of the poor peasants he knew might well engage in open, active rebellion if routine repression disappeared.

Struggle over principles and how to apply them in real life is rife with ambiguity and potential disagreement. Consequently, debates over definitions play a central role in any human society. Clastres (1977, 128ff.) emphasizes that in stateless societies, language (especially coming from the lips of the chief) is a source of power that shapes, identifies, and labels what is of value, what is worth paying attention to, and what shall count in the world of human experience. Alverson and Scott show that this power does not disappear with the rise of the state. Worldviews articulated in language by different social subgroups aim "not just to convince but to control; better stated, they aim to control by convincing" (Scott 1985, 23). The way the Tswana and the villagers of Sedaka talked about their experiences had the potential to transform the material circumstances of their lives.

Language is not the only symbolic code that can be used to define a political position. June Nash (1979) described how disenfranchised Bolivian tin miners manipulated religious ritual to force their employers to pay attention to an alternative understanding of reality. (See EthnoProfile 12.3: Bolivian Tin Miners.) Nash studied the *ch'alla,* a traditional ritual which the miners dedicate to the devil (or *Tío,* as he is called in Spanish). She learned that this ritual had political overtones and that its meaning had changed significantly after the tin mines were nationalized. Before nationalization, the mines had been run privately by a Bolivian elite and non-Bolivian managers who had supported the ritual and had contributed financially to it. Following nationalization, the mines were run by the Bolivian government and Bolivian managers. These people not only withdrew official support from the ritual; they tried to wipe it out altogether.

This change of policy was closely related to the social identity of the new administrators and to their fears that their authority might be challenged on the basis of that identity. The former Bolivian owners and their non-Bolivian managers had a social iden-

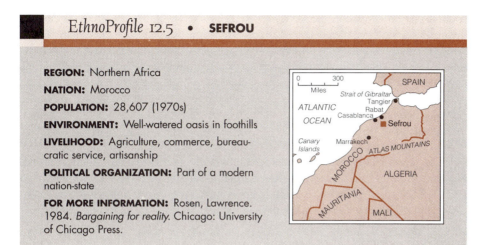

EthnoProfile 12.5 • SEFROU

REGION: Northern Africa

NATION: Morocco

POPULATION: 28,607 (1970s)

ENVIRONMENT: Well-watered oasis in foothills

LIVELIHOOD: Agriculture, commerce, bureaucratic service, artisanship

POLITICAL ORGANIZATION: Part of a modern nation-state

FOR MORE INFORMATION: Rosen, Lawrence. 1984. *Bargaining for reality.* Chicago: University of Chicago Press.

tity clearly distinct from that of the indigenous miners and people. They therefore felt free to encourage the practice of an indigenous ritual that reinforced the distinctness of the mine owners from the mine workers. After nationalization, however, the mine owner became the Bolivian government and the mine technicians were Bolivians. Neither of these groups had unambiguous claims to a social identity that was clearly distinct from the miners and the indigenous people, so they withdrew their support for the ch'alla ritual. The new administrators feared that they, unlike the elite they replaced, might be suspected of sharing the miners' devotion to Tío if they lent their support to rituals honoring him. By repudiating the ch'alla, they repudiated miner identity as well.

Their rejection of the ch'alla had political consequences. Before nationalization, the ritual embodied the harmonious ties linking ruler and ruled. Control by the elite was uncontested, the workers accepted their place, and elite sponsorship of the ritual to Tío certified and reinforced this state of affairs. After nationalization, when threatened administrators attempted to shore up their status and authority by banning the ch'alla, miners ignored the ban, thereby challenging the authority of the mine administration. Performance of the ch'alla now embodied disunity between the two groups rather than solidarity, and it enlisted the power of Tío in support of the workers against the national government.

Bargaining for Reality

Political life involves winning hearts and minds as well as—or even more than—coercing bodies. Anthropologist Lawrence Rosen worked in the Moroccan city of Sefrou. (See EthnoProfile 12.5: Sefrou.) As he listened to his informants discussing and defining their relationships with each other, he realized that none of the traditional concepts they used could be said to have a fixed meaning. Any definition offered by one person would be verbally challenged by another. Rosen concluded that political and social life in Sefrou could not be understood unless one accepted that, for his informants, negotiation was the norm. Rosen (1984) calls this sociopolitical negotiation *bargaining for reality*.

The reality bargained for is not an impersonal, unchangeable set of truths about the world. Like the Tswana migrants, Bolivian miners, and Malaysian villagers, Moroccans aim to persuade one another to accept alternative ways of understanding a particular situation. Persuasive accounts must be *coherent:* they must explain events and processes central to the experience of those to whom they are addressed; they must be expressed in language that other members of society can understand; and they must hang together in a way that is not blatantly contradictory.

The power relationship between men and women in Sefrou illustrates this process. Men view women as less intelligent, less self-controlled, and more selfish than men, and they expect women to obey them. Although women often assent to the male account of this relationship, they do not accept it in all circumstances. Women have developed an alternative account that explains elements in their lives that the male account either overlooks or interprets differently.

Women in Sefrou depend on men—first their fathers and later their husbands—for material support. But marriages are fragile, and women often have to rely on brothers or sons when their husbands divorce them. Consequently, security for women depends on strengthening their positions within their families. In particular, women actively attempt to influence marriage negotiations because marriage automatically rearranges social relationships within the family. Women are eager to protect themselves and their daughters from oppressive demands by a husband and his kin. They view their action as sensible and compassionate, not as misplaced interference. Nor do they accept the men's view that men are superior to women intellectually and morally. Indeed, they often view men as self-centered and childish.

In effect, Moroccan men and women live side by side in different worlds. They share experiences but interpret those experiences differently. Because neither sex has much direct contact with the other during everyday life, these different interpretations of experience do not constantly come into conflict. But there are occasions—such as marriage negotiations—that bring these different sets of understanding into contention. The outcome is reality bargaining, as several different actors attempt to make their definitions of the situation prevail.

Rosen describes one marriage negotiation that he encountered in Sefrou (1984, 40–47). A girl refused to marry the suitor her family chose, and her continued obstinacy had disrupted the harmony of her father's household. Rosen visited the household in the company of a respected male informant who was an old friend of the family. During their visit, the family friend and the girl's mother discussed the betrothal and the girl's refusal to consent to it.

Both parties interpreted the girl's refusal differently. The family friend described the girl's behavior as a typical case of female selfishness and immorality. What other reason could there be for her refusing to obey her father, as dutiful daughters should? He spoke harshly of her and repeatedly asserted that when her father returned they would force her to come to her senses and make the marriage. Her mother never openly contradicted the family friend's assertions. All the while, however, she quietly and insistently continued to make counterassertions of her own. She reported her daughter's reason for reject-ing the match: her intended husband came from a distant city. If she married him she would have to leave her family behind and go live among strangers. It was not that she objected to an arranged marriage; rather, she did not want to marry this particular man because to do so would take her so far away from home. From a woman's perspective, the daughter's anxieties were entirely rational given the powerlessness and isolation that a new Moroccan wife must endure in her husband's family.

As it turned out, the young girl was eventually persuaded to marry the intended spouse, but only after a year and a half of successful resistance. She only changed her mind when she became convinced that consenting to the marriage was an economically sound move, not a submission to patriarchal authority.

So women may agree with the male position in general terms and yet successfully dispute its relevance in a particular situation. Men may get women to comply with their wishes, and yet the women's reasons for doing so may have nothing to do with the reasons men offer to justify their demands. This bears a strong resemblance to the situation in South Africa, where Tswana migrants complied with the wishes of their bosses yet explained their compliance in terms utterly at odds with their employers' understanding. It is also similar to the situation in Sedaka, where rich farmers and poor peasants agreed that combine harvesters hurt the poor and helped the rich but did not agree as to why.

When disputes are settled in this manner, experience is transformed. As Scott ob-serves, "The key symbols animating class relations in Sedaka—generosity, stinginess, arrogance, humility, help, assistance, wealth and poverty—do not constitute a set of given rules or principles that actors simply follow. They are instead the normative raw material that is created, maintained, changed, and above all manipulated by daily human activity" (1985, 309). In a similar way, Rosen refers to such central Moroccan values as intelligence, self-control, and generosity as **essentially negotiable concepts:** "There is an element of uncertainty inherent in these terms, such that their application to any situation by one person can be contested by another" (1984, 43). Bargaining for reality involves just this sort of maneuver: "What is negotiable, then, is less one's view of reality as such than its scope, its impact, and its differential importance" (47).

HISTORY AS A PROTOTYPE OF AND FOR POLITICAL ACTION

When individual actors within a particular cultural and situational context attempt to impose their definition of the situation on those with whom they interact, they draw on elements of a shared tradition of values and beliefs. This shared tradition, however, does not consist of values and beliefs divorced from experience and history. To some degree,

---

essentially negotiable concepts
Culturally recognized concepts that evoke a wide range of meanings and whose relevance in any particular context must be negotiated.

EthnoProfile 12.6 • NORTHERN PERU (RONDAS CAMPESINAS)

REGION: South America

NATION: Peru

POPULATION: Rondas campesinas now operate in more than 3,400 hamlets across Peru's northern Andes

ENVIRONMENT: Mountainous

LIVELIHOOD: Peasant villagers

POLITICAL ORGANIZATION: Originally, community-run vigilante patrols that developed by the mid-1980s into an alternative justice system, filling the vacuum created by an ineffectual central government

FOR MORE INFORMATION: Starn, Orin. 1992. I dreamed of foxes and hawks: Reflections on peasant protest, new social movements, and the rondas campesinas of northern Peru. In *The making of social movements in Latin America*, edited by Arturo Escobar and Sonia Alvarez, 89–111. Boulder, CO: Westview.

people in all cultures continue to reshape—to bargain over—not merely which part of an agreed-on tradition is relevant in a particular situation but also which version of the tradition ought to be agreed on. The combinations they come up with are sometimes surprising.

Consider the development in the northern Peruvian highlands of new rural justice groups, called *rondas campesinas* ("peasants who make the rounds"), beginning in the mid-1970s (Starn 1992). (See EthnoProfile 12.6: Northern Peru [Rondas campesinas].) Rondas consist of armed groups of peasants who walk the paths around their hamlets at night, keeping an eye out for animal rustlers. The rondas began in one small hamlet in the northern Peruvian department of Cajamarca in 1976. During the 1980s, rondas spread hundreds of miles within Cajamarca and surrounding departments. At the same time, their functions were radically expanded: they were transformed into an entire alternative justice system with open peasant assemblies to resolve problems ranging from wife-beating to land disputes. By the early 1990s, rondas operated in 3,400 hamlets in the northern Peruvian Andes.

Five forces spurred campesinos to establish their alternative justice system. First, the theft of animals shot up dramatically with the onset of the Peruvian economic crisis in the mid-1970s. The rise in theft was extremely serious for the poor farmers of the northern Andes, most of whom have small flocks and earn less than $2,000 per year. Second, peasants got no relief from the official justice system. As the economy worsened, many government authorities tried to enlarge their shrinking salaries through bribery, kickbacks, and extortion, and poorer peasants were increasingly unable to pay. Third, the government had only a weak presence in the mountains, providing an opportunity for peasants to develop a new form of community organization. Fourth, country people in northern Peru value toughness and bravery in the face of violence and were able to channel their aggressiveness into the service of order and discipline in the rondas. Fifth, local organizers had outside supporters. In the province where the rondas began, these were activists from the Maoist Red Homeland party. In a neighboring province, peasant catechists trained in liberation theology became early ronda leaders and were defended by priests and nuns as well as the bishop of Cajamarca.

During the 1980s, rondas were transformed from vigilante groups to dispute-resolution groups. Compared to the expensive, time-consuming, humiliating, and ineffective official justice system, the ronda was inexpensive, efficient, effective, and local. By the late 1980s, rustling was virtually eliminated and rondas in some communities were adjudicating over 100 cases a month. The rondas also involve the elaboration of political identity and culture. Songs and poems celebrate the rondas, and festivals commemorate their anniversaries.

To create the rondas, peasants drew on national and local cultural patterns. Peasants had served on patrols to stop thieves on haciendas before the haciendas were broken up in the late 1960s. Men in the hamlets who had served in the Peruvian military incorporated military strategies and forms into the rondas. The peasants also employed local patterns, keeping the ronda patrols under the collective authority of the community. Likewise, when the rondas took on adjudication roles, they adopted some forms from the state bureaucracy, using a table like a judge's bench, rubber stamps, a recording secretary with notarized minutes, and so on. But the openness of the ronda system is very different from the state bureaucracy, for the final decision rests on the president's evaluation of the response of the people attending. Assemblies of the ronda are often held outside, where the event occurred, such as a farmyard. All attending have detailed knowledge of some kind that may be brought into play, and everyone jumps in to attempt to settle the dispute.

But the rondas, for all their effective innovation, are sometimes still enmeshed in old problems. First, they are connected with political parties in Peru, and squabbles involving the parties have weakened the ronda movement. Second, although they have challenged the government's monopoly on the administration of justice, they are not working for the overthrow of the state; rather, they see themselves as the genuine upholders of the law and the Peruvian constitution. Third, although constant rotation in many communities discourages permanent leaders, in some rondas the leaders stay on for many years, hoard power, and begin to show favoritism. Fourth, the rondas perpetuate the problems of patriarchy. Many peasant women march in ronda protests, and in some rondas the women oversee the patrol scheduling. The rondas have also given women a place to censure wife-beating, and a number of offenders have received a stern warning or whipping. Nevertheless, only men patrol; female participation in assemblies is limited and mostly passive; and women are never ronda officers. Finally, there is the problem of violence. The ronderos have learned some of the techniques of the Peruvian police, including whipping with barbed wire or hanging accused rustlers by their arms. But it is important to note that the rondas began as a means of creating peace and order in a violent environment. As rustling has been brought under control, cases of harsh physical treatment have diminished. The leaders of rondas have worked within their communities to prevent the use of excessive force. Starn concludes that, on the whole, the rondas have given Peruvian peasants the vision of an alternative modernity and have renewed among them a powerful sense of independent identity.

NEGOTIATING THE MEANING OF HISTORY

The meanings of the central symbols of any cultural tradition are essentially negotiable. That is, each symbol evokes a wide range of meanings among those who accept it. But what that symbol means in any particular situation, as well as the appropriateness of applying that symbol to the situation, is never obvious. Such matters are cultural dilemmas that people struggle creatively to resolve. In the Moroccan example, nobody denied that daughters should allow their fathers to arrange their marriages. The issue was whether this particular daughter, in refusing to marry a particular man, was rejecting the general principle. From her and her mother's perspective she was not; they would accept an arranged marriage if it did not mean taking her far from her family. The family friend, however, insisted on interpreting her behavior as a challenge to her father's authority.

In the Peruvian example, a central question was: Who are the genuine upholders of the law and the Peruvian constitution? The ronderos and the national government gave different answers. Such powerful national symbols as the law and the constitution carry heavy historical freight. The political use to which such symbols are put can be far from negligible. Leftist political parties and Catholic clergy who had taken up a preferential option for the poor supported the interpretation of the peasants, backing the ronda movement. Power lies essentially in being able to convince others that your knowledge is accurate, that your account counts. If you succeed in so convincing them, you may also persuade them that the only actions that make political sense are those that follow from your account. The rapid spread of the ronda movement suggests that the rondero's account was strongly persuasive to peasants in many areas of northern highland Peru in the conditions of the late 1970s and 1980s.

With the breakup of the Soviet Union in the early 1990s and the subsequent breakdown of the decades-long superpower rivalry between the Soviet Union and the United States, many of the old lessons of history no longer seem enlightening. Those lessons were learned in a world that no longer exists. Some writers have suggested that current events are teaching us "the lesson of Lebanon." This lesson presumably was learned when the United States tried to intervene militarily in Lebanon in the 1980s only to have its troops slaughtered in a terrorist attack. The lesson seems to be that it is difficult if not impossible to identify factions in other societies who are clearly "on our side" or "on their side" in a world without dueling superpowers to define the sides. Current turmoil between factions in the former Yugoslavia, in the former Soviet Union, in Somalia, in Liberia, in Zaire and elsewhere suggest that the United States will have to grapple with future international troubles in a world where finding good reasons to support one faction instead of another will be exceedingly difficult.

KEY TERMS

social organization
power
political anthropology
coercion
legitimacy

autonomy
consensus
persuasion
anomie

alienation
negotiation
essentially negotiable
concepts

CHAPTER SUMMARY

1. Social organization refers to the patterning of human interdependence in a given society through the actions and decisions of its members. Different modes of livelihood do not by themselves shape social forms. We must also consider, say, who takes care of crops and cattle, how it is done, and for whom it is done. This requires that we investigate the power that human beings have to reproduce or to change their social organization.

2. Anthropologists and others have sought laws to explain cross-cultural similarities and differences in social organization. Evolutionists, including Marx, hoped to find those laws in the dynamics of history. Environmental determinists hoped to find them by studying how particular societies adapt to their local environments. Biological determinists looked within the human organism. All these positions assume that certain material factors uniquely determine forms of social organization. They reject the anthropological argument that social relations in any society are ultimately arbitrary because the context of those relations can never be unambiguously defined.

3. The ability to choose implies power. In most societies at most times, power can never be reduced to naked physical force, although this is the Western prototype of power. Power in society operates according to principles that are cultural creations. As such, those principles are basically arbitrary and may differ from one society to another.

4. Western thinkers traditionally assumed that without a state, social life would be chaotic if not impossible. They believed that people would not cooperate unless forced to do so. Anthropologists have demonstrated that stateless societies can maintain order by relying on kinship institutions in the absence of a central coercive authority.

5. People may submit to institutionalized power because they fear punishment, but they may also submit because they believe it is the right thing to do. In many societies, it is probably impossible to separate these two motivations. People may even be willing to give their lives to preserve a meaningful understanding of the world.

6. Those who view power as coercion see political encounters as a form of bargaining or haggling, not for material goods but for control. This perspective assumes that the parties involved are free agents who are not, and should not be, duty-bound to consider the outcome of their actions for anyone but themselves.

7. In stateless societies, social obligations restrict individuals from pursuing their own self-interest to the detriment of the group. In those societies, power is usually seen to be an independent entity to which one may gain access by supplication, not coercion. Likewise, human individuals cannot be coerced but must be persuaded to cooperate. They are not "free" of social obligations, but they are autonomous in that they cannot be forced to do someone else's bidding against their will.

8. In state and stateless societies alike, all human beings possess the power to invest the world with meaning. Regardless of the form of society in which they live, people can interpret their experiences in a manner that "objective" social conditions cannot dictate. This ability, not only to choose an interpretation but also to reject alternative interpretations of experience, lies at the core of human self-identity.

9. Because dominated groups retain the power to invest the world with their own meanings, rulers always face the risk that those they rule may create new persuasive accounts of their experience of being dominated, organize themselves to defend and disseminate their account, acquire a following, and unseat their rulers. Making alternative accounts count is another way of understanding power.

10. Political activity in human society involves not just coercion but also negotiation over the legitimacy of such coercion. Much everyday political life turns on negotiation according to accepted social rules, not the threat of physical force. Politics may even be defined as a set of rules and principles for keeping social order and resolving disputes. Yet the rules and principles always have to be interpreted before they can be applied, and group members may differ in their interpretations. When open rebellion is unrealistic, oppressed peoples may find that everyday forms of resistance can be used to defend their own account of their situation.

11. Debates over definitions play a central role in political life. Interpretations are essentially negotiable, and people may find themselves doing the "right" thing for the "wrong" reasons. When disputes are settled in this manner, experience is transformed.

12. When people bargain for reality, they draw on elements of a shared culture and shared history in order to persuade others of the validity of their position. But they often must bargain over not merely which part of an agreed-on tradition is relevant but also which version of the tradition ought to be agreed on. The results can be surprising. Much political debate concerns which lessons from the past are relevant to the present.

SUGGESTED READINGS

Alverson, Hoyt. 1978. *Mind in the heart of darkness.* New Haven: Yale University Press. *Difficult in places, but important and gripping. A study of how Tswana miners in South Africa maintain a sense of who they are under the most hellish circumstances.*

Arens, W., and Ivan Karp. 1989. *Creativity of power: Cosmology and action in African societies.* Washington: Smithsonian Institution Press. *Contains 13 essays exploring the relationship between power, action, and human agency in African social systems and cosmologies.*

Fogelson, Raymond, and Richard N. Adams. 1977. *The anthropology of power.* New York: Academic Press. *A collection of 28 ethnographic essays on power all over the world. Also contains 2 important essays based on the case studies.*

Keesing, Roger. 1983. *'Elota's story.* New York: Holt, Rinehart and Winston. *The autobiography of a Kwaio Big Man, with interpretative material by Keesing. First-rate, very readable, and involving. We come to know 'Elota by the end of the book.*

Lewellen, Ted. 1983. *Political anthropology.* South Hadley, MA: Bergin and Garvey. *A basic text in political anthropology, covering leading theories, scholars, and problems in the field.*

Making a Living 13

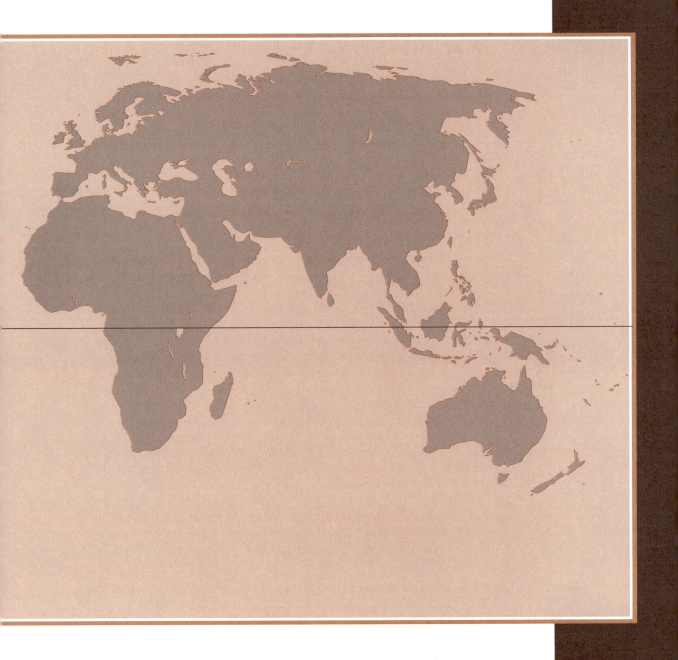

*t*he morning after ethnographer Richard Lee arrived in the Dobe Ju/'hoansi (!Kung) area, his neighbors, including a man named N!eishi, asked him to give them a ride in his Land Rover to get some food. (See EthnoProfile 9.1: Ju/'hoansi [!Kung].) They said there was little left in their area—mostly bitter roots and berries. They wanted to collect mongongo nuts—a staple of their diet and a great favorite—in a nearby grove (Figure 13.1). Lee agreed to take them. "The travel was anything but high-speed, and our destination was anything but near. We ground along for hours in four-wheel drive at a walking pace where no truck had ever been before, swerving to avoid antbear holes and circumventing fallen trees" (1992b, 39).

By the time they stopped, Lee figured they were about 10 miles north of Dobe. Lee was amazed by how fast the Ju/'hoansi, both men and women, were able to gather the nuts. After two hours, they left the grove. He later weighed the food collected in that short time: the women had gathered loads weighing 30 to 50 pounds each; the men, 15 to 25 pounds each. Lee continued:

> That worked out to about 23,000 calories for food for each woman collector, and 12,000 for each man. Each woman had gathered enough to feed a person for ten days and each man enough for five days. Not at all a bad haul for two hours' work!
>
> My first full day of fieldwork had already taught me to question one popular view of hunter-gatherer subsistence: that life among these people was precarious, a constant struggle for existence. My later studies were to show that the Ju/'hoansi in fact enjoyed a rather good diet and that they didn't have to work very hard to get it. As we will see, even without the aid of an anthropologist's truck the Ju/'hoansi had to work only 20 hours a week in subsistence. But what about the fact that N!eishi had come to me that morning saying that they were hungry and that there was no food nearby? Strictly speaking, N!eishi spoke the truth. October is one of the harder months of the year, at the end of the dry season, and the more desirable foods had been eaten out close to Dobe. What N!eishi did not say was that a little farther away food *was* available, and, if not plentiful, there was enough to see them through until the rains came. When N!eishi came to me with his proposition, he was making an intelligent use of his resources, social and otherwise. Why hike in the hot sun for a small meal, when the bearded White man might take you in his truck for ten large ones? (1992b, 40–41).

It is a stereotype of Western culture that human beings who survive off nature's bounty lead lives that, in Thomas Hobbes's famous phrase, are nasty, brutish, and short. This stereotype makes it seem perfectly natural that Lewis Henry Morgan chose to call

the foraging way of life *savagery*. Only recently have anthropologists lived closely enough with foraging peoples to discover the inaccuracy of the Hobbesian position. Lee's Ju/'hoansi informants were well nourished, with balanced diets. What is more, they were choosy about what they ate, unwilling to settle for food they disliked when Lee was there to take them to food they preferred. Such behavior is entirely familiar to us and far from "savage." The Dobe Ju/'hoansi no longer forage as they did in the 1960s. Until recently, however, the Ju/'hoansi were able to live rather well by means of culture in what some see as a marginal environment.

CULTURE AND LIVELIHOOD

People need one another, as well as resources from the wider world, in order to survive, yet there is no obvious blueprint for social organization that all societies are obliged to follow. Particular societies in particular environments must invent ways to make use of the natural and human resources available to them. Their cultures are inventories of inventions that have been tested by time and have been shown adequate to the task. The paradox of the human condition is that although our physical survival depends on our making adequate use of the physical resources around us, our culture tells us which resources to use and how to use them. How people make their living is culturally defined.

In ordinary conversation, when we speak of making a living we usually mean doing what is necessary to obtain the material things—food, clothing, shelter—that sustain human life. Making a living thus encompasses what is generally considered economic activity. However, anthropologists and other social scientists disagree about just what the term *economy* ought to represent. The rise of the capitalist market led to one view of what economy might mean: buying cheap and selling dear. That is, economy means economizing, or "maximizing utility"—obtaining as much satisfaction as possible for the smallest possible cost. This view of economy is based on the assumption of **scarcity.** Many economists and economic anthropologists believe that people's resources (for example, money) are not, and never will be, great enough for them to obtain all the goods they want. Whether this situation is caused by the stinginess of nature, by an innate human desire for self-betterment, or simply by human greed, scarcity is assumed to be a constant of human existence. Economizing, therefore, involves setting priorities and allocating resources rationally according to those priorities.

The assumption of scarcity has not gone unchallenged. Many argue that it is ethno-centric to assume that economic activity means "economizing" for everyone in every society. They claim that the principles central to economic activity in another society may be very different from our own. For them, the job of an economist is to describe the pattern of economic arrangements possessed by each culture. Given this perspective, in the words of Karl Polanyi, the **economy** is best understood as "an institutionalized process of interaction which functions to provide material means in society" (1977, 34).

SUBSISTENCE STRATEGIES

Human beings invent ways of using their relationships with one another and with the physical environment to make a living. *Subsistence* is the term often used to refer to the satisfaction of the most basic material survival needs of human beings, primarily those for food, clothing, and shelter. The different ways that people in different societies go about meeting these needs are called **subsistence strategies.**

Anthropologists have devised a typology of subsistence strategies that has gained wide acceptance (Figure 13.2). The basic division is between **food collectors** (those who gather, fish, or hunt for food) and **food producers** (those who depend on domesticated plants or animals or both for food). Food producers may farm exclusively or herd exclusively or do a little of both. Among those who farm, there are again distinctions. Some farmers depend primarily on human muscle power plus a few simple tools such as digging sticks or hoes or machetes. They clear plots of uncultivated land, burn the brush, and plant their crops in the ash-enriched soil that remains. Because this technique exhausts the soil after two or three seasons, the plot must then lie fallow for several years and a new plot is cleared and the process is repeated. This form of cultivation is called **extensive agriculture,** emphasizing the extensive use of land as farm plots are moved every few years. Other farmers use plows, draft animals, irrigation, fertilizer, and the like. Their method of farming—known as **intensive agriculture**—brings much more land under cultivation and produces significant crop surpluses. Finally, **mechanized industrial agriculture** is found in societies in which farming or animal husbandry has become

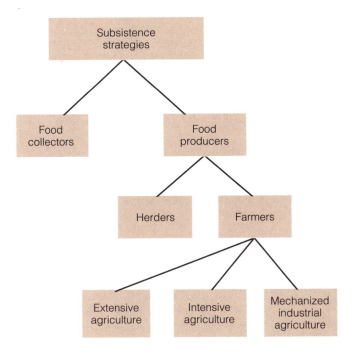

FIGURE 13.2 *Subsistence strategies.*

mechanized along industrial lines. Agribusiness "factories in the field" or animal feedlots transform food production into a large-scale, highly technology-dependent industry of its own.

Many anthropologists used to see a major break separating food collecting from food producing. There is mounting evidence, however, that food producers in some parts of the world continued food collection for many generations, sometimes raising a few crops on the side and occasionally abandoning food production entirely to return to full-time foraging. Archaeological evidence also suggests that, in the past, it was possible for a number of societies that depended exclusively on food collection to settle down and develop more complex forms of social organization. The peoples of the northwest

---

scarcity The assumption that resources (for example, money) will never be plentiful enough for people to obtain all the goods they desire.

economy An institutionalized process of interaction that functions to provide material means in society.

subsistence strategies The patterns of production, distribution, and consumption that members of a society employ to ensure the satisfaction of the basic material survival needs of human beings.

food collectors Those who gather, fish, or hunt for food.

food producers Those who depend on domesticated plants and/or animals for food.

extensive agriculture A form of cultivation that requires moving farm plots every few years as the soil becomes exhausted. It is based on the technique of clearing uncultivated land, burning the brush, and planting the crops in the ash-enriched soil.

intensive agriculture A form of cultivation that employs plows, draft animals, irrigation, fertilizer, and such to bring much land under cultivation, to use it year after year, and to produce significant crop surpluses.

mechanized industrial agriculture Large-scale farming and animal husbandry that is highly dependent on industrial methods of technology and production.

coast of North America are thus only one example of a way of life that at one time was found elsewhere in the world. Nevertheless, once human beings took direct control over production of their food sources and stopped depending primarily on nature's bounty, many new ways of making a living became possible.

PRODUCTION, DISTRIBUTION, AND CONSUMPTION

Anthropologists generally agree that economic activity is usefully subdivided into three distinct phases: production, distribution, and consumption. **Production** involves transforming nature's raw materials into products that are useful to human beings. **Distribution** involves getting those products to the people who need to use them. **Consumption** involves using up the products—for example, by eating food or wearing clothing.

When analyzing economic activity in a particular society, however, anthropologists differ in the importance they attach to each phase. For example, the distributive process known as **exchange** is central to the functioning of capitalist free enterprise. Some anthropologists have assumed that exchange is equally central to the functioning of all economies and have tried to explain the economic life of non-Western societies in terms of exchange. Anthropologists of a marxian bent, however, have argued that exchange cannot be understood properly without first studying the nature of production. They point out that production shapes the context in which exchange can occur, determining which parties have how much of what kind of goods to exchange. Finally, others have suggested that neither production nor exchange patterns make any sense without first specifying the consumption priorities of the people who are producing and exchanging. Consumption priorities, they argue, are of course designed to satisfy material needs. But the recognition of needs and of appropriate ways to satisfy them is shaped by arbitrary cultural patterns. We will examine in turn the arguments of anthropologists who have viewed either exchange, production, or consumption as most central to an explanation of economic life. We will point out the insights that each approach provides as well as the questions it leaves unasked.

Distribution and Exchange Theory

Neoclassical Economic Theory and the Rise of Capitalism   The discipline of economics was born in the early years of the rise of capitalist industry in western Europe. At that time, such thinkers as Adam Smith and his disciples struggled to devise theories to explain the profound changes in economic and social life that European society had recently begun to experience. Their work has become the foundation for neoclassical economic theory in the Western world. **Neoclassical economic theory** is a formal attempt to explain the workings of capitalist enterprise.

Capitalism differed in many ways from the feudal economic system that had preceded it, but perhaps the most striking difference was how it handled distribution. Feudal economic relations allotted goods and services to different social groups and individuals on the basis of status. Because lords had high status and many obligations, they had a right to more goods and services, whereas peasants, with low status and few rights, were allowed far less. This distribution of goods was time-honored and not open to modification. The customs derived from capitalist economic relations, by contrast, were considered "free" precisely because they swept away all such traditional restrictions. As we saw in our discussion of "Sedaka" Village, Malaysia, capitalism also swept away traditional protections. (See EthnoProfile 12.4: "Sedaka" Village.) In any case, distribution under capitalism was negotiated between buyers and sellers in the market.

In Adam Smith's ideal market, everyone has something to sell (if only his or her willingness to work), and everyone is also a potential buyer of the goods brought to the market by others. Individual buyers and sellers meet in the market to buy from and sell to each other—to engage in economic exchange. Ideally, because there are many buyers, many sellers, and no traditional restrictions governing who should get how much of what, prices can fluctuate depending on levels of supply and demand. Distribution is carried out in line with the preferences of individuals. High demand by individuals for certain items raises the price for those items, as many buyers bargain for few goods. This high demand, in turn, entices more people to produce the goods in high demand in order to take advantage of their higher prices. As competition between suppliers increases, however, prices go down, as each supplier attempts to obtain a greater share of the market. Ideally, prices stabilize as suppliers begin offering desired goods at a cost sufficiently high to allow a profit but sufficiently low for buyers to afford.

Market exchange of goods for other goods, for labor, or (increasingly) for cash was an important development in Western economic history. It is not surprising, therefore, that Western economic theory was preoccupied with explaining how the market worked. Markets clearly had a new, decisive importance in capitalist society, which they had not possessed in feudal times. Western neoclassical economics is based on the assumption that market forces are the central forces determining levels of both production and consumption in society.

Formalists   After World War II, formal neoclassical economic theory was adopted by a number of anthropologists interested in explaining economic activities in non-Western societies. These anthropologists, known as **formalists,** recognized that in most non-Western societies there was nothing resembling a "free market." The Ju/'hoansi, for example, traditionally produced food, clothing, and shelter by themselves and for themselves. They had no indigenous markets or money. Exchange took place in a ritual context and followed patterns of kinship and friendship. As in the economy of feudal Europe, distribution was hedged about by restrictions. Similar patterns were found in

production The transformation of nature's raw materials into a form suitable for human use.
distribution The allocation of goods and services.
consumption The using up of material goods necessary for human survival.

exchange The process of distribution in which goods or services are transferred in return for something else.
neoclassical economic theory A formal attempt to explain the workings of capitalist enterprise, with particular attention to distribution.

formalists Economic anthropologists who adopted formal neoclassical economic theory to explain economic activities in non-Western societies.

most of the societies anthropologists traditionally studied. Nevertheless, formalists took the Western capitalist market as their prototype of rational economic organization.

Once in the field, formalists searched for activities and institutions that might represent a metaphorical equivalent of the capitalist market—such as bridewealth exchanges. They analyzed those transactions using the language of formal economic theory. Marriage negotiations, for example, were viewed as market transactions. The bride's family wished to exchange its woman for, say, cattle belonging to the groom's family. Formalists assumed that the law of supply and demand would determine how much bridewealth— or bride*price*—the groom's family would have to pay. More desirable brides—young virgins, for example—could be expected to command a higher brideprice than older, divorced women. If cattle were scarce relative to marriageable women, fewer would be demanded than if young women were scarce and cattle plentiful. The marriage market might be most volatile in societies permitting men an unlimited number of wives. Wealthy older men with lots of cattle might marry all the young women, leaving poorer young men to compete for the remaining, less desirable women. To talk about non-Western economic activity in this way permitted anthropologists to describe non-Western societies in terms that Western economists could understand.

Formalists did not view their undertaking as ethnocentric. They considered formal economic theory to be scientific and therefore unaffected by culture-bound assumptions that might compromise its universal validity. In addition, formal economic theory assumes that individual actors in the capitalist market are *rational*. To suggest, therefore, that non-Western people do not make economic decisions in conformity with the principles of neoclassical theory would be equivalent to calling them *irrational*.

To be **rational** in Western terms is to be concerned first and foremost with one's own individual self-interest. Individual self-interest is defined in terms of the market: to buy cheap, to sell dear, to realize a profit. People in some societies may voluntarily subordinate their individual self-interest to the social obligations of kinship or fealty. But in neoclassical economic terms, any action that benefits others at cost to oneself is, strictly speaking, irrational.

Formalists wanted to accept the axioms of capitalism. At the same time, they wanted to assert that non-Western peoples are rational. As a result, they claimed that people in non-Western societies are basically closet capitalists. That is, their natural attraction to free enterprise has been stifled or short-circuited by traditional social institutions that drain off individual profit for the benefit of the group.

Substantivists Some anthropologists were not persuaded by the formalist approach. They argued that to take self-interested, materialistic decision making in the capitalist market as the prototype of human rationality was both reductionistic and ethnocentric. In the 1960s and 1970s, these anthropologists, known as **substantivists,** pointed out that the capitalist market is a relatively recent cultural invention in human history. Neoclassical economic theory is an equally recent invention, designed to make sense of the capitalist market and its effects.

Substantivists were offended, on theoretical and moral grounds, by what they saw as the formalist attempt to distort non-Western economic life in order to fit it into capitalist categories. They agreed, for example, that marriage transactions involving bridewealth bear a family resemblance to other kinds of exchange, including market exchange. But they asserted that it is bad science, as well as morally repugnant, to reduce one to the other. It may be true, as Igor Kopytoff has recently argued, that people have often been turned into objects for sale in many societies. The most common example is slavery. But Kopytoff also points out that "the slave was unambiguously a commodity only during the relatively short period between capture and first sale and the acquisition of a new social identity; and the slave becomes less of a commodity and more of a singular individual in the process of gradual incorporation into the host society" (1986, 65).

Substantivists suggested that capitalist market exchange is but one mode of exchange. Western capitalist societies distribute material goods in a manner that is consistent with their basic values, institutions, and assumptions about the human condition. So too non-Western, noncapitalist societies have devised alternative modes of exchange that distribute material goods in ways that are in accord with their basic values, institutions, and assumptions about the human condition. In substantivist language, patterns of economic exchange are *embedded* in the societies in which they are found. One cannot understand or explain patterns of exchange apart from this cultural context. Therefore, substantivists argued, although neoclassical theory may be able to account for the functioning of the economy in capitalist societies, it is not suited for analysis of noncapitalist economies.

KARL POLANYI AND MODES OF EXCHANGE   Perhaps the most influential substantivist figure in anthropology was the economic historian Karl Polanyi. Polanyi suggested that three **modes of exchange** could be identified historically and cross-culturally: reciprocity, redistribution, and market exchange.

The most ancient mode of exchange was **reciprocity.** Reciprocity is characteristic of egalitarian societies, like those of foraging peoples such as the Ju/'hoansi. Anthropologists recognize three kinds of reciprocity. *Generalized reciprocity* is found when those who exchange do so without expecting an immediate return and without specifying the value of the return. Everyone assumes that the exchanges will eventually balance out. Reciprocity usually characterizes the exchanges that occur between parents and their children. Parents do not keep a running tab on what it costs them to raise their children and then present their children with repayment schedules when they reach the age of 18.

Balanced reciprocity is found when those who exchange expect a return of equal value within a specified time limit (for example, when a brother and sister exchange gifts of equal value with one another at Christmastime). Lee notes that the Ju/'hoansi distin-

---

rational To think and act in accord with the central principles of one's culture; in Western economic terms, to be concerned first and foremost with one's individual self-interest as defined in terms of the market: to buy cheap, to sell dear, to realize a profit.

substantivists Economic anthropologists who criticized the formalists for being ethnocentric, arguing that economic institutions cannot be explained apart from the particular, substantive cultural contexts in which they are embedded.

modes of exchange Patterns according to which distribution takes place: reciprocity, redistribution, and market exchange.

reciprocity The exchange of goods and services of equal value. Anthropologists distinguish three forms of reciprocity: generalized, in which neither the time nor the value of the return are specified; balanced, in which a return of equal value is expected within a specified time limit; and negative, in which parties to the exchange expect to get the better of the exchange.

FIGURE 13.3 *A classic anthropological case study of redistribution involves the* potlatch *of the Kwakiutl of the northwest coast of North America.*

EthnoProfile 13.1 • **NOOTKA**

REGION: North America

NATION: Canada (Vancouver Island)

POPULATION: 6,000 (1970s)

ENVIRONMENT: Rainy, relatively warm coastal strip

LIVELIHOOD: Fishing, hunting, gathering

POLITICAL ORGANIZATION: Traditionally, ranked individuals, chiefs; today, part of a modern nation-state

FOR MORE INFORMATION: Rosman, Abraham, and Paula G. Rubel. 1971. *Feasting with mine enemy: Rank and exchange among northwest coast societies.* New York: Columbia University Press.

guish between barter, which requires an immediate return of an equivalent, and *hxaro*, which is a kind of generalized reciprocity that encourages social obligations to be extended into the future (1992b, 103).

Finally, *negative reciprocity* is an exchange of goods and services in which at least one party attempts to get something for nothing without suffering any penalties. These attempts can range from haggling over prices to outright seizure.

Polanyi's second mode of exchange, **redistribution,** requires some form of centralized social organization. Those who occupy the central position receive economic contributions from all members of the group. It is then their responsibility to redistribute the goods they receive in a way that provides for every member of the group. The Internal Revenue Service is probably the institution of redistribution that Americans know best. A classic anthropological case study of redistribution involves the *potlatch* of the Native Americans of the northwest coast of North America (Figure 13.3). In the highly stratified fishing and gathering society of the Nootka, for example, nobles "fought with property." (See EthnoProfile 13.1: Nootka.) That is, each sought to outdo the others in generosity by giving away vast quantities of objects during the potlatch ceremony. The noble giving the potlatch accumulated goods produced in one village and redistributed them to other nobles attending the ceremony. When the guests returned to their own villages, they, in turn, redistributed the goods among their followers.

Market exchange, invented in capitalist society, is the most recent mode of exchange, according to Polanyi (Figure 13.4). Capitalism involves an exchange of goods (*trade*) calculated in terms of a multipurpose medium of exchange and standard of value (*money*) and carried on by means of a "supply-demand-price mechanism" (the *market*). Polanyi was well aware that trade, money, and market institutions had developed independently of one another historically. He also knew that they could be found in societies outside the West. The uniqueness of capitalism was how all three institutions were linked to one another in the societies of early modern Europe.

According to Polanyi, different modes of exchange often coexist within a single society, although one mode is generally dominant. The United States, for example, is dominated by the market mode of exchange, yet redistribution and reciprocity can still be found. Within the family, parents who obtain income from the market redistribute that income, or goods obtained with that income, to their children. Generalized reciprocity also characterizes much exchange within the family: parents provide their children with food and clothing without expecting any immediate return.

In the time that has passed since the formalists and substantivists argued with one another, many economic anthropologists have arrived at a compromise position. Stuart Plattner notes that today, economic anthropologists agree that economies are embedded in other cultural institutions and that it is wrong to assume that the economic choices of

---

redistribution A mode of exchange that requires some form of centralized social organization to receive economic contributions from all members of the group and to redistribute them in such a way that every group member is provided for.

market exchange The exchange of goods (trade) calculated in terms of a multipurpose medium of exchange and standard of value (money) and carried on by means of a supply-demand-price mechanism (the market).

FIGURE 13.4 *Bananas for sale in the handicrafts market in Otavalo, Ecuador, spring 1994. Markets can be found in many societies, but capitalism links markets to trade and money in a unique way.*

non-Western peoples are governed by the maximizing "rationality" of capitalism. Nevertheless, many continue to insist that scarcity is an obvious fact of life and that as long as economic anthropologists do not assume that "economizing" behavior exists everywhere, they are perfectly entitled to *look* for it (1989, 14–15).

Other economic anthropologists, however, have decided that the problem lies in the preoccupation with exchange itself. Distribution is an important matter in the economic life of any society, but perhaps exchange is not the prime causal force that both formalists and substantivists took it to be. Certainly, earlier critics of neoclassical economics, such as Karl Marx, argued that exchange could not properly be understood without a prior knowledge of production. People who meet to exchange have different kinds and amounts of resources to use in bargaining with one another. Those differences in resources, Marx argued, are not shaped by the market but rooted in the productive process itself.

Production Theory

For formalist economic anthropologists, the level of production of certain goods depends ultimately on the level of demand for those goods generated by the market. For other economic anthropologists, however, production is seen as the driving force behind economic activity. Production creates supplies of goods to which demand must accommodate, and it determines levels of consumption as well. Anthropologists who stress the centrality of production borrow their perspective on economic activity, as well as many key concepts, from the works of Karl Marx. They argue that this perspective is far more insightful than the one taken by neoclassical theorists of market exchange.

Labor   Labor is perhaps the most central marxian concept these anthropologists have adopted. **Labor** is the activity linking human social groups to the material world around them; human labor is therefore always social labor. Human beings must actively struggle together to transform natural substances into forms they can use. This is clearest in the case of food production. However, material production involves more than food production alone; it includes the production of clothing and shelter and tools. Marx emphasized the importance of human physical labor in the material world, but he recognized the importance of mental or cognitive labor. Human intelligence allows us to reflect on and organize productive activities. Mentally and physically, human social groups struggle together to ensure their material survival. In so struggling, they reproduce patterns of social organization, of production, and of thought.

Modes of Production   Marx saw the productive process as central to human social life, and he attempted to classify the ways different human groups carry out that process. Each way is called a **mode of production.** Anthropologist Eric Wolf has found Marx's work helpful. Wolf defines a mode of production as "a specific, historically occurring set of social relations through which labor is deployed to wrest energy from nature by means of tools, skills, organization, and knowledge" (1982, 75). Tools, skills, organization and knowledge constitute what Marx called the **means of production.** The social relations linking human beings who use a given means of production within a particular mode of production are called the **relations of production.** That is, different productive tasks (clearing the bush, planting, harvesting, and so on) are assigned to different social groups, all of which must work together for production to be successful. Those who use the mode-of-production concept in their work usually apply the term *production* to food collecting as well as to herding, farming, and industrial manufacturing.

The concept of mode of production is holistic, highlighting recurring patterns of human activity in which certain forms of social organization, production practices, and cultural knowledge codetermine one another. Wolf notes that Marx speaks of at least eight different modes of production in his own writings, although he focused mainly on one mode: the capitalist mode.

Wolf finds the concept of mode of production useful. But like most anthropologists inspired by Marx's work, he does not feel bound to accept Marx's conclusions as a matter of course. Wolf suggests that three modes of production have been particularly impor-

---

labor The activity linking human social groups to the material world around them; from the point of view of Karl Marx, labor is therefore always social labor.

mode of production A specific, historically occurring set of social relations through which labor is deployed to wrest energy from nature by means of tools, skills, organization, and knowledge.

means of production The tools, skills, organization, and knowledge used to extract energy from nature.

relations of production The social relations linking the people who use a given means of production within a particular mode of production.

In Their Own Words   **"SO MUCH WORK, SO MUCH TRAGEDY . . . AND FOR WHAT?"**

Angelita P. C. (the author's surnames were initialed to preserve her anonymity) describes traditional labor for farmers' wives in Costa Rica during the 1930s. Her account was included in a volume of peasant autobiographies published in Costa Rica in 1979.

The life of farmers' wives was more difficult than the life of day laborers' wives; what I mean is that we work more. The wife of the day laborer, she gets clean beans with no rubbish, shelled corn, pounded rice, maybe she would have to roast the coffee and grind it. On the other hand, we farm wives had to take the corn out of the husk, shuck it; and if it was rice, generally we'd have to get it out of the sack and spread it out in the sun for someone to pound it in the mortar. Although we had the advantage that we never lacked the staples: tortillas, rice, beans, and sugarwater. When you had to make

tortillas, and that was every day, there were mountains of tortillas, because the people who worked in the fields had to eat a lot to regain their strength with all the effort they put out. And the tortilla is the healthiest food that was eaten—still is eaten—in the countryside. Another thing we had to do often was when you'd get the corn together to sell it, you always had to take it off the cob and dry it in the sun: the men spread it out on a tarp, maybe two or three sackfuls, and they would go and bring the corn, still in the husks, up from the cornfield or the shack where it was kept. Well, we women had to guard it from the chickens or the pigs that were always in the house, but the rush we had when it started to rain and the men hadn't gotten back! We had to fill the sacks with corn and then a little later haul it in pots to finish filling them; that's if the rain gave us time. If not, all of us

women in the house would have to pick up the tarps—sometimes the neighbor-women would get involved in all the bustle—to carry the corn inside. We looked like ants carrying a big worm! The thing was to keep the corn from getting wet.

It didn't matter if you threw out your spine, or if your uterus dropped, or you started hemorrhaging, or aborted, but since none of that happened immediately, it was the last thing we thought of. So much work, so much tragedy and that was so common that it seemed like just a natural thing, and for what? To sell corn at about 20 *colones* or at most at 24 *colones* per fanega [about 3 bushels] of 24 baskets! What thankless times for farm people!

Source: *Autobiografías campesinas* 1979, 36 (translation from the original Spanish by Robert H. Lavenda).

tant in human history: (1) a *kin-ordered mode,* in which social labor is deployed on the basis of kinship relations (for example, husbands/fathers clear the fields, the whole family plants, mothers/wives weed, children keep animals out of the field); (2) a *tributary mode,* "in which the primary producer, whether cultivator or herdsman, is allowed access to the means of production while tribute is exacted from him by political or military means" (1982, 79); and (3) the *capitalist mode.* The capitalist mode has three main features: the means of production are property owned by the capitalists; workers are denied access to such ownership and must sell their labor power to the capitalists in order to survive; and workers' labor for capitalists produces surpluses of wealth (also owned by capitalists) that may be plowed back into production to increase output and generate further surpluses.

An overlap exists between this classification of modes of production and the traditional anthropological classification of subsistence strategies. The kin-ordered mode of production is found among foragers and some farmers and herders whose political organization does not involve domination by one group in the society over everyone else. The tributary mode is found among some groups of farmers or herders living in a social system that is divided into classes of rulers and subjects. Subjects produce both for themselves and for their rulers, who take a certain proportion of their subjects' product as tribute. The capitalist mode of production is the most recent to develop. Its prototype can be found in the industrial societies of North America and western Europe beginning in the seventeenth and eighteenth centuries.

Thus, in some ways the mode-of-production concept simply recognizes the same variation in the "arts of subsistence" that Lewis Henry Morgan recognized in the nineteenth century. Yet the concept of mode of production also highlights certain attributes of subsistence strategies that the traditional anthropological approach tended to downplay. For example, modes of production have as much to do with forms of social and political organization as with material productive activities. That is, the kin-ordered mode of production is distinctive as much for its use of the kinship system to allocate labor to production as for the kind of production undertaken (such as herding). In a kin-ordered mode of production, the *relations of kinship* serve as the *relations of production* that enable a particular *mode of production* to be carried out.

Mode of production and relations of production can be understood as two sides of the same coin. As aspects of human social life that influence one another and have implications for one another, they must be studied together. Anthropologists traditionally have emphasized the important links between a society's social organization (kinship groups, chiefdom, state) and the way that society meets its subsistence needs. This was originally done to demonstrate the stages of cultural *evolution*. Later, the aim was to demonstrate *functional* interrelationships between parts of an individual society regardless of its evolutionary "stage." Both approaches yielded useful information. In both cases, however, the emphasis of the analysis was on the orderly fashion in which societies either changed or stayed the same. Social harmony was understood as the natural state of affairs. Given this assumption, social stability meant that current social arrangements were appropriate and need not change. Social change was possible, but it would take place in an equally orderly fashion, in the fullness of time, according to laws of development beyond the control of individual members of society. Such approaches were therefore bound to be of limited utility for anyone who wanted to show that conflict lay behind social change and that social stability was due to repression of that conflict. This was Marx's goal. It is shared by economic anthropologists who take a marxian perspective.

The Role of Conflict in Material Life Many anthropologists have not been persuaded that social change is orderly or that social organization is by nature harmonious. They find marxian concepts useful in their work precisely because the marxian approach treats conflict as a natural part of the human condition. The concept of mode of production makes a major contribution to economic anthropology precisely because of the very different interpretation it gives to conflict, imbalance, and disharmony in social life.

Marx pointed out, for example, that the capitalist mode of production incorporates the workers and the owners in different and contradictory ways. These groups, which he called *classes*, have different interests, and what is good for one class may not be good for all classes. Capitalists own the means of production (tools, knowledge, and so on) as

In Their Own Words   **SOLIDARITY FOREVER**

Anthropologist Dorinne Kondo, who worked alongside Japanese women in a Tokyo sweets factory, describes how factory managers, almost despite their best efforts, managed to engender strong bonds among women workers.

Our shared exploitation sometimes provided the basis for commonality and sympathy. The paltry pay was often a subject of discussion. . . . My co-workers and I were especially aware, however, of the toll our jobs took on our bodies. We constantly complained of our sore feet, especially sore heels from standing on the concrete floors. And a company-sponsored trip to the seashore revealed even more occupational hazards. At one point, as we all sat down with our rice balls and our box lunches, the part-timers pulled up the legs of their trousers to compare their varicose veins. In our informal contest, Hamada-san and Iida-san tied for first prize. The demanding pace and the lack of assured work breaks formed another subject of discussion. At most of the factories in the neighborhood where I con-

ducted extensive interviews, work stopped at ten in the morning and at three in the afternoon, so workers could have a cup of tea and perhaps some crackers. Nothing of the sort occurred at the Satō factory, although the artisans were, if the pace of work slackened, able to escape the workroom, sit on their haunches, and have a smoke, or grab a snack if they were out doing deliveries or running up and down the stairs to the other divisions. Informal restrictions on the part-timers' movement and time seemed much greater. Rarely, if ever, was there an appropriate slack period where all of us could take a break. Yet our energy, predictably, slumped in the afternoon. After my first few months in *wagashi*, Hamada-san began to bring in small containers of fruit juice, so we could take turns having a five-minute break to drink the juice and eat some seconds from the factory. Informal, mutual support enabled us to keep up our energies, as we each began to bring in juice or snacks for our tea breaks.

The company itself did nothing formally in this regard, but in-

formal gestures of thoughtfulness and friendliness among co-workers surely redounded to the company's benefit, for they fostered our sense of intimacy and obligation to our fellow workers. The tea breaks are one example, but so are the many times we part-timers would stop off at Iris, our favorite coffee house, to sip banana juice or melon juice and trade gossip. We talked about other people in the company, about family, about things to do in the neighborhood. On one memorable occasion, I was sitting with the Western division part-timers in a booth near the window. A car honked as it went by, and Sakada-san grimaced and shouted loudly, *"Shitsurei yarō—rude bastard!"* The offender turned out to be her husband. In subsequent weeks, Sakada-san would delight in recounting this tale again and again, pronouncing *shitsurei yarō* with ever greater relish, and somehow, we never failed to dissolve in helpless laughter.

Source: Kondo 1990, 291–92.

private property. For this reason, nonowners cannot help themselves to whatever they need to produce—say, their own food and clothing. Instead, they are forced to sell their labor power to the owner of the means of production. Their labor and the owner's resources together produce the material goods necessary for survival. Those goods belong to the capitalist, who pays the workers wages for their labor. The workers must then use their wages to purchase the goods they need in the market. In such a situation, the workers' desires (for higher wages with which to purchase more goods) are inevitably opposed to the owners' desires (for lower wages to increase the profit they can keep for themselves or reinvest in tools and raw materials).

This does not mean that warfare is constant between the different classes engaged in a particular mode of production; however, it does mean that the potential for conflict is built into the mode of production itself. The more complex and unequal the involvement of different classes in a mode of production, the more intense the struggle between them is likely to be. Such struggle may not always lead to outright rebellion for sound political reasons, as was the case in "Sedaka" Village, Malaysia. (See EthnoProfile 12.4: "Sedaka" Village.) But we should not be surprised to find the "everyday forms of peasant resistance" that Scott discusses in his analysis of life in Sedaka. When viewed from a marxian perspective, such struggles are clearly not just "healthy competition." Marx was one of the first social analysts, and certainly one of the most eloquent, to document the high level of human suffering generated by certain modes of production, particularly the capitalist mode.

If you look again at Eric Wolf's three modes of production (kin-ordered, tributary, and capitalist), you will see that each mode describes not only what a society's subsistence strategy is but also how people in that society organize themselves to carry out that subsistence strategy. It also accents the lines of cleavage along which tension and conflict may develop—or may have developed historically—between different segments of the society.

Applying Production Theory to Social and Cultural Life Economic anthropologists who focus on production as the prime causal force in material life tend to apply the metaphor of production to other areas of social life as well. They see production as involving far more than short-term satisfaction of material survival needs. If a given *mode* of production is to persist over time, the *means* and *relations* of production must also be made to persist.

For example, farmers produce grain and leave behind harvested fields. They exchange some grain with cattle herders for milk and meat, and they permit the herders' cattle to graze in the harvested fields in exchange for manure they need to fertilize their fields. Consequently, farmers and herders alike end up with a mix of foodstuffs to sustain human life (that is, to reproduce the producers). In addition, each group has what it needs in the coming season to renew its means of production. Both groups will want to ensure that similar exchanges can be carried out by their children; that is, they must find a way to ensure that the next generation will consist of farmers and cattle herders producing the same goods and willing to exchange those goods with one another in the same fashion. Therefore, not only the means of production itself must be perpetuated, but the relations of production as well. The result, then, is the reproduction of society from generation to generation as means of production and relations of production are reproduced.

People also produce and reproduce *interpretations* of the productive process and their roles in that process. Marx used the term **ideology** to refer to the cultural products

---

ideology Those products of consciousness—such as morality, religion, and metaphysics—that purport to explain to people who they are and to justify to them the kind of lives they lead.

of conscious reflection, such as morality, religion, or metaphysics. As used in marxian analysis, ideology refers in particular to those beliefs that explain and justify the relations of production to those who engage in them. For Marx, ideology was not independent of the productive process itself. On the contrary, "men, developing their material production and their material intercourse, alter, along with this their real existence, their thinking and the products of their thinking. Life is not determined by consciousness, but consciousness by life" (Marx [1932] 1973, 164). As a result, marxian economic anthropologists investigate the kinds of ideas, beliefs, and values that are produced and reproduced in societies with different modes of production. As we saw in Sedaka, the class in power usually holds to an ideology that justifies their domination. Those who are dominated may assent publicly to the ideology of the rulers, but in private they are likely to be highly critical and to offer alternative interpretations.

Use of the production metaphor in the analysis of social and cultural life has yielded some important results in anthropology. First, it highlights certain processes and relationships that the exchange metaphor tends to downplay or ignore. For example, exchange theorists are less likely to care why the different parties to an exchange have different quantities of resources with which to bargain. Production theorists, by contrast, are interested precisely in this issue. They aim to show that access to resources is determined before exchange by the relations of production, which decide who is entitled to how much of what. In particular, they reject as naive the assumption that access to valued resources is open to anyone with gumption and the spirit of enterprise. Different modes of production stack the deck in favor of some classes of people and against other classes. This is most clear in the capitalist mode, where owners have disproportionate access to wealth, power, and prestige and where the access of workers to these goods is sharply restricted. Thus, the classes who fare poorly do so not because of any inherent inferiority, laziness, or improvidence. They fail to get ahead because the rules of the game (that is, of the mode of production) were set up in a way that keeps them from winning.

In the second place, a production metaphor provides an especially dynamic perspective on cultural persistence and cultural change. Production theory relates peoples' preferences for different goods to the interests and opportunities of the different classes to which they belong. People buy and sell as they do not out of idiosyncratic whimsy but because the choices open to them are shaped by the relations of production. From this perspective, poor people do not purchase cheap goods because they have poor taste and cannot recognize quality when they see it; rather, their deprived position within the mode of production provides them with very limited income, and they must make do with the only goods they can afford, however shoddy.

Finally, production theory focuses on people as much as or more than it focuses on the goods people produce. It views human beings as social agents involved in the construction and reconstruction of human society on all levels in every generation. Traditions persist, but only because people labor to reproduce them from one day to the next. To speak of the production (and reproduction) of goods, social relations, and ideologies highlights the contingent nature of social life, even as it suggests how traditions are carried on.

Consumption Theory

Consumption is usually understood to refer to the using up of material goods necessary for human physical survival. These goods include—at a minimum—food, drink, clothing, and shelter; they can and often do include much more. Anthropologists have taken one of three approaches to the study of consumption: the internal explanation, the external explanation, and the cultural explanation.

The Internal Explanation: Malinowski and Basic Human Needs

The internal explanation for human consumption patterns comes from the work of Bronislaw Malinowski. Malinowski's version of functionalist anthropology explains social practices by relating them to the basic human needs that each practice supposedly functions to fulfill. Basic human needs can be biological or psychological, and if they go unmet, the society might not survive. In Malinowski's view, all societies have economic institutions concerned with production, distribution, and consumption of material goods. This is because people everywhere share the basic human needs for food, clothing, shelter, tools, and so on. Malinowski proposed a list of basic human needs, which includes nourishment, reproduction, bodily comforts, safety, movement, growth, and health. Every culture responds in its own way to these needs with some form of the corresponding institutions: food-getting techniques, kinship, shelter, protection, activities, training, and hygiene (Malinowski 1944, 91).

Malinowski's approach had the virtue of emphasizing the dependency of human beings on the physical world in order to survive. In addition, Malinowski was able to show that many customs that appear bizarre to uninitiated Western observers are in fact "rational." He did this by explaining how these customs help people satisfy their basic human needs. However, Malinowski's approach fell short of explaining why all societies do not share the same consumption patterns. After all, some people eat wild fruit and nuts and wear clothing made of animal skins, others eat bread made from domesticated wheat and wear garments woven from the hair of domesticated sheep, and still others eat millet paste and meat from domesticated cattle and go naked. Why should these differences exist?

The External Explanation: Cultural Ecology and Ecological Determinism

A later generation of anthropologists were influenced by evolutionary and ecological studies. They provided an external explanation for the diversity of human consumption patterns.

Ecology has to do with how living species relate to one another and to the physical environment. To survive in the long run, a species must find for itself a **niche:** some portion of the natural world on which it can depend for satisfaction of its material needs.

---

ecology The study of the ways in which living species relate to one another and to their natural environment.

niche The portion of the natural world on which a species depends for the satisfaction of its material needs.

Each species must share the material world with many other species. Moreover, the mix of plant and animal species occupying any particular region of the earth, or **ecozone,** varies from one part of the world to the other. A species adapts to the ecozone in which it finds itself when it is able to find a niche that allows it to sustain life. But potential *econiches* must be constructed to make use of the particular mix of living and nonliving resources available in the ecozone. Such resources include edible plants and animals, water, climate, and so forth. *Socioecologists* investigate the features of ecozones to explain why a particular animal population—a troop of baboons, for example—organizes itself the way it does in a particular environment.

CULTURAL ECOLOGY   *Cultural ecology* is an anthropological attempt to apply the principles of socioecology to human beings and their societies. For cultural ecologists, human consumption patterns (as well as human patterns of production and distribution) derive from features of the ecozones in which human populations live. Every human group must learn to make use of the resources available in its ecozone if it is to survive. Hence, the particular consumption patterns found in a particular society do not depend just on the obvious, internal hunger drive, which is the same for all people everywhere; rather, consumption patterns depend on the particular external resources present in the ecozone to which a society must adapt.

One anthropologist who has relied on ecological arguments to explain human consumption patterns is Marvin Harris. Among other things, Harris has been interested in explaining dietary prohibitions found in various cultures. In a well-known article published in 1965, Harris argues that the "sacred cow" of Hindu society was forbidden as food primarily because it made better ecological sense as a draft animal. In his view, the religious prohibition merely emphasized an ecologically sound consumption practice.

Harris also has attempted to explain the dietary prohibition of pork by Jews and Muslims with reference to the ecological requirements for successful animal husbandry in southwestern Asia (1974, 40ff.). In his view, southwestern Asia is too hot and dry to support pigs, which are "creatures of the forests and shaded riverbanks." Pigs thrive on grains and so compete with human beings for food; they are a poor milk source; and they are difficult to herd over long distances. Harris concedes that the taboo on pork is observed in some Muslim areas that are well watered and where pig raising might be successful. But he suggests the taboo is used either for marking off Muslims from non-Muslims (and Jews from non-Jews) or for moral instruction among the faithful, teaching them how to avoid the temptation to indulge in a succulent treat.

These last concessions weaken Harris's ecological thesis. If it were ecologically unsound to raise pigs in southwestern Asia, surely no taboo would be necessary to keep people from raising them. And if the taboo is important in some parts of the Muslim world as a way of marking social distinctions, why might this not be the case in all parts? Harris's critics agree that pigs might suffer in a hot dry climate. They point out, however, that pigs can thrive in such a climate if they are provided with a bit of shade and some mud in which to wallow. In addition, archaeological evidence suggests that pigs were important economically and symbolically in some parts of ancient Egypt before the rise of Islam. They were raised successfully in precisely the ecozones in which they are now prohibited. Finally, although pigs thrive on grain, they are better known in most parts of the world as "living garbage cans." They will consume even human and animal excrement and turn it into meat. Their own feces fertilize their owners' fields, and their grubbing for roots in those same fields breaks up the soil. For all these reasons, pigs are highly valued. Moreover, some Mayan groups in Mexico herd pigs over 70 miles regularly and successfully with the help of dogs, a practice that was also known in ancient times in the Old World. Other Mayan groups find it difficult to raise pigs themselves, but they have not tabooed pork and will eat it when they can (Diener and Robkin 1978, 498). Clearly, dietary preferences and prohibitions cannot easily be reduced to ecological imperatives.

The work of Harris, and others like him, is useful for demonstrating the rationale behind consumption patterns that seem to be irrational from a Western perspective. However, some cultural ecologists tend to assume that because some consumption patterns make good ecological sense, all cultural patterns are determined by the imperatives of ecology. Their approach to human consumption patterns is quite similar to that of the socioecologists who try to explain social organization in primate groups in terms of the interaction between primate dietary preferences and ecological constraints. In the case of primate groups, the connections between diet, ecology, and social organization are often impossible to measure. Cultural ecologists encounter many of the same problems when trying to relate human cultural practices to ecological imperatives.

This is not to say that a consideration of ecological issues is out of place in anthropology; quite the contrary. Anthropologists have always held that a group's culture must provide its members with the minimal resources for physical and social survival; to do this requires an understanding of what the local ecology can provide and how to make use of it. Without a minimal awareness of such matters, no society can survive. Moreover, choosing one way of life over another can have serious ecological consequences for future generations. The widespread felling of trees by western Africa's first farmers produced more than open fields to cultivate: it also increased the breeding grounds for malaria-carrying mosquitos, a development that has had serious impact on the health and adaptation of subsequent generations of western African farmers. Today, we know that the kind of resource consumption favored by capitalist industry has led to widespread destruction of rain forests that not only shelter much of the biodiversity on this planet but also provide the oxygen that sustains life. Nothing prevents adaptive strategies of human societies from being ecologically unsound. Therefore, although we can certainly learn from those societies whose practices make good ecological sense, we have no reason to expect that every human way of life will prove to be equally sensible.

Why do people X raise peanuts and sorghum? The internal, Malinowskian explanation would be "to meet their basic human need for food." The external, ecological expla-

ecozone The particular mix of plant and animal species occupying any particular region of the earth.

nation would be "because peanuts and sorghum are the only food crops available in their ecozone that, when cultivated, will meet their subsistence needs." Both these answers are suggestive, but they are also incomplete. To be sure, people must consume something to survive, and they will usually meet this need for food by exploiting plant and animal species locally available to them. However, we might ask whether the local food sources that people X choose to exploit are the *only* food sources locally available to them. Ethnographic data show that no society exploits every locally available food source to meet its consumption needs. Quite the contrary, consumption "needs" are selective; in other words, they are culturally shaped.

The Cultural Patterning of Consumption   A major shortcoming of both internal and external explanations for human consumption patterns is that they ignore or deny the possibility of choice. Malinowski and many cultural ecologists seem to assume that patterns of consumption are dictated by an iron environmental necessity that does not allow alternatives. From such a perspective, choice of diet is a luxury that non-Western, "primitive" societies cannot afford. Yet to rob non-Western peoples of choice is to dehumanize them.

Marshall Sahlins urges anthropologists to pay close attention to consumption because consumption choices reveal what it means to be a human being. Human beings are *human,* he tells us, "precisely when they experience the world as a concept (symbolically). It is not essentially a question of priority but of the unique quality of human experience as meaningful experience. Nor is it an issue of the reality of the world; it concerns *which worldly dimension becomes pertinent,* and in what way, to a given human group" (1976a, 142, emphasis added).

THE ORIGINAL AFFLUENT SOCIETY   Many in the Western world have long believed that foraging peoples lead the most miserable of existences, assuming that such people spend all their waking hours in a food quest that yields barely enough to keep them alive. To test this assumption in the field, Richard Lee went to live among the Dobe Ju/'hoansi (!Kung), a foraging people of southern Africa. (See EthnoProfile 9.1: Ju/'hoansi [!Kung].) As we saw at the beginning of this chapter, Lee accompanied his informants as they gathered and hunted, and he recorded the amounts and kinds of food they consumed.

The results of Lee's research were surprising. It turned out that the Ju/'hoansi provided themselves with a varied and well-balanced diet based on a *selection* from among the food sources available in their environment. At the time of Lee's fieldwork the Ju/'hoansi classified more than 100 species of plants as edible, but only 14 are primary or major (1992b, 45ff.). Some 70 percent of this diet consisted of vegetable foods; 30 percent was meat. Mongongo nuts, a protein-rich food source widely available throughout the desert environment inhabited by the Ju/'hoansi, alone made up more than one-quarter of the diet. Women provided about 55 percent of the diet, and men provided 45 percent, including the meat. The Ju/'hoansi spent an average of 2.4 working days—or about 20 hours—per person per week in food-collecting activities. Ju/'hoansi bands periodically suffered from shortages of their preferred foods and were forced to resort to less desired items. Most of the time, however, their diet was balanced and adequate, and consisted of foods of preference (56ff.).

Marshall Sahlins coined the expression "the original affluent society" to refer to the Ju/'hoansi and other foragers like them. In an article published in 1972, Sahlins challenged the traditional Western assumption that the life of foragers is characterized by scarcity and near-starvation. **Affluence,** he argued, is having more than enough of whatever is required to satisfy consumption needs.

There are two ways to create affluence. One is to *produce much,* which is the path taken by Western capitalist society; the underlying assumption of capitalism is constant scarcity—people will always want to consume more of everything than there is to go around. The second road to affluence is to *desire little.* This, Sahlins argues, is the option that foragers have taken. Their wants are few, but they are abundantly supplied by nature. Moreover, foragers do not suppress their natural greed; rather, their society simply does not institutionalize greed or reward the greedy. As a result, foragers cannot be considered "poor," even though their material standard of living is low by Western standards. Poverty is not an absolute condition, nor is it a relationship between means and ends; it is a relationship between people. Because the consumption goals, or ends, of foragers are modest, their environment is more than able to satisfy those goals.

The Cultural Construction of Needs The original affluent society of the Ju/'hoansi reinforces the insight that "needs" by themselves are vague. Hunger can be satisfied by beans and rice or steak and lobster. Thirst can be quenched by water or beer or soda pop. In effect, culture defines needs and provides for their satisfaction according to its own logic. And cultural logic is reducible neither to biology nor to psychology nor to ecological pressure.

By adopting this cultural approach to consumption, the distinctions between "needs" and "wants" or "necessities" and "luxuries" disappear. Mary Douglas and Baron Isherwood urge us to "put an end to the widespread and misleading distinction between goods that sustain life and health and others that service the mind and heart—spiritual goods. . . . The counterargument proposed here is that all goods carry meaning, but none by itself. . . . The meaning is in the relations between all the goods, just as music is in the relations marked out by the sounds and not in any one note" (1979, 72–73). For instance, a consumption item's meaning may have to do with its edibility, but this will always be a culturally appropriate edibility. Furthermore, the meaning of any individual item of food cannot be explained in isolation. That meaning only becomes clear when the item is compared with other consumption items that are also marked in terms of culturally appropriate edibility or inedibility.

---

affluence The condition of having more than enough of whatever is required to satisfy consumption needs.

	Class prototype	Clean examples	Unclean examples	Reason prohibited

TABLE 13.1

JEWISH DIETARY PROHIBITIONS

	Class prototype	Clean examples	Unclean examples	Reason prohibited
Earth	Four-legged animals that hop, jump, or walk (that is, cloven-hoofed, cud-chewing ungulates)	Cattle, camels, sheep, goats	Hare, hyrax	Held to be cud-chewing but not cloven-hoofed
			Pig	Cloven-hoofed but not cud-chewing
			Weasel, mouse, crocodile, shrew, chameleon, mole	Two legs, two hands, but go about on all fours
Water	Scaly fish that swim with fins	Carp, whitefish	Shrimp, clams	Possess neither fins nor scales but live in water
Air	Two-legged fowl that fly with wings	Chicken	Grasshoppers	Six legs, cannot walk or fly, and lack feathers

Source: Adapted from Douglas 1966, 41–57.

THE ABOMINATIONS OF LEVITICUS   Consider once again the prohibition against eating pork. For Jews and Muslims, pork is "inedible," culturally speaking. According to Mary Douglas (1966), this has nothing to do with ecological problems associated with pig raising in southwestern Asia, nor has it anything to do with any defects in the digestive systems of Jews or Muslims. Douglas has analyzed the Jewish dietary prohibitions detailed in the biblical Book of Leviticus. She argues that certain animals were prohibited as food because something about them violated the prototypes for edibility recognized in ancient Hebrew culture (Table 13.1). Prototypically "clean" land animals were supposed to have four legs and cloven hooves and to chew the cud; pigs were an "abomination" because they were four-legged, cloven-hoofed beasts who did not chew the cud. "Clean" beasts of the air were supposed to have feathers and to fly with wings; therefore, hopping insects were "unclean" because they had six legs, neither walked nor flew, and lacked feathers. "Clean" water animals were supposed to have fins and scales; shrimp were forbidden because, although they lived in the sea, they lacked fins and scales.

By itself, Douglas argues, a prohibition against eating pork is meaningless and appears to be irrational. However, when the Jewish prohibition against pork is taken together with other Jewish dietary prohibitions and when these are compared with the foods that were permitted, the cultural pattern becomes clear. Douglas and Isherwood write, "Goods assembled together in ownership make physical, visible statements about the hierarchy of values to which their chooser subscribes" (1979, 5). Thus, Jews who shop carefully and purchase only "clean" foods that meet the ritual requirements laid down by their tradition are doing more than procuring the means to satisfy their hunger;

they are also making a social declaration of solidarity with Orthodox Judaism, and the care with which they adhere to the dietary laws is a measure of their commitment. Their need for food is being met, but selectively, and the selection they make carries a social message.

Dietary laws deal with food and drink, and so might still be explained in biological or ecological terms. In fact, many attempts have been made to rationalize the dietary laws in the Bible in terms of hygiene, and we have seen what Marvin Harris has to say about pork prohibition. Such rationalizations are more difficult to construct, however, when we consider the role of banana leaves in the Trobriand Islands.

BANANA LEAVES IN THE TROBRIAND ISLANDS   Anthropologist Annette Weiner traveled to the Trobriand Islands more than half a century after Malinowski carried out his classic research there. (See EthnoProfile 3.3: Trobriand Islanders.) To her surprise, she discovered a venerable local tradition involving the accumulation and exchange of banana leaves (or women's wealth). Malinowski had never described this tradition, even though there is photographic and written evidence that it was in force at the time of his fieldwork. There are probably at least two reasons why Malinowski overlooked these transactions. First, they are carried out by women, and Malinowski did not view women as important actors in the economy. Second, banana leaves would be an unlikely item of consumption, given Malinowski's tendency to label as "economic" only activities that satisfied biological survival needs. After all, you can't eat banana leaves. However, explaining transactions involving women's wealth turns out to be crucial for understanding Trobriand kinship obligations.

Banana leaves might be said to have a "practical" use in that women make skirts out of them. These skirts are highly valued objects, but the transactions involving women's wealth more often involve the bundles of leaves themselves. Why bother to exchange great amounts of money or other goods to obtain bundles of banana leaves? This would seem to be a classic example of irrational consumption. And yet, as Weiner demonstrates, banana bundles play exactly the role Douglas and Isherwood have suggested that consumption goods play in society: "As an economic, political, and social force, women's wealth exists as the representation of the most fundamental relationships in the social system" (Weiner 1980, 289).

Trobrianders are matrilineal, and men traditionally prepare yam gardens for their sisters. After the harvest, yams from these gardens are distributed by a woman's brother to her husband and his male relatives. Weiner's research suggests that what Malinowski took to be the *redistribution* of yams, from a wife's kin to her husband, could be better understood as a *reciprocal exchange* of yams for women's wealth. The parties central to this exchange are a woman, her brother, and her husband. The woman is the person through whom yams are passed from her own kin to her husband and also the person through whom women's wealth is passed from her husband to her own kin.

Transactions involving women's wealth occur when someone in the woman's kinship group dies. Surviving relatives must "buy back," metaphorically speaking, all the yams and other goods that the deceased person gave out to others during his or her lifetime. Each payment marks a social link between the deceased and the recipient, and

In Their Own Words   FAKE MASKS AND FAUX MODERNITY

Christopher Steiner addresses the perplexing situation all of us face in the contemporary multicultural world: given mass reproduction of commodities made possible by capitalism, how can anybody distinguish "authentic" material culture from "fake" copies?

In the Plateau market place, I once witnessed the following exchange between an African art trader and a young European tourist. The tourist wanted to buy a Dan face mask which he had selected from the trader's wooden trunk in the back of the market place. He had little money, he said, and was trying to barter for the mask by exchanging his Seiko wrist watch. In his dialogue with the trader, he often expressed his concern about whether or not the mask was "real." Several times during the bargaining, for example,

the buyer asked the seller, "Is it really old?" and "Has it been worn?" While the tourist questioned the trader about the authenticity of the mask, the trader, in turn, questioned the tourist about the authenticity of his watch. "Is this the real kind of Seiko," he asked, "or is it a copy?" As the tourist examined the mask—turning it over and over again looking for the worn and weathered effects of time—the trader scrutinized the watch, passing it to other traders to get their opinion on its authenticity.

Although, on one level, the dialogue between tourist and trader may seem a bit absurd, it points to a deeper problem in modern transnational commerce: an anxiety over authenticity and a crisis of *mis*representation. While the shelves in one section of the Plateau market place are lined with replicas of so-called

"traditional" artistic forms, the shelves in another part of the market place—just on the other side of the street—are stocked with imperfect imitations of modernity: counterfeit Levi jeans, fake Christian Dior belts, and pirated recordings of Michael Jackson and Madonna. Just as the Western buyer looks to Africa for authentic symbols of a "primitive" lifestyle, the African buyer looks to the West for authentic symbols of a modern lifestyle. In both of their searches for the "genuine" in each other's culture, the African trader and the Western tourist often find only mere approximations of "the real thing"—tropes of authenticity which stand for the riches of an imagined reality.

Source: Steiner 1994, 128–29.

the size of the payment marks the importance of their relationship. All the payments must be made in women's wealth.

The dead person's status, as well as the status of her or his family, depends on the size and number of the payments made, and the people who must be paid can number into the hundreds. Women of the matrilineage collect women's wealth from their husbands, and their own value is measured by the amount of women's wealth their husbands provide. Furthermore, "if a man does not work hard enough for his wife in accumulating wealth for her, then her brother will not increase his labor in the yam garden. . . . The production in yams and women's wealth is always being evaluated and calculated in terms of effort and energy expended on both sides of production. The value of a husband is read by a woman's kin as the value of his productive support in securing women's wealth for his wife" (Weiner 1980, 282).

Weiner argues that women's wealth upholds the kinship arrangements of Trobriand society. It balances out exchange relationships between lineages linked by marriage, reinforces the pivotal role of women and matriliny, and publicly proclaims, during every funeral, the social relationships that make up the fabric of Trobriand society. The system has been stable for generations, but Weiner suggests that it could collapse if cash ever became widely substitutable for yams. Under such conditions, men might buy food and other items on the market, they would no longer be dependent on yams from their wives' kin, and they could therefore refuse to supply their wives' kin with women's wealth. This had not yet happened at the time of Weiner's research, but it could not be ruled out as a possible future development.

The Cultural Construction of Utility   The preceding examples have been approached from the perspective of consumption, but they have much in common with theories of *social exchange*. Social exchange theorists argue that people exchange material goods for esteem or for power: I give you food to eat and in return, at some later date, you will accord me honor or will support me politically. Social exchange theory argues that these trade-offs are motivated by the desire of individuals to maximize their "utility"—that is, their personal satisfaction or pleasure. But just as culture shapes needs, so it also offers standardized ways of satisfying those needs. No social exchange can occur unless the parties to that exchange are able to assess the value of the items to be exchanged. Because of the openness of culture and the ambiguity inherent in many social situations, values and exchange rates may well be bargained over. Such exchanges ultimately rest on cultural principles for assessing value and fairness.

Once consumption is defined as the use of goods and services to communicate cultural values, a new understanding of wealth and poverty is possible. We have noted Sahlins's comment that foragers with simple needs and ample means of satisfying those needs are affluent—rich, not poor. Douglas and Isherwood also refuse to use the sheer amount of material possessions as a universal measure of wealth or poverty. They write: "Many of the countries that anthropologists study are poor on such material criteria—no wall-to-wall carpets, no air conditioning—but they do not regard themselves as poor. The Nuer of the Sudan in the 1930s would not trade with the Arabs because the only things they had to sell were their herds of cattle, and the only things they could possibly want from trade were more cattle" (1979, 17–18). (See EthnoProfile 9.2: Nuer.) Cattle mattered to the Nuer as much for their use as markers of social relations as for their use as food. To have few or no cattle did constitute poverty for the Nuer—as much for the lack of social relationships it indicated as for the lack of food. "To be rich means to be well integrated in a rich community. . . . To be poor is to be isolated" (160).

INSTITUTIONALIZED SHARING   Capitalism not only generates individual fortunes, it depends on them as sources of funds sufficiently great to sustain large private business enterprises. Capitalist societies have passed laws and created social institutions that reward individuals for accumulating wealth. By contrast, noncapitalist societies exhibit economic patterns that prevent individual accumulation; the goal is to spread any wealth that exists throughout the community. This pattern is called *institutionalized sharing*.

People accustomed to capitalist practices are often either incredulous or cynical when it is suggested that institutionalized sharing can be the backbone of economic life. They assume that such widespread "generosity" can only be expected of saintly altruists, not of ordinary human beings. Nevertheless, people in societies with institutionalized

EthnoProfile 13.2 • CREE (SHORT GRASS RESERVE)

REGION: North America

NATION: Canada

POPULATION: About 100

ENVIRONMENT: 3,040 acres of rocky soil and dense aspen brush

LIVELIHOOD: Monthly inadequate relief payments; manufacture and sale of fenceposts; casual ranch work

POLITICAL ORGANIZATION: Traditionally, consensus of adult males announced by chief; today, part of a modern nation-state

FOR MORE INFORMATION: Braroe, Niels. 1975. *Indian and White.* Stanford: Stanford University Press.

sharing are not saints who never experience greed any more than people in capitalist societies are devils who never experience compassion. Both societies, however, make it difficult to get away publicly with practices that undercut established social arrangements.

A pattern of institutionalized sharing can be found among the Plains Cree of North America, studied by Niels Braroe (1975, 143ff.). (See EthnoProfile 13.2: Cree [Short Grass Reserve].) In the past, the Cree were bison hunters living in bands. Each band had a leader who provided his followers with the materials necessary for hunting. This leader was the focus of a redistributive mode of exchange, and generosity in redistribution qualified him to be the band leader. Today, bison are no longer hunted, but the institutionalized sharing of consumption items such as food, clothing, beer, or cigarettes continues. For example, Braroe tells us that "it is not considered improper, as it is among Whites, to ask for someone's last cigarette; to refuse a request, however, is frowned upon" (145). Generosity is further reinforced in ceremonies known as "giveaway dances." The central event in those ceremonies is dancing around the room and giving away such material goods as clothing to other guests. Dancers aim to give away more than they receive. It is an insult to shower someone with gifts in the course of such an event.

The Cree ideal is that generosity should be spontaneous and that contempt for material goods should be genuine. Nevertheless, Braroe's informants sometimes possessed consumption goods or money that they clearly wanted to keep for themselves. Individuals could enjoy such goods in private, but only if their existence were kept a secret. Men sometimes hid beer to avoid having to share it with others. A woman informant once asked Braroe's wife to keep a sizable amount of cash for her so others would not know she had it and demand some. The rule seemed to be that "any visible resource may legitimately be requested by another" (1975, 146), and Braroe reported that direct refusals of such requests were rare.

For the Cree, institutionalized sharing following a redistributive mode ensures that consumption goods are not hoarded but spread out and enjoyed by all in the band. This consumption pattern clashes with that of the capitalist, who views accumulation and consumption by individuals in a positive light. Some individual Cree have earned money off the reserve and have tried to save it in order to "get ahead" (according to capitalist standards). Those people are considered stingy by Cree standards and are resented; they cannot hope to gain a position of leadership in the band.

THE CULTURAL CONSTRUCTION OF THE AMERICAN DIET   American society is capitalist through and through. It must possess an economy that is more tied to material forces than the economies of the Trobriand Islanders or the Plains Cree. After all, capitalism prides itself on its hardheaded realism, its absence of sentiment, and its concern with the bottom line. Surely there is no room in a capitalist society for tastes and preferences that do not maximize efficiency and minimize waste.

Marshall Sahlins disagrees (1976a, 171ff.). He argues that the cultural pattern that shapes American dietary preferences is powerful enough to influence the world markets in foodstuffs. He further claims that Americans, like people in other societies, use dietary preferences to mark social similarities and differences.

Sahlins notes that "the exploitation of the American environment is organized by specific valuations of edibility and inedibility, themselves qualitative and in no way justifiable by biological, ecological, or economic advantage" (1976a, 171). Although we eat both meat and vegetables, meat is more highly valued than vegetables and in fact is the centerpiece of the prototypical American meal. Moreover, we do not rate all meats equally highly. Some cuts of meat that we could consume for high-quality protein we mark as inedible. Beefsteak is the prototypical American meat; it carries with it the connotation of manliness and strength. Pork is also edible, but less prestigious than beef. The meat of other domesticated animals—sheep, goats, rabbits, horses, dogs—is eaten in other parts of the world, yet in America, it either plays an insignificant role in the diet (the meat of sheep, goats, rabbits) or is considered unfit for human consumption (the meat of horses and dogs). Sahlins comments: "Surely it must be practicable to raise *some* horses and dogs for food in combination with pigs and cattle. There is even an enormous industry for raising horses as food for dogs. But then, America is the land of the sacred dog" (171).

Cattle, pigs, horses, and dogs are four important groups of domesticated animals in North America. But the meaning of any one animal cannot be understood apart from the meanings carried by the entire set. These four animal categories, Sahlins argues, can be classified as edible (cattle and pigs) or inedible (horses and dogs). Furthermore, in the edible class, beef is more preferred than pork, and in the inedible class, dogs are more strongly prohibited than horses.

A pattern begins to emerge. Sahlins suggests that the split between edible and inedible marks a split in the kind of social relationships that Americans traditionally cultivate with animals. Inedible horses and dogs are prototypical American "pets," and we usually treat them as honorary members of the human family. Edible cattle and pigs, however, are "livestock," who live apart from human beings and are not treated as members of the family. But our classification system does not stop here. Even when we consider edible animals, we differentiate between the outer muscles, or "meat," and the internal viscera, or "innards." As Sahlins points out, meat is more highly valued than innards. In fact, he suggests, one might read the entire system of classifications as "a sustained metaphor on cannibalism" (1976a, 174). That is, Americans interpret animals' bodies as if they were human bodies. We believe that our inner selves are our "true" selves. Thus, we avoid eating the part of an animal's body that corresponds to the highly valued center of our own bodies. We also avoid eating any part of animals that live in close, quasi-human association with us.

These symbolic associations, Sahlins argues, can account for the higher value we put on steak than on, say, tongue. If price were dictated by supply, the reverse should be the case, because a cow yields more steak than tongue. As he says, "From the nutritional point of view, such a notion of 'better' and 'inferior' cuts would be difficult to defend" (1976a, 176). But such categories are most appropriate for classifying the various subgroups of American society. "Better" cuts of meat are expensive; "inferior" cuts are cheap. It follows from this that the "better" sort of people are the only ones who can afford the "better" foods. Those who must eat "inferior" foods demonstrate that they are indeed inferior. Eating organ meats is metaphorically interpreted as a form of cannibalism. Moreover, according to this cultural logic, those who eat both the innards of permitted beasts and the flesh of prohibited ones must be even more depraved.

In *Meat: A Natural Symbol*, anthropologist Nick Fiddes builds on Sahlins's analysis. Fiddes points out correctly that evidence from anthropology and primatology all suggest that human beings, like their closest relatives, are dietary *omnivores*, adapted to eat a wide range of plant and animal foods. Meat's high status in Western societies, he argues, is due to the fact that meat "tangibly represents human control of the natural world. Consuming the muscle flesh of other highly evolved animals is a potent statement of our supreme power" (1991, 2). The same symbolic role is played by blood sports, such as bullfighting, in which "the entire pageant is constructed to articulate the inevitable victory of brain over brawn, qualities that are regarded as singularly human and animal respectively" (51).

As a result, vegetarianism and the condemnation of blood sports are symbolically similar in that both reject the premise that human beings should dominate nature. Fiddes suggests that the decline of meat consumption and growing popularity of vegetarianism in Western countries in recent years constitutes a symbolic rejection not only of meat eating, but of "the masculine world view that ubiquitously perceives, values, and legitimates hierarchical domination of nature, of women, and of other men, and, as its corollary, devalues less domineering modes of interaction between humans and with the rest of nature" (1991, 210).

A DIALECTIC BETWEEN THE MEANINGFUL AND THE MATERIAL

Production, distribution, and consumption are constant and coexisting aspects of human economic activity. Each phase can be used as a metonym to represent the entire process. Entire modes of livelihood can be erected on such metonyms: witness capitalist society, a monument to the proposition that exchange is—and should be—everything.

Yet each phase of economic activity shapes the others and ultimately cannot be separated from them.

Anthropologist Claude Lévi-Strauss was impressed with the way a focus on exchange helped him make sense of human cultural patterns. Lévi-Strauss saw people exchanging goods, but when he looked at kinship he saw people exchanging people, and when he looked at language he saw them exchanging signs. Yet what does it mean to "exchange signs"? Exchange seems to be rooted in hardheaded economics, so what can we make of "items" exchanged that "speak" of the values they represent?

Metaphorical equations can be read in either direction. Thus, if communication may be read as exchange, then exchange may be read as communication, with hardheaded economics having to accommodate itself to whatever is viewed as meaningful. It is not merely that material goods can be meaningful; equally, what is viewed as meaningful (as stipulated by culture) can have material consequences. If exchange is communication, we should recognize that verbal "exchanges" are rarely problem-free in human society. In the same way, dialogue and negotiation are central to other "exchanges," be these of goods or of people. A dialectic between the meaningful and the material is the underlying basis for the modes of livelihood followed by human beings everywhere.

KEY TERMS

scarcity	consumption	market exchange
economy	exchange	labor
subsistence strategies	neoclassical economic	mode of production
food collectors	theory	means of production
food producers	formalists	relations of production
extensive agriculture	rational	ideology
intensive agriculture	substantivists	ecology
mechanized industrial	modes of exchange	niche
agriculture	reciprocity	ecozone
production	redistribution	affluence
distribution		

CHAPTER SUMMARY

1. Survival requires that people make use of the natural resources in the wider world, and yet our culture tells us which resources to use and in what way. Human beings have devised a variety of subsistence strategies to satisfy their material survival needs. The basic division is between food collectors and food producers. Farmers may practice extensive or intensive agriculture, and in industrialized societies, food production may become mechanized.

2. Human economic activity is usefully divided into three phases: production, distribution, and consumption. In capitalist societies, market exchange is the dominant mode of distribution, yet many non-Western societies have traditionally carried out distribution without money or markets. Some economic anthropologists claim that exchange determines the nature of production and consumption. Others argue that production determines the nature of exchange and consumption. Still others are persuaded that culturally shaped consumption standards determine patterns of production and exchange. Ultimately, a holistic perspective requires that patterns of production, distribution, and consumption be viewed as codetermining one another.

3. Formal neoclassical economic theory developed in an attempt to explain how capitalism works. After World War II, formalist economic anthropologists applied the market model to local activities in non-Western societies that bore a family resemblance to "economics" in Western societies. Formalists assumed that non-Western actors were rational maximizers of their individual self-interest.

4. During the 1960s and 1970s, substantivists pointed out that members of non-Western societies often passed up opportunities to maximize their own self-interest because their economic activities were embedded in cultural institutions. They distinguished three major modes of exchange in human societies: reciprocity, redistribution, and market exchange. Substantivists viewed market exchange, and the maximizing rationality that goes with it, as a recent invention of capitalist societies. By the 1980s, many formalists and substantivists had agreed to compromise.

5. Marxian economic anthropologists view production as more important than exchange in determining the patterns of economic life in a society. They argue that societies can be classified in terms of their modes of production. Each mode of production contains within it the potential for conflict between classes of people who receive differential benefits and losses from the productive process.

6. The internal explanation for consumption patterns argues that people produce material goods to satisfy a basic human need for food, clothing, shelter, and so on. The external explanation argues that consumption patterns depend not on the hunger drive, which is the same for everyone, but on the particular external resources available within the ecozone to which a particular society must adapt. Ethnographic evidence demonstrates that both internal and external explanations for consumption patterns are inadequate because they ignore how culture defines our needs and provides for their satisfaction according to its own logic—a logic that is reducible neither to biology nor to psychology nor to ecological pressure.

7. Particular consumption preferences that may seem "irrational" make sense when considered in the context of other consumption preferences and prohibitions in the same culture. The Jewish prohibition against pork consumption makes sense when considered together with other Jewish dietary rules. The accumulation of banana leaves in the Trobriand Islands makes sense in the context of Trobriand kinship and economic arrangements. Institutionalized sharing among the Plains Cree makes sense in the context of Cree history and traditional social arrangements.

8. Even middle-class North Americans and Europeans, who are committed to economic "rationality" and efficiency, exhibit "irrational"—that is, culturally motivated—consumption patterns, as illustrated by the central role of meat in our diets.

SUGGESTED READINGS

Douglas, Mary, and Baron Isherwood. 1979. *The world of goods: Towards an anthropology of consumption.* New York: W. W. Norton. *A discussion of consumption, economic theories about consumption, and what anthropologists can contribute to the study of consumption.*

Harris, Marvin. 1986. *Good to eat.* New York: Harper and Row. *This is a recent collection of Harris's essays, offering a materialist analysis of why people eat the things they do.*

Lee, Richard. 1992. *The Dobe Ju/'hoansi.* 2d ed. New York: Holt, Rinehart and Winston. *This highly readable ethnography contains important discussions about foraging as a way of making a living.*

Plattner, Stuart, ed. 1989. *Economic anthropology.* Palo Alto, CA: Stanford University Press. *A readable, up-to-date collection of articles by economic anthropologists. Displaying the achievements of formalist-inspired research, it also acknowledges reconciliation with substantivists and recognizes the contribution of marxian analyses.*

Sahlins, Marshall. 1972. *Stone Age economics.* Chicago: Aldine. *A series of important, well-written essays on economic life, written from a more substantivist position. Includes "The original affluent society."*

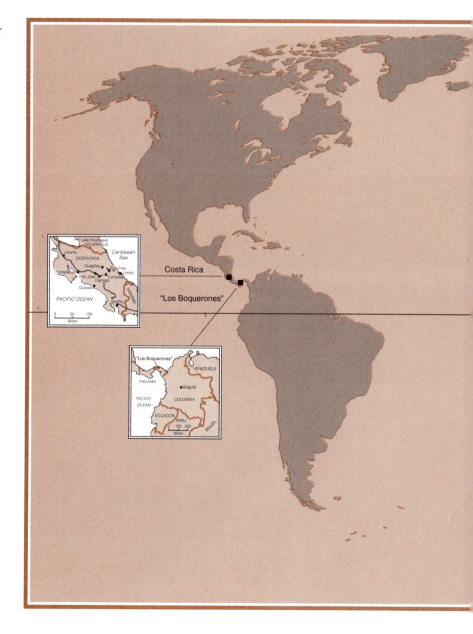

The World System

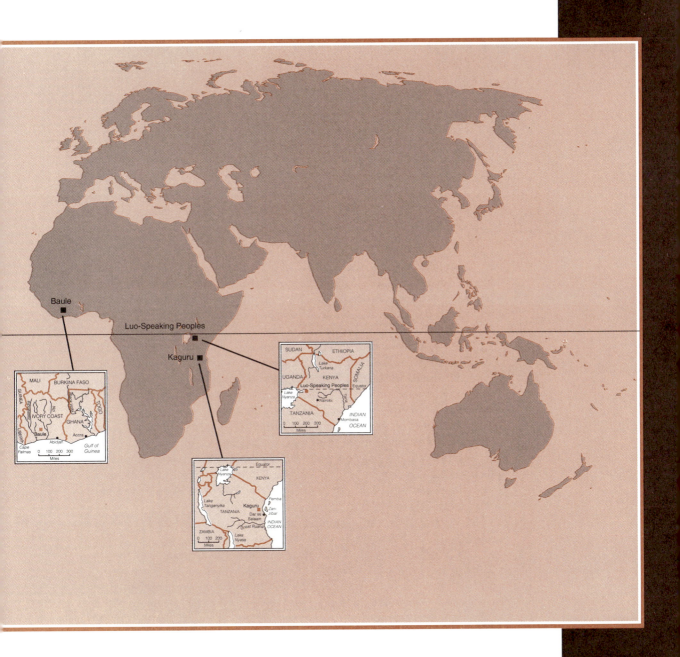

Orlando, Claudio, and Leonardo Villas Boas were middle-class Brazilians who were members of an expedition that explored central Brazil in the early 1940s. Their experiences on this expedition led the three brothers to dedicate their lives to protecting Brazil's indigenous peoples from the ravages of contact with Western society. They were instrumental in persuading the government to create in 1952 the Xingu National Park, a large area in the state of Mato Grosso where indigenous groups could live undisturbed by outsiders. Since that time, they have worked to contact threatened indigenous groups and to persuade them to move to Xingu. One such group was the Kréen-Akaróre, whose existence was menaced by a highway being built through their traditional territory. In February 1973, after years of avoiding outsiders, the Kréen-Akaróre finally gave up. They made contact with Claudio Villas Boas, who had been following them in hopes of finding them before the highway builders did. Shortly after this, Orlando Villas Boas gave a press conference in which he forcefully urged that a reserve be created for the Kréen-Akaróre by the Brazilian government. Anthropologist Shelton Davis tells the rest of the story:

> A month following this interview, Brazilian President Médici signed a decree for the creation of a Kréen-Akaróre reserve. Against the advice of the Villas Boas brothers, however, this decree did not include in the reserve the traditional territory of the Kréen-Akaróre tribe. Further, it made the Santarém-Cuiabá Highway one of the boundaries of the reserve. Within months, this action proved devastating for the remaining 300 members of the Kréen-Akaróre tribe.
>
> In January 1974, less than a year after the pacification of the Kréen-Akaróre, Brazilian newspapers cited a firsthand report on what was happening to the tribe. This report was written by Ezequias Paulo Heringer, an Indian agent commissioned to investigate conditions along the Kréen-Akaróre front. According to Heringer, the Kréen-Akaróre were dispersed along the Santarém-Cuiabá Highway, fraternizing with truck drivers, and begging for food. . . .
>
> Heringer told the Brazilian press that the Kréen-Akaróre had abandoned their gardens and were in a state of sickness, hunger, and despair. . . . Within a year, the population of the Kréen-Akaróre tribe had been reduced from approximately 300 to less than 135. . . .
>
> In October 1974, the Villas Boas brothers commissioned an airplane to transfer the Kréen-Akaróre to the Xingu National Park. At the time of this transfer, it became known that another epidemic was ravishing [sic] the remaining 135 members of the tribe. A Brazilian doctor aboard this airplane reported that the Kréen-Akaróre women were purposely aborting their children, rather than produce offspring who would face the new conditions of the tribe. Since this date, the Kréen-Akaróre have been living next to their tradi-

In Their Own Words   THE ETHNOGRAPHER'S RESPONSIBILITY

French ethnographers Jacques Meunier and A. M. Savarin reflect on the role they can play in Europe to affect the policies of Latin American governments toward the indigenous peoples living within their borders.

At the most fundamental level, the history of thought about primitive people—are they human, overgrown children, or replicas of early stages of Western civilization?—provides a summary of the changes that have taken place in our own culture: the West knows that it can no longer hold exclusive power, but it still considers itself the dominant power. Western ignorance follows from this error. Our taste for exoticism and our morality stem from it, as does the deadly intolerance that seems lodged in our hearts. Centuries of culture and well-intentioned unreasonableness, centuries of humanism have led to the most heinous of all crimes: genocide.

Entire communities forced to abandon their lands, children kidnapped, people treated barbarously, degraded mentally and physically, punitive expeditions launched against them. . . . With genocide, with racism, we confront horror itself. We have spoken of the fragility of traditional societies, of the blind intolerance of our civilization toward the Indians, of the lack of understanding that has led the Amazonians—white, creole, and mestizo—to the organized extermination of the Indians. But there is one question that haunts us, that emerges through the pages of this case like the recurring notes of a flute, forcing us to weigh an unpleasant possibility: aren't we just as guilty of exploiting the Indians, aren't we indulging in a lot of useless discussion? But when we use the word *genocide*, we have no intention of turning ourselves into defenders of a lost cause; we do not see our roles as charity and moralism. We are not writing off the Indians; we do not believe that genocide should be considered an inevitable calamity.

Ethnographers must organize; they must enact plans to safeguard the threatened minorities—this is important. But if they do not capture public opinion, their projects will not produce results. More than anything, ethnographers need to launch an information campaign, a sound and systematic campaign. The general public has the right to know. The right and the duty. To accept this atrocity, to allow these terrible crimes to be committed, is to become an accomplice in them.

Do not misjudge us: our indignation is not mere posturing. We are convinced that it is possible to affect the policy of Latin American governments. Especially since these countries, while dependent on the United States economically, still turn toward Europe culturally. We can say to them without paternalism: the sense Latin Americans have of their countries still comes from Europe. Why shouldn't they learn a respect for their indigenous populations from Europe, just as they have acquired a taste for pre-Colombian antiquities and folklore? In our view, the salvation of the Indian must begin here and now.

Source: Meunier and Savarin 1994, 128–29.

tional enemies, the Txukahamae tribe, in the northern part of the Xingu National Park. (1977, 69–73)

Disease, devastation, and misery have been the all-too-common lot of indigenous peoples who have had to deal with Western society. Recently, however, remarkable things have been happening in Amazonia. In March 1989, the *Anthropology Newsletter* published a report from anthropologist Terence Turner describing how indigenous Amazonians had organized themselves to resist outside encroachment on their traditional lands. They were the people most directly affected by continued destruction of the Amazonian rain forest, and many observers had assumed that their fate would be extinc-

FIGURE 14.1 *To publicize their opposition to a proposed hydroelectric dam complex that threatened to flood their traditional territories, indigenous Amazonian peoples, under the leadership of the Kayapo, engaged in a variety of activities. Here, Kayapo chief Raoni (third from right) and British rock star Sting (third from left) hold a press conference.*

tion. No one could have imagined that these peoples might be leaders in defense of the environment, working successfully with national and international allies. Yet they have done so with great courage and political skill.

Under the leadership of the Kayapo tribe, some 28 indigenous nations of the Central Amazonian region are banding together to construct a huge intertribal village of 3000 people in the path of a proposed hydroelectric dam complex at Altamira on the Xingu River [Figure 14.1]. The dams, if completed as planned, would flood more than 1600 sq kilometers of forest land—the largest man-made lake in the world. The village is conceived as the Indians' own "Altamira Project"—a living community, complete with families and children, in contrast to the drowned forest, dead animals and homeless people that would be created by the Altamira hydroelectric project. A small permanent population will remain at the site to oppose any dam construction. . . .

The integral vision of society and environment embodied by the village is also intended as a political manifesto. In the Indians' view, the environmental, human rights, and specific tribal rights aspects of the Amazonian crisis are integrally interconnected. To them this means that support organizations oriented to these various issues should work together in a common effort, rather than in mutual isolation or opposition as they have tended to do. This was the constant theme of the Kayapo leader, Paiakan, on his recent tour of Europe and North America. . . . Many environmental and other advocacy groups proved receptive to Paiakan's message.

The Indians have realized that they must come together themselves into an effective alliance if they are to expect environmentalist, human rights and indigenous support groups from the outside world to join with one another in a common struggle to save their forest world. Their Altamira village is thus intended simultaneously as a rallying point for the tribes of Amazonia and as an appeal for world support. The boldness and global vision of this project are breathtaking; nothing like such a concerted action by even a few, let alone 28 unrelated Indian societies has ever taken place in the Amazon. The Indians are trying to tell us something important; we should listen. (T. Turner 1989, 21–22)

Peoples like the Kréen-Akaróre or Kayapo, living deep in the Amazonian rain forest, would seem to be far removed from Western influences, yet the shock waves of the Brazilian economic "miracle" reached even them. In this chapter, we deal in a direct manner with how the Western world and the societies visited by anthropologists are interrelated. We will be looking at ourselves as much as we look at the traditional subjects of anthropological research. Through this reflexive exercise, we may learn something of the past and present relationships that link people of all societies to one another. In this way, we can establish a context for contemplating our common fate.

THE GROWTH OF CAPITALISM AND WESTERN EXPANSION

The growth in wealth and power of western Europe coincided with the birth of the "modern" era of Western history. The pursuit of centralized monarchy at home and colonial conquest abroad had begun in the Middle Ages and flourished during the Renaissance and the Age of Discovery. **Colonialism** refers to a social system wherein the political conquest by one society of another leads to "cultural domination with enforced social change" (Beidelman 1982, 2). Since the fall of the Roman Empire, Europe has never been politically unified, which means that, beginning in the fifteenth century, fledgling European states could strike out on their own without being answerable to any central authority. Newly consolidating states pushed into Africa, Asia, and the New World. At the same time, these dynamic Europeans were working out a new kind of society with a new kind of economy whose development was aided by trade and conquest—namely, capitalism.

The term **capitalism** refers to at least two things. On the one hand, it is an economic system dominated by the supply-demand-price mechanism called the market. On the other hand, it describes the way of life that grew up in response to and in service to that market. This new way of life changed the face of Europe. Many changes were

colonialism Cultural domination with enforced social change.

capitalism An economic system dominated by the supply-demand-price mechanism called *the market;* an entire way of life that grew in response to and in service of that market.

financed by wealth brought to Europe from other regions of the globe that were also transformed by their contact with Europeans and the economic transactions that resulted.

The growth of cities represents one significant transformation that resulted from the non-Western world's contact with Western capitalism. To be sure, cities that were products of indigenous civilizations were found in many parts of the world before the arrival of Europeans. By contrast, the colonial city in which capitalist transactions centered was "a conquered place" (Gilsenan 1982, 197). Colonial administrators and merchants dealt with local elites in such places and united there to defend their joint interests against those who remained in outlying areas.

City dwellers see themselves as "modern." In the context of colonialism, however, being modern has often meant nothing more than adopting the practices and worldview of Western capitalism. As a result, the so-called "backward" rural peoples often turn out to be either those who have escaped capitalism's embrace or those who actively oppose it. The colonial city, with the life it represented, came to symbolize everything that was wrong with the colonial order. In contemporary Muslim societies, "in times of crisis the modern city is itself called in question, taken to symbolize forces of oppression or a non-Islamic way of life. . . . For radical and millennial groups the city is a home of unbelief, not of sober, textual Islam. The true believer should, in an image that has great historical resonance, go out from the city, leave as the Prophet Muhammad did the hypocritical and unbelieving citizens of Mecca" (Gilsenan 1982, 214).

Colonial penetration reshaped conquered territories to serve the needs of capitalist enterprise. Cities were centers of commerce, and rural areas were sources of raw materials for industry. Systems set up by colonial authorities to extract raw materials disrupted indigenous communities and created new ones. The mining towns of Bolivia and South Africa, for example, are outgrowths of this process. Labor for such enterprises was recruited, sometimes by force, from local populations. Little by little, in an effort to streamline the system of colonial exploitation, society was restructured.

The Colonial Political Economy

Because the colonial order focused on the extraction of material wealth, it might be said that its reason for existence was economic. Certainly it linked economically communities and territories that in many cases had led a fairly autonomous existence before colonization. Yet this new economic order did not spring up painlessly by itself. It was imposed and maintained by force. For that reason, many anthropologists describe the colonial order as a **political economy**—a holistic term that emphasizes the centrality of material interest and the use of power to protect and enhance that interest. Those who use the term when discussing the colonial order do so, among other reasons, to remind themselves and others not to forget history.

The colonial political economy created three kinds of links: it linked conquered communities with one another within a conquered territory; different conquered territories with one another; and all conquered territories with the country of the colonizers. A particularly striking example of this linkage comes from Wolf, who describes how silver mined in Spanish colonies in America was shipped to another Spanish colony in Asia—the Philippines—where it was then used to buy textiles from the Chinese (1982, 153).

More commonly, colonial enterprises drew labor from neighboring regions, as in South Africa. Here, indigenous Africans were recruited from some distance to work in the mines; money earned in one area was thus remitted for the economic support of families in another area. Again, these linkages did not come about spontaneously. Alverson describes for South Africa a situation paralleled in many other colonies (1978, 26ff.). The British, he argues, could not make a profit in the gold mines of the region without cheap African labor. In the late nineteenth century, however, Africans were still largely able to guarantee their own subsistence through traditional means. They were unwilling to work for wages in the mines except on a short-term basis. Profitability in mining required, therefore, that African self-sufficiency be eliminated so that Africans would have no choice but to work for whatever wages mine owners chose to offer.

This goal was achieved in two ways. First, conquered African populations had to pay taxes, but the taxes could only be paid in cash. Second, the colonial government deliberately prevented the growth of a cash economy in African areas; thus, the only way Africans could obtain the cash needed to pay their taxes was by working for wages in the mines. "The Tswana, along with other African populations, comprised a reserve army of potential labor—that is, labor that it was hoped would exist in inelastic supply and cost industry nothing at all when not being used. [Botswana] and the rural, native reserves in South Africa itself were, and from the capitalist viewpoint still are, social security systems that keep labor alive until such time as it is in demand by the money sector" (Alverson 1978, 34–35). (See EthnoProfile 2.1: Tswana.)

Political independence did not remove Botswana from the clutches of the South African political economy. At the time of Alverson's fieldwork, Botswana was still sending more than two workers to South Africa for every one worker it was able to supply with a job at home. And these workers were not "surplus" migrants whose home communities were eager to get rid of them. "In many ways some Tswana communities have become quasi-societies and quasi-economies, for the absence of men and women abroad has virtually destroyed institutional life and replaced it with nothing except cash" (1978, 62–63). What is true for Botswana has become equally true for ex-colonies elsewhere in Africa, Asia, and the New World.

The Key Metaphor of Capitalism

The capitalist political economy began in Europe, but it soon expanded to enfold a large portion of the earth into a politico-economic world system. There had been expansive empires before the rise of capitalism, but capitalist exploitation was unique because it

---

political economy A holistic term that emphasizes the centrality of material interest (economy) and the use of power (politics) to protect and enhance that interest.

derived from a new worldview. In the words of Eric Wolf, "The guiding fiction of this kind of society—one of the key tenets of its ideology—is that land, labor, and wealth are commodities, that is, goods produced not for use, but for sale" (1969, 277). That is, the world is a market, and everything within the world has, or should have, its price.

The genius of capitalism has been the thoroughgoing way in which those committed to the marketing metaphor have been able to convert anything that exists into a commodity; they turn land into real estate and material objects into inventory. They can also attach price tags to ideas (hence the existence of copyright laws in capitalist societies) and even to human beings. The prototypical slave in Western society is considered "first and foremost a commodity. He is a chattel, totally in the possession of another person who uses him for private ends" (Kopytoff and Miers 1977, 3). Even human beings who are not slaves are nevertheless reduced to their labor power by the capitalist market and become worth whatever price the laws of supply and demand determine; thus, human beings are also turned into objects, and labor becomes a commodity along with beans and cotton. Even when people function as buyers in the market, their actions are supposed to be governed by strict "economizing." They should buy cheap, sell dear, and not allow any personal or social considerations to divert their attention from the bottom line.

To be sure, complex commercial activity was not invented by Western capitalists. Long before western Europe became a world power, stratified state societies in different parts of the world had devised sophisticated socioeconomic systems of their own. In places such as China and India, for example, the use of trade, money, and markets was highly developed by the time the first representatives of Western capitalism arrived on the scene. Elites in such societies were well prepared to take advantage of new economic opportunities offered by Western entrepreneurs, often helping to establish capitalist practices in their own societies and benefiting as a result. However, the consequences of capitalism were often negative for ordinary members of these societies, who lost many traditional socioeconomic supports.

Capitalism was even more devastating for members of small-scale societies existing outside the control of such complex states. Before the introduction of capitalism, land in these societies was not a commodity; its access was controlled and protected. Rights to use land, or **use rights,** might be exchanged, but land ownership, or **land tenure,** was rarely in question, being regarded in most places as an inalienable possession of the social group who made use of it. Before the introduction of capitalism, human beings were identified in terms of a complex web of social identities based on descent, alliance, and residence. Their status may have been low, but they were usually protected from utter destitution by those of high status who were obliged to help them. Before the introduction of capitalism, multipurpose money did not exist, exchanges were hedged about by social restrictions, and there was no single standard according to which anything could be assigned a value.

Capitalism changed all this. When capitalist practices were imposed on non-Western societies through colonial administration, indigenous life was forever altered. To function intelligibly within the capitalist world order, colonized peoples had to begin to see the world as a storehouse of potential commodities. Much of recent world history can usefully be viewed as a narrative of non-Western responses to this new worldview, of the practical actions it encouraged and justified. Some responses were enthusiastic, others were resentful but accommodating, still others were violent in repudiation.

Accounting for Social and Cultural Change

Anthropology was born as a discipline during the heyday of European colonialism in the nineteenth century. Functional anthropology developed in the context of empire. Anthropologists were hired to provide specific information about particular societies under colonial rule. Colonial governments were preoccupied with day-to-day concerns of administration. From their perspective, social change involved the adjustment of conquered peoples to life under colonial rule. They were interested in research that would let them rule with as little difficulty as possible.

Colonial administrations rarely denied the commercial reasons for their existence, yet they also saw their presence as an opportunity to teach their colonial subjects how to become civilized. As we observed in Chapter 4, European anthropologists often played an equivocal role in the colonial setting; they were valued for the expert knowledge they could provide to administrators, and at the same time they were viewed with suspicion because their expert knowledge might easily contradict or undermine administrative goals.

A number of American anthropologists also tried to clarify what their role should be in the expanding world of capitalist colonialism. In two documents, one published in 1936 and another some 20 years later, they urged that the study of change was to be impartial and scientific. Their goal was to discover of laws of culture change. These anthropologists had a broad view of culture change. They considered situations encountered under colonialism, but they also considered situations where contact and change occurred in the absence of political conquest. The latter cases involved autonomous groups whose members were freer to be more more selective about what they selected and rejected. The anthropologists did not see themselves supporting any particular political position in advocating that culture change be approached in this way; however, they were sympathetic to the plight of colonial subjects. Melville Herskovits, in particular, was outspoken in his defense of the right of indigenous African peoples to control their own destinies.

In the years following World War II, European colonial powers were increasingly forced to come to terms with colonial subjects who rejected the role they had been forced to play as students of civilization. The colonial order was no longer a given, and its ultimate benevolence was sharply questioned. This critical attitude persisted after independence was granted to most European colonies in the 1950s and 1960s. It became clear that formal political independence could not easily undo the profound social and economic entanglements linking the former colonial territories to the countries that

---

use rights The right to use, but not own, land for farming or grazing.   **land tenure** Land ownership.

In Their Own Words   THE ANTHROPOLOGICAL VOICE

Anthropologist Annette Weiner traces the history of anthropological challenges to colonialism and Western capitalism, pointing out why the perspective of anthropologists has so often been ignored.

Colonialism brought foreign governments, missionaries, explorers, and exploiters face-to-face with cultures whose values and beliefs were vastly different. As the harbingers of Western progress, their actions were couched in the rhetoric of doing something to and for "the natives"—giving them souls, clothes, law—whatever was necessary to lift them out of their "primitive" ways. Anthropologists were also part of the colonial scene, but what they came to "do" made them different from those who were carrying out the expectations of missions, overseas trade, and government protectorates. Anthropologists arrived in the field determined to understand the cultural realities of an unfamiliar world. The knowledge of these worlds was to serve as a warning to those in positions of colonial power by charging that villager's lives were not to be tampered with arbitrarily and that changing the lives of powerless people was insensitive and inhumane, unless one understood and took seriously the cultural meanings inherent in, for example, traditional land ownership, the technologies and rituals surrounding food cultivation, myths, magic, and gender relations.

All too often, however, the anthropologist's voice went unnoticed by those in power, for it remained a voice committed to illuminating the cultural biases under which colonialists operated. Only recently have we witnessed the final demise of colonial governments and the rise of independent countries. Economically, however, independence has not brought these countries the freedom to pursue their own course of development. In many parts of the world, Western multinational corporations, often playing a role not too dissimilar from colonial enterprises, now determine the course of that freedom, changing people's lives in a way that all too often is harmful or destructive. At the same time, we know that the world's natural resources and human productive capabilities can no longer remain isolates. Developed and developing countries are now more dependent on one another than ever before in human history. Yet this interdependency, which should give protection to indigenous peoples, is often worked out for political ends that ignore the moral issues. Racism and the practice of discrimination are difficult to destroy, as evidenced by the United States today, where we still are not completely emancipated from assumptions that relegate blacks, women, Asians, Hispanics, and other minorities to second-class status. If we cannot bridge these cultural differences intellectually within our own borders, then how can we begin to deal politically with Third World countries—those who were called "primitives" less than a century ago—in a fair, sensitive, and meaningful way?

This is the legacy of anthropology that we must never forget. Because the work of anthropology takes us to the neighborhoods, villages, and campsites—the local level—we can ourselves experience the results of how the world's economic and political systems affect those who have no voice. Yet once again our voices too are seldom heard by those who make such decisions. Anthropologists are often prevented from participating in the forums of economic and government planning. Unlike economists, political scientists, or engineers, we must stand on the periphery of such decision making, primarily because our understanding of cultural patterns and beliefs forces on others an awareness that ultimately makes such decisions more formidable.

At the beginning of the twentieth century, anthropologists spoke out strongly against those who claimed that "savage" societies represented a lower level of biological and social development. Now, as we face the next century, the anthropological approach to human nature and human societies is as vital to communicate as ever. We face a difficult, potentially dangerous, and therefore complex future. A fundamental key to our future is to make certain that the dynamic qualities of human beings in all parts of the world are recognized and that the true value of cultural complexities is not ignored. There is much important anthropology to be done.

Source: Weiner 1990.

had colonized them. The persistence of these ties in the face of political sovereignty came to be called **neocolonialism.**

The study of neocolonialism has led to a new awareness of just how strongly the fate of colonies and the fate of the colonizers have continued to be mutually interdependent. Recognizing the width and depth of this interdependence, scholars have offered new explanations for the "underdevelopment" that characterizes the new nations in what came to be called the Third World.

The Roots of the Neocolonial Order

Coming to terms with the tenacious problems of neocolonialism would seem to require coming to terms with colonial domination itself. The assumption that political independence would allow Latin Americans, Africans, and Asians to become captains of their fate has turned out to be premature.

Anthropologist T. O. Beidelman says, "Colonialism is not dead in Africa if, by colonialism, we mean cultural domination with enforced social change. I refer not only to continued economic and political influence by former colonial powers but also to domination of the poor and uneducated masses by a privileged and powerful native elite fiercely determined to make change for whatever reasons" (1982, 2). Defining colonialism in this way highlights why political independence in the mid-twentieth century made so little economic difference to the new nations of Africa and Asia. It also helps explain why the Latin American nations that became formally independent over a century ago have continued to languish economically. It would seem that political domination is only one option in the growth of a capitalist world system. Cultural domination with enforced social change can occur without political domination if the people of a dominated territory decide on their own to accommodate the wishes of the outside power. But they may refuse to do so or they may lack the means to meet outside needs as fully as the outside power wishes. In either case, the outside power may decide to move in itself, making the changes it sees as necessary for its own welfare, even if local peoples object.

This certainly seems to describe the history of European colonialism in Africa. For nearly 500 years, Europeans traded with Africans along the coast of the continent but were not allowed to penetrate inward. Coastal African societies were profoundly affected by this trade, which led to the rise of new settlements and new African leaders whose power and prestige derived directly from trade with Europeans. Before the arrival of Europeans on the Atlantic coast, the major trade routes connecting Africa to Europe had been across the Sahara to the Mediterranean Sea. European presence on the Atlantic coast served as a new magnet for commerce, substantially redirecting African trade over time. For most of this period, the commodities for which Europeans traded included

---

neocolonialism The persistence of profound social and economic entanglements linking former colonial territories to their former colonial rulers despite political sovereignty.

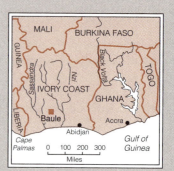

EthnoProfile 14.1 • **BAULE**

REGION: Western Africa

NATION: Ivory Coast

POPULATION: 2,760,000

ENVIRONMENT: Savanna

LIVELIHOOD: Farming (yams in particular) and cloth production

POLITICAL ORGANIZATION: In the precolonial period no state and no clear stratification; today, part of a modern nation-state

FOR MORE INFORMATION: Etienne, Mona. 1980. Women and men, cloth and colonization: The transformation of production-distribution relations among the Baule (Ivory Coast). In *Women and colonization: Anthropological perspectives,* edited by Mona Etienne and Eleanor Leacock, 270–93. New York: Praeger.

human beings destined for slavery in Europe or in New World settlements. As African trading partners searched for slaves in the interior of the continent, profound reverberations were felt far inland, affecting societies who had never seen a European.

The growth of capitalist manufacturing in the late eighteenth century altered how European merchants viewed Africa. They saw the lands of Africa as sources of cheap raw materials for industry and the people as consumers of European manufactures. In the early nineteenth century, England had progressed the furthest in capitalist manufacturing. Hence, England was most interested in the "legitimate" trade in nonhuman commodities with Africa. So it was that England took a lead in abolishing the slave trade with Africa.

As the nineteenth century continued, the industrial development of France and Germany speeded up. Both countries began to compete with England in Africa and elsewhere for the same markets. As this competition heated up, it became increasingly clear that delivery of resources into European hands was too slow and fitful to suit the demands of industry. Solving such problems became a major concern of the Europeans. When European powers began to sign treaties with African leaders in the late nineteenth century, access to resources was a central topic. Once a given European power completely controlled trade within a certain region, it could keep out competitors and make any changes in supply and transportation of raw materials that were required.

Women and Colonization

Colonial administrators were generally convinced that the work of empire would benefit those they dominated—if not now, then in the future. Critics of colonialism deny that any benefits could accrue to a dominated and exploited people. Ethnographic data,

FIGURE 14.2 *Factory production has displaced traditional household-based production of cloth not just among the Baule of Ivory Coast, but throughout Africa. These women work in a textile factory in Lagos, Nigeria.*

however, show that colonial domination did not affect all groups in the same ways. Women are one such group. As we saw in Chapter 13, Trobriand women suffered no loss of status under colonial rule. (See EthnoProfile 3.3: Trobriand Islanders.) Baule women of Ivory Coast in western Africa were less fortunate. (See EthnoProfile 14.1: Baule.)

In precolonial Baule society, according to Mona Etienne (1980), production centered on two products: yams and cloth. Gifts of yams and cloth consolidated marriages, and both sexes worked together in the production of each. Yet the relations of production assigned men responsibility for yams and women responsibility for cloth. Men's traditional control over yams was an outgrowth of the sexual division of labor; men cleared and prepared farm plots for planting, although the women tended the crops. Similarly, women controlled cloth because they raised the cotton and spun the thread from which it was woven, although the men did the actual weaving. Both yams and cloth were indispensable for subsistence as well as for exchange in various traditional social contexts. As a result, the balance of power between men and women was highly egalitarian.

Ivory Coast became a colony of France in 1893. In 1923, the French built in Baule territory a textile factory that sold factory-spun thread for cash (Figure 14.2). Baule men with cash could therefore buy their own thread, and they, not their wives, would control any cloth woven from it. French colonial administrators also encouraged Baule farmers to plant new varieties of cotton as a cash crop. Baule women had traditionally raised their cotton on fields that had been planted with yams the previous year, but these plots were now devoted to growing the new cotton. Cash-crop cotton also required new farming techniques, but for a variety of reasons those techniques were taught to Baule men. Consequently, women's cotton production was reduced considerably. Moreover, because women had to work in their husbands' cash-crop fields as well as the traditional yam plots, they also had less time to spin traditional thread.

The colonial government required men to pay their wives' taxes in cash, a move that seemed to justify the right of Baule men to control production of crops that could be sold for cash. Under colonial rule, cash-cropping became increasingly important. As a result, Baule women found that their traditional autonomous rights to use their husbands' land for their own production gradually eroded, and they became increasingly dependent on their husbands' arbitrary generosity.

There is a final irony in this series of developments. Many Baule women today have become wage laborers in the textile factory in order to earn cash to buy their own cloth, which they can then control. They are aware of the loss of status and power they have suffered over the years, and their discontent has undermined traditional Baule marriage. "The wife-husband production relationship has become a constant source of conflict. Because the production relationship has always been the foundation of marriage, and because cloth and cash now tend to be the measure of a husband's affection and respect, the whole personal relationship is also conflict-laden. Inevitably, many women prefer to remain unmarried and all seek to acquire their own cash" (Etienne 1980, 231). In this way, the traditional Baule mode of production was transformed by contact with the capitalist market. The previously egalitarian relations of production linking women and men (husbands and wives) were destroyed.

VIEWS OF THE POLITICAL ECONOMY

Anthropology identifies four major theoretical perspectives to explain the relationship between the West and the rest of the world: (1) modernization theory, (2) dependency theory, (3) world system theory, and (4) neomarxian theory.

Modernization Theory

The roots of contemporary **modernization theory** can be seen in the unilineal evolutionism of Herbert Spencer and his followers. In brief, social change in non-Western societies under colonial rule was understood as a necessary and inevitable prelude to higher levels of social development. Europe had passed through the same stages of evolution earlier in its history, and contact with Europe was now shaking other regions out of stagnation. Colonization was thus a positive process because it taught backward peoples the skills they needed to move forward. These were capitalist skills that required Western institutions to work properly. By adopting those skills and institutions, it was argued, conquered societies would eventually become "modern" and prosperous independent nation-states.

Spencerian evolutionism was heavily criticized in anthropology and other social sciences in the early twentieth century. As late as 1960, however, we find Spencerian reasoning in economist W. W. Rostow's book *The Stages of Economic Growth* ([1960] 1971). This book codifies the received wisdom of economics that formed the foundation of U.S. foreign aid policies in the 1960s. It thus offers in a single volume the basic principles of modernization theory.

Rostow surveys the history of the world and decides that, economically speaking, known human societies can be sorted into five categories, each of which represents a stage of development. The first, lowest stage is that of "traditional society," which is defined in negative terms. Traditional societies are said to have productive techniques that are poorly developed, and their social institutions are viewed as stumbling blocks in the path of economic growth. Progress thus requires that these blocks be removed if prosperity and modernity are to be attained. Stages two through five chart the steps to "modernity"—defined as a stage of "high mass-consumption."

Rostow conceives of economic growth as if it were organic growth, from youth to maturity to what he calls postmaturity. He describes each new nation-state as if it were an adolescent male undergoing puberty. Young states, like young men, develop according to an inner timetable. They start out ignorant and immature, lacking the knowledge and skills to support themselves properly. In addition, they are unsure of their own identity, and so tend to get involved in fights with one another or with more mature members of the international community. But the passage of time brings wisdom. Rostow has faith that, with sound guidance from their elders, young states will eventually stand beside those elders as self-supporting, even thriving, members of the international community.

Rostow's growth metaphor makes the young state largely responsible for its own success or failure. The only role a mature or "postmature" outside state can play is that of a wise father. That is, established states can provide the advice and the funding to get development off to a good start. After that, the rest is up to the young state itself. If its leaders follow the advice and take advantage of the opportunities provided, their under-developed economy, like an airplane leaving the ground or a college graduate with his first job, should eventually "take off" on its own into self-sustaining economic growth.

Rostow's unselfconscious paternalism and ethnocentrism are illustrated by some of his basic assumptions, perhaps most obviously, by his belief that modernization is an automatic process operating according to eternal laws unaffected by history. Rostow does not see the colonial past of the developing world as playing an important role in the initial modernization of the West. Equally irrelevant are any contemporary relationships that may bind underdeveloped countries to Western states. There is only one path to modernity, the path blazed by the nations of western Europe and North America and recorded in their history. Therefore, if other nations want to share in the same modern prosperity, they must make history repeat itself and follow the same path.

Dependency Theory

Modernization theory is plausible if you accept a metaphor that equates nations with individual organisms and attributes organismic development largely to innate growth mechanisms beyond the reach of environmental influences. But many observers reject such a view. Once colonialism is considered, some argue, modernization theory appears

---

modernization theory Argues that the social change occurring in non-Western societies under colonial rule was a neces-sary and inevitable prelude to higher levels of social development that had been reached by the more "modern" nations.

less and less persuasive. From their perspective, the prosperity of Western nations did not depend on the development of the internal resources of those nations; rather, it was based on the exploitation of cheap raw materials and the captive markets that colonies provided. On this account, the United States differed from European colonial powers only in that the expanding American government did not have to cross oceans to find new resources; it had incorporated the lands and resources of indigenous peoples living within its own borders. In both cases, the West would never have prospered if colonial powers had not expropriated the wealth of other people to fuel their own development.

This view challenges the assumption that nations are naturally autonomous and independently responsible for their own success or failure at modernizing. If colonies and other peoples' resources are necessary for a nation to become modern, then countries without colonies, whose own resources were long ago removed by others, can never hope to become modern. The success of a few has required the failure of the many. Indeed, the "independent" capitalist nations of the world will be prosperous only as long as others are dependent on them for economic direction. This understanding of development forms the basis for dependency theory.

Dependency theory argues that dependent colonies or nations must endure the reshaping of their economic structures to meet demands generated outside their borders. For example, land that could be used to raise food crops for local consumption are planted with flowers or bananas or coffee for export; thus, local needs are pushed into the background. Dependency theorists stress that backward agricultural techniques and careless human overpopulation are not the reasons why people in many so-called "Third World" countries cannot feed themselves; rather, the international capitalist economic order is directly responsible for distorting national economies in these nations.

Dependency theory argues that the development of rich capitalist nations requires the underdevelopment of colonies and less powerful trading partners. Indeed, capitalism deliberately creates "underdevelopment" in formerly prosperous areas that come under its domination. This is the famous **development-of-underdevelopment thesis** of dependency theory. Dependency theorists such as economist André Gunder Frank (1969) argue that the same dependency relationships that link an "underdeveloped" country to a "developed" country are found in the underdeveloped country itself. That is, the economically and politically powerful regions of an underdeveloped country dominate the less powerful areas. Local capitalist elites dominate economic transactions and keep peasants and others dependent on them, down to the level of the smallest village. Therefore, until dependent countries are able to take control of their own destinies and to restructure their economies and societies to meet local needs, underdevelopment will persist.

World-System Theory

World-system theory is associated most closely with the work of sociologist Immanuel Wallerstein and his colleagues. Beginning with *The Modern World-System,* published in 1974, Wallerstein sets forth a global framework for understanding problems of development and underdevelopment in the modern world. Like dependency theorists, Wallerstein is concerned with the history of relationships between former colonies and their former masters. He too argues that the exploitative framework of present-day relations between those states took shape historically and was fine-tuned during the colonial era.

Wallerstein rejects the idea that modern nation-states are independent entities engaged in balanced exchange in a free market; quite the contrary. When European capitalism expanded beyond its borders, beginning in the late fifteenth and early sixteenth centuries, it incorporated other regions and peoples into a world economy based on the capitalist mode of production. Wallerstein deliberately chooses to speak of a world *economy*, rather than a world empire or other political entity. This is because a world economy "precisely encompasses within its bounds empires, city-states, and the emerging 'nation-states.' It is a 'world' system, not because it encompasses the whole world, but because it is larger than any juridically defined political unit. And it is a 'world-*economy*' because the basic linkage between the parts of the system is economic" (1974, 15).

Wallerstein points out that when the European world economy took shape, it was not the only world economy in existence. Perhaps its most important competitor centered on China. Nevertheless, the European world economy was able to surpass the other world economies because it was based on capitalism. "The secret of capitalism was in the establishment of the division of labor within the framework of a world-economy that was *not* an empire" (1974, 127). Banking, finance, and highly skilled industrial production became the specialty of western European nations, which became what Wallerstein calls the **core** of the world economy. The other regions constituted the **periphery** of the world economy, supplying the core with cheap food and raw materials. The core exploited (and continues to exploit) the periphery, draining off its wealth to support highly skilled "free" labor and a high standard of living. The periphery, by contrast, practices various forms of coerced labor to produce goods to support core industries, and the standard of living for coerced workers is generally low.

Wallerstein's model of the world system is functionalist, based on the metaphor that compares a society to a living organism. Functionalism compares various subsystems of society (such as economic and kinship systems) to the various organ systems of a living organism (such as digestive and reproductive systems). Wallerstein's search for a social system for which the metaphor seemed most apt eventually led him to speak of a world system. Only a world system (and not the individual communities within it) shows the necessary integration and self-sufficiency characteristic of a living organism. Wallerstein's analysis can thus be seen as a functionalist analysis raised to a high level. He believes that

---

dependency theory Argues that the success of "independent" capitalist nations has required the failure of "dependent" colonies or nations whose economies have been distorted to serve the needs of dominant capitalist outsiders.

development-of-underdevelopment thesis Argues that capitalism deliberately creates "underdevelopment" in formerly prosperous areas that come under its domination.

world-system theory Argues that, from the late fifteenth and early sixteenth centuries, European capitalism began to incorporate other regions and peoples into a world system whose parts were linked together economically but not politically.

core In world-system theory, the nations specializing in banking, finance, and highly skilled industrial production.

periphery In world-system theory, those exploited former colonies of the core that supply the core with cheap food and raw materials.

the world system is the only social entity in which the relationships posited by functionalist theory actually hold.

Nevertheless, Wallerstein has been criticized for setting forth a model of the modern world in which most of the action is over. For him, the periphery has long since been transformed into a series of specialized segments of the capitalist world economy. There remain only two possibilities for future development. First, various units within the system may change roles; that is, a core state may move to the periphery, or vice versa. Second, the system as a whole may be transformed into something else. This could come about, for instance, by a systemwide socialist revolution.

Neomarxian Theory

The work of Karl Marx and his followers has influenced all three of the theoretical perspectives described so far. Dependency theory and world-system theory both are sympathetic to Marx's insights, and borrow heavily from marxian theory. By contrast, modernization theory notes Marx's existence only to deny the relevance of his work in explaining social change in the modern world.

The anthropological perspective called **neomarxian theory** is based on the work of a new generation of marxian scholars. Although inspired by Marx's work, they nevertheless reinterpret or reject aspects of it when necessary. Of particular note are two French neomarxians, Louis Althusser and Etienne Balibar, whose reinterpretation of Marx offered them a new way of understanding social change in the non-Western world.

Althusser and Balibar (1971) reexamined the concept of mode of production. They concluded that, in the context of the former colonies, economic activity does not clearly represent any one of the classic modes of production. They saw colonial areas as social formations in which capitalist and noncapitalist modes of production had worked out a mode of coexistence. The capitalist mode of production introduced by the colonial power had linked up with indigenous noncapitalist modes of production, modifying them but not transforming them totally. The capitalist and noncapitalist modes linked up in this fashion are described as **articulating modes of production.**

Current Trends

Modernization theory was discredited for many anthropologists when its application seemed to worsen, rather than improve, the lives of the most vulnerable members of non-Western societies. Since the collapse of communism in eastern Europe, many marxian theorists have also had to rethink the bases of their perspective on social change. For their part, ordinary citizens of many so-called "underdeveloped" societies have tried to avoid both traditional capitalist and traditional marxian solutions for their problems, developing in the process a variety of what are called *new social movements*. From vigilante movements (such as the rondas campesinas of Peru) to squatter movements in cities to movements defending the rights of women and homosexuals to movements defending the rain forests, people have attempted to construct cultural institutions that meet their needs in ways that often bypass national governments or development agencies. (See EthnoProfile 12.6: Northern Peru [Rondas campesinas].)

Anthropologist Arturo Escobar (1992) argues that the new social movements in Latin America are struggles over meanings as well as material conditions. They challenge the previously unquestioned "truths" about development and underdevelopment that guided government policies throughout the cold war, whether these concerned the importance of market capitalism or the need for socialist revolution. Escobar sees these new social movements as products of conscious reflection by people who have been marginalized in the "development" schemes of outsiders and who have begun to build alternative forms of "modern" life based on their own values and goals. If some of these alternatives succeed, they may produce less exploitative forms of society in generations to come. That is what Scott (1985) saw as a possible long-term outcome of the everyday forms of peasant resistance he documented in "Sedaka" Village, Malaysia. (See EthnoProfile 12.4: "Sedaka" Village.)

MODES OF CHANGE IN THE MODERN WORLD

We can interpret much of contemporary human history as peoples' attempts to maintain meaningful social life in the face of cultural changes introduced by outsiders. Two major modes of change appear to be at work in the contemporary world. The first involves the power of persuasion; the second involves the power of the gun.

The Power of Persuasion

Although many varieties of modern social change are backed by force, people attempting to introduce change often rely more on tactics of persuasion. Members of non-Western societies have had to deal with two kinds of pressure to change: **sacred persuasion** (brought by religious missionaries) and **secular persuasion** (brought by secular authorities). Although the messages delivered by both means had much in common, particularly during the colonial era, they did at times clash with one another. And although their effectiveness was backed by the force of colonial conquest, sacred and secular persuasion have often led to resistance against its promoters. Christian missionary activity, for example, has produced non-Western converts who have taken the Christian message and turned it into a weapon to fight the domination of the West. Figures such as Archbishop Desmond Tutu in South Africa and liberation theologians in Latin America are some recent examples.

---

neomarxian theory A political economic theory based on the work of a new generation of marxian scholars who, though inspired by the work of Karl Marx, reinterpret or reject certain aspects of Marxist theory when necessary.

articulating modes of production An aspect of neomarxian thought that describes the links between capitalist and noncapitalist modes of production in the Third World.

sacred persuasion The attempt by Western religious missionaries to pressure non-Western societies to change.
secular persuasion The attempt by Western secular authorities to pressure non-Western societies to change.

FIGURE 14.3 *Missionary work has been carried out all over the world.*

Sacred Persuasion: Missionaries in Africa The Christian church was a powerful secular institution when young Western states pushed outward across the oceans to make their first territorial conquests. In the colonies of Spain in the New World, the church became a counterforce to be reckoned with when conquistadors attempted to set themselves up as New World feudal lords with indigenous peoples as their serfs. Missionaries of one sort or another accompanied Western expansion in the Americas, Asia, and Africa (Figure 14.3).

Anthropologist T. O. Beidelman (1982) examined the nature of missionary activity in Africa. He learned that all missionaries were not alike. Some mission stations were large and well funded, others were small and run on a shoestring. Catholic missionaries differed from Protestant missionaries, and the Protestants differed among themselves. In fact, there was often active antagonism between different denominations; they competed over souls to evangelize just as Europeans competed for access to raw materials for industry.

Africans found the celibacy of Catholic priests to be a curious practice. Nevertheless, Catholic missionaries were often able to develop close ties with African converts. Priests were unencumbered by families, well educated, of high status, and often spent their entire careers in a single area. They tended to be more tolerant of African custom, perhaps because they expected to achieve their goals in the long run.

By contrast, Protestant missions were eventually staffed by married couples or families. It was thought that those families would present positive role models for converts, yet in many cases the presence of women and children in mission stations widened the gulf between missionaries and converts. The missionaries felt the need to protect their wives and families from too-easy contact with Africans.

Born-again Protestant missionaries believed that although genuine conversion was an inner experience, it could only be proven by outward behavior. Thus, they tended to demand immediate behavior changes from their converts, taking outward action as an indication of the appropriate inner state. Their prototype of the ideal Christian was based on their own Western experience. Consequently, they often had difficulty deciding

EthnoProfile 14.2 • **KAGURU**

REGION: Eastern Africa

NATION: Tanzania

POPULATION: 100,000 (1960s)

ENVIRONMENT: Varied; about half plateau, some highlands and lowlands, jungle, meadow, savanna, river valley, bush

LIVELIHOOD: Agriculture (mostly maize)

POLITICAL ORGANIZATION: Traditionally some men with influence; now, part of a modern nation-state

FOR MORE INFORMATION: Beidelman, T. O. 1971. *The Kaguru.* New York: Holt, Rinehart and Winston.

whether certain outward cultural forms (including dress, diet, music, smoking, and alcohol consumption), could be acceptable for "true" Christians.

Beidelman observes that the whole reason for the existence of mission work "is the undermining of a traditional way of life. In this the missionary represents the most extreme, thorough-going, and self-conscious protagonist of cultural innovation and change. . . . The missionary, at least in the past, was unashamedly ethnocentric, though he saw the struggle to impose his values as loving and altruistic. He was cruel to be kind. His ethnocentrism and proselytization represent a blend of exclusion and inclusion, domination and brotherhood, and exploitation and sacrifice. Most curious of all, he exalted Western life but loathed many of its features; he felt a parallel fascination and contempt for simpler societies" (1982, 212).

Beidelman focused his attention on the Church Missionary Society (CMS), who had worked among the Kaguru of Tanzania, people among whom he had carried out fieldwork. (See EthnoProfile 14.2: Kaguru.) The CMS missionaries were "born-again Anglican Protestants" who first entered Kaguru territory in 1876, when life among the Kaguru was in turmoil. The Kaguru viewed the first missionaries as "white Arabs." For more than a quarter of a century, their lands had been traversed by Arab caravans linking the eastern African coast and the interior of the continent. The Kaguru had reason to dislike Arabs, primarily because of their slaving activities. Nevertheless, they had developed political and economic relations with the Arabs, and they treated the missionaries in the same way. From the missionary perspective, however, Arabs were evil, not only because they were slavers but also because they were Muslims. The CMS saw its role in eastern Africa as one of wresting control of the region not from Africans but from Arabs.

According to Beidelman, "Christian missions represent the most naive and ethnocentric, and therefore the most thorough-going, facet of colonial life. . . . Missionaries demonstrated a more radical and morally intense commitment to rule than political administrators or business men" (1982, 5). Although the CMS missionaries were ostensibly in Africa to save the souls of Africans, "strictly considered the missionaries were in the field to save themselves. . . . Evangelism was thus as much to build character as to convert. Failure to convert, even for decades, was seen as God's will, as a test of faith, and not as a reason either to abandon an area or to reassess methods" (99–100). Indeed, to some extent the missionaries seemed to expect martyrdom. Beidelman quotes from a missionary's letter home: "The resurrection of East Africa must be effected by our destruction" (65).

Such dedication made missionaries tirelessly devoted to changing the ways of Africans whose lives they viewed as brutal, ignorant, and miserable. Nevertheless, they were of two minds about their potential converts: they saw the Kaguru as childlike, and therefore in need of instruction and guidance, but in their supposed likeness to children, the Kaguru also appeared innocent. Beidelman remarks that it is unclear what the missionaries' real goals were. Did they want to convert the Kaguru totally to the modern Western way of life? Or was their goal a utopian, new Christian society, free of the materialism and corruption that, in their view, characterized the European society they had left behind? In any case, they had exacting standards against which Kaguru converts were to be measured.

In more than one instance, CMS missionaries found themselves at odds with secular colonial authorities. In their early years, when their areas came under German control, "the CMS, because of their alien nationality, continued to view themselves as divorced from the secular sectors of colonial life. Dissociation from government was important to the CMS for two reasons: first, it allowed them to pursue activities unassociated with the secular needs which they considered inimical to spiritual life; and second, that missionaries could struggle in the wilderness unprotected and unencouraged (even thwarted) by government was a sign of divine protection. (Beidelman 1982, 61)

Eventually, the CMS gained converts and established congregations. The missionaries introduced certain practices that the Kaguru embraced, the most important being the religious revival. Revival "could occur only after Africans had been converted and then strayed. . . . Revival allowed a congregation to revalidate publicly certain norms which had been threatened; it also allowed readmission of persons who had been judged unfit for mission life, but whose skills were essential" (Beidelman 1982, 106–7). Revivalism was similar to traditional Kaguru witchcraft confessions. It seems likely that converts had, perhaps unwittingly, carried into their new religion practices developed in the old. Since the 1930s and 1940s, revival has become an important political mechanism among the Kaguru. "Through revival and the resultant assumption of new, superior moral status as 'saved' or 'reborn' Christians . . . local Africans could sometimes compete with local African pastors, catechists, and even European missionaries as the type of Christian most fit to judge and lead others" (108).

Africans and CMS missionaries often had radically opposed views of what the missionary example stood for. The missionaries saw themselves living an austere, altruistic life, with little in the way of material comforts, and they expected their converts to do with even less. Thus, they expected converts to work for the mission for less money than nonconverts, contributing the balance out of their love for God. Such practices were viewed as stingy by many Kaguru, who also thought the missionary talk about brotherhood was hypocritical because however low missionary income was, African salaries were many times lower. "For Africans, the missionaries were failed Europeans. . . . Moreover, Africans saw the CMS as apparently not as well off as competing missions such as Roman Catholics" (Beidelman 1982, 68).

CMS missionaries supported revivalism, and yet they were wary of participating fully in revivals with Africans, lest their own admission of sin damage their prestige and authority. The CMS did not want to get involved in secular matters such as education, yet under the colonial regime it either provided the schools demanded by the colonial administration or lost government support. The CMS encouraged Bible study and direct inspiration by the word of God as set forth in the Bible, without the mediation of priests. But African converts who were literate were then able to read stories in the Bible about God redeeming his people from oppression. They began to identify with the oppressed and to see God as on their side. This was particularly disconcerting to the missionaries, who found themselves identified with the oppressors.

Perhaps the greatest irony revealed by Beidelman's study is that, following independence, Kaguru who rejected the rigorous CMS way of life were asked by the Tanzanian government to live in much the same way. They were to work hard, deny themselves material comforts, and resist the temptation to deviate from authority. "There are new kinds of missionaries afoot in Ukaguru. Some of the sermons now preached by socialist bureaucrats may appear new, but their tactics and aims are not that different from what has passed away" (1982, 209).

Secular Persuasion: Modernizing the Third World   Conquest established the fact of dominance. But to make that dominance profitable, the colonized peoples had to be molded into imperial subjects. This took persuasion. The colonial government relied in part on missionaries to win hearts and minds, but missionaries did not always see eye to eye with the colonial government. If we define colonization as cultural domination with enforced social change, then many nonmission projects were also engaged in winning hearts and minds—if not for God, then for capitalism.

Colonial authorities set about restructuring colonized territories in ways that would make those territories pay their way. To do this, they needed the active collaboration of the people. Sometimes this collaboration was not volunteered and forced labor was employed. Yet other times, colonial authorities sought to persuade their subjects of the utility of conforming with colonial aims. For certain classes of the conquered population, conformity brought new wealth and power. They were taught—and they asked to be taught—how to do things in the Western way. Having learned, they took steps to cajole or threaten others to follow their lead.

Foreign aid and development programs in the postcolonial period continue to follow this pattern. New states request help in industrial, agricultural, or social development from Western nations. Implicitly or explicitly, they are offering to do things in a Western manner if the Western powers will but show them how. Even then, however, things do not always go smoothly. Lynn Morgan (1993), for example, examines how health policy planners in "less-developed" countries have had to perform a tricky balancing act since the late 1940s. Health officials and politicians in these countries who want aid for health projects have been forced to address two audiences at once: local constitu-

EthnoProfile 14.3 • **COSTA RICA**

REGION: Central America

NATION: Costa Rica

POPULATION: 3,000,000

ENVIRONMENT: Tropical forests, central plains

LIVELIHOOD: Varies from banana plantation agriculture to industry, commerce, and so on

POLITICAL ORGANIZATION: A modern nation-state

FOR MORE INFORMATION: Morgan, Lynn M. 1993. *Community participation in health: The politics of primary care in Costa Rica.* Cambridge: Cambridge University Press.

encies and the international funding agencies. Consequently, any development project involves negotiation among international, national, and local groups. In order to qualify for funds, governments and national agencies must propose programs that meet the goals and criteria set by the international agencies. At the same time, however, they must also uphold national interests and deal with local goals. Morgan demonstrates how this attempt to serve two masters has led, in Costa Rica, to contradictions at nearly every level. (See EthnoProfile 14.3: Costa Rica.)

For example, the particular health policy initiatives for "popular participation" that were applied to Costa Rica in the 1970s were rooted in international politics. From the perspective of the United States government, emphasizing "popular participation" in development projects counterbalanced other elements of U.S. foreign policy, such as military training programs or the war in Vietnam. These considerations influenced the policies of such institutions as the United States Agency for International Development (AID), the United States Congress, the World Bank, the International Monetary Fund, and the World Health Organization. Although some saw popular participation as a mechanism for empowering rural communities, or as a way of stimulating democracy as the path to social equity, others, especially after the economic crises of the early 1980s, saw it as a way of getting rural communities to underwrite the costs of health services.

Morgan argues that "in spite of the Agency's [AID] professed commitment to respect national sovereignty and promote self-sufficiency, the U.S. government used its clout to reinforce and strengthen policies compatible with U.S. business and political interests" (1993, 61). Because the health policies were driven more by national and international politics than by input from rural communities, the paradoxical consequence in Costa Rica was that "popular participation" did not involve rural people. Program development, moreover, was undercut more by divisions within the national government than by opposition from rural communities.

Often, the secular powers are most concerned with economic development and it is new ways of making a living that the people are urged to adopt. We can call this *secular persuasion* to the extent that peasants, for example, are not forced to plant new strains of

EthnoProfile 14.4 • "LOS BOQUERONES"

REGION: Central America

NATION: Panama

POPULATION: 350 (1970s)

ENVIRONMENT: Tropical

LIVELIHOOD: Contradictory: farming for use (rice) and sale (sugar)

POLITICAL ORGANIZATION: Part of a modern nation-state

FOR MORE INFORMATION: Gudeman, Stephen. 1978. *The demise of a rural economy.* London: Routledge and Kegan Paul.

crops at gunpoint. Of course, to the extent that all other options are beyond their reach as a result of current social, political, and economic arrangements, the element of force is never totally out of the picture.

THE DEMISE OF A PEASANT ECONOMY   For modernization theorists, the replacement of the "insufficiently developed economic techniques" of "traditional society" by the market techniques of capitalism is a sign of progress. From their perspective, therefore, the demise of a rural economy in an underdeveloped country might be cause for rejoicing. For anthropologist Stephen Gudeman (1978), however, the meaning of such transformations is highly ambiguous. Gudeman's research allowed him to watch as his self-sufficient peasant informants were transformed into a rural labor force at the bottom of the capitalist order in Panama. (See EthnoProfile 14.4: "Los Boquerones.")

In Gudeman's view, this economic transformation involved going from production for use (or subsistence production) to production for exchange (or commodity production). The transformation was triggered by the introduction of a cash crop: sugarcane (Figure 14.4). Traditionally, the peasants raised enough rice and other food crops to tide them over from one harvest to the next. This is the essence of subsistence production: producing what one consumes and aiming to produce only enough of it to make it through the agricultural year. Once food needs and seed for the next season's planting have been met, the peasant need labor no more. The Panamanian peasants who were Gudeman's informants spent much of their "leisure time" celebrating saints' days commemorated in the Roman Catholic religious calendar.

These peasants were independent producers of subsistence goods, and they all produced much the same goods. Rice was the food of choice and the centerpiece of peasant farming, and a loft full of drying rice was the symbol of the just fruits of labor. Rice farming had been practiced by generations of peasants, who passed down their knowledge to their sons. Given this culturally shaped understanding of the earth and crops and weather, the peasants then had to choose how and when and what to plant, as well as when to weed and harvest. Culture provided rules of thumb to help them make

FIGURE 14.4 *As soon as peasants become dependent on the sale of cash crops for their livelihood—such as sugarcane, shown here being harvested on a Brazilian plantation—they become dependent on the capitalist market.*

such decisions. They would discuss the options endlessly with their neighbors, but ultimately the decisions were up to each individual peasant.

In subsistence economies, according to Gudeman, the cultural information pool does not expand. Subsistence production emphasizes not economic growth but production for *use*. The focus is on maintenance, on getting by—"to live, nothing more," as Gudeman's informants put it—in a situation of declining resources. Respectable people were people who were able to achieve this from one year to the next. Panamanian peasants pray to God for the strength to endure such repetitive work and to the saints for help in particular matters. "The Christ figure is a symbol of death and defeat more than resurrection and rebirth" (1978, 44).

But traditional Panamanian peasants had devised only one possible way of making a living on their land. This became clear when commercial sugarcane farming was introduced. The historical change from rice production for use to sugarcane production for exchange illustrates how two different modes of production can rely on different aspects of the natural environment. The choice of cash crop was in some respects decisive: sugarcane so alters the local ecology that land once planted in cane can never be used again for subsistence crops. Nevertheless, Gudeman does not make an ecological deterministic argument to explain the demise of the traditional rural economy; instead, he points out that before sugarcane cash-cropping, before even the establishment of traditional peasant subsistence farming, Spain had conquered Central America and carved up the land. The successors of these original conquistadors continued to own all the land on which Gudeman's peasant informants were merely entitled to use rights. This prior distribution of resources meant that peasants were sharply limited in what they could do with the land they farmed under traditional circumstances. It also meant that whenever a profit-making venture involving the land was in the offing, the landowners would control its development.

And so it was with sugarcane production. Wealthy Panamanian families owned the only two sugar mills to which farmers could sell their cane. Ironically, land reform promised to turn formerly landless peasants into small holders, but the plots they were to be allotted were too small to meet their subsistence needs. They were inexorably drawn into raising more and more sugarcane to sell for cash to buy what they needed. As this happened, the peasants' understandings of labor and time were transformed. Cane cultivation was fitted into the "free" time, the "slack" period that had surrounded the original rice-growing season. In capitalism, time is money, but in subsistence agriculture, time is the surplus left after a person has produced enough food and seed for the next season.

The new relations of production linking mill owners, peasant landowner-producers, and landless peasant laborers were based on the traditional landlord-peasant prototype. In sugarcane production, however, owning the mill was even more important than owning land because the production capacity and schedule of the mills determined the pace and level of local cane production. Gudeman writes: "With their financial command the mills are able to loan money for all stages of crop production. Effectively, they pay for and 'own' the seed, the labour invested and the product itself. At harvest time the peasant must turn over the product to liquidate these advances. Whether the final sums which [peasants] receive are to be termed profits or wages . . . is but a matter of terminology. Effectively all that the peasant as 'owner' does is subcontract his labour, and this, of course, saves the mills a certain amount of administrative cost" (1978, 139).

Production for exchange cannot be justified according to the system of values that peasants use to make sense of production for use: "Cane has 'utility' only when the peasant rids himself of it, the reverse of that which he does with rice" (Gudeman 1978, 121). What is required is a new frame of reference, new understandings about the meaning and end of labor. As soon as peasants became dependent on the sale of their sugarcane for their livelihood, they became dependent on the capitalist market, which had previously ignored them. The consequences are enormous, according to Gudeman: "This minimal shift in productive techniques actually represents and leads to a total economic transformation, for the peasants change their worldly conditions, from being independent, self-sufficient producers to becoming petty capitalists and day labourers" (122). Moreover, "as the peasant plants sugarcane, subsistence no longer refers to producing for consumption, it becomes only the standard of living. And this standard, which previously was defined in relation to others in the countryside and controlled by the individual labourer, now is defined in relation to other strata in Panamanian society and controlled by market prices in relation to the wage in sugarcane. . . . In this fashion a peasantry may become 'impoverished' by moving into capitalism. The 'underdevelopment' of a rural area may develop from the advent of capitalism itself" (140).

When Gudeman returned to the field in the mid-1970s, about a decade after his original study, he discovered that all the land was now owned by the government and devoted to raising sugarcane. In addition, the government had started its own mill. The shift from private enterprise to government ownership, plus a high world sugar price, had totally transformed the village economy. Gudeman calls it a transition from capitalism to state socialism. The government-owned mill controlled all aspects of sugarcane production. Because all available land had been planted with sugarcane, villagers could no longer depend on the countryside to support them. They now depended on the government.

As a result of these changes, Gudeman argues, the villagers can no longer be called peasants because they lack the peasants' self-sufficiency. Their livelihood now depends entirely on the sugarcane market. For every hectare of his land planted in sugarcane, a man receives 70 dollars at harvesttime from the mill. In addition, most men work at the mill; the labor is easier, wages are much higher owing to high world sugar prices, and there are more amenities, market goods, and health and pension benefits. Yet these improvements are fragile. They have been obtained at the price of lost self-sufficiency and seem sustainable only as long as sugar prices remain high. When sugar prices drop, as they must, these former peasants will have little to fall back on.

PEASANT DEFENSES AGAINST THE CHALLENGE OF CAPITALISM   If the situation of Panamanian peasants is prototypical, then Gudeman's picture of "development" in the periphery of the world system paints a dismal future for peasants everywhere in the non-Western world. His informants are an example of a peasantry that has been totally "captured" by the capitalist mode of production. But some neomarxian anthropologists question whether that fate is inevitable. Gudeman himself notes that one factor in the demise of peasant production for use in the village was the lack of institutionalized social relationships linking peasant families with one another. His informants thus lacked an established organizational framework on which they might have relied to defend their interests.

Strong suprafamilial social structures still flourish, however, in other societies of the periphery. It appears, for example, that indigenous kinship structures may sometimes be strong enough to allow peasants to defend their mode of production in the face of capitalist challenge. This seems to be the case among the Luo speakers of western Kenya, whose mode of livelihood was studied by anthropologist Steven Johnson (1988). (See EthnoProfile 14.5: Luo-Speaking Peoples.) In western Kenya, as in the interior of Panama, land is a crucial force of production both for subsistence and for exchange. All land is now privately owned, but peasants in need of land for production can choose how to

EthnoProfile 14.5 • **LUO-SPEAKING PEOPLES**

REGION: Eastern Africa

NATION: Kenya

POPULATION: 3,250,000

ENVIRONMENT: High plateau

LIVELIHOOD: Agriculture; maize, beans, sorghum (formerly, cattle herding)

POLITICAL ORGANIZATION: Traditionally some men with influence; today, elected subchiefs and chiefs, part of a modern nation-state

FOR MORE INFORMATION: Parkin, David. 1978. *Cultural definition of political response: Lineal destiny among the Luo.* New York: Academic Press.

obtain access to it: they can purchase it or rent it, or they can approach landowners who are members of their clan and ask that they be granted a plot for cultivation. This last system of land allocation does not treat land as a commodity, and use rights are distributed on the basis of traditional generalized reciprocity. Access to other forces of production are equally available in the same two ways. For example, ox-plow teams, seed, and even labor may be purchased on the market for cash, or else one may gain access to them without charge from neighbors or relatives.

Johnson argues that among his informants in western Kenya, "the importance of kinship obligations and generalized reciprocity suggest an association with a noncapitalist mode of production" (1988, 15). He describes his research area as a social formation characterized by two articulating modes of production: one capitalist and one noncapitalist. "The point of articulation between capitalist and noncapitalist modes of production is the peasant household where decisions are made regarding which set of social relationships is to be activated at particular points in the production process" (15). Kinship institutions are strong, and peasants remain committed to their kin as well as to ideas of prestige and autonomy that are apt in a kin-ordered mode of production. These sociocultural facts, together with the fact that peasants still exercise some control over the forces of production, have allowed them to prevent the demise of their rural economy despite the penetration of western Kenya by the capitalist mode of production.

The Power of the Gun

As with everything else in social life, the plausibility of theories about the destiny of colonized peoples depends on which aspects of their experiences are emphasized. A deterministic view holds that capitalism is bound to triumph, whether for good or for ill. But such a view is challenged by the last example, in which capitalism's advance seems to have stalled indefinitely. Even more challenging are cases in which the victims of cultural domination resist the dominators and reject the social changes being forced on them. Specifically, these were indigenous peoples who not only cut political ties to colonial or neocolonial rulers, but also attempted to cut economic ties to the entire capitalist world system. Such dramatic actions often involved the use of military force and might reasonably be called, as Eric Wolf (1969) calls them, *peasant wars.*

Wolf examined six cases of peasant revolution in the twentieth century: Mexico, Russia, China, Vietnam, Algeria, and Cuba. To understand these revolutions, he argues, requires looking at the historical developments leading up to them. In all six cases, those developments can be traced to the "world-wide spread and diffusion of a particular cultural system, that of North Atlantic capitalism," which was "profoundly alien to many of the areas which it engulfed in its spread" (1969, 276).

The prototypical situation in these cases is colonialism, understood as cultural domination with forced social change. The dominating cultural system in colonialism was capitalism. As a result, forced social change involved getting local peoples to accept the key capitalist metaphor: that land, people, and things can all be treated as objects for sale on the market. Most peasants who tried to live by this capitalist metaphor were ill equipped to withstand the risks and losses it entailed. Some peasants, however, were not only threatened by capitalism but had sufficient resources to try to resist it, by force if necessary. These were "middle peasants" who owned some land or peasants living in regions on the fringe of control by landlords. They acted not to usher in a new order but to make the world they knew safe for peasants like themselves. Once successful, however, their revolutionary actions made it impossible to return to the way of life they originally set out to defend.

The revolutions examined by Wolf all were waged by armed bands of peasants, but they probably would not have succeeded had not other indigenously organized social groups been fighting with them. Sometimes peasants fought alongside a "paramilitary party organized around a certain vision of what the new society is to be" (Wolf 1969, 296), such as the Bolsheviks in Russia. The Russian revolution was widely viewed as the first successful overthrow of capitalism. It thus became the earliest prototype for revolutionaries seeking to oust capitalists elsewhere. This was the case, for example, in the Chinese and Vietnamese revolutions: "A common Marxist ideology—and especially the Leninist concept of the revolutionary leadership, leading the masses in the interest of the masses—furnished a ready-made idiom in which to cast their own experience of fusion between rebel soldiery and revolutionary leadership" (297). But revolutionary leaders soon discovered that the Russian example could not be slavishly imitated. Thus, in China, for example, Mao concluded that peasants, rather than industrial workers, constituted the oppressed class in whose interest war would be waged.

Peasant revolutionaries were also able to draw on other traditional group structures and use them to organize their armed resistance. The idiom of socialism meshed nicely with communal idioms characteristic of traditional village organization in China and Vietnam, for example. What was revolutionary, however, was taking what had been a village idiom and applying it to relations linking villages with one another and with the army. Indeed, a large part of the subversive power of revolution comes from the way it allows new metaphors to enter social life through armed struggle. That is, it is not enough simply to declare that all people are brothers and sisters. Nor is it enough to preach that peasants, soldiers, workers, and intellectuals are equals. The experience that makes these metaphorical assertions plausible occurs for revolutionaries as they make their revolution. Wolf states, for example, that by the time they achieved victory in 1949, the citizen-soldiers of the Chinese revolution had lived through a variety of practical experiences that had turned ideological claims into reality: "The experience of war in the hinterland had taken them far from cities and industrial areas; it had taught them the advantages of dispersal, of a wide distribution of basic skills rather than a dense concentration of advanced skills. The citizen-soldiers of the guerrilla army had, in fact, lived lives in which the roles of peasant, worker, soldier, and intellectual intermingled to the point of fusion. . . . In China the relation of the peasant to the citizen-army was immediate and concrete" (1969, 300).

Wolf's study of these six peasant revolutions only reinforces the view that non-Western peoples who resist capitalism, with or without violence, have legitimate grievances. The anthropological assumption that all people, including peasants, are human beings, fully capable of recognizing when they are being taken advantage of, would lead us to expect no less. Yet from colonial times to the present day, those in power, whose ways are being rejected, have often experienced great difficulty accepting the humanity of dominated peoples. Ethnocentrism and anxiety about their own interests lead them to assume that because they are dominant, those they dominate must be lesser human beings. Lesser beings should be content with a lesser life and should not complain about their lot, which is suitable for them. If they do complain, the only explanation can be that someone from the outside is stirring them up. Underestimating the humanity of the world's disinherited classes, although comforting to those in power, can be tragically misleading.

Many of the case materials in this chapter demonstrate the human ability to cope creatively with changed life circumstances. They remind us that human beings are not passive in the face of the new, that they actively and resiliently respond to life's challenges. Nevertheless, the example of the Kréen-Akaróre and others like them reminds us that successful adaptation is never ensured. Modes of livelihood that may benefit some human groups can overwhelm and destroy others. Western capitalism has created a world system of powerful interlocking interests that resists easy control. A critical self-awareness of our common humanity, together with concerted practical action to lessen exploitation, may be all that can prevent the modern world system from destroying us all.

KEY TERMS

colonialism
capitalism
political economy
use rights
land tenure
neocolonialism
modernization theory

dependency theory
development-of-
   underdevelopment
   thesis
world-system theory
core
periphery

neomarxian theory
articulating modes of
   production
sacred persuasion
secular persuasion

CHAPTER SUMMARY

1. Modern Western history has been characterized by the rise of capitalism. The achievements of European capitalism were in many cases financed by wealth brought to Europe from other parts of the globe. As a result, other parts of the globe were also transformed.

2. The arrival of capitalism outside the West was often accompanied by the growth of new, commercially oriented cities, which became the focus of intense culture change. Western influence was usually greatest in such cities. The capitalist penetration of non-Western societies was frequently followed by the political conquest of such societies, which were then reshaped to streamline economic exploitation. Indigenous peoples were radically transformed as they lost their autonomy and were reintegrated as component groups within a larger new society.

3. The colonial order may be viewed as a political economy. Colonial empires drew together vast and previously unconnected areas of the world—economically and politically. Although colonies were politically controlled by the colonizers, political independence did not free former colonies from deeply entangling economic ties with their former masters. These entanglements have, in some cases, persisted for over 100 years and are called neocolonialism.

4. The key metaphor of capitalism is that the world is a market and everything within the world—including land, human beings, and material objects—can be bought and sold. Such a view was unknown in noncapitalist societies before Western colonialism, even in those with highly developed institutions. To function intelligibly within the capitalist world order, colonized peoples had to begin to see the world as a storehouse of potential commodities.

5. Western colonialism triggered a series of profound changes throughout the world. During its heyday in the late nineteenth century, early social scientists began to offer theories designed to explain these changes. Today, anthropologists use four major theoretical positions to explain culture change in the non-Western world: modernization theory, dependency theory, world-system theory, and neomarxian theory.

6. Although many varieties of modern social change are backed by force, people attempting to introduce change often rely more on tactics of persuasion. Missionaries accompanied Western colonizers wherever they went and attempted to persuade conquered peoples of the superiority of Western religious worldviews. Secular authorities likewise attempted to persuade conquered peoples of the superiority of capitalist economic and political institutions. Many colonized groups embraced these worldviews and institutions, often with unforeseen consequences.

7. Many anthropologists have assumed that capitalist takeover of traditional societies either has long since occurred or inevitably will occur in the future. Nevertheless, it seems some societies have successfully resisted capitalist takeover, either by maintaining noncapitalist modes of production alongside the capitalist mode or by using military force to eject the capitalists.

SUGGESTED READINGS

Bodley, John. 1988. *Tribal peoples and development issues.* Mountain View, CA.: Mayfield. *An excellent collection of articles—some recent, some dating back into the nineteenth century—providing examples of the effect of the modern world system on tribal peoples.*

———. 1990. *Victims of progress.* 3d ed. Mountain View, CA.: Mayfield. *A very accessible but very depressing documentation of the destruction of tribal peoples throughout the world, all in the name of progress.*

Hobart, Mark, ed. 1993. *An anthropological critique of development.* London: Routledge. *Anthropologists from Britain, Holland, and Germany challenge the notion that Western approaches to development have been successful. They use ethnographic case studies to demonstrate how Western experts who disregard indigenous knowledge contribute to the growth of ignorance.*

Wallerstein, Immanuel. 1974. *The modern world-system.* New York: Academic Press. *A difficult but tremendously influential work that started the world-system approach to understanding and explaining patterns of social change in recent Western history.*

Wolf, Eric. 1969. *Peasant wars of the twentieth century.* New York: Harper and Row. *An important, readable study of the commonalities of this century's major wars of revolution.*

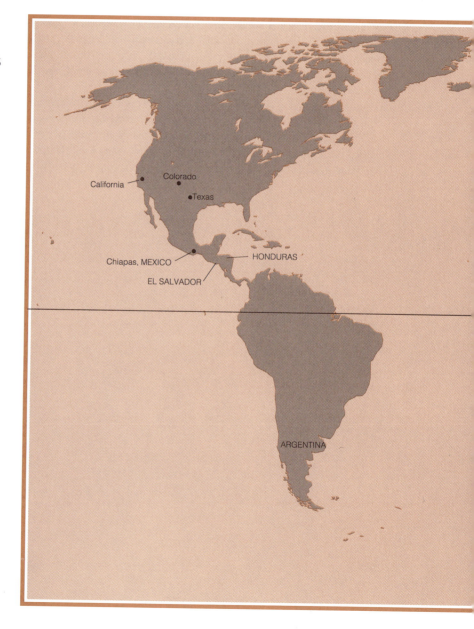

Anthropology in Everyday Life

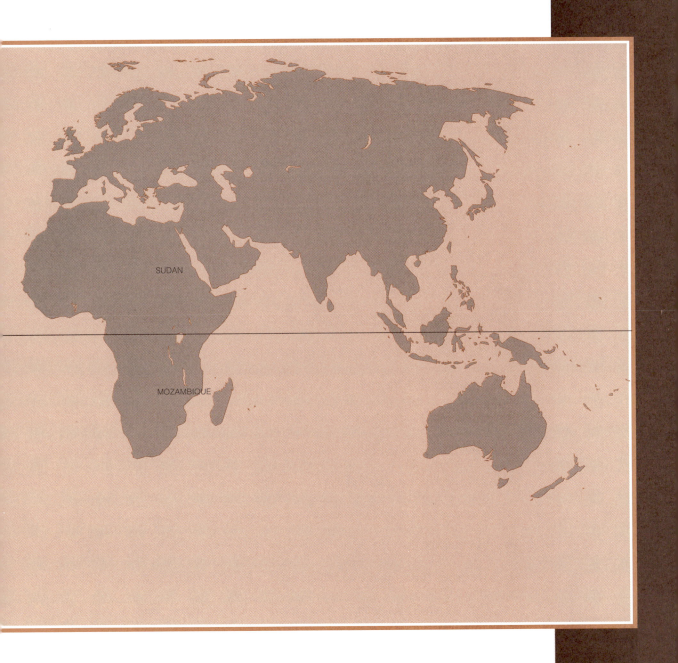

SUDAN

MOZAMBIQUE

many students say that they have found anthropology interesting—very interesting in fact—and that they have learned a great deal about ethnocentrism, other cultures, and even themselves. But they frequently ask what they can do with it. What is the point of it if they don't go on to university teaching? An appropriate response usually comes in three parts.

ANTHROPOLOGY BEYOND THE UNIVERSITY

Our first response addresses the practical concern: Do anthropologists do anything other than teach at universities? The answer is yes. Sir Edward B. Tylor, a founder of anthropology in the early 1870s, called the new field "a reformer's science." The commitment to changing things did not last, however. Anthropology soon concerned itself more with describing and explaining the world rather than changing it. Even so, there were always some anthropologists who believed their discipline had a practical side.

Margaret Mead saw anthropology's practical side throughout her long career. Following her first fieldwork in Samoa in the 1920s, she began to speak out on issues of concern in the United States. She suggested that adolescence in the United States did not have to be as stormy as it was and that perhaps we could learn from the Samoans about the nature of adolescence. Later in her career, she was a columnist for *Redbook,* a widely read magazine.

In the 1930s and 1940s, several American anthropologists played important roles in attempts to reform the U.S. Bureau of Indian Affairs. During World War II, Mead and other anthropologists were actively involved in the war effort. They developed strategies for boosting morale at home, and as the war ended, they helped draw up terms that would allow the Japanese to surrender with as little turmoil as possible.

After World War II, most anthropologists left government work and went back to their universities, becoming more concerned with the details of anthropological theory than anthropology's practical impact. During this period, the discipline grew at a phenomenal rate, but the growth of its practical applications lagged.

Anthropology in the United States was strongly affected by the events of the 1960s. The general distrust of authority at that time was tied to an increasing concern over the uses to which social science data were being put. These concerns increased during the war in Vietnam. For many anthropologists, as for professionals in many other disciplines, the times seemed to demand social action. Coupled with what Erve Chambers calls *four major events,* applied anthropology has become increasingly popular and important (1985, 9).

First, a gradual maturation of the discipline has led to a broader range of concerns, including those associated with regional, national, and even international systems. Second, the peoples with whom anthropologists have traditionally worked have become more sophisticated as they enter into the world system. Consequently, they are increasingly aware of the power imbalance between themselves and anthropologists. As noted in Chapter 3, anthropologists leave the cultures they study; local people cannot. In addition, although anthropologists have taken much from the societies they have studied, they have not always given much in return. Some anthropologists feel that the knowledge they have gained and the careers they have established as a result require greater return than a mention in a footnote. In some places, anthropologists have been called on to remedy this imbalance by demonstrating how their work will directly benefit the local community.

Third, more anthropologists have undertaken work in the United States. This trend is due in part to the difficulty of obtaining grants to support fieldwork outside the United States. (Anthropologists, like other scholars, find that they must sometimes make decisions based on factors that are outside the discipline. Sociopolitical, historical, or economic issues may sometimes prove as important as anthropological theory.) This trend also stems from a concern about our own society's problems and what an anthropological perspective might bring to their solution.

Fourth, over the past 20 years, there have been more new Ph.D. anthropologists and fewer academic jobs. As a result, students and professors realize that "the profession must either shrink or prepare its students for a greater variety of employment possibilities" (Chambers 1985, 10).

In answer to this need, applied anthropology programs have multiplied throughout the United States during the last decade. Today, anthropologists can be found in all sorts of areas. A few are psychotherapists, employing the insights of anthropologist Gregory Bateson and others on family systems and family therapy. Others are cross-cultural social workers. Still others are actively involved in international development, sometimes working with the U.S. Agency for International Development. Their work includes projects dealing with such issues as appropriate technology, fuelwood shortages, agricultural credit, new lands development, feasibility studies for dams and other projects, bilingual education, livestock improvement and range management, and the like (for more examples, see Partridge 1984; van Willigen 1991).

Other anthropologists are in medical anthropology, a new and rapidly growing field. Some applied medical anthropologists are involved in gerontology (Figure 15.1), designing programs for the elderly and doing research on aging in different cultures. Others work in public or community health, medical education, nursing, or hospital planning. Another important area of work is in medical care delivery to distinct ethnic groups. This is related to applied anthropological work in international health, which includes demographics, epidemiology, planning and development of health programs, family planning, environmental health, and the like. Many applied anthropologists are also working on AIDS-related projects.

Some anthropologists have gone into public policy and planning as interpreters, mediators, civil servants, or urban planners. Others have begun to work with indigenous peoples' organizations or with human rights organizations such as Survival International and Cultural Survival, itself founded by anthropologists David and Pia Maybury-Lewis. We examine two cases below in greater detail.

FIGURE 15.1 *Applied anthropologists work in a variety of settings. Here, gerontologist Dena Shenk interviews an informant while carrying out a research project for a local social service agency on the status of the rural elderly.*

Sorghum and Millet in Honduras and the Sudan

Applied anthropologists carry out much work in international development, often in agricultural programs. The U.S. Agency for International Development (AID) is the principal instrument of U.S. foreign development assistance. One new direction taken by AID in the mid-1970s was to create multidisciplinary research programs to improve food crops in developing countries. An early research program dealt with sorghum and millet, which are important grains in some of the poorest countries in the world. This was the International Sorghum/Millet Research Project (INTSORMIL). Selected American universities investigated one of six areas: plant breeding, agronomy, plant pathology, plant physiology, food chemistry, and socioeconomic studies.

Anthropologists from the University of Kentucky, selected for the socioeconomic study, used ethnographic field research techniques to gain firsthand knowledge of the socioeconomic constraints on the production, distribution, and consumption of sorghum and millet among limited-resource agricultural producers in the western Sudan and in Honduras. They intended to make their findings available to INTSORMIL as well as to scientists and government officials in the host countries. They believed sharing such knowledge could lead to more effective research and development. This task also required ethnographic research and anthropological skill.

The principal investigators from the University of Kentucky were Edward Reeves, Billie DeWalt, and Katherine DeWalt. They took a holistic and comparative approach, called *Farming Systems Research* (FSR). This approach attempts to determine the techniques used by farmers with limited resources to cope with the social, economic, and ecological conditions under which they live. FSR is holistic because it examines how the different crops and livestock are integrated and managed as a system. It also relates farm productivity to household consumption and off-farm sources of family income (Reeves, DeWalt, and DeWalt 1987, 74). This is very different from the traditional methods of agricultural research, which grow and test one crop at a time in an experiment station. The scientists at INTSORMIL are generally acknowledged among the best sorghum and millet researchers in the world, but their expertise comes from traditional agricultural research methods. They have spent little time working on the problems of limited-resource farmers in Third World countries.

The anthropologists saw their job as facilitating "a constant dialog between the farmer, who can tell what works best given the circumstances, and agricultural scientists, who produce potentially useful new solutions to old problems" (Reeves, DeWalt, and DeWalt 1987, 74–75). However, this was easier said than done in the sorghum/millet project. The referential perspectives of farmers and scientists were very different from one another. The anthropologists found themselves having to learn the languages and the conceptual systems of both the farmers and the agricultural scientists in order for the two groups to be able to communicate with each other. The FSR anthropologists had the following research goals:

1. To find those things that were holding back the increased production of sorghum and millet so that they could identify areas that needed attention from the agricultural researchers
2. To discover which aspects of new technology the farmers thought might benefit them the most
3. To suggest how new crop "varieties and/or technologies might most easily and beneficially be introduced into communities and regions"
4. "To suggest the long-term implications that changing production, distribution, and consumption patterns might have on these communities" (1987, 74)

The anthropologists began research in June 1981 in western Sudan and in southern Honduras. They were in the field for 14 months of participant-observation and in-depth interviewing, as well as survey interviewing of limited-resource farmers, merchants, and middlemen. They discovered that the most significant constraints the farmers faced were uncertain rainfall, low soil fertility, and inadequate labor and financial resources (Reeves, DeWalt, and DeWalt 1987, 80). Equally important were the social and cultural systems within which the farmers were embedded. Farmers based their farming decisions on their understanding of who they were and what farming meant in their own cultures.

As a result of the FSR group's research, it became increasingly clear that "real progress in addressing the needs of small farmers in the Third World called for promising innovations to be tested at village sites and on farmers' fields under conditions that closely approximated those which the farmers experience" (Reeves, DeWalt, and DeWalt 1987, 77). Convincing the scientists and bureaucrats of this required the anthropologists to become advocates for the limited-resource farmers. Bill DeWalt and Edward Reeves ended up negotiating INTSORMIL's contracts with the Honduran and Sudanese governments and succeeded in representing the farmers. They had to learn enough about the bureaucracies and the agricultural scientists so they could put the farmers' interests in terms the others could understand.

As a result of the applied anthropologists' work, INTSORMIL scientists learned to understand how small farmers in two countries made agricultural decisions. They also learned that not all limited-resource farmers are alike. The poorest third of the Sudanese farmers, for example, have to decide during the cropping season whether to weed their own gardens or someone else's for a wage. If they choose the former, they realize a long-term gain but they and their families go hungry. The latter choice enables them to buy food in the short run but lowers their own harvests later. The decisions farmers make, and the needs they have, are context sensitive.

Together with INTSORMIL, the Honduran and Sudanese governments have increased funding for projects aimed at limited-resource farmers. Staff have been assigned to work with INTSORMIL, new programs have begun, and the research results of the anthropologists are guiding the breeding of sorghum.

Reeves, DeWalt, and DeWalt warn that it is too early to demonstrate gains in sorghum or millet production and use in either country. "Nevertheless, INTSORMIL scientists are clearly coming to accept the farming systems research goals and the value of anthropological fieldwork. The FSR Group has argued that on-site research is both desirable and necessary for the problems of farmers to be correctly identified and that eventually on-farm testing of new plant varieties and technologies will be essential to ensure that farmers are going to accept them" (1987, 79).

The INTSORMIL staff was so impressed by the anthropologists' work that it has begun funding long-term research directed at relieving the constraints that limited-resource farmers face. Rather than trying to develop and then introduce hybrids, INTSORMIL research is now aimed at modifying the existing varieties of sorghum. The goal is better-yielding local varieties that can be grown together with other crops.

In summary, Reeves, DeWalt, and DeWalt point out that without the anthropological research, fewer development funds would have been allocated to research in Sudan and Honduras. More important, the nature of the development aid would have been different.

Lead Poisoning among Mexican American Children

In the summer of 1981, a Mexican American child was treated for lead poisoning in a Los Angeles emergency room. When the child's stomach was pumped, a bright orange powder was found. It was lead tetroxide, more than 90 percent elemental lead. Lead in that form is not found in the three most common sources of lead poisoning in children in the United States: eating lead-based paint chips, living and playing near a smelter where even the dust has a high lead content, and eating off pottery with an improperly treated lead glaze. Under questioning by health professionals, the mother revealed that her child had been given a folk remedy in powdered form—*azarcon.* Azarcon was used to treat an illness called *empacho,* part of the Mexican American set of culturally recognized diseases. Empacho is believed to be a combination of indigestion and constipation.

This case prompted a public health alert that was sent out nationally to clinics and physicians. The alert turned up another case of lead poisoning from azarcon in Greeley, Colorado. A culturally sensitive nurse had read about the Los Angeles case and asked if the mother was treating the child for empacho. She was. Additional questioning in Los Angeles and Greeley turned up what appeared to be widespread knowledge of azarcon in both Mexican American communities. The U.S. Public Health Service decided that an anthropological study of azarcon would be useful.

The Public Health Service in Dallas called Dr. Robert Trotter, who had done research on Mexican American folk medicine. Trotter had never heard of azarcon. Although he checked in all the herb shops where folk medicines are sold in four towns and talked with folk healers, he did not find it in south Texas. Trotter was relieved that the problem seemed to be confined to the western United States.

A short time later, Trotter received a packet of information from the Los Angeles County Health Department, which had discovered that there were several different names for the same preparation. When he went back to the herb shops and asked for *greta,* he was sold a heavy yellow powder that turned out to be lead oxide with an elemental lead content of approximately 90 percent. The shop owners said it was used to treat empacho. Here was confirmation that two related lead-based remedies were being used to treat empacho. Trotter discovered that a wholesale distributor in Texas was selling greta to over 120 herb shops.

Trotter was asked to work in a health education project designed to reduce the use of these lead-based remedies. Because of the complex nature of the problem, he had six different clients with somewhat different needs and responsibilities. The first client was the Public Health Service office in Dallas, which sponsored the first study he did.

The second client was the task force that had been formed to create and implement a health education project in Colorado and California. Task force members wanted to reduce the use of azarcon. In doing so, however, they did not want to attack or denigrate the folk medical system that promoted the use of azarcon. They knew that attacking folk beliefs would produce strong resistance to the entire health campaign and make people ignore the message, no matter how important it was. The task force hoped Trotter's ethnographic data on Mexican American folk medicine could help design a health awareness campaign that would encourage a switch to nonpoisonous remedies.

The goal of the task force became product substitution—to convince people to switch from greta or azarcon to another, harmless remedy for empacho that was already part of the folk medical system. This strategy was based on an old advertising technique: It is easier to get people to switch from one product to another when both products perform the same function; it is difficult or impossible to get people to stop using a product they think they need, regardless of its known danger, unless an acceptable alternative is provided. As Trotter points out, it is easy to get a smoker to switch from Camel filters to Winstons, but very hard to get that person to stop smoking altogether (1987, 148).

The Food and Drug Administration (FDA), Trotter's third client, decided it needed basic ethnographic information on the use of greta. The staff wanted to know who used it, what it was used for, how it was used, and where it could be purchased. The FDA had never considered that lead oxide could be a food additive or a drug, and it needed verifiable data that the compound was being used in this way. As a result of Trotter's research, the FDA concluded that greta was a food additive. It issued a Class I recall to ban the sale of greta as a remedy.

Client number four was the Texas regional office of the Department of Health and Human Services. It needed assistance in creating and carrying out a survey along the United States-Mexico border to discover what people knew about greta and azarcon and how many people used them. Trotter's survey indicated that as many as 10 percent of the Mexican American households along the border had at one time used greta or azarcon. The survey also turned up several other potentially toxic compounds that were in use.

Trotter's fifth client was the Hidalgo County Health Care Corporation, a local migrant clinic. It needed a survey that would compare the level of greta and azarcon usage in the local population in general with the level of usage among the people who came to the clinic. Trotter found that the two groups did not differ significantly in their knowledge about and use of the two preparations; however, the clinic population was more likely to treat folk illnesses with folk medicines than was the population at large.

The sixth client was the Migrant Health Service. It needed to know whether it was necessary to design a nationwide lead project. Based on the research that Trotter and others did, it became clear that such a major project was not necessary; rather, health projects were targeted and health professionals notified in the areas of high greta and azarcon use only.

Because Trotter had several clients, his work led to a variety of outcomes. The health education project resulted in considerable media exposure on the dangers of greta and azarcon. Public service announcements were broadcast on Spanish-language radio stations, special television programs aired in Los Angeles county, and information packets were sent to migrant clinics. Trotter commissioned Mexican American students at the Pan American University to design a culturally appropriate poster warning of the dangers of greta and azarcon. The poster, using the culturally powerful symbol of *La Muerte* (a skeleton) to warn of the dangers, has been placed in over 5,000 clinics and other public access sites (Trotter 1987, 152).

The various health education measures may be judged successful by the fact that, two years after the project began, both greta and azarcon were hard to find in the United States. In addition, the various surveys Trotter carried out led to better screening procedures for lead poisoning. Information on traditional medications is now routinely gathered when lead poisoning is suspected, and several other potentially toxic compounds have been discovered. Health professionals were able to learn about the current use of traditional medications in their areas and about the specific health education needs of their clients.

"Perhaps the most important overall result of the project was an increased awareness of the utility of anthropology in solving culturally related health care problems in at least one segment of the medical care delivery system. . . . Our discovery of the use of greta and azarcon and the subsequent discoveries that similar remedies are causing lead poisoning in Hmong, Saudi Arabian, and Chinese communities have finally demonstrated a clear link between anthropological research and the dominant biophysical side of modern medicine. Anthropological knowledge, research methods, and theoretical orientations are finally being used to solve epidemiological problems overlooked by the established disciplines" (Trotter 1987, 154).

Trotter brought to the project the skills of the anthropologist; his principal focus was on culture. He took a holistic, comparative approach, and he was willing to innovate, to look for explanations in areas that investigators from other disciplines had not thought to look.

Anthropology and Policy

In all this work—and there is much more—the same anthropological perspective illustrated throughout this book has been employed. Applied anthropologists do their work using holism, comparison, relativism, and a concern for particular cases.

Nevertheless, anthropologists are hesitant to make detailed policy recommendations that other professional disciplines make. This may be because anthropologists are particularly aware of the problems in applied work, the problems in trying to make people, or systems, change. Anthropologists are trained to analyze social and cultural systems, but when they are asked how to change them, they begin to ask questions. The questions they ask are based on an awareness of the enormous complexity of human life when it is viewed from ground level. Anthropologists have developed a keen awareness that not everyone makes the same basic assumptions about the world that planners and officials make. They are aware that sometimes technical experts providing help in other cultures know less than the people they are advising or give advice that is culturally inappropriate. Anthropologists realize that no change benefits everyone equally, that some gain as others lose. They also understand that even if they get involved in planning a program, implementation depends on external factors over which they have no control: cash flow problems to the AID office, fear over a congressman's response, political issues, elections, budget reductions, lack of interest, and so on.

Anthropologists believe they have much to contribute in helping build a better world, yet they are also highly sensitive to the kinds of issues that arise when dealing with the complex human systems we have discussed throughout this text. Applied anthropologists are well aware of the ambiguities of the human experience.

Anthropology and Human Rights

Recently, anthropologists have been involved in expanding the understanding of human rights and have participated in organizations for the defense of human rights. In particular, they have contributed to the recognition by human rights legal advocates that the collective rights of groups (such as indigenous peoples) deserve as much attention as the rights of individuals. Ellen Messer observes that anthropologists have examined, and continue to examine, the "contexts of human rights abuses, to understand how the political economic conditions that create cultural customs such as infanticide, underfeeding of women and children, and other abuses of women might be improved and make the customs of less evident utility. They also continue to work with interpreters of local traditions, so that through persuasion and contextualization, and by drawing on the authority of multiple traditions, people might be empowered to improve human rights in their own lives" (1993, 24).

In Their Own Words **GROUP RIGHTS AND INDIVIDUAL RIGHTS**

Citizens of the United States are familiar with the concept of individual human rights, but the concept of group rights is less familiar and may even seem threatening. Marc S. Miller describes what group rights mean and argues that "individual rights mean little without group rights."

The concept of group rights, like those rights themselves, needs defining. Simply, group rights are those rights we enjoy, or are denied, because we are identified in some way with others. For indigenous people (the "target population" for the social scientists who founded Cultural Survival), group rights include the ability of an indigenous society to maintain its language, spiritual practices, economic systems, and so forth. In the absence of these rights, societies die. Group rights also include the rights of women, people of color, elders, and so forth to protection from any discrimination based on their shared membership in a collective identity.

Group rights relate to the rights of individuals, and they involve far more than just a moral assertion that cultures have a right to exist. Rather, group rights are a practical principle in-

volving individuals: without their collective culture to support them, individuals are at risk. As E. P. Thompson and other historians have pointed out, the making of an English working class required the undermining of a previous agrarian, communal culture. For U.S. Indians, Australian Aborigines, and a host of other indigenous peoples, breaking down the patterns of tradition-based human interactions often leads to high rates of unemployment, suicide, alcoholism, and infant mortality.

On a fundamental level individual rights mean little without group rights. It is certainly possible, for example, and all-too-common, for individuals to go to court, one after another to defend the same constitutional rights. But even if each plaintiff has a reasonable chance of winning, the process is inefficient, and each case may leave an unjust law standing or a host of criminals untouched. In rare instances, like *Brown vs. the Topeka Board of Education,* the edifice supporting widespread rights violations may be undermined when the plaintiffs marshall the breadth of resources needed to get to the Supreme Court. More often, the next vic-

tim of the same injustice has to repeat the fight.

It *is* a praiseworthy endeavor to defend the rights of every oppressed individual. Indeed, most rights advocates choose to highlight the cases of particularly endangered individuals to draw attention to a broader denial. This strategy mobilizes tens or hundreds of thousands of well-meaning people in the United States and Europe to defend the rights of perhaps thousands of wronged individuals, sometimes in their own countries, more often in other states. Such work has yielded many significant victories, but like one person's lawsuit, the approach is inefficient and not up to the enormity of rights violations throughout the world.

The strategy underlying a focus on group rights is to mobilize the same tens of thousands of concerned Americans and Europeans to stop the abuse of millions of people throughout the world—and perhaps to prevent more of these violations from ever occurring.

Source: Marc Miller 1993, 1.

Perhaps one of the foremost anthropologically oriented organizations involved with human rights is Cultural Survival, founded in 1972 by anthropologists Pia and David Maybury-Lewis (Figure 15.2a) and dedicated to helping indigenous people and ethnic minorities deal as equals in their encounters with industrial society. Anthropologist Carolyn Nordstrom (1993) writes about the efforts of the Ministry of Education in Mozambique and the Mozambican Woman's Organization to begin programs to assist children and women traumatized, raped, displaced, and impoverished by the 16-year war in that country. She discusses how indigenous healers have come to develop spe-

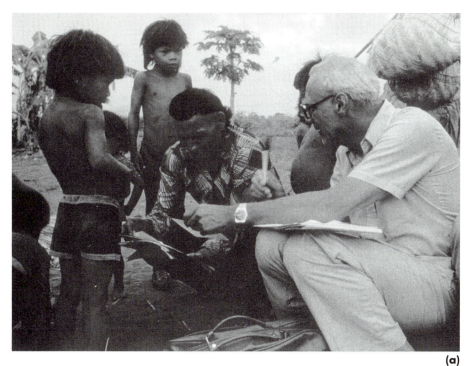

(a)

(b)

FIGURE 15.2 *Anthropologists have become increasingly involved in the defense of human rights. (a) David Maybury-Lewis (pictured here with Xavante informants in Brazil) and Pia Maybury-Lewis founded Cultural Survival, an organization dedicated to helping indigenous peoples and ethnic minorities deal as equals in their encounters with industrial society. (b) In February 1994, forensic anthropologist Clyde Snow investigated the death of peasants following the Mexican army's battle with the Emiliano Zapata Liberation Army in the state of Chiapas.*

cialties in war trauma, "to take the violence out of people," and are being brought into the national health-care system.

Biological anthropologists, most notably Clyde Snow, have also contributed in an important way to the defense of human rights in the world. Snow is a consulting forensic anthropologist who is often called on by police departments, medical examiners, and other law enforcement officials to try to identify human remains and to determine the cause of death. He is helped in this task by his knowledge of (1) human skeletal features to determine sex, age, and population subgroup and (2) the different ways trauma can affect the human skeleton.

In recent years, Snow has been involved in a number of international human rights cases. Beginning in 1984, he worked with the American Association for the Advancement of Science to help the Argentinian National Commission on Disappeared Persons to determine the fate of some of the more than 10,000 people who had vanished during the "dirty war" waged by the Argentine military government against supposed subversives. Snow began his work in Argentina by training a team of medical and anthropology students in the techniques of forensic investigation, both skeletal and archaeological, and then helped them exhume and examine scores of the remains of the *desaparecidos* ("those who have disappeared"). By 1988, only 25 victims had been positively identified, but those identifications helped convict seven members of the former ruling junta and other high-ranking military and police officers (Huyghe 1988).

The Argentine team Snow trained has gone on to investigate sites of massacres in Guatemala, Bolivia, Panama, Iraq, and, most recently, the site of the massacre at El Mozote, El Salvador. Snow himself was in Chiapas in February 1994 to investigate the death of peasants following the Mexican army's battle with the Emiliano Zapata Liberation Army in early January (Figure 15.2b). Snow states, "There are human-rights violations going on all around the world. But to me murder is murder, regardless of the motive. I hope that we are sending a message to governments who murder in the name of politics that they can be held to account" (Huyghe 1988).

UNCERTAINTY AND AWARENESS

Why study anthropology? The second part of our answer is personal.

Studying cultural anthropology brings students into contact with different ways of life. It makes them aware of just how arbitrary their own understanding of the world is as they learn how other people have developed satisfying but different ways of living. In addition, if they are from Western countries that were responsible for colonialism and its consequences, it makes them painfully aware of just how much their own tradition has to answer for in the modern world.

Knowing and experiencing cultural variety gives rise, perhaps inevitably, to doubt. We come to doubt the ultimate validity of the central truths of our own cultural tradition, which have been ratified and sanctified by the generations who preceded us. We doubt because a familiarity with alternative ways of living makes the ultimate meaning of any action, of any object, a highly ambiguous matter. Ambiguity is part and parcel of the human condition. Human beings have coped with ambiguity from time immemorial by

In Their Own Words   INTO THE WARP AND WOOF OF MULTICULTURAL WORLDS

Changes in the contemporary world are producing what anthropologist George Marcus calls "transcultural 'traditional' peoples," whose members live in many different places and whose sense of cultural identity involves a mix of many cultural elements.

The power of global cultural homogenization in the late twentieth century challenges the conventions and rationales by which anthropology has so far produced its knowledge of other cultures. The reorganization of the world economy through technological advances in communication, production processes, and marketing has thoroughly deterritorialized culture. For example, the Tongan islanders of Polynesia that I studied in the early 1970s now constitute a diaspora of communities in locales around the Pacific rim. As many, if not more, Tongans now live permanently in Australia, New Zealand, and the United States as in the islands themselves. One might fairly ponder where both the cultural and geographical center of the Tongan people resides. Their identity is produced in many locales and through the mix of many cultural elements. And their conditions are similar to those of numerous other peoples that anthropologists have traditionally studied. It is no longer just the most powerful, large-scale, and most modern societies, such as the United States and Japan, that exist in international, transcultural science.

Among such transcultural "traditional" peoples, levels of cultural self-consciousness and alternatives increase. The authenticity of performances, rituals, or apparently deep seated norms like those of kinship cannot be merely assumed, either by locals or by visitors such as anthropologists. To some extent, media documentaries have absorbed anthropology's function of presenting vividly the lifeways of other cultures to Euro-American publics that themselves can no longer be considered as homogeneous or mainstream. And, finally, the subjects of anthropological study independently and articulately translate their own perspectives with sensitivity to the effects of different media.

Peoples who in particular have become classic anthropological subjects, such as the Samoans, Trobriand Islanders, Hopi, and Todas of India, know their status well, and have, with some ambivalence, assimilated anthropological knowledge about them as part of their sense of themselves. A recent example was the visit of a Toda woman to Houston. A trained nurse among her people as well as a cultural broker, she was on tour in the United States, giving talks about the Todas, of the sort that anthropologists might have given in past decades. By chance, she was visiting the home of a colleague just as a British documentary about the Todas appeared on the television—a documentary in which the visitor was featured prominently as the filmmaker's prime source of information. The visitor's comments as she watched the program along with my colleague did not much concern the details of Toda culture, but rather dealt with the ironies of the multiple representations of her people—by herself, by anthropologists, and by the British Broadcasting Corporation.

The lesson of this story is compelling. The penetrations of a world economy, communications, and the effects of multiple, fragmented identities on cultural authenticity, once thought restricted to advanced modernity, have increased markedly among most local and regional cultures worldwide. They have thus engendered an ethnography in reverse among many peoples who not only can assimilate the professional idioms of anthropology but can relativize them among other alternatives and ways of knowledge. This does not mean that the traditional task of anthropology to represent distinctive and systematic cultural forms of life has been fundamentally subverted by its own subjects. Rather, anthropology's traditional task is now much more complicated, requiring new sensibilities in undertaking fieldwork and different strategies for writing about it.

Source: Marcus 1990.

means of culture, which places objects and actions in contexts and thereby makes their meanings plain. This doubt can lead to anxiety, but it can also be liberating.

FREEDOM AND CONSTRAINT

Why study anthropology? The third part of our response is, for want of a better word, humanistic.

All human beings, ourselves included, live in culturally shaped worlds, enmeshed in webs of interpretation and meaning that we have spun. It has been the particular task of anthropology and its practitioners to go out into the world to bear witness to and record the vast creative diversity in world-making that has been the history of our species. In our lifetimes, we will witness the end of many of those ways of life—and if we are not careful, of all ways of life. This loss is tragic, for as these worlds disappear, so too does something special about humanity: variety, creativity, and awareness of alternatives.

Our survival as a species, and our viability as individuals, depends on the possibility of choice, of perceiving and being able to act on alternatives in the various situations we encounter during our lives. If, as a colleague has suggested, human life is a mine field, then the more paths we can see and imagine through that mine field, the more likely we are to make it through—or at least to have an interesting time trying. As alternatives are destroyed, wantonly smashed, or thoughtlessly crushed, *our* own human possibilities are reduced. A small group of men and women have for the last century labored in corners of the world, both remote and nearby, to write the record of human accomplishment and bring it back and teach it to others.

Surely our greatest human accomplishment is the creation of the sometimes austerely beautiful worlds in which we all live. Anthropologists have rarely given in to the romantic notion that these other worlds are all good, all life enhancing, all fine or beautiful. They are not. Ambiguity and ambivalence are, as we have seen, hallmarks of the human experience. There are no guarantees that human cultures will be compassionate rather than cruel, or that people will agree they are one or the other. There are not even any guarantees that our species will survive. But all anthropologists have believed that these are *human* worlds that have given those who have lived in them the ability to make sense out of their experiences and to derive meaning for their lives, that we are a species at once bound by our culture and free to change it.

This is a perilous and fearsome freedom, a difficult freedom to grasp and to wield. Nevertheless, the freedom is there, and in this dialectic of freedom and constraint lies our future. It is up to us to create it.

SUGGESTED READINGS

Cultural Survival Quarterly. *A committed voice for the survival of indigenous peoples. A magazine with a relatively wide circulation,* Cultural Survival Quarterly *always publishes provocative and important material.*

Van Willigen, John. 1986. *Applied anthropology: An introduction.* South Hadley, MA: Bergin & Garvey. *A thorough introduction to applied anthropology, including different applied approaches, ethics, and the job search.*

Van Willigen, John, Barbara Rylko-Bauer, and Ann McElroy. 1989. *Making our research useful.* Boulder, CO: Westview Press. *A collection of valuable articles in applied anthropology.*

Wolfe, Robert, and Shirley Fiske. 1987. *Anthropological praxis.* Boulder, CO: Westview Press. *An excellent collection of essays by applied anthropologists about their projects. The articles are written in a consistent format, which makes them especially valuable.*

Bibliography

Adams, Richard Newbold. 1977. Power in human societies: A synthesis. In *The anthropology of power: Ethnographic studies from Asia, Oceania, and the New World,* edited by R. Fogelson and R. N. Adams, 387–410. New York: Academic Press.

———. 1979. *Energy and structure: A theory of social power.* Austin: University of Texas Press.

Ahmed, Syed Zubar. 1994. What do men want? *New York Times,* 15 February.

Akmajian, A., R. Demers, and R. Harnish. 1984. *Linguistics.* 2d ed. Cambridge: MIT Press.

Alland, Alexander. 1977. *The artistic animal.* New York: Doubleday Anchor Books.

Allen, Catherine J. 1988. *The hold life has: Coca and cultural identity in an Andean community.* Washington, DC: Smithsonian Institution Press.

Althusser, Louis, and Etienne Balibar. 1971. *Reading capital.* London: New Left Books.

Alverson, Hoyt. 1977. Peace Corps volunteers in rural Botswana. *Human Organization* 36 (3): 274–81.

———. 1978. *Mind in the heart of darkness.* New Haven: Yale University Press.

———. 1990. Guest editorial in *Cultural anthropology: A perspective on the human condition,* by Emily Schultz and Robert Lavenda, 43. 2d ed. St. Paul: West.

Aufderheide, Patricia. 1993. Beyond television. *Public Culture* 5: 579–92.

Autobiografías campesinas. 1979. Vol. 1. Heredia, Costa Rica: Editorial de la Universidad Nacional.

Avery, Laurence, and James Peacock. 1980. Drama: Aristotle in Indonesia. In *Not work alone,* edited by J. Cherfas and R. Lewin, 181–98. Beverly Hills: Sage Publications.

Bailey, F. G. 1969. *Strategems and spoils: A social anthropology of politics.* New York: Shocken Books.

Barnes, Barry, and David Bloor. 1982. Relativism, rationalism and the sociology of knowledge. In *Rationality and Relativism,* edited by Martin Hollis and Steven Lukes, 21–47. Cambridge: MIT Press.

Bascom, William. 1969. *The Yoruba of southwestern Nigeria.* New York: Holt, Rinehart and Winston.

Basham, Richard. 1978. *Urban anthropology.* Palo Alto, CA: Mayfield.

Bateson, Gregory. 1972. *Steps to an ecology of mind.* New York: Ballentine Books.

Baxter, P. T. W. 1978. Boran age-sets and generation-sets: *Gada,* a puzzle or a maze? In *Age, generation and time,* edited by P. T. W. Baxter and Uri Almagor, 151–82. New York: St. Martin's Press.

Baxter, P. T. W. and Uri Almagor, eds. 1978. *Age, generation and time.* New York: St. Martin's Press.

Beals, Alan. 1962. *Gopalpur, a south Indian village.* New York: Holt, Rinehart and Winston.

Beidelman, T. O. 1971. *The Kaguru.* New York: Holt, Rinehart and Winston.

———. 1982. *Colonial evangelism.* Bloomington: Indiana University Press.

Bellman, Beryl. 1975. *Village of curers and assassins: On the production of Fala Kpelle cosmological categories.* The Hague: Mouton.

———. 1984. *The language of secrecy.* New Brunswick: Rutgers University Press.

Belmonte, Thomas. 1978. *The broken fountain.* New York: Columbia University Press.

Berlin, Brent. 1978. Ethnobiological classification. In *Cognition and categorization,* edited by E. Rosch and B. Lloyd, 9–26. Hillsdale, NJ: Lawrence Erlbaum Associates.

Blanchard, Kendall. 1974. Basketball and the culture change process: The Rimrock Navajo case. *Council on Anthropology and Education Quarterly* 5 (4): 8–13.

———. 1981. *The Mississippi Choctaw at play: The serious side of leisure.* Urbana: University of Illinois Press.

Blanchard, Kendall, and Alyce Cheska. 1985. *The anthropology of sport.* South Hadley, MA: Bergin and Garvey.

Bledsoe, Caroline. 1993. The politics of polygyny in Mende education and child fosterage transactions. In *Sex and gender hierarchies,* edited by Barbara Diane Miller, 170–92. Cambridge: Cambridge University Press.

Bohannan, Laura, and Paul Bohannan. 1969. *The Tiv of central Nigeria.* 2d ed. London: International African Institute.

Brain, Robert. 1976. *Friends and lovers.* New York: Basic Books.

Braroe, Niels. 1975. *Indian and White.* Stanford: Stanford University Press.

Briggs, Jean. 1980. Kapluna daughter: Adopted by the Eskimo. In *Conformity and conflict: Readings in cultural anthropology,* edited by J. Spradley and D. McCurdy, 44–62. 7th ed. Boston: Little, Brown.

Brumfiel, E. M., and T. K. Earle. 1987. *Specialization, exchange, and complex societies.* Cambridge: Cambridge University Press.

Burch, Ernest S., Jr. 1970. Marriage and divorce among the north Alaska eskimos. In *Divorce and after,* edited by Paul Bohannan, 152–81. Garden City: Doubleday.

———. 1975. *Eskimo kinsmen: Changing family relationships in north west Alaska.* American Ethnological Society Monograph, no. 59. St. Paul: West.

Carroll, John B., ed. 1956. *Language, thought and reality. Selected writings of Benjamin Lee Whorf.* Cambridge: MIT Press.

Chagnon, Napoleon. 1983. *Yanomamo: The fierce people.* 3d ed. New York: Holt, Rinehart and Winston.

Chambers, Erve. 1985. *Applied anthropology: A practical guide.* New York: Prentice-Hall.

Chance, John K. 1978. *Race and class in colonial Oaxaca.* Stanford: Stanford University Press.

Chomsky, Noam. 1957. *Syntactic structures.* The Hague: Mouton.

———. 1965. *Aspects of the theory of syntax.* Cambridge: MIT Press.

Clastres, Pierre. 1977. *Society against the state.* Translated by Robert Hurley. New York: Urizen Books.

Colby, Benjamin, and Pierre van den Berghe. 1969. *Ixil country.* Berkeley: University of California Press.

Cole, Michael, and Sylvia Scribner. 1974. *Culture and thought: A psychological introduction.* New York: Wiley.

Collier, Jane, and Sylvia Yanagisako. 1987. *Gender and kinship: Essays toward a unified analysis.* Stanford: Stanford University Press.

Colson, Elizabeth. 1977. Power at large: Meditation on "The symposium on power." In *The anthropology of power: Ethnographic studies from Asia, Oceania, and the New World,* edited by R. Fogelson and R. N. Adams, 375–86. New York: Academic Press.

Cowan, Jane. 1990. *Dance and the body politic in northern Greece.* Princeton: Princeton University Press.

Crick, Malcolm. 1976. *Explorations in language and meaning: Towardsa semantic anthropology.* New York: Wiley.

Csikszentmihalyi, Mihalyi. 1981. Some paradoxes in the definition of play. In *Play and context,* edited by Alyce Cheska, 14–25. West Point: Leisure Press.

Dallmayr, F., and Thomas A. McCarthy. 1977. Introduction to "The positivist reception." In *Understanding and social inquiry,* edited by F. Dallmayr and T. McCarthy, 77–78. South Bend: University of Notre Dame Press.

da Matta, Robert. 1994. Some biased remarks on interpretism. In *Assessing cultural anthropology,* edited by Robert Borofsky, 119–32. New York: McGraw-Hill.

D'Andrade, Roy G. 1992. Cognitive anthropology. In *New directions in psychological anthropology,* edited by Theodore Schwartz, Geoffrey M. White, and Catherine A. Lutz, 47–58. Cambridge: Cambridge University Press.

Danner, Mark. 1994. *The massacre at El Mozote.* New York: Vintage.

Davis, Shelton. 1977. *Victims of the miracle.* Cambridge: Cambridge University Press.

Deng, Francis Madeng. 1972. *The Dinka of the Sudan.* New York: Holt, Rinehart and Winston.

Diener, Paul, and Eugene E. Robkin. 1978. Ecology, evolution, and the search for cultural origins: The question of Islamic pig prohibition. *Current Anthropology* 19 (3): 493–540.

Dorst, John. 1989. *The written suburb: An American site, an ethnographic dilemma.* Philadelphia: University of Pennsylvania Press.

Douglas, Mary. 1966. *Purity and danger.* London: Routledge and Kegan Paul.

———. 1970. *Natural symbols.* New York: Pantheon.

Douglas, Mary, and Baron Isherwood. 1979. *The world of goods: Towards an anthropology of consumption.* New York: W. W. Norton.

Drewal, Margaret. 1992. *Yoruba ritual.* Bloomington: Indiana University Press.

Dumont, Jean Paul. 1978. *The headman and I: Ambiguity and ambivalence in the fieldwork experience.* Austin: University of Texas Press.

Edelsky, Carole. 1977. Acquisition of communicative competence: Learning what it means to talk like a lady. In *Child discourse,* edited by S. Ervin-Tripp and C. Mitchell-Kernan, 225–44. New York: Academic Press.

Elliot, Alison. 1981. *Child language.* Cambridge: Cambridge University Press.

Escobar, Arturo. 1992. Culture, economics, and politics in Latin American social movements theory and research. In *The making of social movements in Latin America,* edited by Arturo Escobar and Sonia Alvarez, 62–85. Boulder, CO: Westview.

Estioka-Griffin, Agnes. 1986. Daughters of the forest. *Natural History* 95 (5): 36–43.

Etienne, Mona. 1980. Women and men, cloth and colonization: The transformation of production-distribution relations among the Baule (Ivory Coast). In *Women and colonization: Anthropological perspectives,* edited by Mona Etienne and Eleanor Leacock, 270–93. New York: Praeger.

Evans-Pritchard, E. E. 1940. *The Nuer.* Oxford: Oxford University Press.

———. 1951. *Kinship and marriage among the Nuer.* Oxford: Oxford University Press.

———. 1963. *Social anthropology and other essays.* New York: Free Press.

———. [1937] 1976. *Witchcraft, oracles, and magic among the Azande.* Abridged ed. Oxford: Oxford University Press.

Fagan, Robert. 1981. *Animal play behavior.* New York: Oxford University Press.

———. 1992. Play, fun, and communication of well-being. *Play and Culture* 5 (1): 40–58.

Fernandez, James W. [1966] 1971. Principles of opposition and vitality in Fang aesthetics. In *Art and aesthetics in primitive societies,* edited by Carol Jopling, 356–73. New York: E. P. Dutton.

———. 1977. The performance of ritual metaphors. In *The social use of metaphors,* edited by J. D. Sapir and J. C. Crocker. Philadelphia: University of Pennsylvania Press.

———. 1980. Edification by puzzlement. In *Explorations in African systems of thought,* edited by Ivan Karp and Charles Bird, 44–69. Bloomington: Indiana University Press.

———. 1982. *Bwiti: An ethnography of the religious imagination in Africa.* Princeton: Princeton University Press.

Fiddes, Nick. 1991. *Meat: A natural symbol.* London: Routledge.

Firth, Raymond. [1936] 1984. *We, the Tikopia.* Reprint. Stanford: Stanford University Press.

Fortes, Meyer. 1950. Kinship and marriage among the Ashanti. In *African systems of kinship and marriage,* edited by A. R. Radcliffe-Brown and Daryll Forde. Oxford: Oxford University Press.

————. 1953. The structure of unilineal descent groups. *American Anthropologist* 55:25–39.

Fortes, Meyer, and E. E. Evans-Pritchard, eds. 1940. *African political systems.* Oxford: Oxford University Press.

Fox, Robin. 1967. *Kinship and marriage.* Harmondsworth: Penguin.

Fried, M. H. 1967. *The evolution of political society.* New York: Random House.

Gamble, David P. 1957. *The Wolof of Senegambia.* London: International African Institute.

Gardner, B. T., and R. A. Gardner. 1971. Two way communication with an infant chimpanzee. In *Behavior of nonhuman primates,* edited by A. M. Schuer and F. Stollnitz, 117–85. New York: Academic Press.

Gardner, Howard. 1982. *Art, mind, and brain: A cognitive approach to creativity.* New York: Basic Books.

Geertz, Clifford. 1960. *The religion of Java.* New York: Free Press.

————. 1972. Deep play: Notes on the Balinese cockfight. *Daedalus* 101:1–37.

————. [1966] 1973. Religion as a cultural system. In *The interpretation of cultures,* 87–125. New York: Basic Books.

————. 1973. *The interpretation of cultures.* New York: Basic Books.

Geertz, Hildred, and Clifford Geertz. 1975. *Kinship in Bali.* Chicago: University of Chicago Press.

Georges, Eugenia. 1990. *The making of a transnational community: Migration, development, and cultural change in the Dominican Republic.* New York: Columbia University Press.

Giddens, Anthony. 1978. Positivism and its critics. In *A history of sociological analysis,* edited by T. Bottomore and R. Nisbet, 237–86. New York: Basic Books.

————. 1979. *Central problems in social theory.* Berkeley: University of California Press.

Gillies, Eva. 1976. Introduction. In *Witchcraft, oracles, and magic among the Azande,* by E. E. Evans-Pritchard. Oxford: Oxford University Press.

Gilligan, Carol. 1982. *In a different voice.* Cambridge, MA: Harvard University Press.

Gilsenan, Michael. 1982. *Recognizing Islam: Religion and society in the modern Arab world.* New York: Pantheon.

Ginsburg, F. 1991. Indigenous media: Faustian contract or global village? *Cultural Anthropology* 6 (1): 94–114.

Ginsburg, Faye, and Anna Lowenhaupt Tsing, eds. 1990. *Uncertain terms: Negotiating gender in American culture.* Boston: Beacon Press.

Gottlieb, Alma. 1988. American premenstrual syndrome: A mute voice. *Anthropology Today* 4 (6).

————. 1989. Witches, kings, and the sacrifice of identity *or* The power of paradox and the paradox of power among the Beng of Ivory Coast. In *Creativity of power: Cosmology and action in African societies,* edited by W. Arens and Ivan Karp, 245–72. Washington, DC: Smithsonian Institution Press.

Gough, Katherine. 1961. Nayar: Central Kerala. In *Matrilineal societies,* edited by David Schneider and Katherine Gough, 298–384. Berkeley: University of California Press.

Greenwood, David, and William Stini. 1977. *Nature, culture, and human history.* New York: Harper and Row.

Gregory, Richard. 1981. *Mind in science: A history of explanations in psychology and physics.* New York: Cambridge University Press.

————. 1983. Visual perception and illusions: Dialogue with Richard Gregory. In *States of Mind,* by Jonathan Miller, 42–64. New York: Pantheon.

Gudeman, Stephen. 1978. *The demise of a rural economy.* London: Routledge and Kegan Paul.

————. 1990. Guest editorial in *Cultural anthropology: A perspective on the human condition,* by Emily Schultz and Robert Lavenda, 458–59. 2d ed. St. Paul: West.

Guillermoprieto, Alma. 1990. *Samba.* New York: Vintage.

Gumperz, John. 1982. *Discourse strategies.* Cambridge: Cambridge University Press.

Gutierrez Muñiz, José A., Josefina López Hurtado, and Guillermo Arias Beatón. n.d. *Un estudio del niño Cubano.* Havana: EmpresaImpresoras Gráficas, MINED.

Handelman, Don. 1977. Play and ritual: Complementary frames of meta-communication. In *It's a funny thing, humour,* edited by A. J. Chapman and H. Foot, 185–92. London: Pergamon.

————. 1983. Presenting, representing, and modelling the world: Toward the study of public events and media events. Photocopied working paper.

Hanna, Judith Lynne. 1979. *To dance is human.* Austin: University of Texas Press.

Haraway, Donna. 1989. *Primate visions.* New York: Routledge.

Harris, Marvin. 1965. The myth of the sacred cow. In *Man, culture, and animals,* edited by A. Leeds and A. P. Vayda, 217–28. Washington, DC: American Association for the Advancement of Science.

————. 1974. *Cows, pigs, wars and witches.* New York: Vintage.

Heider, Karl. 1979. *Grand Valley Dani.* New York: Holt, Rinehart and Winston.

Herdt, Gilbert, ed. 1982. *Rituals of manhood: Male initiation in Papua New Guinea.* Berkeley: University of California Press.

————. 1994a. Introduction. In *Third sex, third gender,* edited by Gilbert Herdt. New York: Zone Books.

————. 1994b. Mistaken sex: Culture, biology, and the third sex in New Guinea. In *Third sex, third gender,* edited by Gilbert Herdt, 419–445. New York: Zone Books.

————, ed. 1994c. *Third sex, third gender.* New York: Zone Books.

Herskovits, Melville. 1973. *Cultural relativism.* Edited by Frances Herkovits. New York: Vintage Books.

Hobsbawm, Eric, and Terence Ranger. 1983. *The invention of tradition.* Cambridge: Cambridge University Press.

Hockett, C., and R. Ascher. 1964. The human revolution. *Current Anthropology* 5:135–47.

Hockett, C. F. 1966. The problems of universals in language. In *Universals of language,* edited by J. H. Greenberg, 1–29. Cambridge: MIT Press.

Hoebel, E. Adamson. 1960. *The Cheyennes.* New York: Holt, Rinehart and Winston.

Hoijer, Harry. 1953. The relation of language to culture. In *Anthropology today,* edited by A. L. Kroeber, 554–73. Chicago: University of Chicago Press.

Holm, John. 1988. *Pidgins and creoles.* Vol. 1 of *Theory and structure.* Cambridge: Cambridge University Press.

Holmes, Lowell. 1989. Concerning Derek Freeman's comment on Holmes's *Quest for the real Samoa. American Anthropologist* 91 (3): 753–58.

Horner, M. 1972. Toward an understanding of achievement-related conflicts in women. *Journal of Social Issues* 28:157–75.

Horton, Robin. 1982. Tradition and modernity revisited. In *Rationality and relativism,* edited by M. Hollis and Steven Lukes, 201–60. Cambridge: MIT Press.

Hudson, R. A. 1980. *Sociolinguistics.* Cambridge: Cambridge University Press.

Hunter, David, and Phillip Whitten, eds. 1976. *Encyclopedia of anthropology.* New York: Harper & Row.

Huyghe, Patrick. 1988. Profile of an anthropologist: No bone unturned. *Discover,* December.

Hymes, Dell. 1972. On communicative competence. In *Sociolinguistics: selected readings,* edited by J. B. Pride and J. Holmes, 269–93. Baltimore: Penguin Books.

Jackson, Michael. 1977. *The Kuranko.* New York: St. Martin's Press.

———. 1982. *Allegories of the wilderness.* Bloomington: Indiana University Press.

Johnson, Steven L. 1988. Ideological dimensions of peasant persistence in western Kenya. In *New perspectives on social class and political action in the periphery,* edited by R. Curtain, N. W. Keith, and N. E. Keith. Westport, CT: Greenwood Press.

Kapferer, Bruce. 1983. *A celebration of demons.* Bloomington: Indiana University Press.

Karp, Ivan. 1978. *Fields of change among the Iteso of Kenya.* London: Routledge and Kegan Paul.

———. 1986. Laughter at marriage: Subversion in performance. In *The transformation of African marriage,* edited by David Parkin. London: International African Institute.

———. 1990. Guest editorial in *Cultural anthropology: A perspective on the human condition,* by Emily Schultz and Robert Lavenda, 74–75. 2d ed. St. Paul: West.

Karp, Ivan, and Martha B. Kendall. 1982. Reflexivity in field work. In *Explanation in social science,* edited by P. Secord. Los Angeles: Sage.

Keesing, Roger. 1982. *Kwaio religion.* New York: Columbia University Press.

———. 1983. *'Elota's story.* New York: Holt, Rinehart and Winston.

———. 1992. *Custom and confrontation: The Kwaio struggle for cultural autonomy.* Chicago: University of Chicago Press.

Keillor, Garrison. 1985. *Lake Wobegon days.* New York: Viking.

Khazanov, Anatoly. 1993. State and violence in the ex-Soviet Union. Paper read at 92nd annual meeting of the American Anthropological Association, November, Washington, DC.

Kondo, Dorinne K. 1990. *Crafting selves: Power, gender, and discourses of identity in a Japanese workplace.* Chicago: University of Chicago Press.

Kopytoff, Igor. 1986. The cultural biography of things: Commoditization as process. In *The social life of things,* edited by Arjun Appadurai, 64–91. Cambridge: Cambridge University Press.

Kopytoff, Igor, and Suzanne Miers. 1977. Introduction: African "slavery" as an institution of marginality. In *Slavery in Africa,* edited by Suzanne Miers and Igor Kopytoff, 3–84. Madison: University of Wisconsin Press.

Krige, E. J., and J. D. Krige. 1943. *Realm of a rain queen.* London: Oxford University Press.

Kuhn, Thomas. 1970. *The structure of scientific revolutions.* 2d ed. Chicago: University of Chicago Press.

———. 1979. Metaphor in science. In *Metaphor and thought,* edited by Andrew Ortony, 409–19. Cambridge: Cambridge University Press.

Kumar, Nita. 1992. *Friends, brothers, and informants: Fieldwork memories of Banaras.* Berkeley: University of California Press.

Kuper, Adam. 1982. *Wives for cattle: Bridewealth and marriage in southern Africa.* London: Routledge and Kegan Paul.

Kürti, Láslö. 1988. The politics of joking: Popular response to Chernobyl. *Journal of American Folklore* 101:324–34.

Labov, William. 1972. *Language in the inner city: Studies in the Black English Vernacular.* Philadelphia: University of Pennsylvania Press.

Lakoff, George, and Mark Johnson. 1980. *Metaphors we live by.* Berkeley: University of California Press.

Lave, Jean. 1988. *Cognition in practice.* Cambridge: Cambridge University Press.

Lee, Richard. 1974. Male-female residence arrangements and political power in human hunter-gatherers. *Archaeology of Sexual Behavior* 3:167–73.

———. 1992a. Art, science, or politics? The crisis in hunter-gatherer studies. *American Anthropologist* 94:31–54.

———. 1992b. *The Dobe Ju/'hoansi.* 2d ed. New York: Holt, Rinehart and Winston.

Lever, Janet. 1983. *Soccer madness.* Chicago: University of Chicago Press.

Levine, Nancy. 1980. Nyinba polyandry and the allocation of paternity. *Journal of Comparative Family Studies,* 11 (3): 283–88.

———. 1988. *The dynamics of polyandry: Kinship, domesticity, and population on the Tibetan border.* Chicago: University of Chicago Press.

Levine, Nancy, and Walter Sangree. 1980. Women with many husbands. *Journal of Comparative Family Studies,* 11(3) [Special Issue].

Lévi-Strauss, Claude. 1962. *L'antropologie structurale.* Paris: Plon. Translated under the title *Structural anthropology* by Claire Jacobson and Brooke Grundfest Schoepf. New York: Doubleday Anchor, 1967.

———. 1955. *Tristes tropiques.* Paris: Plon. Translated by John Weightman and Doreen Weightman. New York: Atheneum, 1974.

Lewellen, Ted. 1983. *Political anthropology.* South Hadley, MA: Bergin and Garvey.

Lewis, I. M. 1967. *A pastoral democracy: A study of pastoralism and politics among the northern Somali of the Horn of Africa.* London:

Oxford University Press.

———. 1976. *Social anthropology in perspective*. Harmondsworth: Penguin.

Lienhardt, Godfrey. 1961. *Divinity and experience: The religion of the Dinka*. Oxford: Oxford University Press.

Little, Kenneth. 1967. *The Mende of Sierra Leone*. London: Routledge and Kegan Paul.

Lutz, Catherine. 1988. *Unnatural emotions*. Chicago: University of Chicago Press.

Lyons, John. 1969. *Theoretical linguistics*. Cambridge: Cambridge University Press.

———. 1981. *Language and linguistics*. Cambridge: Cambridge University Press.

MacCormack, Carol P. 1980a. Nature, culture, and gender: A critique. In *Nature, culture and gender*, edited by Carol MacCormack and Marilyn Strathern, 1–24. Cambridge: Cambridge University Press.

———. 1980b. Proto-social to adult: A Sherbro transformation. In *Nature, culture, and gender*, edited by Carol MacCormack and Marilyn Strathern, 95–118. Cambridge: Cambridge University Press.

Macintyre, Martha. 1993. Fictive kinship or mistaken identity? Fieldwork on Tubetube Island, Papua New Guinea. In *Gendered fields: Women, men and ethnography*, edited by Diane Bell, Pat Caplan, and Wazir Jahan Karim, 44–62. London: Routledge.

Malinowski, Bronislaw. 1929. *The sexual life of savages*. New York: Harcourt, Brace.

———. 1944. *A scientific theory of culture and other essays*. New York: Oxford University Press.

———. [1926] 1948. *Magic, science, and religion, and other essays*. New York: Doubleday Anchor.

Mandler, George. 1975. *Mind and emotion*. New York: Wiley.

———. 1983. The nature of emotion: Dialogue with George Mandler. In *States of mind*, by Jonathan Miller, 136–52. New York: Pantheon.

Marcus, George. 1990. Guest editorial in *Cultural anthropology: A perspective on the human condition*, by Emily Schultz and Robert Lavenda, 254–55. 2d ed. St. Paul: West.

Martin, E. 1987. *The woman in the body*. Boston: Beacon.

Martin, Laura. 1986. Eskimo words for snow: A case study in the genesis and decay of an anthropological example. *American Anthropologist* 88 (2): 418–19.

Marx, Karl. [1932] 1977. *The German ideology*. Selections reprinted in *Karl Marx: Selected writings*, edited by David McLellan. Oxford: Oxford University Press.

Meisch, Lynn. 1987. *Otavalo: Weaving, costume, and the market*. Quito: Ediciones Libri Mundi.

Messer, Ellen. 1993. Anthropology and human rights. *Annual Review of Anthropology* 22:221–49.

Meunier, Jacques, and A. M. Savarin. 1994. *The Amazon chronicles*. Translated by Carol Christensen. San Francisco: Mercury House.

Miller, Barbara Diane. 1993. The anthropology of sex and gender hierarchies. In *Sex and gender hierarchies*, 3–31. Cambridge: Cambridge University Press.

Miller, Marc S. 1993. Behind the words. *Cultural Survival Quarterly* (Summer): 1.

Miracle, Andrew. 1991. Aymara joking behavior. *Play & Culture* 4 (2): 144–52.

Moffatt, Michael. 1989. *Coming of age in New Jersey: College and American culture*. New Brunswick, NJ: Rutgers University Press.

Moll, Luis, ed. 1990. *Vygotsky and education*. New York: Cambridge University Press.

Moore, R. 1992. Marketing alterity. *Visual Anthropology Review* 8 (2): 16–26.

Morgan, Lewis Henry. [1877] 1963. *Ancient Society*. Reprint. Cleveland: Meridian Books.

Morgan, Lynn. 1993. *Community participation in health: The politics of primary care in Costa Rica*. Vol. 1 of *Cambridge studies in medical anthropology*. Cambridge: Cambridge University Press.

Murphy, Robert. 1986. *Social and cultural anthropology: An overture*. 2d ed. New York: Prentice-Hall.

Murphy, Robert, and Yolanda Murphy. 1974. *Women of the forest*. New York: Columbia University Press.

Myerhoff, Barbara. 1974. *Peyote hunt*. Ithaca: Cornell University Press.

Myerhoff, Barbara, and Jay Ruby. 1982. Introduction. In *A crack in the mirror: Reflexive perspectives in anthropology*, edited by Jay Ruby. Philadelphia: University of Pennsylvania Press.

Nanda, Serena. 1994. Hijras: An alternative sex and gender role. In *Third sex, third gender*, edited by Gilbert Herdt, 373–417. New York: Zone Books.

Narayan, R. K. 1974. *My days*. New York: Viking.

Nash, June. 1979. *We eat the mines, and the mines eat us*. New York: Columbia University Press.

Norbeck, Edward. 1974. *Religion in human life*. New York: Holt, Rinehart and Winston.

Nordstrom, Carolyn. 1993. Treating the wounds of war. *Cultural Survival Quarterly* 17 (Summer): 28–30.

Ochs, Elinor. 1986. Introduction. In *Language socialization across cultures*, edited by Bambi Schieffelin, and Elinor Ochs, 1–13. Cambridge: Cambridge University Press.

Ortner, Sherry. 1973. On key symbols. *American Anthropologist* 75 (5): 1338–46.

Ortony, Andrew. 1979. Metaphor: A multidimensional problem. In *Metaphor and thought*, 1–18. Cambridge: Cambridge University Press.

Oswalt, Wendell. 1972. *Other peoples, other customs*. New York: Holt, Rinehart and Winston.

Parkin, David. 1978. *Cultural definition of political response: Lineal destiny among the Luo*. New York: Academic Press.

———. 1984. Mind, body, and emotion among the Giriama. Paper presented in *Humanity as Creator* lecture series, St. Cloud State University.

———. 1990. Guest editorial in *Cultural anthropology: A perspective on the human condition*, by Emily Schultz and Robert Lavenda. 2d ed. St. Paul: West.

———. 1991. *Sacred void: Spatial images of work and ritual among the Giriama of Kenya*. Cambridge: Cambridge University Press.

Partridge, William L., ed. 1984. *Training manual in development an-*

thropology. Special publication of the American Anthropological Association and the Society for Applied Anthropology, number 17. Washington, DC: American Anthropological Association.

Platt, Martha. 1986. Social norms and lexical acquisition: A study of deictic verbs in Samoan child language. In *Language socialization across cultures,* edited by Bambi Schieffelin, and Elinor Ochs, 127–52. Cambridge: Cambridge University Press.

Plattner, Stuart, ed. 1989. *Economic anthropology.* Palo Alto: Stanford University Press.

Poewe, Karla. 1989. On the metonymic structure of religious experiences: The example of charismatic Christianity. *Cultural Dynamics* 2 (4): 361–80.

Polanyi, Karl. 1977. *The livelihood of man.* Edited by Harry W. Pearson. New York: Academic Press.

Rabinow, Paul. 1977. *Reflections on fieldwork in Morocco.* Berkeley: University of California Press.

Redford, Kent H. 1993. The ecologically noble savage. In *Talking about people,* edited by W. A. Haviland and R. J. Gordon. Mountain View, CA: Mayfield.

Reeves, Edward, Billie DeWalt, and Kathleen DeWalt. 1987. The International Sorghum/Millet Research Project. In *Anthropological praxis,* edited by Robert Wolfe and Shirley Fiske, 72–83. Boulder, CO: Westview Press.

Ringrose, Kathryn M. 1994. Living in the shadows: Eunuchs and gender in Byzantium. In *Third sex, third gender,* edited by Gilbert Herdt, 85–109. New York: Zone Books.

Ronan, Colin A., and Joseph Needham. 1978. *The shorter science and civilisation in China. An Abridgement Of Joseph Needham's Original Text.* Vol 1. Cambridge: Cambridge University Press.

Rosaldo, Renato. 1980. *Ilongot headhunting, 1883–1974: A study in society and history.* Stanford: Stanford University Press.

Roscoe, Will. 1994. How to become a Berdache: Toward a unified analysis of gender diversity. In *Third Sex, third gender,* edited by Gilbert Herdt, 329–72. New York: Zone Books.

Rosen, Lawrence. 1984. *Bargaining for reality: The constructions of social relations in a Muslim community.* Chicago: University of Chicago Press.

Rosman, Abraham, and Paula G. Rubel. 1971. *Feasting with mine enemy: Rank and exchange among northwest coast societies.* New York: Columbia University Press.

Rostow, W. W. [1960] 1971. *Stages of economic growth.* 2d ed. New York: Cambridge University Press.

Rowe, William, and Vivian Schelling. 1991. *Memory and modernity: Popular culture in Latin America.* London: Verso.

Ruby, J. 1991. Speaking for, speaking about, speaking with, or speaking alongside—An anthropological and documentary dilemma. *Visual Anthropology Review* 7 (2): 50–66.

Sacks, Karen. 1979. *Sisters and wives.* Urbana: University of Illinois Press.

Sacks, Oliver. 1984. *A leg to stand on.* New York: Summit Books.

Sahlins, Marshall. 1972. *Stone Age economics.* Chicago: Aldine.

———. 1976a. *Culture and practical reason.* Chicago: University of Chicago Press.

———. 1976b. *The use and abuse of biology.* Ann Arbor: University of Michigan Press.

Sapir, Edward. [1933] 1966. *Culture, language, and personality,* edited by David Mandelbaum. Berkeley: University of California Press.

Sapir, J. David. 1977. The anatomy of metaphor. In *The social use of metaphors,* edited by J. D. Sapir and J. C. Crocker. Philadelphia: University of Pennsylvania Press.

Scheper-Hughes, Nancy. 1988. The madness of hunger: Sickness, delirium and human needs. *Culture, Medicine and Psychiatry* 12:429–58.

———. 1994. Embodied knowledge: Thinking with the body in critical medical anthropology. In *Assessing cultural anthropology,* edited by Robert Borofsky, 229–42. New York: McGraw-Hill.

Schneider, David. 1968. *American kinship: A cultural account.* Englewood Cliffs, NJ: Prentice-Hall.

Schultz, Emily. 1984. From Pagan to *Pullo*: Ethnic identity change in northern Cameroon. *Africa* 54 (1): 46–64.

———. 1990. *Dialogue at the margins: Whorf, Bakhtin, and linguistic relativity.* Madison: University of Wisconsin Press.

Schultz, Emily, and Robert Lavenda. 1990. *Cultural anthropology: A perspective on the human condition.* 2d ed. St. Paul: West.

Schwartzman, Helen. 1978. *Transformations. The anthropology of children's play.* New York: Plenum.

Scott, James C. 1985. *Weapons of the weak.* New Haven: Yale University Press.

———. 1990. *Domination and the arts of resistance: Hidden transcripts.* New Haven: Yale University Press.

Shepherd, Gill. 1987. Rank, gender, and homosexuality: Mombasa as a key to understanding sexual options. In *The cultural construction of sexuality,* edited by Pat Caplan, 240–70. London: Tavistock.

Shostak, Marjorie. 1983. *Nisa: The Life and Words of a !Kung Woman.* New York: Vintage Books.

Silverstein, Michael. 1976. Shifters, linguistic categories, and cultural description. In *Meaning in anthropology,* edited by Keith Basso, and Henry Selby, 11–55. Albuquerque: University of New Mexico Press.

———. 1985. The functional stratification of language and ontogenesis. In *Culture, communication, and cognition: Vygotskian perspectives,* edited by James Wertsch, 205–35. Cambridge: Cambridge University Press.

Smith, Andrea. 1994. For all those who were Indian in a former life. *Cultural Survival Quarterly* (Winter): 71.

Smith, G. 1989. Space age shamans: The videotape. *Americas* 41 (2): 28–31.

Smith, M. G. [1954] 1981. Introduction to *Baba of Karo,* by Mary Smith. Reprint. New Haven: Yale University Press, 1981.

Smith, Mary. [1954] 1981. *Baba of Karo.* Reprint. New Haven: Yale University Press.

Smith, Wilfred Cantwell. 1982. *Towards a world theology.* Philadelphia: Westminster.

Spiro, Melford. 1977. *Kinship and marriage in Burma: A cultural and psychodynamic account.* Berkeley: University of California Press.

Starn, Orin. 1992. "I dreamed of foxes and hawks": Reflections on peasant protest, new social movements, and the *rondas campesinas* of northern Peru. In *The making of social movements in Latin America: Identity, strategy, and democracy,* edited by Arturo Escobar and Sonia E. Alvarez, 89–111. Series in Political Economy and Economic Development in Latin America. Boulder, CO: Westview Press.

Stearman, Allyn. 1989. *The Yuquí.* New York: Holt, Rinehart and Winston.

Steggerda, Morris. [1941] 1984. *Maya Indians of Yucatán.* Reprint. New York: AMS Press.

Steiner, Christopher. 1994. *African art in transit.* Cambridge: Cambridge University Press.

Strathern, Marilyn. 1972. *Women in between.* London: Academic Press.

———. 1987. Producing difference: Connections and disconnections in two New Guinea highland kinship systems. In *Gender and kinship: Essays toward a unified analysis,* by Jane Collier and Sylvia Yanagisako, 271–300. Stanford: Stanford University Press.

———. 1992. *Reproducing the future: Anthropology, kinship, and the new reproductive technologies.* New York: Routledge.

Sutton-Smith, Brian. 1980. The playground as a zoo. *Newsletter of the Association for the Anthropological Study of Play* 7 (1): 4–8.

———. 1984. Recreation as folly's parody. *Newsletter of the Association for the Anthropological Study of Play* 10 (4): 4–13, 22.

Tambiah, Stanley J. 1989. The politics of ethnicity. *American Ethnologist* 16 (2): 335–49.

Tannen, Deborah. 1990. *You just don't understand. Women and men in conversation.* New York: Ballantine Books.

Taussig, Michael. 1980. *The devil and commodity fetishism in Latin America.* Chapel Hill: University of North Carolina Press.

Taylor, Julie. 1987. Tango. *Cultural Anthropology* 2 (4): 481–93.

Tedlock, Dennis. 1982. Anthropological hermeneutics and the problem of alphabetic literacy. In *A crack in the mirror: Reflexive perspectives in anthropology,* edited by Jay Ruby, 149–61. Philadelphia: University of Pennsylvania Press.

Trobriand cricket: An ingenious response to colonialism. 1974. Directed by J. W. Leach and G. Kildea. 60 min. Berkeley: University of California Extension Media Center.

Trotter, Robert. 1987. A case of lead poisoning from folk remedies in Mexican American communities. In *Anthropological praxis,* edited by Robert Wolfe and Shirley Fiske, 146–59. Boulder, CO: Westview Press.

Turnbull, Colin. 1961. *The forest people.* New York: Simon and Schuster.

Turner, Terence. 1989. Amazonian Indians fight to save their forest. *Anthropology Newsletter* 30 (3): 21–22.

———. 1991a. The social dynamics of video media in an indigenous society: The cultural meaning and the personal politics of video-making in Kayapo communities. *Visual Anthropology Review* 7 (2): 68–76.

———. 1991b. Visual media, cultural politics, and anthropological practice. *The Independent,* January/February, 34–40.

Turner, Victor. 1969. *The Ritual Process.* Chicago: Aldine.

Valentine, Bettylou. 1978. *Hustling and other hard work.* New York: Free Press.

Valentine, Charles. 1978. Introduction. In *Hustling and other hard work,* by Bettylou Valentine, 1–10. New York: Free Press.

Van Baal, J. 1966. *Dema: Description and analysis of culture.* The Hague: Martinus Nijhoff.

Van Gennep, Arnold. 1960. *The Rites of Passage.* Chicago: University of Chicago Press.

van Willigen, John. 1991. *Anthropology in use: A source book on anthropological practice.* Boulder, CO: Westview Press.

van Willigen, John, and V. C. Channa. 1991. Law, custom, and crimes against women. *Human Organization* 50 (4): 369–77.

Vaughan, James. 1970. Caste systems in the western Sudan. In *Social stratification in Africa,* edited by Arthur Tuden and Leonard Plotnikov, 59–92. New York: Free Press.

———. 1973. Engkyagu as artists in Marghi society. In *The traditional artist in African societies,* edited by Warren L. d'Azevedo, 162–93. Bloomington: Indiana University Press.

Voloshinov, V. N. [1926] 1987. Discourse in life and discourse in art. In *Freudianism,* translated by I. R. Titunik and edited in collaboration with Neil H. Bruss, 93–116. Bloomington: Indiana University Press.

———. [1929] 1986. *Marxism and the philosophy of language.* Translated by Ladislav Matejka and I. R. Titunik. Cambridge: Harvard University Press.

Vygotsky, L. S. 1962. *Thought and language.* Cambridge: MIT Press.

———. 1978. *Mind in society: The development of higher psychological processes.* Cambridge: Harvard University Press.

Wallace, A. F. C. 1966. *Religion: An anthropological view.* New York: Random House.

———. 1972. *The death and rebirth of the Seneca.* New York: Vintage.

Wallerstein, Immanuel. 1974. *The modern world-system.* New York: Academic Press.

Weiner, Annette. 1976. *Women of value, men of renown.* Austin: University of Texas Press.

———. 1979. Trobriand kinship from another view: The reproductive power of women and men. *Man,* n.s., 14 (2): 328–48.

———. 1980. Stability in banana leaves: Colonization and women in Kiriwina, Trobriand Islands. In *Women and colonization: Anthropological perspectives,* edited by Mona Etienne and Eleanor Leacock, 270–93. New York: Praeger.

———. 1988. *The Trobrianders of Papua New Guinea.* New York: Holt, Rinehart and Winston.

———. 1990. Guest editorial in *Cultural anthropology: A perspective on the human condition,* by Emily Schultz and Robert Lavenda, 392–93. 2d ed. St. Paul: West.

Wertsch, James. 1985. *Vygotsky and the social formation of mind.* Cambridge: Harvard University Press.

Whorf, Benjamin. 1956. *Language, thought, and reality,* edited by John B. Carroll. Cambridge: MIT Press.

Williams, Brett. 1984. Why migrant women feed their husbands tamales: Foodways as a basis for a revisionist view of Tejano family life. In *Ethnic and regional foodways in the United States,* edited by Linda Keller Brown and Kay Mussell. Knoxville: University of Tennessee Press.

Wilmsen, Edwin. 1989. *Land filled with flies: A political economy of the Kalahari.* Chicago: University of Chicago Press.

Wilson, Monica. 1951. *Good company.* Oxford: Oxford University Press.

Winn, Peter. 1992. *Americas.* New York: Pantheon.

Witherspoon, Gary. 1975. *Navajo kinship and marriage.* Chicago: University of Chicago Press.

Wolf, Eric. 1969. *Peasant wars of the twentieth century.* New York: Harper and Row.

———. 1982. *Europe and the people without history.* Berkeley: University of California Press.

———. 1994. Facing power: Old insights, new questions. In *Assessing cultural anthropology,* edited by Robert Borofsky, 218–28. New York: McGraw-Hill.

Yanagisako, Sylvia, and Jane Collier. 1987. Toward a unified analysis of gender and kinship. In *Gender and kinship: Essays toward a unified analysis,* edited by Jane Collier and Sylvia Yanagisako, 14–50. Stanford: Stanford University Press.

Credits

(continued from copyright page)

PHOTO CREDITS

Chapter 1 Fig. 1.2a, © Barbara Smuts/Anthro-Photo; Fig. 1.2b, courtesy Carol Worthman, Emory University; Fig. 1.3, Robert H. Lavenda. **Chapter 2** Fig. 2.1, Robert H. Lavenda; Fig. 2.3, UPI/ The Bettmann Archive. **Chapter 3** Fig. 3.1, Robert H. Lavenda; Fig. 3.2, courtesy of the Institute for Intercultural Studies Inc., New York, photo from the Library of Congress; Fig. 3.3, © Napoleon Chagnon/Anthro-Photo. **Chapter 4** Fig. 4.1, The Granger Collection; Fig. 4.2, © Belinda Wright; Fig. 4.3, courtesy Photo Department, Peabody Essex Museum, Salem, Massachusetts. **Chapter 5** Fig. 5.2, Robert H. Lavenda; Fig. 5.5, © J. Greenburg/Photo-Edit. **Chapter 6** Fig. 6.6, © Cordon Art, The M. C. Escher Foundation, Holland. **Chapter 7** Fig. 7.1, courtesy Dr. Michael A. Park; Fig. 7.2, © Robert Frerck/Woodfin Camp and Associates; Fig. 7.3, Reuters/The Bettmann Archive; Fig. 7.4, courtesy Dr. James W. Fernandez, University of Chicago; Fig. 7.5, © Anthro-Photo. **Chapter 8** Fig 8.1, Robert H. Lavenda; Fig. 8.3, J. F. E. Bloss/Anthro-Photo; Fig. 8.4, Motion Picture and TV Photo Archive; Fig. 8.5, © Van Cleve/Tony Stone Images; Fig. 8.6, © Cornell University Press; Fig. 8.7, courtesy James W. Fernandez, University of Chicago. **Chapter 9** Fig. 9.1 (left), © 1898 G. W. James/Southwest Museum, Los Angeles; Fig. 9.1 (right), © Jacques Jangoux/ Tony Stone Images; Fig. 9.5, Dan Budnik/© 1980 Woodfin Camp and Associates; Fig. 9.13, © AP/Wide World Photos. **Chapter 10** Fig. 10.1, Robert H. Lavenda; Fig. 10.2, © Dr. Irven DeVore/Anthro-Photo no. 2764; Fig. 10.3, Robert H. Lavenda. **Chapter 11** Fig. 11.1, © United Nations, photo no. 106414; Fig. 11.2, courtesy Joseph K. Dixon/Museum of New Mexico; Fig. 11.3, Robert H. Lavenda. **Chapter 12** Fig. 12.1, © Donald Smetzer/Tony Stone Images; Fig. 12.2, Robert H. Lavenda; Fig. 12.3, © Elizabeth Harris/Tony Stone Images; Fig. 12.4, © Hugh Sitton/ Tony Stone Images. **Chapter 13** Fig. 13.1, © Dr. Irven DeVore/ Anthro-Photo; Fig. 13.3, neg. no. 411-791 courtesy H. I. Smith/American Museum of Natural History; Fig. 13.4, Robert H. Lavenda. **Chapter 14** Fig. 14.1, © R. Maiman/Sygma Photo News; Fig. 14.2, © Bruno Barbey/Magnum Photos; Fig. 14.3, © Marc and Evelyne Bernheim/Woodfin Camp and Associates; Fig. 14.4, © Sebastian Salgado/Magnum Photos. **Chapter 15** Fig. 15.1, courtesy Jim Altobell, SCSU Public Relations and Publications; Fig. 15.2a, © Crawford/Anthro-Photo; Fig. 15.2b, courtesy Liliana Nieto/Physicians for Human Rights.

TEXT CREDITS

Pages 12, 29, 33, 51, 65, 109, 436, 473, excerpts from *Cultural Anthropology,* 2nd ed. by Emily Shultz and Robert Lavenda, 1990. West Publishing Co. Reprinted with permission. **Chapter 3** Page 61, excerpt from *Yuqui: Forest Nomads in a Changing World* by Allyn M. Stearman, copyright © 1989 by Holt, Rinehart and Winston, Inc. Reprinted by permission of the publisher. **Chapter 4** Page 81, from "The Ecologically Noble Savage," *Cultural Survival Quarterly,* vol. 17, no. 4, Winter 1994. Reprinted with permission. Fig. 4.4 and Table 4.2, from *Political Anthropology* by Ted Lewellen. Reprinted with permission of Greenwood Publishing Group, Inc., Westport, CT. Copyright © 1983 by Ted Lewellen. **Chapter 5** Fig. 5.1, reprinted with special permission of King Features Syndicate; Fig. 5.3, reprinted with the permission of The Free Press, a Division of Simon & Schuster, from *The Religion of Java* by Clifford Geertz. Copyright © 1960 by The Free Press; page 112, reproduced by permission of the American Anthropological Association from *American Anthropologist* 88:2, June 1986. Not for further reproduction; page 120, copyright © 1992 by Houghton Mifflin Company. Reprinted by permission from *The American Heritage Dictionary of the English Language, Third Edition.* **Chapter 6** Fig. 6.2, 6.3, 6.8, from *Culture and Thought: A Psychological Introduction* by Michael Cole and Sylvia Scribner. Copyright © 1974, John Wiley & Sons, Inc.; Fig. 6.4, 6.7, from *States of Mind* by Jonathan Miller. Copyright © 1983 by the Contributors. Reprinted by permission of Pantheon Books, a division of Random House, Inc.; page 156, from *Assessing Cultural Anthropology,* Robert Borofsky (ed.). Copyright © 1993, McGraw-Hill, Inc. Reprinted by permission; page 166, from *Anthropology Today* 4(6), 1988. Reprinted by permission of Royal Anthropological Institute. **Chapter 7** Page 193, reproduced by permission of the American Anthropological Association from *Cultural Anthropology* 2:4, November 1987. Not for further reproduction; page 201, from *Public Culture,* 5(3), 1993. Reprinted by permission of the University of Chicago Press. **Chapter 8** Page 238, from *Custom and Confrontation* by Roger M. Kessing. Copyright © 1992 by University of Chicago Press. Reprinted by permission of University of Chicago Press; page 240, from *Cultural Survival Quarterly,* vol. 17, no. 4, Winter 1994. Reprinted by permission. **Chapter 9** Page 262, copyright © 1994 by The New York Times Company. Reprinted by permission. **Chapter 10** Page 286, excerpts from Chapter 9 of *My Days* by R. K. Narayan. Copyright © 1973, 1974 by R. K. Narayan. Published by Penguin USA. Used by permission of the Wallace Literary Agency, Inc.; page 308, reproduced by permission of the Society for Applied Anthropology from *Human Organization* 50(4) 1991, pg. 369–70; page 312, from *Ethnic and Regional Foodways in the United States,* Linda Keller Brown and Kay Mussell (eds.), University of Tennessee Press, 1984. Reprinted with permission. **Chapter 11** Page 326, from *Lake Wobegon Days* by Garrison Keillor. Copyright © 1985 by Garrison Keillor. Used by permission of Viking Penguin, a division of Penguin

Index

Boldface page numbers indicate glossary definitions.